D0230349

last d

The Modern British Novel

Also by Malcolm Bradbury

Fiction

Eating People is Wrong
Stepping Westward
The History Man
The After Dinner Game: Three Plays for Television
Rates of Exchange
Why Come to Slaka?
Cuts
Doctor Criminale

Criticism

Possibilities: Essays on the State of the Novel
Modernism (editor, with J. W. McFarlane)
The Novel Today (editor)
All Dressed Up and Nowhere to Go
The Modern American Novel
Saul Bellow
The Penguin Book of Modern British Short Stories (editor)
No, Not Bloomsbury
Unsent Letters
Mensonge
From Puritanism to Postmodernism: A History of American Literature
(with Richard Ruland)

THE MODERN BRITISH NOVEL

Malcolm Bradbury

Secker & Warburg
London

First published in England 1993
by Martin Secker & Warburg Limited
Michelin House, 81 Fulham Road, London SW3 6RB

Reprinted 1994

A CIP record for this book is available
from the British Library

ISBN 0 436 201321

Set in 12-point Baskerville
Printed in England by Clays Ltd, St Ives plc

In memory of

Angela Carter, William Golding and Angus Wilson

Contents

Preface

This book is about the British novel – perhaps I had better say the novel as it has developed in Britain – over the remarkable, enormously productive hundred years from the end of the last century to our own present end-of-century. A hundred years is a long time in the history of the novel, and ours has been a century of profound and turbulent change. Not surprisingly, then, all the terms of my title – with the possible exception of the definite article – are contentious, or as we say now contested. "Modern" has a weak and a strong meaning, referring both to an overall period, the "modern" century, ours, and to a distinctive tradition of *avant-garde* literary and artistic experiment. As will soon be seen, I am interested in the intricate relations that have developed between these two. "British" is a term open to many arguments, not least because many of the most important novelists sailing under this flag of convenience are not British at all. Henry James was American, Conrad was Polish, George Moore and James Joyce were Irish, Wyndham Lewis was born on a ship at sea; many of the writers we claim today as part of British writing have names like Ishiguro, Okri, Rushdie, Mo, Kureishi and Zameenzad. Meanwhile many British writers live and think elsewhere, and have seen their tradition very much from the outside. However far we go back the "English" or, to use the now preferred term, "British" tradition has always been in some basic sense international, linked with travel, exile, emigration and exterior influence. And the idea of reading any literature, even one as eclectic and pluri-cultural as the British, in national terms has increased in difficulty in our international, global-village age. Even so, I assume there are certain shaping aspects to a national tradition, though many writers are constantly diverting from it. I have simply been pragmatic here, including writers when they seem important or fundamental to the notion of a shaping tradition (like James, Conrad or Joyce), but not encompassing those who are nowadays best seen in the light of some other lineage – as are, I think, writers like Patrick White, Nadine Gordimer, or Chinua Achebe.

The word "novel" – the term itself suggests it – has always described a loose and baggy monster, a form of fictional prose narrative that contains infinite variety, many different genres, from reportage and social history to fantasy and romance, and reaches from serious exploration of the narrative frontiers to popular gratification and endless generic repetition. The novel – and this is an important part of the story – has changed greatly from the eighteenth century, when it became a key form of public expression in British culture, to our own time, when it is everywhere. It developed radically in the Victorian period (to which so many recent novelists have returned), in the age of Dickens, Thackeray, the Brontës, Trollope, George Eliot; it became social entertainment, moral tract, political criticism, book of etiquette. Then came the "modern" novel, which was in many respects a reaction against the Victorian novel, questioning everything from its patriarchal morality to its notion of the "real." Throughout this century, the borders and frontiers of fiction have been endlessly disputed, and an important part of this story is the thriving argument that has since existed about what the novel is and does. The modern novel has been many things, and functioned at many levels. It would keep D. H. Lawrence poor, and make Jilly Cooper and Jeffrey Archer rich. Novelists are always quarrelling with the idea of the novel. "I have an idea that I will invent a new name for my books to supplant 'novel,'" wrote Virginia Woolf in her diary as she struggled with just this question. "A new – by Virginia Woolf. But what? Elegy?" The frontier here can open in many ways – to lyricism and poetry, reportage and autobiography. We can challenge the idea of the author, the idea of the text, the idea of its representation, the idea of the reader. I shall confine myself to pragmatism: original works of good length that take on and develop fictional powers are what I shall take the novel to be.

The fact is that the idea of the novel has been so disputed because it has become increasingly central to modern British culture, even while that culture has been changing radically. Briefly: this book is a general survey of the development of the novel in Britain through several generations – from the dawn of "the modern novel" to the very plural scene of the present, which we now generally call "postmodern." I regard it as a flourishing period, when the novel changed in spirit, and became a key literary form, challenging poetry and drama for literary dominance, until it too was challenged by the new technological media, film and television, with which it has come increasingly to interact. Over this time it threw off many of its "Victorian" constraints, formal and moral, and became increasingly an exploring, discovering genre, one of the fields of exploration being the question of what the novel itself was. The radical difficulty this presented, in major modern works like Joyce's *Ulysses*, Woolf's *Mrs Dalloway*, or Beckett's *The Unnamable*, is a key part of the history, but hardly the only one. Stephen Spender once claimed that there were two modern traditions – the "modern" one, experimental and *avant-garde*, and the "contemporary," concerned with social questions and the way we live now – and I am interested in both. The two have lived in ceaseless intersection; the story of that intersection, frequently repeated, is a central theme of this book. One of the results of the division is that, in literary criticism (now known as literary theory), most of the attention has fallen on the first half of the century, the period of the "Modern," rather than on the more or less nameless era that has come since. That division has often seemed to imply a fundamental distinction of quality; the second generation was not like the first. It seems to me seriously misleading. Much of the most important writing of the century has come in the second half of it, and it is still coming. The desire to do justice to this is one main motive of this book.

The relative neglect of the post-war period, which is almost fifty years long and contains several generations, has several reasons behind it. It is famously hard to judge our own contemporaries (if only because they might then judge us), though it is done in other countries, like France and the United States. And it has certainly taken a considerable time to grasp who were the important authors, what were the most interesting developments, of the period since 1945, if only because the form was widening and growing more various and it needed time for this expansion to enter critical lore. Moreover the post-war period has not been marked by a great aesthetic debate about the novel comparable to that of the earlier half of the century, in part because the role of writer and critic divided, the writer going off into the marketplace and the critic to the university (which eventually turned out to be much the same thing). The result was that it lacked aesthetic debate, clear tendencies, well-defined milestones. This happened not least because the traditions writers were drawing on were now much more diverse, and if the term "postmodern" means anything it surely refers to a time of interfused styles, mixed cultural layers, oddly merging traditions, multi-cultural pluralism – one reason, indeed, why there is now a significant embarrassment about canons, traditions and national lineages in fiction and culture. In my own view, the post-war period has been a quite remarkable and productive one, insufficiently talked about and recognized. An inspection of the list of authors and titles at the end of this book might suggest the variety, plurality and overall significance of modern fiction, and the way, too, it has grown ever less parochial, ever more eclectic, in its view and vision of the world.

There is also another reason for this neglect: the notion that the decline of the "English novel" goes along with the decline of Britain's place in the world. The idea that the novel, particularly the English novel, is dead has recently revived in currency. The fact is that the novel has been dead in every decade of this century. It was dead in the Edwardian period, the 1900s: "all modern books are bad" says E. M. Forster's Cecil Vyse in *A Room With a View* (1907), "... Everyone writes for money these days." Meanwhile the works of the late Henry James, Joseph Conrad, James Joyce and D. H. Lawrence were appearing. It was dead in the 1920s, when T. S. Eliot said *Ulysses* had shown that "the novel ended with Flaubert and with James," and when, after writing *Mrs Dalloway*, Virginia Woolf noted "I'm glad to be quit this time of writing a 'novel'; and hope never to be accused of it again." We now, of course, acknowledge the 1920s as *the* major period of modern fiction. It was dead again in the Thirties, when Marxist critics and writers saw the novel as a bourgeois prison, though one they themselves found it almost impossible to escape from; Evelyn Waugh, Graham Greene, Henry Green and many more emerged. It was certainly dead by the Second World War, when, said George Orwell in 1940, the writer was to be seen sitting on a melting iceberg: "he is merely an anachronism, a hangover from the bourgeois age, as surely doomed as the hippopotamus." Even so, along with the hippopotamus, the writer somehow survived.

The novel was even deader after 1945. "It is disheartening to think that twenty years ago saw the first novels of Hemingway, Faulkner, Elizabeth Bowen, Rosamund Lehmann, Evelyn Waugh, Henry Green, Graham Greene," Cyril Connolly wrote in his usual twilight mood in *Horizon* in 1947, ". . . but no new crop of novelists has risen commensurate with them." This view persisted through most of the Fifties. In 1954 the *Observer* ran an influential series called "Is the Novel Dead?" which produced the same strikingly discouraging pronouncements: "I do not see, therefore, that the conditions which render fiction a relevant form of expression exist in the present generation," wrote Harold Nicolson. Meanwhile the careers of Angus Wilson, Doris Lessing, Anthony Burgess, Muriel Spark, Iris Murdoch, William Golding, Kingsley Amis, Brian Moore and Paul Scott began; 1954 is generally thought of as the key year for the emergence of post-war British fiction, when three major first novels appeared, one by a future Nobel Prizewinner. "If the novel is truly no longer novel, then many of our critical procedures for discussing it will need revision; perhaps, even, we shall do well to think of another name for it," Bernard

Bergonzi observed in his fine but funereal study *The Situation of the Novel* in 1970; at just this time a new generation of writers from John Fowles to Angela Carter was becoming established. In the 1970s *The New Review* ran a symposium in which nearly sixty British novelists agreed together that there was nothing going on in the British novel; this was when Martin Amis, Ian McEwan and a large group of new writers began their careers. When, as the decade turned, *Granta* magazine started, it devoted its entire third issue in 1980 to mourning "The End of the English Novel." The magazine then went on to publish writers like Ian McEwan, Martin Amis, Julian Barnes, Salman Rushdie, Angela Carter, Bruce Chatwin, Colin Thubron, Jeanette Winterson and John Berger, and by 1983 gave an entire issue over to "The Best of the Young British Novelists." (An event they were to repeat in 1993.) As I write this, the *Guardian* newspaper is once more deeply convinced that the British novel is dead. "British fiction, as everyone knows," writes the literary editor, ". . . is in sad state," while one young contributor who has, I think, yet to write a novel complains that writing novels is "irrelevant, impotent, uncool" compared with regular employment. Plainly things are just as bad as ever, or else we are the victims of a very tired cliché. Perhaps we should all agree that the novel – the British variety in particular, but also the novel in general – is dead, but that somehow a great many remarkable and talented people are writing something peculiarly like it, and discovering themselves and new forms in the process. The abundance has hardly been greater, the quality is rich, fresh new writers appear each year, London remains a world publishing centre, and fiction has a primary role in British life.

The present book takes it for granted that the novel, which has never been one thing but always an infinitely varied form, has survived and is surviving, serving as a major expression of artistic, cultural and intellectual curiosity, exploring the nature of our contemporary narratives and the discovering value of fiction. It also takes it for granted that, for all the pluralism and all the arguments about traditions and canons, the twentieth-century British novel has been in some kind of varied but continuous evolution, and that not just one but several traditions have flourished and continue to do so. I mean this book as a broad, general, accessible survey, a reflection of my interests as a critic but also of my needs as a writer. For writers are, in the end, readers. They need ancestors and traditions, to learn from and to argue with, to perceive the complex and varied nature of creativity and the rich potential of the forms they use. This account could be called both a history of fiction and a fictional history, the way I have found to construct the British past and present of my own form for myself. I am interested, as will be seen, in the generations and cultural eras that make up such a story; I am also interested in the creative explorations and the playful powers of fictions. The result is, I hope, eclectic, even if it is inevitably selective; I can read and enjoy some writers and not others. I believe a writer, if not a critic, should be open in approach, and fascinated by the art of others; and so there is here no single "great tradition" but a variety of traditions and creative options that, for later writers, are likely to cross and interfuse. Since, given the limits of life's reading time, and in the interests of good narrative, selection is inevitable, I have added at the end a much larger list of writers whom I find interesting and important.

Though this is a book about the modern British novel, I consider the novel to be an international form and do not regard British fiction as having been isolated from developments elsewhere. For that reason I hope this study will take its place alongside the several other books where I have explored the broader movements of modernism and Postmodernism. These include *The Social Context of Modern English Literature* (1971), *Modernism 1890–1930* (edited with James McFarlane, rev. ed., 1990), *The Modern World: Ten Great Writers* (1988), *The Modern American Novel* (rev. ed., 1990), *No, Not Bloomsbury* (1987), and, with Richard Ruland, *From Puritanism to Postmodernism: A History of American Literature* (1991). Some parts of this text have appeared, in other forms, in various places, and I have drawn here and there on previous books. I am of course indebted to the very many people – editors and publishers, conference organizers, colleagues, friends – who have encouraged this longstanding exploration by commissioning essays or reviews, debating the arguments with me, or in a variety of other collaborative ways. They include Guido Almansi, Bernard Bergonzi, Chris Bigsby, John Blackwell, Christopher Butler, Robert Boyars, Catharine Carver, Marc Chenetier, Jon Cook, C. B. Cox, Diane DeBell, A. E. Dyson, Jay Halio, Ihab Hassan, Gerhard Hoffmann, Frank Kermode, David Lodge, Derwent May, Blake Morrison, Penny Perrick, Tom Rosenthal, Mike Shaw, Lorna Sage, Vic Sage, D. J. Taylor, Anthony Thwaite, Richard Todd, Kristiaan Versluys, John Walsh, W. L. Webb, Harriet Harvey Wood and Heide Ziegler, as well as many postgraduate students in modern fiction and creative writing at the University of East Anglia. I am specially grateful to many writers who at various times have discussed their work or the novel with me, including Martin Amis, Antonia Byatt, Angela Carter, Margaret Drabble, John Fowles, Kazuo Ishiguro, Doris Lessing, David Lodge, Ian McEwan, Iris Murdoch, C. P. Snow, Salman Rushdie, Graham Swift, Rose Tremain, and Angus Wilson. The dedication refers to three writers who have been especially important to me, and have died recently. But more generally the book is dedicated to all those who go on believing in the art of fiction, and in the future of the novel.

Malcolm Bradbury
Norwich, England, 1992–3

ONE

The Turn of the Novel
1878–1900

It has arrived, in truth, the novel, late at self-consciousness: but
it has done its utmost ever since to make up for lost
opportunities.

> Henry James, "The Future of the Novel" (1899)

The shift to which I refer was gradual, but it took place . . . with
the greatest velocity at about the turn of this century . . . It was
not merely plot, or characterization, or technique, or point of
view, or thought, or symbolic organization that changed; it was
not a matter of irreconcilable meanings, conflicting themes, or
difficult problems. The change in the novel took place at a more
fundamental level than these . . . The process which underlay
the novel was itself disrupted and reorganized. The new flux of
experience insisted on a new vision of existence; it stressed an
ethical vision of continual expansion and virtually unrelieved
openness in the experience of life.

> Alan Friedman, *The Turn of the Novel* (1966)

1.

Just about every historian of British fiction would agree that,
somewhere around the end of the nineteenth century or the
start of the twentieth, there occurred a great "turn of the novel."
The powerful tradition of Victorian fiction – moral, realistic,
popular – began to die, and something different and more
complex came to emerge: the tradition of what we now name
the "modern" novel. The change did not happen only in Britain;
it was part of an international transformation of the arts. Across
Europe, more slowly in the United States, the form of the novel

1

– which had emerged as a major genre of literature only in the seventeenth and eighteenth centuries, then become a crucial companion to the social and emotional expansion of the nineteenth – was moving through a great transition, as was all of Western humanist thought and culture itself. The change was in far more than fiction's subject-matter; deeper structures were reshaping too. The novel was aspiring to become a far more complex, various, open and self-conscious form, one which, in a new way, sought to be taken seriously as "art." The Spanish philosopher Ortega y Gasset, observing this in his "Notes on the Novel" (1949), said fiction had shifted from being an Art of Adventures to an Art of Figures, from an art that told stories and reported life to a form that *created* form.[1] When Virginia Woolf wrote her important, audacious essay "Modern Fiction" in 1919, she considered the modern novel was ready to claim a freedom from old convention that was just like a political revolution. "If a writer were a free man and not a slave, if he could write what he chose and not what he must, if he could base his work upon his own feeling and not upon convention," she argued, in her writers' version of the *Communist Manifesto*, "there would be no plot, no comedy, no tragedy, no love interest or catastrophe in the accepted sense, and perhaps not a single button sewn on as the Bond Street tailors would have it." Life was quite unlike the reality literature encoded; it was, she said, "a luminous halo, a semi-transparent envelope surrounding us from the beginning of consciousness to the end" – and it was the task of the modern novelist to convey this fresh sense of life, with "as little mixture of the alien and external as possible." The modern novel, modern consciousness, would cast off its ancient chains and become free to deal with the strange plotless insubstantiality that was, in Woolf's vision, life or reality itself.

The modern change that came to fiction was not always so revolutionary, and was very much more complicated. For its

---

[1] Jose Ortega y Gasset, *The Dehumanization of Art, and Other Writings on Art and Culture* (Garden City, N.Y., 1956).

coming we can find a great many reasons, and the critics have.[2] There were key social reasons: the growth of urban populations, the acceleration of technological change, the coming of improved education and literacy, the shifting relation of the classes, the expansion of leisure, the gradual increase in personal wealth. There were crucial intellectual reasons: the decline of a religious teleology and of the confident, theocentric, progressive Victorian world view, the rise of science and secular philosophies like sociology and psychology, the coming of a more material vision of life. There were important psychological reasons, as changing notions of the nature of the individual, social life, sex and gender relations, and rising awareness of the distinctive, increasingly mobile and fast-changing nature of experience in a modernizing age gave a new, more fluid view of consciousness and identity. There were important changes in the role of literature itself: the dying of the Victorian "three-decker" novel, designed for libraries and associated with moral uplift, the rise of the literary marketplace and the development of the book as an item of purchase, the restratification of the cultural hierarchies in an age of increasing democracy, otherwise called the "coming of the masses." The explanations are many; all played their part in the changing character of the novel. But however we explain the change, the effects are apparent. The established form of the novel – fictional prose narrative – was acquiring a different kind of writer, a different kind of subject, a different kind of writing process, a different kind of reader, a different social and economic foundation. It was altering in length, appearance, price, and in social, moral and commercial purpose. It was multiplying, dividing its audience, reaching into new kinds of expression, undertaking daring new kinds of exploration, demanding new kinds of attention, claiming new freedoms of method and subject: new rights to social and sexual frankness, new complexities of

[2] See, for example, Alan Friedman, *The Turn of the Novel: The Transition to Modern Fiction* (New York and London, 1966); Raymond Williams, *The English Novel from Dickens to Lawrence* (London, 1970); and Peter Keating's excellent *The Haunted Study: A Social History of the English Novel, 1875–1914* (London, 1989).

discourse and form. Over the course of the twentieth century – also called the "modern" century – this transformation would continue. Changing, sub-dividing, springing from different cultural regions, reaching to very different audiences and new expressive functions, the novel would assume many roles. It would become a relaxing toy of leisure and fantasy, *and* a complex mechanism for imaginative and artistic discovery. It would serve as naive popular entertainment, and would transmit radical, often outrageous or surprising, visions and opinions. Above all it would become a central literary prototype, taking an importance it had never had as *the* literary medium of the age, dislodging poetry, to some degree even sidelining drama – until, later in the century, its dominance was in turn challenged by new technological media that promised or threatened to replace book-based culture with something more immediate, visual, and serial. But even that great change in cultural technology the novel in general seems – so far – to have survived.

In consequence, the "modern novel," an idea constantly discussed as the century closed, became a reality. A distinctive modern tradition developed, marked not just by modern themes, new techniques, wider availability, but by a firm break with past "Victorian" conventions of narrative and literary morality, authorship and readership. But that break was never really to become complete. Many of the Victorian conventions and myths continued to haunt the radical surprise of the modern novel, and Victorian fiction – with its omniscient and godlike voice, its weighty realism, its chronological plotting, its presiding moral confidence, its role as the bourgeois epic – leaves its lasting imprint on British fiction to this moment. In the contemporary novels of Angus Wilson and Margaret Drabble, Marina Warner and David Lodge, Graham Swift and Peter Ackroyd its trace is clear, as the source of a modern social realism or as a traditional text the postmodern writer must unpick. In very self-conscious books like John Fowles' *The French Lieutenant's Woman* (1969) and A.S. Byatt's *Possession* (1990), we observe deliberate acts of homage to its presence, as from their different late-twentieth-century perspectives these authors look back across the bridge between the Victorian and late-modern worlds, the Victorian and the late-modern novel. All these writers, all these books, acknowledge that some epochal change has occurred, in the representation of life, the angle of vision, the notion of Britain and culture. All of them see some continued if perhaps tricky connection between the age of Dickensian fogs and Darwinian crises and the nuclear age, the age of postmodern absurdity and the *nouveau roman*. "The novelist is still a god, since he creates (and not even the most aleatory *avant-garde* modern novel has managed to extirpate its author completely)" writes Fowles in his meta-Victorian novel, which is both loving pastiche and critical parody, "what has changed is that we are no longer the gods of the Victorian image, omniscient and decreeing; but in the new theological image, with freedom our first principle, not authority." Byatt's book shows a greater nostalgia for a denser, richer time, and attempts a fuller possession. But it too deconstructs as well as reconstructs the sentimentalities and gender uncertainties that lay within Victorian solidity. "The [Victorian] writers of the industrial novels were never able to resolve in fictional terms the ideological contradictions inherent in their own situation in society," pronounces the critic Robyn Penrose in Lodge's *Nice Work* (1988), but she soon finds herself in a latter-day version of the same problem, as yet another contemporary fiction explores both the continuing affinity and the literary distance fiction and the world have travelled since the troubled closing of the Victorian age. The modern novel came, but the Victorian novel did not entirely go away; and that is one of the essential secrets of the modern novel.

2.

That some epochal change occurred – in the role of the author, the spirit of the text, the shape of a story, the nature of a fiction – as the Victorian age ended can be more or less agreed. *How* it happened, *why* it happened, what it meant for the future of the novel, remain endlessly disputable. As for just *when* it happened, a variety of audacious dates has been put on offer. In 1899, as the new century turned, Henry James proudly announced the coming of a new "self-consciousness" to the art of fiction: "It can do simply everything, and that is its strength and its life." "On or about December 1910 human nature changed . . .," Virginia Woolf said even more daringly in her essay "Mr Bennett and Mrs Brown" (1924). ". . . All human relations shifted – those between masters and servants, husbands and wives, parents and children. And when human relations change there is at the same time a change in religion, conduct, politics, and literature." Woolf's apocalyptic date is oddly precise, but there is a reason. She pinpoints her great shift in social relations and literary forms, her time of "breaking and falling, crashing and destruction," to the end of the Edwardian period, the beginning of "Georgianism" (as one critic had noticed, the British seemed to have long believed that kings and queens shape writing) – to the month of London's first exhibition of French Post-Impressionist and Cubist paintings, organized by her friend Roger Fry, when Britain saw Modernism's visual face, and "Bloomsbury" went into the ascendant. "It was in 1915 that the old world ended," countered D.H. Lawrence in *Kangaroo* (1923), selecting for his transforming moment the second year of the Great War. He too had good reason: this was the year when apocalyptic signs showed in the sky (Zeppelins) and when his own work was suppressed by the British courts. Writing functions around epochal ideas, and all these key dates make sense. The millennial turn into the new and modern century, when science would reign; the ferment of *avant-garde* activity and new aesthetics that passed right through Europe in the immediately pre-war years; the crisis of war, that fundamental and revolutionary transformation that shattered the *belle époque*, broke down and transformed the European world map, and brought at least one revolutionary new ideology, Bolshevism, to political birth – all are among the important markers of modern European and world history, and of the modern novel.

In literature as in history, what looks sudden is usually born out of a long process. One reason we call the novel by that name is that it is a changing and discovering form, which alters with the new, and the news, and constantly struggles to express our shifting and developing inner and outer life. No one date will ever tell us when the "modern novel," or the "Modern movement," started, any more than we can know for sure when it ended, even though by calling ourselves "postmodern" we clearly assume it has, more or less. What we can do is note the social, historical and artistic changes that made people think in a fresh way about society, culture, art and language, and make them view these things as uniquely "modern" – a condition that has always existed, but that our own age of change and speed-up has highlighted, so that, as Karl Mannheim once said, what makes us modern is that we are always trying "to tell by the cosmic clock of history what the time is." Still, if we start looking for the time of greatest change, we are likely to go hunting a good deal earlier than any of the writers I have quoted. Something was reshaping the world, and the novel, long before 1900, 1910 or 1915. It was in the late Victorian years that what historians have called the "Victorian synthesis" began to dissolve, and the cultural climate began to fragment. The progressive, optimistic view that had marked the earlier Victorian period was coming to an end, and it seemed the age had been not an institution but a revolution, a passage between a seemingly stable rural past and an infinite acceleration. Religious certainty declined under the pressure of the evolutionary theories of Charles Darwin, T.H. Huxley and Herbert Spencer. The fading of the old rural order and the rise of new urban masses, the march of "progress" and "reform," the surge of new technologies and communications, were altering, shrinking and cosmopolitanizing the world. The map of Europe was reshaping (the first German Reich was founded in 1871), and various European empires reaching a point of crisis or internal disintegration. New and revolutionary political movements –

socialism, and the Communist philosophies of Marx and Engels – disturbed the comfortable surface of a bourgeois age. Materialism prospered, but in a climate of great historical uncertainty; it was hard to read where the world was going next. New technologies – the incandescent lamp, the electric street car, the internal combustion engine, the "dynamo revolution" – offered amazing promises of change and prospects for the future; at the same time they indicated that the world was now governed by massive processes that increasingly dwarfed individual lives. Well before the end of the century, there was intense awareness of deep-seated and eternal change, and the idea of a "coming of the modern" became a Europe-wide phenomenon. "Only the day after tomorrow belongs to me," announced Friedrich Nietzsche, the philosopher of the modern. "Some men are born posthumously."

The remaking of human ideas and expectations round the turn of modern centuries is not new. The last decades of the previous century had seen a sequence of revolutions: the American and the French, the Industrial and the Romantic. Now, as the nineteenth century came toward its close, and industrial, technological, and economic development accelerated, a similar restless transformation was in the air. Advance in science, the speeding up of invention and futuristic discovery, the boom in world trade, the rise in European and American imperial and economic power, created a time of innovation. New forms and styles were shaping everywhere. European cities spent imperial wealth on a vast grandiosity; their streets filled with new technologies and architectures, with tramways and electric streetlights, *art nouveau* and *Jugendstil*. The idea of the Modern took on more and more meaning: there was talk of the modern city, modern architecture, modern science, modern man, the modern woman, modern consciousness, the modern soul. Writers and thinkers weighed the "modern" question. "Late-Victorian" sages like Flaubert, John Stuart Mill, Zola, Ibsen, Tolstoy, Kierkegaard and Nietzsche – the world-historical figures the Danish critic Georg Brandes called the "men of the Modern Breakthrough" – aimed to express and explore the

8

distinctive character of the new: its break with past ties, customs, faiths and traditions, its will to bring new consciousness to birth. The belief that a new age was emerging spread across Europe and America; as H. Stuart Hughes says in *Consciousness and Society* (1958), "Nearly all students of the last years of the nineteenth century have sensed in some form or other a profound psychological change."[3] Sociological thinkers like Weber, Durkheim and Pareto explored the underlying systems of the social world. Thinkers in the different realm of consciousness and psychology – William James, Henri Bergson, Sigmund Freud – began reconceiving the structures of the inner life. The Modern could be progressive and "advanced"; it could also be introverted and decadent. But whatever it was, few doubted it was on its way, bringing a decisive break with the past, and new consciousness, new expression, new forms of art.

By the later years of the nineteenth century, especially in Britain, the novel had become a central means of exploration of the state of the nation, the feel of the culture, the relationship between personal and historical life. From mid-century on, as the age of Romanticism began to fade, it had increasingly moved toward realism – a democratizing, empirical way of writing that opened fiction out to social discovery, a wide reportage, a sympathetic responsiveness to the daily feel of ordinary lives. After the liberal revolutions that ran through Europe in 1848, the year of the *Communist Manifesto*, and the powerful impact of Darwin's *Origin of Species* in 1859, Realism became the great movement in art and fiction. Its report grew ever more socially exploratory, analytic, scientific, attentive to new laws of social evolution, the coming of new classes and masses; this was the tendency Zola called "Naturalism." As the century came toward its close, Naturalism too was challenged, by rising aesthetic preoccupations and deepened concern with human consciousness, distrust of the certainties of progress and the laws of social determinism. Thus it began to conflict or

[3] H. Stuart Hughes, *Consciousness and Society: The Reorientation of European Social Thought, 1890–1930* (New York, 1958; London, 1959).

cross over with the movements we call Symbolism, Aestheticism, and Decadence. The Modern movement really came in as
a wave of movements, which oscillated between sociology and
psychology, the progressive and the decadent, the objective and
the subjective, the deterministic and the indeterminate. Its
changes paralleled deep changes in other spheres where uncertainty was emerging: religion and morality, science and medicine, philosophy and physics. This general transition of literary
consciousness was so great and so various that no single date
can ever capture it. But dates can be useful, can sharpen the
meaning of things. That is why, in the hunt for the modern in
the novel, there is much to be said for considering what
happened – or rather did not happen – on 1 November 1878,
and, to be quite precise, at tea-time.

3.

Just two years earlier, an ambitious young American novelist,
Henry James – a child of New York, Albany, Boston, Harvard,
and the cosmopolitan James family – decided to settle in
Europe: indeed in London, the place where, for the novelist
who took social manners and human behaviour as his subject,
there was, he said, the most in the world to observe. Born in
New York in 1843, James had been brought to Europe as a
child for his "sensuous education," returned to see his nation
divided by a terrible Civil War, begun to write in an unhappy
America where the pre-Civil War era of "the American Renaissance" – the age of Emerson, Thoreau, Hawthorne and Melville
– was over. While his American contemporaries of the Reconstruction era, like William Dean Howells, Mark Twain and
Walt Whitman, chose to stay in their plain new nation to write
of its past and future, James, a natural cosmopolitan, began
travelling widely to look for an ideal city of art. He tried Rome,
where earlier American writers and artists had sought escape
from American provincialism and puritanism, and explored his
aesthetic quest in his novel *Roderick Hudson* (USA, 1875), mostly

written in Europe. Rome was somehow *too* aesthetic: he returned home to "try New York," but by 1875 he was back trying Paris – where, through his Russian friend and fellow exile Ivan Turgenev, he met many of the important authors, including Flaubert, Maupassant, the Goncourt brothers, Zola, representatives of the new realist movement of the day. James held himself a realist, but one large theme of his realism was in fact the American romance, above all focused on Europe itself. This is the romance that draws not only Roderick Hudson, but the various characters of his stories in *A Passionate Pilgrim and Other Tales* (1875), and Christopher Newman, the American businessman "stepping forth in his innocence and his might, gazing a while at this poor corrupt old world and then sweeping down on it," who also tries Paris in his first major novel *The American* in 1877.

Late in 1876 James found his European base, decided to make London his home, and settled in Bolton Street off Piccadilly. He was to remain in Britain for most of the rest of his life, and the major phase of his writing. "My choice is the Old World – my choice, my need, my life," he wrote in a letter home, adding:

> For one who takes it as I take it, London is on the whole the most possible form of life. I take it as an artist and a bachelor; as one who has the passion of observation and whose business is the study of human life. It is the biggest aggregation of human life – the most complete compendium of the world.

James had based his "choice" on sound realist reasons. In a claim that upset Howells and Twain, he described American society as "thin," and argued that "the flower of art only blooms where the soil is deep, that it takes a great deal of history to produce a little literature, that it needs a complex social machinery to set the novelist into motion." London offered what the realist needed: a textured society, a world of manners,

11

a "great numerosity" of lives. So James became a British writer: or almost – for, as he rightly explained, "I find myself more of a cosmopolitan (thanks to that combination of the continent and the USA that has formed my lot) than the average Briton of culture." That meant he saw Britain as part of Europe: and Europe as a world of deepened experience which began, he said, as an "enlarged and uplifted gape," and became "a banquet of initiation which was in the event to prolong itself through years and years." The theme of emotional and cultural initiation, entry through art and social complication into the deeper realms of experience, became the key to his fiction. In *Roderick Hudson*, the sculptor Roderick creates a statue of a boy drinking deep from the cup of experience. In *The American*, the symbolically named Christopher Newman, the "great Western barbarian," risks his innocent values to encounter the mannered, deceptive, experienced world of French society. In *Daisy Miller* (1878), the book that made his reputation, the central figure transforms into the young, free, formless American girl, the heiress to all the ages, encountering the miasmic corruptions of Rome. James had found his "international theme," and by *The Europeans* (also 1878) he was confident enough to reverse it, taking a group of sophisticated European travellers on a reverse journey across the Atlantic to plain, puritan New England – as if to show the transaction worked two ways: European experience could learn from American innocence, an American writer could perform equally in the realm of the American and the European novel.

But if London and English life seemed solid and deep, the society in which James settled with such pleasure was hardly settled itself. Nor was the state of the literary form in which he sought to express himself. Certainly, as the 1870s started, the lineage of the Victorian novel – the expansive social form that had developed to explore and challenge the confident urbanizing age of industrial, imperial, world-powerful Britain – seemed secure enough. With the achievement of Dickens and Thackeray, Trollope and Bulwer-Lytton, Disraeli and Mrs Gaskell, it had become the expression of a sturdy, self-critical bourgeois culture in an age of growth, widening commerce, shifting class relations. It dealt, often realistically, sometimes romantically, generally rather sentimentally, with the changing relations of past and present, town and country, class and class, wealth and poverty. It explored religious duties, moral anxieties and social issues, told entertaining and moving stories. At times it attacked the social problems and divisions of the age, and in the 1860s what came to be called "the Condition of England novel" challenged harsh industrialism and moral indifference, social suffering and ideological contradiction. Victorian novels came in prolix variety, but they were generally capacious, multi-narratived and episodic, and made no great claim as works of art. Then, in 1870, the leading figure of Victorian fiction, Charles Dickens, died suddenly at his home at Gad's Hill; the age of Thackeray and Trollope, the Brontës and Bulwer-Lytton, Mrs Gaskell and Wilkie Collins drew to a close. Collins wrote on to attain his greatest fame, though not for his best novels. Trollope kept writing to the decade's end, and in 1875 produced one of his finest and bitterest works, tellingly called *The Way We Live Now*, about an age that was losing all community and values, all but an economic purpose. In 1871 Charles Darwin published *The Descent of Man*, his second challenging account of human evolution, in 1873 Herbert Spencer his *Study of Sociology*; the age was beginning to revolt against itself. And the newer voices exploring the way we lived now saw a world shaped by Darwin and Spencer, Marx and John Stuart Mill – a world of fading religious certainties, evolutionary theories, political transformation, rising scientific discovery, quickening techno-logical growth. In 1872, Samuel Butler published his dystopian fantasy *Erewhon* (it – almost – spells "nowhere" backwards), a deeply ironic vision of an age devoted to money and machines which mocked many of the values of high Victorianism. He went further in his next novel, *The Way of All Flesh*, an attack on Victorian patriarchy, parenthood, hypocrisy and religious com-placency so iconoclastic it could not be published until after Butler's death in 1903 – making it, in effect, the first Edwardian novel. According to George Meredith, it was time to expose the

13

moral tone of the times to the searchlight of what he called "the comic spirit"; he did just that in his novel of Victorian moral hypocrisy *The Egoist* (1879). Many new and different voices sounded in the 1870s, and none more striking than Thomas Hardy, who came to notice with his third novel *Far From the Madding Crowd* in 1874, and whose underlying note was modern tragedy, the tragedy of passage from a religious to a materialist age.

Still, it was plain to see who, after the death of Dickens, was *the* great novelist of the changing late Victorian world. "George Eliot" – Marian Evans – was the moral conscience and artistic arbiter of British fiction. A woman writer working under a man's name, she reinforced the splendid androgyny of the novel, reconciling domestic and public, the sentimental and intellectual, the realist and romantic in one voice. She considered the novel a serious form and claimed it for moral reflection and human sympathy. She was a regional writer with a cosmopolitan mind, a historical novelist with a clear vision of the secular, humanistic process of the present, a writer who understood the great historical transformation of the age. In 1859, the year of *Origin of Species*, she published *Adam Bede*, a work that did much to give British fiction the same spirit of realism that was sweeping through the European fiction of Flaubert and Turgenev and Tolstoy. She explained her kind of art by comparing herself with the Dutch genre painters, realists of the commonplace. "All honour and reverence to the divine beauty of form!" she wrote in *Adam Bede*:

> Let us cultivate it to the utmost in men, women, and children – in our gardens and our houses. But let us love the other beauty too, which lies in no secret of proportion, but in the secret of deep human sympathy. Paint us an angel, if you can, with a floating violet robe, and a face paled with celestial light; paint us yet oftener a Madonna, turning her mild face upward and opening her arms to welcome the divine glory; but do not impose on us any aesthetic rules which shall banish from the region of Art

those old women scraping carrots with their workworn hands, those heavy clowns taking holiday in a dingy pothouse, those rounded backs and stupid weather-beaten faces that have bent over the spade and done the rough work of the world . . .

Eliot's was a realism of the middle ground, less a theory than a progressive social attitude. She explored the common, the customary, the provincial, finding "a course of delicious sympathy" in "faithful pictures of a monotonous homely existence, which has been the fate of so many more among my fellow-mortals than a life of pomp or absolute indigence, of tragic suffering or world-shaking actions." She wrote less of fashionable people or city life than the regions, usually the Midlands, setting many of her stories in the past, though they often showed her characters, especially her strong heroines, aspiring to the freedoms of the present and the future. If she could write felt provincial tragedy in *The Mill on the Floss* (1860), she could deal knowingly and directly with social problems and political reform in *Felix Holt, The Radical* (1866), a "Condition of England" novel that put her with Dickens and Disraeli. In 1872, when she published *Middlemarch*, subtitled "Scenes from Provincial Life," it was acknowledged her powers had reached their peak. The book looked vastly across the Victorian era, surveying the age of the first Reform Bill from the age of the second, capturing the time when liberalism, suffrage, the coming of the railways, the remaking of community, were issues, when the age she wrote in was beginning to take on its powerful shape. In 1876, the year James arrived in Britain, she published what proved her final novel, *Daniel Deronda*, a modern story set in the 1860s. It was her first treatment of the international social scene and political life, and James admired it. It was, he said, "full of the world."

James met Eliot on his previous visit to Britain in 1869, and was smitten. She was the "one marvel" of his visit, and he declared himself "literally in love with this great horse-faced blue-stocking," with "a larger circumference than any woman I have ever seen." He wrote warmly of her work, which he saw as the British equivalent to Flaubert, Turgenev and Tolstoy. She might lack the aesthetic exactness of a Flaubert, the scientific note of a Zola, the vast sweep of a Tolstoy; at times her plots could be mechanical, her devices clumsy. But she was an intellectual writer, who gave fiction emotional seriousness and profound moral reflection, whose concern was with the "rare, precious quality of truthfulness." Where the Victorian novel had often been ill-structured, episodic, a bundle of fragments, she saw the novel as an organic form (even though, he admitted, *Middlemarch* made "an indifferent whole"). Qualities like this would later lead Lord David Cecil, in his *Early Victorian Novelists* (1934), to call Eliot "the first modern novelist" – the writer who in the interests of truth to life and character, broke free of the schematic plots, sentimental moral convention, religious sentiments, and melodramatic devices so characteristic of Victorian fiction, her plots finding their own course through the exacting development of a character or a moral idea. James would have nodded. In the line of British fiction, to which he meant to contribute, she was the great example, the creator of the organic novel, made of truth to life and experience. Not surprisingly he set out to renew acquaintance, and on 1 November 1878 he called on her with a companion at her house in Witley, where she kept a famously unconventional ménage with her literary adviser and sexual partner George Henry Lewes. From James' account in his memoir *The Middle Years* (1917), he clearly had high hopes of the encounter. He knew Eliot, admired her, celebrated her in print. He plainly hoped that some acknowledgement of descent, some apostolic laying on of hands, would occur – that she would recognize, as he put it, that he was doing "her sort of work."[4]

The occasion, alas, did not go as planned. Tea was, James noted, "a conceivable feature of the hour"; it was not served. The visit was brief, then, as James and his companion were

[4] Henry James, *Autobiography*, ed. F.W. Dupee (New York, 1956), contains *A Small Boy and Others* (1913), *Notes of a Son and Brother* (1914), *The Middle Years* (1917). The story is also told in Gordon S. Haight, *George Eliot: A Biography* (Oxford, 1968).

going, Lewes told them to wait a moment, left, and returned with two books, saying, "Ah, those books – take them away, please, away, away!" The books, when inspected outside, proved to be the two volumes of *The Europeans*, James' new novel, which his companion had thoughtfully sent in advance. The episode upset James, though when he recorded it many years later it was to reach a finely Jamesian explanation: "there was positively a fine thrill in thinking of persons – or at least of a person, for any fact about Lewes was but derivative – engaged in my own pursuit and yet detached, by what I conceived, detached by a pitch of intellectual life, from all that had made it actual to myself." So he read what happened as proof of Eliot's purity and high intellectual detachment, an abstraction from the mundane so complete that the custom of writer calling on writer scarcely interested her. Indeed the event confirmed his belief, he said, that she was the one English novelist who possessed "a constant sense of the universal," the secret of her power. She was the novelist as moral perceiver, analytic observer, judge of values, the writer who always responded to the immense variety of life while always knowing the difficulties "with which on every side the treatment of reality bristles." Her characters had minds, their minds had feelings; she put "stirred intelligence" and "moral consciousness" at the centre of literature's actions. What did it matter about tea?

The afternoon probably had a sadder explanation. Lewes was seriously ill, and died later that month. Eliot's last novel was already written; she died in 1880, the last great Victorian novelist. Many of the great Victorian sages – Robert Browning, Herbert Spencer, T.H. Huxley – attended her notable funeral, and an age was done. But the tea-less tea-time had lasting effect on James. The next spring he sat down to write what would prove his best early novel, *The Portrait of a Lady*. It is his first real treatment of Britain, and it is probably no accident that it opens with a famous reference to the British tea-time: "Under certain circumstances, there are few hours in life more agreeable than the hour dedicated to the ceremony known as afternoon tea. There are circumstances in which, whether you partake of

17

the tea or not – some people of course never do, – the situation is in itself delightful." The trace of Eliot shows strongly on the novel, and when James wrote its preface – one of the remarkable series of self-conscious prefaces he sketched for the New York Edition of 1907–17 – he made the debt clear. The book's theme – "a certain young woman affronting her destiny" – comes, he said, from the freedom of action Eliot grants characters like Dorothea Brooke and Gwendolen Harleth, and the way she uses female consciousness as a discovering means for exploring moral and social experience. Just as important is the idea of the novel as an open form rather than a work of plotted convention, its self-discovering design coming from a character set "free" by the author – so in James's story Ralph Touchett sets Isabel Archer financially free to "affront" her destiny, though with ironic results. And when James famously speaks of "the perfect dependence of the 'moral' sense of a work of art on the amount of felt life concerned in producing it," he is plainly thinking of Eliot's dense realism, and claiming his own place in the same tradition. James' homage to Eliot was seriously meant, part of his ambition to be seen as a European realist, not an American romancer. Yet, like the tea-time episode itself, it reveals the considerable gap between them. The fact was that Eliot was a British Victorian writer at the close of her career, James an exiled modern novelist at the start of his.

Over the next four decades – James wrote on till his death in 1916 – his work would change fundamentally, and when he was done the British novel would be a very different creature, not least because of the way he had transformed it. For all her cosmopolitanism, George Eliot wrote from deep inside British culture. James possessed his different cosmopolitanism – what he called the American "joke," which knows that however real and dense European society is, it is not everything, in life or fiction. He knew "reality" in fiction was a created semblance of the real, not a direct representation of it, that the novel did not have to be a "loose, baggy monster," but could also be a fine formal thing, an art of selection, composition, refined aesthetic intelligence. The gap was even apparent in the painterly

18

comparisons each writer employed. Eliot's *Scenes from Provincial Life* followed the manner of past figurative Dutch genre painters: James' *Portrait of a Lady* was done in the fashion of a Whistler or a Sargent, followers of "Impressionism," announced in Paris in the 1870s (his preface explains the book is not intended as "an impersonal account of the affair in hand," but is "an account of somebody's impression of it"). In fact this whole later preface is no statement from a writer of Victorian moral seriousness, but from a self-conscious modern artist first aware of his own creative method. It celebrates Eliot, but deploys an aesthetic language we at once identify as modern: "The spreading field, the human scene, is the 'choice of subject,' the pierced aperture, either broad or balconied or slit-like and low-browed, is the 'literary form'; but they are, singly or together, as nothing without the posted presence of the watcher – without, in other words, the consciousness of the artist," James announces: "Tell me what the artist is, and I will tell you of what he has *been* conscious. Thereby I shall express to you at once his boundless freedom and his 'moral' reference." For James, the morality of fiction is itself an artistic construct, realism an aesthetic project that steeps "the whole matter in the element of reality." Above all the posted presence of the watcher, the artist ever-present in the text, is the guarantee of value. George Eliot's tea-less tea-party may have been an afternoon of Victorian social confusions. It is also as good a place as any for observing the great turn of the novel – the continuity and discontinuity, the bridge and the chasm, that moved fiction out of Victorianism and into the spirit of the modern.

4.

A jaundiced critic once divided Henry James's five decades of work into three phases: James the First, James the Second, and James the Old Pretender. We don't have to agree with the complaint to accept the notion – that James' work was a development through distinct and remarkable stages into an art of high complexity and modern difficulties. The first phase, largely devoted to James' exploration of the "international theme," takes us from the early slight *Watch and Ward* (1871), through the sharp irony of James' very New York novel *Washington Square* (1880), to *The Portrait of a Lady* (1881) – his first great book, recognizably a fiction in transition. *Washington Square* is an ironic tale of female imprisonment, about the romantic dreams of Catherine Sloper, who ends the book trapped and doing "basket-work for life." *The Portrait of a Lady*, though, has Isabel Archer as the young, strong-willed American girl set free, in motion through three different European societies – aristocratic Britain, socialite France, aesthetic Italy. Her search for experience is darkened, her freedom finally trapped, by the aesthetic sterility of Gilbert Osmond and the corrupt cunning of Madame Merle. The method is contemporary realism, what James called "solidity of specification," using exterior representation, authorial omniscience, an objectively "rounded" view of character. But the book is already "modern" in ways Eliot's are not – filled with displaced aristocrats, wealthy American tourists, businessmen and journalists, train timetables and the telegraph. Isabel is a "New Woman," and when she challenges Madame Merle's insistence that we are merely what society says we are, we see James' very American presumption that consciousness precedes social actuality. And in James concern with consciousness – the felt life and experiential consciousness of the characters, and the self-consciousness of the artist, the "posted watcher" in the text – is everywhere an issue. "The centre of interest throughout *Roderick [Hudson]* is Rowland Mallett's consciousness, and the drama is the very drama of that consciousness," James' preface notes of this early novel. The drama of consciousness in its struggle with the weight of society, fed by James' American awareness of the ambiguity of social codes and institutions, would lead his work through the phases that followed, out of his early realism toward the "modern" itself.

George Eliot's death in 1880 effectively marked the end of the Victorian novel. The 1870s had been a time of transition; the

1880s were a time of literary transformation, and writer after writer asserted the need to break free of Victorian conventions. Social theories were changing, rising expectations coupled with economic downturn fuelled political unrest, the logic of positivism and social determinism was increasingly accepted. New writers found the Victorian tradition both aesthetically and morally constraining, and they looked elsewhere, above all to Paris – where, in 1880, two writers well known to James published highly influential works. Guy de Maupassant brought out his frank tale of a fat working-class girl, *Boule de Suif*, and Emile Zola his sexually scandalous *Nana*, as well as the essay *Le Roman expérimental [The Experimental Novel]*, a literary manifesto for the rising trend of Naturalism. Zola used the term "experimental novel" in a different, more scientific, sense than we would now expect. His experiment was sociological and deterministic; he urged that, using laboratory-style methods and documentary and journalistic techniques, novelists should explore systems and processes, the laws of economics, heredity, environment and social evolution, to determine the fate of typical, representative characters. "A symmetry is established," he claimed, "the story composes itself out of all the collected observations, all the notes, one leading to another by the very enchainment of the characters, and the conclusion is nothing more than a natural and inevitable consequence." This was realism schematized; individuals were subject to universal systems, typified general laws; as Zola noted, "A like determinism will govern the stones of the roadway and the brain of man." Naturalism moved away from the liberal and the moral novel, the novel of independent consciousness; it acknowledged genetic drives, the power of heredity, economic determinism, the force of sexual instinct, the *bête humaine*, the animal in man. It perceived the age of the mass, the machine, the crowded and inhuman city; it looked at the ghettos, the age of commodities, rising department stores, the industrial conditions of workers, the visible aspects and processes of the modern itself. It claimed scientific rationality rather than religious or moral wisdom; it

21

was the art of the direct, the frank, the free, the contemporary – the modern tone itself.

For new British writers of the 1880s, Naturalism offered an exploring frankness and set a new mood. George Moore, from Ireland, was a painter as well as a novelist; he studied in Paris, and picked up Naturalism at first hand. "The idea of a new art based on science . . . an art that should explain all things and embrace modern life in its entirety . . . filled me with wonder," he said. He called his clever, erotic novel of bohemian life *A Modern Lover* (1883), presenting the Naturalist spirit as the spirit of the modern itself. *A Mummer's Wife* (1885) mixed determinist assumptions, aesthetic themes and sexual frankness, and was fiercely attacked. In a notorious response, *Literature at Nurse* (1885), Moore assaulted the moralistic and repressive views held by British critics of fiction. For the rest of the decade the "novel" became a field of controversy, not least because sexual representation was central to the issue. Part of the question was frankness in representing sexual activities; this became known as "Zolaism." But, as greater social, emotional and sexual opportunities for women grew, "New Woman" novels by writers like "John Law" (Margaret Harkness), feminist socialist author of *A City Girl: A Realistic Story* (1887), "George Egerton" (Mary Chavelita Bright), "Sarah Grand" (Francis Clark), "Iota" (Kathleen Caffyn), Charlotte Mew and Ada Leverson challenged George Eliot's portrait of passive female suffering with radical different images of women's needs and experience. What Thomas Hardy called "the immortal puzzle – given the man and woman, how to find a basis for their sexual relation," in other words the question of "modern marriage," became a central theme, creating a new explicitness that offended church, press, the lending libraries. The novel again became a place for treating dark social problems or engaging controversial issues, and, following the Naturalist code, it adventured freely into the world of the unexplored, the unexpressed, the unwritten, the unclassed. For George Gissing, the Yorkshire radical whose life was always to be marked by poverty and a sense of exclusion, Naturalism was less a form of art than a bitter social cry, the voice of the unrecorded, the "nether world." "We must dig deeper, get into untouched social strata," he said, and in books like *Workers in the Dawn* (1880), *The Unclassed* (1884), *Demos* (1886), and *The Nether World* (1889) – the very titles reveal their social themes – he did, exploring the facts of "grinding poverty," the pressures of the "competitive system," the bleak trapped lives and the grim struggle of the new urban melting-pot, creating "the working-class novel." For such writers and those who came after, like Arnold Bennett, Somerset Maugham and Robert Tressell, author of *The Ragged-Trousered Philanthropists* (1914), Naturalism marked the opening of the novel into an exploration of the social pains and contradictions of the bourgeois age.

James was no Naturalist. Impressed as he was by what he called its "magnificent treadmill of the pigeon-holed and the documented," he argued that the real adventures of the artistic spirit were precisely what was not reducible to "notes," that the novel's "air of reality" did not come from transcribed facts, that Naturalism was a realism wanting in reality, a simplification of fiction: "The individual life is, if not wholly absent, reflected in coarse and common, in generalized terms." Still, as over the Eighties controversy about the novel grew, he sided with the new trends, arguing that Naturalism had made the novel into a form at last open to artistic argument. As he put it in his key essay "The Art of Fiction" (1884): "Only a short while ago it might have been supposed that the English novel was not what the French call *discutable*. It had no air of having a theory, a conviction, a consciousness of itself behind it – of being the expression of an artistic faith, the result of choice and comparison . . . Art lives upon discussion, upon experiment, upon curiosity, upon variety of attempt . . ." On his own fiction the effect was plain. In 1884 he was indeed himself out on the magnificent treadmill, researching a novel about the political confusion, the social immensity, and the hard detail of contemporary London: "I have been all morning at Millbank prison (horrible place) collecting notes for a fictional scene," he wrote in a letter. "You see I am quite the Naturalist." That novel, *The Princess Casamassima*, and a second, *The Bostonians*, both came out in 1886; they mark a fundamental change in his work, and are the two chief novels of his middle period, James the Second. Both are novels of contemporary society, with strongly political themes. *The Bostonians*, set entirely in contemporary America, deals with the conflicting forces of American culture: art and commerce, North and South, men and women. "I wished to write a very American tale . . . and I asked myself what was the most salient and peculiar point in our social life," he noted. "The answer was: the situation of women, the decline of the sentiment of sex, the agitation on their behalf." The story is an ironically told tale of the battle for Verena Tarrant's soul between a radical New England feminist and a Southern gentleman, a tale of gender war. But it is also a novel about the modern city, about a Boston leaving the age of the old New England social and cultural ascendancy and becoming some-thing new: a Boston divided between "chimneys and steeples, straight, sordid tubes of factories and engine-shops, or the spare, heaven-ward finger of the New England meeting house."

In the same way James' London novel *The Princess Casamas-sima* – probably his most under-estimated work – is a very political novel about the modern city in the age of "horrible numerosities." It portrays an age when the spectre of inter-national terrorism was rising across Europe, as anarchist and Fenian outrages increased, a climate Joseph Conrad returned to in *The Secret Agent* twenty years later. A poor young man, Hyacinth Robinson, is caught up in an international revolution-ary conspiracy; as his name suggests, he finds himself split, between culture and anarchy, wealth and poverty, "Society" and those (some of them from "Society") who want to destroy society. It is a story of London as "the greatest aggregation in the world," a "great grey Babylon," divided between wealth and poverty, those who possess culture and those kept alien from it and who represent "the sick, eternal misery crying out of the darkness in vain." These are Naturalist themes, but in fact James' is less a Naturalist's city than an Impressionist's: "London damp: the way the winter fog blurred and suffused the whole place, made it seem bigger and more crowded, produced halos and dim radiations, trickles and evaporations, on the panes of glass." The impressions – "the assault directly made by the great city on an imagination quick to react" – are, James explains in his preface, primarily those of Hyacinth Robinson, an "obscure intelligent creature whose education should be almost wholly derived from them, capable of profiting by all the civilization, all the accumulation to which they testify, yet condemned to see these things only from outside." James rejects the great Naturalist sweep, and prefers "intensity" ("Without intensity where is vividness, and without vividness where is presentability?" he asks us). He moves close in, using what he called "concentrated individual notation," the world seen through the minds that live in it, so "placing in the middle of the light, the most polished of possible mirrors of the subject." *The Princess Casamassima* is a complex political novel, about strong social ideas and the unfolding of revolutionary events. But it is also about the paradox of culture, which is art and humanity, but also accumulation, wealth and style as power, enfolded in the fog of resentful poverty and exclusion. In fact James creates a modernist city novel, which takes its place with other works – Conrad's *The Secret Agent*, Biely's *Saint Petersburg*, Joyce's *Ulysses*, John Dos Passos' *Manhattan Transfer* – about the vast, fragmentary, many-cultured, many-voiced, Babylonian modern metropolis, which can only be seen as fleeting, synchronic, beyond wholeness or unity.

His novels of the Eighties began to lose James his public. The darkening of his social vision, the fragmentation of his once more solid world, the growing technical complexity and verbal density, the fact that his characters now seemed ambiguous rather than sympathetic, all made him seem difficult, and the reviewers attacked: "I have entered upon evil days," he noted. With his next book *The Tragic Muse* (1890) he returned to a more familiar subject, a portrait of upper-middle-class society, only to reveal how much his view of society had changed – it was no longer a place of experience and moral opportunity, but of concealments, deceptions, hypocrisies and shadows. The book depends on what the social psychologist Erving Goffman

– in his *The Presentation of Self in Everyday Life* (1959) – names "the dramaturgical analogy." In this view of the world the self is an actor and society a theatre, a stage where we present, through changing performances and false masks, the fiction that passes for our so-called substantial self. In the book Miriam Rooth is "a series of masks" – "her character was simply to hold you by the particular spell; any other – the good-nature of home, the relation to her mother, her friends, her lovers, her debts – was not worth speaking of . . . These things were the fiction and shadows; the representation was the deep substance." His fine short stories of this time show how preoccupied James had become with the question of "the real thing" – whether there was a solid observable reality, or whether all is art, artifice, illusion. The qualities James once called the stuff of fiction – "solidity of specification," "accumulated characters," "thickness of motive" – now took on a new ambiguity. Characters grow more self-conscious, less solid; art spreads from the artist to take in his subjects. It was this increasing sense of life's theatricality, as well as the relative failure of his recent novels, that took James off into the unfortunate adventures of writing for the stage. For several years in the early Nineties, thinking his kind of novel was dead, he did his main work for the theatre, an unhappy diversion of his talents which culminated in the failure of his play *Guy Domville* in 1895.

In retrospect this choice seems tragic. For the novel was now moving James' way, departing the Naturalism and political urgencies of the Eighties for the Aesthetic renewal of the Nineties. In 1891 the Zola disciple Paul Alexis availed himself of an important new technology and sent a famous literary telegram to an enquiring Parisian journalist (enquiring journalists were another phenomenon of the age). "Naturalism not dead," he wired. "Letter follows." In the letter that followed, Alexis claimed the scientific, reforming vision marked by Naturalism would come to mark twentieth-century literature. And Naturalism was not dead; Ibsen represented it in theatre (though his later works were already moving toward Symbolism), and young writers in Britain, America and Russia advanced its message. From Gissing and Arthur Morrison (*A Child of the Jago*, 1896) to Arnold Bennett and H.G. Wells, it would be a way of detailing the world of slum and provincial life, the experience of the rising lower middle class and the changes in sexual *mores*, the social problems and aspirations of the age. Even so, the magnificent treadmill was beginning to turn more slowly. Writers were wearying of prolix documentary, and life was proving a commodity in endless supply. Max Beerbohm smartly summed up the fact-sodden Eighties – "To give an accurate and exhaustive account of that period would require a far less brilliant pen than mine," he wrote – and Oscar Wilde in 1889 produced his anti-realist manifesto "The Decay of Lying," complaining about novels "so lifelike that no-one can possibly believe in their probability." In the *fin-de-siècle* shadows, Aestheticism, Art for Art's Sake, Decadence gathered. France again showed the way. In 1884 J-K. Huysmans brought out his mannered portrait of aristocratic decadence *A rebours (Against the Grain)*, which influenced Wilde; in 1890 P.A. Villiers de l'Isle-Adam produced his visionary prose-drama *Axel* ("Live? our servants will do that for us . . . Oh, the external world! Let us not be made dupes by the old slave"). New writers of "consciousness" like Paul Bourget and Edouard Dujardin – deviser of the "interior monologue" developed by James Joyce – came to attention; the philosopher Henri Bergson was elaborating his philosophy of "interior time," interposing between individual and interior world a concept of consciousness and inner memory that would strongly influence fiction (including that of his cousin by marriage, Marcel Proust). In 1890 Henry's brother William published his *Principles of Psychology*, not only an exploration of the new science revolutionizing modern thought – Sigmund Freud in Vienna was already exploring the notion of a secret and recessive unconscious forging human behaviour – but also the source of a famous literary phrase. Arguing that the mind is not the mirror of matter, but has its own motions and structures apprehending experience, James proposed: "In talking of it hereafter, let us call it the stream of thought, of consciousness, or of the subjective life." Interior

27

monologue, stream of consciousness, aesthetic subjectivity, creative intuition, the labyrinthine indirection of meaning, the shifting and impressionistic nature of registered reality – all became key preoccupations of the 1890s. If, as James said in "The Art of Fiction," the only thing we can demand of the novel in advance is that it be interesting, if novels "are as various as the temperament of man, and . . . successful in proportion as they reveal a particular mind, different from others," if the novel, in its broadest sense "a personal, a direct impression of life," was now coming to "self-consciousness," then the brew from which this "modern novel" would come was already forming in the aesthetic climate of the early Nineties.

Other deep changes were transforming fiction too. The lending libraries were losing their moral control, printing and publishing technologies were changing, the commercial marketplace was growing fast. "Cheap fiction" meant a new stratification of the audience (when George Gissing published his *New Grub Street* in 1891, the "nether world" he explored was not the urban poor but the new proletariat of writing itself), and "difficult fiction" grew harder to sell, though it was also increasingly acknowledged as "conscious art." All this increased James' dismay. But in 1897 he returned triumphantly to the novel, with two short, remarkable works, *The Spoils of Poynton* and *What Maisie Knew*. And now, in the changing climate, the point began to be seen, certainly by two of the most promising writers of the next generation, Joseph Conrad and Ford Madox Ford, who recognized *The Spoils* . . . as "the technical highwater mark of all James's work," and developed his methods. Even reviewers, notorious for being late, began to get it; one hailed *What Maisie Knew* as adding "a whole new conception of reality to the art of fiction." Not everyone welcomed late James, James the Old Pretender; even his friends admitted his gift for difficulty. Conrad agreed the man in the street would never read him; his good friend Edith Wharton, who generously diverted some of her own royalties to subsidize the badly selling New York Edition, said even she couldn't read the final works, even though some people thought she had written them.

Thomas Hardy felt he had "a ponderously warm manner of saying nothing in infinite sentences"; his once good friend H.G. Wells later attacked him viciously. The sense of difficulty was understandable. Some – not all – of the late books that followed are labyrinthine and indirect; his method of dictating them did not always help. But the important thing was that James' "painting" was losing its direct mimesis, becoming ever more an "impression," stressing, like contemporary painters, the dominance of the medium over the content, the way of seeing over the subject. The novel, James now emphasized, was not a reported "adventure." It was a composition, an "affair," a "doing" that composed its own vision, its illusion of reality. Realism had not left his work entirely, but the observed reality was no longer that of a moral community, an agreed common culture. It was a refracted thing, seen through angles of vision, through the evolving consciousness of its perceivers. And it was not so much a "dense society" that set a novelist in motion, but the "Things, always the splendid Things," that in *The Spoils of Poynton* make up "the sum of the world." Culture dissolves into possessions, commodities, *objets d'art*, generally with a price-tag attached. Similarly, sexual relations are not a sphere of romantic discovery but are complex transactions about things, rights, possession.

James' new, fragmentary, darkened world of experience comes out clearly in *What Maisie Knew*, the most cunning of his new novels. The title tells all; the key to the tale, the preface explains, is the young girl Maisie, the "central vessel of consciousness," through whose eyes the story is seen. What she knows or in childish "innocence" does not know – all she sees, feels, senses, registers or avoids – is what we get by way of story. The adult reader can intuit those things, above all sexual things, that Maisie does not know, though by the end we are not clear how much knowledge she possesses. For knowing is itself ambiguous, and the book itself refuses to provide its reader with a complete "knowledge." This is a tale of innocence not learning from but corrupted or blocked by experience; by limiting his tale to one "knowing" consciousness James has upturned the social spread and moral breadth of his earlier fiction. Innocence is a toy – Maisie is used as a token, a plaything, a message, by her adulterous and corrupt parents – and experience is not wisdom, which means innocence is itself an ambiguity. That theme passed on to the great ghost story James would tell as the century ended, *The Turn of the Screw* (1898). James was now fascinated with what one critic calls "the haunted house of Victorian culture," the shadow world behind the social façade that other writers like Stevenson (*Dr Jekyll and Mr Hyde*) and Wilde (*The Picture of Dorian Gray*) were exploring, and Gothic and the ghost story were becoming ever more popular as the age examined its own hidden spaces. James accepts many of the Gothic conventions: the strange country house, the governess, ambiguously placed between the master, her charges, and the other servants, her responsibility for protecting "innocence" while harbouring romantic dreams, her acceptance of mysterious duties. The great change he makes is to make this a "psychological" ghost story, based on odd angles of perception and ambiguous states of mind and emotion, as well as on the dangerous border between childish "innocence" and adult sexuality. The tale is deceptive; as the second narrator Douglas says, "The story *won't* tell . . . not in any literal vulgar way." The governess narrator may be repressed or deluded, and the story is filled with blanks and indirections, and finally refuses the conventional finality of fiction (it creates an "incomplete signification," as the modern critics say). In fact it leaves us, as James would say, within "the beautiful difficulties of art." Its ambiguities point to the problems of many later modern fictions and modern creativity – how "whole" is a story? how much of it should be told? where and why does closure come? is completeness desirable, since life and consciousness do not have concluded shapes? how do we make stories appear "true"? As James wrote his essay "The Future of the Novel" in 1899, looking round him as the century turned, he had good reason to say that the novel was at last coming to self-consciousness, and becoming a complex, speculative and modern art.

And if so he was becoming the modern master, the writer who had gone through the passage from realism and Naturalism, and come to aestheticism and now, increasingly, to Modernism. Living now at Rye in Sussex, he produced, over the turning of the century, and in a great creative burst, some of his most remarkable works. By now he had accepted he would never be a popular novelist, but he would be a discovering one. He produced the wry mannered social comedy of *The Awkward Age* (1899), the baffling ambiguity of *The Sacred Fount* (1901) – a work of incomplete investigation about the problem of reading and decoding human relations that has rightly been compared with the French *nouveau roman*. There was the symbolist *The Wings of the Dove* (1902), with its famous techniques of grammatical indirection ("She waited, Kate Croy, for her father to come in . . ."), with its implication for the indirectness of all human subjectivities and all human relations, but also the far more accessible *The Ambassadors* (1903), the tale of Lambert Strether, the man who comes to Europe in quest of a young artist and learns at last to see, to discover the nature of the impression, and so to live, learning the book's lesson: "Live all you can; it's a mistake not to." He returned to and rewrote the international novel in *The Golden Bowl* (1904), with its central image of the cracked bowl of loving human relations, which is related to similar cracks in all objects of desire. Here the social depth of Europe, the discovering innocence of America, turn back on themselves: the European aristocrat has the name of Prince Amerigo, while wealthy Americans collect and commodify the arts of Europe. In their different ways these books express the indirection of James' late discourse, "those sentences which delay exact significance to the end and even leave it problematic then, casting the reader on his impressions like a boat surrendered to a stream" – the discourse that is not just a way of telling the story, but *is* the story.[5] In all of them, as he said in his preface to *The Ambassadors*, there are hence two fundamental stories: "There is the story of one's hero and then,

[5] Millicent Bell, *Meaning in Henry James* (Cambridge, Mass., and London, 1991).

thanks to the intimate connection of things, the story of one's story itself."

"I sat for a long while with the closed volume in my hand going over the preface in my mind and thinking – that is how it began, that's how it was done," Conrad wrote on receiving the first volumes of the New York Edition, which came out along-side the final novels. James was now unmistakably the Master. What he sought to do was apparent not just in the fiction he wrote, but in what he wrote about fiction – in the key essays "The Art of Fiction" (1884), "The Future of the Novel" (1899), and "The New Novel" (1914); in these prefaces to the twenty-four-volume New York Edition (1907–17); in the extraordinary records he kept in his notebooks of his "germs" and "*données*," now available to us.[6] His late novels, as some contemporaries saw, are modern because they present a late nineteenth- and early twentieth-century world adrift from the old anchors and certainties, filled with anxieties of consciousness and unexpected structures of discovery. It is a world of impressionism, but also hard materialism, *belle-époque* lives and sudden wealth, business-men and tycoons and poor European princes, rising cultural anxieties about the blankness of experience and the cultureless void on which culture or meaning is overlaid. In all this James had come a long way from George Eliot's tea-less tea-time of 1878, his later books amending, subverting, or creatively mis-reading his earlier vision of realism. He had found, as he said, that the house of fiction had many windows, and reality was to be seen from many standpoints. The novel was no plain report on life, and its rules were born from within, from the potential of creative making. Novelists do not report but create, discover and compose and dramatize, and it is art that makes life and creates importance. Stories are not external tales, but self-investigating explorations, done through characters who are themselves consciousness in motion. Language is not what we see through; it is what we see with. James died in 1916 (shortly

[6] F.O. Matthiessen and Kenneth B. Murdock (eds.), *The Notebooks of Henry James* (New York, 1947).

after becoming a British citizen), and by then the importance of his work had come clear. Conrad and Ford had become his successors, and then a new generation of writers like Gertrude Stein, Virginia Woolf and Dorothy Richardson. His works, they saw, offered a double vision of fiction; they carried realism onward into modernism, and restored modernism to its origins in realism. It was also an international fiction, that contributed not just to the British novel but to the modernity of the novel in general. As Gertrude Stein, an American working over in Paris, claimed, perhaps it really took an American to see how modern he was: "Henry James is a combination of two ways of writing and that makes him a general a general who does something. Listen to it." Many writers did: the sequence from the James who wrote in homage to George Eliot to the James written to in homage by so many modern novelists is one of the key stories not only of British but of modern world fiction.

5.

Listening to James was important to many British novelists from the 1890s on. But there were other modern masters in his generation to listen to, some of a much more native kind. In 1914, D.H. Lawrence was in Germany and Italy, struggling to find the new fictional method that would let him write his great culture-reading novel *The Rainbow*. He wrote to a friend: "Have you got Lascelles Abercrombie's book on Thomas Hardy? . . . I am going to write a little book on Hardy's people." Lawrence did write his *The Study of Thomas Hardy*, though it was never completed and only appeared posthumously in *Phoenix* (1961).[7] But it had its deep impact on *The Rainbow* – one of those works where a writer, seeking to create a tradition for his own purpose, greedily rewrites and reinterprets another. Hardy thus became one of the great antecedents of modern British fiction, as indeed

[7] See Edward D. McDonald (ed.), *Phoenix: The Posthumous Papers of D.H. Lawrence* (London, 1961).

he did of modern poetry, and for Lawrence he marked the passage out of Victorian fiction to his kind of novel, just as James did for Conrad and Ford. James and Hardy belonged to the same literary generation, started their major work in the 1870s, and shared a mutual influence in George Eliot. Beyond that, they seemingly had little in common, and the paths away from them also seem to divide. Neither admired the work of the other. James spoke of "good little Thomas Hardy," but found his novels technically naive; Hardy said "James' subjects are those one could be interested in when there is nothing larger to think of." This was not surprising, for if they shared some common influence in George Eliot they drew on quite different sides of her work. James was the cosmopolitan who chose his own relation to the British tradition; Hardy was the provincial writer who by art and instinct extended what he saw as an already founded heritage, of themes, concerns, communities, communal language. The son of an American Swedenborgian whose "native land" was the wandering James family, and the builder's son from Dorset who lived and largely wrote from within the confines of the West Country, came to writing from different places, and developed different destinies for themselves, finally becoming probably the two great opposites of the late nineteenth-century novel in Britain. James had his "international theme" and Hardy had his indurant Wessex. James was the formalist, the writer of what Mark Schorer calls "technique as discovery," while Hardy wrote grainily about an ordinary world people recognized and hardships and sufferings they daily faced. James challenged and tested the role of the storyteller; Hardy accepted it, writing in an omniscient, choric, sometimes God-like way in what he considered a Godless world. James saw fiction as a discovery of knowledge, a careful apprehension of experience, and hungered for the sensations of "felt life," reached through art. Hardy felt experience as the ominous weight of life itself, and brooded tragically or stoically before it, making his characters not so much discover experience as suffer it. James let his plots discover themselves from their infant germs; Hardy subjected his characters to his inexorable plots, those plots to cosmic ironies. James' novels claim the freedom of form; Hardy's are schematically made, are written, as one admirer, Marcel Proust, observed, with the solid geometry of the master stonemason.

If Lawrence rightly considered Hardy to be a "modern" writer, it was for reasons quite different from those we tie to James. It had to do with his vision of a modern fate, a vision Lawrence quarrelled with but entirely understood. As E.M. Forster once said, "The fate above us, not the fate working through us – that is what is eminent and memorable in the Wessex novels"; Hardy had largely resolved the nature of the human condition, acknowledged the human irony, before he began his books. It was his aim of making fiction the field of a modern metaphysic, however arguable, that for Lawrence made him a writer to contend with. Hardy started off in a familiar world of culture, nature and British history, and turned it into drama, metaphor and crisis, making his Wessex not only a large regional landscape but a primal scene, a place of nature and of culture, of eternity and of social change. When, in late life, he produced his "Wessex Edition," he too divided his novels into three groups – very different, though, from those applied to James. There were the novels of "Character and Environment," the "Romances and Fantasies," the "Novels of Ingenuity," and Wessex was stage to all. He might write of it joyously, as in *Under the Greenwood Tree* (1872), his story of the Mellstock choir, a pleasant rural comedy with a sub-title that shadows George Eliot, "A Rural Painting of the Dutch School." But it could equally be the field for a very modern tragedy, as in *Jude the Obscure* (1895). With his third novel *Far From the Madding Crowd* (1874) he laid full claim to his region, making it what William Faulkner, constructing his own distinctive region of Mississippi in the next century, called his own "postage stamp of soil," on which all kinds of story could unfold. The writer – Hardy explained, when he tried to draw his novels together for the Wessex Edition – needs a "territorial definition of some sort to lend unity," a place part real and part dream, which would permit "a deeper, more essential, more transcendent handling."

For "that which is apparently local should be really universal," he said, expressing the faith of the local-colour movement that played so large a part in late nineteenth-century fiction right across Europe. But Wessex was not just an indurant land of nature; as Raymond Williams has said, it was a "border country . . . between custom and education, between work and ideas, between love of place and experience of change."[8]

Lawrence was surely right. From *Far From the Madding Crowd* onward, Hardy was a "modern" novelist, even if the mostly tragic fortunes of modernity were to be played out on a pastoral Wessex stage. That book's title, from Gray's "Elegy in a Country Churchyard," makes Hardy's claim to pastoral clear at once. This is a tale set in a space apart, and the name of the central character, Gabriel Oak, the long-enduring sheep farmer, tells us that some at least of the characters are imbued with nature's spirit. But it is plain that Wessex is a wide stage, onto which come figures and influences from the world elsewhere; it is also plain that the nature Hardy is reflecting on is not the illuminating guide and wise friend of the British Romantic poets. It is prehistoric, born of a druidic, pagan past. It is subject to the cosmic workings of an indifferent and irrational universe, a place of vast transitions and modernizing change, suffering the shifts of consciousness that move us painfully from one historical age to another. Hardy may not have been a highly educated writer; that shows in the heavy hand of some of his prose. But he was widely read, above all in the writers of nineteenth-century pessimism: Darwin, Spencer, Mill, Schopenhauer, von Hartmann, the philosophers of the age of blind evolution, random process, the Unconscious Will. With the publication of Darwin's *Origin of Species* (1859) and *The Descent of Man* (1871), conceptions of progress had turned to theories of chance, humanist hopes into cosmic anxieties, eternal purpose into random selection. In an age caught between God and science, continuity and unbidden change, new troubled speculations about individuality and process began to arise. As

---

[8] Raymond Williams, *The English Novel from Dickens to Lawrence*, cited above.

William James would observe in 1895: "the visible surfaces of heaven and earth refuse to be brought by us into any intelligible unity at all. Every phenomenon that we could praise there exists cheek by jowl with some contrary phenomenon that cancels all its religious effect on the mind. Deity . . . rolls all things together to a common doom." Hardy could have written this, it may well have been guided by his pervasive, gloomy vision; but, for many more than Hardy, this was the age of "pessimism."

Over three decades and fourteen extremely various novels – comedies, tragedies, romances, tales of ingenuity – Hardy went on to explore the British world under the gaze of that dark vision. *The Return of the Native* (1878), the first of the great novels, is set back in the 1840s; like many Victorians Hardy constantly returned to the historical novel. The book is dominated by the primal scene of Egdon Heath, with "its lonely face, suggesting tragic possibilities," which will emerge. On the heath, individuals are "solitary atoms of life," and live in a dangerous natural and cosmic space: "Above the plain rose the hill, above the hill rose the barrow, and above the barrow rose the figure. Above the figure was nothing that could be mapped elsewhere than on a celestial globe." Individuals like the "figure," Eustacia Vye, either struggle aspiringly up from nature into that larger space, or, like the cosmopolitan traveller Clym Yeobright ("Mentally he was in a provincial future, that is, he was in many points abreast with the central town thinkers of his date"), are blindly returned to nature, with their burden of "modern nerves." They live in a universe neither moral nor immoral, but unmoral ("there may be consciousness, infinitely far off, at the other end of the chain of phenomena, always striving to express itself, and always baffled and blundering, just as the spirits seem to be," Hardy once wrote). They perform some evolutionary task, Darwinian or Lamarckian, but it is not clear by what need or to what end; meanwhile the mind is "adrift on change, and harassed by the irrepressible new," for the eternal space is also a changing history, a passage, Hardy says here, "from the bucolic to the intellectual life." His pessimism was not entire, nor was it universal. When readers disliked the grimness of *The Return of the Native*, he gave them one of his light romantic works, *The Trumpet Major* (1880), set back in the Napoleonic Wars. Still, it was that pessimism, that sense of the futile evolution of history, that awareness of life's struggle and humanity's ironic fate, that made him one of the deepest as well as most dissenting voices of late-Victorian fiction.

Like James', Hardy's work was plainly changed by the changed fictional climate of the 1880s. No more than James could he be a conventional Naturalist; his view of irony, fate and chance was distinctive, and nothing like Zola's environmental or genetic determinism. It came from a kind of cosmic brooding, an innate pessimism, which Lawrence correctly saw as a tragic metaphor of the human condition. He certainly did not write a fictional documentary, and observed that " 'realism' is not art." His fiction was architectural, poetic, symbolistic, and at times surreal, and utterly distinguished from most Naturalism by the cosmic vastness of the stage on which it is set. Naturalism, too, was generally an affair of cities, crowds and masses; it could be said that Hardy returned it to the world of nature it had, after all, come from. But even while he espoused its sexual frankness, Hardy was not concerned, as such, with the *bête humaine*; indeed it was precisely the struggle of consciousness away from the animal about which he wrote best.[9] For all their tales of sexuality, erroneous desire, misplaced passion, and modern marriage leading to modern divorce, for all that the aspirations of his characters are repeatedly held in check by the failure of the evolutionary struggle for growth and survival, that struggle is always felt within, by the living and self-conscious mind, as it develops its own desires and dreams, its hungers of consciousness, its distinctive individualisms. Admittedly, while humankind has consciousness, the forces that

---

[9] What was the *bête humaine?* Zola gave one important explanation in the preface he wrote for *Thérèse Raquin* (1867): "I had only one desire: given a highly sexed man and an unsatisfied woman, to uncover the animal side of them and that alone, then throw them together and note down with scrupulous care the sensations and actions of these creatures. I simply applied to two living bodies the analytical method that surgeons apply to corpses . . ."

control it have not, or at least they reject human intention. In *Two on a Tower* (1882), he attempted to treat this lyrically, aiming to set "the emotional history of two infinitesimal lives against the stupendous background of the stellar universe." But with the final group of late novels – *The Mayor of Casterbridge* (1886), *The Woodlanders* (1887), *Tess of the D'Urbervilles* (1891), *Jude the Obscure* (1895) – which form the major era of his work, he acknowledged that for his central theme the real mode was tragedy.

In these books themes that plainly belong to the age of Naturalism emerge as something larger. Here Wessex, as a choric stage, dissolves into a general modernizing process. And these are stories of isolated individuals, struggling for consciousness against the changing world: modern tragedies, works of ironic fatality, temperamental passion. The drunkenness, intemperate anger and stubbornness that eventually destroy the aspiring Michael Henchard in *The Mayor of Casterbridge* can be seen as Naturalist forces as much as tragic inner flaws, and chance and circumstance conspire in his downfall; but so does the historical cycle and the rise of the new order represented by Farfrae. *The Woodlanders* is an oddly sunny book for late Hardy, and his own favourite, but it too is about a world blighted by destiny, blind chance, corrupted growth, failed sexual relations. Above all there is the "Unfulfilled Intention": "Here as everywhere, the Unfulfilled Intention, which makes life what it is, was as obvious as it could be among the depraved crowds of a city slum. The leaf was deformed, the curve was crippled, the taper was interrupted; the lichen ate the vigour of the stalk, and the ivy slowly strangled to death the promising sapling." Tess of the D'Urbervilles is, as the subtitle defiantly says, "a pure woman," a victimized social heroine of nineteenth-century fiction, trapped between nature and public morality – a familiar Naturalist theme – but equally the victim of "the Unfulfilled Intention." As both Durbeyfield and D'Urberville, she is divided both in her social and her genetic inheritance, and she equally suffers from "the mutually destructive interdependence of flesh and spirit." Seduced and betrayed, she finally hangs for murder, in what Hardy sees as a tragic cycle: "The President of the Immortals (in the Aeschylean phrase) had ended his sport with Tess." *Jude the Obscure* is also about the "deadly war waged between flesh and spirit," and is "a tragedy of unfulfilled aims." Jude Fawley is again seeking to evolve from a primitive to a civilized existence, only to be defeated by what seem eternal forces. Some are social, born of the pressures of class and the limits of education, "the artificial system of things"; others are larger powers − crossed destinies, the competing energies of survival and destruction, nature as rank abundance and nature as rank deceit, "man and senseless circumstance," which has its way in the end.

But, as Lawrence, reading Hardy for his own purposes, noticed, these "modern tragedies" are important and modern not simply for their sense of social victimization, nor their vision of cosmic gloom and life's little ironies. Their strength lay in the instinct of the modern itself − Hardy's sensuous understanding of the living struggle of human consciousness, the battle of the human flesh and spirit, and the metaphysical force with which he saw the relation between the world of social experience and individual felt experience of being, both in society and in nature. Hardy's work was praised, or blamed, for its Olympian detachment, its highly plotted narrative, its familiar philosophizing: "What," asked Edmund Gosse in his review of *Jude*, "has Providence done to Mr Hardy that he should rise up in the arable land of Wessex and shake his fist at his Creator?" But Lawrence noticed something different, an intense intimacy between the author and the inner life of his created characters. Tess herself acknowledges the world to be "a psychological phenomenon"; meanwhile Hardy intimately follows her as she intensifies "the natural processes around her until they seemed part of her own story." Similarly Jude Fawley's fate may be plainly plotted from without, but it is also deeply felt from within, as a state of consciousness. As a child growing up toward adult awareness, Jude looks out from under his straw hat and feels life as "a sort of shuddering": "All around you there seemed to be something glaring, garish, rattling, and the noises and glares hit upon the little cell called your life, and shook it, and warped it." Hardy's novels, especially the late ones, were, as Lawrence saw, about the struggling aspiration of human consciousness and its vital energy to grow away from nature or Wessex and become more than it is. In the event that aspiration is stifled, by social convention or moral conditioning, by blind change and universal fatality, or else by what in *Tess* is called "the chronic melancholy which is taking hold of the civilized races with the decline of belief in a beneficent Power." By Lawrence's more modern, more vitalist, more Nietzschean view of things, this means that what holds his characters, and the world of nature and society, back from emergence and realization is on the one hand their own "weak-life flow," and on the other Hardy's flawed metaphysic, his post-Darwinian pessimism. At the same time they contain the essential struggle, the energy and desire of human consciousness and human evolution to pass from the pre-modern to the modern age. Lawrence's own books could therefore take up the story, and they do, only to develop, in a process of evolutionary return, toward tragedy, the tragedy of consciousness that invests his own late books forty years on.

This is Lawrence's Hardy, but it points us to what was so modern in his work. For modernity is indeed one of Hardy's most essential themes, especially in the late fiction. *Jude the Obscure*, his last and most powerful novel, is the story of the endeavour to reach a new awareness, through social advancement, through education, through new emotion. Jude, with his orphaned, suffering, struggling consciousness, is an uprooted modern self, seeking a new culture that will lift him out of primal nature into spirituality and civilization, from Arabella to Christminster. Sue calls herself a "modernist", and is Hardy's vision of the "New Woman," educated, sexually tense, strangely fragile, potentially destructive, making her break with the past yet haunted by fatality. Both of them see themselves as "pioneers," only to find the time is not yet ripe: "Our ideas were fifty years too soon to be any good to us." "We are horribly sensitive, that's what's wrong with us," explains Jude. It is a

41

novel of lost roots and rapid motion, of parts of the culture in contrast and conflict, of quick passage, by train, from one world to another. Jude begins obscure, and ends obscured; his life and desires are not completed but curtailed, his significance is never fulfilled – or not in the novel that bears his half-cancelled name, though later fiction would be filled with Judes no longer obscure. Hardy sees him as a modern hero, Sue as a version of the modern heroine, but both live in a world that returns them to fatality and insignificance. In a parable of human wishes aborted, the story ends on the grim spectacle of child suicide, a sign of the "coming universal wish not to live." This is almost too apocalyptic, except that modern fiction since has again and again returned, like Hardy, to cosmic irony and darkness.

It is relevant that Hardy's own hopes for the novel as a form were aborted too. *Tess* was his endeavour to write of a publicly victimized woman, and not surprisingly it was attacked as such: "if this sort of thing continues, no more novel-writing for me," Hardy noted in his journal. Yet *Jude*, his novel not of the New Woman but of the New Man, struggling against "men and senseless circumstance," was a yet greater challenge, with its ironic contrast "between the ideal life a man wished to lead and the squalid real life he was fated to lead." It was widely read, and widely attacked, in part for its sexual frankness – the famous hog's pizzle thrown at Jude by Arabella – and its decadent "morbidity" – the killing of the young children by "Father Time," who obviously embodies that spirit of *fin du globe* that Max Nordau attacked in his book *Degeneration*, published in the same year. Hardy's novel was assaulted as immoral by the critics ("Even Euripides, had he been given to the writing of novels, might well have faltered before such a tremendous undertaking," said one), rejected by the lending libraries, condemned by the church, burned by an Anglican bishop; "the experience completely curing me of further interest in novel-writing," Hardy explained later in a bitter preface. There was in fact one more notable novel, *The Well-Beloved* (1897), which was admired by Proust, but it had mostly been written in 1892. Thus from 1895 to his death in January 1928,

Hardy concentrated on poetry, the form in which he felt happiest, and here he did some of his finest work. His *Wessex Poems* came out in 1898; today he is acknowledged as among the most important of our early modern poets. It seems ironic, if not Hardyesque, that, just before the novel really began to lay full claim to its new freedoms, just before James' career opened out into its late phase, Hardy's collapsed – meaning that he will always be seen as essentially a late-Victorian novelist. As his career in fiction ended, H.G. Wells' began, and the story of those Judes who no longer felt so obscure began to be written. But the essential onward link was indeed with Lawrence, who was able to convert Hardy's vision of social, sexual and vitalist aspiration, of the new self struggling toward birth out of the historical culture, into a new modern myth. Hence "where *Jude* ends *The Rainbow* begins," it has been said.[10] By the end of the century James had already begun one tradition of exploratory modernity in the novel, the novel as self-consciousness, the novel as "affair." Hardy had bequeathed another, more communal and choric, its sense of crisis differently affirmed, and that went on too, through Lawrence and into contemporary fiction, including that of David Storey, John Berger and Raymond Williams, writers for whom the struggle of consciousness out of nature, into culture, has been essential to the modern British novel.

6.

By the mid-1880s, the state and nature of the novel was a matter of public argument. James' essay "The Art of Fiction" (1884) was a reply to a lecture by Walter Besant, and proposed a much wider and more open view of the genre: "We must grant the novelist his subject, his idea, his *donnée*; our criticism is applied only to what it makes of it." This essay in turn provoked a reply, or rather "A Humble Remonstrance," from a

---

[10] In Ian Gregor, *The Great Web: The Form of Hardy's Major Fiction* (London, 1974).

young Scots novelist, Robert Louis Stevenson, who wanted to widen the definition further. The remonstrance was probably humble because James had gone out of his way to praise Stevenson's romance of the year before, *Treasure Island* (1883), as "delightful, because it seems to me to have succeeded wonderfully in what it attempts," and the two writers in fact became close friends. But Stevenson was keen to establish that what he was attempting, the "romance," was indeed as import-ant and central to fiction as the "solidity of specification" and "the intense illusion of reality" commended by James. Romance, action and escape were also essential fictional materials: "The novel which is a work of art exists, not by its resemblances to life, which are forced and material, as a shoe must still consist of leather, but by its immeasurable distance from life, which is designed and significant, and is both the method and the meaning of the work." As a Scot, Stevenson was a follower of Scott and the romance tradition, and he was in reaction against the social and moral emphasis of what even the American James called "the English novel." He was also a Scot in revolt, against the Presbyterian realism of his Edinburgh childhood, and during the 1870s he had won a reputation with accounts of his adventurous European travels. He delighted in the world of daydream and fantasy as a means of escape into the life of the imagination: "Fiction is to grown men what play is to a child," he said. He made his love of the wonderworld of story plain in his early collection *The New Arabian Nights* (1882), while *Treasure Island* – a story of, as James nicely put it, "murders, mysteries, islands of dreadful renown, hairbreadth escapes, miraculous coincidences and buried doubloons" – proved one of the most successful novels of its day, and made even the boys' book seem worthy of serious attention. When *Kidnapped* (1886), set in the Jacobite Rebellion, appeared, James was again warm in his praise, saying the book showed a high "imagination of physical states." *Kidnapped* merged the boys' book with the Scots historical romance; seeing the story from the standpoint of the boy David Balfour, Stevenson was able to give the book a dream-like motion and a sense of adventurous action that still renders it legendary.

Though he admitted that his novels, which were enormously popular, had a considerable element of "Tushery," Stevenson was determined to establish that he was no naive storyteller but a self-conscious artist. In fact, so prolix and various were the subjects of his writing that, right up to his death at the age of 44, he still seemed to be in search of his essential style and theme. Nonetheless he was enormously productive, the exemplary popular novelist, a writer who created or reconstructed a wide variety of different fictional genres. There was the genre of the regional romance, developed in *The Master of Ballantrae* (1889), *Catriona*, sequel to *Kidnapped* (1893), and the unfinished *Weir of Hermiston* (1896), which conferred on Scots historical writing a whole new identity. There were works of fantasy, children's tales, stories of travel and high adventure, like *The Black Arrow* (1888). Indeed there were many Stevensons, from the author of the thrilling boys' book to the artist of complex literary sophistication. His claims for "romance," as a primal space for imaginative discovery, and indeed as a region where action and intellect, technique and flamboyant fantasy, highly literary and highly popular forms could happily lie down together, did a great deal to reverse the drive toward realism and Naturalism that had shaped most serious fiction ever since the 1850s; the cause of "romance" influenced not simply the popular novelists – the Hentys and the Haggards – but James and Conrad. Throughout the twentieth century Stevenson has continued to win important admirers, not the least of them that master of postmodern fantasy and early magic realism, Jorge Luis Borges. Meanwhile his own life became an adventurous travelling romance, a search – like his fictions – for worlds elsewhere, which led him finally to Samoa, as distant as possible from the Scots origins he both honoured and revolted against; here he died suddenly of a brain haemorrhage in 1894.

But no book was more important to modern fiction, nor more revealing of the divided nature of its author's imagination, than the book that became one of the most successful, expressive

works of the 1880s, *The Strange Case of Doctor Jekyll and Mr Hyde*
(1886). In it Stevenson went back into the tradition of Gothic
romance, with its awareness of mirrored lives, threatening
doubles, strange powers released by the abuse of science, which
lead the mind out of the world of reality and reason and into
darkness, duplicity, otherness, metamorphosis. But, just as
James was, Stevenson was looking inside "the haunted house of
Victorian culture," and this tale of the *homo duplex* – the man
split between a respectable public self and a hidden, violent and
animal double – was a fable that touched some of the deeper
moral anxieties of the age. The book's essential message is
"Man is not truly one, but truly two," and it touched many
chords. It acknowledges the Naturalist concern with the animal
in man, the *bête humaine*, but it equally shares the decadent
fascination with narcissism so strong in Aestheticism. Jekyll
himself expounds on "the profound duplicity of life," and the
book engaged with increasing scientific curiosity about the
unconscious self, the hidden *id*, unspoken in an age of repression
and strict morality, that Freud would soon explore. If the theme
is sensational, the subject is psychological, the technique complex. This is, like many Gothic novels, the story of an investigation, and prefigures the rising popularity of the detective
story; in fact Arthur Conan Doyle would introduce the public
to his "unofficial detective" Sherlock Holmes, man of medicine,
science, and deduction, chasing strange crimes in the London
fog, in *A Study in Scarlet* the next year. So the plot involves yet
more doubling: the lawyer Utterson, who investigates the
mystery, explains "If he be Mr Hyde . . . I shall be Mr Seek."
There is yet another doubling: beneath the social surface of
bourgeois London life lies a darker world, and the city of
civilization hides in its heart dark secrets and criminal selves.
Creating his doubled world, Stevenson was introducing late-
Victorian culture to one of its strongest themes, one which
would obsess the dying of the century and the entire spirit of
Decadence itself, and compound its sense of unease. The theme
of the doubled self in the doubled city would appear in its
Decadent form in Oscar Wilde's *The Picture of Dorian Gray*

(1891), where the ambiguity is brought into the centre of art itself. In Wilde's version, Dorian becomes ever more corrupt in life, but holds on to his golden youth. Meanwhile his portrait in the attic ages and decays, art expressing the reality as the reality turns into art. The portrait becomes the double; when it must be destroyed ("It had been like a conscience to him . . . He would destroy it"), Dorian himself ages and dies.

Stevenson's importance lay in his challenge to realism, his clear proof that the age of documentary Naturalism was also open to myth and exotic fantasy. His defence of the "romance" and his re-exploration of Gothic were important campaigns of the 1880s, and encouraged the proliferation of forms that followed as the popular market for fiction expanded. It was because of the enormous success of *Treasure Island* that H. Rider Haggard embarked on *King Solomon's Mines* (1885), a boys' tale of male quest through the adventurous landscape of Africa. Haggard's book – there would be many more of the kind, from the adventures of G. A. Henty to the novels of Kipling – depended on the fact that the late-Victorian age was one of expanding imperial horizons, as an ever greater part of the world map came under Western political, economic or imaginative domination. As a result what Martin Green calls "dreams of adventure, deeds of empire" became key fables of the age.[11] Both in Britain and the no less imperialistic USA, tales of manly or boyish adventuring into the unknown and the dangerous – into distant landscapes, new frontiers, far-off wars and tribal conflicts – became a highly popular form, and the lost city, the missing treasure, the hidden tomb, the undiscovered tribe, the law of the jungle and the call of the wild, recaptured their place in fiction. What Stevenson called "romance" need no longer be set in history; it could follow the

[11] Martin Green, *Dreams of Adventure, Deeds of Empire* (London, 1980): "My argument will be that the adventure tales that formed the light reading of Englishmen for two hundred years and more after *Robinson Crusoe* were, in fact, the energizing myth of English imperialism." See also Alan Sandison, *The Wheel of Empire: A Study of the Imperial Idea in Some Late Nineteenth Century and Early Twentieth Century Fiction* (London and New York, 1967).

reaches of Empire, the tracks of exploration, the battlegrounds of imperial wars. "Romance" was no story of love, but of adventure and travel, an exploration, a voyage into mythic space, a tale of discovery or heroism. The new boys' papers promoted it, in part as an antithesis to the "morbid realism" and the *fin-de-siècle* sensibilities that seemed to be infecting life, and fiction, at home. When Nordau's *Degeneration* appeared in 1895, many read it as a warning against the kind of novels Hardy and Wilde wrote, to which works of spirited adventure, like Rider Haggard's, offered a very welcome contrast.

"Ah! this civilization, what does it all come to?" asks Allan "Hunter" Quatermain, the African explorer and Haggard's narrator in *King Solomon's Mines*, putting the big question of the day. His answer – escape into nature in the form of the African wild – proved so popular Quatermain came back in fourteen more tales, a frontiersman almost as popular as Fenimore Cooper's "Leatherstocking," that free spirit who had wandered the American frontier a hundred years before. In the second story, *Allan Quatermain* (1887), Haggard spelled out his message of nature against modern civilization ever more clearly. "Nineteen parts of our nature are savage, the twentieth civilized, but the last is spread out over the rest like the blacking on a boot, or the veneer over a table; it is on the savage that we fall back in emergencies." Haggard, like his fellow writers of the modern adventure, Henty and Kipling, was maybe not so far from Naturalism after all. And as for the "emergencies" in question, Elaine Showalter is no doubt right to suggest that one of them is indicated by the very title of *She* (1887); they were women.[12] This was Haggard's most successful novel, and the story of a quest for the eternal woman, Ayesha, the white queen of the mysterious African land of Kor, "she who must be obeyed." With her secret of eternal life, she constructs an everlasting matriarchy, an ageless female principle. But though she must be worshipped, she can be challenged and defeated when things go too far. Like

[12] See Elaine Showalter, *Sexual Anarchy: Gender and Culture at the Fin de Siècle* (London, 1991).

Dorian Gray, she finally perishes from her own eternal beauty, burned up in her own flame. However, the rules of romance are generally permissive. When her story proved enormously successful, she managed to reappear for the sequel, *Ayesha*, in 1905.

7.

The fictional arguments that raged through the 1880s – about Realism and Naturalism, Aestheticism and Romance – were really part of a larger issue of the time: the very nature and spirit of the "modern" or the "new" itself. When Walter Pater in his study *The Renaissance* (1873) talked of "modern sensations," or George Moore called his novel of 1883 *A Modern Lover*, or that same year Georg Brandes celebrated the "men of the modern breakthrough," people knew more or less what was meant: an alertness to the fragile moods of a time of change, a sense of transition and transience, a new manner of behaviour, a fresh reaching out to the forces that would shape the future. By the end of the decade, as a new century loomed closer, the issue intensified. "New" was the new word of 1889. Right across Europe belief grew that thinkers like Ibsen, Zola, Nietzsche, Weber and Durkheim were opening wide the doors to a time of transformation, a "new age." That was the year Europe saw *Ghosts*, Ibsen's powerful play about the way the past can taint the sunlit hopes of the present. It was the year Nietzsche went mad, still publishing his apocalyptic works: "Only the day after tomorrow belongs to me." In that year the French celebrated the Centennial of the French Revolution by erecting the Eiffel Tower, which the historian Roger Shattuck has described as "in its truculent stance . . . the first monument of Modernism."[13] It was a work of mechanical abstraction, later much celebrated by those who called themselves "Futurists," built to dominate a great Exposition of a kind with which the century had grown

---

[13] See Roger Shattuck, *The Banquet Years: The Origins of the Avant Garde in France, 1885 to World War I* (New York, rev.ed., 1968).

familiar, designed to display the emerging technologies that marked the new stage the industrial revolution had reached, and were bringing fresh inventions and systems into every city, street and home. Indeed the hero of the Exposition was not a Frenchman at all, but an American, Thomas Alva Edison, "the Wizard of Menlo Park," the "Magician of the Century," inventor of the telegraph, the phonograph and the electric tramway. Edison's incandescent bulbs lit up the fair, as they would light the streets of most of the European cities before long; meanwhile that year Edison was developing the Kinetoscope, the source of modern film. Evidently the modern meant not just new sensibilities but new technologies. Hence "future fiction" – in the wake of Jules Verne – was becoming the rage, and Edison appeared in that too. In 1886 Villiers de l'Isle Adam, aesthete and influence on Oscar Wilde, in his novel *L'Eve future (The Future Eve)*, has Edison inventing a female android to give the hero, a British nobleman, the sexual solace he cannot find in human form. As the American historian Henry Adams, a tireless visitor to the great exhibitions of the end of the century, observed, the human race was moving from the age of the Virgin to the age of the Dynamo, and from the universe to the multiverse.

The "new" came even to Britain. Admittedly the British book of 1889 was Jerome K. Jerome's *Three Men in a Boat*, a suburban clerkly comedy that would lead on to George and Weedon Grossmith's *The Diary of a Nobody* (1892), the very ordinary and politely bourgeois story of Mr Pooter, of The Laurels, Brickfield Terrace, Holloway. British suburbanism flourished, but "The Red Flag" was written, after a dock strike. Ernest Vizetelly, publisher of Zola and Maupassant, was sent to prison for foulness; but George Gissing published his Naturalist classic *The Nether World* and G.B. Shaw his *Fabian Essays*. Aestheticism declared itself with Wilde's *The Decay of Lying*, which asserted that "Art is our spirited protest, our attempt to teach Nature her proper place." "The Nineties began in 1889 and ended in 1895," Richard Ellmann has noted, writing of the space between Wilde's triumph and his trial. "At least the Wildean Nineties did so, and without Wilde the decade would never have found its character."[14] In 1889 a writer James dubbed "the infant monster" came from nowhere (in fact from the imperial outpost of Lahore, India) with several already published books hot and ready for British reissue; so Rudyard Kipling won sudden fame with *Plain Tales from the Hills* and *Soldiers Three*. That year a Polish sea-captain calling himself "Joseph Conrad" resigned command of the *Otago* and, awaiting a vessel to take him up the Congo, rented a villa in Pimlico and began work on an imperial romance about the Malay archipelago, *Almayer's Folly*. The "new" in fact was everywhere: "The range of the adjective gradually spread until it embraced the ideas of the whole period, and we find innumerable references to the 'New Spirit,' the 'New Humour,' the 'New Realism,' the 'New Hedonism,' the 'New Unionism,' the 'New Party,' and the 'New Woman,'" reports Holbrook Jackson in his brilliant book *The Eighteen Nineties* (1913).[15] It meant many things, from the Victorian and Celtic Twilight to the New Jingoism, from Decadence to "future fiction." The "new arts" were forever in the news: there were many more newspapers, and the "New Journalism" flourished in a decade that saw the yellow press as well as the *Yellow Book*. This was a time of dawns and twilights, aubades and nocturnes. Naturalism continued, reinforced by the new socialism and the new sociology, dealing with all that went unexplored and unacknowledged: poverty, prostitution, the provinces. But it intersected with the arts of a time intensely self-conscious about style, mannerism, fragile sensation, veiled symbols, sexual ambiguities. This was, said Jackson, a "decade of a thousand movements," of Naturalism and Impressionism, Aestheticism and Symbolism, the "novel" and the "romance," which generally meant a division not just in form but in the literary marketplace, for the "novel," like

[14] Richard Ellmann, *Oscar Wilde* (London, 1987). Also see John Stokes, *In the Nineties* (New York and London, 1989), and Malcolm Bradbury, David Palmer and Ian Fletcher (eds.), *Decadence and the 1890s* (London, 1979).

[15] Holbrook Jackson, *The Eighteen Nineties: A Review of Art and Ideas at the Close of the Nineteenth Century* (London, 1913; reissued 1988, with an introduction by the present author).

"aestheticism," stood for high art and "romance" for popular literature.

For other things were new. The entire marketplace of the novel was shifting, as the lending libraries declined in influence and the cheap book increasingly appeared on the new bookstalls meaning that novels could now be slim and elegant productions from opulent publishers or cheap volumes sold from the news agencies. The number of new novels doubled over a decade that saw the rise of the literary agent and the growth of literary commerce, at which some writers were good and others were not. So there was what George Gissing announced as "New Grub Street" in his novel of that title in 1891. Now the poverty Gissing naturalistically examined was literary poverty, as various kinds of writers in different ways confronted the facts of literary commerce (the hero Edward Reardon refuses to supply "good, coarse, marketable stuff for the world's vulgar," while his wife protests that "Art must be practised as a trade, at all events in our time. This is the age of trade"). Meanwhile in the wake of new theories of consciousness, like those of William James in 1890, Naturalism was losing a good deal of its faith in the purely scientific or analytical vision. In 1894 George Moore produced his best book yet, *Esther Waters*, the moving story of a London servant girl with an illegitimate child, which immediately provoked comparisons with Hardy's Tess. It has Naturalist impulses, but Moore had now really broken with Naturalism. He complained that Zola was too concerned "with the externalities of life," that Naturalism was a "handful of dry facts instead of a passionate impression of life in the envelope of mystery and suggestion," that art's aim was "not truth but beauty." Other writers explored Naturalism less as a deterministic method or a social protest than an aesthetic in itself. In 1898 Arnold Bennett came to literary notice with his *A Man from the North*, the story of a provincial young man like himself who comes from the Potteries to an indifferent London to write and seek his sexual freedom. Bennett's method is self-consciously flat and banal, but then he was, he explained, "the latest disciple of the Goncourts," in other words a Naturalist. He also insisted on his strong aesthetic standpoint, and collectively rejected his Victorian antecedents for lack of artistry in almost Jamesian language: "As regards fiction, it seems to me that only within the last few years have we absorbed from France that passion for artistic shapely presentation of truth, and that feeling for words as words, which animated Flaubert, the Goncourts, and Maupassant . . . An artist must be interested in presentment, not in the thing presented. He must have a passion for technique, a great love for form . . ." – in other words those qualities that Virginia Woolf accused Bennett of not having when she joined battle with him twenty years later.

The fact was that during the 1890s, a time of aesthetic reconsideration, many things – Naturalism and Symbolism, Socialism and Decadence, the "thing in front of us" and "presentment . . . not the thing presented" – were shading into each other, as the novel took on a fresh generic variety and a widening variety of tones, themes, audiences. The whole map of literature widened, just like the Empire itself. This was very visible in the treatment of London, James' "biggest aggregation." In 1890 the explorer and journalist H.M. Stanley wrote about the Belgian Congo in his powerful report *In Darkest Africa*. That year General William Booth, founder of the Salvation Army, also new, countered with *In Darkest England and the Way Out*, showing London's East End as another dark continent awaiting the ministrations of the explorer and the missionary ("As in Africa it is all trees, trees, trees with no other world conceivable, so it is here – it is all vice and poverty and crime"). "Darkest London," already there in James and Stevenson and Gissing's "nether world," became a motif of fiction. It was the world of slum life Arthur Morrison naturalistically explored in *Tales of Mean Streets* (1892) and *A Child of the Jago* (1896), and W. Somerset Maugham in *Liza of Lambeth* (1897); Jack London, the American Naturalist, would stalk through it again in his *People of the Abyss* (1903) to show life as endless Darwinian struggle. But in the age of the "impression" London also offered many other shades: the foggy urban world of the crime and detective fiction into which Sherlock Holmes adventured as he penetrated "the lowest portions of the city," but also the crepuscular mists of the urban nocturne, painting in prose – Wilde, Herbert Crackenthorpe, Aubrey Beardsley – what Whistler painted in pastel. Then there was the green London that William Morris prospects in *News from Nowhere* (1890), a reformist Utopian work in which, in the arcadian twentieth century, the fogs, poverty, and industrial problems of present London have somehow gone: "The soap-works with their smoke-vomiting chimneys were gone; the engineers' works were gone; the lead works were gone . . .". Writers now "reasserted the romance of London in their new-found love of the artificial," Jackson notes; and the London they explored could equally be a world of grim poverty and Darwinian struggle or a flickering city of strange impressions, glimpses, contrasts, a rich urban artifice. Like Dr Jekyll, the detective story and the ghost story drew together different worlds, wealth and poverty, surface and underside, opening out windows from one to the other. London, like so much else in the decade, was mirrored, doubled: the great world capital of empire and trade was also the heartland of poverty, crime and anarchy, representing at once civilization, art and artifice, and its secret sharer, darkness and disorder.

This was the image brought together at the decade's end by Joseph Conrad in *Heart of Darkness* (1899), which draws on most of these motifs. Conrad, the Polish sea captain whose spoken English stayed so poor he would be briefly picked up as a German spy in the Great War, began as a novelist of Empire when he published *Almayer's Folly* (1895) and *An Outcast of the Islands* (1896), two stories of the distant Malayan archipelago where nature met culture. *Heart of Darkness*, his symbolist novella about the ambiguity secreted in the imperial mission, brings all this much closer to home. The story starts on the Thames in the port of London; this is "the biggest, and greatest, town on earth" and also "this monstrous town," which, says the narrator, Marlow, suddenly, "has been one of the dark places of the earth." The story then moves through a circuitous, labyrinthine descent from this river to another, the Congo, in "darkest Africa," and through the layers of indifference, futility, corruption, barbarism and inhuman cruelty to empty evil, the world of "exterminate the brutes," and "the horror, the horror." From here on, Conrad's fiction would construct a universe in which everything is mirrored and doubled, as London mirrors and refracts the Congo: courage and cowardice, faith and betrayal, culture and nature, individualism and tribalism, light and darkness. In each mirror is a glimpse of the abyss and a need to preserve the fidelity of the surface. This moral and metaphysical ambiguity is one mark of the writing of the 1890s, one of its chief gifts to the Modernist vision. "Man is not truly one, but truly two," Jekyll had said in Stevenson's Gothic fable of his *homo duplex*. Wilde's *Dorian Gray*, a work both of the New Aestheticism and the New Hedonism, converts these Gothic materials into a fable about art and reality. Such Gothic deceptions became an essential part of the popular writing of the 1890s, which produced two of the great fables of modern Gothic sensationalism from the haunted house of late-Victorian culture. George du Maurier's *Trilby* (1894) is set in bohemia, the world of Parisian artists, where the threat comes with Svengali, who uses a popular science, Mesmerism, as his instrument of control over others. But it is when the conventional young solicitor Jonathan Harker unwisely chooses to do some conveyancing work in darkest somewhere, and travels to Transylvania, land of Vlad the Impaler ("It seems to me that the further East you go the more unpunctual are the trains," he is soon complaining), that the dark shadows just beyond the edge of culture find their strongest popular treatment. Transylvania, in Bram Stoker's *Dracula* (1897), is another land at the heart of darkness, where the writ of modern reason does not run: "the old centuries had, and have, powers of their own that mere 'modernity' cannot kill," Harker learns. The vampire, culled from old fictions, strikes back; it takes a mirror, a Christian cross, decapitation and a stake through the heart to lay the fear of the undead, which still satisfies the living today. Or the ghost may be just across another border: "No one would have believed in the last year of the nineteenth century that human affairs were being watched keenly and closely by intelligences greater than man's and yet as mortal as their own," began H. G. Wells' *The War of the Worlds* (1898), a "scientific romance" about an invasion from Mars. The age of scientific reason and social analysis was also the age of the sensational romance, the mythology of a time filled with a sense of contradiction, uncertainty and transition, and perturbed by what lay at its borders, or in the future. So it provided the "new" popular culture which would pass on, a mythology endlessly to be rewritten, into our modern mass media – born out of Edison's Kinetoscope of 1889.

8.

It has often been pointed out that, if the writing of the early 1890s was given to arts of mannered style, evanescent impression and veiled meaning, and opened into labyrinthine uncertainties about civilization and darkness, the self and the other, then this had – as in the contemporary work of Freud and Breuer themselves – a great deal to do with a growing sense of sexual ambiguity. As Elaine Showalter has put it, "when sexual certainties broke down, fictional certainties changed as well."[16] For now both feminism and a half-veiled gay writing flourished, and a good deal of high-minded eroticism entered literature, as in Wilde's *Dorian Gray*, where the innocent face conceals not just corruption but sexual ambiguity, in Aubrey Beardsley's work, not least his pornographic *Under the Hill*, or in *My Secret Life*, which was simply written by Anonymous. Beyond this was a fundamental change in the refracted image of the sexes themselves. Naturalism had frankly explored the power of the sexual instinct ("I simply applied to two living bodies the analytical method that surgeons apply to corpses," in Zola's version), and faced, as in Hardy's *Jude*, the "marriage question." Strong feminist works, most importantly Olive Schreiner's *The Story of an African Farm* (1883), had been part of

---

[16] Elaine Showalter, *Sexual Anarchy*, cited above.

the Naturalist campaign of the 1880s. Now "New Woman" fiction – that term was invented by the popular novelist "Ouida" in the 1890s – looked at the way women, offered greater independence by improving educational and work opportunities, changing *mores* and better birth control, began, in life and fiction too, to claim more control of their lives and aspirations. This then was another essential "modern" theme, explored in works like Sarah Grand's *The Heavenly Twins* (1893) and "George Egerton's" stories *Keynotes* (also 1893). Egerton, having lived in Scandinavia and imbibed the influence of Ibsen and Hamsun, wrote about women's lives in a newly passionate prose: Mona Caird, in *The Daughters of Danaus* (1894), explored the struggles of women who attempted to produce serious art; Ellen Hepworth Dixon produced her feminist *The Story of a Modern Woman* (1894). And "New Woman" fiction also included works like Hardy's *Tess*, Moore's *Esther Waters*, and Gissing's *The Odd Women* (1893). Writers male and female were arguing, if in different voices, much the same issues: modern marriage, free love, the nature and balance of the sexual instincts, the imprisonment of moral codes, eroticism and "New Hedonism." When Grant Allan, who proselytized for the latter, published his *The Woman Who Did* (1895), a fiction of free love, it was quickly countered by "Victoria Cross" (Vivian Cory) in *The Woman Who Didn't* (also 1895), which put the case for female purity; book talked back to book. These were fundamental themes of the late-Victorian dissolution, and they duly passed their concerns onward to more powerful writers from H.G. Wells and D.H. Lawrence to Virginia Woolf, May Sinclair, Dorothy Richardson and Rebecca West.

But often the choice was simpler, and the readers of the time were offered a choice of male or female worlds: worlds of empire and adventure, or worlds of social and domestic pressure at home. For once, this was an age when it was women writers who wrote bitter realism and men who wrote romance. Above all there was Rudyard Kipling, the "Imperial Laureate," the first British writer to be awarded the Nobel Prize. In our own plain and post-imperial times, it is sometimes hard to see why he was regarded by so many as the most important and representative British writer of the age, but no writer was more closely in touch with the energies that were making the age what it was. On the one hand there was the vast commercial and governmental task of empire, on the other there were the oily jobs of the machine age; Kipling wrote about both, celebrating daily things and routine work. Born in Bombay in 1865, he was schooled in Britain, then returned to India as a journalist. He knew the Empire not as a traveller, but as one who lived its workaday life and lived its daily pan-racial relations. It was in India that he laid the solid grounding for the career that followed; when he moved back to Britain in 1889 to earn his living as a writer, he had seven books, mostly of short stories, already finished. They include some of his finest work; James was right to call him the "infant monster." These include complex stories of sexuality like "Without Benefit of Clergy," and "The Man Born to be King" (1888), about two rogue adventurers who try to set up a version of the Empire in "Kaffiristan," finally with grim and ironic results. The two voice imperial high dreams, but expressed in the vernacular; Kipling's vernacular language often has a power like Mark Twain's of expressing a vision of the world comically undermining the one that has been politely written down. Like Twain, it offers us the sense of a well observed, honest and half-comic vision; from this comes the jangling, popular voice of his fiction and poetry, which would sound out over the following decades. The novel he wrote on return to England, *The Light That Failed* (1890), is really a fable about his literary choice. It is set in the Sudan and in London: the world of war and action, and the world of art and bohemia. The central character, a painter and an adventurer, loses his sight, and this dangerously returns him to the world of action; the fable seems to represent Kipling's own choice, of public forms over private ones, the world of doing over domestic and aesthetic life. From then on his tales of adventure, action and work began to dominate the decade. Stronger in the short story than the novel, he could write modernist fiction, as his story "Mrs Bathurst" proves. But his two great treasures lay in childhood life – he had the statutory unhappy childhood of so many writers – and India (to which, in fact, he did not return, living in Britain and the United States). So he could create the unhappy, wonderful, above all tribal world of school and childhood in *Stalky & Co.* (1899), of India in what is probably his best book, *Kim* (1901). He wrote many excellent stories, like "Wireless" and "Mary Postgate"; his Indian stories for children – *The Jungle Books* (1894, 1895) and *The Just So Stories* (1902) – won him youthful audiences that never left him after. Altogether, his sense of the struggle of life, the battle for experience, the ways of tribes and races, the dangerous adventure of the age of the Gatling gun and the Imperial mission, made him central to his unsettled, expanding age.

At the same time his artistic grasp began to diminish. James had the highest hopes of this "infant monster"; his mind changed later. "I thought he perhaps contained the seeds of an English Balzac, but I have given that up in proportion as he has come down steadily from the simple in subject to the more simple – from the Anglo-Saxons to the natives, from the natives to the Tommies, from the Tommies to the quadrupeds, from the quadrupeds to the fish, and from the fish to the engines and screws." What's more, he complained, his work had "almost nothing of the complicated soul or of the female form or of any question of *shades*." Kipling did write simply, but he wasn't simple; his best work possesses a clear aesthetic subtlety. But he lacked Conrad's moral subtlety, and firmly belonged to the imperial age, the age of the race and the tribe, of the savage and the white man's burden, the age of the machine. Still, he wrote with a sense of social and psychological complexity, an awareness of the power of the natural and the savage, and a view of life through the eyes of the underdog, seen against the importance of a great empire and the worth of the rule of law. When he wrote across the races, it was sometimes with condescension, but at others with real sympathy and understanding. His fiction is born in romance, but filled with a distinctive Naturalism; he possessed the pessimism of the age, its abiding anxiety about the future, and he understood the burden of ordinary daily life and work, the subjection of the footsoldier to the regiment or the machine, the life of "engines and screws." More than most, he understood the power of the machine, and wrote finely about the craftsmen and engineers of the time of technical change, when machines made machines. As Holbrook Jackson also observes, he also gained his power from a deep shift in the spirit of the 1890s. For around 1895, the era that had begun with Wilde, aestheticism and decadence shifted toward something else. Wilde's trial and imprisonment in 1895 – which coincided with the publication of Nordau's *Degeneration*, and the silencing of Thomas Hardy in fiction – was a crucial moment: "The aesthetic cult, in his nasty form, is over," announced *The News of the World*, though perhaps so too was the Victorian age. According to Jackson, the decade fell into two clear halves, the first "remarkable for a literary and artistic renaissance, degenerating into decadence; the second for a new sense of patriotism degenerating into jingoism," and ending in "that indulgence of blatant aspirations," Mafeking Night in 1899.[17] Yet, he adds, the impulse of the decade had always been double. If there was *fin de siècle*, there was also *aube de siècle*; if there was "degeneration," there was also "regeneration." Many writers were themselves versions of *homo duplex*. In the same year as *Dorian Gray*, Wilde could write *The Soul of Man Under Socialism*. Writers who understood the "beautiful difficulties of art" also produced commercial successes, like Stevenson or Du Maurier. Kipling himself was aesthete as well as imperial laureate, experimental prose writer as well as conservative jingoist: another complicated voice of the Modern.

And so was another new author who, in 1895, seemed to come from nowhere and became not just one of the most popular writers of the day, but the voice of things to come. H.G. Wells, born in 1866, the son of a cricketer-shopkeeper and a lady's maid, was a Jude who had no intention of being obscure. He got his technocratic education at the Royal College of Science, coming under the influence of T.H. Huxley, and a

[17] Holbrook Jackson, *The Eighteen Nineties*, cited above.

political education from Socialism. Then in the year of *Jude* he published his *The Time Machine*, a work of what was then called "scientific romance" or perhaps "future fiction," and we know simply as "SF." What Wells showed was that there were directions the mind – and the romance – could travel in other than spatially, through the Empire, down the Congo, backward into the historical past. Utopian and dystopian predictions existed in plenty, most recently in Edward Bellamy's *Looking Backward* (1888) and William Morris's *News from Nowhere*, but they were mostly versions of pastoral, and lacked scientific insight or a real gift for historical anticipation. Prophecies of future war had also been increasing in number (there was, for instance, the famous *The Battle of Dorking* [1871], by Sir George Tomkyns Chesney), and works about the cities of the future.[18] But Wells' was a work of the age of Edison and Eiffel, which perhaps owed most to Jules Verne; above all he brought to the form a distinctive scientific clarity. He could foresee the heat-death of the solar system, and propose "a fourth dimension" in which his "Time Traveller" could bicycle forward to the year 802,701, to find a world divided between an aesthetic class and an eternal underclass, the Eloi and the Morlocks. This was Wells' political theme, already important, and to develop through the novels, social fantasies and anticipatory works of the next decade. As G.K. Chesterton, who also tried the form in his *The Napoleon of Notting Hill* (1904), would say, Wells' "first importance was that he wrote adventure stories in the new world the men of science had discovered," and he had the capacity to excite his readers about the hopes and dangers of the future. Indeed he virtually invented science fiction in its modern form, and in its modern variety – as futuristic exploration, as satirical fable, as scientific prophecy, as grim warning.

Wells was a serious novelist, who set off on his work with high artistic ambitions. During the 1890s he became a close friend of Henry James, Joseph Conrad, Stephen Crane – writers we would plainly acknowledge as "moderns." Wells saw himself

[18] See I.F. Clarke, *The Pattern of Expectation, 1644–2001* (London, 1979), for details.

as a modernist too, but in a very different way. He wrote in popular forms for a popular audience, often inventing extravagant action and excitement. For the genre he opened with his early work was popular scientific romance, a fiction not of modern techniques but of the modernizing process itself. If he was a Socialist, it was not of an arcadian, William Morris kind; what he believed in was reform through science and politics, through free thought, free love, evolutionary biology, political foresight, space travel, the coming world state. He envisioned a world where technology was changing everything, from the relation of the sexes and the races to the accessibility of the solar system to space travel, and dispensing with Old England and the Victorian age. The books he wrote up to the turn of the century – *The Island of Doctor Moreau* (1896), *The Invisible Man* (1897), the disturbing invasion prophecy *The War of the Worlds* (1898), which depicted not only Martian invasion but technological warfare, *The First Men in the Moon* (1901), and more – were filled with amazing inventions, extraordinary machines, scientific discoveries, future wars. But though their content was frequently highly fantastic, they drew, excitingly, on real scientific and military possibilities: spaceships, killer rays, collisions of competing world powers. They foresaw remarkable prospects – there was a strong note of social optimism – but also new terrors – world war, social collapse, racial conflict. Henry James admired Wells, and even offered to join in "doing Mars" with him; it remains one of literary history's most unlikely collaborations. As the century turned, his attention moved closer in, to contemporary English life and the potential of personal and social change, though his themes were never less than world-historical. As he would write in *A Modern Utopia* (1905): "The almost cataclysmic development of new machinery, the discovery of new materials, and the appearance of new social possibilities through the pursuit of material science, have given enormous and unprecedented facilities to the spirit of innovation." The story of the new sorts of lives evolving in the age of change and innovation – the lives of the ordinary "new" young men and women, the Mr Kipps and Mr Pollys and Ann Veronicas, typical figures seizing modern opportunities – became an exemplary form of Edwardian fiction. If, as James said, the novel as the century turned was coming to a new self-consciousness, it was clear there would be many shapes to the shape of fictional things to come.

9.

By 1900 many elements of the modern novel in Britain were already in place. It was becoming a voice of modernity, and had shaken loose from many of the elements that had seemed to confine it: the lending libraries, dutiful and religious morality, even the confident notion of grand authorial omniscience. It had claimed the right to freedom and frankness of expression, an issue that would ensure many conflicts and censorings over the next days; it had also begun to claim another freedom, the aesthetic right to complexity and obscurity we associate with Modernism. It was developing an *avant-garde* independence from the popular audience, but also using popular techniques to reach deeper into that audience. It was reaching outward, into documentary and social and journalistic concerns, and it was reaching inward, into the recesses of consciousness and psychology that would give it a whole new language of awareness. It was spreading in subject-matter, into the realms of boyish and imperial adventure. It frequently looked backward, in a decadent world-weariness, to the wonderlands of the past, but it also looked forward, into the techno-wonderland of the age of things to come. It was beginning to leave behind those crises of religious and moral conscience, those dramas of damnation or redemption, that filled the pages of much Victorian fiction; its new dramas were dramas of social and sexual relations, modern marriage, generational struggle, represented less in the discourse of religion or morality than that of sociology or aestheticism. It had begun to break, in several different ways, with the conventions of realism and familiarity, of subjectivity and objectivity, of time and space, that governed most previous fiction. In an age when the old gods were indeed dying, and new powers and convictions were to be summoned, it came to seem, at best, to be itself a form of human discovery, creative evolution, a quest for knowledge in an age when what was knowable was itself becoming indeterminate. By the turn of the century, writers had increasingly come to see that, as Frank Kermode has put it, "a text might have to stand in a new relation to reality to be truthful."[19]

The novel was becoming a radical art, but also an important new commodity, an adventure in the marketplace. Books got cheaper, literacy grew, adventurous themes raised the interest of the reading public, and the number of new novels published jumped, from 381 in 1870 to 1,825 in 1899. As authors like Haggard and Henty, Wells and Bennett, Chesterton and John Buchan demonstrated, writing novels became a fine way to earn a crust, a grand and profitable adventure: "The last decade of the nineteenth century was an extraordinarily favourable time for new writers . . ." Wells was to say; "Below and above alike there was opportunity. More public, more publicity, more publishers and more patronage." This began to drive a wedge, all too familiar now, between the novelists who saw fiction as an art, an affair of high impressions and fine technique, like painting, and those who saw it as a profitable and influential commodity, like soap. By the 1900s, said Ford Madox (Hueffer) Ford, fiction in Britain was counterpoised between the artistic and the blatantly commercial. Henry James watched his reputation soar and his royalties diminish; Arnold Bennett, who made a fortune from writing, could declare, "I am a writer, just as I might be a hotel-keeper, a solicitor, a doctor, a grocer, or an earthenware manufacturer" (no doubt making the kind of commodity the characters in James could not bear to mention). But even popular writers do not usually like to admit they are writing down to the market; what they are doing, of course, is elevating the market up to them by going down to it. Bennett

[19] See Frank Kermode, *Essays on Fiction: 1971–82* (London, 1983).

freely wrote "art," and rubbish; and he, and Wells, and many more, thought that just as much as James they were undertaking a "modern experiment." This matter famously came to a head in 1915 (Lawrence's "year the old world ended") in a quarrel between James and Wells, those former friends who had once thought of "doing Mars" together. James' late essay "The New Fiction" – originally titled "The Younger Generation" in the *TLS* in 1914 – had taken a sweep of his literary contemporaries, and he complained the novel was dissolving into artless art, an art of "saturation" by life. Wells, like Bennett, was one of the saturators mentioned in the piece, and took his revenge in his novel *Boon* (1915), a work totally unremarkable for anything but this, by satirizing James' late fiction: "It is like a church lit but without a congregation to distract you, with every light and line focused on the high altar. And on the altar, very reverently placed, intensely there, is a dead kitten, an eggshell, a bit of string." James defended his view of fiction, replying, "It is art that *makes* life, makes importance, for our consideration and application of these things, and I know of no substitute whatever for the force and beauty of its process." Wells retorted he preferred to be seen as a journalist, not an artist: "To you, literature, like painting, is an end, to me literature like architecture is a means, it has a use."[20]

To this episode, many ironies attach. Wells had already in effect left the novel behind, and was into the future of science and the world state; he lived on till 1946, to see Hiroshima and the Mind at the End of Its Tether. James was also leaving the novel behind; he died the next year. The Great War had begun, and after it novels would be written in new ways, neither with Wellsian optimism nor the Jamesian sense of the labyrinthine complexity of society. The work of D.H. Lawrence, named in the controversy, would be censored, and many of the most important novels to follow would come out of *avant-garde* exile.

[20] This splendid quarrel is recorded in Leon Edel and Gordon N. Ray (eds.), *Henry James and H. G. Wells: A Record of Their Friendship, Their Debate on the Art of Fiction, and Their Quarrel* (London, 1958). Stephen Spender's comments are in his *The Struggle of the Modern* (London, 1963).

Generally the future of fiction would confirm the viewpoint of James; the highest value of modern fiction is as a form of challenging discovery, not as an instrument of saturation or report – the newer media can give us that in plenty. There is generally no shortage of records of life, people with a pen and a story; there is a general dearth of real artistic explorers, makers of radical form and imagination. But the argument opened up then was destined to be repeated over and over, in other similar quarrels: Virginia Woolf *v.* Arnold Bennett, D.H. Lawrence *v.* John Galsworthy, and to become, as Stephen Spender put it, an ongoing conflict between "moderns" – the aesthetic explorers – and "contemporaries" – the recorders, explorers and critics of contemporary life. The issue has lasted beyond the wars of Modernism, and remains, a powerful oscillation in the history of the novel, to this day. Iris Murdoch distinguishes between "crystalline" (neo-symbolist) and "journalistic" novels; David Lodge sees the late modern novelist eternally returned to the crossroads, ever choosing between the paths of realism and experiment.[21] If as the new century came there was indeed a new age for the novel coming in Britain, it did not point a single direction, did not declare a single aesthetic, did not claim a single audience, or emerge from a single tradition. What had been willed to the modern novel was not a tradition but a mixture of traditions, not a clear fictional culture but a multi-layered variety of them, not a clarified view of life but a confusion of visions, impressions, social apprehensions, future feelings. The twentieth century would not have a style; it would be an age in ceaseless quest for a style, an aesthetic battlefield. As the inheritors of James' "self-consciousness" found and showed over the years ahead, what they had been bequeathed was a confusing, various, rich bundle of prospects that would lead to the multi-faceted, multi-layered, multi-cultural fictional phenomenon we call the novel today.

[21] Iris Murdoch, "Against Dryness" (1961), and David Lodge, "The Novelist at the Crossroads" (1969), both reprinted in Malcolm Bradbury (ed.), *The Novel Today: Contemporary Writers on Modern Fiction* (London, new edition, 1990).

TWO

The Opening World
1900–1915

Millennium! Millennium!
The wondrous world that is to come.

> William Ford Stanley, "Millennium! Millennium!" (1903)

It was – truly – like an opening world . . . For, if you have
worried your poor dear brain for at least a quarter of a century
over the hopelessness of finding, in Anglo-Saxondom, any traces
of the operations of conscious art – it was amazing to find these
young creatures not only evolving theories of writing and the
plastic arts, but receiving in addition an immense amount of
what is called "public support".

> Ford Madox Ford (Hueffer), *Thus to Revisit* (1921)

1.

The "opening world" Ford Madox Ford, formerly Ford Madox
Hueffer, is here recalling – as he gazes backward across the
deep murderous trench of the Great War, across a time when
everything, even his own name, has changed – is the patch of
London years between 1908 and 1914, a major era of the
experimental arts in Britain. It was, everyone agreed, a Modernist wonderland – a time when British philistinism and
provincialism wonderfully dissolved, and for a brief few years
new arts, new ideas, new movements were everywhere. "Europe
was full of titanic stirrings and snortings – a new art coming
into flower to celebrate or announce a 'new age,'" recalled
another famous survivor of the era of experiment and wartime,
Wyndham Lewis, the writer, painter, and founder of Vorticism,

67

in his bitter memoir *Blasting and Bombardiering* (1937). What had happened, he claimed, was that between 1908 and 1914 an entire new school was in formation, right across Europe. It was more significant than the Romantic Revolution, not just recreating the arts but transforming all the philosophical rudiments of life, and heralding great social and political changes. And then, he reports, "down came the lid – the day was lost, for art, at Sarajevo." His was one of many reports. "It was an age of noise, and every new effort had to be announced with a blare of trumpets," recalled another recaller, R. A. Scott-James, who was also looking back from the Depression disappointments of the 1930s, when all this was a distant past: "It was a sort of *mi-carême* festival of big drums and little tin whistles and fancy dress. A new show of Post-Impressionist pictures had much the same character and purposes as the marches of flustered suffragettes on Whitehall." "If we had no Offenbach to set everyone whirling frantically to tunes in which mad gaiety blended with the tom-toms of death," declared, even more extravagantly, another participant, Douglas Goldring, "there was nonetheless a close resemblance between the last days of the Third Empire and the London which woke with a hangover to face the deluge of blood in 1914." This, said Virginia Woolf, was the time when everyone behaved differently, thought differently, voted differently, felt differently, and – very importantly – loved differently. In fact human character changed. "The first signs of it are recorded in the books of Samuel Butler, in *The Way of All Flesh* in particular; the plays of Bernard Shaw continue to record it." But it all came to a peak, she famously said, in December, 1910.[1]

If almost every survivor seems to have a story to tell about the pre-war Modernist wonderland, when so many careers, ideas, and -isms, so much artistic activity in so many spheres,

[1] Ford Madox Ford, *Thus To Revisit* (London, 1921); Wyndham Lewis, *Blasting and Bombardiering* (London, 1937); R. A. Scott-James, "Modern Accents in Engish Literature," *The Bookman* (NY), Sept. 1931; Douglas Goldring, *South Lodge* (London, 1943); and Virginia Woolf, "Modern Fiction" (1919), in Leonard Woolf (ed.), *Collected Essays of Virginia Woolf* (London, 4 vols., 1966–7).

came to the boil, that partly has to do with the extraordinary stir of excitement the British version of the Modern revolution generated, the extraordinary new personalities it threw up, the fact that the whole idea of an era of New Arts in philistine Britain – all artists knew as an act of ultimate faith that Britain was philistine – came as a shock of surprise. Ever since 1895, the year of Wilde's trial, of Hardy's withdrawal from fiction, of Wells' emergence, the tide of experiment that had been seen at the opening of the decade, with Aestheticism and Decadence, had appeared to be ebbing fast. "The decade of [the Nineties] began with a dash for life and ended with a retreat," Holbrook Jackson said in *The Eighteen Nineties*, which appropriately appeared in 1913, reminding the new generation of experimentalists that others now forgotten had been most of this way before. The *avant-garde* and decadent arguments, the mannerist forms and elegant styles, the sexual frankness and ambiguity, the surging sense of modern transition, that had quickened the early Nineties all seemed well past, leaving the mauve decade marooned as a time of lost possibilities, evanescent moments, eternal transition. The careers, and in quite a number of cases the lives, of the main participants had faded fast too. In 1900 Nietzsche, who had called on the 1890s to "transvalue their values," died mad in Jena, and never saw the age of the Superman he had tried to summon; that same year Oscar Wilde died in lonely disgrace in Paris; Emile Zola, having fought the battle of the Dreyfus case, died there two years later, suffocated by the fumes of a charcoal stove. The new century that everyone called "modern" came, but, as W. B. Yeats explained in a famous comment, "everybody got down off his stilts; henceforth nobody drank absinthe with his black coffee; nobody went mad; nobody committed suicide; nobody joined the Catholic Church; or if they did I have forgotten."[2] The *fin de siècle* was over, like the *siècle* itself, and a plainer, less decorated, more confidently, perhaps smugly modern twentieth-century age dawned. Then, in 1901, the Victorian Era, which had been closing for such a

---

[2] W. B. Yeats, "Introduction" to *The Oxford Book of Modern Verse* (Oxford, 1936).

long time, did truly close. Queen Victoria, the very image of Britain, died, after over sixty years on her imperial throne. Edward VII succeeded her; the "Edwardian Era," Britain's brief *belle époque*, began.

Except in the diary of country ladies, Edwardianism would never really have a good literary press. As Richard Ellmann rightly said, "the phrase Edwardian literature is not often heard," and when it is, it is generally in a note of Bloomsbury disparagement.[3] It has never been a period held notable for its writing, though this considerably mistaken impression is largely due to the excitement the age that followed next – Hueffer/Ford's "opening world" – has had for literary historians, who rightly see in it the roots of Anglo-American modernism, fanning out into William Carlos Williams and the future of the American arts. But the fact is that much that was important for the modern movement in fiction and poetry – James' late phase, Conrad's finest fiction, the founding work of James Joyce, Virginia Woolf, D. H. Lawrence, the growth of poetic Imagism – was initiated in the Edwardian age, even though some of the most significant was not actually published then. It has simply not been considered to typify it, because in so many cases the publications or the recognitions did get delayed, as is common with those arts that call themselves *avant-garde*. What instead has been thought to typify it were just those things many of the new writers were in revolt against – the last gasps of Victorian moralism, the formal social conventions and hypocrisies, the bourgeois-philistine mood, the culture of commercialism and the literature of profit. Certainly these were commercial, material, imperial times, when Kipling sounded and British power and trade still ruled the world. They were also reforming times, an era of political upheaval, welfare attitudes, income tax and state intervention. Quite a lot of the fiction seemed formed out of a happy mixture of the two, a radical adventure in commercialism, as the boom-careers of writers like H. G.

---

[3] Richard Ellmann, "Two Faces of Edward," in R. Ellmann (ed.), *Edwardians and Late Victorians* (New York, 1960).

Wells and Arnold Bennett, G. K. Chesterton and Rudyard Kipling, showed. Typical books seemed to be brooding works of distant travel – W. H. Hudson, R. B. Cunningham-Grahame – or boyish or manly adventure by Henty and Deeping and Merriman and Le Queux. Women writers produced pieces of well-done tosh – there was Elinor Glyn's *Three Weeks*, sex on a tigerskin in the age of imperialism, Florence Barclay's *The Rosary*, a sentimental tract, Marie Corelli's *The Treasure of Heaven*. But far more biting women writers were emerging: Ada Leverson produced the sharp social satire *The Twelfth Hour* (1907), May Sinclair a grim glance at marriage in *The Helpmate* (also 1907), and Virginia Woolf, around this same time, began her first novel. It was an age of the bluff bookman, and bookish people found writers like G. K. Chesterton, who linked his Catholicism to the detective story in the "Father Brown" tales, and parodied *fin-de-siècle* pessimism in *The Man Who Was Thursday* (1908), W. H. Hudson, author of the lush, and pleasing, Venezuelan romance *Green Mansions* (1904), Walter de la Mare, John Masefield, Hugh Walpole, John Galsworthy or Hilaire Belloc among the great glories of English literature. They were not, though often they were good. Meanwhile James and Conrad struggled for an audience, while James Joyce, who had more or less completed *Dubliners* in 1904-5, was decisively silenced by the caution of British and Irish publishers. When the liberal politician C. F. Masterman, in his influential *The Condition of England* (1909), suggested that the Condition of England and the Condition of the English Novel were related, both seemed to give cause for concern.

That the Condition of England and the Condition of the English Novel were indeed related – and in more complicated ways than is sometimes supposed – was shown in a brilliant essay by Frank Kermode, "The English Novel, *Circa* 1907."[4] In Edwardian times, he notes, there was much popular commercial writing, but also much talk about matters of technique and purpose in the novel, and broad consideration of how much

[4] Collected in Frank Kermode, *Essays on Fiction, 1971–82* (London, 1983).

further the novel could go in the direction of art, innovation, and sexual frankness. The social, sexual, generational and class issues that stirred the late-Victorian era still remained at the forefront of fiction. Samuel Butler's *The Way of All Flesh* (posthumously published in 1903) and then Edmund Gosse's *Father and Son* (1907), both clear, critical farewells to the pre-Darwinian age and the rule of the Victorian paterfamilias, made it plain that the theocentric age was over, a secular one in progress, and what came next was an age of machines, materialism, and money. These books were seized on by many younger writers, who agreed that sons, and daughters too, were in revolt against the Victorian fathers, and that the time had come for an end to reticence, a return to the heart, a new equation of feeling. In intellectual circles religion had mostly given way (apart from Chesterton and Belloc) to science and socialism, as H. G. Wells made plain in his novels, and Bernard Shaw in his plays. New writers like E. M. Forster, whose first book *Where Angels Fear to Tread* appeared in 1905, might acknowledge that they belonged to "the fag-end of Victorian liberalism" but they looked for a new view of life and culture, based on personal relations, the reform of the heart, on passion and paganism. The "Condition of England" concerned many writers. H. G. Wells explored it, with brilliant satire, in his *Tono-Bungay* of 1909; Forster confronted it in his balanced, liberal moral comedy *Howards End* of 1910. Liberalism, as a Whig programme of progress and reform, was dissolving, as the nation split betwen commercial and imperial Toryism and a spirit of scientific socialism; and this was the time of what historians call "the strange death of Liberal England." But as it declined as a public politics, liberalism was emerging as something more, or else, as the "liberal imagination," a critical, reforming desire to examine and reconceive the nature of public and private life, confront what Forster called the "inner darkness that comes with a commercial age," and challenge the cultureless, philistine Condition of England itself.

In Edwardian times there was no shortage of writers called "modern." The difference between the "Edwardian" writers and those, many of the same generation, who achieved influence after was a disagreement about where the heart of the modern lay. Thus Joseph Conrad, writing his strange version of imperial romance, did not at the time seem notably modern, while, to the critics confronting what Henry James in his preface to *The Golden Bowl* (1904) nicely described as the "marked inveteracy of a certain indirect and oblique view of my presented action" the late great novels that were now appearing seemed works of contorted and willed obscurity. On the other hand H. G. Wells – now directly portraying Edwardian life with its commercial enterprise, its new social types and possibilities, and speaking up for the new classes, the new men and women, and the new spirit of sex, all of this seen in a light of a great world-historical vision – seemed a prototype of the modern. So did Arnold Bennett and John Galsworthy, exploring the social texture of a changing age that had now left Victorianism well behind. James and Conrad wrote aesthetically, indirectly, from within; Wells and Bennett and Galsworthy wrote from without, as vivid, objective, "realist" observers of a time in rapid change. They were materialist writers for materialist times, recorders of its new opportunities and dulling limitations, its sexual and emotional aspirations and its moral and class hypocrisies. Commerce and free love, business and socialism, were all modern. This was a time of department stores and aeroplanes and new opportunities, calling for adventurous writers. In *Tono-Bungay*, Wells celebrated "the romantic element in modern commerce": "We became part of what is now quite an important element in the confusion of our world, that multitude of economically ascendent people who are learning how to spend money," his narrator explains: "With enormous astonished zest they begin *shopping* . . ." New technologies were modern. The car and its goggled driver ("a short figure, compactly immense, hugely goggled, wearing a sort of brown rubber proboscis, and surrounded by a tableland of motoring cap"), the aeroplane and the destroyer are there in *Tono-Bungay*; cars moving at 60 m.p.h. allow the Wilcox family to hurtle across the old pastoral England without noticing it in *Howards End*; trains of virgin

newness which move as smoothly "as British gilt-edged securities" symbolize the age for Ford Madox Ford in his retrospective war novel *Parade's End* (1924). This was an age of statism
and social planning, and the businessmen, bureaucrats, mandarins and scientific social thinkers, the people who "adminis-
tered the world," appear again and again in the fiction of Wells,
Galsworthy, Forster, and Hueffer/Ford. And so do new young
men from the lower classes seeking their rightful place in
culture, from Wells' Mr Polly to Forster's Leonard Bast, along
with the new young women demanding will and independence,
like Wells' Ann Veronica. Masterman defined the "Condition
of England" as a set of contradictions, where it seemed impossible to reconcile old interests and new politics, past institutions
and new vitality, the instincts of individualism and the demands
of welfare, the desires of culture and the needs of the nation-
state in a time of fast change, political uncertainty, and rising
international competition. He called on writers for a new,
overarching cultural vision – something that a good many
writers, from the socialist Wells to the liberal Forster to the
Nietzschean D. H. Lawrence, did not fail to provide.

A great deal was stirring, then, in the brief Edwardian period,
between 1901 and 1910. But what the Edwardians had really
not decided, as many of their successors more confidently did,
was the meaning of the word "modern," the kind of artistic
claim and commitment it seemed to require. In 1904 James
Joyce (that Irish Edwardian, who set his most famous novel on
a June day in this same Edwardian year) began *Stephen Hero* –
a *Kunstlerroman*, or fictional "portrait of the artist," a type of
novel that had flourished greatly in the Decadence – as in
Huysmans' *A rebours*, Wilde's *Picture of Dorian Gray*, Thomas
Mann's *Buddenbrooks*. The story of the artist emerging from the
material world of bourgeois reality has many dimensions, but
one of them, said Joyce, was to enter the unknown arts, and be
"modern," or "vivisective." "The ancient method investigated
law with the lantern of justice, morality with the lantern of
revelation, art with the lantern of tradition," Joyce's young
artist Stephen Dedalus explains. "But all these lanterns have

magical properties; they transform and disfigure. The modern method examines its territory by the light of day." Examining "by the light of day" meant both a voyage into the "unknown arts" and a changed and radical conception of the artist: "I will tell you what I will do and what I will not do," Joyce has Stephen say in a later, aesthetically more refined version of the book, *A Portrait of the Artist as a Young Man* (1916): "I will not serve that in which I no longer believe, whether it call itself my home, my fatherland, or my church: and I will try to express myself in some mode of life or art as freely as I can and as wholly as I can, using for my defence the only arms I allow myself to use, silence, exile and cunning." The price of Joyce's artistic revolt was soon clear – silence and exile. The stories of *Dubliners*, offered to publishers in 1905, were rejected for indelicacy and possible libel. Set in galley in 1912, they were again suppressed, and did not appear until 1914, when modernist small press culture began to emerge, and the artist could declare his claim to an experimental modern vision.

What was missing in British culture, according to Hueffer/ Ford, was the "critical attitude," and so in 1908 he founded his excellent *English Review*, devoted to "the arts, to letters, and to ideas," a sequence, he acknowledged, of almost hopeless causes, to promote just that. It seems odd now, when there is too much of it, that everyone then was asking for criticism. It was "criticism, on other than infantile lines," that James cried for, and this was one reason he wrote the prefaces to the New York Edition, which appeared alongside his late great novels. Conrad requested something similar, growing ever more irritable with the "inconceivable stupidity" of a childish reading public that could only tolerate clear plots and simple endings. D. H. Lawrence and Virginia Woolf had both begun writing fiction by now, he in 1906, she in 1908; both were experimenting with forms of fiction where consciousness and psychology created not clear plots and simple endings, but a structure and texture distinct and belonging only to itself. Around this same time, a new, "harder" poetry was beginning to emerge, as the romantic shell and the divine afflatus were cast off, and the poem became a node, an event in language. And, just as the "inner" poem was beginning to throw off the case of the "outer" one, so an "inner novel" was beginning to be disclosed. "Story," "plot," and "description" were the stuff of the outer novel; but "Yes, yes – but is this *all*?" Henry James was begging the reader to ask. "These are the circumstances of the interest – we see, we see; but where is the interest itself, where and what is its centre, and how are we to measure it in relation to *that*?" Most Edwardian readers did not yet know the answer, but in fact it lay in some variant of the word "form." You could also try "design," "pattern," "technique," "revelation," "epiphany" or "consciousness." It may not quite have been what Arnold Bennett was after when he told his tales of Bursley (though he was interested in the question), or H. G. Wells when he explored that great new romp called modern life. But it was at the centre of what was increasingly being named "the art of fiction," which assumed, along with James, that part of the essential subject of the novel was the story of its own making or becoming. And the age of "the art of fiction" was clearly in the air when, in May 1910, King Edward VII died, King George V ascended to the throne, and the Georgian age began.

2.

It was no doubt of all this Virginia Woolf was thinking when she pronounced, in her essay " Mr Bennett and Mrs Brown" (1923), that "in or about December 1910 human character changed," and along with it everything else, including religion, politics, conduct, values and literature. Up to 1910, she explained, there was no British novelist from whom a new writer could learn his or her serious business. James was an American, Conrad was a Pole, Dostoevsky was a Russian, and Joyce simply remained invisible above his unpublished handiwork, paring his fingernails. The leading British novelists were Arnold Bennett, H. G. Wells and John Galsworthy, and they had educated the public into understanding what the novel was

– a material thing, made of flat realities, exteriorly seen characters, broad social history, plainly charted plots. Going to them to learn how to write modern fiction, she said, was "like going to a bootmaker and asking him to teach you how to make a watch." Their books had nothing to do with the way in which life was really known and felt, certainly not as she herself knew and felt it. "Is life like this? Must novels be like this?" she demanded. By 1910 it seemed clear, if the lessons of Cubist painting, of Einstein's relativity, or of Dostoevsky's novels were any guide, that life was not really like this at all; it was filled with angles, recesses, indeterminacies, fragments. After attending the exhibition of French Post-Impressionist paintings ("Manet and the Post-Impressionists") organized by Woolf's friend Roger Fry at the Grafton Galleries, in December 1910, which included works by Van Gogh, Cézanne, Picasso and Matisse, even Arnold Bennett seemed inclined to agree: "Noting in myself that a regular contemplation of these pictures inspires a weariness of all other pictures that are not absolutely first-rate ... I have permitted myself to suspect that, supposing some writer were to come along and do in words what these men have done in paint, I might conceivably be disgusted with the whole of modern fiction, and I might have to begin again."[5] Novels, then, did not necessarily have to be like "this." In that year, 1910, Bennett's own *Clayhanger* and Wells' *The History of Mr Polly* had appeared, and they were two of the stronger works of Edwardian realism. But so had E. M. Forster's most important pre-war novel *Howards End*, where realism is shot through with symbolism, and Hueffer's *A Call*, a novel of the telephone. Then in 1911 came D. H. Lawrence's sensuous first novel *The White Peacock*, Katherine Mansfield's volume of subtle and highly Chekhovian stories *In a German Pension*, and a first novel, *Dolores*, later to be disowned, by another new writer, I. Compton-Burnett, who would duly turn the old Victorian world into an eternal stage set for her biting modern art. Hueffer now

[5] "Jacob Tonson" (Arnold Bennett), "Neo-Impressionism and Literature," *The New Age*, 8 December 1910; reprinted in Arnold Bennett, *Books and Persons* (London, 1917).

published his volume of essays, *The Critical Attitude*, and Virginia Woolf was herself becoming widely influential as a very critical literary critic, the modern equivalent of her father Leslie Stephen (in its way Bloomsbury too belonged to the fag-end of Victorian liberalism). A new generation of "Georgians" was already emerging, leaving the Edwardian novel behind in its "unreality," and, said Woolf, with "a sound of breaking and falling, crashing and destruction," starting to break free.

So 1910 became a folkloric Bloomsbury date, and it was certainly the year when Bloomsbury itself, famous for its intellectual and aesthetic novelty and high sensitivity, started to acquire both its name and its artistic identity. But Fry's exhibition was essentially a reminder to the largely uncomprehending British ("The mild tragedy of the thing is that London is infinitely too self-complacent even to suspect that it is London and not the exhibition which is making itself ridiculous," wrote Bennett) that the *avant-garde* tendencies and aesthetic enquiries that had been growing from the later nineteenth century had really not expired. The first decade of the century had been a flourishing, discovering period for the international Modern movement, which grew ever more international by the day. It was born in an appetite for transformation, the need to transcend and triumph over the past, following the Nietzschean imperative to create the world anew, in an endless sequence of creative discovery. By 1908 a modern *avant garde* had plainly emerged, covering a new bohemian map that spanned from Moscow to Chicago, Rome to Oslo, Trieste to Dublin. It had resolved itself into a complex web of tendencies and causes, some of them closely inter-related, others deeply hostile to each other. In Paris by 1908 Pablo Picasso had painted "Les Demoiselles d'Avignon," Cubism had been declared, Gertrude Stein had begun the uncertain adventure of writing Cubist prose, and Proust had started *A la recherche du temps perdu*. In Germany, the art critic Wilhelm Worringer had defined "abstraction" rather than "empathy" as the key of modern art, and Expressionism had begun. In Vienna Musil, Schnitzler and Hoffmannsthal were writing, and Freud had published *The*

78

Psychopathology of Everyday Life. In Italy Marinetti had started announcing Futurism; in February 1909 the *Futurist Manifesto* appeared, calling for the destruction of the cities and the art of the past ("Flood the museums!"), and celebrating new forms based on the automobile, the aeroplane and war. In pre-Revolutionary Russia, where Chekhov was writing his late plays, it found its parallel in Constructivism. All these movements were claiming history for themselves: announcing new psychologies of creation, new principles of form, new modes of perception, new attitudes to the future in the age of brute modernity, and declaring that artistic styles were not derived from accepted practices and conventions, but had to be newly sought and freshly made. The Modern movement was in essence an international affair, founded on exile, the movement of the arts, ideas and forms from one bohemia to another. And even in "philistine" but imperial and hospitable pre-war Britain it now was starting to find a homeless home. Marinetti toured the country, declaiming his outrageous manifestos, and many artistic expatriates and exiles from elsewhere, drawn by its imperial vitality, were starting to flood in. In 1908 Ezra Pound arrived from the United States, determined to start a "mouvemong" on the French model, and he found a group of poets, now well remembered as "the Forgotten School of 1909," to support his search for the "new poetic," which in itself was a link with the Symbolist campaigns of the 1890s.[6]

From 1908 on, then, signs of the modern change, the movement spirit, began to stir in Britain. Late in 1908, the continentalized Hueffer, determined to rouse the commercial and philistine age into a "critical attitude," risked everything he had – and quite a bit others had too – to begin his monthly magazine *The English Review*. He explained it as "sort of *aube de siècle* Yellow Book," and Pound called it "the EVENT of 1909–10"; it could best be described as at once the last of the Great Victorian Reviews, and the first of the Modernist little

[6] This is fully detailed in Malcolm Bradbury and James McFarlane (eds.), *Modernism, 1890–1930* (Harmondsworth, rev. ed., 1989).

magazines. Hueffer's aim, too, was to start a new movement, as he later flamboyantly explained:

> ... the old literary gang of the *Athenaeum-Spectator-Heavy Artillery* order were slowly decaying. Young lions were not only roaring but making carnage of their predecessors. Mr Wells was then growing a formidable mane, Arnold Bennett if not widely known was at least known to and admired by me ... Experimenting in forms kept Conrad still young. Henry James was still "young James" for my uncle William Rossetti and hardly known by the general public. George Meredith and Thomas Hardy had come into their own only very little before ... It seemed to me that if a nucleus of writers could be got together with what of undiscovered talent the country might hold, a Movement might well be started. I had one or two things I wanted to say ...[7]

This was a largely Edwardian cast, and he printed almost all of them, but he also wanted to introduce in the paper, edited from over a greengrocer's shop, his "young lions," those writers he liked, being Francophile, like everyone else, to call "Les Jeunes." This seemed the fond dream of an old Nineties movement man; but, as he explained, "Les Jeunes" really existed and were only waiting to be discovered:

> Les Jeunes, as they chronologically presented themselves to us, were Mr Pound, Mr D. H. Lawrence, Mr Norman Douglas, Mr [F. S.] Flint, "H. D.", Mr Richard Aldington, Mr T. S. Eliot ... in our Editorial Salons they found chaises-longues and sofas on which to stretch themselves while they discussed the fate of already fermenting Europe. So, for three or four years, culminating in the London season of 1914, they made a great deal of noise in a city that was preparing to reverberate with the echoes of blasts still greater. They stood for the Non-Representational in the Arts; for *Vers Libre*; for symbols in Prose, *tapage* in Life, and death to Impressionism.

[7] Ford Madox Ford, *Return to Yesterday: Reminiscences 1894–1914* (London, 1931).

Over the two years of his editorship the paper comfortably printed, side by side with the Edwardians, nearly all the above, and the magazine marks a moment of strong literary transition. The movement came, the critical attitude flourished. Hueffer's instincts were right, and he had chosen his moment well. In the sphere of the literary arts, there was – truly – an "opening world."

3.

Virginia Woolf's sound of "breaking and falling, crashing and destruction," was therefore real enough. By the four years between the beginning of Georgianism and the outbreak of the Great War, the "modern spirit," the sense of *avant-garde* adventure, of new forms opening new windows on a changed world, had once again begun to take hold. New and powerful influences, Dostoevsky and Chekhov, Ibsen and Nietzsche, Bergson and Sorel and Freud, began affecting British writing. For the moment London was recognizably a major centre of artistic cosmopolitanism, and writers and forms flooded in, in what is now remembered as a period of high cultural hospitality and internationalism rare in the modern British arts. Everyone slipped off to Paris. Hueffer came to see himself as German, or French, indeed anything but English. Then there were the expatriates and exiles: Conrad and Gaudier-Brzeska from Poland, S. S. Koteliansky from Russia, Yeats, Shaw and George Moore from Ireland (Joyce took his exile further afield, to the old Habsburg port of Trieste); James, Pound, "H. D.", and later the quiet T. S. Eliot from the USA; Katherine Mansfield from New Zealand, and Wyndham Lewis from God alone knew where (he was appropriately born on a ship at sea). Lawrence made Nottinghamshire sound like a place of exile, followed German literature with passion, and began, like Joyce, on the path of wandering. Now more and more little magazines, generally with strange typographies and abstract covers, began their insecure publication; more and more movements and manifestos appeared (Imagism, Vorticism), calling in their different ways for energy, explosion, destruction and recommencement, aiming to blast down the past in the hope of blessing the future. The arts were in a mood of rebellious warfare, and their flamboyant putsches, campaigns and counter-putsches won public attention.[8]

Woolf's term for this, "Georgian," was perhaps less than satisfactory. She was speaking of a double revolt, against "Victorianism" and "Edwardianism," but in fact the new movements and tendencies split in many directions, in which Georgianism – everything now was an "ism" – was just one voice. In 1912 came Edward Marsh's *Georgian Poetry*, printing a variety of poets and generations, and claiming that the Georgian period might "take rank in due time with the several great poetic ages of the past." To D. H. Lawrence, who was both in it and reviewed it, the new "Georgian" spirit was one of Nietzschean hope: "The nihilists, the intellectual, hopeless people – Ibsen, Flaubert, Thomas Hardy – represent the dream we are waking from. It was a dream of demolition . . . But we are awake again, our lungs are full of new air, our eyes of morning." Others were less sure. Georgianism in verse was soon challenged by Imagism, which was then challenged by Vorticism, each of them with a different view of the distilling form – "image," "vortex," or whatever – of the new. Dreams of the great demolition, the crashing and falling, continued. When Wyndham Lewis started a Vorticist manifesto-magazine in 1914 he called it *Blast*: and in a volley of brief, violent curses and benedictions he blasted the Victorians, rejected Romanticism for Classicism, Georgianism for something harder, tougher, more to do with machines than nature, and blessed the age of the abstract vortex and the cleansing modern explosion. The new excitements intensified year by year, and some of those who had called themselves simply moderns now knew they were Modernists, claiming that a most momentous

[8] A good recent record of this era is Julian Symons, *Makers of the New: the Revolution of Literature, 1912–1939* (London, 1987). Also see Frank Swinnerton's bluff but interesting *The Georgian Literary Scene* (London, 1938).

transformation was fully under way. Small groups gathered, experimental enclaves flourished, hard experimental art-works multiplied, and new small presses and little magazines appeared to exhibit the *avant garde*, printing works by writers whose work seemed to have been shamefully denied, from the new feminists to the exiled James Joyce. Hueffer, who once called himself an "Impressionist," in the manner of Conrad, now called himself a "Vorticist," and used Vorticist methods for his novel *The Good Soldier*, a section of which in turn appeared in *Blast*. *The Egoist*, once a feminist magazine, now had acquired Pound as literary editor; it promoted the movement of "Imagism," and then in 1914, over 24 episodes, ran Joyce's *A Portrait of the Artist as a Young Man*. It was a rare and remarkable period in British writing, in prose and poetry, and in painting and sculpture and dance, all of which linked together in common cause. A pre-war Modernist wonderland did exist, and it was indeed like an opening world.

Even so, it is quite possible that all this could have been a brief and seasonal adventure, were it not for one terrible fact. The pre-war writers did not know they *were* pre-war writers, though sometimes it seems they half-intuited what was to come. The *avant garde*, for all its modern prophecies, was not aware of what it was really *avant*. 1914, the year of Joyce's *Dubliners* and the serialization of *A Portrait* . . ., saw the excitement reach its peak. Then in August, between the first and second issues of *Blast*, the real blasts sounded. The collapse of the imperial Europe, following the assassination of the Habsburg Archduke in Sarajevo, started; the Great War began. Soon the vortex of new energy ran free, and the young were all transforming themselves into Good Soldiers. Many, including T. E. Hulme, voice of the hard new classicism, and Gaudier-Brzeska, who had declared in *Blast* "The War is a great remedy," died at the front. The abstract metallic explosions, the bursting mechanical violence, the new kinetic energy, became realities; the bombing of the old art cities, the flooding of the museums, that the Futurists had called for turned into fact. Over several literary generations writers had been prophesying the coming of the

New Age, the violent end of an epoch, the rule of the destructive element, a war of the worlds. Now an era that thought it was beginning also found that it was ending, that even the spring-time new hopes were dashed. An era in culture, the arts and civilization was now in crisis, as Henry James, now at the close of his life, saw. He wrote his story "A Dream of Armageddon," and reflected in a letter of August 1914 to his friend Howard Sturgis "the plunge of civilization into this abyss of blood and darkness . . . is a thing that so gives away the whole long age in which we have supposed the world to be, with whatever abatement, gradually bettering, that to have to take it all now for what the treacherous years were all the while really making for and *meaning* is too tragic for any words." Indeed, he noted, "the war has used up words." It was a notion that would re-surface grimly after the Holocaust of the Second World War. The words, of course, would come in time. But the realization that they would have to be new words, that the war had drained most of the old ones of signification, that a different language, pared of most of the old romantic and cultural associations, would have to be found, grew as the terrible Great War went on. So it was that the War itself completed what pre-war Modernists had begun to imagine: the sweeping away of Victorianism, and Edwardianism. Georgianism, its eyes full of morning, went too. The war smashed romanticism and senti-mentalism, naive notions of patriotism and imperial adventure; they did not outlast the conflict. But, paradoxically, some of the complex aesthetic ideas that had stirred in the years between 1910 and 1914 – "hardness," "abstraction," "collage," "frag-mentation," "dehumanization" – and the key themes of chaotic history, Dionysian energy, the "destructive element," did help to provide the discourse and forms of the world to come.

1915 – the year the war settled into the futility of trench warfare, and Zeppelin airships arrived to bomb London – was the culminating year, both in the war and in the transition of the arts. Some of the key books of the years of experiment appeared, marking a deep change in fictional climate. Conrad's emphatically titled *Victory* came out; so did John Buchan's classic spy story, *The 39 Steps*. Hueffers' farewell to the *belle époque*, the book that he had intended to call *The Saddest Story* (in accordance with its famous opening line, "This is the saddest story I have ever heard"), appeared under the new wartime title of *The Good Soldier*. Virginia Woolf's long-delayed first novel appeared at last as *The Voyage Out*, and Dorothy Richardson opened her long experimental sequence "Pilgrimage" with the volume *Pointed Roofs*. D. H. Lawrence, who had proved himself a writer always interested in apocalyptic moments and signs, the leap from the ruins, the personal resurrection, found the growing darkness of his vision confirmed. Before the War, he had started his most ambitious project so far, *The Sisters*, aided by his reading of Thomas Hardy. Now he divided it into two, to take account of what was happening. "I knew I was writing a destructive work . . .," he explained later, "And I knew, as I revised the book, that it was a kind of working up to the dark sensual or Dionysic or Aphrodisic ecstasy, which actually does burst the world, burst the world-consciousness in every individual. What I did through individuals, the world has done through the war. But alas, in the world of Europe I see no Rainbow." In 1915 the first segment of the book, which was called *The Rainbow*, the rainbow being an apocalyptic sign, appeared. It was a work both of crisis and Dionysic sensual ecstasy, developing both in optimism and pessimism on from Hardy. The critics were shocked, perhaps in part by its apparent indifference to the War itself. One thousand and eleven copies were seized and destroyed by the police, and it was banned under the Obscene Publications Act. "The world is gone, extinguished," Lawrence bitterly noted, already planning the path of post-war exile; "It was in 1915 that the old world ended." Many of the fruits of the pre-war experiment had come to birth. So had a new world, bitter and empty, made out of cultural disorder and European ruins. It might be a modern, but it was no longer an opening, world.

4.

It is hardly surprising that the immediately pre-war years became folkloric, for the participants and then for the later critics; so much that is important to the idea of modern literature stirred into existence then. In retrospect, said Wyndham Lewis, looking back from 1937, when he had himself become the "Enemy," at odds with most of what happened thereafter to the Modern movement, it would all appear "an island of incomparable bliss, dwelt by strange shapes labelled 'Pound,' 'Joyce,' 'Weaver,' 'Hulme' . . . As people look back at them, out of a very humdrum, cautious, disillusioned society . . . the critics of the future will rub their eyes. They will look, to them, so hopelessly avant garde!, so almost madly up and coming! What energy! – what impossibly spartan standards, men will exclaim! . . . *We are the first men of a future that has not materialized!*" Whether this is self-serving or not, it is certainly true that we cannot write the history of modern fiction without looking with some care at many of his strange shapes. And there is no doubt that one of the strangest, and most representative, was the one then labelled "Hueffer," though later known as "Ford." Hueffer/Ford always had a gift for metamorphosis, and this brought him into close contact with nearly everything that was interesting and significant about the Modern movement. Lewis, whom he discovered, called him "a flabby lemon and pink giant, who hung his mouth open as though he were an animal at the Zoo inviting buns – especially when ladies were present" (they often were); H. G. Wells, first his friend, then his enemy, described him as "a great system of assumed persona and dramatized selves." Indeed it was true his manner often appeared a disguise, and there somehow seemed to be two or more of him. He was the British writer incarnate, but he was also German, or French. Sometimes he was the foreign bohemian adrift among British philistines; sometimes he was the last British Tory, condemned to travel the great wilderness know as "abroad." At various times he was the Last Pre-

Raphaelite, the first Impressionist, a Post-Impressionist, a Vorticist, and a soldier of the Parisian "Revolution of the Word." He wrote extensively about the "critical attitude," but was not a theorist (his companion of the 1920s, Stella Bowen, described him as "a writer – a complete writer – and nothing but a writer"). He collaborated with Conrad, wrote well on James, and had literary friendships (though they often turned, as such things do, into enmities) with most of the major figures of the era – Conrad, James, Hardy, Wells, Pound, Lawrence, Violet Hunt, Rebecca West, May Sinclair, Joyce, Stein, Jean Rhys and Robert Lowell, helping many of them to publication. He was close to every major movement, from Pre-Raphaelitism to Dada, over the fifty years of his writing life. He wrote over eighty books in innumerable genres, children's stories to advanced poetry, from the early 1890s to 1939, the year of his death; thus his writing life more or less matched the main span of Modernism.

He both enacted Modernism's story, and told it – not always accurately, but he was an "Impressionist" – in many books of criticism and reminiscence. He was born in 1873, in a Pre-Raphaelite bohemian household; his father was a German music critic just arrived in Britain, his mother was daughter to the painter Ford Madox Brown. At eighteen, as the Nineties started, he published his first book *The Brown Owl*, a fairy story that owed something to Stevenson, and by 1898, after several more books, met the still little-known Conrad. They collaborated on three commercial novels, *The Inheritors* (1901), *Romance* (1903) and *The Nature of a Crime* (1924), and Hueffer also had a hand in *Heart of Darkness* and *Nostromo*, two of Conrad's finest works. Drawing on the theories of Flaubert, Maupassant and James, they agreed together on the method of "Impressionism": "We accepted the name of impressionists because we saw that life did not narrate but made Impressions on our brains," he later explained. "We in turn, if we wished to produce an effect of life, must not narrate but render impressions."[9] He was also

[9] Ford Madox Ford, *Joseph Conrad: A Personal Reminiscence* (London, 1924).

writing novels of his own, and making important literary friendships, with Henry James, H. G. Wells, John Galsworthy and Stephen Crane, the American author of *The Red Badge of Courage*, now living in Britain. Most of these were gathered together, as if for experimental literary security, in the same general area of Kent and Sussex; they visited each other frequently – James on his bicycle, Crane with his six-gun – and formed an important seedbed for the cultivation of the modern, a meeting-place for many of its main ideas and, indeed, its future quarrels.

Between the century's turn and the coming of war, Hueffer – a writer's writer who wrote every day – produced almost forty books, from memoirs and children's books to historical and social novels. Several were in the typical Edwardian form of the "Condition of Engand" novel, explorations of the contemporary social order and its conflicts. But he explored them with "impressionist" techniques, as he did, more surprisingly, the historical romance – above all his fine *Fifth Queen* trilogy, about Katherine Howard, which he completed in 1908, just as he was founding *The English Review*. That magazine brought him into close contact with an entire new generation of writers, including Pound, Lewis, and D. H. Lawrence, all of whom he "discovered": "Ford Madox Hueffer discovered I was a genius," Lawrence wrote, " – don't be alarmed, Hueffer would discover *anything* if he wanted to." He championed the new because it *was* new, original, innovative; the process helped make his own work new. He began to see that an experimental bridge could be built between the older writers of the 1890s and the younger innovators, even those at odds with his own literary philosophy. A declared Impressionist, he gladly published those like Pound who cried "Death to Impressionism." Though he had total contempt for the Novel With a Purpose ("A novel should render, not draw morals"), he published Wells, who after 1900 wrote little else – and before he was done Hueffer wrote Novels With a Purpose too (his post-war "Parade's End" sequence had, he said, for its purpose "the obviating of all future wars"). He believed in Flaubertian French perfection, but he advanced expressionistic neo-Nietzscheans like D. H. Lawrence. He saw and wrote of an age of looming sexual chaos, but assisted New Feminist writers like Violet Hunt (translator of Casanova, and author of the interesting novel of the life of working women, *The Workaday Woman*, 1906), Rebecca West, Stella Bowen, and later Jean Rhys. Sometimes his assistance went a very long way, and led to various unconventional *ménages*; generally he received either too little or too much in the way of gratitude. It didn't matter; what counted was "perfection," the "critical attitude," the "serious artist," the "spirit of modern life." In 1912, he finally and grandly announced his farewell to literature, to leave the field to newer writers "whose claim or whose need for recognition and what recognitions bring was greater than my own."

Fortunately, and typically, he soon changed his mind, and so in 1913, on his fortieth birthday, he resolved to give himself one last chance. "I had always been mad about writing – about the way writing should be done and partly alone, partly with the companionship of Conrad, I had even at that date made exhaustive studies into how words should be handled and books constructed," he explained, but "I had never really put into any novel of mine *all* that I knew about writing." That aim went into his new book, which proved his finest, his great contribution to the New Novel. He followed the method of Conrad and later James by dictating some of his story, which doubtless added to its hesitancies and indirections, its air of fracture and tension. Excited by Vorticism, he borrowed its "hard" technique, and made the book polished, "like a steel helmet." Responding to the mood of the time, he made his theme the dying of the European *belle-époque* world, which he presented with bitter irony. He gave the book an ambiguous, American narrator, Dowell, a deceived husband, who declares "Six months ago I had never been to England, and, certainly, I had never sounded the depths of an English heart." The novel's theme is sounding the false beat of the pre-war English heart, and the book contains its own ominous warning. Hueffer ensured that the chief events occur on 4 August of various years – the date of the outbreak of the Great War, which came as he worked on the novel.

The book, *The Good Soldier*, therefore appeared in 1915, along with other key books of the pre-war modern movement. The peak of his experiment, it was also the end of an era. Despite its title, it is a novel not of war but pre-war. Set mostly in the German spa town of Nauheim (in enemy territory by the time the book appeared), the story is about a man of honour corrupted by sexuality and the social deceits and hypocrisies which surround and disguise it. Two central couples, the British Ashburnhams, the American Dowells, have *mariages blancs*, unconsummated marriages; for different reasons the wives want to protect their sexual sanctity. They pretend to "heart disease" so that, at the spa, various polygamous arrangements can be made. Ashburnham, who seems especially honourable, is the British "good soldier." But married love is conducted through surrogates and intricate systems of deception. Only Dowell, the cuckold narrator, seems unaware of them; the story he tells as it were deceives him. His method of indirect narration also deceives us ("I have, I am aware, told this story in a very rambling way so that it may be difficult for anyone to find their path through what may be a sort of maze. I cannot help it . . . when one discusses an affair – a long, sad affair – one goes back, one goes forward . . ."). If, as he says, the book's social world is "secret," "subtle," "subterranean," the workings of the sexual world are more obscure still; one critic of the book has remarked that its sexual activity seems always the echo of an echo – now you see it, now you don't. The innocent Dowell is left to unravel the impressions and deceits confronting him. The word "impression" is crucial to the story – there are "all-round impresssions," "first impressions," "false impressions." The baffled decoding of impressions – learnt from James and Conrad – gives the difficult fragmented technique. *The Good Soldier* has been called the best French novel in the English language; it is easy to see why. It is what the French critic Roland Barthes calls *scriptible*; we are always aware of the self-conscious method of the writing, the writerly nature of the text. In Jamesian terms (which Hueffer adopted), the story is an "affair," the telling is a "treatment," the method displays James' "baffled relationship between the subject-matter and its emergence." James here was referring to Conrad, but Hueffer takes matters one step further, making his narrator the victim of the story he tells. But in a world of false social surfaces, where everything is deliberately unspoken, it takes an art of great indirection to get to, well, the heart of the matter.

The Good Soldier, one of the culminating books of the pre-war modern movement, was Hueffer's last novel as Hueffer. When he came back from the front he changed his name to Ford; domestic troubles were part of the reason, but, as he rightly said, all identities had changed in the War. He still had twenty more years of writing life, some thirty more books to bring to print, including the excellent "Parade's End" sequence (1924–28), of which more later on. But part of its importance is that it explores the difficult passage, through the battlefields of the Somme, from pre-war to post-war Britain, and suggests why the Condition of England was no longer an easily available subject, why modern forms continued to fragment. By now he was an exile in France; for the "opening world" had plainly closed by now, the London experiment had virtually died, and Britain had banned, silenced or alienated many of its finest and most demanding writers. He would never live permanently in Britain again, and his main work hereafter was done in France, amid the experimental excitements of the 1920s. And by now the modern novel had ceased to be an "affair"; it had become the expression of an historical crisis. The future had indeed materialized, but not in the way its prophets had expected. Hueffer/Ford died in France in 1939, when the Modern experiment was as good as over. Hueffer had seen one half of it; Ford had seen the other. Each had written a major modern work: Hueffer the pre-war *The Good Soldier*, and Ford the post-war "Parade's End." His own reputation had declined by now, but he had done what he meant to do – bring a French perfection to the English novel, and support the changing experiment of British writing. He had crossed with nearly everything that was significant, and midwived many of the main achievements, from start to finish, from Conrad's *Nostromo* and Lawrence's *The White Peacock* to Stein's *The Making of Americans* and Joyce's *Finnegans Wake*. He had written good books and bad ones, and, as he confessed, not done all he intended. But in Modernism's discontinuous continuity he still remains a central figure.

5.

If the young Ford Madox Hueffer who met and collaborated with Joseph Conrad in 1898 was not always to remain Hueffer, the forty-year Polish émigré his path had crossed with had certainly not always been Joseph Conrad. The disorders of imperial middle Europe had brought about his change of name and cultural identity, and they left their mark on all his work. He was born Josef Teodor Konrad Nalecz Korzeniowski, the child of Polish gentry in 1857 in the Russian-occupied Polish Ukraine, a "country that was not a country." His father Apollo was a romantic nationalist who fought against the Tsarist domination, and when he was sent into Russian penal exile he took the young child with him. From this time onward "Conrad" would always remain to some degree exiled and stateless; so would the fiction he came to write. As he grew up he wandered in Europe – he moved to France, went to sea, fought a duel, engaged in gun-running, spent a fortune, attempted suicide. To avoid conscription in the Russian army, he joined the British merchant navy, and sailed the seaways of the imperial and mercantile world, from the Pacific to South America, the British coastal ports to the Congo. That gave him British citizenship, but never quite perfect English; the fiction he started now would always have, in language as well as vision, a touch of the foreign and the exiled about it. Nonetheless, in a time that was turning to the imperial romance, he evidently possessed perfect exotic material, and a chance meeting with John Galsworthy on an Eastern voyage led him to think of writing a novel. He began a tale about outcast

Europeans in the Malayan archipelago, based on personal experience, which he carried about the world; it appeared in 1895 as *Almayer's Folly*. In 1896 he followed it with another similar story of the Pacific, also about Europeans split between two worlds, *An Outcast of the Islands*. Both were romances, but both have a haunting sense of life on its frontier, of existence as isolation and extremity. And a distinctive Conradian note is already struck in a passage in the second novel where he speaks of "the tremendous fact of our isolation, of the loneliness impenetrable and transparent, elusive and everlasting; of the indestructible loneliness that surrounds, envelops, clothes every soul from the cradle to the grave, and perhaps, beyond."

Then in 1898, just round the time Hueffer met him, he produced a quite different kind of book. Today it is uncomfortably dated by its title, *The Nigger of the "Narcissus"*, but it remains a work of unmistakable modernity, the beginning of his major fiction. The story of a homeward voyage from Bombay to London, it tells of nihilistic forces set loose on the ship during the passage, and of the final, necessary restoration of order. Like many of Conrad's later books, it is also a myth – possibly influenced by Herman Melville's remarkable sea-fable "Benito Cereno" (1856) – about an unreliable and doubled world. It was the first of many tales he would set on merchant vessels, seen as microcosms of the social, moral, indeed metaphysical world, where the need for order and discipline conflict with wilderness and threat, not only from the "terrible sea" and the anarchy of life, but from the inner ambiguity of human nature itself. Shipboard society becomes a space where the "essential" values – honour, duty, courage, fidelity ("Those who read me know my conviction that the world, the temporal world, rests on a few simple ideas; so simple they must be as old as the hills," Conrad observed: "It rests notably, among others, on the idea of Fidelity") – are tested to extremity. Pervading the stories is a fearful scepticism, the awareness that civilization soon finds its limits, light turns into darkness, virtue and courage are always at risk, behind every face there is a secret sharer, behind every man there is a darker double. When David Daiches hailed

Conrad as "the first important modern novelist in English," it was because of the distinctive timbre of his metaphysical vision, which means that "the world of significance he creates is at the furthest remove from the world of public significance created by the great Victorian and eighteenth-century novelists." Like the Russian fiction of Dostoevsky, whose work Conrad claimed to detest ("I don't know what Dostoevsky stands for or reveals, but I do know he is too Russian for me," he said, in a remark that peculiarly resembled the complaints of some critics about his own novels), his novels implanted into social or romantic themes an existential crisis. And with that modern spirit went a modern method, part-born from this alien, metaphysical tone of his writing – a method always indirect, deferring, bred of his dark conviction that he wrote of a gloomy unstable universe in which, as he said, "no explanation is final."

So quite as famous as *The Nigger of the "Narcissus"* is its preface, now taken as one of the most important manifestos of the modern way in fiction. Perhaps stung by H. G. Wells' charge of "obscurity," probably influenced by Stevenson's defence of the "web . . . or the pattern" at the heart of fiction ("a web at once sensuous and logical, an elegant and pregnant texture: that is style, that is the foundation of the art of literature"), Conrad made the case for a novel that unified form and content by searching inwardly, self-consciously for its own logic and coherence. A famous phrase declares the symbolist credo: "A work that aspires, however humbly, to the condition of art should carry its justification in every line." A novel should have the magical suggestiveness of music and the plastic arts, should be "an impression conveyed through the senses." And the task of the novelist was to "render." "My task which I am trying to achieve is, by the power of the written word to make you feel – it is, before all, to make you *see*. That – and no more, and it is everything. If I succeed, you shall find there according to your deserts: encouragement, consolation, fear, charm – all you demand – and, perhaps, also that glimpse of truth for which you have forgotten to ask." The aim of art, just like that of life, "is inspiring, difficult – obscured by mists. It is not in the clear logic of a triumphant conclusion; it is not in the unveiling of one of those heartless secrets which are called the Laws of Nature." Art grew not from statement or narrative completeness; it grew from rendering, figuration, "impressions," the pursuit of the symbol. If some unhappy readers thought this simply produced novels that were themselves obscured by mists, others felt this was indeed what James called the new self-consciousness of fiction.

What Conrad had in mind perhaps grew a little clearer when he set off directly for the heart of his darkness. *Heart of Darkness*, the powerful long novella of imperialism he published in magazine form in 1899, and collected in the volume *Youth* in 1902, starts in the gloomy light of London, the imperial city; it returns safely back at last to the drawing-rooms of social fiction. Between comes a cunning allegory of light falling into darkness, a descent through the heart of Africa into human horror and the black places of the soul. In 1890 Conrad had taken part in the new scramble for Africa, sailing to the imperial Belgian outpost in the Congo; he returned ill, shaken, morally outraged by the cruelties and corruption he had seen. "Before the Congo I was only a simple animal," he said. The story follows his experience almost exactly, taking its narrator, Marlow, on a "night journey" from London, via a sinister Brussels, to the grim Congo and the "Inner Station" – a journey that moves from civilization through futility and carelessness to evil, darkness, exploitation, and "the earliest beginnings of the world." In the Congo Marlow finds his tragic double, Mr Kurtz, an idealist who had dreamt of bringing civilization to Africa, been drawn into its savagery – "The wilderness had patted him on the head" – and comes to the ultimate abyss, declared in his dying cry of "The horror! The horror!" Kurtz bequeaths Marlow a moral dilemma; when he returns to London he has to report his death to Kurtz's *fiancée*, "the Intended," who asks what his last words were. Marlow chooses a saving lie over a revelation of the moral anarchy he has seen: "The last word he spoke was – your name," he says. But the story contains a second story, of its own telling. Marlow recounts it all, on a

ship in a London port, to a chosen audience, an Imperial trio:
a Lawyer, an Accountant and a Director of Companies, to
whom he reveals that London too has been, is, one of the earth's
dark places. Marlow – the angled, ironic narrator who first
appeared in the earlier story "Youth" – is the key to the tale.
He is, Conrad explained, a man "with whom my relations have
grown very intimate in the course of years . . . He haunts my
hours of solitude when, in silence, we lay our heads together in
great comfort and harmony; but as we part at the end of a tale
I am never sure that it may not be for the last time." He is,
effectively, the storyteller as method, not just the experiencer of
the tale, but its constructor, interpreter, investigator, decoder,
an intruded presence between tale and reader. He has his own
view of story: "The meaning of an episode is not inside like a
kernel but outside, enveloping the tale which brought it out
only as a glow brings out a haze, in the likeness of one of those
misty halos that sometimes are made visible by the spectral
illumination of moonshine." This may sound like a defence of
Romanticism, but the point, of course, is that "episodes" do not
have one simple meaning, but are refracted. This was what
readers otherwise admiring of Conrad often challenged. "Is
there not also a central obscurity, something noble, heroic,
beautiful, inspiring half-a-dozen great books, but obscure,
obscure?" asked E. M. Forster. To others this became the
essence of modern fiction itself, what James, also writing of
Conrad, called the baffled relation between the story and its
emergence, which made the novel not an action but an "affair."

A novel should be not a "superficial how" but a "fundamental
why," suggests Marlow, when he returns, one of several narrators, to tell the story of *Lord Jim* (1900). Jim, the hero who fails
to be a hero, abandons his vessel, the *Patna*, loaded with
pilgrims en route for Mecca, when he thinks it is sinking, and
so violates a fundamental law of duty and responsibility. The
ship is rescued, and his cowardice and shame exposed, at an
official enquiry. But this fails to satisfy Marlow, who sees Jim
as "one of us" and looks for what this tells us about human
nature: "Why I longed to go grubbing after the deplorable

details of an occurrence which, after all, concerned me no more than as a member of an obscure body of men [sailors] held together by a community of inglorious toil and by fidelity to a certain standard of conduct, I can't explain," he tells us: " . . . Perhaps, unconsciously, I hoped I would find that something, some profound and redeeming cause, some merciful explanation, some convincing shadow of an excuse." The book changes from seafaring adventure into a psychological and metaphysical investigation, and develops not to a final resolution but to a deep uncertainty about human complexity. Marlow teases the story backward and forward, seeking the essence among the multiplied meanings of Jim – coward and hero, outcast and *tuan*, the man who tries to redeem his moral crime by confronting the "destructive element," and finally meets the positive and negative faces of his own self in an apparently senseless act of sacrifice. The book's time-scale, and its viewpoint, move back and forth, through indirections and curious retellings. These indirect methods are of the essence, functioning in the story just as Marlow does: to fill out an expanding world of values and ambiguities against which Jim is tested, and has tested himself, and which leaves him and the story "inscrutable at heart," real and yet disembodied.

Later in life Conrad would describe his art as lying "almost wholly in my unconventional grouping and perspective," explain that he was concerned for "effects" rather than "mere directness of narrative." Complexity was becoming the essence of his novels; like his own Captain Giles in *The Shadow Line* (1917), Conrad had chosen to be an expert in "intricate navigation." If readers found them difficult, as they did, this was not only because of oblique tactics – his breaking of conventional time-codes, his refusal of safe endings, his multiplication of viewpoints – nor because of his sense that life and human action were enigmatic, "inscrutable at heart." There was also something that could aptly be called "foreign" about his writing, a double vision, displayed in the spirit of irony – a spirit seemingly at odds with the best hopes and public themes of the Edwardian age, when in fact he produced his finest work.

Nostromo (1904) is often thought his best novel, an ultimate fable of New World imperialism. It is set in the imaginary South American republic of Costaguana – otherwise "the dung coast," dominated by its silver mine, the ever-ambiguous symbol of New World adventuring – and written in the mode of what we now call "magical realism." Conrad gives his imaginary land a complex Borgesian history, drawn, he says, from Don José Avellanos' *History of Fifty Years of Misrule*, a lost work whose pages float away across the harbour in the course of the novel. "I am in fact the only person in the world possessed of its contents," Conrad says in the preface, ". . . I hope my accuracy can be trusted." It has to be, since, as he also says, "There was not a single brick, stone, or grain of sand in its soil I had not placed into position with my own hands." Like the New World itself, Costaguana is an invented space of history and myth: it is pastoral, virgin land, the placid gulf, an American dream, a half-blank page on which history is still to be written, "a twilight country . . . with its high shadowy Sierra and its misty campo for mute witness of events flowing from the passions of men short-sighted in good and evil."

It also has a very modern politics, and if its history is still being written, many try to write it: the old colonists and the new European adventurers, who bring the usual mixtures of idealism and materialism, buccaneering exploitation and liberal dreams, social reform and violent revolution, hope and depravity, "violent efforts for an idea and sullen acquiescence in every form of corruption." "Liberals! The words one knows so well have a nightmarish meaning in this country," we learn; all the causes prove to have "a flavour of folly and murder," and no one survives very long. Western civilization intrudes with its apparent principles of order and reason, bringing the steamship company, the railroad, the exploitation of the San Tomé silver mine, otherwise known as "material interests." "Silver" is the novel's key word, intricately coded into the book. It is a moral ideal, and a source of European and North American wealth; a dream of redemption and the corrupting instrument of an age of capitalism and individualism. The source of identity, it destroys everyone – Charles Gould, Decoud, above all Nostromo, "our man," the Man of the People, the figure of "unbroken fidelity, rectitude and courage" whose fidelity and bravery are corrupted and rendered an artifice: "Nostromo had lost his peace; the genuineness of all his qualities was destroyed." Nature and civilization becalm each other, producing a collapse of ideals and dreams, love and will, creating indifference and nihilism. *Nostromo* is a dark book – in its vision of human nature and desire, its view of modern history, its doubt of all political systems. At the end the United States still waits in the wings ("We shall run the world's business whether the world likes it or not"), and the name of the corrupted Nostromo still rings ambiguously over the dark gulf. This is the work of a man who sees that history does not work by progressive liberal evolution nor by revolution, that idealistic virtues and political dreams rarely survive pure but betray or are betrayed from within or without: an ironist indeed.

His next book, *The Secret Agent* (1907), brought that irony far closer to home. He turned to a British subject, given him by Hueffer, with a Russian flavour, explaining his conception like this: "The vision of an enormous town presented itself, of a monstrous town more populous than some continents and in its man-made might as if indifferent to heaven's frowns and smiles: a cruel devourer of the world's light. There was room enough here to place any story, depth enough for any passion, variety enough there for any setting, darkness enough to bury five millions of lives." The "monstrous town" is London, the darkness holds grim political secrets as well as obscure and furtive lives. The theme is anarchism, the central situation based on a bizarre and futile attempt made in 1894 on Greenwich Observatory – the sailor's sanctuary, the place where the temporal mean is set – when the terrorist had been blown up by his own bomb. This was the stuff of the sensational novel and the detective story; Conrad described his task as one of "applying an ironic method to a subject of this kind." The irony he applied is universal: there is irony of character (all the figures in the book are somehow examples of paradox, contradiction and futility), irony of plot (nothing ever works out as intended), irony of narrative perspective (the outcome of the story is an emotional nihilism), irony of existence (life, as Mrs Verloc discovers, is not worth looking into). Anarchism unwraps into the empty void of its own nihilism, and is in any case the product of safe bourgeois values; the book distances all the human agents, even the gentle simpleton Stevie, and spares neither civilization nor the revolutionary aspirations that threaten it. Frank Kermode describes the book as "a story with an enormous hole in the plot"; other critics have seen it as a novel without a hero, and a work without a perspective. But as Thomas Mann saw, when he wrote the preface for the German translation, the perspective is that of irony itself. It was a work neither of political liberalism nor revolutionary utopianism, both tempting attitudes of the day; it uses what Mann calls the method of "the tragic grotesque," the viewpoint of dismayed distance, the modern tone. There was one further irony; Conrad had subtitled the book "a simple tale," and hoped his melodrama would lift his disappointing sales; it did not. Chesterton was affronted enough to counter the book with his *The Man Who Was Thursday*; it may well have stimulated Wells, to whom it is dedicated, to write his more buoyant version of the monstrous town in *Tono-Bungay*. Conrad explained the book to Galsworthy as "an honourable failure . . . I suppose there is something in me that is unsympathetic to the general public . . . Foreignness, I suppose."

And "foreignness," the fact that not all the world is to be seen under Western eyes, was the theme of his next novel, *Under Western Eyes* (1911). This surely is Conrad's real masterpiece, even though it has its obvious imperfections, enough to drive its author to a nervous breakdown after writing it. It is an exile's book, in which he returns to the source of his own exile, Russia, that land of heroic romance and empty futility, tyranny and anarchy, "spectral dreams and disembodied aspirations," a work that links his fiction back to Dostoevsky and forward to Nabokov. Conrad added a preface to the book after the Bolshevik Revolution of 1917, explaining its underlying prophecy: an autocratic state founded on total moral anarchism had now been upturned by its "imbecile opposite," a proletarian and utopian revolution that went for destruction as the first means to hand. The book unlocks the hidden implication behind many of his other novels – that, if you happen to see the world with not quite Western eyes, not with the conventional assumptions of British liberalism or good-hearted reform, political order is generally a thin film on the top of chaos, and political sentiment quickly leads to a world of guilt and treachery. For all that he dismissed the works of Dostoevsky (just being translated in Britain as his book appeared), his fiction, and the tradition of the Russian novel, is imprinted on this novel: in the divided ideology, split between conservatism and revolution, in the romantic turmoil of soul, and the search for a metaphysic between contradictory, violent extremes. Razumov, the book's central character, directly recalls the Raskolnikov of *Crime and Punishment*, with his introspective and tormented consciousness, and his need to confess and purge the crime he has committed; both writers deal with the theme of the psychological purging of the self in a world that itself lacks all moral substance – a modern existential theme that has been central to the modern novel.

But there is one essential and fundamental difference, which makes the book into a dual text (as Nabokov's *Ada*, imprinting the landscape of Russia on America, the Russian novel on the American novel, is a dual text). The vivid tale of Razumov's student life, his encounter with revolution, and his betrayal in Saint Petersburg, and then his confession and expiation among the revolutionary exiles of the city of exiles, Geneva, is a Russian story. But the story is told to be interpreted and read under Western eyes. The book's narrator, a British teacher of languages in Geneva, is a latter-day Marlow, trying to tell and read the tale that has come his way. "To the teacher of languages there comes a time when the world is but a place of many words and man appears to be a mere talking animal not much more wonderful than a parrot," he tells us at the start; words are, he confesses, "the great foes of reality." It is his distance from the inner secrets of so many words that make him a less than reliable narrator, for though he is a student of many grammars there is much he cannot see with his "Western eyes." Thus the book layers two stories, from two narrative traditions, two different political and moral cultures. There is the language teacher's story, and that of Razumov, which he draws from his written confessions or his partial witnessing of events. Thus the story is filled with hidden secrets, which he doubly attempts to decode: making what sense he can of Razumov's tale, and making the experience understandable to readers who have only Western eyes. He uses Razumov's diary to extend his eye-witness material, but also develops and comments on it. The difficulty, not always narratively successful, becomes part of the virtuosity of the telling. It was not entirely surprising that British readers had some trouble with Conrad's "obscurity." When his own narrator has such problems in reading and interpreting a tale so dense with confusions and secrets, when that story concerns a different and alien world with a different sense of history, then it takes care and time to read with Western eyes a story that questions the gaze of Western eyes.

Conrad's obscurity, in short, was more than a technical obscurity; it had also to do with a challenge to Western culture his readers took some time to accept. Nonetheless they did accept it; with his next novel, *Chance* (1913), Conrad had at last his first popular success. Thereafter his audience magically widened. His last group of books – *Victory* (1915), *The Shadow Line* (1917), *The Arrow of Gold* (1919), *The Rescue* (1920), *The Rover* (1920) – satisfied the audience at last; where earlier books had runs of less than three thousand five hundred copies, *The Rescue* had a first run of twenty-five thousand. By now he had returned, largely, to sea stories, and his famous obscurity seemed to have turned into a dense and satisfying Romantic haze. His technique had muted, turning into what one great admirer, Virginia Woolf, called "old nobilities and sonorities . . . a little wearily reiterated, as if times had changed." In his final years he became one of Britain's most famous writers, revered abroad, offered a knighthood (mysteriously refused) in

1924; he died later that year. His greatest importance as a writer had lain in two things. One was the vision of a world of disorder, which challenged our sense of humanity and politics, and demanded an obscure new faith. The other was his obscurity itself, or rather what he made of it as a meaning for the writing of fiction. His best books remain those that, as the painter Max Ernst recommended, make the audience "a spectator at the birth of the work." Or, as Mark Schorer put it: "The virtue of the modern novelist – from James and Conrad down – is not only that he pays so much attention to his medium, but that, when he pays most, he discovers through it a new subject-matter, and a greater one . . . the final lesson of the modern novel is that technique is not the secondary thing it seemed to Wells, some external machination, a mechanical affair, but a deep and primary operation; not only that technique *contains* intellectual and moral implications, but that it *discovers* them."[10] And if by the close of the Edwardian period the novel was beginning to be acknowledged not simply as a mimetic but an autotelic form, that is, an internally coherent struggle to construct, from its own discovering means, its own discovering expression, Conrad indeed remains of profound importance.

6.

Edwardian readers who had difficulty with the obscurity and pessimism of Joseph Conrad plainly had none with the bright brash new world of H. G. Wells. By the early years of the century he had no more belief in the value of the obscure novel. "I have never taken any great pains about writing," he explained. "Long ago, living in close conversational proximity to Henry James, Joseph Conrad, and Mr Ford Madox Hueffer, I escaped from under their immense artistic preoccupations by

[10] Mark Schorer, "Technique as Discovery," in *The World We Imagine: Selected Essays* (London, 1969).

calling myself a journalist." In 1900, the year of *Lord Jim* and Freud's *Interpretation of Dreams*, he stepped away from his scientific romance to publish *Love and Mr Lewisham*, the story of a very ordinary schoolmaster caught between Great Ideas and the Instinct of Sex. This was the first of a row of novels Wells produced rapidly over the Edwardian period, all with somewhat similar themes, all about the excitement of life in a time of change and promise. Wells was above all readable; he was the novelist of ordinariness and familiarity, which he made excitingly unordinary and unfamiliar. His stories were mostly based on autobiographical materials, born out of the lower-middle-class London suburban world from which he came, tales of aspiring, opportunity-seeking young men and women who were taking on the adventure of social, educational, commercial, and sexual self-transformation. The basic plot is plain: a young person from modest beginnings is helped by political awareness, scientific knowledge and sexual openness to face the widening prospects of life, challenging convention and the stuffy inheritance of the British past in the process. There is usually a Big Idea on hand – Science, Evolution, Socialism, Feminism, Free Love, Modernity, or just a great new commercial invention. Some of the stories, like *Kipps* (1905) or *The History of Mr Polly* (1910), are larky and Dickensian, and Wells brought a welcome note of comic relief to the general solemnity of fiction. Others, like *Ann Veronica (1909)*, a portrait of a free new woman who takes what she wants, or *Tono-Bungay* (also 1909), a remarkable analysis of contemporary British culture, are more deeply serious. The Wellsian message is also unmistakable. If we are timid or unlucky, we return to the prison of convention or dull domesticity, but the real promise is the rule of positive evolution, stated in *The History of Mr Polly*: ". . . when a man has once broken through the paper walls of everyday circumstance, those unsubstantial walls that hold so many of us securely prisoned from the cradle to the grave, he has made a discovery," Wells tells us: "If the world does not please you, *you can change it.*"

Wells, we know, along with Arnold Bennett, John Galsworthy, and some others, wrote the Edwardian novel. But what then was the Edwardian novel? Plainly it was not the new self-conscious fiction James, Conrad and Hueffer were commonly expounding. But this did not mean its authors were ignorant of the claim that the novel was, as James said, an "affair." Wells had kept good company with "the immense artistic preoccupations" of these writers, and had given some considerable support to them; for example, he hailed Stephen Crane's highly Impressionist *The Red Badge of Courage* (1895) as a new kind of writing, "the expression in art of certain enormous repudiations." He sustained his friendship with Conrad, who dedicated *The Secret Agent* to Wells as "the historian of ages to come" (he likewise dedicated *Nostromo* to John Galsworthy, who had indeed encouraged him to begin writing). Wells believed he was constructing a radical experiment in fiction, as did Galsworthy and above all Bennett, who had signalled himself as "the latest disciple of the Goncourts," had devoted himself during the 1890s to what he called "conscious pleasure in technique," and always asserted there was no conflict between experimental artist and commercial literary adventurer. The experiment was above all a revolt against Victorianism, the nineteenth-century notion of the novelist. The question was the direction in which that revolt led the new writer. While the authors of "immense artistic preoccupations" followed the course of Impressionism, the Edwardians felt they had inherited the sweeping, reforming spirit of Naturalism. For a period in the 1890s the two seemed to be reconciled. By the early twentieth century the choice seemed to be between the one or the other: on the one hand "the beautiful difficulties of art," which dissolved materiality in fiction, and on the other the reforming passion born of Nietzscheanism, which moved on beyond Darwinian pessimism to a new evolutionary optimism. If the Symbolists claimed "art," the Edwardians claimed life: as Wells put it, imperially, "Before we have done, we will have all life within the scope of the novel."

"Life," from the Naturalists on, obviously meant more than just life, ongoing existence. It meant evolutionary energies, people seen in their environment and history, as representatives of the workings of the world; it was love and death and sex and marriage, plainly and frankly, objectively and critically seen. It was material mass, houses and goods and class relations, detail on detail amassed and considered and ordered. It was material in another sense, the telling facts of social activity and human behaviour the writer had noted, by being there and finding out. It was the world with all its facts challenged and its statements investigated, everything checked and taken down in evidence. It was literature supported by the investigative skills of journalism, the scepticism of science; it was not sentimental, or if it was sentimental it was in the interest of radical expectations. Readers then and since agreed that life was, indeed, just like this.[11] One thing was clear; it was not seeking a Flaubertian perfection of art. "Literature is not jewelry, it has quite other aims than perfection, and the more one thinks of 'how it is done' the less one gets it done," said Wells: "These critical indulgences lie along a fatal path . . ." "What I'm trying to render is nothing more or less than Life," explains George Ponderevo, the very self-conscious narrator of *Tono-Bungay*. Arnold Bennett entitled an entire section of *The Old Wives' Tale* (1908) "What Life Is" – the answer was in fact a long, slow, melancholy decline into age and death – and insisted his first concern was with life's feel and texture, "the interestingness of existence." Amongst other things it was clear that what life required of the writer was not aesthetic wholeness or even Conradian incompleteness but a plain openness. "I fail to see how I can be other than a lax, undisciplined storyteller," asserts George Ponderevo. "I must sprawl and flounder, comment and theorize, if I am to get the thing out I have in mind." Where James said that art made life, these writers purposefully insisted that life, observed, made art. And when Virginia Woolf said that the novel is not like that because life is not like that, she

---

[11] "I can feel with this [Wells' creative energy] strongly, as I felt strongly with Lewisham many years ago making schedules for exams: the first character in fiction I ever fully identified with." Raymond Williams, *The English Novel from Dickens to Lawrence*, cited above.

was arguing against writers who had already made their own confident declaration of what life actually is.

But equally this was not a return to the middle ground of Victorian realism, even though these novels do often inspire reference back to Dickens or Hardy. For Wells, the open "sprawling" method was a way of dealing with the shapelessness and lack of social coherence that was Edwardian England, when "all that is modern and different has come in as a thing intruded or as a gloss upon [the] predominant formula." As he put it himself, the traditional English novel has been formed within a fixed social frame; now, with "the new instability," that frame had splintered and itself become part of the picture. As Raymond Williams explains it, the Victorian novel was created out of community, a social and moral compact that linked individual and social life; in the Edwardian period the communicable society had dissolved, and individual and society lived in a fluid and atomized world. If the Edwardian novel carried realism forward, it carried it into new social conditions. God the benevolently omniscient narrator was still there, but now He was God the Scientist, God the Sociologist, God the Journalist. He was interested in progress, evolution and social change, and was always a meticulous external observer of the world as it worked. In Edwardian fiction – and it goes on being written still – the observer is everywhere, a presence between writer and reader. "The opening chapter does not concern itself with Love – indeed that antagonist does not appear until the third – and Mr Lewisham is seen at his studies," begins *Love and Mr Lewisham*, telling us about Mr Lewisham at his studies. "Those privileged to be present at a family festival of the Forsytes have seen that charming and instructive sight – an upper middle class family in full plumage," announces Galsworthy the novelist at the start of *The Man of Property* (1906), going on to tell us that these observers would see a spectacle "not only delightful in itself, but illustrative of an obscure human problem"; in fact they would have "a vision of the dim road of social progress." "On an autumn afternoon of 1919 a hatless man with a slight limp might have been observed

ascending the gentle, broad declivity of Riceyman steps,"
commences Arnold Bennett's *Riceyman Steps* (1923), and this
positioned observer is kept busily moving and, of course,
observing, for the rest of this objectified novel.

In Edwardian fiction, chapters concern themselves with
topics, obscure human problems are illustrated, visions of the
dim road of social progress are regularly offered. Characters are
seen from the exterior, their dominant characteristics signalled
("a hatless man with a slight limp"), as if they exist more for
their social representativeness than any felt life within. They
live unconsciously as symptoms of a larger case, become what
D. H. Lawrence, writing on Galsworthy, called "a subjective-
objective reality, a divided being hinged together, but not
strictly individual." "A character has to be conventionalized,"
Bennett explained: "You can't put the whole of a character in a
book, unless the book were of inordinate length and the reader
of infinite patience. You must select traits . . ." "I have come to
see myself from outside, my country from outside – without
illusions," says Ponderevo. The result of this is a distinctive
way of writing fiction, no less fictional, of course, than any
other. It is, as Virginia Woolf fairly says, material realism –
dense with social life, rich in illustrative detail, filled with
exteriorized observations which are also generalizations, dealing
with social types in a transforming political order. It also
mirrors a sense of change as an involuntary and formless
growth. In many of the novels of the Nineties, and in the fiction
of James and Conrad, individuals, living in a world of "things"
or "material interests," are often drawn back into an existential
subjectivity. In Edwardian fiction, the individual, though often
solitary and exposed, is generally caught up completely in the
padded mahogany furniture, the busy streets and commerce, of
an age of materiality. It could be said that "Edwardian fiction"
not only revived realism, but ensured its survival as a means of
twentieth-century writing. Like the work of Dreiser in the
United States, it created a dialectic with a more abstract
modernity that has remained powerful in the evolution of
modern fiction.

That said, it becomes apparent when we look more closely at the best Edwardian fiction – and it seems fair to take Galsworthy's *The Man of Property* (1906), Bennett's *The Old Wives' Tale* (1908) and Wells' *Tono-Bungay* (1909) as eminent examples – that "Edwardian fiction" was never a single thing, as those who challenged it later sometimes suggested. John Galsworthy's *The Man of Property* – which by a very appropriate process of dynastic evolution turned first into the three and then the nine volumes of "The Forsyte Saga" (1906–34) – is a still readable family saga that details the disintegration of the property-owning middle classes from the mid-1880s to the 1930s, and it chronicles a significant social change. "*The Forsyte Saga* has great importance as the mirror of the British high bourgeoisie," observes Herr Birenbaum, a character in Angus Wilson's novel *No Laughing Matter* (1967), which both pastiches and parodies the form. If, as has so often been said, the English novel is first and foremost the burgher epic, then this is that form in a kind of self-conscious disintegration. The Forsytes start as the representatives of the rising class of their age: "the middlemen, the commercials, the pillars of society, the corner-stones of convention," the people whose wealth and security makes everything possible, "makes your art possible, makes literature, science, even religion, possible. Without the Forsytes, who believe in none of these things, where should we be?" Galsworthy catches them at the peak of their power, which is corrupted from within by the possessive code of property, and threatened from outside by what usually threatens such things – adulterous love and divorce. Like Thomas Mann in his remarkable *Buddenbrooks* (1900), Galsworthy at first seemed to write the story of the collapse of the bourgeois age, as historical forces undermine it, and his observation at first is detached and highly ironic. And perhaps, if there had been a major social revolution in Britain, Galsworthy would have been its great chronicler. But Britain remained and remains a bourgeois society, and as the sequence evolved the tone grew less critical, as the characters became more attractive to the readers and clearly to their author. The critique of a class turns into a family saga, following the family over three generations, through peace to war and uncomfortable peace again. Because the fundamental world remains whole, there is no crisis of form (as there is in Mann's fiction), and Galsworthy stayed an Edwardian novelist into post-Edwardian times. He became the great chronicler of middle Britain, and as such won the Nobel Prize for literature in 1932.

Bennett's social history has quite different cultural roots. He was above all the self-made author, the solicitor's son from the Five Towns who watched the dissolution of the weighty, moral, confining Victorian age through the eyes of someone who has been carried upward by social change and his own effective career. The story of an age in motion from limited provincial lower-middle-class life to the promises and disappointments of the "newfangled days" is the heart of his theme as a serious writer, the most memorable part of his large human comedy. He belonged to the age of regional realism, that opening out of the wider world to honest literary treatment that was one urgent justification for Naturalism; he brought the spirit of the Goncourt brothers to the British literary provinces, and British provincial fiction has depended on this ever since. But he divested the task of much of its theory, in accordance, no doubt, with his own claim that "The novelist should cherish and burnish this faculty of seeing crudely, simply, artlessly, ignorantly." At best this made him a novelist of deep social honesty, at worst an aspiring vulgarian. In 1902 he produced two utterly contrasting works. One was *Anna of the Five Towns*, the story of a miser's daughter in the Potteries of his childhood, intimately charting a process of social change from the 1880s to the present; the other was *The Grand Babylon Hotel*, a high-life fantasy obviously written to display sophistication and frankly written for money. His work went up and down in quality, but onward and upward in commercial success; he admitted he had set out to become "an engine for the production of literature," and he made his literary fortune. In that same year he moved to Paris, which provided him with the essential contrast of one of his finest books, *The Old Wives' Tale*. It began, his preface tells us, in Paris in 1903, in the Naturalist way; observing a ridiculous old woman in a Paris restaurant, he realized she had once been slim and beautiful. To explore her story, he gave her a sister, also fat; one of the sisters would live "ordinarily," fulfilling a life of provincial virtue, the other would become a Parisian and a whore. "Neither has any imagination," he noted. "The two lives would intertwine." Constance and Sophia Baines, daughters of a Bursley draper, with their two very different, ageing lives, were born from these thoughts. The story of dutiful Constance, who stays at home, and rebellious Sophia, lured by a travelling salesman to Paris, becomes a long, loving chronicle over the forty years from the 1860s to the 1900s; at first a shared heredity and environment appear to produce two quite different destinies, but they unwind, over the slow and erosive passage of time, and through the later stages of the industrial revolution and through the French empire, to one common human fate. The novel skilfully bridges not just British provincial and French experience, but French techniques and a British subject-matter, the commonplace Staffordshire world becoming ever more brighly lit in the gaze from Paris. As Henry James admiringly said, this was all done clearly and effortlessly and became the method of "saturation," achieved with a power of demonstration "so familiar and quiet that truth and poetry . . . melt utterly together." It also showed the limitations of the method of "hugging the shores of the real." But it is not when he hugs the shores of the real – as he so successfully did here, and again in *Clayhanger* (1910) and *Riceyman Steps* (1923) – but when he sets sail on the sea of the fanciful that Bennett is disappointing; and "hugging the shores of the real," disclosing the novel as a felt moral and social history, is, as John Updike has said, one of the essences of fiction.

Bennett, of course, did not see his art as artless; and no more did Wells when he wrote *Tono-Bungay*, the book in which he put the largest part of his vision, and which lies at the heart of his claim on fiction. It owed, he said, something to Balzac, certainly a good deal to Dickens, and, in its comedy of impertinence, something also to Mark Twain, who also wrote of the age of the entrepreneur and advertising – above all in the mocking comedy of *A Connecticut Yankee in King Arthur's Court* (1889), where the era of the machine and the bomb violently intrudes into the timeless chivalric wonderland of Camelot, so reassuring to Victorian imaginations. In Wells the land of timeless Englishness is the "Bladesover System" – "great house, the church, the village, and the labourers and the servants in their stations and degrees . . ." – in which nonetheless change moves unseen, even though "all that is modern and different has come in as a thing intruded or as a gloss on this predominant formula, either impertinently or apologetically." This is really the principle of the novel, which takes the "predominant formula," equally found in fiction, and subjects it to impertinence and rewriting. For, as the narrator George Ponderevo tells us, this is a story of "this immense process of social disintegration in which we live"; the "ordered scheme" is going. Bladesover has been "outgrown and overgrown," and a "modern mercantile investing civilization" has rapidly taken its place. The book that Ponderevo now writes is thus "something in the nature of a novel," its apparent formlessness resembling the condition of England itself. Formlessness is in fact not just the method of the book, but its central metaphor. "I suppose what I'm really trying to render is nothing more or less than Life – as one man has found it." George tells us in the now familiar way, adding, "I want to tell – *myself*, and my impressions of the thing as a whole, to say things I have come to feel intensely of the laws, traditions, usages, and ideas we call society, and how we poor individuals get driven and lured among these windy, perplexing shoals and channels." So his book is "just an agglomeration," "not a constructed tale." It is the lively, funny story of George's Uncle Edward Ponderevo, a Mr Toad-like entrepreneur and adventurer, "the Napoleon of domestic conveniences," who pursues wealth, fame, power and social position by peddling a worthless, maybe even harmful, patent medicine that offers to cure the new ailments of the changing age. As Uncle Teddy deceives a society that has already begun to deceive itself, George himself turns into a scientific inventor, a figure out of Wells' earlier future fiction who is involved in the invention of a flying machine, a radioactive compound called "quap," and at last a "destroyer" on which everyone can sail away after the collapse of the artificial Tono-Bungay empire. Like the earlier scientific romances, the book contains an important social allegory about the splits, divisions and conflicting, potentially destructive forces of an age dissolving into the future.

Tono-Bungay is, of course, a "Condition of England" novel, and one of the finest, a panoramic satire of its age. Its random energy is portrayed best in its portrait of London itself, in a version that contrasts interestingly with Conrad's in *The Secret Agent*. Here is "the richest town in the world, the biggest port, the greatest manufacturing town, the Imperial city – the centre of civilization, the heart of the world!" The "whole illimitable place" teems with "suggestions of indefinite and sometimes outrageous possibility, of hidden but magnificent meanings," but it is also a tentacular chaos, spreading, teeming, "unstructured" and "cancerous." "Factory chimneys smoke right against Westminster with an air of carelessly not having permission, and the whole effect of industrial London and of all London east of Temple Bar and of the huge dingy immensity of London port, is to me of something disproportionately large, something morbidly expanded, without plan or intention," George reports, creating an analogy between the city and the activities of the two Ponderevos themselves. "All these aspects have suggested to my mind . . . the unorganized, abundant substance of some tumourous growth-process . . . To this day I ask myself will those masses ever become structural, will they indeed shape into anything new whatever . . ." London too is formless, but filled with chaotic energies, which Wells presents with a delighted wonder, opening the story up to include science and shopping, the building of fortunes and the building of houses, loveless marriages and so "freer" sexual relations, social contrast and the implicit danger of war. But, for all that it needs reform, modern life remains a great and "impertinent" adventure. And it is on further formlessness that the book ends: "I fell into a thought that was nearly formless," George declares, as he departs the shores of Britain on his "destroyer," looking for something else new. The solution, of course, lies where Wells himself would put it, in science, machinery and invention. "I decided that in power and knowledge lay the salvation of my life; the secret that would fill my need; that to these things I would give myself," he concludes.

This could, in its way, be taken as Wells' own farewell to the real experiment of the novel, even though he wrote a good many more. *Ann Veronica*, also published in 1909, created a public scandal with its story of a free woman seeking free love; he retrieved his comic reputation with *The History of Mr Polly* in 1910, another story about the little man breaking loose. However Wells was increasingly giving himself elsewhere, to science, political prophecy, world visions, and the bounds of the novel were proving too small. *The New Machiavelli* in 1911 is an endeavour to write a political novel about the making of the state: "The state-making dream is a very old dream indeed in the world's history," says its narrator: "It plays too small a part in novels." The book deals with the struggle between a Great Idea and a Great Love, with feminism and the transformation of the modern family, with military policy and apocalyptic warnings – all to come true – about war with Germany and the break-up of Empire; it has a chaotic force, but none of the aesthetic care that was shaping other novels of the modern. That year Wells declared his position in a lecture on "The Contemporary Novel," in which he attacked the cult of "artistic perfection," separated himself from the self-conscious artists, and urged that the task of fiction was to deal with "political questions and religious questions and social questions." Here was the basis for the famous quarrel of 1915 with Henry James; for Wells was, in effect, now taking on the whole idea of the "literary imagination" itself, and the way in which it stood apart from "the world." The "world," as Wells saw it, meant science and technology, politics and history, the formation of new societies and the shaping of the new world order. The novels he wrote, and continued to write, if with diminishing force, toward the year of his death in 1946, were, as he said, frankly instrumental, means in a larger argument. It became an argument between literature and science ("the two cultures"), between pessimism and optimism, between the moral crisis of progress and progress itself. It was part of a split in the fortunes of the modern novel which was also a split in British culture itself, one to which writers would continually return. To understand the novels of Wells, and Bennett and Galsworthy, you had merely to read them and perceive their view of life, society and politics. But to understand the work of James, Conrad, Woolf and Joyce, you needed to grasp an entire conception of art itself, and its distinctive modern task.

7.

If the British novel and the British culture of 1910 seemed split and in need of reconciliation, then it was offered one kind of answer in the work of E. M. Forster, whose *Howards End* – with its epigraph of "Only connect . . ." ("Only connect the prose and the passion") – appeared that year. Forster, who said he belonged to "the fag-end of Victorian liberalism," the late-Victorian dissenting intelligentsia whose members included "philanthropists, bishops, clergy, members of parliament, Miss Hannah Moore," possessed an Arnoldian desire to see life steadily and see it whole. He had been (like many of the Bloomsbury Group, with whom he was half-associated) at Cambridge, and come under the influence of the philosopher G. E. Moore, who emphasized "aesthetic states" and "personal relations" as the standards of life; he had read and been shaped by the works of Samuel Butler, with his "undogmatic outlook," and George Meredith, who urged that "the cause of comedy and the cause of truth are the same." By 1910 he had already published three social comedies – *Where Angels Fear to Tread* (1905), *The Longest Journey* (1907), and *A Room With a View* (1908) – which challenged social dullness and philistinism, sexual convention and the undeveloped English heart, and emerged as an important comic voice of a new humanism. His moral comedy was illuminated by a sharp liberal intelligence and a symbolist inclination, and these three were novels of new feeling. But it was plain that with *Howards End* a new ambitiousness had entered his fiction, and that here was a work that confronted Masterman's "Condition of England," and not with the larky splendour of Wells' *Tono-Bungay* but with an urgent desire to relate and unify a formless culture split in many directions: between class and class, culture and commerce, materialism and idealism, head and heart, muddle and mystery, society and consciousness, or culture seen as cancerous and formless and culture as meaning and wholeness.

The question at the heart of *Howards End* was "Who shall inherit England?" – a question to which it gave complex answers. "Does she belong to those who have moulded her and made her feared by other lands, or to those who have added nothing to her power, but have somehow seen her, seen the whole island at once, lying as a jewel in a silver sea, sailing as a ship of souls, with all the brave world's fleet accompanying her towards eternity?" the book asks. Like Wells, it acknowledges that something new is happening to England: in the "Age of Property," a new "civilization of luggage" is advancing, and modern discontinuity is accelerating, driven by commercial enterprise, new industrialism and technology, and the potential clash of world imperialism. Here too there is a tentacular growth, as the "red rust" of London's suburbia spreads over the land and sprawls toward Howards End, the ancient farmhouse that is the central symbol of the novel. Forster embodies this split world in a story of two families. There are the Wilcoxes, energetic people, male-dominated, rushing by car round the nation to do the work of Empire; and there are the Schlegels, represented by two sisters – the intelligent Margaret, the impulsive Helen – who are emancipated, humane, of foreign stock, and devoted to ideas. They take from their German father a sense of idealism and a faith that materialism can be dissolved by "the mild intellectual light," and "In their own fashion they cared deeply about politics, but not as the politicians would have us think; they desired that public life should mirror whatever is good in the life within." The book's theme is

116

the relation of these two, and of both to a third. For at Howards End lives Mrs Wilcox, different from them all. She has faint mystical properties, is linked not with the busy present but with the yeoman past, and attached to some of the book's main "symbols" – the house Howards End, with its Druidic spirit, the wych-elm tree, and the hay in the meadow – though these symbols are carefully contained within the human: "House and tree . . . kept within the limits of the human. Their message was not of eternity, but of hope on this side of the grave."

The novel is the story of these two families, who are drawn toward each other through various personal relationships, but become divided. When Mrs Wilcox dies she wills Howards End to Margaret, hoping for a reconciliation. Margaret eventually marries the widower Mr Wilcox, and an ambiguous unity is achieved. Meanwhile her sister Helen has had an affair with a lowly Wellsian clerk, Leonard Bast, and had an illegitimate child. At first Mr Wilcox refuses to give any help. But the story ends with Mr Wilcox ill, Margaret triumphant, and Helen's child likely to inherit Howards End. Barely told, the story sounds schematic, but the book is a complex and ironic comedy, and in Forster's world nothing is simple. For this is a world split in many ways, between the whole and the part, the eternal and the "flux," "infinity" and "panic and emptiness," the note of spiritual anarchy that sounds out of Beethoven's Fifth Symphony. And Forster gives the novel a large panoramic sweep. It is deeply set in the Edwardian period (it *is* an Edwardian novel) and amid the forces active in it: the economic race with Germany, the process of imperial expansion and commercial growth, the technological destructions of the motor car, the intellectual pressures shifting people from liberalism to socialism. In the three main settings of the book – the metropolitan intellectual world of the Schlegels, the commuter world of the Wilcoxes, the clerkly suburbia of Leonard Bast – change is moving fast. A key theme of the novel is moving house and rebuilding; Wickham Place, where the Schlegels live, is to be pulled down for flats ("Can what we call civilization be right if people mayn't die where they were born?" asks Mrs Wilcox), and "the civilization of luggage" is nearing Howards End, as the nearby railway station shows ("The station . . . struck an indeterminate note. Into which country will it lead, England or Suburbia? It was new, it had island platforms and a subway, and the superficial comfort exacted by business men . . ."). Margaret looks for "infinity" in King's Cross station, and hopes to "live in fragments no longer"; but she too lives the life of "gibbering monkeys," and zig-zags "with her friends over Thought and Art." Motion and muddle threaten any idea of culture or the infinite, and Margaret sees that the places of solid life are "survivals, and the melting-pot was being prepared for them. Logically, they had no right to be alive. One's hope was in the weakness of logic." Forster's endeavour is to reconcile two worlds not naturally akin, the worlds of "life by time" and "life by value," and recognizes – it is an essential part of his comic vision – that they rarely converge.

As the American critic Lionel Trilling was later to see, Forster is one of the great novelists of modern liberalism, a writer of checks and balances, who extends his liberal scepticism even to the most cherished of liberal principles, like the Wellsian faith in progress or science. In *Howards End* nothing is eternally reconciled; history upsets eternity, muddle upsets mystery, and panic and emptiness question the symbols of wholeness that float through the book. The will to vision, the liberal wish for right reason, the claim of the holiness of the heart's affections – all are consistently confronted with ambiguity. The same scepticism applies to his style, which is always dialectical. Forster had not dispensed with realism and familiarity, but opened it out to wider things. So poetry resides with comedy, symbolism with realism, and, says Trilling, where "the plot speaks of clear certainties, the manner resolutely insists that nothing can be so simple."[12] *Howards End* lies, "liberally," midway between Wells' assertively progressive novel, the carrier of history, and the symbolist novel of late James or Woolf, the

[12] See Lionel Trilling, *E. M. Forster* (Norfolk, Conn., 1943; London, 1944). And also see the essays of his collection *The Liberal Imagination: Essays on Literature and Society* (New York, 1950).

118

carrier of form, between social and moral comedy and something more symbolist or metaphysical. The book works in a double form – an attempt to connect not only the prose to the passion of life, but realism to the "musicalization" of fiction. And so one way the book can be read is as Forster's attempt to reconcile, through his distinctive comic humanism, the two directions in which the novel was now pulling: toward social and political realism, and pure wholeness of form. "Yes – oh dear, yes – the novel tells a story," Forster was to say in his admirable study *Aspects of the Novel* (1927), and that means it must satisfy realism, familiar recognition, and story's narrative "and then . . . and then . . ." But the novel can also be a form of "pattern" and "rhythm," and reach for "expansion": "That is the idea the novelist must cling to. Not completion. Not rounding off but opening out." By the time Forster returned to the public with his novel of Empire *A Passage to India* in 1924, the world of his Edwardian novel had already dissolved. British empiricism and German idealism had not met, or not in the way he imagined; the civilization of luggage, and "panic and emptiness," were here to stay. Symbolism has become more ambiguous, confronting a greater nullity; the machine of civilization persistently breaks down and turns into stone, and not just the political world but the earth itself resists wholeness. Keeping his saving comic irony, his belief in the moral world of personal relations, Forster had passed from being a liberal novelist to a Modernist. Thereafter, from 1924 till his death in 1970, he wrote no more novels, saying that the world his fiction comprehended had gone. But he also had a striking influence on his successors; writer after writer, from Christopher Isherwood to Angus Wilson and Doris Lessing, has since returned to the mode of the liberal novel. And this still left *Howards End* a classic of pre-war liberal fiction, *A Passage to India* a classic of Modernist fiction: two of the more important British novels of the century.

8.

"How do you know I'm not dead?" Forster asked D. H. Lawrence in 1922, when Lawrence was saying that all the English were dead. "Well, you can't be dead, since here's your script," Lawrence replied: "But think you *did* make a nearly deadly mistake glorifying those *business* people in *Howards End*. Business is no good." Forster's sceptical humanism was in the opposite spirit to Lawrence's passionate apocalypticism, and yet these were two writers who shared a great deal in common. Both were novelists who were seeking to unite the spectrum of the English soul, Forster under the roof of Howards End, Lawrence under the apocalyptic sign of his rainbow. The "red rust" of suburbia spreading toward Howards End resembles the "hard cutting edges of the new houses" that sprawl in "a dry, brittle, terrible corruption" across the countryside at the end of *The Rainbow*, and both books seek a great new social and emotional union. The pagan Italians who redeem the undeveloped English heart in *A Room With a View* in turn resemble the various figures, Italians, Indians, gypsies, who attempt to rescue the dead soul in so many of Lawrence's novels. And, from start to finish of his writing life, Lawrence too wrote the "Condition of England" novel. But it was an England in a different condition, seen from a different social standpoint, needing a different redemption. Hence it called for a different, a new kind of novel: a sensuously radical document, a "bright book of life," a work that could "get the whole hog." "I am man alive, and as long as I can I intend to go on being man alive," Lawrence declared. "For this reason I am a novelist. And being a novelist, I consider myself superior to the saint, the scientist, the philosopher and the poet, who are all masters of different bits of man alive, but never get the whole hog." That meant the novelist was a prophet: not Wells' scientific and political prophet, not Forster's tolerant humanist, but an emotional, visionary Nietzschean prophet, a prophet of the new imagination. Hence, he said, "Each work of art has its own form, which has no relation to any other form." Forster understood this, and acknowledged Lawrence as "the greatest imaginative novelist of his generation." He was not alone: among many writers and thinkers of the day, if not with the general public or the censor, it was widely agreed that in Lawrence England had found its difficult modern genius.

Once again it was Hueffer at *The English Review* who found him. According to his version, he one day received from an unknown Nottinghamshire author and provincial schoolteacher a short story, "Odour of Chrysanthemums," about the death of a miner in an accident. This is not quite accurate; in fact Lawrence's friend Jessie Chambers had sent Hueffer some poems, which got him into print. But Hueffer had seen in his new author, the son of an Eastwood collier and an educated mother, that precious thing a "working-class writer," a writer equivalent to Arnold Bennett in his power to capture the ordinary working life of his origins, and the story duly appeared in the review. Hueffer and his then companion Violet Hunt introduced Lawrence to London literary life, and he also read the manuscript of the novel Lawrence had been working on since 1906, saying that although it "sins against any canon of art as I conceive it," it presaged a great future. He directed the book toward Heinemann, from whom it appeared in 1911 as *The White Peacock*. It was hardly the working-class romance Hueffer thought it was; but then it took editors, publishers and critics a long time to come to grips with the difficult, poetical, deeply individualized spirit of Lawrence's writing. The book is set on home ground, the Nottinghamshire-Derbyshire border, but the miners' lives, the bleak pitheads, the grim red houses that would sprawl in later fiction are not here. It is a story of provincial intellectual life, set close to the fecund world of the Moorgreen reservoir, where an ancient fertility is under threat. The sensual writing of the opening lines, written in an inward, vividly felt prose, displayed its freshness: "I stood watching the shadowy fish slide through the gloom of the mill-pond. They were grey, descendants of the silvery things that had darted away from the monks, in the young days when the valley was lusty. The whole place was gathered in the musing of old age. The thick-piled trees on the far shore were too dark and sober to dally with the sun, the weeds stood crowded and motionless." The code of words is already Lawrentian: the grey dying of a lusty age, the crowding of the weeds and the failure of the trees to dally with the sun. There is a stirring sense of revolt, emotional "jerking awake," in what follows. The characters are ordinary, but radical, self-educated and bookish, like the people of the world from which Lawrence came. Other seeds of dissolution are here too. For another code of the book is the voice of prophecy, as Lawrence draws in the figure of Annable, the educated gamekeeper, a "man of one idea: – that all civilization was the painted fungus of rottenness." If Annable seems something of an intrusion into the book, and dies before the tale is done, he is already a sign of the urgent passion that would make Lawrence into the bitter prophet of his age. He is also the antecedent of Lawrence's late gamekeeper hero, the Mellors of *Lady Chatterley's Lover* (1928), his last real novel and the book where, in his exile, he would return once again to the Nottinghamshire landscape to make his historical reckoning.

The Trespasser (1912), Lawrence's second novel, was part-written with Helen Corke, and remains something of a botched conception. It is based on her story of an affair with a music teacher on the Isle of White (Corke published her version as *Neutral Ground* in 1934), but its interest now lies less in the affair and its erotics, or the sexual radicalism of the New Woman. The key figure is Siegmund, the music teacher, a Wagnerian hero who is suicidally trapped between erotics and death, and hungering for "a breaking of the bonds, a severing of blood-ties, a sort of new birth." As his name and nationality suggests, the book is full of Germanic echoes. Lawrence had a powerful self-education, like many of his heroes, and had been reading avidly in continental ideas. But where most of his contemporaries were looking to the French, where Bennett was seeking his "Naturalism," or Hueffer his Flaubertian notions of "rendering" and "impersonality," Lawrence was exploring elsewhere. He concerned himself with Nietzschean ideas of will, dissolution and renewal, with German Expressionist notions of inward and self-revealing form ("He doesn't see, he envisions," explains one critic about the Expressionist artist: "He doesn't decipher, he experiences"). There was the basis for a literary argument here, since most of his literary friends were Francophile and Russophile – his editor Edward Garnett, for instance – and looked in his novels for an objectivity and formalism he had already begun to distrust. (Hueffer did find *The Trespasser* "execrably bad art," though Garnett was more encouraging.) Something else developed from his German interests; he thought of becoming a lektor in Germany, and began visiting Ernest Weekley, the Professor of Modern Languages at Nottingham University, and so met his wife, Frieda von Richthofen Weekley. In 1912, close to the time *The Trespasser* appeared, the two eloped together to Germany.

Frieda, Germany, and the state of independent artistic exile Lawrence now found himself in had everything to do with the making of *Sons and Lovers*, the highly autobiographical novel he now finished with her assistance. It would prove his first mature book, and many critics still regard it as his best. It promises in its first half to be a powerful, realistic and socially evocative story of British provincial life in the mining village of "Bestwood." It starts off in grainy realism ("The Bottoms succeeded to Hell Row") though without the familiar Naturalistic distance, but it soon turns into a war of archetypal emotions, as the educated miner's wife Mrs Morel transfers to her sons her sense of aspiration for both higher and deeper things. Frieda, and the artistic exile that Lawrence now found himself in, undoubtedly had a great deal to do with *Sons and Lovers*. The struggles of parents and children, flesh and spirit, are presented in an immediate, felt language and with a kind of sensuous physical apprehension not seen before in British fiction: ". . . the dusky, golden softness of this man's sensuous flame of life, that flowed off his flesh like the flame from a candle, not baffled and gripped into incandescence by thought and spirit as her life was, seemed to her something wonderful, beyond her." Written out of the senses, the book has all the intensity of an autobiographical charge: indeed it is, in Expressionist terms, an "I-drama," a tale of coming to being. And the work is also vividly sexual. "I never did read Freud, but I have heard about him since I was in Germany," Lawrence observed. He had indeed; Frieda had been through psychoanalysis, and she was guiding the struggles of the rewriting, and giving new meaning to the psycho-sexual struggles of the book and the portraiture of, especially, the women characters. The book's essential theme became something much more than autobiographical realism, even if that was how many of its readers read it. It was the story of the attempted escape of Paul Morel, through the struggles of his own individuation, from the binding relationship with his mother to sexual self-discovery, from the deathly psychic web where a divided consciousness and culture had trapped him into a different realm. The discovery is essentially pursued through the process of writing or rather rewriting the book; and a myth that lay well beyond familiar realism thus took on Oedipal force, as the struggles of mothers who are lovers of their sons, sons who are lovers of their mothers, push onward toward the making of a whole identity. Whether new consciousness is truly achieved is not completely clear. Lawrence called the book a tragedy – "the tragedy of thousands of young men in England . . . The name of the old son-lover was Oedipus. The name of the new one is legion" – and seemed to suppose he had left the ending still pointing toward death and extinction: "He is left in the end naked of everything, with the drift towards death. It is a great tragedy." By the end of the book Lawrence feels the need to place Paul behind him. But the text on the page surely points toward rebirth, self-discovery, coming through. In front of Paul the city of Nottingham shimmers: "But no, he would not give in. Turning sharply, he walked towards the city's golden phosphorescence. His fists were shut, his mouth set fast. He would not take that direction, to the darkness, to follow her. He walked towards the faintly humming, glowing town, quickly."[13]

[13] The story has been excellently told in John Worthen's *D. H. Lawrence: The Early*

This, perhaps, is because *Sons and Lovers* has another key theme – the casting off of the past, of mother, class and home, to forge the birth of the artist. Like Joyce's *A Portrait of the Artist as a Young Man* – written around the same time, though not published till 1916 – it is about the artist who through an Oedipal break is self-exiled from his own past and his maternal birth, and re-born in separation and apprehensive openness into a dubious freedom, facing new books, new worlds, new forms and new emotions to come. And the form of the novel had itself been born through such a struggle: "I tell you it has got form – *form*; haven't I made it patiently, out of sweat as well as blood," he wrote urgently to his editor Garnett, who in fact saved the book, when Heinemann turned it down, by taking it to another publisher, Duckworth: "If *you* can't see the development – which is slow, like growth – I can." It was this search for new and inwardly energized form that became the preoccupation driving his work in a different direction from Joyce – not toward the self-consciousness of experimental modernist epic, but into the deep envelope of feeling, the great felt psycho-myth of cultural and sexual relations, and a distinctive mythology of creation through disintegration, which became both the source and the inner myth of the novels themselves. In Italy with Frieda, and feeling free of the limitations of his origins, he began a remarkable new burst of production, starting on many things – *The Lost Girl* (1920), much important poetry, but above all a large new project he called *The Sisters*, which went through four hard-worked drafts over 1913–14. "It is very different from *Sons and Lovers*; written in another language almost," he wrote to Garnett. "I shan't write in the same manner as *Sons and Lovers* again, I think – in that hard violent style full of sensation and presentation." In another letter he declared the theme of the project; it was to be "the relationship between men and

---

Years 1885–1912 (Cambridge, 1991), which in turn has been able to benefit from the autobiographical materials of Lawrence's posthumously published novel *Mr Noon* (Cambridge, 1984), and from the uncensored texts of the novels in their new "definitive" Cambridge editions.

women. After all, it is *the* problem of today, the establishment of a new relation, or the readjustment of the old one, between man and woman." Through version after version, the book struggled into existence. Lawrence was discarding nearly all his mentors, including Garnett. He began the idiosyncratic study of Hardy, following out the struggle of consciousness in his characters, even as he rejected the controlling plots. He read and dismissed Bennett: "Tragedy ought to be a great kick at misery. But *Anna of the Five Towns* seems like an acceptance – so does all the modern stuff since Flaubert. I hate it." "Tell Arnold Bennett that all rules of construction hold good only for novels which are copies of other novels," he wrote his agent. "A book which is not a copy of other books has its own construction, and what he calls faults, he being an old imitator, I call characteristics." What he was doing lay beyond explanation, and he told Garnett that the book was "like a novel in a foreign language I don't know very well – I can only just make out what it is about."

By mid-1914 the book was called *The Wedding Ring*, and he was comparing the spirit of it with Marinetti's Futurism, which he had been following with excitement. He wrote to Garnett, who disliked the draft, explaining that what should be under-stood was that he had dispensed with previous forms, above all with the old, conventional idea of character, "the old-fashioned human element," in favour of a Futurist "inhuman will," or "physiology of matter." "I don't so much care about what the woman *is* – what she IS – inhumanly, physiologically, materially – according to the use of the word: but for me, what she *is* as a phenomenon (or as representing some greater inhuman will), instead of what she feels according to the human conception . . . You mustn't look in my novel for the old stable *ego* – of the character. There is another *ego*, according to whose action the individual is unrecognizable, and passes through, as it were, allotropic states which it needs a deeper sense than any we've been used to exercise, to discover are states of the same single radically unchanged element." But where Marinetti and the Futurists were seeking vitality within mechanism, Lawrence

126

was looking toward something almost the opposite: he was a prophet of the redeeming flesh, seeking an "inhuman" vitalistic energy born out of blood rhythms, states of consciousness, the solar plexus – in other words, something nearer the eternal human unconscious. But what, he said, was important about his new novel was that it no longer followed the rule of development through individual characters, but through the relation between individuation and the collective motions of consciousness: "the characters all fall into the form of some other rhythmic form, as when one draws a fiddle-bow across a fine tray delicately sanded, the sand takes lines unknown." If *The Wedding Ring* was a move toward a greater self-expression, it was also a move toward a greater abstraction, indeed a post-humanist form of writing.

At last the book split into two parts, one becoming *The Rainbow* (1915), the other *Women in Love* (1920) – an Old Testament and a New. Lawrence had written his study of Hardy, and also read Thomas Mann's dynastic *Buddenbrooks*; both may have encouraged his late decision to drive his new story backward over several generations. So *The Rainbow* became a historical novel, the story of three generations of the Brangwyn family, from the pastoral, creational age of the 1840s and through into the deathly, decultured modern world. The book opens at Marsh Farm to traditional, indeed Biblical rhythms, filled with fertility and sensuousness: "They felt the rush of the sap in spring, they knew the wave that cannot halt, but every year throws forward the seed to begetting, and, falling back, leaves the young-born on the earth. They knew the intercourse between heaven and earth, sunshine drawn into the breast and bowels, the rain sucked up in the daytime, nakedness that comes under the wind in autumn." But the powers of historical change are there, as canals, railways, collieries come, planting dead mechanism into the land. And the powers of change are also there in the eternal division of consciousness between the men, rooted in their soil, and the women, who "looked out from the heated, blind intercourse of farm-life, to the spoken world beyond . . . They strained to

127

listen," reaching toward "the magic land ... where secrets were made known and desires fulfilled." Possibly with hints from *Howards End*, *The Rainbow* merges two kinds of novel, the historical novel and the novel of consciousness, and works in two different languages. One retains many of the solid elements of realism, and deals with the familiar workings of the world; the other is concerned with sexual dialectics and the flow of human consciousness, and requires a sensualized, symbolist mode of expression.

Many readers have sensed a crossover point in the novel, where one language yields dominance to the other, realism to psycho-symbolism. Frank Kermode calls the method "palimpsest," meaning that the writing is less chronological and developmental than "layered" – "historical chapters" interweave with "symbolic" chapters, time and timelessness merge into each other, especially in moments of erotic stasis or emotional arrest, and each new generation revisits the experience of the past in the form of a revised commentary. What unites the language of realism and the language of sensuality and symbolism is a third voice, the language of prophecy. For, as Kermode also points out, the book is held together by another scriptural code founded on the Apocalyptic types: the myth of crisis and rebirth, of last things and first, Genesis turning to Revelation. Lawrence's largest theme is the modern dying of the world, and the birthing of the new individual and a new sensual creation out of the crisis of the age. This is symbolized by the book's overarching image, the rainbow itself, which takes on a sequence of meanings, as salvation, religious architecture, cultural union, sexual congress, finally the architecture of consciousness itself. At the end, which was to be the beginning of the second book, Ursula Brangwyn – the modern woman who inherits the story, as well as the sensual rebellion and the chaotic sterility of modern times – has passed "outside the pale of the old world," and is looking for "a new germination." The key image takes its last form: "She saw in the rainbow the earth's new architecture, the old, brittle corruption of houses and factories swept away, the world built up in a living fabric of Truth, fitting to the overarching heavens."[14]

The book about crisis – a crisis of history, consciousness, sexuality, gender, and literary form – appeared in 1915, a time of crisis. Lawrence claimed the book was "written and named in Italy . . . before there was any thought of war." This was not quite so; he revised the book further in wartime, darkening some passages to suit, but it still ends on a note of promise. The crisis became personal; soon after publication (by Methuen), the book was seized for obscenity, and banned with the publishers' consent. In wartime conditions, when literary experiment no longer seemed urgent, Lawrence found few defenders. Meanwhile, as a tubercular non-combatant with a German wife, he was harried and persecuted by the authorities, and refused a passport for the United States. All this and the deathliness he saw everywhere convinced him that the apocalyptic signs were real, that the book was an accurate prophecy. "It was in 1915 the old world ended," he said, and "What I did through individuals, the world has done through war." His sense of crisis, his bitterness, his dismay with history, his sense of universal death-flow, a "process of active corruption," his weariness with humanity, his belief in the dominance of the mechanical – all this went into the rewriting of *Women in Love* he undertook in 1916, recasting most of the material (the book was re-issued, expurgated, by Martin Secker in 1921). His wartime experiences entered the story, the hard futurist dimension of the book intensified, and, though it remains set in the immediately pre-war world of Britain and Europe, it moves inexorably toward the age's dance of death, its chosen oblivion in the snow. Lawrence was always to insist that the two works were one, and made an organic whole, and there is great unity of theme: the apocalyptic dissolution of an older order, the struggle of consciousness through sexual and gender relations, the summoning of a new age and its destructive and bitter birth. But

---

[14] See Frank Kermode, *Lawrence* (London, rev. ed., 1985), and his essay "Lawrence and the Apocalyptic Types," in *Continuities* (London, 1968).

The Rainbow retains a deep texture of realism, while *Women in Love* – he thought of calling it *Dies Irae*, or *The Last Days* – is a vastly more radical work, a full-blown experiment in uniting experience with doctrinal passions, a post-humanist novel of the unstable ego, of disintegrative form and emotion, a tale of the tragic present. He himself called it "purely destructive, not like *The Rainbow*, destructive-consummating." For all the connections, *The Rainbow* remains a pre-war novel, and *Women in Love* – written, like so many of the key works of Modernism, across the war – is a post-war novel, filled with the wound of war and the renewed encounter with disintegration; it is discussed again later. Lawrence, unable "to write of England any more," despairing of the white soul, sought his dark gods, his apocalypse, his sexual and sensual salvation, the phoenix of rebirth elsewhere, leaving behind the coffin of England. He became an exile, to Italy, Sardinia, Australia, New Mexico, Mexico, and France, where he died in 1930. He did return to Britain and his Nottinghamshire countryside for a final summation in his "Condition of England" novel, *Lady Chatterley's Lover*, a last cry of disaster and sensual rebirth. Published in Italy, the book too was exiled, and stayed banned in Britain to the 1960s – when it returned to British culture, along with its author's reputation as, at last, a major revolutionary maker of modern British fiction.

9.

Perhaps what was most remarkable about the fiction of the immediately pre-war years was not simply the individual achievements (many of which had been separately born a good deal earlier) but the sudden convergence – in a single time, and in so many fields of activity, from poetry and painting to philosophy and music – of so many radical ideas of art and the artist. With them, too, went another notion, that of the artist as the self-exile. No writer was to display all this more plainly, deeply or mythically than James Joyce. If the artist could now be his or her own hero, indeed Stephen Hero, then "silence, exile, and cunning" – the means and methods Stephen Dedalus prescribes for himself when he makes his famous *non serviam* in *A Portrait of the Artist as a Young Man* – increasingly came to seem the foundations of the necessary rebellion: the means of experiment, the source of the long critical distance and the great struggle with culture, form and language the modern writer, unaccepted by his own society, needed to undertake in order to break open the meaning of his history, his origins and his world. It was in the year of his exile, 1904, that almost everything in Joyce started, and to which almost everything came back. Even his greatest work, *Ulysses* (1922) – which T. S. Eliot said explored the panorama of futility and anarchy which was post-war history – is set on a single day, now called Bloomsday, 16 June, in that same year of 1904, when Joyce was still only twenty-two. It was the year of choice, of sudden creativity; the year of his meeting with Nora Barnacle ("she'll stick to him," they said), the year of his artistic vocation, the year he finally left Ireland "to forge the uncreated conscience of my race." In that year, writing quickly, he sketched out many of the short stories of *Dubliners*, the poems of *Chamber Music*, and began *Stephen Hero* (written in 1904–6, posthumously published in 1944), the artist's autobiography that eventually turned into *A Portrait of the Artist as a Young Man*. But between these beginnings, when the largest part of Joyce's projects for a lifetime were to take shape, and the ultimate moment of publication fell a very large gap. A version of *Dubliners* was ready for publication in 1905, but twice rejected, in London and then Dublin, because of anxieties over obscenity and libel; the book did not come out until 1914. *Stephen Hero* went through various drafts, emerged in new form from the revision of 1911 as *A Portrait of the Artist . . .*, and was serialized in *The Egoist* in 1914–15. But Lawrence's problems with *The Rainbow* made publishers anxious; it appeared in an American edition only in 1916, then an English edition in 1917. Also around 1904, Joyce sketched a tale about a Wandering Jew in Dublin, which he returned to in 1914. So began the great project of *Ulysses*, a book written and published in exile. Serialization began in 1918, but not until 1922 did it finally come out in a limited edition from a Paris bookshop, banned for some long time in Britain, the USA, above all in the Ireland it was about. It could be said that the Dublin of 1904 spawned almost all of Joyce. It could also be said that if, after 1904, he made a stateless exile of himself – in Pola, in Trieste, in Rome, Zürich, Paris – the Irish-English culture he grew up in also made an exile of him.

Hence, of all the English-language writers, Joyce seems most to exemplify the myth of the modern, rebellious, fractured journey into the "unknown arts," the orphan birthing of the new. But that journey had started even earlier, in the late nineteenth-century climate of Naturalism and Impressionism, Decadence and the Celtic Twilight. From the symbolist aesthetic debates of that time (and the influence of W. B. Yeats) came many of the arguments of *Stephen Hero*, which shows his interest in the spirit of a Paterian aestheticism. But he was also drawn toward Naturalism, and it was his admiration for the "modern" and "vivisective" spirit of Ibsen (he learned Danish to read him) that began his quarrels with the authorities and his break with the Catholic Church. Explaining his intentions for *Dubliners*, he phrased them in highly Naturalist terms: "My intention was to write a chapter in the moral history of my country and I chose Dublin for the scene because the city seemed to me to be the centre of paralysis," he explained: "I have written it for the most part in a style of scrupulous meanness and with the conviction that he is a bold man who dares to alter the presentment, still more to deform, whatever he has seen and heard." In fact the style is frequently poetic, the intention symbolist, the spirit not one of "scrupulous meanness" – though realism remains the essential code. The fifteen stories are linked in a cycle where the connections come not from the separate reported lives but from an overall view of Dublin's stasis and paralysis. Hence all these lives are in some way trapped – by limitation, circumstance, inarticulacy, historical inertia, a failure to act on dreams and possibilities. Paralysis occurs "literally" in the first story, "The Sisters," about a dying priest, and carries through to the last image of the last story, "The Dead," of the snow that is "general all over Ireland" and hems in all lives. In "The Dead," Gabriel Conroy has a glimpse of something larger, as he observes his wife on the stairs, listening to music, "with grace and mystery in her attitude as if she were a symbol of something." But the image is one of love lost in death, of living and dead becoming one; meanwhile the solid world itself fades to nothingness and nullity, "dissolving and dwindling." But if the characters cannot reach freedom or a full revelation, that task passes elsewhere, to the visionary revelation of the story itself, which radiates naturalist events with symbolist implications.

In fact the unspoken figure of the stories is already the artist, the priest of sensation, revelation, ecstatic discovery, who sees such ordinary things of life in sacramental, symbolist or transcendental terms, and this story too had to be told. Joyce began it in *Stephen Hero*, about the artist-hero Stephen Daedalus as, he stressed, a young man. Stephen shares Joyce's history: born in the 1880s in shabby-genteel late-Victorian Dublin, the first city of Ireland, second city of the British Empire, seventh city of Christendom, and in a state of "paraplegia" after the fall of Parnell. Born of a spendthrift father and a religious mother, he goes to Clongowes seminary, following his mother's desire to see him become a priest, but resentment of discipline, dissent and even his bad sight change him. At sixteen, he commits a "cardinal sin" of the senses, has an emotional and sensory rebellion, and seeks to create "life out of light." So he rebels against the maternal religion by becoming a priest of art, both intensely engaged in and apart from what he sees. "The spectacle of the world in thrall filled him with the fire of courage. He at last, though living at the farthest remove from the centre of European culture, marooned on an island in the ocean, though inheriting a will broken by doubt and a soul the steadfastness of whose hate became as weak as water in siren arms, would lead his own life according to what he recognized as the voice of a new humanity, active, unafraid, and unashamed." He also realizes that "though he was nominally in amity with the order of society into which he had been born, he would not be able to continue so." Joyce gives him the name of Daedalus (later Dedalus) after the "fabulous artificer" who built the Minoan labyrinth and escaped on wings he had himself constructed, and is hence a "a symbol of the artist forging anew in his workshop out of the sluggish matter of the earth a new strong imperishable impalpable being." This is the basis for his new vocation, his secular, symbolist priesthood. The key word that links the two vocations is "epiphany": "By an epiphany he meant a sudden spiritual manifestation, whether in the vulgarity of speech or gesture or a memorable phrase of the mind itself. He believed it was for the man of letters to record these epiphanies with extreme care, seeing that they themselves are the most delicate and evanescent of moments."

The two basic versions of this tale are two variant autobiographies of the young artist in pursuit of the modern. Both are *Kunstlerroman*, stories about artistic emergence or aesthetic discovery, much practised at the time in works like Huysmans' *A rebours*, Mann's *Buddenbrooks*, Lawrence's *Sons and Lovers*, and Proust's *A la recherche du temps perdu*, a good deal of which was written contemporaneously with *A Portrait of the Artist* . . . But the difference between the versions itself displays the subtly shifting nature of these developments in Joyce himself. Each is a search for the supreme artist: "the artist who could disentangle the subtle soul of the image from its mesh of defining circumstances most exactly and re-embody it in artistic circumstances chosen as the most exact for its new office, he was the supreme artist." Both question existing concepts of fictional creation: "When we come to the phenomena of artistic conception, artistic gestation and artistic reproduction I require a new terminology and a new personal experience," says Stephen in *A Portrait* . . . But that meant that the work itself had to be commensurate with just this ideal. The first version was an uncomfortable mixture of Naturalism and Impressionism, autobiography and exposition – a third-person omniscient picaresque tale based on the ballad "Turpin Hero," external and social rather than inward and psychological. But Joyce was now beginning to acknowledge that art stands beyond the autobiography and personality of the artist, and should grow from its own psychology of creation. Stephen himself is seen acknowledging this, accepting that while art may begin as artistic cry it must turn into epic and dramatic narrative – so that the artist starts to refine himself out of existence, producing pure form, and "The mystery of aesthetic like that of material creation is accomplished. The artist, like the God of creation, remains within or behind or beyond or above his handiwork, invisible, refined out of existence, indifferent, paring his finger-nails." By now Joyce is already beginning to see the book that followed, and Stephen is cast in his role as the eternal aesthete. So, in the revision that becomes *A Portrait*. . . the method becomes psychological, fluid, and self-conscious. It begins in a world of childish consciousness which is also a Modernist synaesthesia: "Once upon a time and a very good time it was there was a moocow coming down along the road and this moocow that was down along the road met a nicens little boy named boy tuckoo . . . His father told him that story . . ." The technique follows the various human stages of internal awareness by which life is not so much recorded as apprehended. The human senses and the various discourses of awareness begin to inter-seam with one another, giving a coherence to the developing language itself, which generates a complex web of motifs, images, symbols. The result of this aesthetic growth is accept-ance ("Welcome, O life!") but also exile, as Stephen, doing what Joyce had done in 1902, finally sets off to his artistic exile in Paris, in order "to forge in the smithy of my soul the uncreated conscience of my race."

There were, in fact, two exiles. Joyce himself would return to Dublin, witness the death of his mother, and then depart again, on the second, permanent, exile of 1904. This return is what we learn of in *Ulysses*, in which the next aesthetic step on the journey is taken. For that novel is not a work of symbolist naturalism, like *Dubliners*, nor even a psychological lyric, like *A Portrait* . . . It is, as Joyce explained, a work written "from eighteen different points of view and in as many styles, all apparently unknown or undiscovered by my fellow tradesmen." Though Stephen the artist is still present, reading the signatures of unknown things, he is a character among characters, a consciousness among consciousnesses. Other principles of creation and generation – Leopold Bloom's, and his wife Molly's – take a central place. Everything that happens – and everything happens, birth and death, defecation and menstruation, masturbation and lovemaking, past and present, history and historylessness – occurs on a single day. Myth has come in, through the story of Homer's *Odyssey*, both the material for parody and the source of new and deeper mythmaking. The methods of the modern interiorization of story – "interior monologue," "free association," "stream of consciousness" – consort with the linguistic devices that make a text self-consciously a text. Above all *Ulysses*, like *Finnegans Wake* to follow, was a fable of creation in process, a text seamlessly at work reading the signs of the world. "If it is not a novel, that is simply because the novel is a form which will no longer serve;" wrote T. S. Eliot, "it is because the novel, instead of being a form, was simply the expression of an age which had not sufficiently lost all form to feel the need of something stricter." It was another stage of aesthetic self-discovery and self-begetting creation, expressionistically born, like the novels Lawrence was writing at around the same date. *Ulysses* – which is discussed more fully later – was to become not just Dublin's book but everybody's, in fact the Novel of the Century in the age of the Death of the Novel. The phrase that Samuel Beckett, who carried on Joyce's lineage, used to explain it is famous and central: "His writing is not *about* something; *it is that something itself*." It applies to what Lawrence was trying to do, and others in the period around 1914, when it seemed the novel had indeed "lost all form" and had to win, out of creation itself, a new one. And, for the moment at least, this was the "modern novel."

THREE

The Exciting Age
1915–1930

"I don't see that it would be possible to live in a more exciting
age," said Calamy. "The sense that everything's perfectly
provisional and temporary – everything, from social institutions
to what we've hitherto regarded as the most sacred scientific
truths – the feeling that nothing from the Treaty of Versailles to
the rationally explicable universe, is really safe, the intimate
conviction that anything may happen, anything may be
discovered – another war, the artificial creation of life, the proof
of continued existence after death – why it is all infinitely
exhilarating."

"And the possibility that everything may be destroyed?"
questioned Mr Cardan.

"That's exhilarating too," Calamy answered, smiling.

Aldous Huxley, *Those Barren Leaves* (1925)

Ours is essentially a tragic age, so we refuse to take it tragically.
The cataclysm has happened, we are among the ruins, we start
to build up new little habits, to have new little hopes. It is
rather hard work: there is now no smooth road into the future;
but we go round, or scramble over the obstacles. We've got to
live, no matter how many skies have fallen.

D. H. Lawrence, *Lady Chatterley's Lover* (1928)

1.

So large was the change in fiction's tone and temper after the
Great War ended that it is best to start off with a roll-call. In
the middle of the war, in 1915, the year he said the old world
ended, D. H. Lawrence published *The Rainbow*, and Ford
Madox Hueffer brought out *The Good Soldier*, just before leaving

for the Front himself. Virginia Woolf signalled her forthcoming career as a novelist of the Twenties with her first novel *The Voyage Out* (Lytton Strachey praised it as "very un-Victorian"), and Dorothy Richardson began her long thirteen-book experimental sequence "Pilgrimage" (collected together in four volumes in 1967) by publishing its first volume or "chapter," *Pointed Roofs*. This was a work which Woolf described as inventing "a sentence which we might call the sentence of the feminine gender," and May Sinclair called "stream of consciousness going on and on" (as, to be frank, it rather did); between them these two books marked the beginnings of a distinctive feminist modernism. Then in 1916, the year when Henry James died, James Joyce's aesthetic and psychological novel of voyage into the unknown arts, *A Portrait of the Artist as a Young Man*, came out in book form in New York, and was reprinted in Britain the next year by the small Egoist Press. In that year, 1917, Conrad published *The Shadow Line*, and Norman Douglas *South Wind*. It was a year of experiment in poetry – T. S. Eliot printed his first volume *Prufrock and Other Observations*, and W. B. Yeats *Wild Swans at Coole* – and in publishing. Small *avant-garde* magazines and presses were multiplying, and Leonard and Virginia Woolf began the Hogarth Press, which would sponsor many important and experimental works over the next decade, from Eliot, Rilke, Freud, Rebecca West, Gertrude Stein, Italo Svevo and more. In 1918, the year the War ended, Wyndham Lewis published his hard Vorticist novel *Tarr*, and "Rebecca West" (Cecily Fairfield), best known as a polemicist, turned to fiction with a topical novel about shellshock, *The Return of the Soldier*. "Bloomsbury" declared itself a major power with what has been called "the first book of the Twenties," Lytton Strachey's *Eminent Victorians*: a mocking demolition of four Victorian sages (Cardinal Manning, Thomas Arnold, Florence Nightingale and General Gordon), a celebration of the witty deconstructive present, a firm repudiation of the past.

1919, a year when writers were already starting to look round in disillusion at the post-war age, saw Virginia Woolf's second

novel *Night and Day*, and, possibly even more importantly, her
influential essay "Modern Fiction," where she demanded a new
realism based on consciousness: "Life is not a series of gig-
lamps symmetrically arranged; but a luminous halo, a semi-
transparent envelope surrounding us from the beginning of
consciousness to the end," she wrote; "Is it not the task of the
novelist to convey this varying, this unknown and uncircum-
scribed spirit, whatever aberration or complexity it may display,
with as little mixture of the alien and external as possible?"
Ronald Firbank published his ornately decadent *Valmouth: A
Romantic Novel*, and May Sinclair her experimental, autobiographical *Mary Olivier*. In 1920 Conrad brought out *The Rescue*,
Katherine Mansfield produced her first collection of very
Chekhovian short stories, *Bliss*, and from a New York private
press came Lawrence's *Women in Love* – which, he explained,
"does contain the results in one's soul of the war." In 1921
Lawrence's book appeared in Britain, and Aldous Huxley, who
was satirized in it, published his clever first novel, *Crome Yellow*,
about the psychoses of the post-war intelligentsia. Galsworthy
completed the first trilogy of "The Forsyte Saga" with *To Let*,
set in the post-war world and acknowledging that "The waters
of change were foaming in, carrying the promise of new forms
only when their destructive flood should have passed its full."
But Galsworthy now stood for an older spirit in a fiction that,
like post-war poetry, was prepared to be rebellious, experimental, "new." That grew plain in 1922, Modernism's year – the
annus mirabilis of the modern movement, Harry Levin has called
it. In Paris Proust died that year; however on 2 February, his
fortieth birthday, James Joyce brought out, in a half-hidden
limited edition of a thousand signed copies from a small
English-language bookshop, his vast novel *Ulysses*. For all it was
banned in Britain and the USA, the book dominated experimental fiction for the rest of the Twenties. T. S. Eliot, whose
crisis-laden modernist poem *The Waste Land* appeared the same
year, spelt out the work's meaning in an essay, "Ulysses, Order
and Myth" (1923), saying Joyce had finally broken the mould
of the old novel: "The novel ended with Flaubert and with

James." Referring to his use of the framework myth of *The Odyssey*, he said: "No one else has ever built a novel on such a foundation before . . . In using the myth, in manipulating a continuous parallel between contemporaneity and antiquity, Mr Joyce is pursuing a method which others must pursue after him." Joyce, he claimed, had found "a way of controlling, of ordering, of giving a shape and a significance to the immense panorama of futility and anarchy which is contemporary history . . . Instead of the narrative method, we may now use the mythic method. It is, I seriously believe, a step toward making the modern world possible for art . . ."

Virginia Woolf, whose own *Jacob's Room* appeared that year, considered the book "underbred," but she did recognize Joyce's importance in the making of "modern fiction." That year, too, Lawrence published *Aaron's Rod*, and Katherine Mansfield the fine-tuned stories of *The Garden Party*. Two notable novels about the war experience, a key theme of the Twenties, William Gerhardie's *Futility* (set in Russia around the time of the Revolution) and C. E. Montague's *Disenchantment*, also came out, and their titles said it all. Of course the "old" novel had not ended with Flaubert and James; it has not ended still. Wells, Galsworthy and Bennett still remained the leading literary novelists, and in 1923 Bennett published his excellent and highly realist *Riceyman Steps*. But the campaign for "modern fiction" now intensified, and Woolf fiercely attacked him and his fellow materialists in her essay "Mr Bennett and Mrs Brown," where she suggested he saw everything and understood nothing, and announced the great change of 1910. By now it was growing much easier to see what she meant. In 1924 – the year of Thomas Mann's *Buddenbrooks* and Ernest Hemingway's *In Our Time* – E. M. Forster published his finest, most innovative and final novel, *A Passage to India*, Ford Madox Ford opened his remarkable four-volume experimental sequence about wartime, "Parade's End," with *Some Do Not . . .*, Michael Arlen won fame with his smartly modern *The Green Hat*, and Firbank published the very camp *Prancing Nigger*. All were modern in their different ways: modern in form, modern in subject and smartness, modern in their awareness of psychoanalysis, decadent cynicism or Spenglerian despair. In 1925 Virginia Woolf published her finest novel to date, *Mrs Dalloway*, showing she had made good use of the Joycean lesson, Lawrence his novella *St Mawr*, Aldous Huxley *Those Barren Leaves*, and I. – Ivy, it turned out – Compton-Burnett her *Pastors and Masters*, which converted the patriarchal Victorian family into a timeless *mise-en-scène* for the eternal tragi-comedy of domestic life.

New American fiction, especially from expatriate Paris, was increasingly influencing European writing. Three important experimental works, Gertrude Stein's word-novel *The Making of Americans*, John Dos Passos' expressionist city novel *Manhattan Transfer* and F. Scott Fitzgerald's *The Great Gatsby* all came out that year, and over the next two or three years Hemingway and Faulkner made their mark. And in Britain too, by the second half of the Twenties, a fresh, distinctively post-war generation, mostly born in the twentieth century, was changing the tone and spirit of the novel. Modern conventions were now becoming commonplace. When, in 1927, E. M. Forster published his study *Aspects of the Novel* and said "Yes – oh dear, yes – the novel tells a story," as if this were just the smallest part of its work, modern writers and readers now knew just what he meant. In 1926 a young Oxford undergraduate Henry Green (Henry Yorke) published his experimental, "sightless" novel *Blindness*, and Rose Macaulay a witty tale of a "modern" independent woman, *Crewe Train*. In 1927 Virginia Woolf published *To the Lighthouse*, the storyless story of a trip untaken to a Hebridean lighthouse, Rosamund Lehmann her psychological story of a girl's growing up, *Dusty Answer*, and Elizabeth Bowen *The Hotel*. All these were novels where sensibility ("pattern," "rhythm," "poetry") rather than story were in charge, part of what Woolf saw as a "feminization" of the novel that was to flourish in the following years. The *avant garde* prospered, as writers fled Victorianism, puritanism and their parents for the independent country of art, and bohemian communities themselves became common subjects in fiction. There was Hemingway's story of lost-generation Montparnasse *The Sun*

Also Rises in 1926, and Lawrence showed the wandering bohemia of Twenties artists in many of his fictions. 1927 saw Wyndham Lewis' vast artistic satire *The Childermass*, and Jean Rhys' story of drifting and writing on the Left Bank, *Postures* (later called *Quartet*). Bohemia led to sexual scandal; in 1928 Lawrence brought out *Lady Chatterley's Lover* – a tale of shattered bohemian lives in the modern "tragic age," a book so sexually frank it had to be published privately in Italy, and "Radclyffe Hall" her novel of lesbianism *The Well of Loneliness*, which was banned and not reissued until 1949. Popular fiction flourished now, above all the thriller and the cerebral detective story. In 1928 the Dantean scholar Dorothy Sayers set Purgatory aside to unravel a number of mysterious deaths at which *Lord Peter Views the Body*, and Agatha Christie ingeniously solved *The Mystery of the Blue Train*.

As the decade began to close, a large group of brilliant new writers appeared, very much the products of the post-war climate. In 1928 Evelyn Waugh emerged with his black-comic novel of the age's "bright young things," *Decline and Fall: An Illustrated Novelette*; Christopher Isherwood published *All the Conspirators*, about, he said, the Second "Great War," by which he meant the war of the old and the young, which led the way on to the work of the "Auden Generation." In 1929 Graham Greene appeared as a novelist with his historical novel *The Man Within*, starting a fictional career that would last eight decades. The decade closed with a sudden burst of disillusioned war fiction, Richard Aldington's *The Death of a Hero*, Robert Graves' *Goodbye to All That*, and many more; the futility of the Great War now seemed ever more apparent, and the post-war generation felt somehow betrayed. Henry Green published his "industrial novel" *Living*, a mixture of experimentalism and social conscience, and John Cowper Powys *Wolf Solent*. Then in October 1929 the American stock market crashed, the Depression which had already begun was confirmed, and the entire mood changed. "The modern decade" became the dislocated, lost decade; George Orwell condemned it from the Thirties as "a period of irresponsibility such as the world has

never before seen" – though he would also condemn his own
decade in much the same way. The excitement of Modernism,
the aesthetic excitement that had peaked between 1922 and
1929, began to fade, grim fears for the future grew, Europe
entered an era of new and terrible disorder, and writers looked
to society, reality, and political commitment. It grew harder
now to acknowledge the achievement of the immediately post-
war decade, even though so much new writing had begun in it.
Yet it was another period of the "New Arts," and quite as
important as any. It was also the time when the "modern
novel" ceased to be a shock of surprise, and became an artistic
convention.

2.

I have given this roll-call to show how deeply the flavour of
literary culture changed over the Twenties, the decade of the
general triumph of the "modern." Many of the epic books at
the heart of the Modern movement – *Women in Love* and *Ulysses*,
A Passage to India and *Parade's End*, *Mrs Dalloway* and *The
Childermass* – came out at this time, and were paralleled with
similar work in French, German and American fiction. The
concept of the novel, the very language of fiction, changed, and
it seemed that the experimental spirit that had been developing
from the 1880s on was now fully confirmed. In fact the tone of
modern experiment had altered greatly in the wake of the war;
the mood was no longer that exhilarated excitement in new
forms and *avant-garde* possibilities that Hueffer could celebrate
as "the opening world." "Modern" became a widespread term,
though it now seemed less to suggest an exciting adventure,
more a dark historical necessity. The "modern" experiment
took on a bleaker, more decadent, more fragile, even more
terminal mood. If it stood for a breaking of reticences, a freeing
of forms, a poetic opening out of the inwardness of narrative, a
new voyage into consciousness (as it was to Virginia Woolf), it
was also a dismayed reaction to the fragmentation of culture, to

a catastrophic history, to the pervasive sense of psychic crisis, to modern violence and dislocation. The difference between the experimental expansiveness of Woolf's first novel *The Voyage Out* and the psychic fragility of *Mrs Dalloway*, where Clarissa's crisis is intimately linked with the shellshocked mind of Septimus Smith, is telling. The "post-war novel" had arrived, and lives as well as novels, history as well as literary form, had been modernized during the war. If the new modern epics were often works of deep inner fragmentation (fragments shored against the ruins, as Eliot said in "The Waste Land"), of broken myths and history aestheticized into form, that was because the very nature of culture and its myths had deeply changed over wartime, and had to be rewritten, pared down, recovered, reconstructed.

So, as a post-war generation used the arts to survey and catch at a different and shattered world, Twenties experiment took on a character all its own. Today we see the Twenties as the first truly modern decade we have behind us – modern not just in its art-forms, but because in life and fiction alike we see modern lives lived in modern ways. It was, as Strachey's *Eminent Victorians* showed, an age of the "younger generation," who saw Victorianism far behind in the past, and thought they had passed through a great and terrible historical initiation. The moral certainty, the monumental attitude, the progressive view of history, the sense of cultural stability, that still remained in the experimental works of the Edwardian and early Georgian era had now largely gone. War, battlefield slaughter, the loss of a whole part of a generation, political uncertainty, historical doubt, sexual freedom, psychic tension, the sense reported in Aldous Huxley's *Those Barren Leaves* that "everything's perfectly provisional and temporary," the belief in what Lawrence's *Lady Chatterley* named a "tragic age," gave a feeling of passage through a momentous change. The war *was* modernity, and modernity meant not just free verse, stream-of-consciousness prose, fragments shored against the ruins, the revolution of the word, abstraction, surrealism or Dada, but also life speeded up, flattened out, stripped of something. It meant radio and cinema and the telephone, the new popular technologies, the accelerated pace of daily life, the culture of a generation that was already rejecting its parents. As Isherwood said of his *All the Conspirators*, the motto of the day was "My Generation – right or wrong." But the age declared itself less through politics or passion for reform than through *avant-garde* rebellion, self-conscious independence of style and *mores*, revolution of the sensibility. Style meant form, meant fashion, meant self-conscious initiation, a new manner of being, and the new tastes, the new amusements, the new public roles and identities all became part of the changing style of the arts themselves. Sexual *mores* had changed greatly; there was new independence for women, as the trimmed figures and capped hairdos showed. There was a search for vitalism, primitivism, passion, a faith in the unconscious and the libido, a rejection of "puritan" codes.

To be "modern" meant many different things. It indicated the abstract difficulty, the fragmentation and syncopation of free verse or the stream-of-consciousness novel, but also the generational revolution in morals and values, the mood of decadent disenchantment, that came so often from the young. As Hemingway in *The Sun Also Rises* had his "lost generation," Evelyn Waugh had the "bright young things" of *Decline and Fall* and *Vile Bodies*, while among their elders the topic of the Younger Generation "spread like a yawn." For to be modern also meant disenchantment with history, living for the instant, life seen as just like the Big Wheel at Luna Park in Waugh's *Decline and Fall*: "They're all trying to sit on the wheel, and they keep getting flung off, and that makes them laugh, and you laugh too." Or it was the headlong rush toward disaster, the "faster, faster" of the parties, instant love affairs and motor races of his *Vile Bodies* (1930), which ends, like several Twenties novels, and many in the early Thirties, with an apocalyptic premonition of future war. A cynical rejection of all that was romantic, traditional, or "Victorian" linked with harder styles, hero-less stories, and pacey, flickering narrative to change and speed up the narrative voice of Twenties fiction. This owed not a little to the coming of the most modern, and popular, type of narrative of all: first silent cinema, with its narrative method of montage and rapid cutting, and then in 1927, in a sudden technological acceleration, the sound movie, with its dialogue as well as visual action. All of these things entered the spirit of modern style in writing, became steps in making the modern world possible for art.

It is useful to distinguish two "modern" generations in Twenties fiction, each with a different impact on the lineage of the modern British novel. One is the Modernist generation, who really represent a radical development of the experimental writing that had begun before the turn of the century and seemed to peak as War began; the second was the younger generation of writers who established themselves during the Twenties, for whom modern experiment was already a birthright. By around 1915 there was already a growing consent in intellectual, artistic and literary circles that a modern revolution, of form and sensibility, was transforming the arts. The fiction of James and Conrad, Ford, Lawrence, Joyce and, soon, Woolf was seen to come from an era that had come to acknowledge the power of the evolutionary modernizing processes foreseen by Marx and Darwin, the new imperative of Nietzsche, the impassioned modern consciousness of Dostoevsky ("Confound all these young fellows," Galsworthy wrote, "how they have gloated over Dostoevsky"), the sexual unconscious of Freud. A variety of movement names were found for what was happening – Post-Impressionism, Expressionism, Imagism, Vorticism, or, said the philosopher T. E. Hulme, "let us agree to call it classicism" – and ideas like Worringer's "abstraction," Fry's "significant form," Joyce's "epiphany," Eliot's "impersonality," Woolf's "luminous halo," were increasingly accepted. Writers increasingly saw the artist's own vision and consciousness, rather than some exterior reported reality, or some eternal law of story, as art's prime source, regarded narrative not as reporting or telling but "presenting" or "rendering," considered that art followed the self-made laws of its own aesthetic goals. If this *was* the Modern revolution, it could indeed be argued that in Britain it was largely done by 1915. A good many artists saw it like this, going off to Paris in the Twenties to find the stateless capital of Bohemia, where experiment ran freer, sexual mores were franker, censorship less, the parties and the drinks better, and the *avant garde* had its own best home. But the social changes of the Twenties transformed the literary environment, the mood of post-war crisis induced its own new decadence, and, without necessarily being *avant-garde*, writers back at home were also developing their own new arts. In this, they had, at least for a time, the leadership of experiment's British outpost, "Bloomsbury," and a general culture that self-consciously accepted that the world, and modern society, had been transformed and modernized by the war.

For, whether you wrote in *avant-garde* Paris or at home, it was clear enough that the War did represent, or serve as the great metaphor of, an epochal transition. Pre-war fiction – for all its interest in the "new," the "abstract," the "inhuman" – generally had the spirit of liberal humanism as its companion. It accepted progress in history, human development, the advance of the spirit as the motors of culture, and sought to see it "whole." Even if the human self was proving to have deep recesses of unconscious behaviour, or was submitted to the blind powers of heredity, environment or libido, or the dehumanizing forces of modern mechanization, there was a faith in the rounded character and the general density of personal life. But war seemed to abstract and empty life itself, creating a landscape of violence and uncertainty in which the human figure was no longer a constant, the individual self no longer connected naturally with the universe, the word no longer attached to the thing. Culture now seemed a bundle of fragments, history no longer moved progressively, but cyclically, toward a Viconian eternal return – or more likely toward Spenglerian decline; no wonder history was, as Stephen Dedalus says in *Ulysses*, a "nightmare from which I am trying to awake," or Eliot's "immense panorama of futility and anarchy." Life came randomly to consciousness, so that, said Virginia Woolf in "How It Strikes a Contemporary" (1923), the modern writer "cannot

147

make a world, cannot generalize." The ancient echo that Mrs Moore hears in the caves of *A Passage to India*, which says "Everything exists, nothing has value," sounded for many writers of the Twenties, helping to create that "twilight of the gods" feeling, that "destructive element," that George Orwell and Stephen Spender read in post-war literature. If abstraction, collage and fragmentation provided the mode of many works in the Twenties, if many of them were parodic versions of previous forms, this surely had something to do with crisis and cataclysm. As a result Modernism now began to look, especially in European writing, less like joyous experiment than grim prophecy, and pre-war discovery turned into post-war disillusion.

From the 1890s onward, it is true, fiction had been filling with prophecies of future wars, often linked with belief in (or fear of) the limitless powers of science and speculation about the social or racial future of the planet. There were Wellsian Wars of the Worlds, imaginary battles of or invasions by European powers, wars between machines and men.[1] Similarly fiction had expressed rising suspicions of a universal anarchy underlying culture, that "destructive element" that Conrad speaks of in *Lord Jim*. The metaphor of life as warfare underlay a good deal of Naturalism; even literature was often seen as a kind of modern warfare. The term *avant garde* is after all a military analogy, and it was scarcely an accident that Wyndham Lewis should title his pre-war Vorticist magazine *Blast*, and declare that "Dehumanization is the chief diagnostic of the modern world." But the uneasy sense of prophecy that preceded the Great War bore only small relation to the reality. When it came, it proved more terrible, more dehumanizing, than any prophecy, more violently destructive than any dystopian fantasy, more damaging to the European political and social order

---

[1] A brilliant study of all this is I. F. Clarke's *Voices Prophesying War: Future Wars 1763–3749* (Oxford and New York, rev. ed., 1992). Clarke's bibliography lists an enormous number of titles, some by "serious writers," others popular fantasies, others by military men, accelerating in quantity as 1914 approaches. Since 1914, of course, the genre has multiplied and become part of the convention of science fiction.

than any prediction. The writers who were there to record it, at or away from the front, found they had to forgo all lyricism, sentimentality, or romanticism, that the language of impression, macabre irony, abstraction, fragmentation and dehumanization frequently served them best to express their own sense of powerlessness.[2] The war was a crisis not simply for the subject-matter of fiction – heroism and bravery, the value of individual life and social history – but for its very power of representation. It is understandable that many critics have found this the epochal moment when literature took on modern sensibility, as social representation was fragmented, language decentred, reality de-realized. So John McCormick, in his *American Literature: 1919–1932* (1971), argues that the war "smashed all the Stendhalian mirrors," forcing literature to shift away from representation of society toward a shattered representation of the self; Frederick J. Hoffman says in *The Mortal No: Death and the Modern Imagination* (1964) that – though all war depersonalizes – the Great War, with its mass slaughter without victory, challenged every traditional idea of warfare, and overthrew the decorums within which all writing of war and death had previously been contained. But the most vivid comment is by the German critic Walter Benjamin: "men returned from the battlefield grown silent – not richer but poorer in communicable experience," he notes. "A generation that had gone to school on a horse-drawn streetcar now stood under the open sky in a countryside in which nothing remained unchanged but the clouds, and beneath those clouds, in a field of force of destructive torrents and explosions, was the tiny, fragile human body."[3]

[2] "The passage of these literary characters [the soldiers who wrote about the war] from pre-war freedom to wartime bondage, frustration and absurdity signals just as surely as does the experience of Joyce's Bloom, Hemingway's Frederic Henry, or Kafka's Joseph K. the passage of modern writing from one mode to another, from the low mimetic of the plausible and the social to the ironic of the outrageous, the ridiculous, and the murderous," writes Paul Fussell in *The Great War and Modern Memory* (London and New York, 1975), p. 312. And he quotes H. M. Tomlinson's comment that "the parapet, the wire, and the mud" are now "permanent features of human existence."

[3] John McCormick, *American Literature, 1919–1932: A Comparative History* (London,

The deep change plain in the temper of post-war fiction clearly deserves such an explanation, even though some, at least, of the shifts of style and vision often commented on were clearly present in the novel well before the war. But the war and its historical and psychological impact was one of the chief stories the post-war writer was forced to tell. For one reason or another, most of the leading modernists – Joyce, Woolf and Lawrence, Pound, Eliot and Yeats – did not take up arms or go to the front. Even so the fiction of the Twenties was indeed dominated by the war novel; by 1930, it's estimated, some seven hundred books had been written on the war. Even in the works of writers who had not directly seen the battlefront horrors the war is omnipresent, appearing as wound, cultural fracture, violence and intrusion, modern revolution (Gerhardie's *Futility* is about waiting for the one in Russia), the moment of severance, the confirmation of the modern as a state of cultural crisis. In Woolf's *Mrs Dalloway*, war has destroyed the mind and peace of Septimus Smith, who is a surrogate of Clarissa Dalloway herself; in *To the Lighthouse* it is the great destructive vacancy at the book's centre, blankly removing many of the characters. It is there in the home-based fiction of Rebecca West and Elizabeth Bowen. War and its wound destroys the past and the identity of Christopher Tietjens in Ford Madox Ford's "Parade's End", which takes the story to the battlefront. It brings the castrating wound that, literally and symbolically, sterilizes Sir Clifford Chatterley in *Lady Chatterley's Lover* – a book that is, Lawrence tells us, dominated by "the false inhuman bruise of war," and already senses the next one. Sir Clifford writes stories too, "clever, rather spiteful, and yet in some mysterious way, meaningless," but "curiously true to modern life, to modern psychology, that is." Lawrence acknowledges this new style even as he tries to subvert it with a

1971); Frederick J. Hoffman, *The Mortal No: Death and the Modern Imagination* (Princeton, 1964); and Walter Benjamin, "The Storyteller," in *Illuminations* (London, 1973). Also see Holger Klein (ed.), *The First World War in Fiction: A Collection of Critical Essays* (London, 1976).

language of vernacular sexual "tenderness"; that is the reason for his famous "frankness." But clever, spiteful stories, curiously true to modern psychology, certainly did dominate the Twenties. Impersonal dehumanized techniques – Wyndham Lewis celebrated them as the method of "the Great Without" – went along with the sense of the human creature as an absurd machine of being, irrationally split between thought and passion. Harder, sharper, more detached methods matched the sense of transitoriness, accelerating pace, the "faster, faster," the collapse into danger or death. Directly or indirectly, the wound of war was everywhere in the post-war novel, explaining the note of sharp generational change, historical weariness, waste-land vision and rootless psychological tension so plain in much of the best fiction.

Some of the finest of these books were by writers who, having already established pre-war literary reputations, produced their classic works, works of most extreme disturbance, across the bridge of the war: Joyce's *Ulysses*, Forster's *A Passage to India*, Proust's *A la recherche du temps perdu* (*Remembrance of Things Past*), Gertrude Stein's *The Making of Americans*, Thomas Mann's *Buddenbrooks*, Franz Kafka's *The Trial*, in fact some of the key texts of early Twenties Modernism. These works, begun in one historical climate, finished in another, offered their monumental lessons (if not their actual monumentalism) to younger writers. And by the mid-Twenties Modernism had become, in effect, an institution. Stein, Pound and Ford gave their masterclasses in Paris; in Britain "Bloomsbury" was now less an outrage than an influential cultural élite; the Modernist T. S. Eliot edited the leading respectable literary magazine, *The Criterion*. Works like Percy Lubbock's *The Craft of Fiction* (1921) and Forster's *Aspects of the Novel* (1927) treated Jamesian notions of "point of view," "pattern," "rhythm" as agreed literary convention. Hence for newer writers like Aldous Huxley, Evelyn Waugh, Ronald Firbank and Michael Arlen, most too young for the war, the modern was no obscure artistic "affair," but a condition of life to be reported. The age of great Modernist epics or anti-epics – *Women in Love*, *Ulysses*, "Parade's End", *A la recherche du temps perdu, Buddenbrooks* – was thus also an age when life became fragile, love became brittle, art became amusing, style became manner, when everything was an "experiment." Being "modern" meant being close to the sharpest tastes of the age – the flappers and car rides, the nightclubs and parties, the yawning boredoms and weary affairs, the orgies and cynicisms, the despair and the *nada*, for immersion in the present, giving oneself to the intensifying if senseless pace of history, was one way of dealing with post-war things, of telling by the clock of history what the time was. This helped create the smart exoticism of Arlen, the febrility of Firbank, the mixture of involvement and satirical detachment in Huxley or Waugh, where the very senselessness and loss of meaning becomes a sad comedy. And then, around 1930, when new terrors showed on the horizon, history became not a post-war amusement but a pre-war horror, and exile and violence came to seem the universals of contemporary life, the "Modern" grew boring. Or rather, in fiction, it began to turn into something else, the contemporary realist novel of the surreal dark twentieth century.

3.

Twenties poetry had the shock of Eliot's "The Waste Land," Twenties fiction had the shock of Joyce's *Ulysses*. Despite, maybe because of, its Parisian publication, and its famed difficulty and obscurity, it became the book serious modern writers (and readers) had to take in, learning its lesson and imbibing its influence. It was a compendium of the modern genres, a stylebook for the age; banned from Britain and the United States, it was smuggled into both disguised as *The Complete Works of William Shakespeare*, which it was as big as. And, coming from an Irish exile, printed by a Dijon printer, and published by a small Paris bookstore, it helped establish "modern English literature" as something quite independent of a single nation, as Hugh Kenner has observed. If it was not an

English novel, nor an American novel, it was not quite an Irish novel either. The famous last words of the book, Molly Bloom's great erotic cry of sexual and human acquiescence "yes and I drew him down to me so he could feel my breasts all perfume yes and his heart was going like mad and yes I said yes I will Yes." are not quite the last words. They are followed by a byline, "Trieste–Zürich–Paris 1914–1921," the byline of a modern literary exile. *Ulysses* is the great novel of Dublin, but it is about a Wandering Jew, based on another famous wanderer, Ulysses, and written by another wanderer, who having finally chosen Paris as his home died in Zürich. This was certainly a novel written across the war. Our first glimpse of it goes back to a postcard of 1906 ("I have a new story for *Dubliners* in my head. It deals with Mr Hunter") sent by Joyce from Rome to his brother Stanislaus. But this germ for a short story about a Jewish cuckold in Dublin, to which he later adds the title "Ulysses," was not to find its way into *Dubliners*. In early 1914 Joyce was encouraged by the successful London serialization of *A Portrait* . . . to think of extending the story of Stephen Daedalus, and setting his Stephen Hero in a larger myth. By now Joyce was in Trieste, the Adriatic outlet of the dying Austro-Hungarian empire, teaching languages, and learning them. He had made many cosmopolitan literary friendships with, for instance, Italo Svevo, the sardonic Triestian modernist who wrote *The Confessions of Zeno*, had become in effect a middle-European writer who wrote in the press on the affairs of the region, and was writing a play aptly called *Exiles*. When war broke out from events very close to hand (Trieste is not so far from Sarajevo), he was immersed in the difficult working out of his book, and professed indifference. By 1915 Stanislaus was interned in Austria, and he himself, paroled by the Austrians, moved to new exile in neutral Zürich, haven, as Tom Stoppard readers will know, to revolutionary exiles of many dispositions, including Lenin, Tristan Tzara, founder of the movement of Dada, and Joyce himself, brooding a revolution of his own.

In Zürich a good deal of the novel *Ulysses*, that great

paperchase, was written, and Joyce expressed many of his underlying ideas to Frank Budgen, a friend he made there. He recorded them in *James Joyce and the Making of "Ulysses"* (1934), a study that makes it clear how the work changed enormously in the writing, taking in new narrative, new schemata, becoming an ever more ambitious and elaborately coded text. By now it was no longer another tale for *Dubliners*, or even a supplement for *A Portrait* . . .; it had become a major new project, the book of books. When early chapters were serialized, in Britain and the USA, in 1918, Virginia Woolf read them and acknowledged that, in an age of materialist fiction, "Mr Joyce is spiritual; he is concerned at all costs to reveal the flickerings of that innermost flame which flashes its messages through the brain . . ." The book was, she said, "important," "difficult," and "unpleasant." The "unpleasantness," the concern with bodily functions, with defecation and urination and menstruation, led to its banning; the serial instalments were never completed. When the war ended, Joyce briefly returned to Trieste.

Then in 1920 he met Ezra Pound, who had helped get the work published and arranged financial support for him. He suggested Joyce move to Paris, explaining that it was "the cheapest place last year," and he already had a large *avant-garde* reputation there. It was the best of advice; later that year Joyce came to Paris, then alive with post-war experimental tendencies, Dada and Surrealism, and, with its cheap franc and its available wine, attracting young writers from Britain and the United States, tired of Victorianism, Anglo-Saxonism, Puritanism and, in America, Prohibition. It was the ideal place both to finish *Ulysses* and publish it in an environment that could accept it. Moving from apartment to apartment, Joyce completed the book, now acknowledged as the greatest Modernist novel of the century, at 5 Boulevard Raspail in October 1921. He had met the American bookseller Sylvia Beach, who thought him a genius, and the book that could no longer be published in Britain or the USA appeared from her small bookstore Shakespeare and Company in the Rue de l'Odéon. The death of Proust that year had left an experimental vacancy. Joyce filled it, and *Ulysses* was hailed both as a great work of experimental Paris and a major emblem of the Modern movement.

It is still worth asking how its vast reputation arose. At first glance *Ulysses* is not a contemporary novel. It is set back on one long June day and night in the distant Dublin of twenty years before, just at the point when its author departed the city, more or less for good. It was already an historical novel, about a Dublin that no longer existed, except in Joyce's own vivid memory and through his own meticulous research. Friend after friend had checked every detail, answering the questions that the writing had thrown up. The Imperial Dublin in which the book was set was over and done with; in the year of publication the Irish Free State was declared. History, in the book, is omnipresent, yet history is the nightmare from which Stephen Dedalus (the spelling of his name had changed) is desperately trying to awake, into another realm entirely, the transubstantiated realm of art. This, perhaps, is why the story is held tight to one single day in Dublin, the city of paralysed stasis, and why the narrative code is not sequential, as in most novels, but synchronic. But history, under another rule, is there nonetheless: as immediate sense-data, as newspaper report ("Sufficient unto the day is the newspaper thereof"), contemporary popular song, endless Nationalist demands for republican political engagement, which Stephen Dedalus and Leopold Bloom (as Hunter had become) hear but are not engaged by, having their own other interests. History lives over again in the meticulous detailing of the city's advertising signs, its tramway routes, its water and sewer system ("through a subterranean aqueduct of filter mains of single and double pipeage constructed at an initial plant cost of £5 per linear yard"). For the immediacy of life and the transformations of art are the contradictory, countervailing powers in this story. As Anthony Burgess says, *Ulysses* is a great comic novel which achieves "the solemnization of drab days and the sanctification of the ordinary."[4] Joyce had so

---

[4] Anthony Burgess, *Here Comes Everybody: An Introduction to Joyce for the Ordinary Reader* (London and New York, 1965).

carefully prized his accuracy, stored his memories, checked his facts that, he claimed, if the Dublin of 1904 were destroyed, it would be possible to recreate it from the book. But this Dublin is more than Dublin, as Eliot's London in "The Waste Land" is more than London. Joyce remarked that "if he could get to the heart of Dublin he could get to the heart of all the cities of the world"; and *Ulysses* is an exemplary modern city novel, one of those works of experiment where the city, any city, becomes an open space for the flickering collage that is modern experience. But above all it is a modern city where, as Eliot said, history is amended by myth: a classic myth of home and homelessness, of sons lost and fathers found, of faithful/faithless wives and cuckold/loving husbands, of departure and return. The myth teases the commonplace city; the commonplace city challenges but gives human substance to the modern myth.

Back in Zürich, Joyce had wisely told Budgen his elaborate mythic intentions. In selecting Ulysses as his heroic prototype (rather than Jesus, or Hamlet, or Faust), he had picked a complete man with a complete and rounded life, a man who was son and father, husband and lover, soldier and family man, hero and victim, someone who would transfer into the very contemporary figure of Leopold Bloom, the ordinary yet also marvellously rich Jewish advertisement canvasser whose local wanderings are set in counterpoint to those of Stephen Dedalus, the modern artist–aesthete. But Joyce was not aiming to retell the story of the wily Ulysses in modern-day terms; his aim was to create a complex system of correspondences. Each separate chapter of the book had, he explained, an exact Homeric parallel, and was written in its own distinctive language. Each episode had a linguistic and stylistic character appropriate to its subject; the book was also an epic of the parts of the human body, and structured with musical and colour codes. It was thanks, then, to Budgen, and later to Stuart Gilbert, another respectful and loyal interpreter, that modern readers/interpreters (one did not just read *Ulysses*) were made to understand that the dense social, domestic and sexual detail of this encyclopedic book was deep-coded with complex systems of parallelism and correspondence: that the novel was both a reasonably open, though difficult, story of Dublin life and a very hermetic text, awaiting its professorial exegetes.[5] Joyce laid down other guides to an interpretation, as Eliot did with "The Waste Land," a poem with footnotes. Thus he wrote in a letter: "It is an epic of two races (Israelite–Irish) and at the same time the cycle of the human body as well as a little story of a day . . . It is also a sort of encyclopaedia. My intention is to transpose the myth *sub specie temporis nostri*. Each adventure (that is, every hour, every organ, every art being interconnected and interrelated in the structural scheme of the whole) should not only condition but even create its own technique . . ." Of the many things that seemed new about *Ulysses*, one was its power to construct and interweave an entire universe inside itself. Joyce told Budgen that the English language was wonderfully rich in words, but they were not all the right ones; hence the book is filled with linguistic invention. He also said that the problem was not so much finding the right words, but putting them in the right order; so it is also filled with multiple types of discourse, distinctive and self-created grammars. The resulting constructions – the unusual verbal amalgams, the literary echoes, parodies and pastiches, the allusions and the lists, the quotations, interlocutions and interrogations – made *Ulysses* the great word-book of Modern literature. Unlike, say, Gertrude Stein's *The Making of Americans* (1925), another "text" (the term became inevitable) of "the Revolution of the Word," Joyce's novel is unrandom, God-like, self-consciously made throughout. It is one reason why part of the Modernist tradition is made of hermeneutic texts: texts as interpretation, that continue to require interpretation. Joyce was not only constructing a modern book; he was constructing, with it, the modern deconstructive reader.

[5] See Frank Budgen, *James Joyce and the Making of "Ulysses" and Other Writings* (London, rev. ed., 1972 [originally published 1934]), and Stuart Gilbert, *James Joyce's "Ulysses"* (New York, rev. ed., 1952 [originally published 1930]). Harry Blamires, *The Bloomsday Book: A Guide Through Joyce's "Ulysses"* (London and New York, 1966), is also recommended.

But this is not the only way we can read *Ulysses*: it is made in many layers, constructed in many registers. There is no shortage of ordinary Naturalism ("Mr Leopold Bloom ate with relish the inner organs of beasts and fowls. He liked thick giblet soup, nutty gizzards, a stuffed roast heart, liverslices fried with breadcrumbs, fried hencods' roes. Most of all he liked grilled mutton kidneys a fine tang of faintly scented urine"), even though it is so mannered and careful in its making that it does not read like innocent Naturalism. There is, thanks to the vividly given consciousness of Stephen Dedalus, a portrait of the artist as a slightly older man, a great deal of Aestheticism, and the lore of Aestheticism ("Ineluctable modality of the visible: at least that if no more, thought through my eyes. Signatures of all things I am here to read, seaspawn and seawrack, the nearing tide, that rusty boot. Snotgreen, blue-silver, rust: coloured signs. Limits of the diaphane"), but it is not quite the Aestheticism a late nineteenth-century reader would recognize. Modern readers read popular romances (and so does Molly Bloom), so the intonations of Ouida and Paul de Kock ("nice name he has") are there ("The hero folded her willowy form in a loving embrace murmuring fondly *Sheila, my own*. Encouraged by this use of her christian name she kissed passionately all the various suitable areas of his person which the decencies of prison garb permitted her ardour to reach"), though this is not the level of writing we are asked to believe in. Innumerable popular languages – the languages of newspaper reporting, political speechmaking, advertising, commercial jingle ("What is home without/Plumtree's Potted Meat?/ Incomplete./ With it an abode of bliss") – are incorporated into the collage, as is the endless chatter of Dublin, that city of gabbers. The different registers, brought together, all function just off register, making a text that shifts freely between representation and pastiche or parody. Language opens out into gaps and fractures, allusion and borrowing, so that we must read this writing as writing, not, as with so many novels, simply looking through the word to the world it seems to stand for. The world itself becomes a book, and a book to be read.

Yet the work never ceases to be other than vividly real, because it never loses touch with character or the density and physicality of the human self. The great and mythic triad of characters – Stephen, now mourning the accusing death of his mother; Bloom, formerly Virag, alas Henry Flower, Wandering Jew, cuckold husband, good Samaritan; Molly, the unmothering mother, the unfaithful wife, weaver of the web of myth, sometimes claimed as the most deeply felt female character in fiction – are themselves both psychologically deep and multi-layered, fragmentary, floating on sensation and consciousness, fed by their random thoughts and their half-conscious dream worlds. Collectively, they form a psychic unity, of father, mother, and surrogate son, of husband, wife, and eternal desire.[6]

The dominant role taken by *Ulysses* in the making of modern fiction (and for that matter modern criticism) is testament to a deeply changing conception of literature, and it had many implications, forward and back. The idea of the novel as a self-creating artefact was vindicated, giving a new sense of tradition to the line of literary self-consciousness that had developed from James. Most serious modern novelists, faced with the task of creating a twentieth-century fiction, feel the need to confront *Ulysses* – not just as the day-book of Dublin perpetuated, but the book of the modern genres in their relation and juxtaposition. As Eliot suggested, it seemed to mark the end of the Old Novel, to propose that the modern century summoned a different fictional discourse. Whether true or not (and many writers have found it possible to reconstruct some effective linkage with the novel of nineteenth-century realism), the book proposed a challenge to literary practice that has never gone away. Joyce remained resident in Paris for twenty years, and became there the exemplary author of an age of expatriate writing, when novelists and poets from Britain and Ireland, the United States and Russia, and many more countries sought less to write a literature of nationality than of a new *avant-garde*

---

[6] I have discussed *Ulysses* in more detail in Chapter 7 of *The Modern World: Ten Great Writers*.

internationalism. With *Ulysses* written and published, he went on in 1923 to start the open-ended project he called simply "Work in Progress," publishing influential segments in various magazines over the 1920s; only late in the day was the text finally given the title *Finnegans Wake*. When he was asked how long *Ulysses* took to write, he said five years, and a lifetime. "Work in Progress," *Finnegans Wake*, took sixteen years to produce, the second half of a lifetime, and Joyce was to suggest that if it took that long to write it should also take that long to read. But *Finnegans Wake* challenges interpretation at a level beyond *Ulysses*, as it was meant to; one critic has aptly described the book, and the reading of the book, as a "life sentence." It was, exactly, a work in progress, a dreamlike adventure in writing itself that, being cyclical, has no clear principle of closure. If *Ulysses* can be reasonably described as a "stream of consciousness" (the stream, of course, is carefully managed and metered), then *Finnegans Wake* is the great flowing river itself, moving onward yet eternally renewing itself from the source. If *Ulysses* grew out of wandering exile, *Finnegans Wake* grew out of the concentration and distillation of the *avant garde* in its own chosen capital city, and flourished on its controversies; when many critics attacked the project for its obscurity, Eugene Jolas rallied the troops of his "Revolution of the Word" to produce *Our Exagmination Round his Factification for Incamination of "Work in Progress"*, which Shakespeare and Company published in 1929, offering, long before the work was complete, one of the now many guidebooks to the riddling novel that was not to appear until seventeen years to the day after publication of *Ulysses*; it came out in New York on 1 February 1939.

From its opening pages, *Finnegans Wake* promises an endless cycle of return: "riverrun, past Eve and Adam's, from swerve of shore to bend of bay, brings us by a commodius vicus of recirculation back to Howth Castle and Environs," it begins. The river is the Liffey, Dublin's river, but is also Life, and it starts in Genesis, or Paradise, on its journey of Viconian renewal. Down it everything flows, or everything that, using the multi-referential resources of human language, Joyce could manage to incorporate or coalesce into its cycle of motion and stillness, birth and death, beginning and ending and beginning again. The flow is a flow of language, but it is a new and self-composing language, a connective tissue of semiotic relations and punning release. Every word in the book is a word in the making, and alludes or refers in multiple directions. Each letter is a sign and a promise: thus HCE = Howth Castle and Environs = H. C. Earwicker = Here Comes Everybody. The letters throw up a cast of characters: Earwicker the Father, Anna Livia Plurabelle (ALP) the Mother, and the sons Shem ("the penman") and Shaun, all of whom have multiple and often contradictory stories and functions, spinning off in many directions. Language exists in the condition of Babel; this is a polyglot text in which all languages known to the author merge into one. In one sense the work seems to reject the role of author, replacing him with the book. In another sense this book can belong to one author only, and be his own private mode of speech. *Finnegans Wake* is the hermetic text of the Modern movement, at once the most complete and incomplete of the modern novels, the book of books, the book beyond books, which we do not so much read as decode.

Where *Ulysses* disseminated its radical methods here and there through modern writing – variously affecting the fiction of Virginia Woolf, John Dos Passos, William Faulkner, André Gide and so many more – *Finnegans Wake* functioned differently. It has been suggested that where *Ulysses* is a key text of Modernism, the later novel is the key early text of Postmodernism, the era of multi-culturalism, depthless juxtaposition, parodic quotation, collage. In more than one sense, the work really was a Wake, a party for the end of something. Significantly it appeared in the year Europe collapsed again, and in that collapse the Modern movement itself began to die – its writers thrown into yet newer exiles, its *avant garde* dissipated, its cultural vision thrown under new political questioning, its key figures reaching the end of their writing lives. But more than Modernism was dying in 1939; so was the Europe of the first half of the century, whose radical art this had been, whose crisis

161

it had come to express. Later that year, the Second World War began, and *avant-garde* Paris was vacated. Joyce's most obvious successor and fellow Irish exile, Samuel Beckett, who helped him transcribe *Finnegans Wake*, joined the French Resistance; the novels he in turn wrote during and after the war are works of radical silence, of language frequently attenuating to nothing, of lost names and voiceless voices, of an eternal waiting for the messages that do not arrive. The world after the Wake was a darkly different world, and Joyce too found himself once again in flight. In 1940, with the German occupation of Paris, he returned again to neutral Zürich, where *Ulysses* had once taken shape. Here, on 13 January 1941, he died of a perforated ulcer, leaving many serious writers to think they would always be writing in the wake of his Wake.

4.

For part of modern British literature at least, Paris in the Twenties was to become the centre of continuing *avant-garde* development. As Ezra Pound, who moved there from London ("an old bitch gone in the teeth") in 1920, put it, it became the post-war "laboratory of experiment in the arts." Where London seemed to shrink back toward provinciality, Paris, where living was cheap and the excitements of post-war culture flourished, attracted innumerable English-language writers to the *avant-garde* ferments of Montparnasse. Many came from the United States, finding the Left Bank an invaluable extension of Greenwich Village, and with them they brought their own bookshops, magazines, small presses, and social community, which proved one of the essential supports for Joyce. The post-war movements, Tristan Tzara's Dadaism and André Breton's Surrealism, extensions of Modernism into post-war chaos and the age of psychoanalysis, flourished – along with strident manifestations, dramatic manifestos, and parades that stopped the traffic asking "Do you want to slap a corpse?" Young American writers like Ernest Hemingway, William Carlos Williams and

Robert McAlmon arrived from 1920 on to learn the Modernist lesson from Stein, Pound and Joyce, and British writers from "Bryher" to Jean Rhys came there too. Marcel Proust, writing in his cork-lined room on the Boulevard Haussmann, extended right through the war the multi-volumed novel of time and subjective memory that he had begun in 1909 and called *A la recherche du temps perdu*; he was still writing it to the day of his death in 1922. The arrival of James Joyce in 1920 made these two into contrasting monuments of the modern spirit in the novel, though they affected not to know of each other: "I regret I do not know M. Joyce's work," said Proust; "I have never read M. Proust," remarked Joyce. When Proust was buried, in the French way, with full military honours, Joyce was present at the great funeral; thereafter he largely inherited Proust's mantle as the *doyen* of fictional experiment.

Also among the mourners that day was Ford Madox Ford. He had finally dropped the Germanic name of Hueffer, not though in wartime but in 1919, after his demobilization from the British army, when, he claimed, writers were let go last, along with window-cleaners. He had returned in dismay to what he claimed was an increasingly philistine Britain that was pulling down Regent Street, and losing sight of the great experiment of the pre-war years. There was also the embarrassing fact that he was being pursued by not one but two Mrs Hueffers, and he wished to restart his life with a new companion, the writer and painter Stella Bowen. So he too moved to France, and came to Paris in 1922, too late to meet Proust in the flesh, but just in time to attend his funeral, and consider the momentous question of the Proustian succession. In Ford's eyes, Proust had been the true fictional historian of his age, the creator of what he called, approvingly, "the ponderous novel," and Proust's death, he asserted grandly in his memoir *It Was the Nightingale* (1934), was what "made it certain I should again take up a serious pen." The future of the ponderous novel needed to be ensured, and he declared there was now work to be done. That work included creating and editing the excellent magazine *The Transatlantic Review*, which would print some of

Gertrude Stein's *The Making of Americans*, some of Joyce's *Work in Progress*, and early pieces by Hemingway. But the chief project that came from Proust's funeral was his own four-volume *roman fleuve*, "Parade's End," started in 1922, and completed in New York in 1927. Initially it was to consist of three novels, *Some Do Not . . .* (1924), *No More Parades* (1925), and *A Man Could Stand Up –* (1926), but, pressed by a friend to reveal "what became of Tietjens," the hero, he added a fourth, *The Last Post* (1928). He explained the project thus: "The work that at that time – and now – I wanted to see done was something on an immense scale, a little cloudy in immediate attack, but with the salient points and the final impression extraordinarily clear. I wanted the Novelist in fact to appear in his really proud position as historian of his own time . . . The 'subject' was the world as it culminated in the war." He meant it as a work of Impressionist "rendering," a book written "without passion," but also as something he had long despised, the Novel With a Purpose: "I sinned against my gods to the extent of saying that I was going . . . to write a book that would have for its purpose the obviating of all future wars."

"Parade's End" did not, we know, obviate all future wars, but it did fulfil the aim, which he called "Proustian," of writing an epic novel about "the public events of a decade." His first thought was to use the method by which "all the characters should be great masses of people – or interests," in which case we might well have had an expressionist sequence like John Dos Passos' *USA* (1934). But he then changed his mind, deciding to focus the story round a single central character who suffers the tribulations of war and peacetime. Experience of the Front had produced what he called the "singular conclusion" that what preyed most on non-professional soldiers at the front was not the horrors ("you either endure them or you do not") but "what was happening at home." What Ford saw happening at home between 1912 and 1918 was a vast change in the social and moral order, in public values, gender relations, class attitudes. So he created his suffering hero Christopher Tietjens, the "mealsack elephant," the "last Tory," a Christian gentleman with an English estate and an oddly Germanic name, someone who had a place in peace and war: a *"homo duplex,"* he explained, a "poor fellow whose body is tied in one place, but whose mind and personality brood eternally over another distant locality." Officer and gentleman, country squire and Whitehall mandarin, Tietjens indeed could intersect with most realms of British life in peace and wartime: "I seemed to see him stand in some high places in France during the period of hostilities taking in not only what was visible but all the causes and all the motive powers of infinitely distant places." The representative of a feudal and social inheritance, a man of "clear Eighteenth Century mind," living out the contradictions of that code to their ultimate conclusion, he carries history, and suffers for it. Whether the novel really owes much to Proust, as its author claimed, is doubtful – though it is a Modernist work, concerned with inner psychology, time-shift and the involuntary operations of the memory. It is certainly a "Condition of England" novel, at a time when that form seems at the end of its tether, and what the Hungarian Marxist critic Georgy Lukacs would call a "historical novel": a novel, that is, which carries the contradictory processes of an age and the struggles of class in an evolving culture. The result is that "Parade's End" is a panoramic epic, or anti-epic, engaged with history in a way that, say, Virginia Woolf's novels, even her panoramic *The Years*, could never be. Ford uses modern methods, but he sustains many of the nineteenth-century interests of fiction: in public life, the social web, the state of the nation. The techniques then are techniques for presenting large-scale dispositions of experience and historical time, of bringing the large and the small into relation. "Parade's End" is an historical allegory with a psychological centre, a "Condition of England" work about an individual whose psychic and social collapse and fragile renewal *enacts* history.

Despite impressive competition – C. E. Montague's *Disenchantment* (1922), R. H. Mottram's "Spanish Farm" trilogy (1924–26), Richard Aldington's *Death of a Hero* (1929), and more – "Parade's End" is as a result surely the finest English novel we have to deal, both directly and indirectly, with the Great War and its effects. Indirect, angled, fractured in technique, it tells of the collapsing of a culture and the closing of an epoch, of a society that is pushed into fragmentation and passes through fundamental revolution as the guns boom on the front. If this is an Impressionist novel, it is not Impressionism as either Proust or Woolf would define it: not Proust's "inner book of unknown symbols," Woolf's "the atoms as they fall." The aim is not to bring the story under the control of some metaphor, or produce a sense of aesthetic luminosity, but to tell a social allegory about the fate of an age, and draw the elements of history together before a total disunity sets in. So the book tells two stories, set side by side. One is the social story, the story of "the public wants of a decade," which involves the replacement of the old ruling class by the new mandarins, the careerists and climbers, and of a felt, historic national identity with the cult of National Efficiency, all of this encouraged by the war. The other is the psychological story, the story of the collapse of a representative individual, the British gentleman as sacrificial victim, who goes to battle, passes through the purgatory of the front, and progresses, through madness and memory loss, into the new post-war world, where he has to learn to live again. Ford is able to manage this because he takes as the centre of his "affair" a character who wants to hold these two worlds in relation, though the result is an unbearable strain; indeed he suggests that he is the last man who would try to do so. Tietjens is the good gentleman who bears the burden of his class – "Our station in society naturally forms a rather close ring," he observes – but, as an old feudalist, is also separated from its values. He is the last of his line, a figure of romance caught at the point of extinction, and after him there will be no more men "who do not." To some extent he is an absurd and comic figure, with a perverted creed, masochistically sustaining his own identity while questioning the society he lives in.

In Ford's allegory of change, his agony precedes the war; indeed the strains already there in the bodies politic and sexual make the war a necessary purgatory. The crisis is there from the novel's beginning, in 1912, and comes from the false, unhappy marriage Tietjens has made with his unfaithful wife Sylvia, pregnant by another man. That "chivalric" act not only throws his heritage into doubt, but provokes Sylvia, one of fiction's more frightening and vengeful immoralists, into challenging his chivalry in every way possible, as she tries to bring him down to human scale. This same assault on the chivalric disposition (caught symbolically when the car driven by General Campion hits the horse Tietjens is riding) intensifies when the story moves, by sudden time-shift, from the relatively secure world of 1912 to the world at war – a war of mismanagement, bureaucracy, corrupt politics and red tape, where the enemy is less the opposing Germans than the "swine in the corridors of Whitehall," his own government, the High Command, and Sylvia, now entrenched with the General's party in France. Three wars – world war, social war, sex war – are intimately related; "War is inevitable as divorce," Tietjens says prophetically at the start, and the two are aspects of each other. But the war turns the cycle, and bleakly begins to open a new life for Tietjens. He collapses toward madness and amnesia, but at last is able to make the break with his own past, and find a life beyond chivalry, glory, and parades. In the historical allegory, the aristocrat gives way to the bureaucrat, the chivalric to the mechanical, the age of values and convictions to the age of individual survival. Finally, like Guy Crouchback in Evelyn Waugh's "Sword of Honour," the equivalent trilogy for the Second World War, Tietjens halts his epic pilgrimage, and makes ironic peace with what is.

It is matched in the ironic tone of the text itself. Ford's technique of "aloofness," the concern with registration he drew from Flaubert, sets the story at a distance. It begins on a note of objective social realism, capturing the Georgian social scene of 1912. "The two young men – they were of the English public official class – sat in the perfectly appointed railway carriage," runs the famous opening: "The leather straps to the windows were of virgin newness; the mirrors beneath the new luggage racks immaculate as if they had reflected very little; the bulging upholstery in its luxuriant, regulated curves was scarlet and yellow in an intricate, minute dragon design, the design of a geometrician in Cologne. The compartment smelt faintly, hygienically of admirable varnish; the train ran as smoothly – Tietjens remembered thinking – as British gilt-edged securities . . ." These two young men are administrators of a well-managed, very British world ("If they saw a policeman misbehave, railway porters lack civility, an insufficiency of street lamps, defects in public services or in foreign countries, they saw to it either with nonchalant Balliol voices or with letters to the *Times*, asking with regretful indignation, 'Has the British This or That come to *this*?' "), but the imagery tells us it is already dissolving. The train has a brittle newness; there is a hard foreign abstraction to the decor. This is a world of surfaces without depths, of hypocrisies laid over sexual corruptions, the England of National Efficiency and Imperial statistics. Soon the knackers' cart comes round the corner, and, by the Modernist device of time-shift, the action dissolves to the battlefront of 1917, with a war-wounded Tietjens lost amongst the chaos he had once thought to control. From social realism the method moves toward greater Impressionism, representing the fragmentation of war, society, consciousness itself. In *It Was the Nightingale*, Ford tells us that it is the nature of War to take away all confidence in social substance: "A social system had crumbled . . . Nay, it was revealed to you that beneath Ordered Life itself was stretched, the merest film with, beneath it, the Abysses of Chaos. One had come from the frail shelters of the Line to a world that was more frail than a canvas hut." This dissolving world justifies the fragmentary method: time-breaks, flashbacks and flashforwards, rapid cuts from scene to scene to generate a cumulative impression, or relate the world of the front to the world of "money, women, testamentary bothers" back home. In *No More Parades*, Tietjens is buried, gassed, wounded, and his own inner realities begin to dissolve. *A Man Could Stand Up* – cuts between battlefield and the Armistice, between amnesia-stricken Tietjens and the life of his new female friend, who is also a "New Woman," Valentine Wannop.

Tietjens has lost his old values, his old heaven, his world of parades. "Feudalism was finished; its last vestiges were gone. It held no place for him," he reflects. In the final volume, *The Last Post*, which Ford was never sure whether to keep in the main sequence, Tietjens is only partly glimpsed as a character, and the end of the feudal world is shown; an entire social heritage gives way to an age of individualized values in which there are no more chivalries, no more parades, though perhaps a vague agrarian hope.

"Parade's End" is, no doubt, a very British version of Modernism, indirect yet social, complex yet accessible, a large cultural history as well as a work of consciousness (but then so are the novels of William Faulkner). And it shows Ford, like his hero, making a transition from one age to another: from the age of the modern novel as an "affair" to one of a fiction made fragmentary by the very history of cultural collapse it concerns itself with. As in Ezra Pound's poem "Hugh Selwyn Mauberley," the methods of collage, juxtaposition, and fragmentation are now techniques for creating the distance, hard irony, disorder and historical dismay suited to a darkened age, and led on to the note of "fictional indifference" that marked much Twenties and then Thirties writing. Ford played a serious part in British Modernism, significantly influencing other writers from Jean Rhys to Graham Greene and Evelyn Waugh. In Paris in the Twenties, in American universities during the Thirties, he advanced the cause of experiment, still writing prolifically, but never again with the force that produced *The Good Soldier* just before the War, "Parade's End" just after it. He died, after a lifetime of involvement in the Modern movement, in June 1939, in Deauville in France, just a few weeks before the beginning of the Second World War his novels did not obviate. So much, he would doubtless have said, for Novels with a Purpose; always a true Modernist, he never really believed in them anyway.

5.

Meanwhile, if Paris in the Twenties had Montparnasse, London had Bloomsbury. It was no area of boulevard cafés and zinc-topped bars where writers stopped to write a little and discuss the Revolution of the Word, no centre of salons and small presses and dramatic moments and manifestations. It was a postal district, around the British Museum, mostly noted for bookshops and Georgian terraces. Bloomsbury did not interrupt the opera with noise and protests, or invite you to slap a corpse; it generally lived behind closed Georgian doors, and disappeared to cottages in Sussex in the summer. The intellectuals and writers who increasingly chose to live in this part of London were largely an established network of friends, an already known élite who now commanded many of the magazines and the presses and set the critical tone. Bloomsbury, in fact, was a distinctive caste, though also a state of mind. It stood for what was *avant-garde* and experimental, not just in writing and publishing, but in sexual relations, economics, painting, politics, philosophy, biography and interior design. But it was unquestionably a social as well as an artistic phenomenon, an educated social caste that could read its genealogies back to the heart of the Victorian intelligentsia, to Thackeray and the Clapham Sect, to the Pre-Raphaelites and Pater. If Lytton Strachey's *Eminent Victorians* typified the great quarrel it conducted with the Victorian past, this frequently resembled a family quarrel, of sons and daughters against fathers and mothers, conducted in public. Bloomsbury was amongst other things a shared social and family background, a web of family relations, friendships, a network of complex sexual liaisons, an élite with a body of agreed social and cultural assumptions and standards. Essential to this was an "aesthetic" attitude to the world itself, which involved a celebration of the "modern." Bloomsbury had its own tribal assumptions about creative personal relations and emotional states, and about the aesthetic deliverances art afforded. It helped to have read Walter Pater, who emphasized the power of impressions and of "quickened, multiplied consciousness." It was wise to have gone to Cambridge, perhaps been an "Apostle" there, and certainly to have studied with or read the philosopher G. E. Moore – whose *Principia Ethica* (1903) reminded a whole generation that "By far the most valuable things we know or can imagine are certain states of consciousness, which may roughly be described as the pleasures of human intercourse and the enjoyment of beautiful objects."

Bloomsbury was unmistakably descended from the liberal, critical Victorian intelligentsia, and knew its own cultural authority. With its "taste for truth and beauty," its freedom and frankness of personal and sexual relations, its powerful intellectualism, it was a revolt against the Establishment that soon became a new, formidable Establishment itself. It had taken shape before the War, when Roger Fry supported the new Cubist painters and developed his philosophy of "significant form," and Virginia Woolf, daughter of Sir Leslie Stephen, took over his role as a major literary critic. It had Fry and Clive Bell as its Post-Impressionist aestheticians, Lytton Strachey as its biographer-historian, Maynard Keynes as its economic thinker, Bertrand Russell as its philosopher, Duncan Grant, Vanessa Bell, "Carrington" and Mark Gertler as its painters, Lady Ottoline Morrell as one of its chief social patrons, E. M. Forster, to begin with, as its novelist, Virginia Woolf as its literary, critical and social conscience. Being a daughter, Virginia had not gone to Cambridge, which outraged her; but she wrote and thought much as if she had. When she, her sister Vanessa, and her brothers Thoby and Adrian, settled in 1904 at 46 Gordon Square, north of the British Museum, "Bloomsbury" began to acquire a local habitation and a name. Virginia called it "the most beautiful, the most exciting, the most romantic place in the world," where "Everything was going to be new; everything was going to be different." In literary terms, what was to be "new" and "different" she explored in her criticism, much of it for *The Times Literary Supplement*, where she took particular interest in the past and future of the novel, looking back at the

British fictional tradition, but equally at the cosmopolitan heritage of Dostoevsky, Chekhov, James and Conrad. Her brilliant, if at times mannered, critical essays, written over the following years, were key works of modern interpretation, and, collected under the title of *The Common Reader* (1925), they much affected the Twenties. But Woolf was no common reader; this was a subtle and specialized journey in quest of her own new and rigorous notion of "contemporary fiction" and "the modern novel." Many of her ideas of a new "poetic" modern fiction were thus largely formed before she completed her own first novel *The Voyage Out*, begun in 1908, accepted for publication in 1913, not published till 1915. As she explained: "It is not that life is more complex or difficult now than at any other period, but that for each generation the point of interest shifts, the old forms put the interest in the wrong places, and in searching out the severed and submerged part of what to us constitutes form we seem to be throwing fragments together at random and disdaining the very thing we are trying our best to rescue from the chaos." The search for a new form elicited from fragments, the opening of a new expressive awareness, the creation of a transformed and poeticized contemporary sensibility, was also a struggle of consciousness. It was also, importantly, a sexual battle, part of the "fight between the fathers and the daughters."

Bloomsbury – which has been sentimentalized and exoticized in recent literary commentary, to the point of excess[7] – both expanded and constrained British literary culture, and some of the literary exile and political and artistic anger that shaped the

[7] As Noel Annan nicely put it in *The New York Review of Books* in 1978: "It seems that almost everyone who ever spoke to the denizens of Gordon Square has found an amanuensis. As the critical studies and reminiscences mount, you are seized with panic and exhaustion and go down on your knees begging to be spared yet another account of the Pattle sisters, of Sir Leslie [Stephen] groaning, of the Midnight Society and the Apostles in 1900, and of the familiar anecdotes repeated in every account. Yet what we are witnessing is the documentation in detail of a kind never before seen in English letters: so that by the time it is completed we shall know more about the members of the Bloomsbury Group than of any other set of people in literary history . . ."

British writings of the Twenties and the Thirties was plainly an attempt to get away from it. D. H. Lawrence came close to, then vehemently rejected, Bloomsbury in his troubled wartime years. That goes into *Women in Love* (1920), his exploration of "the results in one's soul of the war." This is, like all Lawrence's books from here on, a modernist work – a radical work born out of artistic turmoil, written not so much to narrate its story as to distil, in moments of neo-symbolist concentration, the merging moments of sexuality and radical purging – but also a darkly prophetic one, well summarized (it is difficult if not impossible to summarize) by John Middleton Murry.[8] It is the novel where Lawrence breaks loose from ideas about the novel as anything other than "the bright book of life," where fiction is made to invigorate and enflesh essential ideas, instinctualism becomes an incantatory prophecy about life in a sterilized and tragic age, as Birkin struggles through "decay and decomposition" and "dark, potent secrets" to a new subconscious unity of the sensual and spiritual, and the role of the writer is "leadership." But though it is essentially a major modern text of social and sexual dissolution, *Women in Love* is also a savage satire on British literary and artistic culture, following a theme that would recur through many of his impassioned works of the Twenties, from *Saint Mawr* to *Lady Chatterley's Lover*, as Lawrence seeks to explore what has poisoned the springs of creation and consciousness. Old personal scores are settled; a number of the characters are identifiable, including Bertrand Russell, Murry, and Lady Ottoline Morrell; and Bloomsbury, in both its social tone and its aesthetic idealism, is "a menagerie of apeish degraded souls," who display the enervation both of British

---

[8] "It is easy enough to understand Lawrence's intention in *Women in Love*: to present first the contrast between a man who immolates himself to the mechanism of modern civilization and one who is in dynamic revolt against it; and also to present the fatal influence on the man–woman relation of the inward sterility of Gerard [Crich], and the gleam of hope in the 'love' that is based on Ursula's response to the vitality with which Birkin conquers his own despair. The theme is profound and prophetic. But much of its working out is mysterious . . ." John Middleton Murry, review of F. R. Leavis, *D. H. Lawrence: Novelist*, *TLS*, 1955; reprinted in John Gross (ed.), *The Modern Movement* (London, 1992).

social *mores* and artistic values, failing to respond to the tragic implication of the tragic age. "Comes over one an absolute necessity to move," Lawrence announced now, and spent most of the Twenties in a wandering exile, through Italy, New Mexico and Mexico, looking for the presence in the world of a new primitive soul, natural and animal. His bitter charges about the decay of the English soul and spirit, alike in its intellectuals and its working class, would resound through his fiction of the decade through to his death in Vence in 1930. If *The Lost Girl* (1920), which Virginia Woolf reviewed, suggesting that Lawrence was reverting to the spirit of Arnold Bennett, and new-found works like *Mr Noon* show him capable of continuing to write a distinctive social history of Britain, other novels insistently direct their observation at the British aesthetic intelligentsia as symbol of the decline of the Western mind and spirit: the stories of *England, My England* (1922), the political prophecies of *Kangaroo* (1923), the historical despair of *Lady Chatterley's Lover* (1928) and the sexual resurrection of *The Virgin and the Gypsy* (1930) all pursue the theme. No doubt there was an element of class hostility in this (to return among the writers of the 1950s), but above all it was an argument about culture; the Bloomsbury compound – aestheticism, sensitivity, self-awareness, liberal social reformism – summoned Lawrence's resentment and despair.

Not surprisingly, Bloomsbury hardly took to Lawrence, though Woolf would admit his powerful originality and contribution to the new psychology of the novel. There were different reservations about Joyce. In 1918 he offered *Ulysses* to the Hogarth Press, but it was hard to find a printer who would risk it. In any case, Virginia Woolf, who had praised *A Portrait* . . ., did not like it, finding it naturalistic and sensual, filled with too much of "the alien and external": "the scratching of the pimples on the body of the bootboy at Claridge's," in fact. Later she acknowledged its "greatness" – though greatness "of the inferior water" – and drew on it for *Mrs Dalloway*, perhaps even hoping to suggest what its true experiment should have been. But Bloomsbury did like Proust: not Ford's creator of "the ponder-

ous novel," but the Proust who had rescued form and consciousness from the dross of materialism, pursued the modern quest
for "significant form." It was Roger Fry – who disliked novels
that were choked with "criticisms of life, of manners or of
morals," which most novels are – who introduced Proust in
Britain before the war, as he introduced the Post-Impressionist
painters. He drew him to Woolf's attention: "Oh, if only I
could write like that!" she wrote back enthusiastically. "I try.
And at the moment such is the astonishing vibration and the
saturation and intensification that he procures – there's something sexual in it – that I feel I *can* write like that, and seize my
pen and then I *can't* write like that. Scarcely anyone so
stimulates the nerves of language in me; it becomes an obsession." At work on *Mrs Dalloway*, she notes in her journal: "I
wonder if this next lap will be influenced by Proust? I think his
French language, tradition, &c., prevents that: yet his command of every resource is so extravagant that one can hardly
fail to profit, & must not flinch, through cowardice."

Likewise E. M. Forster celebrated Proust in a key section of
Aspects of the Novel (1927), observing the importance for the low,
recalcitrant form of the novel of his use of "rhythm" and
"pattern," those neo-musical elements that, stitching a work
together from within, gave it aesthetic harmony. Forster was
not quite Bloomsbury, but very close to it: he shared similar
social and intellectual origins in "the fag-end of Victorian
liberalism," a Cambridge education, a belief in the primacy of
personal relations, and a neo-symbolist view of art – "the one
orderly product our muddling race has produced," "the only
material object in the universe which may possess internal
harmony." But he also believed that, oh dear yes, the novel
tells a story, that, unlike poetry, it must respond to the laws of
narrative, acknowledge the interest of society and history,
incorporate "the immense richness of material which life provides." Here he fell out with Virginia Woolf, who reviewed
Aspects of the Novel and made her difference plain. He had
written "The novelist who betrays too much interest in his own
method can never be more than interesting; he has given up the

creation of character and summoned us to help analyse his own mind . . ."; she disagreed, rejecting the "assumption that fiction is more intimately and humbly associated to the service of human beings than the other arts . . . though it is impossible to imagine a book on painting in which not a word should be said about the medium in which a painter works, a wise and brilliant book about fiction, like Mr Forster's, can be written without saying more than a sentence or two about the medium in which the novelist works. Almost nothing is said about words . . . In England at any rate the novel is not a work of art." That was the true Bloomsbury argument: what Woolf meant to do, in her long critical campaign, was exactly to make the novel in England a work of art, a work of self-conscious method.

The difference between them was not great; background, close friendship and generation linked them. But, though only three years separated their ages, Forster would remain an exemplary figure from the early part of the century, an Edwardian and Georgian writer who wrote nearly all his fiction before the First World War and then became a Modernist, a liberal humanist novelist for whom the essence of fiction lay in its concern with manners, morals and humane values, though he also knew it must aspire to wholeness of form. And he did achieve one magnificent Modernist work. After completing *Howards End* in 1910, he had difficulty in developing the next stage of his fiction. He tentatively started the novel *Arctic Summer*, but never completed it; he wrote *Maurice*, which he did complete but, since it was a frank story of a homosexual revolt against family, friends and culture, it could only come out posthumously in 1971. Then in 1912–13 he visited India, which had a profound effect on him, and began a novel about it, which he also set aside, finding the subject too vast for the governing imagination (when the book came at last, this would be its theme). The war, which he spent largely doing Red Cross work in Alexandria, also blocked it, but widened his experience of the non-British world. In 1921 he returned to India and took up the novel again, now conscious of new influences, Proust above all. "I learned ways of looking at character from him.

The modern subconscious way. He gave me as much of the modern way as I could take," he later told an interviewer; the "modern way" was undoubtedly the use of rhythmic composition and symbolist structure for the linear and social plot. Walt Whitman's all-embracing poem "A Passage to India," about the great westering dream of American democratic imperialism ("The earth to be spann'd, connected by network/ The races, neighbours, to marry and be given in marriage/ The oceans to be cross'd, the distant brought near/ The lands to be welded together"), gave him his title. *A Passage to India*, the book he had struggled with right across the war, appeared at last in 1924.

A Passage to India is his most ambitious work, and surely one of the classic modern English novels, a work both of modern chaos and modern aesthetic order. The echo in the Marabar Caves ("ou-boum") levels all meanings to one, declares "Everything exists; nothing has value," enforces that "twilight of the double vision" in which the Janus-face of the universe is visible, where its horror and smallness are simultaneously known, where we can "neither ignore nor respect Infinity." At the same time Forster's aspiration for rhythmic wholeness draws together the book and makes it a symbolist unity. This is the work that most embodies the neo-symbolist aspirations of *Aspects of the Novel*, giving it an imaginative texture different from the pre-war novels. Yet many of the same liberal themes continue: here once more are those powers in social life and nature – the claims of public and private, seen and unseen, social conventions and personal desires and relations which divide the universe and produce the need for reconciliation. Forster's basic moral sympathies are here too: the book is based in the testing-ground of human relationships, in the need of the liberal mind, of "good will plus culture and intelligence," to overcome the grids of interest, ignorance and custom that divide individual from individual and race from race. So are his basic literary methods, the moving between poetic evocation of mystery and the comic world of human muddle, maintaining both a symbolist and a social mode of fiction. But the balance has changed. For some critics, *A Passage to India* is Forster's most affirmative book, his declaration that "unity and harmony are the ultimate promises of life," according to Wilfred Stone. Others have seen the opposite: a novel about the final gap between chaotic human life and the intractable infinite.[9] What is clear is that Forster's social observation is fuller and finer than before, his sense of human mystery is deeper, his theme of far greater vastness. This is surely the best novel by an Englishman to deal with the weight of the Imperial experience, and the confusing, spiritually demanding nature of the world its imperial net is laid over.

So on one level – yes, oh dear yes – the novel tells us a story, a social and political story told in a spirit of comedy and human muddle, about the life of the British Raj, the strict, bloodless conventions of British behaviour, the rituals of class, the rules of behaviour and racial duty. The British mean well, and do their task – "to do justice and keep the peace" – effectively. They hold "bridge parties" with the Indians, but they dissolve into misunderstanding; even those who try harder, like the mystical Mrs Moore or the liberal schoolteacher Fielding, fail to encompass the sum that India represents. "Nothing embraces the whole of India, nothing, nothing," says the young Hindu doctor, Aziz. Sects and races are divided among themselves; so is the earth itself: "The fissures in the Indian soil are infinite: Hinduism, so solid from a distance, is riven into sects and clans, which radiate and join, and change their names according to the aspect from which they are approached." The "extraordinary" awaits, and India invites cosmic meanings. But Beauty is absent, Nature rejects Romantic engagement: "not the unattainable friend, either of men or birds or other suns . . . not the eternal promise, the never-withdrawn suggestion that haunts our consciousness; . . . merely a creature, like the rest, and so debarred from glory." The human never quite touches the infinite: "Trees of poor quality bordered the road, indeed the whole scene was inferior and suggested that the countryside

[9] See, for example, Wilfred Stone, *The Cave and the Mountain: A Study of E. M. Forster* (Stanford and London, 1966), and James McConkey, *The Novels of E. M. Forster* (Ithaca, N.Y., 1957).

was too vast to admit of excellence. In vain did each item in it call, 'Come, come.' There was not enough god to go round." Mrs Moore and Fielding try hard; Forster as novelist tries harder, seeking to incorporate everything, not with a Whitman-esque barbaric yawp, but with a wry sense of human comedy, which sees how we generally fail when we seek to grasp diversity.

The human plot – set largely round the city of Chandrapore, evidently in the 1920s – hinges on Adela Quested, who comes to India to marry, has doubts when she sees what Indian service has made of her fiancé, and tries to see more. She goes on an expedition with her fiancé's mother Mrs Moore to the Marabar Caves, arranged by the friendly Indian doctor Aziz. In one cave she thinks she is sexually attacked by him (in an early draft she is); meanwhile Mrs Moore hears her echo, and suffers her "twilight of the double vision." Adela accuses Aziz of attempted rape, and though she retracts this at the trial the incident sows discord and exposes the political stresses and the racial crisis in the country. While Fielding seeks for personal and political reconciliation, Mrs Moore, haunted by her glimpse of the eternal abyss, dies on the way home, and Adela returns to Britain unwed. Both stories seem to fail, but, as Lionel Trilling once wisely remarked about the book, "The characters are of sufficient size for the plot; they are not large enough for the story – and indeed that is the point of the story."[10] Progressing through three large blocks of experience – Mosque, Caves and Temple – and through circle after circle of the Indian infinity, the story, following various heavenly invita-tions, moves away from its human plot toward the goal of "completeness not reconstruction," "expansion, not com-pletion." It opens – through the figure of the Hindu mystic Professor Godbole, the Hindu ceremony, and the strange return of the spirit of Mrs Moore among the Indian crowds – on a hint of wholeness. What it does not offer is the certainty of it. At the close of the book, the earth still says "No, not yet," and the sky

[10] Lionel Trilling, *E. M. Forster* (Norfolk, Conn, 1943: London, 1944).

says, "No, not there." The echo at the edge of Fielding's consciousness persists: "Everything echoes now; there's no stopping the echo. The original sound may be harmless, but the echo is always evil." The two aspects of the novel – the social realism, the comedy of the human plot, and the patterned, symbolist hunger for the "one orderly product" – remain in suspension, and that too is the point of the story. Forster avoids the closure of the realist plot, but he equally avoids the closure of the symbolist plot; both material realism and symbolism ask, in their different ways, for everything to be included, and Forster did neither. *A Passage to India* – Forster's last brilliant work of fiction, for though he lived until 1970 he produced no more novels – remains a humanist novel, accepting its own contradiction and its own dualism, as the novel so often has: the world is both a mystery and a muddle. This did not quite suit Virginia Woolf, even though she admired the book for its modernity, and acknowledged it was going in the right direc- tion: "though it is true there are ambiguities in important places, moments of imperfect symbolism, a greater accumula- tion of facts than the imagination is able to deal with, it seems as if the double vision which troubles us in the earlier books is in process of becoming single," she wrote. But Forster, she had to confess, was a materialist novelist, "too susceptible to the influence of time": in other words he felt the need to admit social life, history, and contradiction into his universe. Forster was good, but he was still not quite Bloomsbury.

6.

If Virginia Woolf had problems with Forster's view of the novel ("too susceptible to the influence of time"), it was not surprising he had a reverse problem with hers. "You're in a very special position, I feel; you seem to be experimenting in the direction of poetry, and might carry fiction into a region where it will glow and contract," he wrote. Forster's critical judgement on her books was one she highly valued; he in turn had to confess, as others of her friends, like Lytton Strachey, also did, that they missed from them many of the thicker densities of life. "Elegant arabesques," said Strachey, while Forster observed, "she is always stretching out from her enchanted tree and snatching bits of the flux of daily life as it floats past, and out of these bits she builds novels." He, it seemed, still respected the old novel; she wrote the "new" one, the insubstantized novel. He was an Edwardian, she a "modern," who came later to fiction, in a different spirit, beginning her work at a time when the day of the material novel was over, or at least incapable of conveying any meaningful sense of life as it had become. As for Woolf's own sense of life, it was clear, vivid, subjective; it sparkled in moments, shifted between mind and mind. "Examine for a moment an ordinary mind on an ordinary day," she said in "Modern Fiction" in 1919. "The mind receives a myriad impressions – trivial, fantastic, evanescent, or engraved with the sharpness of steel. From all sides they come, an incessant shower of innumerable atoms; and, as they fall, as they shape themselves into life of Monday or Tuesday, the accent falls differently from of old . . ." Not all of us would say that this is the life of the ordinary mind on an ordinary day; it is more like the life of an aesthete's mind on a symbolist day. For Woolf's atoms are more than random or contingent; they form into glimpses, sudden revelations, which become the essences of fiction, the basis for a quite different sort of story, about an utterly different "that." "For the moderns 'that,' the point of interest, lies very likely in the dark places of psychology," she explained: "At once then, the accent falls a little differently, the emphasis is on something hitherto ignored; at once a different outline of form becomes necessary, difficult for us to grasp, incomprehensible to our predecessors." Thus the novelist's task was to dematerialize what was material, de-create form as it had been, make the novel a self-creating species, writing a decomposition as well as a composition. Maybe what she was seeking was not even a novel at all "I have an idea that I will invent a new name for my books to supplant 'novel'," she put in her diary in July 1925, as she planned *To the Lighthouse*. "A new — by Virginia Woolf. But what? Elegy?"

In fact Woolf's kind of "insubstantized" novel can be traced back, maybe to Walter Pater, certainly to William James' insistence in *Principles of Psychology* (1890) that reality was not an objective given, but was subjectively perceived through consciousness. From then on, in experimental poetic fiction, we find "consciousness" constantly interposed between the world and the individual "subject," creating a new kind of gaze. Sometimes this produces psychological realism, sometimes a highly aesthetic or poetic self-consciousness; mostly it produces a merger between the two. As Dostoevsky became better known in Europe, as James exerted his influence, as Freud and Bergson came to be generally read, the claims of the psycho-aesthetic vision intensified. The claims of aesthetics to provide an overview of human, especially modern, experience were put forward with missionary energy, and Bloomsbury founded its distinctive secular religion on aligning sensitivities of art and form with intensity in personal relationships. The idea of a "new" composition spun from a sensitive authorial consciousness whose own psychology was so finely attuned as to produce a symbolist metamorphosis, an aesthetic epiphany, underlies many of the novels of sensibility, psychology and poetry that began appearing in the second decade of the century – when there was a growing revolt against the scientific positivism of Wells and Shaw, and many fresh notions of the need to evaluate experience through consciousness. In 1913 the first two volumes of Proust's eight-volume *A la recherche* . . . came out, to Bloomsbury interest. In 1914–15, twenty-four instalments of Joyce's *A Portrait of the Artist* . . . appeared in serial form in the British magazine *The Egoist*, and won Woolf's admiration. In 1915, the year of Woolf's own first novel *A Voyage Out*, Dorothy Richardson's *Pointed Roofs* appeared, the first "chapter" of her *roman fleuve* "Pilgrimage," quickly followed by several more (*Backwater*, 1916; *Honeycomb*, 1917; etc.), which Woolf found exciting, though egotistical and hence formless. What links all these together is that they are simultaneously psychological and experimental novels, their structure won from orders drawn from interior rather than historical time. As Richardson justly pointed out, not all these books could have influenced each other: "An interesting point for the critic who finds common qualities in the work of Proust, James Joyce, Virginia Woolf and D.R. is the fact that they were all using the 'new method' though differently, simultaneously."[11] Something else must have linked them together, a new attitude to art and literature itself.

There was also something else – feminism, or at least a concern with the development of a distinctive feminine, or differently engendered, vision. *The Egoist*, the magazine where much experimental new work, including Joyce, Eliot and Pound, appeared, where the poetic movement of Imagism was announced, was a feminist paper, first called *The New Freewoman*. Richardson herself was a "New Woman" who had broken with her once wealthy family, taught in Germany, been a suffragette, worked in London as a typist, had the almost statutory affair with H. G. Wells. *Pilgrimage*, the slowly, seamlessly unfolding tale of Miriam Henderson, is virtually autobiographical, following out an independent, struggling life like the author's over the course of the years through thirteen deeply felt "chapters." Richardson defined her aim as "to produce a feminine equivalent of the current masculine realism," but rejected the narrative methods of established novelists, who "left out certain essentials and dramatized life misleadingly. Horizontally. Assembling their characters, the novelists developed situations, devised events, climax and conclusion. I could not accept these finalities." It was another important feminist novelist and critic, May Sinclair, who, in *The Egoist* in 1918, took a key phrase from William James to describe what she was doing. This was, she said, the method of "stream-of-consciousness," depending on "moments tense with vibration, moments drawn out fine, almost to snapping point." Woolf, who thought her methods less egotistical and far more refined, did not relish the compari-

---

[11] All this is usefully recorded in Leon Edel, *The Psychological Novel: 1900–1950* (New York and London, 1955) and Morris Beja, *Epiphany in the Novel: Revelation as Art* (Seattle and London, 1971).

sons made between her work and Richardson's, but she increasingly acknowledged the centrality of the feminine vision. In *To the Lighthouse* she would look beyond the men who "negotiated treaties, ruled India, controlled finance," to sensibilities, female sensibilities, distinctively attuned to "little daily miracles, illuminations . . ." And female radiating characters like Clarissa Dalloway and Mrs Ramsay helped point the way to the "new" novel – the novel of flowing consciousness, "moments tense with vibration," life's shimmer, psychological intensity, released from the rule of time and identity. Perhaps, she suggested in her *A Room of One's Own* (1929), and yet more forcefully in *Three Guineas* (1932), it was because women were not supposed to write novels that they could break free of convention, beyond social constraint into what she elsewhere called "queer individuality." In any case, she promised in her essay "Women in Fiction" (1929), women writers could be less absorbed than men in facts, and no doubt in the future they "will look beyond the personal and political relationships to the wider questions which the poet tries to solve – of our destiny and the meaning of life."

In Woolf's vision, the modern novelist was free: but free to do what? In her two key essays "Modern Fiction" and "Mr Bennett and Mrs Brown" she spoke for the writer released from traditional views of time, identity and reality, and stressed three elements of new fiction: the novel, through the withering away of old conventions, becomes more "itself"; it manifests a new mode of perception; it reveals the real spirit of "life" once dross and materiality have been discarded. Life is, she says, "a luminous halo, surrounding us from the beginning of consciousness to the end," and this the novelist should convey, with "as little mixture of the alien and external as possible." But if the novelist was concerned with "consciousness," what Woolf meant by that term was not quite what other novelists made of it. For some, from James to Joyce and Faulkner, the method of consciousness served to reveal the contingency, the chaos, the underlying stress, of a life from which all wholeness and coherence had gone, and displayed the problem of finding order in a disordered age. In James it is the ordeal of fine minds in a specific social environment, and a partial instrument of understanding; in Lawrence it is the means to break up the "old stable ego" and explore the energies, vitalistic or deathly, that pass among individuals in an apocalyptic time. In Joyce stream-of-consciousness is both aesthetic (Stephen's reflections) and subterranean (Molly's soliloquy), and by *Finnegans Wake* it has become a dreamlike substratum of myths, images, and linguistic associations. In Woolf, consciousness is flowing, poetic, feminine, above all painterlike and aesthetic – the means by which art can enter the realm of intuition, imaginative pattern, heightened responsiveness, a reverie of the *ego* rather than an emanation of the *id*. In her novels consciousness flows, not only backward and forward in time, and spatially, from this place to that, but among and above the characters, who often share a strange intuitive relation to some common symbol: the lighthouse, the waves. And consciousness does more than apprehend the "shower of innumerable atoms," or "the luminous halo"; it reaches to the edge of eternal revelation, to moments of vision, "little daily miracles, illuminations, matches struck unexpectedly in the dark." Woolf can create flux in its terrifying enormity, as with Septimus Smith in *Mrs Dalloway*, who, shellshocked in war, accepts that "it might be possible that the world itself is without meaning," or Eleanor in *The Waves* who acknowledges that atoms that "danced apart and massed themselves" might hardly construct "what people called a life." From the start her novels never lack pain or melancholy, her note of "elegy." But the quest does point to some symbolist wholeness; consciousness can ultimately reveal form, penetrate the curtain. Thus the reflection of Mrs Ramsay in *To the Lighthouse*:

> there is a coherence in things; a stability; something, she
> meant, is immune from change, and shines out (she glanced
> at the window with its ripple of reflected lights) in the face
> of the flowing, the fleeting, the spectral, like a ruby; so that
> again tonight she had the feeling she had once today, of

185

peace, of rest. Of such moments, she thought, the thing is
made that endures.

It is the vision remembered in turn by Lily Briscoe, ten years
on: "In the midst of chaos there was shape; this eternal passing
and flowing (she looked at the clouds going and the leaves
shaking) was struck into stability. Life stand still here, Mrs
Ramsay said."

Woolf pursued this quest for the revealed shape in the midst
of chaos through eight novels, written over five decades. Her
first book, *The Voyage Out*, began as *Melymbrosia* as early as 1908;
her last, the mature *Between the Acts*, appeared just after her
death by suicide in 1941. From 1915 on she kept a detailed,
vivid diary recording – along with much else of her daily life
and thought – the progress of this endeavour toward "some
queer individuality." One of the great compositional records, it
does much to illuminate not just her own, but the modern,
creative instinct in an age of critical self-consciousness. With
her third novel, *Jacob's Room* (1922), a meditation on the life
and the room of a dead soldier ("Let us suppose that the Room
will hold it together," say her notes), comes the breakthrough;
she remarks "I have found out how to begin (at 40) to say
something in my own voice." Critics agree in seeing the group
of books that followed – *Mrs Dalloway* (1924), *To the Lighthouse*
(1927) and *The Waves* (1931) – as the centre of her work, the
heart of her contribution to Modernism. *Mrs Dalloway* – originally called *The Hours*, and set over seventeen chimed hours of
one day in London in 1923 – is a portrait of a fifty-two-year-old
society hostess preparing a party. Her gift is to "kindle and
illuminate," despite illness, sexual loneliness ("Narrower and
narrower would her bed be"), intimations of death. Juxtaposed
with her story is that of Septimus Smith, a spirit from a different
London, racked and broken by the War. His death by suicide
coincides with Clarissa's party, and resonates through the final
scenes. Otherwise the two do not come directly together, other
than by the flowing motions of the prose, the rhythms of

consciousness that move through the city, pick up the crowds, the walkers in the street, the nursemaids in the park, the moments from various individual pasts that distil in the present. As she wrote it, from 1922 to 1924, Woolf recorded its joys and depressions in her diary. She shows the need for a planned design, then the need to upturn it; she records the discovery of "my tunnelling process, by which I tell the past in instalments, as I have need of it," she declares her final conviction that the book has passed beyond mere accomplishment: "it seemed to leave me plunged deep in the richest strata of my mind. I can write and write and write now: the happiest feeling in the world." All this is matched in the rhythm of the book, which plainly progresses through a series of inner aesthetic gratifications, concluding with the obvious sense of artistic fulfilment in the famous final sentence: "For there she was."[12]

One critic has nicely called Clarissa a "metaphysical hostess," a figure who distils the experience of others and is an equivalent to form and life itself. So is Mrs Ramsay (based on Woolf's own mother) in her next book, *To the Lighthouse*. She is a pulsing, radiating centre of life, a "lighthouse" herself, a unified sensibility, living "in beauty":

> Mrs Ramsay, who had been sitting loosely, folding her son in her arm, braced herself, and, half turning, seemed to raise herself with an effort, and at once to pour into the air a rain of energy, a column of spray, looking at the same time animated and alive as if all her energies were being fused into force, burning and illuminating (quietly though she sat taking up the stocking again), and into this delicious fecundity, this fountain and spray of life, the fatal sterility of the male plunged itself, like a beak of brass, barren and bare.

The book's two episodes, an evening and a morning ten years apart, split by an interlude which sets those ten years of history

[12] I have discussed *Mrs Dalloway* more thoroughly in Chapter 10 of *The Modern World: Ten Great Writers*.

into a parenthesis, describe a world with Mrs Ramsay and a world without her. Like *A Passage to India* the book is structured as a triptych: the first part, "The Window," is gently celebrative; the second part, "Time Passes," evokes the decay of the house over the period of the Great War, during which two of the Ramsay children die, and Mrs Ramsay; the third, "The Lighthouse," treats a world of absence, redeemed by art. A lighthouse trip is achieved, Lily Briscoe finishes her painting: ". . . she drew a line there, in the centre. It was done; it was finished. Yes, she thought, laying her brush down in extreme fatigue, I have had my vision." The human has passed into the aesthetic; out of blobby experience a harmony has been captured, some answer to Lily's large question "What is the meaning of life?" The aesthetic is also an intuitive metaphysic, culminating in a unity called form. What Lily may be presumed to do is draw together the multiple moments of vision that make the novel. Woolf is never a narrative novelist, and this is a book of constant stases, moments of visionary gazing, contemplation, rapture: Charles Tansley seeing Mrs Ramsay's beauty plain; Lily perceiving human thought as a scrubbed kitchen table in a tree; Mrs Ramsay going on a spit of land "which the sea is slowly eating away, and there to stand, like a desolate sea-bird, alone." In different ways the task of "merging and flowing and creating" is assigned to all parties; as the characters halt for moments of reflection and veneration, the narration enriches this with an elaborate iconography, in which, however, "nothing was simply one thing." The novel ends on Lily's brushstroke, which finally becomes a composition; so, while the flux may be the flux of human consciousness, it reaches a coherence not of life or thought but of aesthetic completion. Pattern emerges, the pattern of art, the Cézanne-like shape in the midst of chaos, giving form to the absences, vacancies and obscurities of the human world.

Woolf followed the book with a squib, *Orlando* (1928), a playful exercise in androgyny. She herself called it an "escapade," though it proved curiously successful commercially. But "as usual I am bored by narrative," she wrote in her diary in

1929. So started the next major project, an emerging new book that was first called *The Moths* and finally appeared as *The Waves* (1931). She noted: "I am not trying to tell a story . . . A mind thinking. They might be islands of light – islands in the stream that I am trying to convey: life itself going on." Life going on, as it moves against narrative, against the steady dead beat of the clock, against history's familiar line of progress, against all that was dead and material, against conventional notions of human identity and personality: this was what her new work was trying to convey. *The Moths*, or *The Waves*, would be a prose poem, a flow, a novel beyond the novel, a work where every atom is saturated, a "combination of thought; sensation; the voice of the sea," a book written to a rhythm, not a plot. Six identities merge into a common lyrical and elegiac rhythm of experience, and the book is the culmination of one of her central themes – her near-erotic fascination with a world beyond personality and individuality, which is also the world of death. This is her plainest use of the stream-of-consciousness method, and her most abstract novel, a novel that was hardly a novel at all, but a post-naturalist, post-impressionist writing, displaying both her power of innovation and formal composition, and an era of consciousness in disarray. When the book came out, Woolf's place as a major Modernist writer was, in effect, secured. After Joyce, whose *Ulysses* came to stand as the great English-language classic of Modernist fiction, this middle group of Woolf's novels are where we look next to see the heart of the Modernist spirit in British fiction. With Proust, Mann, Joyce and Faulkner, Woolf had become one of those significant novelists who, seeing the novel lying in the ruins of its past, somehow found the way to build a new one.

Hence, in his great critical study *Mimesis* (1953), written in wartime, Erich Auerbach could look back and read her as the representative writer of what he calls "modern realism," the maker of a new mimesis in which "exterior events have actually lost their hegemony; they serve to release and interpret inner events."[13] There were limitations of which she herself was

[13] In this superb chapter "The Brown Stocking," Auerbach identifies many of the

189

conscious; as she said, "My only interest as a writer lies, I begin to see, in some queer individuality, not in strength, or passion, or anything startling." She also increasingly came to see that what she had done was to feminize Modernism, producing a writing on one hand formal, crystalline and complete, on the other intensely personalized, internalized, emotionalized ("when we speak of form we mean that certain emotions have been placed in the right relations to each other"). Hence, as critics have increasingly noted, her contribution was not only to Modernism's experimental adventure, which began to expire in the Thirties as political issues rose (she resisted, saying that art was in jeopardy when "rage and personal grievances" came into it, while accepting that the idea that the artist was "absolved from political duties" in order to have "freedom of mind, security of person, immunity from practical affairs," was now fundamentally challenged). It was also to the making of a new feminine novel, the writing of "Shakespeare's sister." Indeed she was a leading figure in a new tendency that developed powerfully during the Twenties in the work of May Sinclair, Dorothy Richardson, Katherine Mansfield, Rebecca West, Jean Rhys, Rosamund Lehmann, Elizabeth Bowen and more. For the "new methods" had released into fiction a deepened psychology, a more profound female portraiture, a richer discourse of inner life, a vital sense of aspiration – and a conviction that there is no presiding rule, no "proper stuff of fiction," that "the story might wobble, the plot might crumble, ruin might seize upon the characters. The novel, in short, might become a work of art."

During the Thirties, when personal stories increasingly

---

central features of her method: the disappearance of the objective narrator, and exterior reality as something generally valid and recognizable; the use of multiple subjective consciousness to present an impression of everything perceived and felt; the contrasting use of "exterior" and "interior" time; the reduction of exterior life through cutting away historical events or even major episodes in individual lives; the presentation of interior life through a randomness "neither restrained by a purpose nor directed by a specific subject of thought"; and the use of the "random moment" as the *mise-en-scène* of action. Erich Auerbach, *Mimesis: The Representation of Reality in Western Literature*, trans. Willard Trask (Princeton and London, 1953).

yielded to public and political ones, Woolf produced two more novels, *The Years* (1937) and *Between the Acts* (1941), works of panoramic historical intention, but less fundamental originality. The waning of art was in fact a theme of the age, and the air of crisis that had touched her work became more intense. In January 1941, with a new war going on round her, she noted in her diary James Joyce's death – "Joyce about a fortnight younger than I am." She recalled reading *Ulysses*, in its blue and white cover, with "spasms of wonder, of discovery, and then again the long lapses of intense boredom . . . And now all the gents are furbishing up their opinions, and the books, I suppose, take their place in the long procession." She wrote her essay "The Leaning Tower," a reflection of the decline of art in an age of politics, and a challenge to the younger generation who had found important historical issues, but had not written great books. Her own tragic death followed just after, in March, when, shattered again by the new war, she drowned herself in the river at Rodmell. Her own books, with their aesthetic intensity, high poetry, felt femininity, their struggle to complete identity both in art and life, were indeed, as she put it herself in *To the Lighthouse*, forms beyond experience, "one of those globed compacted things over which thought lingers, and love plays." And they too now took their own much argued, though increasingly respected, place in "the long procession," where history and criticism would go on doing their complicated work.

7.

The fiction of high aesthetic intensity, of inwardly felt "globed compact things" that offer through art a wholeness not there in life, was never the only aim of the contentious Modern movement. According to Ortega y Gasset's famous essay, a prime feature of Modern fiction was its move toward dehumanization – its departure from romanticism, realism and humanism toward perspective, abstraction, ironic observation, defamiliarization, away from the centrality of the human figure. Lawrence saw his novels firmly moving away from human representation in the direction of the greater inhuman will. In Woolf's *To the Lighthouse*, Mrs Ramsay's presence is replaced by her absence, and in *The Waves* individual identities give ground to the endless rhythm of life and death itself, a world beyond the self: "The difference we make so much of, this identity we so feverishly cherish, was overcome," Woolf wrote at the end of that book. In Joyce's *Ulysses*, human figures yield ground to the verbal life of the busy text they inhabit; even in Forster's humanistic *A Passage to India*, individuals are like "dwarfs shaking hands" in the obscure mystery of the landscape, and the human plot gives way to the symbolic one. As in painting, the represented human figure was losing its place at the centre of the world, the romantic self yielding to modern collectivity and impersonality.[14] "The primal artistic impulse has nothing to do with the rendering of nature," the German art critic Wilhelm Worringer wrote in *Abstraction and Empathy* in 1908; "It seeks after pure abstraction as the only possibility of repose within the confusions and obscurity of the world-picture . . ." All this, as critics have often noted, increasingly led at least one part of modern fiction in the direction of a pervasive irony, reflecting the sense of fading identity in a nihilistic, destructive and depersonalizing age. It was not surprising that this spirit of irony intensified in the post-war years, responding to the incongruity and horror of life with a vision of the modern as the age of meaninglessness and absurdity. Detachment, abstraction, impersonality, not realism or romantic subjectivity – surely these were the essen-

[14] Wyllie Sypher offers a brilliant study of this in his *Loss of the Self in Modern Literature and Art* (New York, 1962), which draws the lesson that in the age of collectivity, science and the vanishing individual any new humanism "must come to terms with our sense of the anonymity of the self, must therefore get beyond any romantic notions of selfhood. The importance of recent painting and literature is here, for both suggest that we must no longer confuse humanism with romantic individuality or with an anthropomorphic view that put the self at the centre of things. I take the phrase from Jean Grenier's essay on the disappearance of man from art: 'We now walk in a universe where there is no echo of "I".' The image of the self held in past eras has been effaced from the universe in which even nature seems an abstraction."

tials of the modern method in the age of the machine and mechanical war?

That was certainly the view of "the Enemy," Wyndham Lewis, proponent of the Vorticist method of "the Great Without." Born in 1882, educated at the Slade School of Art, then in Munich and Paris, Lewis was both painter and writer, and an active power in the early international Modern movement. Back in London in 1909, he was taken up by Hueffer/Ford for the *English Review*, and after that played a key part in the pre-war British *avant garde*. A central moment was his split with Roger Fry and his Post-Impressionist Omega Workshop; Lewis was attracted by the violent energy of Marinetti and the Futurists, and set up his own Rebel Arts Centre – from which, with the support of Pound, came Vorticism, celebrating the radical mechanical vortex of energy at the centre of art, and its magazine *Blast*. By 1911 he had started a Vorticist novel, *Tarr*, set in Paris' artistic bohemia, about the war between the artist and the rational philosopher, displaying many of his essential ideas about art in the age of the modern machine. Like other important works of the time, it was completed in wartime, when Lewis served on the front as a gunner, serialized in *The Egoist* in 1916–17, published in 1918. *Tarr* is an art of "polished and resistant surfaces," a comedy of machines, in which the characters are automata, human mechanisms seen in absurd performance. They acknowledge this themselves: "Deadness is the first condition of art," announces Tarr. "The second is the absence of soul, in the human and sentimental sense . . . good art must have no inside." The hard external manner is stark, what many would call "modern":

> Tarr possessed no deft hand or economy of force: his muscles rose unnecessarily on his arm to lift a wine-glass to his lips: he had no social machinery at all at his disposal and was compelled to get along as well as he could with the cumbrous one of the intellect. With this he danced about it is true: but it was full of sinister piston-rods, organ-like shapes, heavy drills . . .

From the start Lewis rejected "fiction from the inside," the interiorized novel of psychology that romanticized conscious-ness, as did Virginia Woolf's. "The *external* approach to things (relying on the evidence of the *eye* rather than on the more emotional organs of sense) can make 'the grotesque' a healthy and attractive companion," he explained; "Dogmatically, then, I am for the Great Without, the method of external approach."

As the dismaying Twenties developed, and the Modernist excitement turned to something else, Lewis' hard aesthetic detachment shifted to a plainer satirical disgust. He claimed that the pre-war rebellion had lost its direction, and Blooms-bury's ascent in the Twenties increased his disputatious rage. He became "the Enemy," the adversary of false experimental traditions, scoffing at the clownish age. Like Lawrence, he saw the Twenties as a time in crisis, unable to reconcile mechanical and human, reason and passion. Unlike Lawrence, he rejected the Romantic solution, the retreat into primitivism, intuitional-ism, vitalism and "the wild body." He condemned the novels of Joyce, Lawrence, Stein and Woolf alike for what he saw as their sentimentalization of experience and consciousness. And his answer was comedy; modern literature should be satirical or comic, meeting dehumanization with dehumanization. "The root of the comic," he says in *The Wild Body* (1927), following Bergson, "is to be sought in the sensations of a thing behaving like a person. But from that point of view all men are necessarily comic; for they are all things, or physical bodies, behaving like persons." Two remarkable works – *The Childermass* (1928), an abstract comedy of ideas set on the arid steppe at the threshold of heaven, and *The Apes of God* (1930), a bitter satire directed at a Britain "dead as mutton," above all at the contemporary artistic scene and especially the Bloomsbury intelligentsia, that "general rabble that collects under the equivocal banner of ART" – put the method into practice. These are works of vivid prose, powerful social observation, hard satirical rage. This is satire that enjoys all the Swiftian mechanics of disgust. Thus, from *The Apes of God*, this passage about the aged Lady

Fredigonde Follett, symbol for the whole culture, rising from her chair:

> The unsteady solid rose a few inches, like the levitation of a narwhal. Seconded by alpenstock and body-servant (holding her humble breath), the escaping half began to move out from the deep vent. It abstracted itself slowly. Something imperfectly animate had cast off from a portion of itself. It was departing, with a grim paralytical toddle, elsewhere. The socket of the enormous chair yawned just short of her hindparts . . .

Lewis – who remains an under-estimated writer, in part because his political ironies at the expense of the fashionable Left led him too close to Fascism for a time, and who kept on writing through the Fifties – is a novelist of extraordinary force, at his best capable of the rage of a Lawrence at the progressive enfeeblement of the culture, at his worst a writer who is chaotically prejudiced, painfully personal and shrill. But he also stays important for what he exemplifies: the rise of detached, objectively satirical methods and forms as a way of representing the grim modern experience in art. For the method of "the Great Without" was what many modern writers saw the point of. Robert Musil's "man without qualities," Italo Svevo's weatherless heroes, Kafka's self-victimizing victims, belong to a new age of ironic texts and characterless characters, writers of a world where the human was emptying out as the subject of art.

Sean O'Faolain, in *The Vanishing Hero* (1956), his interesting study of some of the best writers of the Twenties and Thirties (Joyce, Woolf, Hemingway, Faulkner, Aldous Huxley, Evelyn Waugh, Graham Greene, Elizabeth Bowen), explains that "The one constant in them all is the virtual disappearance of that focal character of the classical novel, the Conceptual Hero."[15]

---

[15] See Sean O'Faolain, *The Vanishing Hero: Studies in Novelists of the Twenties* (London, 1956).

In his view, the novel of the Twenties sees the end of earlier fictional humanism and of the socially approved hero, who becomes instead the anti-hero, the self-creator, the nonentity, the rebel, the misfit or the "galvanized puppets of their authors' transcendental ideas." And the humanist framework of the novel was indeed weakening, not only because of the movement toward symbolism and poetic fiction, or toward Lawrence's "inhuman self," but for more directly historical reasons: the war itself had eroded heroism in the scale of its mass slaughter, and the post-war weakening of public values, and social and psychological stability, accelerated the process. Heroes were falling off their monuments in the Twenties, and public values decaying; Wyndham Lewis was doubtless right to see that one of the mechanisms for dealing with this was a new comedy of manners and of ideas, which in fact the novelists of the Twenties give us in considerable profusion. There were the bright social comedies of Michael Arlen, the camp comedies of Ronald Firbank, above all the fiction of Aldous Huxley, the most underlyingly serious of them. Huxley, born in 1894, grandson of the Darwinian T. H. Huxley, wrote four fine novels over the Twenties – *Crome Yellow* (1921), a brilliant debut, mocking Lady Ottoline Morrell's Garsington and filled with invention and wit; *Antic Hay* (1923), a highly satirical portrait of London's cynical bohemia; *Those Barren Leaves* (1925), which was set among expatriates in Italy; and *Point Counterpoint* (1928), a novel of ideas about writing a novel of ideas. A presiding theme is the very nature of the modern itself. "Living modernly's living quickly," explains Lucy Tantamount in *Point Counterpoint*: "You can't cart a wagonload of ideals and romanticisms around with you these days. When you travel by airplane, you must leave your heavy baggage behind. The good old-fashioned soul was all right when people lived slowly. But it's too ponderous nowadays. There's no room for it in the airplane." The good old-fashioned soul disappears from Huxley's novels; these are characters who are quite used to crisis. "I don't see that it would be possible to live in a more exciting age," says Calamy in Aldous Huxley's *Those Barren Leaves* (1925): "The sense that

196

everything's perfectly provisional and temporary . . . the feeling that nothing . . . is really safe, the intimate conviction that anything may happen, anything may be discovered – another war, the artificial creation of life, the proof of continued existence after death – why it is all infinitely exhilarating."

It was little wonder that Huxley's novels came to be seen as works of modern cynicism. His characters appeared powerless to act, their relationships incapable of taking shape, their ideas circular and pointing to eventual futility. These are novels of ideas that set no store by the salvation of ideas. When, in *Point Counterpoint*, Philip Quarles sets out to write a book for the times, it is indeed a novel of ideas. "Novel of ideas . . .," he notes. "The chief defect about the novel of ideas is that you must write about people who have ideas to express," in other words intellectuals, who are disappointing and futile in their own ways. Quarles also thinks it a good idea to put a novelist in the novel ("He also justifies experiment. Specimens of his work may illustrate other possible or impossible ways of telling a story"), which of course is just what Huxley himself had done; these books are nothing if not self-conscious. As for the ideas themselves, they generally turn on notions of crisis and desires for primitivism, the products of an age of lost ideals and universal boredom in which barbarism and Freudian libido become solutions to an intellectual sterility (which is why, of course, the ideas turn into comedy). Huxley knew well he was one of the people he was himself satirizing, living in a "pointless landscape" (or what D. H. Lawrence, himself satirized in *Point Counterpoint* as Rampion, called the "slow suicide of inertia"), in a world where things are either exciting or boring, when humanity is a wearisome condition. Behind them is a sense of the failure of history and the collapse of secular progress, so that only irrational solutions are possible. Perhaps it was inevitable that Huxley's next and most famous book would be *Brave New World* (1932), written when the processes Huxley was writing about had gone yet further. A dystopian, anti-Wellsian novel about the future, set in the seventh century AF (After Ford), a Butler-like satire on a world where science, mechanism and reason have triumphed over human nature, it makes clear that, though Huxley's novels were regarded as indifferent and cynical, the underlying pain, anxiety and humanism were real enough. And Huxley spent his later years in the USA, as a modern thinker rather than a novelist, watching, as his eyesight failed, a good many of his bleaker predictions and prophecies come true in the age of science and mechanization.

Still, there was no doubt who the writer was who distilled modern comedy, and best caught the mood of the later Twenties. Evelyn Waugh, born in 1903, the son of Arthur Waugh, the literary journalist and publisher's editor, was a schoolboy at Lancing during the Great War, and so belonged to the distinctively post-war generation. He went up to Oxford in 1922, the year of *Ulysses* and *The Waste Land*, the peak year of the Modern movement, and in it he took a great interest; indeed the influence of Eliot is plain on his work, and he later took the title of *A Handful of Dust* (1934) from his famous poem. Toward the end of the decade he began writing fiction, and his work reflected this. He had also been reading Hemingway, a younger American writer then working experimentally in Paris, whose very post-war story of futility, modern pain and "the lost generation," *The Sun Also Rises*, with its tight, understated and economical prose, appeared in 1926, around the time Waugh began writing. His interests were eclectic. He admired Max Beerbohm, whose witty if highly romantic comedy of Oxford life, *Zuleika Dobson*, appeared in 1911; the novels of P. G. Wodehouse, with their utterly distinctive, timeless, comfortingly British comic world, supported by the excellent Jeeves; the novels of Ronald Firbank, whose *Valmouth* appeared in 1919 and his *Prancing Nigger* in 1924 (he died in 1926). Waugh was a writer in search of a distinctive modern style, and he found one. Writing on Firbank just after he had published his first novel *Decline and Fall* (1928), in an essay in 1929, he explored the modern technique of Firbank's fiction. Effect, he noted, was presented without cause; his art balanced "the wildest extravagances and the most austere economy"; presentation was done through dialogue rather than characterization, extravagant action, and the pace and cross-cutting of film. And, like Lewis, Waugh had evidently read his Nietzsche and Bergson, whose ideas are expressed by Professor Silenus in *Decline and Fall*, where he speaks of a world of the purely mechanical, uninvaded by the mischief that is called man. Waugh is a writer who has been consistently under-estimated because his work seems to offer no intellectual analysis of the modern condition, but simply represents it as an absurd situation. But that was the point: he had found his modern style, entirely distinctive and original. It was an absurdist humour; indeed he can be taken as the chief creator of the spirit of black humour in modern British fiction. His early novels (written, as Edmund Wilson once remarked, in the spirit of Jowett's advice to the British gentleman: "Never apologize, never explain") are remarkable for the completeness of their comic vision, the pure anarchy of their world, the concentration of their modern comic form.

Decline and Fall: An Illustrated Novelette is a brightly modern picaresque comedy about the adventures of an innocent young man, a twentieth-century Candide, from the time he is unjustly sent down from his Oxford college to the time just over a year later when he returns to it, having been witness to a modern world fantastic in its nature and challenging to all his liberal assumptions. Meantime everything has happened to him, and also nothing. He has taught at a rogue school, met a great variety of confusingly anarchic characters, spent a "very modern night of love" with Margot Beste-Chetwynde, a society lady who doubles as a brothel-keeper, gone to prison, and been mysteriously released. He finally discovers the "still small voice" of conscience, which means that he doesn't really belong in the anarchic modern world at all, and ends back exactly as he began. But he too is not a hero, as Waugh carefully explains in the text: "the whole of this book is really an account of the mysterious disappearance of Paul Pennyfeather, so that readers must not complain if the shadow which took his name does not amply fill out the important part of hero for which he was originally cast." He is not a hero because this is not a world for heroes, and also because the disappearance of the human element is part of the story of the modern world – as Professor Silenus, the voice of modernity, explains: "What an immature, self-destructive, antiquated mischief is man!. . . on the one side the harmonious instincts and balanced responses of the animal, on the other the inflexible purpose of the machine, and between them man, equally alien from the *being* of Nature and the *doing* of the machine, this vile *becoming!*" Silenus sees the problem of art as "the elimination of the human element from the consideration of form."

And so in his way does Waugh. His achievement was indeed the creation of a complete style, an impassive, ethically neutral, modern comic form. The writer stands at the centre of his comedy, omniscient but evasive, surrounded by his own distinct universe of outrage and absurdity. His world passes by as an impression, a mad collage without psychological depth, flickering, quickly rendered, made with short scenes, rapid pace, comically vivid and yet characterless characters whose lives and reality do not detain us. His characters deliberately lack deep psychology, and live in a world that operates according to whim, chance or fortune, an anarchic "modern" universe beyond moral law. Waugh's later work gives a history to this state of modern alienation and human meaninglessness. His early work simply represents it, as a plain state of affairs. And while in *Decline and Fall* Paul can simply leave the anarchic world, in the next novels there is no escape. In *Vile Bodies* (1930) the worlds of black comedy and contemporary history exactly overlap. Despite his name, Adam, the central character, is no innocent, and has to manage his survival within the world of vile bodies, "faster, faster," mad motor races, flimsy affairs, brief marriages, economic chaos, dead religion, a "radical instability of the world order." The vision is of the last days, the impulse is toward herd-suicide; the novel closes on a war between unspecified parties on "the biggest battlefield in the history of the world." And so it was onward into Waugh's remarkable fiction of the Thirties, which is discussed in the next chapter.

The fiction of the Twenties can be seen in two ways: as a

consolidation of the Modern movement, the realization of a series of artistic developments that had been taking place over twenty-five years; or as its opposite, the product of an apocalyptic moment that had fractured all traditions, even the Modern one, leaving the writer with a new kind of task, as Lawrence claimed in his wartime and post-war comments. "Ours is essentially a tragic age, so we refuse to take it tragically," begins his *Lady Chatterley's Lover* (1928), the book in which he attempted to take the age both tragically and comically (it is filled with satirical social observation), and his largest culture-reading of the post-war age. "The cataclysm has happened, we are among the ruins, we start to build up new little habits, to have new little hopes . . . This was more or less Constance Chatterley's position. The war had brought the roof down over her head. And she had realized one must live and learn." This had been the theme of his writing since *Women in Love*. In *Aaron's Rod* (1922), which starts with the end of the war, in *Kangaroo* (1923), a political novel set in Australia, and *The Plumed Serpent* (1926), a mythic romance set in Mexico, he had sought new transformations, looked for new social orders, new forms of leadership, new depths of primitivism, to salvage the age or the individual. These are novels of a long search through darkness and the irrational that has been bred, as much as anything, by the war itself. *Lady Chatterley* . . . was his last major work of fiction, written and published in Italy, and in its full form it was kept from British and American audiences until the 1950s. In it he returned home again, to the English Midlands and its natural and social landscape, to the "Condition of England" novel, and to much of the spirit of his earlier writing, except that his world is now entirely dominated by the "bruise of the false inhuman war." This has cancelled "all the great words," love, joy, happiness, even sex: "the last of the great words, it was just a cocktail term for an excitement that bucked you up for a while, then left you more raggy than ever."

Lady Chatterley . . . is a dark fable of social and sexual sterility, a story of the "gap in the continuity of consciousness" that makes the modern person a creature of mechanism rather than feeling, producing the thin post-cataclysmic sensibility that forms the flavour of the novel, and against which Mellors, the good soldier–survivor, revolts. The book went through three distinct drafts, playing the story in different ways, and offering, in the earlier versions, some promise of a political solution to the crisis afflicting an England divided between the classes, between the industrial and pastoral, the mechanical and passional, and flowing toward death. In the decisive final version this is withdrawn, and the bad time is coming still; it is only the language of intimate personal tenderness, and the vernacular sexual language of that tenderness, that offers an answer, though one that itself does not satisfy; the end is still nigh. The apocalyptic message is strong, here as in much else that came from the later Twenties. It can be long argued whether the darkened apocalyptic mood of Twenties Modernism represented an essential spirit or, as some American writers like William Carlos Williams argued, a gloomy European diversion away from its artistic promises. Later critics, notably George Orwell, came to question this Twilight of the Gods feeling in a different way, as an aesthete's attempt to reject history by substituting art for real politics, though in the end history was to prove no better muse. What is true is that during the Twenties the direction of fiction sharply changed, and the Modernist adventure that had been growing from the later nineteenth century generally took on a new apocalyptic note. The fact remains that some of the greatest, and also the most various, works of modern British fiction came from the moment, and they have retained their power over the fate and fortune of the novel ever since.

FOUR

Closing Time in the Gardens
1930–1945

Nina looked down and saw inclined at an odd angle a horizon of
straggling red suburb; arterial roads dotted with little cars;
factories, some of them working, others empty and decaying; a
disused canal; some distant hills sown with bungalows; wireless
masts and overhead power cables; men and women were
indiscernible except as tiny spots; they were marrying and
shopping and making money and having children. The scene
lurched and tilted again as the aeroplane struck a current of air.
  "I think I'm going to be sick," said Nina.
  "Poor little girl," said Ginger. "That's what the paper bags
are for."

Evelyn Waugh, *Vile Bodies* (1930)

"Nothing dreadful is ever done with, no bad thing gets any
better; you can't be too serious." This is the message of the
Forties from which, alas, there seems no escape, for it is closing
time in the gardens of the West and from now on an artist will
be judged only be the resonance of his solitude or the quality of
his despair.

Cyril Connolly, "Editorial," *Horizon* (Dec 1949/Jan 1950)

1.

It was one of the implications of the post-war Modern movement that the Crisis of the Word and the Crisis of the World
were intimately linked. This is why, when we revisit many of
the great works of the early 1920s, we can scarcely miss the way
they seem shaken into being by crisis and change, the disaster
of war and the feelings of historical chaos and futility that
followed it, which gave them both their mood of despair, loss

203

and exile, and their artistic tactics of fracture, fragmentation, and linguistic crisis. Yet, in the early Twenties, the consequence of this visible "crisis" is frequently a new adventure into form, an excited rediscovery of art, a rejection of the decadence of history for the lasting value of aesthetic space. During the rest of the decade, this aesthetic but despairing view of "modern" writing, the famous "Waste Land" sensibility, penetrated a good part of the serious literature of Europe – though in the United States a more optimistic view of the alliance between futuristic progress and modern form was often felt. By the decade's end, when it became even clearer how little the war had achieved in creating European stability or worthwhile social change, the climate of historical dismay, impotent outrage, and anxious pessimism greatly increased. It was made plain in a whole sequence of war, or rather anti-war, books – Edmund Blunden's *Undertones of War*, Siegfried Sassoon's *Memoirs of a Fox-Hunting Man* and R. C. Sherriff's *Journey's End* in 1928, Richard Aldington's *Death of a Hero*, Robert Graves' *Goodbye to All that*, Henry Williamson's *The Wet Flanders Plain*, Erich Maria Remarque's *All Quiet on the Western Front* and Hemingway's *A Farewell to Arms* in 1929, Frederic Manning's *Her Privates We*, H. M. Tomlinson's *All Our Yesterdays* and Hašek's *The Good Soldier Schweik* in 1930, and so on – which indicated all the war had done was to leave its survivors and successors in a shattered, unmanageable, directionless world. Novels like Waugh's *Decline and Fall*, Lawrence's *Lady Chatterley's Lover*, both published in 1928, were already exploring the still more terrible thought that the age lay *entre deux guerres*, between two world wars; and in 1929 a friend of W. H. Auden was "talking excitedly of a final war." Younger novelists, like Waugh, Christopher Isherwood (*All the Conspirators*, 1928) and Graham Greene (*The Man Within*, 1929), and the poets who would soon be known as "the Auden generation," writers who had been born in the first years of the century, and inherited the Twenties from the deeds of their elders, were already writing of and in a shattered, historically hopeless, morally damaged world. And, much as those same elders had felt themselves in

204

revolt against the Victorians, so they felt their own revolt was one against the Edwardian and early Georgian age. They consciously belonged to a new generation, with a new and damaged history. And, claimed Isherwood in his fictionalized autobiography *Lions and Shadows: An Education in the Twenties* (1938), "we young writers of the middle 'twenties were all suffering, more or less subconsciously, from a feeling of shame that we had not been old enough to take part in the European war."

The mood of generational change was plain well before the Twenties were over. "Only from about the year 1926 did the features of the post-war world begin to emerge – and not only in the sphere of politics," wrote T. S. Eliot in January 1939, in a sad final editorial for his review *The Criterion*, when the war these new writers had imaginatively prospected was about to begin: "From about that date one began slowly to realize that the intellectual and artistic output of the previous seven years [the peak years of Modernism] had been rather the last efforts of an old world, than the struggles of the new." By the mid-Twenties, the great "Shock of the New" had already passed: "modern" experience and material was now familiar matter in art, fashionable as bobbed hair, and the opening of a Museum of Modern Art in New York in 1929 marked a clear acceptance of what was once thought *avant-garde* and totally outrageous. The *avant garde* was already set to become a modern institution, and a number of the writers whose work began from small presses in Paris were turning into popular authors. A writing of civilized misery, historical sterility and class uncertainty became common; as Erich Auerbach said in *Mimesis* (1953), one increasingly found in writing "a hatred of culture and civilization, brought about by the subtlest artistic devices culture and civilization have developed, and often a radical and fanatical urge to destroy."

But, as the Thirties dawned, the note of ominous disorder and historical nervousness grew ever stronger. This is what W. H. Auden, the poet whose tight economy and wit of image did so much to give a language to the Thirties, indicates in his famous "diagnostic" poem "1929": "It is time for the destruction of error./ The chairs are being brought in from the garden,/ The summer talk stopped on that savage coast . . ./ In the sanatoriums they laugh less and less,/ Less certain of cure; and the loud madman/ Sinks now into a terrible calm." 1929 was a key date for obvious reasons – the year in which a condition of political modernity perhaps seventy years in the making suddenly jolted forward toward totalitarianism, dictatorship, rearmament, disaster. Politics were back: in a climate of deep social and economic unease, a General Strike and a growth of poverty, Labour's second Government came to office in Britain that year. Then a decade that had opened with one historical crisis, the uneasy armistice at the end of a Great War, ended on yet another, the coming of the Great Crash; in November that year the American stock market failed. By the end of the year, and on more than the calendar, the Twenties were over, their moral, stylistic and psychological credit exhausted, their tinsel settling to earth – as one of their best interpreters, F. Scott Fitzgerald, observed. Capitalism seemed to be entering a terminal decline; economic realities – if anything to do with economics can ever be called a reality – took over. And so did totalistic political solutions: Stalin's Bolshevik Russia radiated its powerful ideological and modernizing influence, a Germany enfeebled by punitive war reparations, inflation and class disintegration bred a new era of national socialism, Nazism, and in Mussolini's Italy the highly Futuristic movement of Fascism rose. All modern histories were now globally interconnected, and the European crisis was reflected and repeated in Britain itself. In 1931 the nation came off the Gold Standard; in 1932 unemployment peaked at 2.8 million, Oswald Mosley founded the British Union of Fascists, and Communist Party membership multiplied. In 1933 Hitler became German Chancellor, and the Communist International prophesied "a new round of revolutions and wars." In 1934 Fascists took over in Austria; in 1936 came the Spanish Civil War – the war which, thanks to outside intervention, became the battlefield of the "modern" ideologies, the harbinger of the greater European war that emerged fully-fledged in 1939.

By 1930 the Twenties was already a distinct decade, slipping away into history. But it quickly seemed the Thirties was shaping up to be another equally distinctive decade, a trough between Great Crash and future crisis. In the event, its cycle would last almost exactly ten years too, from the Slump of autumn 1929 to the outbreak of World War in autumn 1939. This time there was no doubt at all that the war had been imaginatively prefigured; matters of peace and war, violence and disorder, politics and ideology, dominated most of the writing of the decade. The writers of the Twenties had thought of themselves as a generation, probably a "lost" generation. The writers of the Thirties soon saw themselves as one too: the "Thirties Generation," or, eventually, taking the name of the most influential of the "diagnostic" poets (poetry played a big part in the writing of the decade), the "Auden Generation." For, just like the decade itself, notable for its terrifying massing of groups, armies, crowds, parades, causes and ideologies, it was their instinct to be collective – one reason why so many modern studies of this time treat them collectively.[1] For the novel at least, the term "Auden generation" is plainly too narrow; but it does help remind us that the generational, collective climate in writing was not simply a matter of the grouping tendencies of the decade. It also came from the intimate networking of writers, who so often shared backgrounds – schools, famous universities (Oxford and Cambridge, or Oxbridge), friendships, partners, homosexual brotherhoods – in common, and frequently commented on, or collaborated in, each other's work. We think of the Thirties as an age of "proletarian" writing, and important figures like Lewis Grassic Gibbon, Walter Greenwood, James Hanley, Walter Brierley, Sid Chaplin and others wrote fine working-class fiction during

[1] See, for instance, Samuel Hynes' *The Auden Generation: Literature and Politics in England in the 1930s* (Princeton, 1976), and Valentine Cunningham's wonderfully capacious *British Writers of the Thirties* (Oxford and New York, 1989), as well as the many memoirs by Christopher Isherwood, Stephen Spender, John Lehmann, Louis MacNeice, Cyril Connolly, George Orwell, Graham Greene, Evelyn Waugh, Henry Green and others.

the decade. It seemed the social origins of literary writing were changing, and there were other writers, above all C. P. Snow and William Cooper (Harry Hoff) who were exploring society from the near-Wellsian standpoint of the provincial, grammar-school, scientifically trained meritocracy, while regional fiction grew in importance. The fact remains that never before in British writing had a particular cadre, the socially connected, well-educated, public-school and university intelligentsia, been so obviously influential. A large proportion of the dominant authors were sons or daughters of doctors, army officers, literary journalists, academics, Anglican ministers, or earlier writers. The world of their social and educational background – Waugh's Oxford, Isherwood's Cambridge, Greene's Berkhamsted school, Orwell's St Cyprian's – became part of the literary landscape, one reason, no doubt, why narratives set in lesser-known schools and redbrick or new universities provided some of the key contradictory myths of the fiction of the Fifties.[2] If anything, in these leftwing and political times, British fiction narrowed rather than widened in social source, though it broadened widely in other ways – through travel, through increased consciousness of European and world politics, through extensive social observation, through large-scale historical "diagnosis." But the shared social culture and background does so much to explain the private cadences and allusions of quite a lot of writing, to the point where Cyril Connolly once suggested that the writers of the period were held in a state of permanent adolescence, still eternally at their prep and public schools. One result of this was a pervasive note of class guilt, as

---

[2] In his *Children of the Sun: A Narrative of "Decadence" in England After 1918* (London, 1977), Martin Green offers an interesting list, noting that of the writers, artists and political figures he deals with, many went to similar prep schools, and similar or the same public schools: "Waugh and [Tom] Driberg went to Lancing: [John] Betjeman, [Louis] MacNeice, [T. C.] Worsley, and [Anthony] Blunt went to Marlborough. And to Eton went . . . [George] Orwell, [Harold] Acton, [Brian] Howard, [Robert] Byron, [Cyril] Connolly, [Henry] Green, [Anthony] Powell, [Oliver] Messel, [Alan] Pryce-Jones, [John] Lehmann, [Ian] Fleming, [Randolph] Churchill and [Guy] Burgess. From there most went on either to Oxford or Cambridge." Humphrey Carpenter also follows the Oxford story in *The Brideshead Generation*. Also see my *The Social Context of Modern English Literature* (Oxford/New York, 1971).

social and economic change, a conviction of long-term historical crisis, and generational anger was applied to that most elegant and intricate of human artifices, the British class system, which has given so much to the nature of the novel. An air of social anxiety, political instability, liberal dismay, crypto-exile, runs through the writing of an era, as an old establishment sought to disestablish itself, and find a different place in, a fresh angle on, history.

2.

No wonder that this was the age of the "writer's dilemma," and that, whatever the writer's origins, the belief that a new literary accounting was necessary grew widespread. It was a time when, as Jean-Paul Sartre proposed in *What Is Literature?* (1947), writers hesitated between proclaiming the new world and being the gravediggers of the old, when "Historicity flowed in upon us." The Thirties was a nightmare decade, and produced a nightmare literature, a daydreaming on the edge of the real world, where even the fabric of daily commonplace experience – schooldays, family life, suburban domesticity – generally acquired a surreal aspect of estrangement and horror. In Graham Greene's distinctive and intensely autobiographical universe, as in Isherwood's, there are always corruptions in the dorm, deceits in the passageways, strange creatures beneath the garden, a gun in the bathroom cupboard. Writing filled with sinister, Gothic images ("the hooded women, the hump-backed surgeons,/ And the Scissor Man," of Auden's "The Witnesses"). Writers assumed poses of disguise and self-concealment, found themselves ever crossing both sides of the social, moral and sexual borders, thought of themselves as exiles or spies in their own countries ("Our hopes were set still on the spies' career," wrote Auden, ever good with a line; one result of all this was the spy scandals and Moscow flights of the Fifties and the Sixties). They hid names and backgrounds behind pseudonyms; the Etonian Eric Blair who turned into the proletarian George

Orwell, and was scarred by the birthmark of his origins, was by no means the only dramatic self-transformer. They surveyed their landscape with an aerial detachment (Auden saw himself as "the helmeted airman"), and travelled to live their lives in secret abroad. These detached aerial views oscillated with painful psychological frankness; Auden revealed his "neural itch," Stephen Spender was suitably described as "redeeming the world by introspection."

Meanwhile History itself had taken over from the artist as the great experimentalist, and writers felt passive before it. If the serious writers of the Twenties had generally seen themselves as a vanguard, advancing, individualistically, aesthetically, apolitically, under the banner of the experimental arts, those of the Thirties often saw themselves as inert agents driven by "inevitable," "necessary" forces beyond their own individuality, requiring collective homage (what, asked Louis MacNeice, "would we have history say/ Of us who walked in our sleep and died on our Quest?"). In the Twenties History was a fool that knew nothing, a nightmare from which the artist was trying to awake. In the Thirties the writer was, it seemed, inescapably inside the nightmare, so that novelty in literature increasingly came from a "diagnostic" or "psychological" response to the strangenesses, terrors and irrationality of the historical world. From this chaos, politics seemed, for a time, to offer an escape. In a recurrent Thirties enterprise writers "took sides," fighting each other, and the bourgeois class from which they generally came. The aesthetic revolts of the Twenties turned into the class wars and ideological confrontations of a new decade when (as the new critical magazine *Scrutiny* ironically observed) the question "Under Which King, Bezonian?" was endlessly asked. "As an Englishman I am not in the predicament of choosing between two evils," Evelyn Waugh answered when the *Left Review* polled writers' allegiances during the Spanish Civil War. "I am not a Fascist nor shall I become one unless it were the only alternative to Marxism. It is mischievous to suggest such a choice is imminent." But this was bold and unusual; for most writers the choice *was* imminent, already made for them by History, in advance. Most looked Left, going "forward from Liberalism" via anti-Fascism to Communism and the Party, or somewhere "committed" close by. Especially later in the decade, some (Julian Bell, John Cornford, Christopher Caudwell) forgot preliminaries and were militant Marxists from the start. Others looked Right, like T. S. Eliot, with his Anglo-Catholic/Classicist/Royalist sympathies, or Wyndham Lewis. Others (like Waugh and Greene) looked up, to God, especially when Catholic, searching beyond left and right or right and wrong to good and evil.

According to Stephen Spender, in his very typical, and very liberal, polemical work – *Forward from Liberalism* (1937), the death of liberalism and hence the forthcoming alliance between the writer and Marxism was the crucial issue. "The Individual has died before . . .," resignedly announced MacNeice in his "Epitaph for Liberal Poets." If this was true (there were many writers who never did feel it was), then it is also notable how variously un-Marxist much of the best writing of the decade finally is. For one thing, many of these writers had actually started their careers in the Twenties, and done their literary apprenticeship with *Ulysses* and "The Waste Land," the poem disturbingly read out at Oxford in Waugh's powerful retrospect of the doubled Twenties-and-Thirties era, *Brideshead Revisited* (1945). The fiction of the Thirties echoes with Joycean sounds – in early Isherwood and Henry Green, in Samuel Beckett and Malcolm Lowry, who freely confessed he was "Joyced with his own petard" – just as the poetry is filled with Eliotic remnants. Modernism and Thirties writing existed in uneasy coalition right through the decade, and Bloomsbury remained a power in the land well into the Fifties. T. S. Eliot's *Criterion* published, in January 1930, Auden's charade "Paid on Both Sides," generally seen as the first testimonial statement of Thirties writing, and, for all its "classicist" line, went on supporting the new writers (even printing Hugh McDiarmid's "Hymn to Lenin"). Leonard and Virginia Woolf's Hogarth Press published the Michael Roberts anthologies *New Signatures* (1932) and *New Country* (1933) which set out the younger writers

211

collectively; and it also brought out many of their books (Isherwood's, Henry Green's), thanks largely to John Lehmann, the supporter of "new writing" who worked for the press. Quarrels came: Eliot challenged the Marxists and ideologists; Virginia Woolf expressed her criticism of the new Leftists looking out from their leaning tower, built on parental gold, in a forceful last essay of 1940 "The Leaning Tower."

Similarly, the new writers found Modernism a "distortion" or an "irrelevance," Eliot a "reactionary," and Woolf's fiction of the Thirties over-aesthetic, precious and "unsocial" ("elegant arabesques," as even Lytton Strachey put it). But certain links were plain; in a way it was the darkness in Modernism that excused the "dream of violence" of the "new" Thirties writing. So when Spender wrote his study of modern writing *The Destructive Element* (1935), he took his title from a potent phrase of Conrad's, and, in a convenient rewriting, acknowledged a basic continuity between the Modern movement, with its Twenties note of Waste Land sensibility and Spenglerian decline, and his own contemporaries. However, where the Moderns wrote "subjectively," in an age without belief or clear values, the new generation, he claimed, had produced a writing that was "objective and social." Later, after the Marxist God had failed, he observed in his autobiography *World Within World* (1951): "perhaps, after all, the qualities that distinguished us from the writers of the previous decade lay not in ourselves, but in the events to which we reacted." Perhaps so: the pervasive note of a good deal of Thirties writing is not, finally, its political engagement but the spectacle of its liberal experimentalists trying and failing to be engaged. "Writers were scared now, and very rightly too," Pamela Hansford Johnson once brusquely commented. "For the first time since 1918 they had to face the fact that *they personally* might be starved, degraded, tortured, murdered. They had to write for their lives: and in the face of that necessity, 'art for art's sake' became to them temporarily without meaning." This may be too hard, but much Thirties writing is a battlefield of liberal anxiety, where crisis in history and politics is also a crisis of self and identity. This then led on to that distinguishing air of secrecy, self-concealment, wander-lust, exile, infidelity, existential crisis, seediness, inauthenticity and betrayal, all perhaps to be solved by "commitment," political, religious, psychoanalytic, existential, that runs through so much of the writing of the whole decade. In fact we can already find in Thirties writing much of that dark existential disquiet, about the lost soul caught in the sink of history, that would return in much writing after the new, "absurdist" crisis of the Second World War.

One useful marker of the transition from Twenties to Thirties is the passage from the very Twenties word "modern" to the very Thirties word "new." During the Twenties all that was experimental was also "modern"; in the Thirties nearly all the various magazines and anthologies that attempted to capture the changing climate sported the word "new" somewhere in the title. In 1932 Michael Roberts' famous anthology *New Signatures*, printing poetry by Auden, Spender, Cecil Day Lewis, William Empson, and others, proclaimed editorially that this was not just work of a "new" generation, but a fresh unesoteric poetry where "imagery taken from contemporary life consistently appeared as the natural and spontaneous expression of the poet's thought and feeling." That year F. R. Leavis published *New Bearings in English Poetry*, emphasizing a different but no less radical lineage, focused on Eliot; his wife Q. D. Leavis published her *Fiction and the Reading Public*, looking at the impact of the new mass culture on the novel; and they both started the Cambridge critical magazine *Scrutiny*, which became a central voice of what would be called "New Criticism." Oxford, better known for writers than critics, came out with the Left-wing *New Oxford Outlook*. In 1933 Roberts produced his second anthology *New Country*, adding "new" prose by Isherwood and Edward Upward, and a marked steer to the Left; the editorial announced that as the writer sees "his interests are bound up with those of the working-class, so will his writing clear itself from the complexity and introspection, the doubt and cynicism, of recent years." (It never did.) That year Geoffrey Grigson started *New Verse*; in 1934 H. E. Bates and others began *New*

Stories. In 1936, as the Spanish Civil War began, the "new" endeavour was pulled together in John Lehmann's elegantly produced *New Writing*, later extended into *Folios of New Writing* and *New Writing and Daylight*. Publishing poetry, fiction, criticism and reportage, displaying a strong leftward emphasis as well as a strong European dimension, it printed much that was remarkable: Isherwood's *The Nowaks*, Edward Upward's *The Border Line*, Rex Warner's *The Wild Goose Chase*, George Orwell's *Shooting an Elephant*, notable working-class writing by James Hanley, George Garrett, Sid Chaplin and B. L. Coombes, important European work by Boris Pasternak, Bertolt Brecht, Ignazio Silone and Jean-Paul Sartre. These would provide valuable funds when, in 1940, with war begun, the venture developed into *Penguin New Writing*, a cheap paperback magazine with many of the same writers, and large wartime sales, which kept the creative and reportorial record of the dark years and the period of Cold War, rationing and austerity that followed. It closed in 1950.

3.

What, then, was "new"? Plainly quite a lot of the best writing of the Thirties was not, if only because it was "modern." It was a writing that came directly from change, responding to the rising political disorder, ideological confrontation, and crowd frenzy of what had become an age not of the *avant garde* but of the cumulative modern masses. It aspired in its own way to be a "mass," or at least a "public," writing, as Lehmann explained in his Penguin volume *New Writing in Europe*, published in 1940, where he sought to place it in what was now a historical perspective. He recorded the growth, in the early 1930s, of "a group of poets and prose-writers who were conscious of the great social, political and moral changes going on around them, and who became increasingly convinced that it was their business to communicate their vision of this process, not merely to the so-called highbrow intellectual public to which their

214

predecessors had addressed themselves, but to the widest possible circles of ordinary people engaged in the daily struggle for existence." "New writing," he said, marked an extension of the Modernist rebellion past the crisis of 1929–31. This "cracked the world of the twenties beyond repair," demanding a fresh awareness of historical realities and progressive aims, a move beyond aesthetic humanism to social realism and reportage, a need to search for a "proletarian" writing (and *New Writing* encouraged a good many working-class writers, though never to the point where they dominated). The result was often a strange, uneasy marriage between "Bloomsbury" and "public writing," aestheticism and social realism. The chief "new writers" frequently emerged both as bourgeois and anti-bourgeois, scientists and subjects of their own experiment, diagnosticians and their own patients, in what Auden called "this country of ours where no-one is well." Reportage, sociology, "mass observation" provided one important discourse; so did the new gurus of psychoanalysis, above all Georg Groddeck and Homer Lane, specialists in various forms of the "neural itch." "New writing" was the product of a decade essentially, "inevitably," preoccupied with itself, and in that very fact it proved to be what it intended to be, "symptomatic."

"New writing" was not alone in its distinctive characterization of the nightmare decade, in which history became a machine, society a battlefield, and neurosis the typical inner condition. Writers left and right explored chaos, the "destructive element," and the systems, rational and irrational, that might control it. They travelled, everywhere, until they generally became foreign travellers at home, or proto-Europeans in their own land. Isherwood, the passive camera, went to homosexual – which also, as the wheel of history turned, proved Fascist – Berlin; others, from Greene to Waugh to Malcolm Lowry, went to Abyssinia, Mexico, or wherever the age's borderlands – frontiers of right and left, God and dialectical materialism, civilization and barbarism – lay. The dangerous border, the risky frontier, the barbed-wire fence, the local revolution, indeed became the grand metaphors for the age, and the view from the air, or some other angle of detachment, became ever more important. Meanwhile Lawrence's "bad time coming" and Waugh's "biggest battlefield in the history of the world" ran like a lode-bearing seam through the literature of the era, moving from surreal fantasy toward historical actuality. "*It's going to happen*," George Orwell wrote in *Coming Up for Air* in gloomy 1939. "All the things you've got at the back of your mind, the things you're terrified of, the things you tell yourself are just a nightmare or only happen in foreign countries." In the time of nightmare, writers, and writing itself, increasingly aspired to action: travelling, flying, hiking, climbing, bicycling, and going – as by 1936 many were ready to do – to war. With the Spanish Civil War, Thirties writing, and especially "new writing," found both its moment and its crisis. Many went to report or participate, a significant number died, and others, like George Orwell, returned disillusioned, the agreed ideological certainties already half-dissolved.

"I proceed like a somnambulist," Adolf Hitler, who dominated the decade, once declared. So, in its later half, did most of the writers of the Thirties. Lehmann meant his *New Writing in Europe* to show, he said, how "the seed which lay at the heart of the whole movement, – to put it shortly, the idea of a *public* writing, of speaking to the people and with the people in their struggle for a better world, – reached its full flowering during the early part of the Spanish [Civil] War." But he also says that it was now the programme began to collapse – "the real disintegration started before the War was over" – and the spirit of the Thirties changed into something else. History did this too. In March 1938 Hitler assumed the powers of War Minister, and marched into Austria; Mussolini won international support for his annexation of Abyssinia; Franco was beginning to triumph in Spain; in the Soviet Union that spring, Stalin's show trials revealed him as yet another totalitarian dictator. The troubled fantasies and prophecies that already filled poetry and fiction became actuality; dictators and generalissimos were taking charge; jackboots and strutting armies, street parades and saluting masses, rolling tanks and overflying bombers dominated not just imaginative fiction, as they already had, but European reality. In the autumn of 1938 Chamberlain went to Munich and won his famous piece of paper; German troops entered the Sudetenland. Right across Europe, air-raid shelters were dug, gas-masks issued, doors broken down; midnight arrests took place, books were burned – those of the German Nobel prizewinner Thomas Mann in his own country, as he joined the flight of displaced persons, persecuted races and literary exiles for the United States. "If I were asked," Lehmann writes, "I would say the first date in the disintegration [of the Thirties consensus] was the Munich agreement of September 1938, the second the final overthrow of the Spanish Republic in the following spring, and the third the outbreak of international war in September 1939, – or the Russo-German pact which preceded it." As he said later in his memoir *The Whispering Gallery* (1955), a hangover had set in, and now the best books were those that illuminated "not the cruelties of fascism and the perversions of fascist thinking, but the equally menacing ideals that fanatical left-wing idealism could lead to." The coming of war and new militarization completed the process. By the time Lehmann summed up the "new," it had already transmuted into something else: a reportage of battle, the struggle of shaving through the blitz, the fear of universal totalitarianism. Lehmann turned his eyes from Russia to America, as did a good number of Thirties writers. By early 1939 Auden and Isherwood had already joined the rising tide of European exiles departing Europe for the States, and their later work largely became a revisionist version, a fundamental rewriting, of their writing of the Thirties. It was not very long before the Thirties turned from an age of political progress to the "low dishonest decade."

This changing viewpoint can be read in the very form of the fiction of the period. The Thirties had begun with a hunger for historical realism. But, as J. A. Morris convincingly argues, the political and military developments of the later decade, and the gradual collapse of the Marxist argument for "proletarian realism," released many of the under-movements that were always apparent in the writing of the decade: satire, allegory, parable, fable and fantasy.[3] Modern history now seemed less a conflict of clearly defined ideological forces than a mass psychosis. The novels of Kafka were translated into English, by Edwin and Willa Muir, across the decade: *The Castle* in 1930, *The Trial* in 1937, *America* in 1938. In a world itself grown – the term found extensive employment – "Kafkaesque," Kafka seemed, of all the moderns, the most relevant, his strangely gothicized and psychological forms the most useful, his extreme inner exile the most telling of prophecies. "Balzac carried a cane on which was written the legend: I smash all obstacles," he had written in his diary: "my legend runs: every obstacle smashes me." He had expressed, ambiguously, a wish to suppress his books at his death in 1924. Now the suppression his executor Max Brod had refused was happening; his books were banned in Germany, then in his own Czechoslovakia, occupied in 1938, and he was one of the age's many silenced writers. By the decade's end his metaphysical fantasy of modern exposure and absurdity entered much new writing. 1938 saw the publication in Paris of Jean-Paul Sartre's novel *La Nausée* (*Nausea*), perhaps the first true work of modern existentialism ("The word remains on my lips; it refuses to go and rest upon the thing"), Samuel Beckett's work of philosophical absurdism *Murphy*, and Lawrence Durrell's surrealist *The Black Book*. Graham Greene published his most existential novel *Brighton Rock*, Rex Warner his surreal fantasy of persecution *The Professor*, Edward Upward his no less surreal fable of the bourgeois spirit *Journey to the Border*, Eric Ambler his thriller *Epitaph for a Spy*; and the year also saw Auden and Isherwood's play *On the Frontier* and Spender's *The Trial of a Judge*. 1939 brought not only war and the summative masterwork of the Modern move-

---

[3] J. A. Morris, *Writers and Politics in Modern Britain, 1880–1950* (London, 1977), which argues: "Indicative of the shift from commitment to an inward-looking, self-questioning debate on where man stood in society, in the world or even in the universe, is the variety of literary styles to appear in the late thirties . . . By the late 1930s and early 1940s generic terms such as allegory, satire, parody, fable, pastiche had become increasingly applicable."

ment, Joyce's *Finnegans Wake*, but Orwell's grim war prophecy *Coming Up for Air*, Isherwood's *Goodbye to Berlin*, and Henry Green's ironic fantasy *Party-Going* ("what targets – what targets for a bomb"). And in 1940, Arthur Koestler published his truly Kafkaesque novel of the modern Marxist state *Darkness at Noon*, intimately linking the world of inner and outer crisis ("when the two officials of the People's Commissariat of the Interior were hammering on Rubashov's door, in order to arrest him, Rubashov was just dreaming that he was being arrested").

When an earlier generation of writers confronted the coming of the Great War, some at least saw it as heroic on the one hand, or cleansing and futuristic on the other. The mood across Europe as the Second World War approached was quite different. In his autobiography *World Within World* (1951) Stephen Spender emphasizes the mood of emotional and aesthetic passivity, taking a telling note from his diary: "Peter Watson travelled from Paris to Calais a few days ago in a troop train. The compartment was crowded with soldiers. They sat all the way in absolute silence, no one saying a word." The passivity resembled the sense of an art swamped by events that had grown through the decade – in, for instance, the deliberately enfeebled, flatly observing, camera-eye of Isherwood's Berlin stories. For the age of historical enormity, journalism, reportage, the diary and the memoir seemed the only proper instruments; in fact they would occupy many of *Penguin New Writing*'s pages in the wartime years. The First World War provoked new vortices of artistic energy; the Second did not – perhaps because, as the poet Keith Douglas said, the same horrors cannot be written twice. A fiction long haunted by images of the barbed-wire frontier, the marauding raid, the aerial bombardment, the shattered factory, plastic false teeth, ersatz sausages, the food queue, the ration book, the gas-mask and fumbling Waste Land lusts – "the slogans, the enormous faces, the machine-guns spurting out of bedroom windows" that Orwell had foreseen in *Coming Up for Air* – turned into reported actuality, as the sirens sounded over London, the air-raids began, and soldiers went to war. All this was background to

219

Orwell's essay "Inside the Whale" (1940), written as War began, where he claimed that an age of totalitarianism had silenced writing, and shown "the impossibility of any major literature until the world has shaken itself into a new shape." Looking back across writing since the Great War, he observed three possible postures for the writer. One was Modernism, with its Twilight of the Gods feeling, which he found "reactionary"; another was the "committed" writing of the Thirties, which he challenged for its "orthodoxy-sniffing"; the third was quietism, the response of the writer who, imprisoned in the womb of history, trapped inside the whale, makes a passive, obscene, impotent protest, as the American writer Henry Miller, much admired by Orwell (who borrowed his jacket to go to Spain), had done. The age of liberalism was over, in the time of totalitarian dictatorships and the militarized state: "The literature of liberalism is coming to an end and the literature of totalitarianism has not yet appeared and is barely imaginable," he wrote: "As for the writer, he is sitting on a melting iceberg: he is merely an anachronism, a hangover from the bourgeois age, as surely doomed as the hippopotamus."

By one of the better fortunes of modern history, this was to prove excessive. Universal totalitarianism did not prevail, however much the grim modern century pointed toward it; and one of the first works of the post-war era was Orwell's own *Animal Farm* (1945), a satire on totalitarianism addressed to liberal readers. But the gloom he expressed was widespread. It had been encouraged by the murder of writers in Russia and Germany, the exiling of many more, the sudden deaths of yet others – including Yeats, Freud, Joyce and Virginia Woolf, now seen as some of the key figures of the Modern movement. "Periods end when we are not looking," wrote Cyril Connolly (who actually aimed to rescue the situation by bringing over a hundred writers and intellectuals from the USA) in his magazine *Horizon* in August 1941; "The last two years have been a turning point; an epidemic of dying has ended many movements." But it was not only Modernism that was reaching its dying fall. So was the political writing of the Thirties. Orwell was only early in renouncing Communism for patriotism. Committed writers were now exiling themselves from history, uncommitting their commitments; six of them famously announced their ideological withdrawal from the church of Marx in *The God That Failed* in 1949. Others fell silent, or audibly theorized about silence. Evelyn Waugh best caught the mood in *Work Suspended* (1941), a novel under way as war began he symbolically left unfinished – "all our lives, as we have constructed them, quietly came to an end," says the narrator; "Our story, like my novel, remained unfinished – a heap of neglected foolscap at the back of a drawer." But not all novels remained unfinished: a number of writers, including Graham Greene and Henry Green, Elizabeth Bowen and V. S. Pritchett, and indeed Orwell and Waugh, produced some of their best work in or around the war. The war and the blitz made Greene's seedy Greeneland seem entirely natural, and it reinforced the shattered fragility of Bowen's writing. New writers of war appeared, mostly in short fiction – Alun Lewis, Denton Welch, J. Maclaren-Ross. Nonetheless something seeped from writing as the war began, and in quite different ways from in 1914; the Forties is for good reason the least remembered literary decade. Like the historical Thirties themselves, the fictional Thirties ended in dismay, disorder, lost causes and weary apostasies. They soon became Auden's "low dishonest decade," Orwell's "scenic railway ending in a torture chamber," Leavis's "Marxizing decade," a decade effectively defeated by the history it had hoped to seize. And so strong was the general air of collapse that, when the task of the novel resumed in post-war conditions, it resembled the task of beginning all over again.

4.

The great break between Thirties fiction and post-war writing seems in retrospect a pity, for a good deal of important fiction, a good many important writers, emerged from the surprising variety of the anxious decade. It was no doubt the concern with history, society, and the public self that made the age one that appeared drably committed to reportorial realism; ironically enough, much of its best work is a deviation from that form. The realism that the Thirties writers and critics so often argued for was not, in fact, the middle-ground social and moral realism of George Eliot, nor even the sociological documentary of Zola and Gissing, or the progressive materialism of Bennett and Wells. It was shaped by a changed and more ideological brand of argument: the Marxist case for "proletarian writing" or "Proletcult," the sociological argument for "mass observation," or the journalistic argument for "reportage." The growth of a mass audience, the impact on the arts of the age of mechanical reproduction, the pressure of film, the weight of history and travel into history, all played their part. So, particularly, did the Marxist argument about the need for the bourgeois writer to accommodate to progress and the people after the false aesthetic adventure of Modernism. This was a fashionable opinion, to be found even among some former Modernists in the United States and elsewhere, and it was strongly put in several works of polemical criticism in Britain. So the Marxist critic Ralph Fox, himself a novelist, argued in his *The Novel and the People* (1937) that lack of the dialectical philosophy had led fiction off on a false trail; he advised writers to follow the practice of ancient tyrants who "mingled at night-time with their subjects, carefully disguised as common men," if they were to return to the "active life" of the age, and called for a new epic of the age of history. The no less Marxist Edward Upward argued in *The Mind in Chains* (1937) that the writer could no longer share the life of a bourgeois class that could not solve the problems confronting it, and only if he moved to the progressive side of the conflict "will it be possible for his writing to give a true picture of the world."[4] The "true picture" frequently meant a populist picture, or a proletarian picture; in

[4] Ralph Fox, *The Novel and the People* (London, 1937: reissued 1979); C. Day Lewis (ed.), *The Mind in Chains: Socialism and the Cultural Revolution* (London, 1937).

fact it more or less came to mean what the Hungarian Marxist critic George Lukacs would call "contemporary realism," or "the realism of the future," deriving from the alliance between the writer, the working class and the revolutionary objectivity of History, the great progressive machine that knew exactly what it was doing.[5]

And a significant body of "proletarian writing" – by no means all of it by proletarian writers – did appear, much of it in the earlier Thirties, when unemployment peaked and national and regional social problems predominated; one result of this was not just a new and bitter social and political documentary but a powerful strengthening of regional and industrial fiction. The vivid Scots novels of Lewis Grassic Gibbon (*A Scots Quair*, 1932–34) with their powerful vernacular voice, the Salford fiction of Walter Greenwood (*Love on the Dole*, 1933), the sea stories of James Hanley (*Boy*, 1931), the Durham mining stories of Sid Chaplin, the Derbyshire miner Walter Brierley's *Means Test Man* (1935) or the Welsh miner Lewis Jones' *Cymardy* (1937), are works that come closest to a serious working-class fiction, extending the tradition of *The Ragged-Trousered Philanthropists*. But a good deal else under the "proletarian" banner followed the propagandistic and melodramatic formulae – hard facts, gross and evil bosses, heroic workers – of what Arthur Koestler called "the pink novel," the work of "a period in which novels read like dispatches by war-correspondents from the fronts of the class struggle. The characters seemed to be flat, two-dimensional beings, fighting their shadow battles against a lurid background. People in the pink novel had a class-dimension (length), plus, say, a sex-dimension (width); the third, irrational

[5] George Lukacs, *The Meaning of Contemporary Realism* (1957: London, 1963). "A correct aesthetic understanding of social and historical reality is the precondition of realism . . .," he says: ". . . it may appear that critical and socialist realism are virtually indistinguishable. But in spite of the similarities, there are important qualitative differences. These derive from that hard-and-fast perspective of the future, that 'true consciousness,' which socialist realism by definition possesses . . . In no other aesthetic does truthful depiction of reality have so central a place as in Marxism."

dimension (depth) was missing or atrophied."[6] Another significant part of "working-class fiction" was the writing of bourgeois writers who, following Lawrence, frequently looked to working-class, or rural, men and women as the embodiment of vigour, libido or cultural alternative, as did writers as various as Malcolm Lowry and Christopher Isherwood, J. B. Priestley and H. E. Bates, Sylvia Townsend Warner and Mary Webb. (The great parody of the overlush darling buds of May-ness this sometimes produced was Stella Gibbons' *Cold Comfort Farm* [1932], an ironic juxtaposition of smart metropolitan Lambeth and the world of phallic shoots and something nasty in the woodshed.) Undoubtedly the writer who gave most sense and strength to the idea of honest social realism was George Orwell (one reason why his work had such an impact on the younger writers of the 1950s). He merged many of the fundamental period elements: the Naturalistic reportage of the working-class novel and a high awareness of that complex structural ladder in British society that is called "class"; experience of travel and that of hard descent into "ordinary" working life; the historical urgency and socialist polemic and the aesthetic concern of one fearful for the misuse of language; radical sympathies and a blunt John Bullish Englishness – all of this dramatized in the complex character of his invented self, "George Orwell." Good prose might be a window pane, as Orwell claimed, but he also knew that realism is never simply life observed, but something constructed, structured, argued, placed, to create its consensus about, to assemble its agreed working model of, "the real." His persuasive, elaborate, plainspeaking codes of resemblance were managed objects, but they constructed an effective renewal of the realist and descriptive tradition itself.

Generally, though, the realism the Thirties talked much of was not a realism of social report but a realism of history; and since history itself was surreal, absurd, nightmarish, and threatening, so too was much of the fiction. Hence what most good

---

[6] Arthur Koestler, "The Novelist's Temptations," in *The Yogi and the Commissar and Other Essays* (London, 1945).

fiction of the time betrays is an anxiously unstable relationship with realism, and it often turns into a formal or an emotional revolt against it. The pervasive unreality of the modern historical realities concerned most of the writers of the day. "As imagined thrillers, even as authentic revelation of the Chicago underworld or the international drug traffic serialized in the Sunday newspapers, the Moscow Trials might pass; but as part of the everyday lives of ordinary people, they were disconcerting," Malcolm Muggeridge observed in his impressionistic study *The Thirties* (1940). "The policeman on his beat, scrutinizing doorways, bundling along a drunk and incapable; the horseguards, spendid and immobile in Whitehall; Cabinet Ministers assembling in Downing Street . . . Was it possible that they too might become terrible and strange? In their ways, secret and bloodthirsty?" In the imagination of Thirties fiction, a great deal grew terrible and strange, became a kind of collective landscape – a "menacing dream-experience," Rosamund Lehmann called it – shared by writers left and right, materialist and religious. *It's a Battlefield*, Graham Greene titled one of his novels of seedy desolate London in 1934. The panorama of suburbia and decay Nina sees from the plane in Waugh's *Vile Bodies* (1930) – which closely resembles Auden's panorama of "Smokeless chimneys, damaged bridges, rotting wharves and choked canals" of "Get There If You Can," published in the same turn-of-decade year – was to turn into the typical Thirties fictional landscape. In Orwell's work, suburbia, spreading over England, becomes intricately linked with the disorders of elsewhere, "the things you tell yourself are just a nightmare or only happen in foreign countries." Engagement and disdain, commitment and detachment, become common codes: the daily world grew nearer, but also further away, a world of ersatz sausages, Bakelite ashtrays, cheap music, arterial roads, abandoned pitstocks, rusting machinery and decaying vicarages. In an age of the mass, crowds and mob motion fill many novels: gathering for strikes or protests, aimlessly watching a film or a parade. Human figures grew cheaper, bodies more vile: little Lord Tangent had already been disposed of, at a tangent, in two or three brief sentences of Waugh's *Decline and Fall*, but now sudden death and random violence became commonplace material, popular Gothic. So did ominous travels, journeys to world frontiers, dangerous quests, soldiers at checkpoints, threatening military machines, walls of barbed wire, the strange landscapes of Rex Warner's novels. Aeroplanes flew over with lethal or absurd cargoes, like the dog dropped from the air to explode on the rooftop terrace in Aldous Huxley's *Eyeless in Gaza* (1936). The world was littered with violence and casualties, from the wounded of the Great War or the clubbed strikers of Grassic Gibbon's *A Scot's Quair* to the many psychological victims of the age. For a sense not just of social crisis but psychic danger filled the novel. Most writers shared, it seemed, a guilty self-suppression, a sense of betraying or having betrayed. Psychology offered a solution, or if not a solution then an explanation, or a mythological accountancy, for the errant desires, the vulnerable passivities, the lack of moral focus, the unheroic selves of the day, and in some writers like Graham Greene seediness, lovelessness and betrayal became a metaphysical modern condition. Indeed one result of all this was a heightening of the metaphysics of fiction in the face of absurdity, Pascal's "endless territory of death." So realism merged with surrealism, objective reportage with subjective confession, to construct the style of the "new" fiction in what was inescapably a nightmare age, and it left the modern novel with an enduring legacy.

5.

If there really was a distinct Thirties fictional climate, which significantly shifted the direction of the new or modern novel, then one of the writers who most evidently embodied it was Christopher Isherwood, who, while still a student at Cambridge in the mid-Twenties, was – according to Spender – already presciently being considered "the Novelist" of his generation, just as his friend Auden at Oxford was being considered "the

Poet." At Cambridge Isherwood was to produce the most famous piece of unpublished fiction to come out of the period, the sequence of stories he wrote in collaboration with another friend, Edward Upward, called "Mortmere" (the matricidal implication is deliberate). Collaboration was another common concern of the Thirties, when individual voices wondered if they were enough; Isherwood would produce some of his most interesting work with Auden, using the common ground of Expressionist poetic drama. As Isherwood tells it in *Lions and Shadows*, the Mortmere tales were "a dream, a nightmare, about the English," set in an "anarchist paradise" which was "a private place of retreat from the rules and conventions of university life." The chief surviving fragment is Upward's "The Railway Accident" (finally published, after much private circulation, in his *The Railway Accident and Other Stories*, 1969), and it shows the intended spirit of surreal fantasy very clearly. This is fiction that reaches out of a failing bourgeois world to the gap in the pavement, the door in the wall, that would lead into an "other world" of fiction that could be superimposed on the real one. "Mortmere" already displays that distorted, half-psychological, half-political texture of prose that would become so familiar in the Thirties, when distinctive moral and existential domains (Greene's Greeneland) were so often laid over the almost familiar "real" world. It is also appropriate that "Mortmere" is an aborted, uncompleted work. So, in fact, were all Isherwood's early fictions, which, according to his own account, always came from something much larger – a massive unfinished project that history, or personal weakness, never allowed him to complete.

When he left Cambridge, Isherwood planned another large-scale project, an "immense novel" that would be called *The North-West Passage*. All that survives is the intention: it would be a large portrait of the post-war generation, seen from the standpoint of the "Truly Weak Man," the anti-hero making his indirect and deviant journey toward the America of life. If it remained unwritten, that was part of the point; the modern writer was indeed the Truly Weak Man, no longer in control of life. Nonetheless it was undoubtedly this that spawned his first two published novels, *All the Conspirators* (1928) and *The Memorial: A Portrait of a Family* (1932). Both return to many of the "Mortmere" themes, above all the struggle with the repressive mother and domestic and bourgeois life. In *All the Conspirators* the young would-be artist Philip Lindsay struggles against the conspiracy of the old with his new, distinctly neurotic, conspiracy of the new. The method now is not surreal but naturalistic, but various Modernist devices are also used; as Isherwood commented, "there were several 'thought-stream' passages in the fashionable neo-Joyce manner which yielded nothing, in obscurity, to the work of the master himself." Thirty-five years later, Isherwood, now in Hollywood, returned to his phase of his life and writing in the retrospective novel *Down There On a Visit* (1962), and targeted the key theme and flavour of both of these novels in defining his own character: "Perhaps his strongest negative emotion is ancestor hatred. He had vowed to disappoint, disgrace and disown his ancestors." The second, better, novel *The Memorial* treats the same de-monumentalizing theme with somewhat more sympathy. Isherwood confessed a debt to E. M. Forster, who dealt with large themes in terms of personal relations, and called this a "potted epic . . . disguised as a drawing room comedy." This is another novel of attempted escape from the monumentality of the past, an anti-war book in which all those left behind by the war become the modern wounded, "living on in a new world, unwanted, among enemies." The novel ends by following out Isherwood's own course, as its anti-hero escapes to the Berlin of the Weimar period. During the writing of the book Isherwood, on Auden's enthusiastic recommendation, made the same journey, which in the event was to prove a voyage toward his most fundamental material. For the land of homosexual freedom, sun worship, oiled male bodies and Weimar decadence, his natural destination, was also the place where contemporary history was unfolding. Isherwood remained in Berlin from 1929 to 1933; over that period Nazism rose, and Hitler became Germany's chancellor. A relationship could be forged between the figure through which he perceived himself, that of the weak and enfeebled modern writer, and the rising crisis of the age.

Another large project was planned, a novel called *The Lost*, which would deal with life in Weimar Berlin over the five years up to Hitler's coming to power. This too was never finished, but the shattered fragments from the larger idea would produce Isherwood's major work. Over the course of several years there emerged a network of novels and stories – *Mr Norris Changes Trains* (1935), *The Nowaks* (in *New Writing*, 1936), *Sally Bowles* (1937), *Goodbye to Berlin* (1939) – which were at last collectively presented as *The Berlin Stories* in 1946. They formed an essential narrative of the Thirties, though the main material belongs to the dying of the Weimar age, the Modernist decadence. Lehmann (who plainly thought the work brilliant, but felt it could do with ideological improvement) accounts for it in *New Writing in Europe* as a work whose "implication" is revolutionary, even though Isherwood disappointingly avoids dealing with "revolutionaries" and "almost invariably prefers, on the contrary, to take eccentric and fantastic characters as his central pivots, the extreme products of the anarchy and pathological condition of modern society." Yes indeed. Lehmann also uncomfortably admits that "one is forced to read the last few pages [of *Mr Norris* . . .] shaking with laughter. While this is a source of disappointment to one part of Mr Isherwood's public, I cannot help suspecting it is the secret of his popularity with the other." It is also, of course, the secret of success, but in the Thirties History was not to be laughed at, and historical satire not always an easily understood form. The point about all these stories is that they are rendered on a note of almost neurotic passivity, with a first-person, plainly autobiographical narrator variously rendered as "William Bradshaw" and "Herr Issyvoo," who describes himself as "a half-hearted renegade from my own class, my feeling muddled by anarchism talked at Cambridge, by slogans from the confirmation service, by the tunes the band played when father's regiment marched to the railway station, seventeen years ago." He is ostensibly the reporter, or, more passively still, "a camera." "I am a camera with its shutter open, quite passive, recording, not thinking," he notes in *Goodbye to Berlin*. "Recording the man shaving at the window opposite and the woman with the kimono washing her hair. Some day all this will have to be developed, carefully printed, fixed." Meanwhile, though, it stays, as intended, provisional, immediate, almost improvised. As the German critic Walter Benjamin wrote in his *Small History of Photography* in 1931: "'In our age there is no work of art that is looked at so closely as a photograph of oneself, one's closest relatives and friends, one's sweetheart,' wrote Lichtwark back in 1907, thereby moving the inquiry out of the realm of aesthetic distinctions and into social functions. Only now this vantage point can be carried further." Isherwood, we can say, does.[7] The camera, of course, does not simply record; it is an object from the age of mechanical reproduction, challenging the authority of art by its instantaneous collusion with its subject. It has lenses, angles, shutter speeds; it quotes from reality, renders life as instant; it snaps, magnifies, distorts, frames and excludes, creating, here, a variety of mixed and almost random images from an age of surreal absurdity, when life is already reportage and will soon be history. So beyond the woman in the kimono and the man shaving, or the English nightclub whore Sally Bowles, the fastidious British adventurer Mr Norris, with his wigs and whips, the wandering expatriates seeking decadence, the gay young men seeking the sun, the Nowaks and the Lindauers, are the racial tensions, the rising hatreds, the glimpse of the baton

[7] It was as if Isherwood was deliberately reflecting the condition examined by Walter Benjamin in his famous essay "The Work of Art in the Age of Mechanical Reproduction" (1936: reprinted in *Illuminations* [London, 1970]): ". . .that which withers in the age of mechanical reproduction is the aura of the work of art. This is a symptomatic process whose significance points beyond the realm of art . . . Unmistakably, reproduction as offered by picture magazines or newsreels differs from the image seen by the unarmed eye. Uniqueness and permanence are as closely linked in the latter as are transitoriness and reproducibility in the former." He later adds that mankind's self-alienation "has reached such a degree that it can experience its own destruction as an aesthetic pleasure of the first order. This is the situation of politics which Fascism is rendering aesthetic. Communism responds by politicizing art."

and the concentration camp; a nightmare evolution from reality to decadence to violence is unfolding.

"Youth always demands its nightmares," Isherwood noted in 1939, ". . . Germany supplied them." Without any artistic formality history suddenly enters the passively visual narrative. "Berlin was in a state of civil war," we suddenly learn in *Mr Norris* . . . "Hate exploded suddenly, without warning, out of nowhere; at street corners, in restaurants, cinemas, dance-halls, swimming-baths; at midnight, after breakfast, in the middle of the afternoon. Knives were whipped out, blows were dealt with spiked rings, beer-mugs, chair-legs or leaded clubs; bullets slashed the advertisements on the poster-columns . . . Frl. Schroeder's astrologer foretold the end of the world." By the end Hitler is in power, Mr Norris has become that primal figure of the age, the double agent, daily life goes on in its usual daily snapshots in the cafés – and Herr Issyvoo, "smiling," is ready to leave, his last photographs taken and ready to be developed. What makes these Berlin tales remarkable is not only the radical historical moment they capture through fragments, a moment which entered the English imagination as the sign of the way the world was moving, and provided the landscape of nightmares to come. It is also their frank aesthetic passivity, which emerges as an apparently flat reportage rendered to us by a narrator whose very passivity is a product of the way history is affecting artistic consciousness. They mark Isherwood's move out of an interest in Modernist mannerism to an endeavour in what came to be "reportage," but was also an experiment in self-cancelling autobiography set in history, the writing of a time when, Isherwood said, "everyone must be his own guinea-pig." They also made him a writer peculiarly dependent on the history to which he might bear witness, and when he moved to peculiarly historyless California in 1939, his subject largely died. Walter Allen once called Isherwood the great disappointment of the modern novel. But this is not because of the half-aborted tales he produced in the Twenties and Thirties; it was because his later life never allowed him the same peculiar intimacy between historical crisis and the neurotically conceived artistic self. Isherwood remained a camera: his next book, *Prater Violet* (1945), deals with an *émigré* European film-maker, and the making of a film, a story of the moving picture; he himself became an important Hollywood screen-writer. But the later fiction is work essentially of personal narrative rather than historical diagnosis. *The World in the Evening* (1954) deals with what is really sexual boredom in the Cold-War, comfortably alienating USA. *Down There on a Visit* (1962) returns him to his old life in the 1920s and 1930s, but acknowledges his role as essentially that of the tourist in history. *A Single Man* (1964), a work of vivid present-tense neurosis, is a tale of a historyless America and the portrait of a single man who cannot build a full identity and has chosen not to mature. Isherwood, as he knew himself, stayed eternally a novelist of the Thirties, a novelist whose work was focused and historicized by a decade.

The same is true of Edward Upward, the "Chalmers" of *Lions and Shadows* and the collaborator on "Mortmere." The first of the Auden group to join the Communist Party, he published various important short stories and worked slowly on his novel *Journey to the Border*, which appeared in 1938. This is another work from the nightmare world, showing the influence of "Mortmere," the story of a neurotic young tutor, working for a rich British family, who finds the familiar social world distorted to the point of surreal extremity. But, though Upward feels obliged finally to justify his point in *The Mind in Chains* that neurosis might disappear if one took the standpoint of the workers, the book's essential theme is not political but psy-choanalytical, indeed neurotic. The "border" was the final place of Thirties fiction (and Auden and Isherwood published their related play *On the Frontier* in the same year), the bridge not simply between self and history but between identity and neurosis, reality and unreality; it is the margin of consciousness itself. The force of the book lies in the (Kafkaesque) way the worlds within and without erode each other, and the border tested is that of fictional realism itself. Upward, still Marxist, returned to fiction in the 1960s, with the novels about the

historically struggling poet Alan Sebrill that form the trilogy
"The Spiral Ascent" (*In the Thirties*, 1962; *The Rotten Elements*,
1969; *No Home But the Struggle*, 1977). It is a serious yet finally
laboured work of modern realism, recording Sebrill's sequence
of battles to balance art and Party membership through the
political and emotional vagaries of the Thirties, wartime and
the Cold War years. But this time the subject failed to yield a
strong imaginative form of expression, unlike Doris Lessing's
The Golden Notebook, one of the most notable of post-war novels,
and a work in which the struggles of art, Marxist politics,
sexuality and consciousness generate a radical literary form –
which happened to appear in the same year as Upward's first
volume, and showed the stylistic transition from age to age.

6.

Journey to the Border, though, remains one of the key works of the
psycho-political allegory that fascinated the later Thirties,
when, in fact, the novel was moving away from and not toward
what Upward called "the true picture." For, as Irving Howe
has said, from the Russian Revolution to the end of the Thirties,
the political novel had passed from being a work of revolutionary excitement, Utopian possibility and proletarian promise to
a work of psychosis, terror and victimization, following a dark
descent, "an increasingly precipitous fall into despair."[8] An
important indication of this is the fiction of Rex Warner, the
poet and classicist who, as the decade closed, wrote three
powerful allegorical novels, *The Wild Goose Chase* (1937), *The
Professor* (1938) and *The Aerodrome* (1941), which expressionistically explored the rising power of the masses and the machine,
of modern totalitarianism and tyranny. These are political
novels in more than a proletarian, and certainly more than a
British, sense, dealing with the ideas, the powers and the

[8] Irving Howe, *Politics and the Novel* (New York, 1957; London, 1961), a work that
follows the course of the political novel on a European scale.

political structures of an age of European tragedy; "I do not aim at realism," Warner observed. *The Wild Goose Chase* is a "fable" of ethical and existential quest, filled with strong scenes, flavoured with the spirit of Marx and Freud, influenced by Kafka. *The Professor*, the most notable of these works, is set in an imaginary Eastern European country threatened by its neighbours and Fascist forces within (the situation closely resembles that in the Czechoslovakia of the day), and which is another borderland, a dream world of terrible actuality, where moral and political drama is set against inexorable and hideous fact. The central character, Professor A., is a world-famous scholar who believes in the Greek *polis*, the liberal democratic state which can summon the high values of civilization to resist the barbarian at the gates. But it, and he, are about to be overthrown, as he is summoned to take leading political office. It is a fable of his defeat as "metal was to be proved harder than his flesh, stupidity and fanaticism more influential than his gentlest syllogisms"; the age of force beyond civilization prevails. *The Aerodrome* was written in wartime, and allegorically shows the corruption of War. Militaristic Fascism from the nearby aerodrome overlays the seemingly familiar world of the British village; images of nature yield to those of the machine, man yields to metal, honour yields to power, love to cold political reason. At the same time this is a story of domestic crimes and tragedies, drawing on the structures of Greek tragedy as well as those of the Expressionist drama of the day. But these novels are also contemporary political fables, in that they are about the modern *polis*, the state that threatens human reason and life's complexity with violence, terror and power.

Of similar power and importance are Arthur Koestler's *The Gladiators* (1939), *Darkness at Noon* (1940) and *Arrival and Departure* (1943), three political novels by a Hungarian-born journalist and former member of the German Communist Party who had been imprisoned in both Spain and France before he escaped to Britain in 1941. Koestler described his fiction as being about whether a noble End justifies the use of ignoble Means, and about the relentless logic in both Marxism and

234

Fascism which ensures that its own intellectual leaders are sacrificed "in the death camps of Utopia." *Darkness at Noon*, the most notable of them, written first in German, tells the story of the Bolshevik Rubashov, who confesses to crimes he has not committed in Stalin's totalitarian state. In a world where victims collude with executors in the belief that "Everyone with a goal in front is forced to its baleful track," Rubashov no longer knows whether he is in an actual history or an eternal nightmare, and he is finally brought to the point, under questioning, where nightmare and reality actually merge and he becomes capable of Doublethink. This is a psychological as well as an ideological tale, but also a vividly precise, historically exact political story about the lies, slogans, betrayals, imprisonments, interrogations, tortures, psychological deceptions, false confessions and executions that had become the standard weapons of the totalitarian state, as well as about the "grammatical fiction" of modern ideology, which destroys the I in the We. Here we see the modern political novel acquiring a terrible new meaning, as the intellectual life corrupts itself, and revolutionary politics become not a matter of hope but of moral despair. George Orwell, in a notable essay on Koestler, indicated his importance: "One development of the last ten years has been the appearance of the 'political book,' a sort of enlarged pamphlet combining history with political criticism, as an important literary form," he said, adding that its most remarkable writers had been European "renegades from one or another extremist party, who have seen totalitarianism at close quarters and known the meaning of exile and persecution." And he noted the difference between Koestler and other Left-wing writers, who "have always wanted to be anti-Fascist without being anti-totalitarian."

There is no doubt that Koestler's work in turn influenced Orwell's late fiction, the two anti-Utopian political satires *Animal Farm* (1945) and *Nineteen Eighty-Four* (1949), which are likewise stories of the harsh, recognizable realities of totalitarian states, and their horrifying promise of a post-humanist future in which the jackboot comes down on the human face forever.

The link between the two writers was, personally and artistically, close, though Orwell was as patriotic as he was socialist, as deeply English as Koestler was European. But Orwell's writing and ideas were interwoven by a European and internationalist view of history and politics, to a degree surely unusual in British fiction. "What I have most wanted to do throughout the past ten years is to make political writing into an art," he explained in 1946. "My starting point is always a feeling of partisanship, a sense of injustice." He wrote, he said, "because there are some lies I want to expose, some fact to which I want to draw attention" – though he did add that the work must be "also an aesthetic experience." "So long as I remain alive and well I shall continue to feel strongly about prose style, to love the surface of the earth, and to take pleasure in solid objects and scraps of useful information," he also observed: "The job is to reconcile my ingrained likes and dislikes with the essential public, non-individual activities that this age forces on all of us." The result of all this is a complicated balancing of a fictional tradition bred from the "Condition of England" novel and the work of the Naturalists – he admired Gissing and Kipling, Wells, Bennett and Galsworthy – with a fiction of political experience and intellect: a kind of novel which is often highly traditional, but which could, and would, leave realism behind and move toward moral and anti-Utopian satire. Orwell saw himself not as primarily a novelist but a political writer, a writer of engrained Englishness who has rebelled against Britain as "a family with the wrong members in control," and a social history he felt the moral need to change. Born Eric Blair in British India in 1903, the son of a colonial official, and so belonging, as he explained it with his familiar precision, to the "lower upper middle class," he was returned to England for his schooling. At prep school, then as a scholarship boy at Eton, he acquired, he said, much of the snobbery of his class, but also a sense of social displacement and loneliness that marked him after, politically, emotionally, stylistically. In 1921 he went to Burma as a colonial policeman, and was divided again, "stuck between my hatred of the Empire

I served and my rage against the evil-spirited little bastards
who tried to make my job impossible." He came back in 1927
to a Britain in the aftermath of the general strike, and determined to fulfil his ambition to be a writer. A period of economic
deprivation and vagrancy followed in which he worked in Paris
hotels and tried to survive in the London of the Depression, all
this recorded in the neo-documentary *Down and Out in Paris and
London* (1933). With this he became no longer Eric Blair but
"George Orwell," a name he took partly to spare his family,
but also as a badge of escape and rebellion ("the only thing to
do in the world of twentieth-century barbarism was to rebel").

His first novel *Burmese Days* (1934) returned to his experience
in Burma, and his anti-hero Flory is significantly scarred with
an ugly birthmark, signifying his own anxious curse of birth
and class and his "outcast" state. He published three more
novels over the decade, *A Clergyman's Daughter* (1935), *Keep the
Aspidistra Flying* (1936) and *Coming up for Air* (1939) – novels of
considerable but not the highest quality, in part because their
purpose is sometimes too plainly instrumental. But with them
are interwoven two crucial non-fiction books: *The Road to Wigan
Pier* (1937), a journey into the working-class Condition of
England which is also a work of intense self-analysis, and
Homage to Catalonia (1938), his remarkable account of his
experiences in Spain with the POUM forces during the Civil
War (in which he was almost fatally wounded) and from which
he returned in disillusion both with Communist tactics and the
attitude of the British left-wing intellectuals – the "orthodoxy-
sniffers" – who had supported them. It was as much from such
works, and his critical and political essays, as from fiction that
there came the rigorous, spiky, critical, collective identity that
was Orwell. He had been down and out in Paris and London,
followed the road to Wigan Pier, fought in Spain, made his
political homage to Catalonia. He had modulated the old
Etonian Eric Blair into the plainer George Orwell, and made
himself a central and deeply immersed recorder of the economic,
social, political and historical problems of the age. Half in
resistance to aestheticized writing, he had perfected his famous

plain style, the no-nonsense manner that united the British common sense and decency with the revolutionary propagandist so easily that his voice sounded as if it were the truth frankly declaring itself. He had known poverty and pain, challenged imperialism and capitalism, tried several forms of social identi- fication, and come to speak not only for the unemployed and deprived of Depression Britain but for the new half-life of Thirties British suburbia, with all its respectable constraints and limitations. He had come to a radical, vivid, often deeply idiosyncratic yet loving reading of his culture in its contradic- tion and variety, while seeing that culture in a world-historical frame as part of an ongoing and universal crisis. Out of this he had come to devise both a form of writing and a form of politics, a sometimes strange, frequently volatile mixture of radical socialism and intimate identification with lasting British decen- cies, a liking and loathing. His realistic writing is experienced and plain ("good prose is like a window pane") and he believed in the task of telling the historical truth against the orthodoxy- makers. His pursuit of a critical social representation – he saw a "death of society," a Britain ruined by class, poverty, sterility and unemployment, where what had collapsed was not just an economic but a cultural structure – never lost sight of the dense experience of British life, of which he was a compelling reporter. Glimpses of that life at its best are to be seen: in rural life, in the traditional working-class home, in comic seaside postcards, in the "Great Peace" of Edwardian society, all now subject to inexorable erosion and decay. Present realities are judged from a double perspective: one that of the historical past, which sees current reality in the light of historical continuity or disconti- nuity, the other that of the political future, which turns the real into instant history, a quickly passing and apocalyptic world.

Orwell's Thirties novels are works of rebellion, against class limitation, money-centred capitalism, and the sterile erosion of British culture itself, portraits of a dying society, a failing nation, in which social detail and milieu, rather than the fortunes of the protagonist, finally dominate. *Keep the Aspidistra*

Flying is a story of a would-be rebel, Gordon Comstock, a character who prefigures some of the angry rebels of fiction twenty years later. He has ambitions to be a poet, but above all is in revolt against society, advertising, and that flag of British lower-class respectability, the aspidistra in the window, as well as against "the futility, the bloodiness, the deathliness of modern life." He takes a downward path ("He wanted to go down, deep down, into some world where decency no longer mattered; to cut the strings of his self-respect; to submerge himself, to sink") which is also a willing self-degradation. "The sense of disintegration, of decay, that is endemic in our time, was strong on him," and he reads in his fellow human beings "The great death-wish of the modern world. Suicide pacts. Heads stuck in gas-ovens in lonely maisonettes. French letters and Amen Pills. And the reverberations of future wars." The rebellion is incomplete, and like many of his successors in fiction he becomes a creator of the advertising slogans he has despised ("It was what, in his secret heart, he had desired"). In *Coming Up for Air* (1939), told in the first person in a grainy and even comic vernacular, the horrors underlying the social surface have come even closer, the angry disgust and violence are yet plainer: "Everything's streamlined these days, even the bullet Hitler's keeping for you." Orwell warningly wrote it when he knew war was coming, and the book mingles this apocalyptic knowledge with images from an idyllic Edwardian Thames Valley childhood which cannot be recreated, and a few glimpses of hope in the common decencies of ordinary people. It was written close to the essay "Inside the Whale," where he was already developing his "totalitarian hypothesis" that the two oligarchies of Communism and Fascism would come together, and that the writer was being returned to a grim passivity, trying to write amid the ruins. Nonetheless just after war started he began to incubate a large English family saga, to be called either *The Lion and the Unicorn* or *The Quick and the Dead* – which, like so many books of the time, was never written.

What was written instead during wartime was *Animal Farm: A Fairy Story*, though it did not appear until 1945. He had conceived the original idea in 1937 in Spain, and he wrote it over a period of three months in late 1943 and early 1944, at a time when the Russians were beginning to throw off the German advance, when Churchill, Roosevelt and Stalin met in Teheran to plan the Nazi overthrow, and Stalin stood high in British popular esteem. The book is a plain allegory of the betrayal of the Russian Revolution by Stalin and his cohorts, of the treacherous treatment of Trotsky, the purges and Show Trials, and the exploitation of the populace for party survival and advantage. Publishers whether left or right were unwilling to publish; T. S. Eliot at Faber acknowledged the book's Swiftian power, but said that the house did not believe that "this is the right point of view from which to criticize the political situation at the present time." These infuriating delays and obstructions in fact favoured the book, which appeared as the war closed, so that instead of dramatizing the recriminations of the Thirties it captured the atmosphere of liberal crisis and the new fear of continued totalitarianism that outlasted the conflict. "*Animal Farm* is the first book in which I tried, with full consciousness of what I was doing, to fuse political purpose and artistic purpose into one whole," Orwell said; and now a work that in wartime might have been read solely as political polemic could be seen as something more. It carried forward, as few political works from the Thirties did, the moral as well as political energy that could be salvaged from the Thirties; it also attacked some of its darker illusions. It united satirical and political rage with the vivid near-timelessness of mythic writing, helped in this by the old satiric form of the animal fable. It expressed itself less as political venom than moral vitality. It took the official versions and authorized texts of modern ideology and subjected them to ultimate scepticism; oppressive fictions become the fictions they are, set against "human" (here animal) decency. Orwell held on to his socialist hope in a revolution that could truly transform society; but the book was essentially a liberal text, about the need to raise people over systems, ordinariness against power, decency against historical inevitability, scepticism against authority, prose against propaganda. And the publication of

Nineteen Eighty-Four (1949) reinforced the point that Orwell's later fiction was not simply a warning against Stalin, but about the corruptions of power, the weaponry of propaganda, the structure of terror, the nature of authoritarianism, the use of scapegoats and victims, and the defeat of language itself. These books may have been the last novels of the Thirties; but they also became in effect the first British post-war novels, a fundamental line of continuity between the fiction of the Thirties and the writing of a post-Holocaust future.

7.

Even so, it was as well for the fortunes of modern British fiction that not every writer set out to accept bourgeois guilt, see history through the eyes of the workers, or provide Upward's "true picture of the world." One of the most notable writers of the age was Evelyn Waugh, a writer never considered distinguished for his political virtue, finally a lasting goad to the Left. Waugh, to my view, was a major modern writer, though in a quite different way from Joyce, with his intricate new discourse, or Woolf, with her complex vision of consciousness. His power lay in a pure vision of comedy so complete that it became a compelling modern style, a style that seemed to spring fully-grown from the early fiction and served him well until the 1960s. Comedy is more than a mode of amusement; it is a vision of life in both its romantic possibility and its darkness and grim absurdity. It is a high self-consciousness of style, of the play of form and language, and Waugh constructed it in its mode of modern satire, through which the compulsive claim of history itself can be challenged through a mixture of anarchistic delight in ephemeral follies and sheer indifference to externally imposed fictional and ideological orders. In later life he chose to dramatize this by inhabiting the mask of testy colonel which he analyses (and mocks) so well in *The Ordeal of Gilbert Pinfold* (1957). Pinfold is the man who presents himself to others as infuriated by all that has happened in his own lifetime ("His strongest tastes were negative. He abhorred plastics, Picasso, sunbathing and jazz – everything that had happened in his own lifetime . . . There was a phrase in the 30s: 'It is later than you think,' which was designed to cause uneasiness. It was never later than Mr Pinfold thought"). Yet to begin with Waugh was a modernist stylist, who at Oxford in 1922 had been greatly taken by the vogue for literary experiment, was concerned with the transition out of Victorian form, and wrote an admirable book on Dante Gabriel Rossetti on that theme. There is a clear influence of Hemingway on his early work, while his essay on Firbank is an analysis of the modern method of narrative, noting how his books are "almost wholly devoid of any attributions of cause to effect; there is the barest minimum of direct description; his compositions are built up, intricately and with a balanced alternation of the wildest extravagance and the most austere economy." Both writers taught Waugh the modern value of stylized dialogue, descriptive economy, and cinematic pace. Waugh's novels are, needless to say, a radical critique of the age about which he wrote; they also contain a dense social history of the period from the early 1920s to the age of the post-war Welfare State. Indeed they embody the climate and discomfort of the times as deeply as do Isherwood's or Orwell's. But in them what is plainly a dark moral vision converts into a delighted comic anarchy; if the age has condemned itself to barbarism, the barbaric age deserves a vision of itself in which comic outrage is a norm.

Reviewing *Vile Bodies* (1930), Waugh's first novel of the Thirties, Rebecca West identified its highly radical technique. It was, she said, "a further stage in the contemporary literature of disillusionment"; its narrative method, conducted largely through tight, monosyllabic dialogue, did "something as technically astonishing as the dialogues in Mr Ernest Hemingway's *A Farewell to Arms*, so cunningly does he persuade the barest formula to carry a weight of intense emotion." The debt to Hemingway's *In Our Time* and *The Sun Also Rises* is clear, not only because of the hard new dialogue but for the lost-generation subject-matter, though here the situation is played less as modern tragedy than absurdist comedy. The Bright Young Things are (as usual) in rebellion against their elders, convention, and the older world of "Anchorage House," a revolt of the "amusing" against the "bogus" which is, as one critic puts it, "not experimental, but fashionable," part of "a revolution of manners, stabilized, popularized, flattened out." There is also, as the slightly sinister Jesuit priest Father Rothschild explains, "a radical instability in our whole world order," though also "a fatal hunger for permanence." The novel begins on a cross-channel ferry with all the main characters suffering, "unhappy about the weather" ("to avert the terrors of seasickness they indulged in every kind of civilized witchcraft, but they were lacking in faith"), and ends with a fantastic World War between unnamed powers, "the biggest battlefield in the history of the world." Salvation of various kinds is on offer: there is Father Rothschild's Catholicism; the evangelism of Mrs Melrose Ape (based on Aimée Semple Macpherson) and her tattered choir of angels; Shepheard's Hotel in Dover Street where, "parched with modernity," the Bright Young Things can go and "draw up, cool and uncontaminated, great healing draughts from the well of Edwardian certainty." Meanwhile they seek satisfaction in action and fun, the endless round of parties (Agatha Runcible "heard someone say something about an Independent Labour Party and was furious that she had not been asked"), travel, speed ("faster, faster"), sexual carelessness and "vile bodies" ("Masked parties, Savage parties, Victorian parties . . . dull dances in London and comic dances in Scotland and disgusting dances in Paris – all that succession and repetition of massed humanity . . . Those vile bodies. . ."). Civilization is running rapidly off the rails; politics are surrealistically in chaos (they were), Prime Ministers keep changing (they did), and, as the hero Adam Fenwyck-Symes murmurs, "things can't go on much longer" (they didn't). Waugh implies, but does not state, his deep disenchantment with the smart, metropolitan, cynical world where "certainty," "permanence," "faith" and "honourable people" are all set in the past. But he identifies with the comic follies of the present, and the comic spirit of the book is, it has been said, a "joyfully insolent defiance of reason and right."

Waugh's novels always give us a detailed social history of their period of writing, and in the next book, *Black Mischief* (1932), the Bright Young Things are already changing ("Everyone's getting poorer and it's making them duller"), the barbarism of the world increasing. The novel is chiefly set in "Azania" (based on Abyssinia, which Waugh had recently visited, writing a travel book), one of the modern borderlands that fascinated the Thirties imagination. Here Basil Seal, the book's insolent and amoral hero, a natural survivor, meets the Emperor Seth – Chief of Chiefs of the Sakuyu, Lord of Wanda and Tyrant of the Seas, Bachelor of the Arts of Oxford University – who, trying to shake off the jungle that surrounds him, believes in Western Progress: "I have been to Europe . . . I have read modern books – Shaw, Arlen, Priestley . . . at my stirrups run woman's suffrage, vaccination, and vivisection. I am the New Age. I am the Future." It need hardly be said that progress brings nothing but trouble. "I think I've had enough of barbarism for a bit," Basil admits at the end, after he has inadvertently eaten his fiancée at a cannibal feast ("I'd like to eat you," he has unwisely said to the ill-named Prudence), and seen the death of Seth; but progress offers no better. "The story deals with the conflict of civilization, with all its attendant and deplorable ills, and barbarism," Waugh wrote in a letter of explanation to the Catholic Church he had now joined; "the plan of my book throughout was to keep the darker aspects of barbarism continually and unobtrusively present, a black and mischievous background against which the civilized and semi-civilized characters performed their parts; I wished it to be like the continuous, remote throbbing of hand drums, constantly audible, never visible . . ." At the end Sonia Trumpington complains "I've got a tiny fear that Basil is going to turn serious on us too"; and this now increasingly applied to Waugh himself. And, though he explained in his next travel book *Ninety-Two Days* (1934) that he had become interested in "distant and barbarous places, and particularly in the borderlands of conflicting cultures and states of development, where ideas, uprooted from their traditions, become oddly changed in transplantation," it is clear that the border was closer to home.

That is apparent in his next novel, *A Handful of Dust* (1934), which Waugh thought his best; it is. It takes its title from "The Waste Land" ("I have seen fear in a handful of dust") and is a modern Gothic comi-tragedy. The shape of the fable is clear. The aptly named hero Tony Last is in every way the last of his line. He loses his son and heir in a hunting accident, his wife by divorce, his loved ancestral home by deception, and ends his search for the ideal city in the South American jungle endlessly reading Dickens to the mad, and ominously named, Mr Todd. The agents of destruction, mother and son, are called the Beavers, who administer the new world, taking a commission on everything, preying on the misfortunes and boredoms of Society. Society itself has new fads: osteopathy, reducing diets, fortune-telling and maisonette flats are the vogue. Hetton, the house Tony loves, is itself no ancestral mansion, but a Victorian pile rebuilt in 1864 ("I'd blow it sky-high," says one observer), and he is no aristocrat, though his wife Brenda is. But she is seen by her London friends as "the imprisoned princess in a fairy story," and takes John Beaver as her lover. Hetton and everything Tony associates with it – Victorian architecture, Victorian marriage, the Victorian nursery – have no value in the age of chrome plating and easy adultery, and are fated to be lost: "hard cheese for Tony," but "nobody's fault." Barbarism, indifference and the rule of the jungle prevail, and Tony is subjected to an ever-accelerating cycle of horrors: "for a month now he had lived in a world suddenly bereft of order; it was as though the whole reasonable and decent constitution of things, the sum of all he had experienced or learned to expect, were an inconspicuous, inconsiderable object mislaid somewhere on a dressing table; no outrageous circumstance in which he found himself, no new, mad thing brought to his notice, could add a jot to the all-encompassing chaos that shrieked about his ears." The book, for all its grim and Gothic material, remains wonderfully funny, but it establishes a new sympathy for its protagonist and indeed for Brenda; suffering is now implicated in absurdity. Its fable is condemnation of the moral chaos of the world; the book, Waugh said, dealt "entirely with behaviour. It was humanist and contained all I had to say about humanism" – presumably that human nature is beyond the explanation of the humanist, that it led to egotism and the endless vanity of human wishes, the deception of secular dreams. But what was tragic to the moralist was still rewarding to the comic writer; the mixture of these two things makes it Waugh's most subtle book.

With his next work of fiction, *Scoop: A Novel About Journalists* (1938), Waugh left behind this intricate structure and returned to high farce. A satire on the modern press and exotic press travel to foreign wars, it remains one of the best novels on the modern media ever written. The book's action takes place in a world of dangerous international politics, finance and intrigue, all seen through the eyes of one of his most innocent and Candide-like heroes, William Boot, a writer of small newspaper pieces about nature ("Feather-footed through the plashy fen passes the questing vole . . .") who lives in a world of "change and decay." Boot is sent by error to cover the war in Ishmaelia (Abyssinia again, but now changed in meaning by the Italian occupation), and, like his precursor Paul Pennyfeather, he undergoes a fantastic series of adventures, visits "lush places," falls in love, meets pure evil, and finally gladly returns to the place of change and decay where it all began. But Waugh was no longer satisfied by satire; no longer a bright young thing attracted to modernity, he craved to write a more intimately serious book. He intended the book that was eventually published as *Work Suspended* (1941) to mark the end of his youth, and of an era; it did, far more dramatically than he suspected. The story is set in what proved to be the last days of peace, in a London of vanishing houses, rising flats, crude commercial travellers and communist fellow-travellers. The story, very close to autobiography, is told by Waugh's first first-person narrator, John Plant, a writer of detective stories, and deals with intimate things: the death of a father, falling in love, the birth of a child

("To write of someone loved, of oneself loving, above all of oneself being loved – how can these things be done with propriety? How can they be done at all?") It is about altering social and artistic conditions, about a man who is robbed of an ordered life because he is deprived of the things that make it possible; it expresses a direct dismay with the world. In the event war prevented the completion of the book, and this is another of the aborted works of the age. Plant adds his postcript, explaining that the new life he had sought was given him "not by my contrivance . . . all our lives, as we had constructed them, quietly came to an end. Our story, like my novel, remained unfinished – a heap of neglected manuscript at the back of a drawer."

In fact it took two more books to complete this phase of Waugh's work. He dealt with the Phoney War period in *Put Out More Flags* (1942), a satire where the Bright Young Things, now ageing and growing responsible, make their peace with war. Then he grasped at the entire period of the *entre deux guerres* in *Brideshead Revisited: The Sacred and Profane Memoirs of Captain Charles Ryder* (1945). The book, which is hardly comic, was partly written on war service in Yugoslavia, and shows a gluttonous appetite for the past ("I piled it on rather," he admitted) and for the glories of Oxford and British country-house life. It is also his first explicitly Catholic novel. But it is also something else: a complex social and moral history of an entire period which runs from youthful hope and artistic promise through decline to death, from Arcadia to that of which Arcadia reminds us, the *memento mori*. The social history covers the General Strike, the disorders of the Thirties, the rise of the press barons making politics and war, the ascent of the common man. It is a story of people falling apart "into separate worlds, little spinning planets of personal relationships," of an era when "man had deserted his post and the jungle was creeping back into its old strongholds," of the nomadic, aesthetic, decadent and dandified life of art and the yearning for social and religious security. Charles Ryder, who tells the story, and who Waugh stressed was not himself ("I am not I"), is ultimately used by a higher plotter for higher ends. The central image is of the great baroque house Brideshead, with its small chapel. Waugh by now plainly thought that what was already there in England was better than anything that reform or revolution could bring to it, and the book is suffused with historical nostalgia. But Brideshead is an image not solely of English aristocratic life but Arcadia itself, the paradisal, innocent world of beatific vision, which does not however yield grace. The house and its meanings end up, as most meanings in Waugh do, in another, chaotic, wartime world, as an army camp with a lunatic asylum at its gates, "quite remote from anything the builders had intended," but still an indirect, ambiguous symbol of an essence. If *A Handful of Dust* is Waugh's finest, most completed novel of the period, *Brideshead Revisited* is the great social recapitulation, clearing the ground for Waugh's embittered encounter with the post-war world to follow.

8.

If Waugh seemed to spring fully-fledged as a writer with a style, Graham Greene seemed to spring fully-fledged as a writer with a subject, a vision, a world of his own so distinctive that it came to be called Greeneland ("that last-chance waterfront where the vultures clatter down like thunder from heaven on the tin roof beneath which a drunken doctor and corrupt police chief exchange brown concubines and confidences about losing their faith at preparatory school," one critic calls it). Greene, who was born in 1904, the son of the headmaster of Berkhamsted School, always believed that writerly imagination, like misery and faithlessness, started in childhood; and his own certainly did. The imprint of young unhappiness and a youthful attempt at suicide laid a version of life over his fiction – the fiction of an ever distinctive world of "misery's graduates," spies and adulterers, betrayers and sinners, where temporal disorder is universal, civilization never on offer, redemption ambiguous and death certain, which, shifting from one form to another, he would always write. One striking thing about Greene in retrospect (he died in 1991) is the sheer scale of his production: over twenty-five novels, over fifty books, several plays and important film scripts, like *The Third Man* (1950), with its famous chase through the sewers of life, which would change directions in modern cinema. Greene was influenced by several strands of Modernism, and possessed particular admiration for Conrad and Ford, though also for much more popular writers like John Buchan, Marjorie Bowen and Eric Ambler, who opened up many of the landscapes of his work. But he was essentially a writer formed in the Thirties, and his writing gradually rejects Modernist mannerism for a vividly metaphoric realism, drawing on journalism, travel writing and popular forms. His work, with its spyings and treacheries, seedy landscapes and dangerous frontiers, its wastes of moral and political confusion and its high metaphysical anxieties, its European and internationalist texture, always remained born out of that decade, even though more than any other novelist he would carry forward the vision through the era of the Cold War and the superpower age and right into the New World Order. Some of his best books belong there, though also some of his worst. His first novel *The Man Within* (1929), written when he was a recent Catholic convert, is a historical novel which opens out some of his essential themes – betrayal, pursuit, the manhunt, the inner burden of guilt and anxiety – but remains slight; his next two novels were failures and were later withheld from the Collected Edition. But over the Thirties his fiction realized the forms it needed for itself, and the sequence of novels he produced just before, around and immediately after the war – *Brighton Rock* (1938), *The Confidential Agent* (1939), *The Power and the Glory* (1940), *The Ministry of Fear* (1943), *The Heart of the Matter* (1948) and *The End of the Affair* (1951) – surely form the recognizable centre of his fiction.

Greene's first successful novels – artistically as well as commercially – were in fact his "entertainments," borrowings from the popular and sensational forms from the crime novel to the psychological thriller which, in the Thirties, suddenly acquired a moral, political and metaphysical relevance. He called his first really successful novel *Stamboul Train* (1932) an entertainment (it was written for money); the book borrowed from Agatha Christie's *The Mystery of the Blue Train* (1928) and elsewhere those ever more familiar themes of crossing risky frontiers and the borders of civilization, of espionage and sudden arrests, seduction and meetings with strange emissaries of foreign powers, all born from a Europe in terrible unrest, which flavoured so much of the fiction of the Thirties, from Isherwood to Elizabeth Bowen (*The House in Paris*, 1935). *A Gun for Sale* (1936) – another "entertainment," though now meant more seriously – is the story, set in a world fearful of war, of a harelipped political assassin, Raven, who says "There has always been a war for me," and whose complex amoral mixture of loyalty and treachery gives the novel not only its dark flavour but a metaphysical theme. David Lodge has noted how in Greene's work "the properties of realism – the sharp visual images presented through cinematic devices of montage and close-up, the catalogues of significant particulars, the keen rendering of sensation, the touches of local colour laid on with so skilled a hand – seem to cluster around the nucleus of some ambiguous moral concept which is 'the heart of the matter' and which is represented by some word or words recurring as insistently as a drumbeat." In *A Gun for Sale* the word is "betrayal," in his next novel *It's a Battlefield* (1934) it is "justice," in *The Confidential Agent* (1939), Greene's third entertainment, it is "trust," in *The Heart of the Matter* (1948) it is "pity," in *The Human Factor* (1978) it is "gratitude." They indicate the deepening moral and metaphysical thrust of his writing, indeed its emerging religiosity. They remind us too of Conrad, by whom he was technically and morally influenced, and *It's a Battlefield* – set around the police investigation of a political crime, in a vividly rendered, grimly desolate contemporary London which is indeed a social, political and moral battlefield, and concerned, Greene said, with the inadequacy of human justice – is Greene's most direct homage to him.

For, like Conrad, Greene was becoming a novelist of the

gloomier moral flavours, of fidelity and infidelity, trust and betrayal; after all the writer was at heart, he said, "a man given over to an obsession." Also like Conrad, he was a writer who never seemed quite at home with the familiar, and who sought out the dark places of the earth. Even when he wrote of English life – the desolate London of the political rally in *It's a Battlefield* or in parts of *England Made Me*, seedy bedsitter Nottingham in *A Gun for Sale*, the Brighton of the pre-war razor gangs in *Brighton Rock* (1938) – it appeared a foreign and distanced place, part of a larger European map, increasingly a world map, of pain and compassion, guilt and sin, betrayal and obscure redemption. It feels, increasingly, an abandoned world, a ruined place where life is damned or fallen, though there is always "someone who has betrayed one's natural distrust of human nature, someone one has loved." Bridging the gap between popular and serious writer, storyteller and experimentalist, he was progressively coming to see the novel as a narrative for telling stories of heroes or, more often, anti-heroes who, in the dark and confusing passages of modern history, faced some difficult yet eternal trial, succeeded or, more probably, failed in some existential and metaphysical quest. It was a journey without maps in a landscape where the secret agent and the private detective, the spy and the traitor, stalked through the mean streets of an ill-lit world, where kindness and compassion frequently led to self-betrayal and despair, where, it has been said, characters have discovered a sense of sin but not set their feet on the way of salvation, and where life is a gamble with a death that has its own obscure yet strangely radical theology of hell and redemption. With this comes a Conradian understanding, even a sympathy or moral identification, with those who have not managed to keep faith, or have committed treachery.

Brighton Rock is the novel where the theme of faith emerges clearly in Greene's fiction, as it does in Waugh's with *Brideshead Revisited*. It started as yet another entertainment, with the seventeen-year-old racecourse hoodlum Pinkie a villain from the same world as Raven; but by setting the book in a world in which good and evil become a common country, apart from conventional right and wrong, the themes of salvation and damnation are significantly released ("She was good, he'd discovered that, and he was damned; they were made for each other"). This is played against structures taken from the crime novel and the thriller movie, with an element of chase and detection; it shares with *noir* fiction like Patrick Hamilton's the notion that life is throughout a dingy world ("Why, this is Hell, nor are we out of it," says Mr Drewitt in the book). Ida, who thinks otherwise and believes in "human nature" ("Bite all the way down, you'll still read Brighton," she says, comparing life to Brighton rock, "that's human nature"), is thus not the novel's heroine, but a blowsily good-hearted figure of farce; Rose, who supports Pinkie throughout, despite his cold evil ("no more human contacts," he dreams), much as Pinkie accepts his own damnation, is the moral focus. The novel surprises, even shocks, because of the moral frame in which its action is interpreted; at times, indeed, it becomes difficult to grant the author his Greenean God on which so much depends. These are lawless roads, where the hunter is a narrower human being than the hunted, the rule of law is less than the rule of salvation and damnation, and the marked man can become the alien or demonic hero, dependent at the last on the "strangeness of the mercy of God." If, as Greene said, he had learned from Marjorie Bowen to write of a world of "perfect evil walking the world where perfect good could never walk again," here was the book to prove it. With his next, *The Confidential Agent* (1939), Greene offered another, and far less weighty, entertainment that really goes back to Conrad and *The Secret Agent*, though it draws on the Spanish Civil War for its political atmosphere and its angle of foreignness. But with *The Power and the Glory* (1940), "the only book I have ever written to a thesis," Greene's religious theme returned in all its force.

Basing the novel on his travels in revolutionary Mexico over two months in 1938, Greene here extraordinarily creates the physical, moral and religious landscape of central America in a period of cruel anti-clericalism. It is a fitting Greenean setting to the drama of his nameless whisky priest, the seedy lover and alcoholic who fails as a man but succeeds in his office, so that at once he descends into darkness and ascends into martyrdom. He is one of the central characters of Greene's fiction, one, he said, that "had emerged from some part of me, from the depths." His failings are many, but they teach him human love; he can still fulfil his function, and in Greene's interpretation become that much more the saintly man. For increasingly Greene was turning to the paradoxes of his Catholic religion, the metaphysical ironies and enigmas of faith, the portrait of a Pascalian, absurd world from which God seemed absconded, but in which obscure acts of faith constitute something midway between a humanist and a religious – in other words an existential – salvation. There was another entertainment, *The Ministry of Fear* (1943), now most notable for its evocation of London in the Blitz; but the larger theme returned again in *The Heart of the Matter* (1948), a novel set in expatriate Africa in wartime, in which the colonial policeman Scobie attempts to take on the world's evil and suffering, and finally dies by suicide. Set in a West Africa where "Heaven remained rigidly on the other side of death, and on this side flourished the injustices, the cruelties, the meanness that elsewhere people so cleverly hushed up," where love is a response to human unattractiveness, where what Scobie offers up to God is his own damnation, this is one of the most complete of the "Greeneland" social, moral and metaphysical landscapes, a central work that, lacking the sensationalized crime aspects of *Brighton Rock*, or the political persecution of *The Power and the Glory*, becomes the interpretation of a psychology. With these three novels Greene had laid out his central themes, established his distinctive flavour, and turned what had begun as sensational popular fiction (his work was never entirely to lose that flavour) into the novel of existential crisis. And what had begun as a fiction written, as he said, against "the economic background of the thirties and that sense of capitalism staggering from crisis to crisis," a fiction in which the social order has been destabilized and existence is lived according to hellish rules, had become a universal theme, a bleak overall accountancy of the twentieth-century condition, a metaphysical setting. The fictional world has become a universe, with Greene its neo-divine creator – the maker of its plots, the deviser of its obscure governing moral and metaphysical rules, the dispenser of its strange spiritual destinies, working in collusion with a yet higher plotter still. This created some of the fictionalist ambiguities of his next novel *The End of the Affair*, a book strangely split between the human and divine author, so that the first is able to assign a miracle to the second. Greene's highly ordained, metaphysically terrible, historically seedy universe was in place, all ready to sustain him over more than thirty more years of influential and central writing.

9.

"What a decade!" wrote George Orwell in 1940, in what looked like a relieved farewell to the entire Thirties: "A riot of appalling folly that suddenly becomes a nightmare, a scenic railway ending in a torture chamber." The obituaries on the "low, dishonest decade" started almost at once. If the times had a dominant form, it was elegy; and the striking poetic elegies Auden wrote for the deaths of two of the great "Moderns," Sigmund Freud ("To us he is no more a person/ But a whole climate of opinion") and W. B. Yeats ("In the nightmare of the dark,/ All the dogs of Europe bark,/ And the living nations wait,/ Each sequestered in its hate"), just as he left for the United States appeared to sum up the prevailing mood. Dismay and the funereal note were now clearly dominant in the arts. In the pages of *Horizon*, Cyril Connolly announced that it was "closing time in the gardens of the West," and mourned the dying not just of one but of two eras of writing: the Modernist era, and the "new writing of the Thirties." There was, he noted, an intimate link between "the Twilight of the Arts and the twilight of a civilization," and, though this artistic as well as historical gloom might have seemed the personal pessimism of a legendary decadent, it was widely shared by others. In *Penguin*

New Writing in 1942, John Lehmann complained that "this war has found no writer in prose and verse to interpret it with anything like . . . depth and power," and saw writing in general decline, virtually mute; so did most commentators. War and a new patriotic feeling had not made writing flourish. The Forties started out with *Finnegans Wake* and *No Orchids for Miss Blandish*, the terminal experiment and the seedy grim thriller. Where fiction was written, its map of contemporary life was almost universally one of frustration, bewilderment, maladjustment, disintegration, anxiety. Kafka and his heirs cast their influence wide, from the political novels of Koestler, Warner and Alex Comfort (*The Powerhouse*, 1944) to the entertainments of Graham Greene, which became now a report from the unfamiliar on the entirely familiar, and so on into the popular thriller – now a widely read form of escape from yet grimmer actuality. Meanwhile the terminal mood of the commentators reinforced the belief that all the darker aspects of Thirties fiction – the death of the hero, the self-cancelling of the author, the growing conviction of the irrelevance of art in the age of great History, vast masses, and the age of mechanical reproduction – had all the time been signalling the end of literature, the death of the novel itself, just as Orwell's "Inside the Whale" prophesied. The decade of the Thirties may have started in realism, but it ended in surrealism; no wonder it handed on to the writing that did actually follow an intense awareness of a grotesque and absurd world which has never since disappeared from the climate of fiction.

This apocalyptic reading of the end of the arts was, of course, understandable, even though in time it proved too grim. Modernism had faded, and the movement had been robbed of some of its dominant figures; the later sadness in Woolf's work, the terminal mood of *Finnegans Wake*, reflected not just personal dismays but experiment's fading fortunes. Even so, the spirit of experiment had by no means departed entirely from fiction. One of the more striking novelists of the Thirties was Henry Green (Henry Yorke), whose insistently fictionalist, very textual works have lately attracted the attention of deconstructionist critics because of their playful linguistic texture, their verbal idiosyncrasy and enigmatic spaces. But his early *Living* (1929) was, for all its textural complexity, an important industrial novel set around a Birmingham foundry-works, part of the reincorporation of the industrial world into literature that went on developing during the Thirties. Then came *Party-Going* (1939), a remarkable work about a party of rich young people befogged, in society, stasis, and the arbitrariness of words themselves, as well as bad weather, in a very Saussurian railway station. *Party-Going* was plainly a Thirties political novel, a work of social criticism by a writer on the Left; but it was also a mannerist work about a crisis of expression and moral obscurity. Like many books of this date it prefigured the war, and some of Green's best work came with wartime, in which he served as a London fireman. *Caught* (1943), about London in the air-raids, is one of the most vivid and effective of British wartime novels; *Loving* (1945), by contrast, is a dense and complex fable set in a castle in neutral Ireland, while *Back* (1946) is about a soldier back from the wars. The Forties were Green's most productive decade, and seven novels appeared between 1939 and 1952. His fiction hovers between realism and pure text, a writing of dense texture and narrative incompleteness; it has remained important to writers and lovers of self-conscious fiction ever since, as an important expansion of the Modern experiment.

"Experiment," then, certainly did outlast the Thirties. There was, for example, Malcolm Lowry, author of *Ultramarine* (1933; revised ed., 1962), a youthful novel about a bourgeois young man who ships as a deckhand on voyage to the Far East, and who is looking both for human solidarity and for his own artistic solitude and identity.It is filled with Expressionist scenes and strong literary echoes; typically the manuscript was stolen and had to be rewritten, for Lowry was the unluckiest of writers. Even after publication Lowry wrote it again, trying to incorporate it into the larger adventure of his fiction, his "voyage that never ends." Lowry actually drafted a good deal of his fiction over the Thirties, though most of it was not published until much later, quite a lot of it after his death in 1957. So there was the much more Expressionist *Lunar Caustic* (1962), a wild, jazz-like evocation of the modernist city, based on his experience of being hospitalized for drunkenness in New York's Bellevue Hospital, and there was *In Ballast to the White Sea*, unpublished and destroyed in a fire in 1944. Then there was the book Lowry started in Mexico in 1936 as a political parable, and which turned through many rewritings into one of the great mythic novels of the age, *Under the Volcano*; published at last in 1947, it was to become one of the most important of post-war novels. Samuel Beckett – who had worked as amanuensis to Joyce, and translated part of *Finnegans Wake* into French – was born as a writer into the climate of Modernism. He published the clever playful stories of *More Pricks Than Kicks* in 1934, and then in 1938 a major absurdist novel *Murphy* – in which Murphy enters the Magdalen Mental Mercyseat, a mental hospital roughly equivalent to the solipsistic space of his own mind ("life in his mind gave him pleasure, such pleasure that pleasure was not the word"). In 1942–44, while working with the Resistance in France, he produced his next novel *Watt*, which opened the way toward a new and productive phase of his writing, and the central part he played in the post-war literature of "absurdity." Also in 1938, Lawrence Durrell, likewise working in Modernist Paris, published *The Black Book*, a surrealist work that was banned in Britain, a rhetorical flux of images of death and rebirth, obsessed with the evolution of consciousness from its regressive state in a world of nightmare realities. Durrell too was to become one of the most important of post-war writers, and, like Lowry and Beckett, he continued the experimental tradition into his novels of the Fifties and Sixties.

And there were other ways of writing history, and other ways of reading the history of the novel. Anthony Powell was a notable writer of the 1930s: his *Afternoon Men* (1931) is a splendid novel about the Bright Young Things entirely comparable with the fiction of his friend Evelyn Waugh, while *Venusberg* (1932), a cinematic and surreal comedy about the affairs of a Baltic country (Finland), remains one of the overlooked classics of the period; Powell, later, would become one of the great recorders of the social, moral and artistic history of the century. C. P. Snow produced in *The Search* (1934) a fine novel, about the provincial life of a lower-middle-class young man who has chosen science as his vocation, that developed the tradition of Wells and Bennett, and would form the basis of his later social fiction; his friend H. S. Hoff produced three novels under his own name before turning into the post-war writer "William Cooper." Joyce Cary wrote four excellent novels based on his African colonial experience over the Thirties, the finest of which are *Aissa Saved* (1932), *The African Witch* (1936) and *Mister Johnson* (1939). Henry Williamson wrote several notable nature novels (*Tarka the Otter*, 1927; *Salar the Salmon*, 1935), and a key war novel (*A Patriot's Progress*, 1930); he also got unpleasantly close to Nazism.

Around or soon after the end of the Thirties, all these writers started work on major *romans fleuves*, long-flowing sequences that suggested that some significant line of connection and development linked the inter-war, the wartime and the post-war world. So there now began to appear Snow's eleven-volume "Strangers and Brothers" sequence (1940–70), which would duly track the coming of the post-war welfare state and the atomic age. Cary's "Gully Jimpson" trilogy (*Herself Surprised*, 1941; *To Be A Pilgrim*, 1942; *The Horse's Mouth*, 1944) would follow the fate of British artistic bohemia in its story of a wild and inventive artist, and it was succeeded by a second important trilogy in the Fifties (*Prisoner of Grace*, 1952; *Except the Lord*, 1953; *Not Honour More*, 1955), the story of a religious upbringing and its consequences. William Cooper traced the development of an autobiographical hero who moves from provincial life to the world of metropolitan power in his four-volume "Scenes from Life" sequence (*Scenes from Provincial Life, 1950; Scenes from Married Life*, 1961; *Scenes from Metropolitan Life*, 1982; *Scenes from Later Life*, 1983). Anthony Powell would produce one of the key narrative records of the century in his splendidly funny and wonderfully well-observed twelve-volume "Dance to the Music of Time" sequence (1951–75), and Henry Williamson would go on to write the even vaster fifteen-volume "A Chronicle of Ancient Sunlight" (1951–69), a record of an autobiographical hero, a "passionate pilgrim of our age," that epically covers the period from the close of the Victorian age to the Sixties. These *romans fleuves* are more than retrospects, though most of them are about the remembrance of things past (most of these writers, even the more realistic, acknowledged the importance of Proust); they were to represent a continuity of style that would help define the social material and the public scope of subsequent fiction.

Meanwhile another essentially continuous body of human experience, the world of love, sexuality, and loneliness, was explored in the fiction of several very notable women writers. Most of them began work during the Twenties, developed during the Thirties, and had considerable influence on writing after the War. Rose Macaulay, a writer of great wit and observation, producer of thirty-six books, some of them satires on the literary world, did some of her finest work in the 1930s – for instance her Spanish Civil War novel *And No Man's Wit* (1940) – and continued to write fiction into the 1950s. The Anglo-Irish novelist Elizabeth Bowen established herself with her first novel *The Hotel* in 1927, and with *The Last September* (1929), a felt, poetic novel about the Irish Troubles in the early Twenties. She wrote several powerful novels over the Thirties, above all *The House in Paris* (1935) and *The Death of the Heart* (1939), about the impact of public on private worlds, centred on individual female sensibilities in a socially shattered world, and concerned, as she said, with poetic truths caught in non-poetic statements. Bowen's manner was self-consciously feminine, fragmented, concentrated in sharp moments, good on loneliness ("I have isolated, I have made for the particular, spot-lighting faces or cutting out gestures that are not even the faces or gestures of great sufferers"). It particularly suited the experience of wartime; her Forties short stories like "Mysterious Kor," and her war novel *The Heat of the Day* (1949), set in a time of bombings, conspiracies and double agents, when the disorder always implicit in her best novels is a clear reality, are among her finest work. Rosamund Lehmann first established herself with *Dusty Answer* (1927), a bold story of schooldays lesbianism; then, during the Thirties, she was active with her brother John Lehmann in the "new writing" movement, and continued to publish a significant, strongly realistic fiction of the crises of sexuality and solitude. Her fiction, too, powerfully extended across and beyond the war, and her two late books, *The Ballad and the Source* (1944), a child's perspective on adult sexuality, and *The Echoing Grove* (1953), a subtle treatment of adultery, remain among her best.

And then, above all, there was Jean Rhys, born in the West Indies, and a friend in Paris of Ford Madox Ford. He wrote the preface to her first story collection, *The Left Bank* (1927), noting her knowledge of "many of the Left Banks of the world," and became one of the subjects of her *Postures* (1928). Rhys moved to London in 1927, and produced her novel *After Leaving Mr Mackenzie* (1930), a vivid portrait of sexual drifting and half-survival in Paris and London. The theme of the woman identityless and adrift, floating like flotsam in a random social world, became the chief subject of her Thirties fiction. Then, after *Good Morning, Midnight* (1939), about another woman drifting in Paris, Rhys was silent, "disappeared," for twenty-seven years till the 1960s – when she produced the remarkable *Wide Sargasso Sea* (1966), her complex rewriting and recoding of *Jane Eyre*, exploring its "hidden" story, the life of the crazed Creole wife locked away in the attic of Thornfield Hall, providing her with a past, a history of dislocation and loneliness, an aberrant identity, missing from the original novel. Her work, like that of the Australian Christina Stead and the Canadian Elizabeth Smart, came from the sense of endless displacement, as a colonial and as a woman, and offered a bohemian answer to it; it greatly influenced the women writers of the Sixties, providing them with a missing culture of creativity. Like certain elements of the Modernist tradition, the tradition of feminine experimentalism also outlasted the war.

There was an even more glorious way to deal with the ominous idea of History that sounded through the Thirties.

And that was flamboyantly to set it aside, substituting a quite different era and idea of history for it. This is what Ivy Compton-Burnett does in her remarkable novels, which are among the finest of the period. Compton-Burnett had published her first novel *Dolores* in 1911, but she later disowned it; her last novel was published after her death in 1969. This made a career of twenty remarkably similar novels, her mature work starting with her second book *Pastors and Masters*, which came out in 1925, one of the peak years of Modernism. Modernism was what, on the face of it, Compton-Burnett seemed to have little to do with; her work over forty years scarcely changed in subject or background, and each of her books is set in a fixed historical time and a ritualized fictional space. The time is that less of late-Victorian life than the late-Victorian novel, which Compton-Burnett does not reject but subvert, preserving it in an eternal stasis, for repeated decoding. This is the eternal world of Samuel Butler's *The Way of All Flesh* and Edmund Gosse's *Father and Son*, and Butler's deep irony and Gosse's sense of patriarchal crisis are both essential elements of her method. The titles of some of her novels suggest both their world and their highly dramatic material of conflict: *Brothers and Sisters* (1929), *Men and Wives* (1931), *A House and Its Head* (1935), *A Family and a Fortune* (1939), *Manservant and Maidservant* (1947), *A Father and His Fate* (1957), *A Heritage and Its History* (1959), *The Mighty and Their Fall* (1961), and so on. This is a completely patriarchal, hierarchical world, where the landed gentry rule forever, though they generally hold their ancestral estates in reduced and difficult circumstances. The social rules and customs are precise; these patriarchs and masters have butlers and governesses, menservants and maidservants, imperious wives (often several), unreliable children and normally rebellious dependents. Society is totally important, though never in the Thirties sense of that word. So is history, though here it means the weight of the past and the power of custom, not Marx's revolutionary process. In this world religion is observed, and other classes do not normally impinge; indeed almost everything outside the designated family space – the classic space of Greek tragedy – is excluded, and the main powers of change are social, sexual and generational. Struggles for love, power and influence, and for fortune, precedence and inheritance dominate; the crimes and sins are the classic ones, of pride and hatred, of bigamy, incest, murder, child abuse and fraud. The dissecting, deconstructive irony that Compton-Burnett brings to this realm of domestic comedy and tragedy is generally shared by the very self-aware participants themselves ("What a day it has been!. . . There is material for an epic. The fall of Lavinia; the return of Ransom; the uplift of Ninian," says Hugh in *The Mighty and Their Fall*). And material for an epic, moral and ironic, comic and tragic, there is indeed.

Suppose, Compton-Burnett's novels suggest to us, that on or about December 1910 human nature did *not* change, and all human relations, "those between masters and servants, husbands and wives, parents and children," did *not* shift, as Virginia Woolf had claimed in her famous essay of 1924 – one year before the special world of Compton-Burnett emerged. That world is a stylized version of the eternal drama of human experience, which has been carefully placed in one selected phase of historical evolution. Compton-Burnett had, we know, read Engels' *The History of the Family*, and she seems to have turned it into a universal landscape. And if history has been stylized, so has her literary method. Almost everything is represented in the form of abbreviated, self-knowing dialogue, a dramatic ritual that is shared by all of the characters, whose lives are consciously presented as purified forms of social art. It is the distance that makes all the difference; this is family life rendered totally unfamiliar, made universalized and emblematic, a consensual fiction. Compton-Burnett's books are neither realistic nor social, and they are not historical either. They treat the "past" as if it were the "present," "history" as if it were "modernity," one fiction laid over another. But they are intensely modern in form, and seamed with contemporary experience, even as they insist on remaining fictions and refuse competition with reality. As Angus Wilson once put it, "In the age of the concentration camp, when from 1935 to 1947 or so, she wrote her very best novels, no writer did more to illumine the springs of human cruelty, suffering and bravery." And as another critic (Wolfgang Iser) has observed, "the more artificial her technique of presentation, the more possibilities she unfolds." Compton-Burnett is a wonderful reminder of the fact that fiction is a power on its own account, and that, even amid the omnipresent historical realities and social arguments of the Thirties, the Victorian novel, if sufficiently decoded, was by no means dead. It was a heritage and a history, a father and a fate, a family and a fortune, there to be struggled with, so that a very modern writer, if sufficiently cunning, could question it and then re-create it as a form of contemporary moral and human truth. Like many of the novelists who succeeded in outlasting the oppressive historical pressure of the Thirties, Compton-Burnett challenged simple and doctrinal history; instead she rendered history as radical style. It was a style that went on to serve her, with little change, right through into the Sixties, by which time she had become a leading novelist of a totally different age.

FIVE

The Novel No Longer Novel
1945–1960

It may happen in the next hundred years that the English
novelists of the present day will come to be valued as we now
value the artists and craftsmen of the late eighteenth century.
The originators, the exuberant men, are extinct and in their
place subsists and modestly flourishes a generation notable for
elegance and variety of contrivance. It may happen that there
are lean years ahead in which our posterity will look back
hungrily to this period, when there was so much will and so
much ability to please.

Evelyn Waugh, *The Ordeal of Gilbert Pinfold* (1957)

The situation of the Western novel during the past forty years
has been precisely one in which a large amount of local
movement has been evident, but no overall development since
the achievement of Proust and Joyce and the other major
innovators of the early twentieth century . . . If the novel is truly
no longer novel, then many of our critical procedures for
discussing it will need revision; perhaps, even, we shall do well
to think of another name for it.

Bernard Bergonzi, *The Situation of the Novel* (1970)

1.

There is no doubt that the Second World War was as terrible a
fracture in the twentieth-century experience as the First had
been. In fact its impact on world history, human consciousness,
and artistic expression was ultimately far greater than that of
the conflict of just twenty-five years before. After war's outbreak
in 1939, nightmarish fantasies far greater than any writers of
the Thirties had dared imagine soon began to unfold. On the

biggest battlefield in the history of the world, tanks rolled, jackboots marched, overflying bombers and unmanned rockets smashed great cities with mass aerial bombardments. Vast regions of Europe saw occupation by foreign troops; the knout and the lash took over, and the intentions and deeds of totalitarian regimes proved far more terrible than the grimmest prophets had foreseen. By the war's end in 1945, many of the great European cities were gutted by bombing or land offensive, large regions of the continent lay in ruins, industrial activity ceased, harvests went unreaped, all frontiers were unsettled and many of Europe's peoples were displaced. Shattered survivors and returning prisoners of war wandered a landscape of senseless borders and broken regimes. As Donald Watt put it: "Rejoicing was doled out in small bundles which were instantly engulfed in horror about the past and the present and usually in grim foreboding about the future too . . . realism, if not actually disillusionment, was the order of the day." Worse was to come: the unbelievable facts about the deportations, massacre and genocide that had occurred in Nazi concentration and extermination camps like Buchenwald and Auschwitz only now began to emerge. The Nuremberg Trials of Nazi war crimes in 1946 revealed the apocalyptic scale of the "final solution" planned by the Third Reich. Six million Jews had perished in a terrible "Holocaust." Millions more, Jewish and non-Jewish, had been deported or used as slave labour. Nor was the conscience of the Allies clear. As a result of Anglo-American research into the atom and its power, the war ended with another, no less terrible holocaust, the dropping of atomic weapons on the cities of Hiroshima and Nagasaki in August 1945, which led to the Japanese surrender.

Thus the end of the war was the beginning of the Atomic Age; human beings now had the power of universal self-annihilation. Now began what W. H. Auden, writing his "diagnostic" poems in New York, called in 1947 "the Age of Anxiety." Forty years further on, Martin Amis was still saying that he wrote in the overpowering time of "Einstein's Monsters," the nuclear age ("It is the highest subject and it is the lowest subject. It is disgraceful, and exalted. Everywhere you look there is a great irony: tragic irony, pathetic irony, even the irony of black comedy or farce; and there is the irony that is simply violent, unprecedentedly violent. The mushroom cloud over Hiroshima was a beautiful spectacle, even though it owed its colour to a kiloton of human blood . . ."). The Holocaust and the nuclear cloud dominated the sensibility of the period; and, as political tensions continued, and the hot war turned into a cold one, the post-war into the non-peace, the mood of anxiety, horror, and apocalyptic peril increased. In 1946 Winston Churchill announced that an Iron Curtain had descended across Europe, from Stettin to the Adriatic, as new totalitarian regimes were imposed right across central and eastern Europe; in 1947 the term "Cold War" was coined. If there had been – as writers in the Thirties used to say – a "mind of Europe," it was now a mind grimly divided and conflicted. Europe was not only cut in half geographically, by wire fences, armed guards and concrete walls, but ideologically, split between the influence of two vast atomically weaponed super-powers, the United States and the Soviet Union. Each represented a fundamental twentieth-century ideology, born out of the historical making of the modern: democratic liberal capital-ism and totalitarian Communism, the one-party state. The "post-war world" was born, in a web of confrontations, crises, and conspiracies; the spy story seemed the exemplary tale of the times. And this long stasis did not end (if it has ended) until forty-five years later – when Marxist ideology and its command economies collapsed, the Berlin Wall came down, and the "new world order" started, with its own changed and wounded illusions about future history.

From 1939 to 1989 is a period half a century long, as long as that covered by the entire rise and decline of the Modern movement. However the second half of the century was every-where proving quite unlike the first. The rise and fall of Fascism led to a new ideological order which grimly extended many of the darkest aspects of what had seemed defeated, the growth of new scientific discovery simply intensified the risks of annihilation, and even the power of space travel had a military meaning. Much of the progressive optimism that had fed the idea of modernity began to fail; as the second half of the century turned into a grim stand-off, the human hopes and ideological Utopias of the Thirties (the "low dishonest decade") now appeared at best naive illusions, at worst treacheries and betrayals. If Europe's capitals, economies and political systems lay in ruins, so did its intellectual, ideological, metaphysical and cultural values: its ideas of the self, the state, politics, history, art, good and evil. Reinhold Niebuhr expressed the metaphysical shock when he warned that modern liberal morality could no longer cope "with the ultimately religious problem of the evil in man." In countries that had been defeated or occupied (and this meant a very large part of Europe), the intellectual, cultural and political tradition had to be constructed afresh. Accusations of treachery, the *trahison des clercs*, were widespread; the figure of the tainted intellectual remained a potent symbol for the rest of the century. Ezra Pound, one of the heroic organizers of Modernism, was in a mental hospital in Washington, unfit to plead on a treason charge after broadcasting from Mussolini's Italy during the War. In France, where leading writers like Céline were seen as collaborators, questions of allegiance and "commitment" became central. Events in Eastern Europe made the question more urgent. Stalin's armies had, in the emollient phrase of the day, "liberated" many countries, and the resulting puppet regimes were suppressing intellectual argument, silencing, imprisoning and murdering writers, in the interests of history's great revolution. Many – not all – who in the Thirties had been on the progressive or revolutionary Left withdrew their allegiance. A notable sign of the new mood was the volume *The God That Failed* in 1949, where six writers, including Spender, Koestler, André Gide and Ignazio Silone, explored their rejection of Marxism and totalitarianism – as Orwell and others had already done in the years just before the war.[1]

[1] Richard H. Crossman (ed.), *The God That Failed* (London, 1949): "In this book, six intellectuals describe the journey into Communism, and the return," Crossman writes in the Introduction, adding that their conversion to Communism was "rooted

The post-war world knew it was post many things. It was post-Holocaust, post-atomic, post-ideological, post-humanist, post-political, and indeed, some declared, post-Modern – for it was not surprising that this now ever more influential term should already be in play by this date.[2] Modernism was over, even tainted; the deaths of Joyce, Woolf, Yeats and Freud had reinforced the feeling. In critical circles, it was already being historicized, defined, monumentalized, given its name and structure; it was no longer *avant*, as it had always meant to be, but *arrière*. Meanwhile the new dominant tone in Western thought became one of chastened liberalism – a guilty, vigilant "new liberalism" not always distinguishable from conservatism. The times called, said Lionel Trilling, in *The Liberal Imagination* (1950), for "moral realism" – a renewed awareness of the danger of history, the unreliability of human nature, a return to "the tragic sense of life." As some turned to religion, Trilling looked to literature. It was no longer politics, now largely discredited for its ideological simplicities, but the novel, with its awareness of difficulty, contradiction, ambiguity, that spoke to the difficult age. But many writers now felt nearer to muteness: if the outbreak of war had brought many close to passive silence, its ending only seemed to prolong that silence in perpetuity. "We come *after*," said George Steiner in his *Language and Silence* (1967), "and that is the nerve of our condition. After the unprecedented ruin of humane values and hopes by the

---

in despair – a despair of Western values," and their return was shaped in part by the refusal of Soviet Communism to respond to Western intellectual values. The book takes its place with Hannah Arendt's *The Origins of Totalitarianism* (1951), Friedrich Hayek's *The Road to Serfdom* (1944), Arthur Koestler's *The Yogi and the Commissar* (London, 1945) and Lionel Trilling's *The Liberal Imagination* (New York, 1950) as primary influences on the intellectual atmosphere after the War.

[2] As Margaret A. Rose usefully records in her *The Post-Modern and the Post-Industrial* (Cambridge, 1991), the term "post-modern" had been used by Arnold Toynbee in his *Study of History* in 1939 to define the period inaugurated by the Great War of 1914–18, and was used by others including Irving Howe and C. Wright Mills to define the post-war intellectual and social climate, and indeed the reaction against Modernist abstraction. It has thus, like many such terms, virtually reversed in meaning as the "postmodern period" went on, from a reaction against Modernism to a kind of ambiguous continuity with a difference.

political bestiality of our age." "No poetry after Auschwitz," warned Theodore Adorno, conscious that the aestheticization of life might breed the evil in history. "There is nothing to paint and nothing to paint with," Samuel Beckett, a key figure of writing after Modernism, told Georges Duthuit in the late 1940s. When the post-war arts did begin to emerge, as they did, they often found language, form and literary humanism inadequate to deal with the horrors committed, and the nihilism and meaninglessness they invoked. Thus they were frequently marked with a spirit of absurdity and extremity, an air of nihilism, an instinct toward minimalism – as if human nature had betrayed itself, human character had collapsed. If, after 1945, there was a felt "postmodern condition," these were the things that notion implied.

2.

It was no wonder that the most influential expression of Western philosophy over the post-war years was Existentialism: the thought of Kierkegaard, Heidegger, Husserl, Jaspers, but above all Jean-Paul Sartre – the French philosopher whose vision of human anguish, forlornness and despair in *L'Etre et le néant* (*Being and Nothingness* 1943) had expressed, from the very heart of wartime and the German occupation, a philosophical vision based as much on the anguish, forlornness and terror of the contemporary historical situation as it was on the fading tradition of humanism and idealism in European thought. In this vision of things Sartre was not alone. His fellow Frenchman Albert Camus had similarly explored, in *The Myth of Sisyphus* (1942), the sense of overwhelming absurdity that afflicted the human condition in an age of futility and inhumanity. And Sartre and Camus were not only philosophers; they were novelists and playwrights, whose fictions sounded the depths of the philosophical issues they explored. As early as 1931, Sartre had begun *La Nausée*, which was published in 1938, and translated variously as *Nausea* and *The Diary of Antoine Roquentin*:

269

a plainly "absurdist" work, about a hero who cannot pass from existence to essence, and who randomly records his sense of life's meaninglessness and contingency. Then during and immediately after the war, he produced the trilogy *Les Chemins de la liberté* (1945–49, translated as *The Roads to Freedom*, 1947–50), which carried its hero Mathieu from a condition of nothingness – *le néant* – to the moment when, gun in hand, he is able to assert "Freedom is exile, and I am condemned to be free." Meanwhile Camus too had published a novel in wartime: *L'Etranger* (1942, translated variously as *The Outsider* and *The Stranger*), set in Oran, Algeria, and about a sensual and directionless anti-hero, Meursault, who commits an aimless modern crime to test the limits of his own being. In 1947 came another novel, *La Peste* (*The Plague*), which is an allegory of the German occupation; an outbreak of bubonic plague attacks Oran, and the hero Dr Rieux – who acknowledges that he too suffers from the "present sickness," and is "sick and tired of the world he lived in" – still tries to counter meaninglessness, death and bureaucratic opposition with humanism. This was the theme too of Camus' philosophical study *The Rebel* (1951), in which he confronted the impact of Nazism's "nihilist revolution" on the age, and sought to summon a humanist rebellion into being.

The international impact of Existentialism in the post-war years undoubtedly owed much to the fact that both these two influential writers and philosophers came from a country which had suffered wartime occupation, and had seen both a brave resistance and a *trahison des clercs*, an intellectual collaboration by some important writers and thinkers. Existentialism was a philosophy, but it was also a literature – a variety of novels, stories and powerful plays – and a lifestyle. Its writings bore a similar message: sombre, absurdist, a vision of the emptiness and cruelty of existence, the loss of significance in experience, the inner vacancy of self. And it also summoned up an endeavour of humanist recovery, in which the writer was centrally implicated. In 1947 Sartre published his study *What Is Literature?*, a book that had great influence on the writing of the day. In an argument not unlike that of Orwell's "Inside the Whale," it identified post-war writers as the "third generation" of twentieth-century literature, following on from two earlier generations whose task had clearly failed – the bourgeois Modernists of the period before 1914, who had aestheticized art, and the writers of the inter-war Surrealist revolution, unable to decide whether they were the proclaimers of a new world or the gravediggers of an old. Both were bourgeois voices of modern catastrophe, writers from what he called the age of the fat cows; now "in the time of the lean cows they have nothing more to say." Sartre took it that the writer possessed a fundamental and revolutionary intellectual responsibility – though he did, in a notable passage, exempt British writers, who, living in a society that had never seen writers as intellectuals, "make a virtue of necessity and by aggrandizing the oddness of their ways attempt to claim as a free choice the isolation that has always been imposed on them by the structure of their society." The writer's task now was, he held, nothing less than recovery of the word itself, the re-creation of meaning. "The war of 1914 precipitated a crisis of language," he said: "I would say the war of 1940 has revalorized it." He called for a renewal of the sign, in effect a new realism, based on an existential, a political, indeed a Marxist commitment. And he counted first on the novel, for "The empire of signs is prose." Like many empires at this time, Sartre's did not last for too long. He focused literature on language, hoping to show that, by an act of "commitment," writers could replenish the sign with meaning. When later movements – Structuralism, Post-Structuralism, Deconstruction – had done with this, the "revalorization" lay seriously challenged. For the present, though, Existentialism seemed the intellectual necessity of the generation. It might depend on an obscure act of "good faith," but it expressed a rejection of aesthetic obscurity, a reaction against the view that art was now doomed to silence, a revolt into humanism.

It is not hard to see now why Sartre's "existentialist realism" – or the general search for a return to realist expression –

271

appeared important after wartime horrors so enormous that they called out for representation: a naming, a record, a history. In a France where writers lived in the gloomy aftermath of Occupation, resistance and collaboration, the fiction of Sartre, Camus, Malraux and others confronted absurdity with art as a mode of renaming and potential moral action. In a now divided Germany, where under Nazism books were burned and propaganda had entirely destroyed the credit of the word, the writers who, in 1947, formed *Gruppe 47*, including Günter Grass and Heinrich Böll, saw their task as replacing lie with truth, the falsehood with the reality. (It is this story that is allegorically told in Grass's *The Meeting at Telgte* (1979), about writers meeting after the Thirty Years' War to "bring back the long war as word butchery".) In Italy, where Fascism had ruled and the Allied invasion had left extensive destruction, writers like Ignazio Silone, Cesare Pavese, Alberto Moravia and the young Italo Calvino looked to "neo-realism" to tell the story of wartime crisis and post-war poverty and chaos. In the United States, existential realism also developed in the fiction of black writers such as Richard Wright (*The Outsider*, 1940), who saw the "absurdity" and alienation of their situation, and above all in the fiction of those Jewish-American writers like Saul Bellow, Edgar Lewis Wallant, Bernard Malamud and Norman Mailer, who felt compelled to confront in their fiction the Holocaust and the moral crisis of humanism it implied. In Britain, where the wartime experience and the profound social change that followed it called for record, many writers followed Orwell and others in their search for a return to the honest word. When later critics (like Bernard Bergonzi in *The Situation of the Novel* 1970) began to reflect that the novel was "no longer novel," this revival of realism was chiefly what they meant.

The history of twentieth-century literature is often nowadays written in two broad strokes: there was Modernism and there was Postmodernism, two large periods of the twentieth-century experiment. This seriously misleads and abbreviates. Throughout the century there had run a sustained, though ever-changing, tradition of realism. Against this, both Modernism and Postmodernism reacted (the *avant garde* needed a tradition to outrun), though frequently the two dissolved into each other, producing, for instance, the surrealism of the Thirties. Most writers who revolted against realism – James, questioning the novelists who were too devotedly "hugging the shores of the real," Woolf, challenging the materialism of the novel – also professed it, though in a new form. James argued for "solidity of specification" and the art that makes life, Woolf asked us to "Examine life on an ordinary day." Their arguments and experiments explored realism's borders, debated its phenomenology, challenged its veracity, rejected its unpsychological materialism; but they also professed their own search for a fresh reality. The Modernism that developed after the Great War was itself an endeavour to capture the new and changed reality, a search for a pared-down, fragmentary language of new authenticity, its Revolution of the Word matching the Revolution of the World. After 1945, the situation seemed to be exactly reversed. Language had been a weapon of War, and had been corrupted by it; now truth, documentation, record, the recovery of the damaged sign, were what was needed. The hard facts of history needed telling, moral assessment had to be made. In 1949 George Orwell closed his anti-utopian fable *Nineteen Eighty-Four* with a grim appendix about the fate of words under totalitarianism, warning that the corruption of language is the corruption of thought itself. He explained the system of "Newspeak," which controlled society, Ingsoc, by taking control of the word itself through the techniques of Doublespeak, Newthink and Crimestop: "The purpose of Newspeak was not only to provide a medium of expression for the world-view and mental habits proper to the devotees of Ingsoc, but to make all other modes of thought impossible."

The return to realism that formed one powerful trend in the post-war novel internationally came partly from the endeavour to make other modes of thought possible. Shaped by the need to return damaged words to honest meanings, restore signification, name reality in a world where it was no longer the familiar friend but the dangerous enemy, it represented less a rejection of modernist experiment than a need to re-articulate Nietzsche's "sixth sense," the awareness of the power of history, in fiction after the Holocaust and the birth of the nuclear age. This would provoke its own reaction, as philosophers and theorists returned to the language questions posed by earlier twentieth-century scholars from Saussure to Wittgenstein and Carnap. By 1953 the movement of "Structuralism" was already challenging Sartrean Existentialism, and Roland Barthes, in *Writing Degree Zero*, was writing that, far from representing reality, "Literature is now openly reduced to the problematics of language, and indeed that it is all it can now be." The post-war return toward representation was a significant moment in the development of fiction, but it provoked, in a changed philosophical frame, a new version of the fictionalist arguments that had grown among writers since the end of the nineteenth century. So Vladimir Nabokov, in a note to his *Lolita* (1955), observed that "reality" is "one of the few words that mean nothing without quotes," and added, "It is childish to study a work of fiction in order to gain information about a country or about a social class or about the author." A dialogue or dispute, more often a complicated interpenetration, of these elements – "realism" and "experiment," "novel" and "anti-novel" – developed, and would have much to do with the direction of fiction over the following years. But even the "fictionalist" novels that developed from this were often responses to the horrors of history, the crisis of authenticity, the problems of representation that affected the post-war era; many of them dwelt on the wartime experience, which still haunts fiction to this day.

3.

Despite Sartre's wry words about British writing, the Second World War was as great a watershed for Britain as for other European countries. The British mainland had remained uninvaded through the conflict, but the threat came close; the nation emerged from the conflict a victor, but a badly depleted one, facing bleak times ahead. The War had united rather than divided it; the accusations of intellectual betrayal common in other countries did not apply, though the spy scandals of the Fifties and the Sixties, and the general sense of intellectual uncertainty felt elsewhere, showed that some continuities had shattered and that the ideological conflicts of the time equally touched British life. The long destructive air-raids had left its major cities deeply damaged, its housing stock depleted, its reserves and resources almost spent, and the wartime atmosphere long outlasted the war. When the American critic Edmund Wilson came to tour European ruins in the late Forties, he felt Britain, with rationing, austerity and state organization, seemed like a defeated power. It was no longer the same nation it had been in the Thirties, and its map of politics and ideology had greatly changed. The common endeavours of wartime brought unstoppable demands for social change, and as the war ended Britain passed through a quiet but still fundamental social revolution, a shifting of social power and political values marked by the election in 1945 of the Attlee Labour government, committed to the birth of the new "Welfare State" and the "nationalization" or state control of many sectors of the economy. The Beveridge Plan initiated the programme of post-war "cradle to grave" social welfare, the Butler Education Act of 1944 opened doors of educational opportunity. Heavy taxation flattened incomes, the power of the trades unions greatly increased, the wartime bureaucratic apparatus largely stayed in place.

In the immediate post-war years, austerity ruled: coal shortages, steel shortages, food shortages, housing shortages, even travel shortages. ("Long ago in 1945 all the nice people in England were poor, allowing for exceptions," wrote Muriel Spark at the start of her 1963 novel *The Girls of Slender Means*.) With foreign travel restricted, even the travelling writers of the Thirties had mostly to remain at home. Horizons narrowed; Britain was losing its economic power and its vast imperial role. What it lost in power it sought to hold in moral influence. As the symbolically austere Sir Stafford Cripps, Labour Chancellor of the Exchequer, put it: "The world crisis is . . . in my view basically a moral rather than a political or economic crisis" – using a word and emphasis that would resound through the Fifties. But British moral empire hardly compensated for the decline in world role and economic strength. Meanwhile Europe, the scene of recent terrors, hardly beckoned, though there were already proposals for a "United States of Europe." Economically, politically, intellectually, Britain looked to the United States; and American Marshall Aid played a fundamental role in reviving Britain's and Europe's fortunes, in due time creating the modern version of a capitalist liberal economy, in other words a consumer mass-society, which began to emerge during the Fifties, when Harold Macmillan assured the British they had never had it so good. The youth culture and pop culture were not yet born; Britain was struggling to understand her reduced world role, most evidently in the Suez crisis of 1956. Intellectual doubts and guilts raged, and the issues sounded by Existentialism and American "new liberalism" sounded in Britain too. As in the USA, the post-war period saw the emergence of a new, anxious, self-critical liberalism, guilty about the revolutionary ideologies of the Thirties, conscious of the continuing threat to democratic systems, marked as much by its own self-doubt as its power to make a moral judgement on the age of extremity.

Unsurprisingly, at the war's end pessimism was widespread. "England as a great power is done for," Evelyn Waugh wrote in his diary in 1946, ". . . the loss of possessions, the claim of the English proletariat to be a privileged race, sloth and envy, must produce an increasing poverty . . . until only a proletariat and a bureaucracy survive." Others of more liberal viewpoint looked with more hope at the world of Beveridge, Butler and the Welfare State. But a mood of populism, austerity and bureaucracy seemed to encourage dullness and anti-intellectualism, and, except in official forms of public celebration like the 1951 Festival of Britain, the arts seemed out of place. Magazines folded in dismay, dark reports came in quickly. It was soon noted that, where the end of the Great War had been followed by the Modernist explosion, nothing similar was emerging after 1945. Cyril Connolly, always the elegant pessimist, took his pessimism even further. In *The Unquiet Grave* (1944) he noted: "Flaubert, Henry James, Proust, Joyce and Virginia Woolf have finished off the novel. Now all will have to be re-invented from the beginning." In 1946, in his magazine *Horizon*, he complained there was no sign of this happening, "not because of a decline in talent, but on account of the gradual dissolution of the environment in which it ripens." By 1947 he was growing ever more impatient. "It is disheartening to think that twenty years ago saw the first novels of Hemingway, Faulkner, Elizabeth Bowen, Rosamund Lehmann, Evelyn Waugh, Henry Green, Graham Greene . . . but no new crop of novelists has risen commensurate with them," he wrote. Art was not properly supported, the reading bourgeoisie were disappearing, and "such a thing as *avant garde* has ceased to exist." "There is an intimate connection between the Twilight of the Arts and the twilight of a civilization," he warned. The "twilight of the arts" account of the post-war situation continued through most of the Fifties; and it was certainly true that in austere post-war Britain the *avant-garde* spirit that had flourished three decades earlier showed little sign of returning.

This post-experimental gloom was, it should be said, internationally widespread, not least in the United States, where critics like Malcolm Cowley and John Aldridge were making similar comparisons and drawing similar conclusions: the age of experiment was over, literature seemed incapable of recovering from the war. In Britain critics who sought to discover a new literary generation or a new *Ulysses* expressed constant disappointment. Many important writers from the 1920s and 1930s continued to write, including (besides those Connolly mentioned above, all still writing) George Orwell, Ivy Compton-Burnett, Joyce Cary, L. P. Hartley, Anthony Powell, Christopher Isherwood, Aldous Huxley, C. P. Snow, the brilliant short-story writer V. S. Pritchett and more. What was absent was the next generation; the young writers who did emerge seemed, Waugh sourly observed, like bespectacled,

277

state-aided, production-line specimens, and the post-war mood appeared just as austere as grim Stafford Cripps himself. The new generation emerging from the expanding number of universities had a redbrick hue to it, and looked more inclined to moral seriousness than dandyism, criticism rather than creation. They were encouraged to solemn rigour by literary-critical magazines like *Scrutiny* and *Politics and Letters*, which for a time appeared far more exciting than the literary journals, and mostly invited them to cast away childish Bloomsbury things – including, some suspected, literature itself.[3]

The literary pessimism that grew in the Forties long outlasted its season; some of it goes on to this day. Fed by strong feelings of cultural transition and insecurity, an image of the British novel started to emerge in some quarters that strangely resembled that of post-war Britain itself. As it sank giggling into the sea, its power fading and its economic base in disarray, it looked back to exploit what it had most of: the past. It still managed to produce quality fiction of a traditional kind, the novel's equivalent of the Burberry raincoat or Harris tweed; from time to time the odd stylish innovation occurred, fiction's equivalent of Carnaby Street or The Beatles. But, ignoring the demanding transformations of the Modern movement and the aesthetic and philosophical issues reshaping fiction elsewhere, its writers "hung on," to traditional plot, character and subject, defiantly refusing the aesthetic challenge of the day. In fact, though Modernism had indeed begun to fade, as much because it was deeply intertwined with the perceptions and ideologies of a now discredited period as because its leading figures had departed the scene, the aesthetic standards it set became ever more influential. Now criticism began to reconstruct the "Modern tradition," burnish its monuments, give it its name, order and significance, distil its aesthetic implications; the *avant garde* became an academic institution. The novel, above all the "modern novel," began to replace poem and play as exemplary

---

[3] An interesting and personal report on all this is Martin Green's *A Mirror for Anglo-Saxons* (London, 1960), by a post-war pupil of F. R. Leavis.

literary object, and the fiction that was now being produced often seemed regressive by comparison. It marked a return to an older concept of fiction, to realism, materialism, empiricism, linearity, against which the Modern movement had been in revolt. It reverted to humanism, rediscovered provinciality, rejected the shock of the new, returned to hugging the shore of the real. No longer a project for imaginative adventure and linguistic discovery, the British novel was "no longer novel." As Waugh put it, a golden age of writing was now followed by a silver one, notable not for radical invention but "for elegance and variety of contrivance." Meanwhile, so this line of argument continued (it still does), fiction elsewhere – in the United States, France, Italy, later Latin America – carried on the great modern experiment. That was the view of post-war British fiction that started to become dominant critical currency, with the result that to this day criticism has been inclined to over-emphasize the realism and anti-experimentalism of British postwar fiction, overlook its variety, and neglect the substantial rewriting of the tradition actually taking place.[4]

Certainly the atmosphere in post-war British fiction was not that of an opening world. Aesthetic debate narrowed, serious British critics – for whom, it seemed, the only good novelist was a dead novelist – paid scant attention to new fiction ("The most discouraging thing about writing novels . . . for a young novelist in this country," complained one young novelist who turned to drama, David Storey, "is the fact that they have no importance, I mean they have no intellectual currency"). The three best books on post-war British fiction were by American critics, all of whom perceived it going through imaginative withdrawal symptoms. Frederick R. Karl, in his *A Reader's Guide to the Contemporary English Novel* (1959), noted that "we have been

---

[4] There are some interesting comments on this in Neil McEwan's *The Survival of the Novel: British Fiction in the Later Twentieth Century* (London, 1981), where the author rightly notes: "Our fiction is strong in fantasy, in scandal and sexual humour, in eccentric forms of life, in philosophical and intellectual comedy, in its radical social irreverences; and in its attitude to genre, its parodies, and its attitude to the verbal nature of the novel." Such a view has been slow to emerge.

279

reminded with alarming frequency that the English novel of the last thirty years has diminished in scale," its novelists implying that "the experimental novel . . . is no longer viable and retreat is perhaps expedient . . . The contemporary novel is clearly no longer 'modern.'" James Gindin in his survey *Postwar British Fiction: New Accents and Attitudes* (1962) saw post-war fiction as chiefly concerned with representational themes of social class and conduct, though he rightly emphasized the strong Existentialist flavour of much of the writing. Rubin Rabinowitz, in his *The Reaction Against Experiment in the English Novel, 1950–1960* (1967), thoroughly documented the withdrawal from Modernism of younger British novelists, and their return to an older tradition of the novel. In his wider, later study *The Situation of the Novel* (1970), the British critic Bernard Bergonzi likewise judged that post-war British writers had settled for "the ideology of being English," had accepted "the nineteenth century as a going concern," and were failing to write the "fiction of the Human Condition" being explored elsewhere. From these accounts it could be judged that the British fiction of the Forties and Fifties rejected formal experiment and became a workaday object of representation, artistically and socially provincial in tone. Its characteristic tale was the story of a working-class or lower-middle-class young man wandering, in a state of anguish and alienation, along a canal bank in Nottingham or Wakefield; its typical method was that of nineteeth-century reportorial realism; if asked, its writers firmly dismissed the challenge of form.[5]

[5] See Frederick R. Karl, *A Reader's Guide to the Contemporary English Novel* (New York, 1959; rev. ed., London, 1963); James Gindin, *Postwar British Fiction: New Accents and Attitudes* (London and Berkeley, Calif., 1962); Rubin Rabinowitz, *The Reaction Against Experiment in the English Novel, 1950–1960* (New York, 1967); and Bernard Bergonzi, *The Situation of the Novel* (London, 1970). Karl's book in fact deals with writers of several generations, including Graham Greene, Evelyn Waugh, George Orwell, Henry Green, Joyce Cary and Elizabeth Bowen, as well as with "the Angries." It is a useful study, which concludes that British fiction has elected to be "restrictive rather than extensive, to bring back character and plot rather than to seek the inexpressible; in brief, to return to a more self-contained matter while retaining, however, many of the technical developments of the major moderns." Gindin's study is intentionally concerned with the novel of conduct and class, and

These are useful studies of the time, and there is considerable truth in the judgement. But the argument was always far too narrow, and is now long past its sell-by date. British fiction had not "returned" to realism; it had been there throughout the century. Though it frequently betrayed narrowly national or provincial implications, it was not apart from developments taking place elsewhere. The need to record the social changes of the post-war world drove many young writers to the pen; the political anxieties and alienations of a time of moral and ideological confusion, and afterwards of affluent conformity, plainly entered fiction; there was much concern with the social origins of writing, and a search for a vernacular renewal of language. But the portrait of post-war British fiction as generally devoted to sociological realism is far too simple, and depends not only on which writers the critics chose to emphasize but on the kind of reading their books were given. While these debates and doubts were occurring, British fiction in the later Forties and above all the Fifties was in fact passing through a significant revival; this is when most of the main post-war directions, many of the most important fictional careers, began. And, far from moving in one single direction, the novel was moving in many – toward realism, but also new forms of experiment; toward provincialism and regionalism, but a changed internationalism; toward social representation, but moral allegory, fantasy, gothic, metafiction. In Britain as elsewhere, what was happening was the emergence of a period where no one movement dominated, no single style or aesthetic manner prevailed, the multiplicity of heritages and influences

---

the tradition of the social theme in British fiction, and acknowledges the multiplication of perspectives on social experience. Rabinowitz particularly explores the revolt against "Bloomsbury" that developed in British fiction in the post-war years. Bergonzi is concerned with the late twentieth-century crisis of humanism and identity which is expressed in the post-war novel, and the way in which British writers have retained a concern with liberal values, by comparison with American "comic-apocalyptic" fiction, with their fundamentally different presumptions about the nature of self and society. All these books are valuable studies that played an important part in shaping a discussion of British fiction at a time when it was largely neglected by British critics themselves.

writers had to hand multiplied, the imaginary museum of the modern arts expanded. Cultural layers changed and grew confused; the emergence of the mass media and the technological and consumerist revolution changed the nature of culture and publishing, and what Al Alvarez called an age of "No-Style" emerged.

Within this there were distinctive British directions. By the Fifties, the British novel was increasingly reflecting two things. One was a desire to reconstruct the novel as a form of humane liberalism, which meant recapturing some elements from the past of the British tradition, often bypassing the Modern movement in the process. The other was a need to face the spectacle of the age, the era of anxiety, modern barbarism and evil, which transformed that tradition, and meant acknowledging many of the most powerful and troubling aspects of the Modern movement, such as the work of Dostoevsky or Kafka. Many of the most interesting works of the early post-war years – from Malcolm Lowry's *Under the Volcano* (1947) to George Orwell's *Nineteen Eighty-Four* (1949), from Angus Wilson's *Hemlock and After* (1951) to William Golding's *The Lord of the Flies* (1954) – dealt, in various forms, from realism to political allegory, documentary to mythic experimentalism, with that dilemma of continuity and crisis. The return to social realism was one element in a much larger story, as, over a period of large-scale aesthetic, cultural and social change, British fiction began to take on its post-war shape.

4.

There could be no doubt about which was the first British post-war novel. On 17 August 1945, in the month atomic bombs annihilated Hiroshima and Nagasaki, and the Japanese surrender brought six years of fighting to an end, George Orwell's *Animal Farm: A Fairy Story* was published. The book was a clear break with Orwell's Thirties fiction, and, as its subtitle makes clear, it was no work of ordinary realism. Nor was it written from "inside the whale," in a state of resigned passivity. It is a classic political allegory in the form of an animal fable, the story of a great revolution of the oppressed and suffering animals on the decaying (and very English) Manor Farm. What starts as an egalitarian revolution turns into a totalitarian order, run by an apparatus of propaganda, terror and betrayal. Orwell meant the book not as an anti-revolutionary novel, but as a warning of how modern revolutions go wrong, basing this on Stalin's rise to power in the Thirties. It is a hard and bitter satire on revolutionary illiberalism, with its one-party states, its unprincipled leaders and corrupted *apparatchiks*, its management of thought and its exploitation of the masses, all this written with a liberal's rage and a Swiftian bitterness and certainty. But the story, about the past, had a far more immediate meaning, as right across Eastern Europe the processes he described began to unfold. Orwell's is one of the great modern political satires, and a book of great topicality whose meanings spread far beyond Britain. No less potent was the book that followed it, *Nineteen Eighty-Four*, which came out in 1949, just one year before Orwell's early death from tuberculosis, and is set in the Britain of only forty years on. This too was hardly a work of conventional realism, as the shock of displacement in the famous opening line indicates: "It was a bright, cold day in April, and the clocks were striking thirteen." In fact it is a work about the destruction of common-sense realism and the defeat of ordinariness, the corruption of language by force and power, as "Big Brother" takes command. The ordinary working world of the small hero Winston Smith is destroyed by the new reality, which takes the form of a modern terror directed against all that is familiar – love, friendship, brotherhood, even the clock of time itself. *Nineteen Eighty-Four* is a dystopian novel (the genre would grow) given much of its strength by Orwell's deep political understanding of the mechanisms of terror, psychological invasion, and brainwashing by which the new reality is introduced. Among the strongest mechanisms is the corruption of language itself, the replacement of communal and inherited speech by "Newspeak," the corrupted language of "justice" and "progress." Both Orwell's books are very British books, and they depend on a commonsense notion of a shared language; but they explore the general condition of the age. The word "Orwellian" was soon added to the word "Kafkaesque" to describe the development of many a state, many a public vocabulary, the world as it developed up to and beyond 1984, and in many countries Orwell's post-war novels took their place in the *samizdat* undercover writing of the times. For British writers, their meaning was slightly different; Orwell renewed the tradition of decent liberalism, and restored the value of commonplace language. Along with E. M. Forster (no longer writing fiction, but publishing widely), Orwell became a fundamental influence on the cultural mood, and his novels helped shape not only the spirit of post-war realism but the fiction of moral allegory and dystopian anxiety that was to follow.

If Orwell was a writer from the Thirties who handed a grim vision of the post-war world on to his successors, so, in a quite different way, was Evelyn Waugh – a writer who had no liking at all for the post-war age, and took a comically pugnacious stand against it. With *Brideshead Revisited* (1945) he made his lush farewell to the inter-war years, irrevocably lost in the chaos of wartime. Then in 1947 came a political satire, *Scott-King's Modern Europe* (1947), the story of a British history teacher who is invited to attend a bogus national festival in the revolutionary state of Neutralia. He witnesses a revolution and has various sinister adventures; finally he returns to his school just in time to discover that it is now proposing to "fit its boys for the modern world." Scott-King objects, pointing out that not fitting anyone for the modern world is "the most long-sighted view it is possible to take." Waugh too did not intend to fit himself for the modern world, and took up a grandly aristocratic position that disdained almost all its works, from the new egalitarianism and liberal notions of progress to the processes of Americanization and homogenization that followed the war. Meanwhile he observed what was happening with comic delight; and there was no shortage of happy subjects. When he was invited to Hollywood to discuss an aborted screen version of *Brideshead*

Revisited, he was taken to visit Forest Lawns, the fanciful theme-park cemetery whose commercial founder had become, as Waugh delightedly put it, "the first man to offer eternal salvation at an inclusive charge as part of his undertaking service." The result was *The Loved One: An Anglo-American Tragedy* (1948), a brilliant black comedy of American innocence and European experience set round American burial customs. Hollywood's "Whispering Glades" cemetery, with its depthless borrowing of motifs from European culture ("The Wee Kirk O' The Heather") and its absurd cosmetician, Mr Joyboy, has a comic counterpart in the nearby pet cemetery, which offers equivalent services for our animal friends ("Dog that is born of bitch hath but a short time to live . . ."). Waugh's wonderfully Gothic text and his delighted reaction to the bland, plasticated, film-set modern California, the new Arcadia where death was unreal and culture did not even go skin-deep, is more than condescending. Other writers were to find deeper treasures in the transatlantic voyage; to Waugh it became an emblematic visit to the world of the modern unrealities, founded on the failure to confront all that mattered to him – history, culture, identity, faith, death and the Last Things.

By now Waugh's Catholic faith was becoming a more overt element in his fiction, a consolation set against the late modern chaos. From that, then, came the pietistic *Helena* (1950), his dullest and most devotional novel, a story of the British saint's discovery of the True Cross. But from it also came the most important of his postwar works, the trilogy "Sword of Honour" (*Men at Arms*, 1952; *Officers and Gentlemen*, 1955; *Unconditional Surrender*, 1961). In it Waugh set out to do for the Second World War what Ford Madox Ford's "Parade's End" sequence had done for the First, and there are plain echoes of the earlier work. Waugh's Guy Crouchback is, like Ford's Tietjens, a chivalric hero, an old-fashioned Christian (though Catholic) gentleman with an estate and the wish to go to a just war on a true crusade. Instead what he finds are ignominious episodes, political treacheries, corrupt alliances, while at home his unfaithful wife Virginia, who owes something to Ford's Sylvia, has an affair with the commonplace Trimmer. The true crusade proves false in almost all respects. When the Russo-German Pact is signed, putting Fascism and Communism in alliance, Guy thinks the real and true enemy is "plain in view, all disguise cast off. It was the Modern Age in arms." But the British-Soviet alliance corrupts this, the true cross turns into the Sword of Stalingrad, the conflict into "the people's war." Betrayals continue, as the British support Tito in Yugoslavia, and everywhere in the Mediterranean campaign retreats and disasters corrupt the heroic dream. In the end Guy resignedly accepts that the history of the world does not seem to progress according to an understandable divine intention, and, a stoic Christian gentleman, makes his disappointed peace with what is – even taking back Virginia, with her "faint, indelible signature of failure, degradation, and despair," and accepting her child by Trimmer as his own. Unlike Ford's, Waugh's sequence is plainly a comedy, one more tale of romantic failure in a corrupted, declining, ignominious world. Like his friend Anthony Powell's delightful "Dance to the Music of Time" sequence, the work is often inconsequential in structure, taking a fine rambling delight in chronicling British class attitudes and the great gallery of British wartime types – eccentric heroes, bureaucrats, spivs, spies and traitors. But it is also shaped by a myth of historical decline and failed quest, which involves Guy accepting a world where redemption does not come in history, through war, society, or love, a world more chaotic and absurd, or unintentional, than he imagined. It is a notable book; indeed, along with Olivia Manning's "The Balkan Trilogy" (1960–65) and "The Levant Trilogy" (1977–80), another picaresque voyage through chaotic wartime events, set first in a collapsing Romania and then in Egypt, it can be reckoned the best British fiction to come from the front, on which Waugh himself served with an appropriate mixture of heroism and eccentricity.

There was one other important and profoundly revealing post-war novel, *The Ordeal of Gilbert Pinfold* (1957), a work of almost undisguised confession. Its central character, Mr Pinfold, is a middle-aged, dandyish and self-conscious writer who, like his creator, has adopted the mask of testy don and eccentric colonel, and feels an aristocratic dislike of all that has happened in his own lifetime. He considers he lives in a declining age of letters, and that he writes novels "quite external to himself." On a cruise to the Far East, he finds himself subjected to persecution by a variety of strange and accusing voices, attacking him for every kind of sin and deviance, and threatening him with death and disaster. Finally he surmounts his ordeal, which is a paranoidal near-madness, recovers his reason and "modesty," his carapace of disguise, and realizes now that "a mocking slave always stood beside him in his chariot reminding him of his mortality." The mocking slave called; Waugh died suddenly in 1966. *The Ordeal of Gilbert Pinfold* is certainly not a work quite external to the author's self; it is an agonized and often highly ironic late-life confession. Waugh had been through a similar experience of hallucinatory paranoia, his self-induced persecution often closely resembling attacks made on him by liberal critics who opposed his dislike of the modern world and the people's "long revolution." He had had the gall to satirize the age of egalitarianism, regard it not as a time of social justice but an age of decline and fall. In fact all Waugh's books, from *Decline and Fall* onward, share a similar vision. In the early works he stood outside the crisis, presenting it pure; in the late ones the author is implicated, and endures like Crouchback or suffers paranoidally, like Pinfold, so that comedy becomes imbued with a sense of personal tragedy. What is important is that Waugh's sense of historical nihilism, leavened by his quirky version of the Catholic faith and British recusant history, gave him his absurdist comic vision – his assumption that, in the light of eternity, history is a folly, the idea of progress absurd, the barbarian always at the gates. From this came the dark grim humour of absurdity that was his great gift to fiction; Waugh revived an essential comic tradition of the novel that went back to Swift, Sterne and Fielding, and gave it a mocking place in the post-war world, challenging many of its liberal expectations and illusions. In the biting social satire of Angus Wilson, the Catholic irony of

Muriel Spark, the social observation of Simon Raven, the happily prejudiced social comedy of Kingsley Amis, the trace of Waugh is to be found. So it is in the nihilist black humour of much of the best American fiction of the Sixties, and the dark uneasy satire of much British fiction of the Eighties.

But the writer from the Thirties who had the most pervasive influence on post-war writing was Waugh's co-religionist Graham Greene. He was a writer of Sartre's "second generation," a literary contemporary of Malraux, Mauriac, and Bernanos; but his impact, and the larger part of his writing life, was to belong to the third. That was partly a matter of longevity and productivity, but also a matter of sheer imaginative vitality and power. Green was one of the most various of novelists, and by the time he had done he had worked in nearly all the genres – the spy novel and the thriller, the novel *noir*, the religious romance, the political novel and the social comedy – and converted them into powerful currency for the post-war age of historical chaos and metaphysical darkness. His free use of popular forms, his near-parodic use of genre fiction, often led critics to think he never found a real form for his fiction, an aesthetic to call his own. He himself has Rowe, his central character in *The Ministry of Fear* (1943), reflect on this during the course of a heavy bombing raid on London: "You used to laugh at the books Miss Savage read – about spies, and murders, and violence, and wild motor-car chases, but dear, that's real life . . . The world has been remade by William Le Queux." Greene's fiction presumed the world had been remade by the thriller writers; like Waugh he saw history as debased, corrupted and senseless, life at odds with the divine and the eternal, betrayal and guilt everywhere, turning innocents into murderers, loving husbands into spies. Unlike Waugh, he saw this less with total dismay than with a kind of world-weary knowingness, the eye of the initiate who has always possessed this peculiar secret. His world of seedy landscapes, depressed lives, failed loves, political and sexual faithlessness, divided loyalties, moral and metaphysical guilt, was plainly a Catholic one, but over the course of time it came strangely to match the spirit of the age of existential anguish, and increasingly the ideological and the geographical map of the Cold War world itself. His stained and agonized realism moved toward the centre of modern writing as the years went by, even as his work shifted to take fascinated account of the new ideological divide, and the chaos of lives everywhere caught up in the great superpower game. A Catholic who could sympathize with Communism, to the point where he evidently presumed some shared identity between the two, a writer who regarded sinners as capable of sainthood, disloyalty as pointing to some higher loyalty, he finally succeeded in turning his own distinctive and vastly international Greeneland into a close simulacrum of the Cold War world itself. Through it he then became an indefatigable traveller, capturing its trouble-spots and primary points of conflict, its textures and aromas and local colours, making them real places in a densely imagined metaphysical world.

Even so Greene's post-war novels were not, as he said, works of realism, and they spend little time on the detailed social manners common to much British fiction, though anxious class attitudes and ideas of social duty are in them everywhere. Nor are they, in most cases, religious novels, rather works written in the shadowy moral and geographical wasteland of religion's aftermath. Greene once explained that the significance of the religious novel was that it sustained the human factor in fiction – "with the religious sense went the importance of the human act" – and that was the drift of his post-war work. His first novel after the war's end was *The Heart of the Matter* (1948), set in the Sierra Leone he had known as a British intelligence officer during the War. His story of the colonial policeman Scobie, the weak man who sins out of human compassion, and so is led to adultery, blasphemy and suicide, still sustains the form of the religious novel, but this is already a work set in a drab and dying empire, political and metaphysical, where the moral and social law is in decay. Next came *The End of the Affair* (1951), which too is a version of religious novel, as the epigraph from Léon Bloy – "Man has places in his heart which do not

289

yet exist, and into them enters suffering, that they may have existence" – suggests; indeed it is a theological detective story. But the story, told by a writer-narrator, Bendrix, is also a deeply self-conscious fiction about the nature of fiction. A cynical humanist, having an affair with a married woman, Sarah, he becomes convinced that she has yet another lover whom he jealously sets out to pursue and detect. The rival proves to be God, whom Sarah has turned to in sexual guilt; He is the higher plotter in whose games of sin and redemption, sinners and saints, Bendrix can only have an irrevocably minor role. The story turns into a struggle between the higher and lower plotter, which Bendrix loses. "We are inexorably bound to the plot, and wearily God forces us, here and there, according to his intention, characters without poetry, without free will, whose only importance is that somewhere, at some time, we help to furnish the scene in which a living character moves and speaks . . .," he resentfully concludes, accepting that the only way to confront the deviousness of God's love is with his hate. This is the one book where Greene comes close to disclosing his aesthetic of the novel, the terms of his metaphysical myth. In a sinful world, the novelist acts like God, perhaps with or against Him, but creating human lives, moral law and the terms of justice and compassion, a divine as well as a secular plot. Greene's closest examination of the hunger for doctrine and the desire for eternity becomes his closest look at the complexity of narrative ("If this book of mine fails to take a straight course, it is because I am lost in a strange region; I have no map," Bendrix notes); his most blatantly Catholic novel also proves his most meta-fictional.

But for the moment the book was the end of that affair. There is a writer in Greene's next novel, *The Quiet American* (1955), but he is no elaborate explorer of narratives. He is a reporter, covering the French colonial wars in Indo-China, later Vietnam, recording the imperial withdrawals of the day, and telling the story of Pyle, the quiet American, innocently doing guilty things in the interests of long-term political aims. The book extends Greene's metaphysical concerns, dealing with his distrust of innocence, which implies lack of knowledge of personal and political evil; it is also very plainly about its author's own dividing loyalties in the age of Cold War ideology. It observes the naivety of Western liberalism in the face of Third World resurrections, and remarkably prophesies the disastrous American campaign in Vietnam a decade on. Thus *The Quiet American* opens a new sequence of books which, in various styles and tones, were to take their subject-matter from Greene's enquiring journeys to the places of political turmoil, Third World crisis, and ideological confrontation, over which he would then set his own distinctive preoccupations with guilt and innocence, violence and heroism, liberal optimism and obscure religious faith. The next book, *Our Man in Havana* (1958), set in Batista's Cuba, is a comedy at the expense of the British Secret Service. Wormwold poses as a secret agent in order to acquire a pony for his daughter, and becomes comically (and finally tragically) involved in the complicated mechanisms of Cold-War spying, which he identifies as belonging "to the cruel and inexplicable world of childhood." *A Burnt-Out Case* (1961), set around a leprosy colony in the Congo, marks a return to religious concerns. It explores the now burnt-out, once-famous Catholic architect Querry – his name a cross between "quarry" and "query" – and was, Greene explained, "an attempt to give dramatic expression to various types of belief, half-belief and non-belief." So were the remainder of his novels, if with various degrees of seriousness and comedy.

A Burnt-Out Case is indeed serious, considering the sinful world out of which creation arises; the next book, *The Comedians* (1966), is an explicit reflection on comedy, set in "Papa Doc" Duvalier's corrupt regime in Haiti, where, under the dictator and his grim secret police, evil is rampant and terror universal. Goodness here becomes so absurd that the individual can only act as an absurd comedian. As the character Brown explains: "We are the faithless; we admire the dedicated . . . for their integrity, their fidelity to a cause, but through timidity, or lack of sufficient zest, we find ourselves the only ones truly committed – committed to a whole world of good and evil, to the wise and the foolish, to the indifferent and the mistaken." But there is a final, absurd revolution of the comedians, and the book itself was effective enough to provoke "Papa Doc" into an extravagant denunciation of Greene's work and political attitude. Surviving within the world of modern politics was an increasingly important theme. *The Honorary Consul* (1973) then turns to the South American dictatorships and the activities of guerrillas in Argentina and Paraguay, deals with a bungled kidnapping, and considers the morality of political terrorism. *The Human Factor* (1978), plainly based in part on the case of Kim Philby, the very British spy who fled to Moscow, is a compassionate account of the story of that primary modern figure, the double agent. Greene gives his central character Castle a history not unlike his own; and the novel intertwines the themes of religious and political faith and disloyalty, as Castle, who defects to Moscow, seeks to travel onward beyond God and Marx to the land of peace of mind. The most notable of other late books is *Monsignor Quixote* (1982), which is a reflection on two of his fundamental interests: divided loyalties, and the form of the novel. It is a rewriting of the great comic source story from which all Western novels sprang, Cervantes' *Don Quixote*, set in a contemporary Spain where the Don and Panza are Catholic priest and Communist mayor, the windmills are the modern ideologies. The two travellers debate their metaphysical and materialist positions, and find that they may be riding in the same direction after all.

Greene died in 1992, after eight decades of writing, still a writer the British tradition found quite hard to deal with. His work had never quite resolved into one single shape or form, yet it was always distinctively Greene-ian, constructing, no matter what in the world it dealt with, a pervasive atmosphere, social, political, metaphysical, religious. It remained in essence international, reaching into entire foreign continents of modern experience as well as into the dark or more anxious places of the human condition, a journey without maps, or else with imperfect ones. Yet there remained, for all the exiled and deliberately disloyal aspects of it, a distinctive Britishness, an awareness of origins; unlike some modern fiction, the writer's air of exile was never total. His work disputed with contemporary liberalism, though unlike Waugh's it remained politically progressive; it challenged innocence, confronted evil, and acknowledged the human disorder. For all its variety, his fiction collectively amounted to one of the most solid and complete of modern writing lives. During it he had moved from the grim era of Depression social and political crisis, through wartime horrors, to a no less dark and deadly world of superpower rivalry, and from a writer of thrillers and entertainments to a central explorer of modern issues and dilemmas of faith and justice. Many found his religion and his politics – idiosyncratic Catholicism blending with a no less idiosyncratic strain of Marxism – and his ironic vision of Western liberal intentions worrying; others felt dismayed by his vision of a world where compassion often led to self-destruction, the survival of the human factor often seemed an arbitrary matter, and good causes generally had strange effects. But his perspective on a modern world where maps are never safe and ideologies are never entirely just provided a convincing and complete vision of later twentieth-century life. Other critics found his work notable but lacking in a defined artistry, and well outside the development of the British novel; Greene himself was satisfied, when asked, to be known as "a good popular writer." In fact his range, over his more than fifty books, was remarkable, and in British fiction he left his trace everywhere. Writers who otherwise have little in common have a common influence in him – Malcolm Lowry and John Le Carré, Muriel Spark and P. D. James, Anthony Burgess and Ian McEwan, Brian Moore and Len Deighton, David Lodge and Martin Amis. He shaped the future of the dark crime novel, which captured the seediness of the world at war, and spy fiction, which explored the duplicities and conspiracies of the cold-war age. He also influenced the future of the experimental religious novel – the work of Murel Spark, for example, a writer who shared his paradoxical sense of God as plotter and the implications this bore for the paradoxical relations of author to novel. At their very best, his books assume the density and the moral and political wisdom of Conrad, or the religious intensity of Mauriac. Greene was, I think, a major writer, author of some books that were great, some that were feeble, but all fed by a large imaginative vision, almost too large for his own interpretation of it, of the difficult and often meaningless age of decay and ideological disorder, bleak history and the troubled human factor, through which he lived.

5.

But was Modernism truly dead now, had the *avant garde* ceased to exist, as critics like Connolly claimed? There were, undoubtedly, few signs of strong experimental passions among the newer writers who began emerging from austere Welfare-State Britain. Perhaps, though, the truth was that the Modern experiment was not dead, but alive, and well, and living in exile, where it was gradually turning into something else, the beginnings of a new era of experiment. In Paris as the war ended, Samuel Beckett – an Irishman now beginning to write in French, and so doubly at an angle to the British tradition – was already working on what would prove some of the most important writing of the post-war era, though its importance would take a little time to surface. Beckett had first gone to Paris from Ireland in the late Twenties, and worked with Joyce, before publishing (in London) an important study of Proust; his Modernist credentials were plain enough. He taught again in Ireland, wandered Europe during the Thirties, then chose to be in France during the wartime occupation. Two works published in London during the Thirties had begun to establish his experimental career: the bleakly comic stories collected together in *More Pricks Than Kicks* (1934), and the more ambitious novel *Murphy* (1938), a work of elaborate playfulness that could be compared with Flann O'Brien's *At Swim-Two-Birds*, another brilliantly playful novel from an Irish writer that came out the following year (both books acquired a significant

294

following). Beckett kept writing even while working with the Resistance and risking arrest from the Gestapo, and produced the novel *Watt*, a work whose central character is a question always encountering a negative answer (Knott). This did not see print until 1953, in Paris, by which date Beckett had already produced most of his major fiction, for after 1950 his attention began increasingly to move to the stage. He had by now turned to French for his literary language ("It was more exciting for me," he explained), and put these books into English only later. This key body of work included *Mercier et Camier* (not published until 1970) and the trilogy *Molloy* (Paris, 1951, New York, 1955), *Malone Dies* (Paris, 1952, New York, 1956) and *The Unnamable* (Paris, 1953, New York, 1958). Also from this period came the aptly titled *Texts for Nothing* (Paris, 1955, New York, 1967) and that most powerful of post-war plays, *Waiting for Godot*, initiating the "theatre of the absurd." As Christopher Butler has put it, these were works from "after the wake" (*Finnegans Wake*), and form a brilliant, purist progress, or regress, on from Modernism, intensifying its irony and intellectual comedy to the point of making a new and absurdist fictional world, or text.[6] As works from Modernism's afterlife, it became appropriate to call them too, in time, "postmodern."

Beckett's fiction grew by a kind of fundamentalist reduction, gradually reducing the familiar human and social content of fiction, while at the same time questioning the nature of language, the status of the word, the basis of the fictional act itself, and the status and powers of the imagination to imagine. *Murphy*, the first novel, starts sombrely ("The sun shone, having no alternative, on the nothing new") and its "hero" Murphy, the "seedy solipsist," spends a good deal of time in his rocking-chair. But this is still a work of very Irish black humour, with clear debts to Sterne, Swift and Rabelais, and for all its caged

---

[6] See Christopher Butler, *After the Wake: An Essay on the Contemporary Avant Garde* (Oxford, 1980), which examines this phenomenon across most of the arts. Also interesting is John Fletcher, *Claude Simon and Fiction Now* (London, 1975), which draws some important parallels between developments in French fiction and the work of some contemporary British novelists.

setting, in the Magdalen Mental Mercyseat in East London, a work of plenitude and punning. It is set in a defined place, London; has a defined central character, Murphy, with a variety of bohemian friends and obscure sexual contacts; it has even something like a continuous plot, about Murphy's quest for success in life and his chesspiece-like movement toward self-extinction. The novel ends with his death, or rather continues beyond – to Murphy's remains, intended to be flushed down a toilet at the Abbey Theatre, Dublin, but in fact scattered among the butts and vomit of a London pub floor, to the last sequence where the kite-flying Mr Kelly tries to discover where seen and unseen meet. Murphy is a split being, and this is a tragi-comedy of Cartesian anxieties, making the human conscious-ness and intellect a comic manifestation. If the body, like the poor, is always with us, it is the life of the mind that gives Murphy pleasure – so much pleasure that pleasure is not the word. The author's pleasure is equally plain, as he parodies logic, language, and literary form. *Watt* – that question seeking an answer – takes parody further. Watt is blocked by a succession of quandaries (how do you feed a dog, or name an object?) in the caged, surreal confines of the house of Mr Knott, but he comically survives amid the negatives. Thereafter the terms of minimal survival are a basic theme of Beckett's work, as, increasingly, a sense of late modern, or absurd, tragedy arises – the vision grows more purgatorial, the characters become "lost ones," caught in an obscure, parodic quest, painfully struggling to maintain human motion in a world of travail without result: otherwise the human condition.

"If it begins to mean something, I can't help it," Beckett once wrote. That applies to the trilogy, which, following the course of his developing vision of absurdity, is marked by the slowing down of narrative itself, as we move from character to his absence, and from naming to unnaming. *Molloy* contains a double quest. Molloy, poor, old, impotent, caught in a scarcely defined landscape with a minimum of objects (a bicycle, a few stones in his pocket, and so on) is hunting for his mother. Meanwhile Moran, a private detective, is hunting Molloy. Both quests are parodic and circular, without real progression or a sequence that is really a sequence. Things do change: Molloy loses his bicycle and crutches, and is left to crawl on, observing, "But I am human, I fancy, and my progress suffers, from this state of affairs, and from the slow and painful progress it had always been, whatever may have been set to the contrary, was changed, saving your presence, to a veritable calvary, with no limit to its stations and no hope of crucifixion." Words also change; Moran's narrative finally returns to its first sentence, with negatives added. More quandaries of narrative form the theme of *Malone Dies*, where Malone, dying, tries to fill his time with fictional time, which disposes the facts differently (as, perhaps, all writers do), the act of writing serving a combinatorial function rather like the stones that Molloy had tried to permute in the earlier novel. With *The Unnamable*, language comes near to silence, and begins to lose most of its signifying powers: the hero disappears, and only words make him. Over the whole course of the trilogy the landscape dissolves away, the material world is reduced down to a small number of permutable objects ("To restore silence is the role of objects"), human motion slows, to a kind of eternal mental imprisonment as well as physical arrest. The "heroes" grow ever more disembodied and identityless: characterless characters. As writing moves toward silence, the character or author becomes an identityless agent producing text without certainties or plain purpose. Language comes closer to babble or gabble, and takes on the nature of an imperfect or obscure memory incapable of being precisely invoked, meanwhile asking us to consider whether there is identity at all, and how writing comes out of it.

The result is an agonized comedy of writing itself, one that asks some of the deeper questions of modern fiction's enquiry. Beckett's work plainly belonged to the era of Existentialism, though its apprehension of the absurdity of the world went further, toward the fading of signification explored by later Structuralist critics like Roland Barthes. A key phrase from *Molloy* – "There are no things but nameless things, no names but thingless names" – was tuned to the same mood that produced

Barthes' view that modern literature is "openly reduced to the problematics of language," his case that fiction was a text written against "the essential enemy, the bourgeois norm," and his notion of the theoretical Death of the Author, which considers that the writer does not write but is written, by the problematics of language itself. In Beckett, too, the author grows authorless, text grows texty and unreliable, and his multiple "writers" are made to write by, report to, forces outside themselves. At the end of *Molloy*, writing denies itself. Moran writes: "Then I went back into the house and wrote, It is midnight. The rain is beating on the windows. It was not midnight. It was not raining." Malone, trying to write the story of his own death, ends in the silence of writing itself. *The Unnamable*, a monologue spoken in limbo, incorporates but also rejects the writing written earlier in the trilogy: "All these Murphys, Molloys and Malones do not fool me. They have made me waste my time, suffer for nothing, speak of them when, in order to stop speaking, I should have spoken of me and me alone." It ends: "it will be the silence, where I am, I don't know, in the silence you don't know, you must go on, I can't go on, I'll go on." Beckett indeed went on too, mostly into drama and stage monologue, but also, in 1961, to *How It Is* (Paris, 1961; London, 1964), one further step. At its centre is a naked being crawling forward through mud in a world of minimal names and objects (mud, sack, can-opener, cans), toward negation. The book depends on the permutation of a limited set of signs that sometimes turn into gabble ("quaqua"). The story is untrue, but there is a kind of survivalist's humanism in the book, a minimal signification: "something happened yes." Or, as another later piece of the short prose put it: imagination dead imagine.

Though Beckett – who was awarded the Nobel Prize in 1969, in, of course, his absence – should properly be called either an Irish or a French writer (it's been said that to understand him a green Eire passport is required) he had considerable impact on post-war British fiction, and on late modern fiction everywhere. Indeed, along with Jorge Luis Borges and Vladimir Nabokov, two other late Modernists who wrote on into the post-war circumstance, he could be said to express nearly all that was central to serious fictional "postmodernism," despite the many developments that followed, especially in French and American fiction. For sympathetic British writers from Iris Murdoch to Anthony Burgess, to whom his trace adheres, it has probably been his pained, vestigial humanism that means most. But for many writers of fiction he has suggested the difficult yet crucial path of experiment in an age when existence itself seemed to be challenged, the human subject or identity put in doubt, the power of language to speak to reality brought under question. His concern with the dominance of language moves away from the path of representation favoured by most British (and other) novelists. But he has been an essential contemporary reminder that realism is not a stable entity, that the novel is a construct made by a fictionalizing imagination, out of a language whose referential and perceptual powers are subject to self-cancellation. If the novel is a narrative, a "going on," that narrative is a progression ever constituting, questioning, and destroying, or deconstructing, itself. Certainly, from the moment in the early Fifties when *Waiting for Godot* was staged in Britain, and the trilogy was translated during the decade, Beckett became perhaps the best example of *avant-garde* writing there was. "He is there, looming large and inescapable on the literary landscape; the games which he has been playing with words for over thirty years have become matters of immediate relevancy to us," John Fletcher wrote in the mid-1960s: "His extraordinary hero roams about in our consciousness, a haunting and troublesome shadow." In later reduced circumstances, Beckett did what Joyce did: fiction, this closely examined and explored, could never be quite the same again.

Meanwhile another graduate of the experimental Paris of the Thirties, Lawrence Durrell, also took an interesting post-war direction. In Paris Durrell had worked with Henry Miller, imbibed a great deal from the movement of Surrealism, and with *The Black Book* (1938) produced what Miller describes as "a good little chronicle of the English death . . . a book Huxley could have written if he were a mixture of Lawrence and

Shakespeare." It contained the same mixture of sexual "real-ism" and social surrealism as Miller, and was not published in Britain because of its obscenity. The tradition of surrealism and fantasy, eroticism and psycho-sexual occultism, continued into the sequence of novels known as the "Alexandria Quartet" – *Justine* (1957), *Balthazar* (1958), *Mountolive* (1958) and *Clea* (1960) – which reflected his experiences during the war and after in Egypt. The sequence, a flamboyant reminder of the exotic and erotic sources of fiction, and of storytelling's roots in the Arab world, was a complex series of mirror novels about highly elaborate sexual relationships set in Alexandria. Durrell said the buoyant and inventive sequence was based on the Freudian rubric that every sexual relationship involves four people, and described it as "a four-dimensional dance, a relativity poem," "a four-card trick in the form of a novel" which "might raise in human terms the problems of causality or indeterminacy." Durrell's determined attempt to render the novel "spatial" rather than temporal generates a perspectivized form of narration, aided by the fact that the novels have various narrators and many of the characters in the sequence are themselves novelists or writers whom we see in the act of writing. Later on, Durrell's highly decadent spirit was to turn into an ever more elaborate, orientalized exoticism; there is no doubt that his mixture of erotic and exotic made much of his appeal for many of his readers. His later sequences – *Tunc* (1968) and *Nunquam* (1970), set in a Turkish harem, and *The Avignon Quintet* (1974–85) – are less successful, though they develop another aspect of his very narcissistic fiction: his notion that the novel is not only a sexual but a cultural, indeed a metaphysical, meeting place, which can open the door to occult forms of knowledge beyond Western rationalism.

Then there was Malcolm Lowry, another writer from the Thirties who had taken his experiment yet further afield, to Mexico and then Canada. His youthful *Ultramarine* (1933: reissued in revised form 1963), about a middle-class young man who ships as a deckhand on an Asian voyage, and is taunted but at last accepted by the crew, was a Thirties novel, but it laid down a key theme that Lowry was to continue to develop to the end of his life, the notion of the mythic or romantic voyage into the spirit, the long creative voyage that never ends. After various adventures on his own long wandering voyage, Lowry settled in the Thirties in Mexico, and here began a vast epic about the Faustian damnation of his hero, an alcoholic consul in Cuernavaca, Mexico, whose abuse of his "magical powers" brings about his death in a *barranca* at the hands of a local Fascist gang. This much redrafted work, *Under the Volcano*, came out at last in 1947; it is arguably the best novel to appear in Britain in the immediate post-war period. Set on the Day of the Dead in 1938, right after the signing of the Munich agreement, it was meant as a mid-century tragedy of contemporary urgency. The story of Geoffrey Firmin, the alcoholic British consul who spirals down to death in an atmosphere of historical crisis, political corruption, infidelity and sexual despair, and romantic self-destruction, clearly had a historical allegory behind it (Lowry wrote his publishers that it was a parable about "the universal drunkenness of mankind during the war, or during the years immediately preceding it, which is almost the same thing"). But also, like *Ulysses*, it was meant as a multi-significant text, filled with "borrowings, echoes, design-governing postures," as Lowry put it. In other words it was a work of what contemporary critics call "intertextuality" – laden with allusions to other texts and codes drawn from astronomy, the Kabbala, writers like Dante, Melville and Joyce: a hermetic work requiring interpretation. The Joycean echoes are strong: the novel is set on a single day, depends on a complex management of consciousness, functions through a variety of styles, and each chapter is structured to a set of complex codes. Indeed, as Lowry also informed his not readily comprehending publishers, it is "so designed, counterdesigned and interwelded that it could be read an indefinite number of times and still not have yielded all its meanings or its drama or its poetry." Altogether he meant it, he said, as "a prophecy, a political warning, a cryptogram, a preposterous movie, and a writing on the wall"; all these things are there, seaming this complex novel. Movies play a big part, cryptic signs are everywhere; meanwhile the struggles of world powers are building to war between the liberal democracies and the totalitarian states, and this has its parallels and sinister echoes in Mexico. Yet, in Modernist fashion, the book is structured less with than against historical time, its deliberate stasis opening up its metaphoric and mythical aspects; the destructive cycle is an eternal human state as well as an historical condition.

Complex as the book was, Lowry did not intend his creative journey to end there. He wanted it as part of a vast and ambitious scheme – "The Voyage That Never Ends" – in which it would be an inferno, followed by a purgatorio and a paradiso. The whole constantly varied project grew to incorporate six or seven books, meant to explore different versions of the creative imagination struggling with the world, and introducing the "Modernist" themes of the violation of fiction by reality, the need for a text to remain eternally unfinished. Books already written and published – a rewritten *Ultramarine*, and *Under the Volcano* – would be a part of the great open scheme; so would books written but not yet published, like *Lunar Caustic* (which appeared posthumously in 1968), and books that had been written but lost, like *In Ballast to the White Sea*, which he hoped to rewrite. *Under the Volcano* would stand in the middle, referred to in the others, and be written not by Lowry but by Sigborn Wilderness, one of the fictional *alter egos* Lowry gave himself. Like Beckett – but according to a quite different creative drama, of much more romanticism and an endless, ever-growing plen-titude – Lowry was always concerned to incorporate one book into the next, refract book against book, make his writing life one continuous narrative. Sadly, things went in a different direction. Lowry returned from Canada to Mexico, ran as he usually did into difficulties, and wrote up this experience as *Dark as the Grave Wherein My Friend is Laid* (posthumous, 1968), a disappointing variant on the earlier novel. The last project, as the plan changed yet again, was *October Ferry to Gabriola* (posthumous, 1970). Set in Canada, where he was now living and writing, this dealt again with expulsion from the paradisa-ical garden, and the corruption of the wilderness: an interesting book, but without the power of his masterpiece. Lowry's sudden death from drugs and alcohol in 1957 cut off the ever more elaborate creative project he was still devising. To this day he remains an under-valued author, a writer's writer, as fascinating for the ideas, the elaborate creative adventures, the hyper-ambitious projects he set out to explore. But the one novel, *Under the Volcano*, confirms the seriousness and importance of his experiment, and his place in the late modern tradition.

6.

There were important experimental tendencies alive in post-war fiction. There is, though, no doubt that there were powerful *anti*-experimental tendencies too. In 1959 William Cooper (Harry Hoff) published an essay, "Reflections on Some Aspects of the Experimental Novel," which explained his literary credo. "During the last years of the war a literary comrade-in-arms [C. P. Snow] and I, not prepared to wait for Time's ever-rolling stream to bear Experimental Writing away, made our own private plans to run it out of town as soon as we picked up our pens again – if you look at the work of the next generation of English novelists to come after us, you'll see we didn't entirely lack success for our efforts," he observed, adding, "We had our reasons for being impatient. We meant to write a different kind of novel from that of the thirties and we saw that the Thirties Novel, the Experimental Novel, had got to be brushed out of the way before we could get a proper hearing."[7] If this is somewhat confusing – the identification of the "Experimental

---

[7] William Cooper, "Reflections on Some Aspects of the Experimental Novel," *International Literary Annual, No. 2*, ed. John Wain (London, 1959). Cooper went on: "Putting it simply, to start with: the Experimental Novel was about Man-Alone; we meant to write novels about Man-in-Society as well. (Please note the 'as well'; it's important. We had no qualms about incorporating any useful discoveries that had been made in the course of Experimental Writing; we simply refused to restrict ourselves to them.)" Other similar comments can be found in statements by Pamela Hansford Johnson, Angus Wilson, Kingsley Amis and Philip Larkin. See Rubin Rabinowitz, *The Reaction Against Experiment in the English Novel*, cited above, note 5.

Novel" with the "Thirties Novel" is odd, especially since both Cooper and Snow had been Thirties novelists – the point he is making is not. There *was* a strong thrust in post-war fiction away from the Modern movement, and toward a more socially descriptive form of writing. It was largely distinct from the impulse to realism (which usually meant political realism) that had been so strong in the Thirties, being prompted largely by response to the new social and cultural changes that were altering post-war Britain. As Connolly had rightly sensed, many of the foundations, both aesthetic and economic, that had supported the Modernist arts in Britain were now weakening, and the long cultural and social dominance of Bloomsbury was coming to its end. To post-war writers, many drawn from very different social origins and educations (lower-middle or working-class backgrounds, grammar-school and redbrick-university educations), it appeared that a distinct social class had appropriated the realm of modern high culture. As Lawrence had warned, the notes of British Modernism generally sounded in an upper-middle-class accent, and "experiment" had come to seem the preserve of a social as well as an artistic élite. One significant part of the "reaction against experiment" therefore came from the desire to draw art from a different social and regional source. The class factor was unquestionably an element in the changing climate of post-war literary culture; and Stephen Spender in an *Encounter* article of the Fifties noted the emergence of "a rebellion of the lower middlebrows" which had "an aroma of inferiority about its protest," along with a strong distrust of the metropolitan and international literary scene. It need hardly be said that these challenges and resentments were often quite blind to the range and complexity of the Modernist impulse, and frequently resulted in a crude narrowing of the meaning of Modernism to "Bloomsbury" itself. As Angus Wilson remarked later, when the inevitable reaction against this reaction came, many of these literary attitudes derived from "reasons which are really extraneous to the novel but something to do with the social battle inside England, and should never have played a part in deciding the form."

As I have indicated already, there were other important reasons for the large change of direction, the mood of reconstruction, in post-war British fiction as it hesitantly emerged after 1945. One was a growing recognition that the Modernist revolt against the Victorian and the realistic Edwardian novel had itself grown out of a generational battle, a war of children against fathers, that had passed long since. The rebellion into the "modern novel" meant that much of the long tradition of British fiction, including the regional and provincial tradition, appeared to have been ejected from the accessible past of the novel, and there was every reason to suppose some of it might be reachable again. So the debate of the early twentieth century – Spender's battle of the "moderns" and the "contemporaries" – now resumed, but with the key terms reversed. Now it was the "moderns" who represented the tradition, the "contemporaries" who were trying to create the fresh heritage. In 1950, Angus Wilson, just beginning his career, wrote a pastiche of Virginia Woolf's essay "Mr Bennett and Mrs Brown," and asked us to consider the problem of "Mrs Green" – living in the country, with "her good tweeds, her untidy grey hair, her interesting beauty," and her preoccupation with the behaviour of the servants, the pattern of the clouds and the distant problem of the poor. Mrs Green was the Woolfian heroine, half highbrow and half middlebrow, refining life into poetry, and excluding the forces outside the realm of her sensitivity and the human and moral jungle beyond. Wilson was later to retract his satire, acknowledging the influence of Woolf on some of his own work, where, indeed, figures much like Mrs Green (Meg Eliot in *The Middle Age of Mrs Eliot*) become Wilsonian heroines, their lives transformed by new conditions where the protection of class and literary aesthetics no longer completely serves them. He also acknowledged that the post-war revolt against aesthetic fiction had its own limits, and argued that the real task of the post-war writer was that of uniting the panoramic diversity of the traditional British novel of Dickens or Trollope with the psychological depth and aesthetic completeness of the experimental Moderns. An essential point of these arguments was that post-war writers clearly felt that, despite all that had happened in recent history (and art), British culture retained some fundamental and deep-seated continuities, which allowed them to reconstruct the links between contemporary writing and the pre-modern, panoramic, moral novel of the past. The results grew ever clearer; as Wilson acknowledged in 1961: "The traditional English novel as practised by the great Victorians – the novel with strong social implications, the novel of man in the community rather than man in isolation or in coterie, the novel, above all, of firmly constructed narrative and strong plot rather than verbal and formal experiment – has made a triumphant return in England in the last ten years."[8]

The signs of this return began early, in two youthful novels by a writer who would establish himself a decade later as one of the most important, the most explicitly unexperimental, the most self-consciously English of post-war poets. In 1946 Philip Larkin published a fine first novel, *Jill*, set in an Oxford of very un-Brideshead-like flavour during the gloomy opening years of the war, and dedicated to a fellow undergraduate, Kingsley Amis. Its central character is a clumsy working-class boy from Lancashire whose romantic dreams and social fantasies are contrasted with his own northern background and the daily realities; the story ends in an equivocal acceptance of the ordinary. In 1947 Larkin followed with a second work, *A Girl in Winter*, about a girl from an unnamed foreign country who works in a provincial British public library. She too has high expectations of the place she has come to and the people she meets, but finds herself coming to terms with the simple and unromantic ordinariness and contingency – "the flat landscape,

---

[8] See Angus Wilson, *Diversity and Depth in Fiction: Selected Critical Writings* (ed. Kerry McSweeney, London, 1983), especially the title essay and the two essays on Woolf. Wilson makes the point that the return toward a more social and narrative fiction was "a logical result of the interlocking of subject and form rather than any dogmatic devotion to the traditional English novel. If stream-of-consciousness, interior monologue of the more orthodox kind, cinematic treatments of time and other experimental forms are less used – and for my part I believe that this is only a temporary rejection of over-exploited devices still rich in promise – it is because their defects of cumbrousness and monotony have become apparent."

wry and rather small" – of British life. These are works of realism as social understatement, and the books are filled with an essential refusal to romanticize; the realistic spirit is not a protest, hardly an interpretation, to some degree an affirmation, but above all a vision – a way of precisely painting the half-forlorn yet much-valued texture of British life and landscape. When Larkin left the novel for poetry, publishing his major collection *The Less Deceived* in 1955, the same world – the undeceived eye, the flat universe, the customary practices of daily life – would become the stuff of his unromantic verse. In fiction and verse, Larkin had found a flat, observant, daily way of writing that would be accepted by others as a primary post-war idiom.

However Larkin's two novels, which are fine but self-consciously slight, would scarcely have had the influence they did had they not been reinforced over the years by a number of other fictional debuts that brought a new tone of voice to the English novel. One of the most important was that of Angus Wilson, a slightly older writer who had begun writing fiction at the end of the war, following a breakdown, and published his first satirical short story in 1946. More stories – sharp, clever, often savagely malicious tales about the post-war order, which had left its chief characters, the pre-war bourgeoisie, its shabbily genteel men, its indomitable women, adrift on the sea of social change and post-colonial decline – appeared during the late Forties, and were collected together in two volumes, *Such Darling Dodos* (1949) and *The Wrong Set* (1950). They were novels in miniature, filled with vivid characters and satirical social observation, bitingly pointing in two directions: against the old bourgeoisie, trying to hang onto their old class attitudes, privileges and gentilities, and against the cleansing new bureaucrats who were administering the post-war period. Wilson's was a brilliant debut, and in 1952 he turned to the novel, with *Hemlock and After*, a story about the ambiguities of modern liberalism. It tells the story of a well-known writer and "moral scourge," Bernard Sands, who tries to establish, with government help, an official artistic centre at Vardon Hall (it could

well have stood for the post-war novel itself). But fine liberal
and reforming intentions fail under the complexity of human
nature, problems of madness and evil, and Sands, forced to
confront his own unacknowledged homosexuality, realizes his
own life has been built on, exactly, sand.

During the Fifties, Wilson developed into one of the most
important of post-war British writers, both because of his own
gifts as a "moral scourge" and because of his panoramic if not
Dickensian sweep (appropriately, he eventually wrote a notable
book on Dickens). Wilson was a moralist, but he also saw the
instability of the moral life, just as he saw the underlying crises
of the liberal progressive spirit. In *Anglo-Saxon Attitudes* (1956) –
a large and panoramic novel which took its title from Lewis
Carroll's *Through the Looking Glass*: "He's an Anglo-Saxon
messenger – and those are Anglo-Saxon attitudes. He only does
them when he's happy" – he explored the British hypocrisies
and moral self-deceptions, setting his story around an archaeological dig for the tomb of an Anglo-Saxon bishop, which has
been an occasion for fraud. The story as a whole is a social and
psychological archaeology of the way British goodwill frequently leads to the refusal to face the hard realities. The theme
returns in his next novel, *The Middle Age of Mrs Eliot* (1958),
about a middle-aged married woman, Meg Eliot (whose literary
name is doubtless intentional), of Virginia Woolf-like characteristics, whose ordered life is suddenly thrown into chaos when
her husband is killed at a foreign airport in a random incident
of international terrorism. Mrs Eliot then has to rebuild, in her
changing England, a quite new life for herself; the story is the
story of her courage, and, by implication, of the way in which
literature encloses us, and narrow British lives must change to
face the contemporary crises and the modern chaos. So far,
Wilson's novels had shown him as a wide-reaching, realistic
recorder of contemporary social life, and his fiction owed as
much to George Eliot as it did to Dickens in its sense of moral
urgency. But as the Sixties began, Wilson signalled a sharp
change in his work (and he was not the only writer to do so).
In 1961 he wrote *The Old Men at the Zoo*, a nightmare invasion

fantasy set in the future, about the release of evil in the life of a bureaucratic institution. Wilson, always an intelligent, never a simplistic, writer, wrote the book, he said, in reaction to the "tyranny of neo-traditionalism in English novel-writing," and opened the way to the much more experimental, text-examining spirit of his later work, discussed in the next chapter.

But where had the "tyranny of neo-traditionalism" come from, and what was the usable tradition available to the British novelist dispensing with the era of modern experiment? Here the literary critics helped; in critical debate interest in the social, the moral and the representational lineage of the novel was growing ever stronger. F. R. Leavis was now the most influential British critic, and the spokesman for the "New Criticism." In 1948 he published *The Great Tradition*, a study of the British novel. Today, in an era of theoretical abundance and wide-ranging interpretation, the book looks narrow and idiosyncratic; but it constructed and interpreted a clear, distinctive line of social and moral realism running through the centre of the British novel – from Jane Austen to the Dickens of *Hard Times*, and on to George Eliot, Henry James and Joseph Conrad, culminating in D. H. Lawrence, whom Leavis saw as the major modern novelist. Leavis was concerned to establish the importance of the novel as a critique of life and culture, and also to suggest that its historical vigour had now been compromised: by Bloomsbury's aestheticism and mannerism, by Marxist sociologizing, and by the corruptions of popular mass culture. Other books reinforced the point. In 1950 the American critic Lionel Trilling (he had written a notable book on E. M. Forster, a writer whose influence was strong in the Fifties) published *The Liberal Imagination*, a book written in revolt against the ideological certainties and political emphasis of the Thirties. Trilling looked to literature, above all to the novel, as the great expression of humanist scepticism; it was higher than politics, deeper than a social report, a form that saw the world in its human multiplicity and variety, and was capable of grasping the contradiction and ambiguity that lay beyond the limits of ideology and certainty. "The novel, then, is a perpetual quest for reality," he wrote in a key essay, "Manners, Morals, and the Novel," "the field of its research being always the social world, the material of its analysis being always manners as the direction of man's soul." He admitted that the novel in this form had never really established itself in America, and equivalent books in the USA (Richard Chase's *The American Novel and Its Tradition* [1957], for instance) stressed the difference between the European "novel" and the American "romance," born in the era of Gothic. If the novel of society, manners and morals had been neglected in the American tradition, it was, though, alive in the British. The European novel, the novel not just of Fielding and Dickens but of Balzac and Tolstoy, had always taken social and historical existence seriously, seen manners as an aspect of morals and metaphysics, and in its care for character and society it was an expression of the liberal imagination itself, the voice of life's complexity, and the struggles of culture and anarchy that made for creative understanding. In 1953 the debate extended with the publication, in translation, of Erich Auerbach's remarkable wartime book *Mimesis: The Representation of Reality in Western Literature*, an extraordinary study of the arts and practices of fictional representation. If you were a student of literature then (and I was) realism, the moral value of the novel, the modes of social representation, were what you talked about, the demands you made on fiction.[9]

The recovery of the novel as a moral and humanist form was therefore a presiding theme of fiction as the Fifties started, and a new generation of writers did show signs of emerging. The

[9] It is important to stress again that this was by no means identical to the political realism of the Thirties, and in many respects was a reaction against it. If social and political urgencies remained powerful, the powerhouse of history now generated a quite different kind of light. As Stephen Spender put it in *The Creative Element* (1953), reflecting on post-war literary "liberalism": "The point really is that a moral view of society can be stated without any concern for political action of any kind, whereas directly politics enters in, social action and taking sides are involved." In the Thirties, he says, one had to accept "the modern consciousness of politics as a universal fate." Now it was possible to see an independent significance in literature itself, without taking a totally "aesthetic" stance or supposing that literature and politics were not somehow intertwined.

mood was reinforced when, in 1950, William Cooper brought out his *Scenes from Provincial Life*, a work of regional realism and strong social feeling that suitably took its title from the subtitle of George Eliot's *Middlemarch*. Cooper's lyrical comic work was not, in fact, a contemporary novel at all; it was set in a provincial city (plainly Leicester) at the dying of the Thirties, over the period between the Munich agreement and the outbreak of war. It was, amongst other things, a story of how close the reality of England had come to invasion and defeat; it also implicitly distinguished between those who had departed from Britain in 1939 and those who remained and experienced its fate and fortunes. The story is told in retrospect by Joe Lunn, a young science teacher at the grammar school, who has literary ambitions, and deals with a group of friends, nonconforming provincial intellectuals, some homosexual, who are convinced there will be a German occupation of Britain of which they will be early victims, and are planning exile to the United States. But they also see themselves as remote from the great events, and the day-to-day world of provincial life, the problems of love-affairs and jobs and local pleasures, eventually become far more important than history. They remain just where they are, amid commonplace life and ordinary Englishness; fortunately for the story, and human life itself, history was to reinforce their choice. Like Larkin's, this is a work of appreciative realism, a lyrically comic celebration of the ordinary over the extraordinary, the day-to-day over the grand march of history. It celebrates the tones and morality of ordinariness, preferring scepticism to romanticism, sense to sentimentality, comedy to the grand manner. Later the story went to three more volumes, following the later development of Joe Lunn's life – first as a wartime scientific adviser to the government, where he has a hand in the planning of the atomic bomb, then into his post-war life as a writer and a married man. *Scenes from Metropolitan Life* (completed in the 1950s but not published because of libel problems until 1982) takes us into the post-war world, the metropolis, the corridors and clubs of Whitehall, the heart of the "Establishment." *Scenes from Married Life* (1961) is,

311

unusually in contemporary fiction, a celebration of marital happiness as well as an exploration of the private side of a public life in which Joe is now an important figure; *Scenes from Later Life* (1983) brings him close to retirement in the late Seventies. All these stories are told, by Joe, with an appreciative sense of the commonplace, and a distinctive comic good humour and hopefulness prevails.

It is notable that realism here is not, as so often in modern fiction, being used for the task of protest, but to celebrate the plain flat virtues of ordinary English life. Cooper, himself a scientist and a government adviser, confessed himself a warm admirer of H. G. Wells: "I loved it, enshrining Wells' message of optimism," Lunn says in *Scenes of Later Life* of Wells' *The History of Mr Polly*. The links between these two writers are significant. Cooper shared Wells' scientific hopefulness, his sexual vitalism, above all his feeling that British society was changing in favour of the career open to talents. Both told stories of the "new men" with scientific educations. Cooper, who has written some eighteen novels, brought out two, *The Struggles of Albert rVoods* (1956) and *Memoirs of a New Man* (1966), about "goings-on in the world of science and technology." Behind his books there is a hopeful story of social ascent: from province to metropolis, ordinary origins to public influence, science to faith in social progress. Like his friend and "comrade-in-arms," C. P. Snow, with whom he worked in Whitehall, and who appears as "Robert" in several of these books, he had some claim through his wartime government work (which included involvement with the British atomic bomb) and his bureau-cratic activities to be an architect of post-war Britain. Cooper's light-hearted comic realism helped set the tone for a whole sequence of novels that, over the following decade, explored tradition and change, class and classlessness, provinciality and metropolitanism, optimism and alienation, considering English life with a fresh and exploratory curiosity. John Braine called the book "seminal": other writers, like Alan Sillitoe, David Storey, Stanley Middleton and Stan Barstow, reflected its influence. Fiction in this tradition explored the story of a Britain that was gradually emerging from austerity to growing confidence and greater wealth, changing in its fundamental class relations, witnessing the rise of new working-class affluence and meritocratic prospects. It reflected the decline in political and ideological hostilities, and the growth in social consensus, that came in the early 1950s, until the Suez crisis of 1956 brought the emergence of a new political agenda, stimulated the growth of the Youth Culture, and encouraged the rise of the New Left which pointed the way to the Sixties.

A similar story of the new men and the rise of social hope was told, in a far more solemn public voice, by C. P. Snow in his "Strangers and Brothers" sequence (1940–70), a very Wellsian tale of modern history and social ascent presented in the manner of a Victorian one. Snow's eleven-volume social, political and moral record of Britain from the First World War to its own present is told by Lewis Eliot, former provincial outsider, eventually lawyer, academic, scientist, bureaucrat, government adviser, and member of Harold Wilson's Labour administration in the Sixties. Its basic theme begins as early as Snow's novel *The Search* (1934), about a young lower-middle-class scientist who makes his way from Leicester to London and from drabness to society. The volumes of "Strangers and Brothers" are modern history seen from the inside, an account of the intentions and conflicts of the teachers, academics, lawyers, politicians, scientists and bureaucrats who over the troubled and often anarchic march of history hope to make reason, justice and progress prevail in human affairs, and who eventually shape and administer the changes of post-war Britain. Key volumes target the central moments of this process. *Time of Hope* (1947) deals with the Wellsian spirit of provincial life just before the Great War, and Eliot's desire for fame and success in London. Other stories deal with post-war tasks and crises. *The Masters* (1951), about contention inside a Cambridge college when a new master is to be appointed, deals with competing versions of life and value, and has been called "a paradigm of the political life." *The New Men* (1954) is about the problems of scientific doubt and moral conscience that attend

313

the birth of the British atomic bomb. *Corridors of Power* (1964) addresses the effect of the Suez disaster on the Conservatives, and other volumes face the conflicts of public and private life, of reason and rising unreason. Chaos, evil and the sense of mortality are never far away. But essentially the shape of the sequence is a progress. "I had kept an interest in success and power which was, to my friends, forbiddingly intense," Eliot confesses in *Homecomings* (1956); so he does, and the voice of the telling follows the history of the hero, moving from the private to the public man.

It is sometimes said that the saga novel, a form of great popularity in the Fifties, reflecting, perhaps, a desire for renewed continuities, is innately conservative. But that is hardly the spirit of Anthony Powell's sequence "A Dance to the Music of Time," which started out in 1951 with *A Question of Upbringing*, ended with *Hearing Secret Harmonies* in 1975, and covered a similar span of historical time to Snow's. Powell's long narrative, which is now best read as one continuous tale spread over much of a century and across twelve books, is about the decline of the British aristocracy and the fragmentation of the Victorian world through various eras of crisis, especially the war, to be observed in flashes, through many tones and voices, and with play and irony. Nick Jenkins' long story (which Kingsley Amis called "the most important effort in fiction since the war") takes us on from, in effect, the period when naturalism dissolves into modernism, through the years of "great changes," and out into the postmodern world. Against the survivor Jenkins is set the formidable destructive figure of the rogue Kenneth Widmerpool, who stalks ever-wider horizons of success and power, and who emerges chameleon-like in various positions of suspect influence at different points in the history (at one stage he becomes a latter-day university vice-chancellor of weirdly radical opinions, at another a possible spy). As narrator, Jenkins himself is a chameleon too, moving polymorphously through the styles of writing that emerge over his lifetime, meanwhile seeking his own distinctive and secret harmonies from the polyphonic music of time. By contrast with Snow's sequence, where the voice takes on an ever more public aspect, the author becoming ever more an authority on what is real, Powell's remains stylish human comedy that never settles for a single clear voice, while always remaining intimate with historical actuality and the social and human existence of its characters. And quite as formidable was Doris Lessing's sequence "The Children of Violence," which ran through five volumes between 1952 and 1969. Her story of Martha Quest is a story of a woman's absence from history, and Martha's gradual acquisition of a place in it – through Communist politics in Rhodesia, through the struggles of gender – though Lessing's goal of exploring "individual conscience in relation to the collective" is a struggle toward both being and obliteration, in which realism's voice grows ever more unstable.

But, for the moment, British fiction did seem, as Trilling suggested, a repository of social reality in literature, and writers seemed to agree with Angus Wilson that "No sharpening of the visual image, no increased sensibility, no deeper penetration of individual consciousness . . . could fully atone for the frivolity of ignoring man as a social being." Cooper was right: his own spirited social comedy, and Snow's more heavily public record, did help give voice to the British fiction of the Fifties, and the revival of the "liberal" novel. For the moment, the new British fiction seemed easy to characterize. It was anti-experimental and anti-romantic, anti-ideological and eminently realistic. It was devoted to the commonplace and the ordinary, much concerned with characters, manners, histories, social practices; it valued characters, felt with "real" lives. The older preoccupations of the British novel had reasserted themselves, and the novel was now less a formal or metaphysical enquiry than a practical, popular form of expression. Some of its emphases were also provincial in a rather less desirable sense. The homage to the longer tradition of British fiction that now resumed led writers like Cooper and Snow to express the belief that the work of Joyce, Woolf and Dorothy Richardson had damaged the fortune of fiction, that "stream-of-consciousness" had diverted the flowing river of the novel, that the task of fiction was that of plain social chronicle. This rejection, as writers later began to see, had its price in narrowing representation, and in diminishing the aesthetic and psychological springs of modern fiction. It was more than Modernism that was being rejected, but many of the depths behind fiction's surfaces; the challenge of life beyond the text, the challenge of the word inside it, the multiplicity of narrative and the contention of genres and human voices would have to be returned to again.

7.

So was there, now, a trend emerging, did we have something that might even be called the Fifties novel? Many did not think so. In August 1954, the *Observer* newspaper undertook a now familiar exercise, and ran a series of articles on the subject "Is the Novel Dead?" Inaugurating the debate, Sir Harold Nicolson argued magisterially that, since the novel was scarcely more than two hundred years old, it was plainly no more than "a transitory response to certain conditions." As he explained: "The ancients did not write novels since they were so busy with art, politics, administration and war that they never achieved the special type of tranquillity in which the art of fiction becomes creative and relevant." Now, in the untranquil world, the novel had again become irrelevant. In one of the many replies, Alan Pryce-Jones suggested that the Ovidian gloom might possibly be overdone: "it needs only one or two outstanding novels to appear for us to be told that English fiction is in the beginning of a remarkable revival." A little cursory investigation might have suggested that it was; the truth was that the Fifties was a remarkable era of first novels and beginning careers, many of which would become extremely notable. In 1950, the year of *Scenes from Provincial Life*, Barbara Pym brought out her social comedy *Some Tame Gazelle*, and a new writer called Doris Lessing published her *The Grass Is Singing*, a novel about settlers in South Africa that has rightly been called a work of "radical realism"; she followed it during the decade with several volumes of her powerful "Children of Violence" sequence (1952–69). In 1951, the year of the "Festival of Britain," Nicholas Mosley published *Spaces of the Dark*. In 1952 Angus Wilson emerged as a novelist with *Hemlock and After*, Paul Scott, novelist of the dying Indian empire, brought out *Johnnie Sahib*, and Thomas Hinde *Mr Nicholas*. In 1953 Ian Fleming started the career of James Bond in *Casino Royale*, and John Wain published *Hurry On Down*, a realistic picaresque novel far more critical in tone than Cooper's. Here the "anti-hero" Charles Lumley revolts against his grammar-school and university upbringing and the conventional life it promises him, and goes "down" in society, in a clear echo of Orwell's *Keep the Aspidistra Flying*. Lumley comically sustains his revolts and tries to purge the taint of class by taking various jobs – as window-cleaner, hospital orderly, chauffeur, and nightclub bouncer – to end up in the fashionable occupation of a radio comedy scriptwriter. This was an "outsider" story, a type popular at the time, but Lumley has to admit the battle fought between self and society has ended neutrally, in "a draw." Wain's later novels, always interesting, though frequently ponderous in manner, return to these themes, examining convention, the limitations of middle-class marriage, the problems of artistic life in a philistine society. One of the best, *The Contenders* (1958), deals with, and celebrates, anti-cosmopolitan artistic life in the Potteries ("It's because the provinces accept dreariness that London can boast of its brilliance"), and displays a clear debt to Arnold Bennett, another writer whose fortunes revived in the Fifties. "Does one person in a hundred thousand know what he really believes or what he really ought to do?" Wain asked in *A Travelling Woman* (1959), explaining the spirit of his air of revolt; but he made it plain he saw no easy escape from the web of ordinary conventional life. And he also stressed his realist convictions: "A serious novel is an invented story about the truth, not a fantasy," he declared.

1954, the year of Harold Nicolson's funerary sermon on the death of the novel, in fact saw three quite remarkable debuts. Kingsley Amis published *Lucky Jim*, Iris Murdoch *Under the Net*, and William Golding *Lord of the Flies*, all of them remarkable (and highly various) first novels by writers who would acquire great influence. For the rest of the decade the signs of fictional revival would continue. In 1955 came Nigel Dennis' *Cards of Identity*, Dan Jacobson's *The Trap* and Ruth Prawer Jhabvala's *To Whom She Will*. In 1956 came Anthony Burgess' *Time for a Tiger*, and Roger Longrigg's satire on modern advertising *A High-Pitched Buzz*. 1957 saw Muriel Spark's *The Comforters*, John Braine's *Room at the Top*, Colin MacInnes' *City of Spades*, Keith Waterhouse's *Billy Liar*, Hugh Thomas' *The World's Game*, and Christine Brooke-Rose's *The Languages of Love*. In 1958 Alan Sillitoe brought out *Saturday Night and Sunday Morning*, and John Berger *A Painter for Our Time*; 1959 saw V. S. Naipaul's *Miguel Street*, Andrew Sinclair's *The Breaking of Bumbo*, even the first novel of the present author. 1960 saw David Storey's *This Sporting Life*, Raymond Williams' *Border Country*, Edna O'Brien's *The Country Girls* and Stan Barstow's *A Kind of Loving*. In the years immediately after, John Fowles, Margaret Drabble, and John Le Carré emerged. Not too surprisingly, Harold Nicolson's gloomy reflections were quickly replaced by a different kind of argument. Now the talk was all of a Fifties literary revival and the emergence of a post-war movement; the issue was no longer whether the novel was dead but what kind of contemporary life it was living. In 1954 the *Spectator* identified a "New Movement" in poetry (its poets included some of the novelists above) notable for its self-elected modesty and irony and its refusal of romanticism. Following the Royal Court Theatre production of John Osborne's *Look Back in Anger* in 1956 (the year of the Suez crisis), there was much talk of a "new British drama," the "theatre of anger." Similar attempts were made to categorize the "Fifties novel," the most common description being that it was the fiction of "the angry young men." This was somewhat narrow, since a lot of the authors were not angry, many were not young, and a lot of them were women.

The fact was that the fiction that began emerging over the middle and later Fifties was highly various – as would become ever plainer when these emerging careers began to grow to full flower. But things need names and trends need spotting, and there were several useful indicators. There was indeed a trend toward realism in some, though certainly not all, of these writers. There was an inclination toward acknowledging the relationship between contemporary fiction and the long if not necessarily the great tradition of the English novel. Cooper and Snow paid their homage to Wells, Angus Wilson to Dickens, Wain to Arnold Bennett (as did, a little later, Margaret Drabble), Kingsley Amis to Henry Fielding, Golding to R. M. Ballantyne, Sillitoe to Lawrence, Charles Reade and Robert Tressell, Storey to Lawrence, and so on – though, on the other hand, Wain also paid his homage to Flann O'Brien, Iris Murdoch dedicated her first novel to the French surrealist Raymond Queneau, and there was a very considerable influence from contemporary American fiction and above all from the French existentialists, who had a great impact upon the themes and emotions of British Fifties writing. The class-base of writing had certainly shifted, and a good number of these writers came out of the new meritocracy, from lower-middle-class or working-class origins, with a corresponding decline in upper-middle-class fiction – though writers like Simon Raven and Andrew Sinclair wrote well about Cambridge, and a number of the novels set on redbrick university campuses, that site of contemporary social and cultural transition, were by writers educated at Oxbridge. In the wake of Cooper and Snow, there was a marked movement away from metropolitan themes toward provincial subjects, and in fact a serious revival of the regional novel. There seemed to be a note of anti-Establishment protest, and there was a fiction of the "outsider" (Colin Wilson's pseudo-philosophical book with that title appeared in the politically transitional year of 1956), though often, like *Hurry On Down*, the rebellion ended in a "draw." Some writers were plainly writing political fiction, and several nailed their colours to a left-wing mast in the volume *Declaration*, edited by Tom Maschler in 1957, after the Suez crisis of 1956; however a number of others seemed to take (for writers) an unusually benign view of the contemporary social order. If this was a "movement," it was a highly unstable one, with many directions to it. For the moment, though, it would do. In the mid-Fifties it seemed there was a distinctive spirit to the post-war British novel, and critics more or less knew what it was. In fact no sooner had the trend begun to come clear than it began to dissolve, in the changed climate after 1956, and by the end of the decade British fiction was already plainly turning the cycle into "the Sixties."

8.

There were several good reasons why Kingsley Amis' *Lucky Jim* – a remarkably funny book which had been round sixteen publishers before it got into print in 1954 – came to seem the exemplary Fifties novel. The story of Jim Dixon, the young history lecturer in a provincial university who is inwardly and comically at odds with the Bloomsburified academic, artistic and social culture of his elders, captured a powerful contemporary mood. In many respects the book is a traditional romantic comedy: Jim, the comic innocent, trapped in someone else's culture, who always sees that the emperor wears no clothes, receives the comedy's ancient blessing, good luck and good fortune, just like his predecessor in fiction, Henry Fielding's Tom Jones. Amis was plainly a very English writer, and he said so.[10] Its innovation, then, lay not in its form but its spirit, tone and voice. Like Wain's Charles Lumley, though at a higher level of comedy, Jim is a meritocrat who is lifted by social opportunity out of his familiar culture into one he cannot accept or indeed understand; like Salinger's Holden Caulfield in *The Catcher in the Rye* (1951), he undercuts with his innocent eye and his vernacular voice the culture and social pretensions of those

[10] He too challenged the claims of the "experimental novel": "The idea about experiment being the life-blood of the English novel is one that dies hard. 'Experiment' in this context boils down pretty regularly to 'obtruded oddity,' whether in construction . . . or in style; it is not felt that adventurousness in subject matter or attitude or tone really counts." (Quoted in Rabinowitz, cited above, note 5.)

who represent the dominant world. An academic in a provincial university, he fails to accept the academic values of his seniors, above all those of his head of department Professor Welch (who announces himself on the telephone as "History speaking"). Finally, when he has disgraced himself with a wonderfully drunken lecture on the topic of "Merrie England," which he explains never was, he makes his revolt plain, and departs for comedy's literary reward of a good job and the nicest girl, out there in the ordinary commonsense working world. The force and the comic strength of the book lie in the cultural and linguistic substitutions it performs: commonsense prose replaces literary prose. The romantic university novel, once shifted out of Oxbridge, turns into the "campus novel," set in a world where culture is not taken for granted but struggled for, and where rapid social transitions are taking place. Dixon's values are ordinary and provincial, his education is narrow, his engagement to his academic subject totally incidental ("the medieval papers were a soft option in the Leicester course"), his values entirely empirical. Words like "culture," "art," "form," and "academic" sound offensively in his ears; and his theory of life and society is that "nice things are nicer than nasty ones." Throughout the book cultural notions normally framed in one language are deftly rewritten in another ("He remembered a character in a modern novel . . . who was always feeling pity moving in him like a sickness, or some such jargon. The parallel was apt; he felt very ill").

If Dixon is, as the reviewers said, an intellectual rebel, it is not against contemporary British society or culture, but against genteel high culture, aestheticism and bohemianism, the hangover of Bloomsbury. Art is the adversary of real life; Jim's enemies always end up looking like André Gide and Lytton Strachey, while his friends have commonplace lives, ordinary troubles and unpretentious attitudes. If Jim's cultural indignations ("filthy Mozart") sometimes sound like barbarian prejudices, they might better be compared with Mark Twain's mock-naive comic response when, as an American "innocent abroad," he visited the sites of European high culture ("when I

321

had seen one of these martyrs I had seen them all"). Dixon represents the contemporary truth-teller, and his innocent language is an empirical morality, in which honesty is better than self-deceit, common sense better than pretension. Amis was himself a university teacher of literature when he wrote the book, a literary critic and a fine anti-romantic poet, also interested in jazz, detective fiction and the spy story. His novels thus have built into them a sense of serious – or at any rate a literary-critical – purpose. As one tradition is held in disrespect, there are many signs of the making of another. He described himself as "writing novels within the main English-language tradition . . . about understandable characters in a straight-forward style," and his books contain many implied homages to the elements of that tradition, both to its moral realism and to its cleansing spirit of comedy.

Amis' second book, *That Uncertain Feeling* (1955), is set (maybe in homage to his friend Philip Larkin) around a Welsh public library; the story of an adultery that finally affirms the value of domestic ordinariness, it also manages some useful satire at the expense of Dylan Thomas and the Welsh romantic tradition. Then (ironically enough, since Somerset Maugham had described the new writers of the Fifties as "scum") Amis won the Somerset Maugham Travelling Prize, which had the aim of sending the British writers abroad to widen their horizons. Abroad certainly did not widen Amis', and *I Like It Here* (1958) is a fictional record of the results. This is about a writer, Garnett Bowen (a name itself laden with literary allusions), who goes, like his creator, to Portugal, suffers at the hands of foreigners, and meets the deadly world of "bloody abroad." Bowen is no exiled Modernist; he feels Portugal could be improved if moved to somewhere like Eastbourne. He is in fact a hero of Fifties prejudices, anti-upper-middle-class, anti-Bloomsbury, anti-London, anti-Modernist, anti-foreign. *I Like It Here* is often read as a novel of British Fifties insularity, and the "here" that its hero likes is, of course, contemporary Britain. Perhaps it is an insular book (Amis indicated his books were about "what it means to be English"); but its tone is ironic, and the hero has his own limitations, confessing to a deep-seated fear of a nameless journey into the unknown. It is also a decidedly literary text, filled with – as we have learned to say nowadays – "intertextual" jokes about the Moderns, Conrad, Joyce, and Proust; while Bowen is persistently plagued by an expatriate writer with the Jamesian name of Strether, who speaks the banalities of life in long experimental sentences. Happily his traveller's reward comes; Bowen discovers in Lisbon the grave of honest Henry Fielding. This permits another literary homage, to the eighteenth-century author who showed the novel could express "a moral seriousness that could be made apparent without evangelical puffing and blowing." And Amis possessed his own moral seriousness, displayed almost instinctively as comedy. Indeed he was as strong a comic stylist for his generation as Waugh had been for his. At the time it seemed his comic spirit was based on almost the opposite social premises, prejudices and moral feelings; later in his career the similarity between the two writers became ever more obvious.

But if Amis could be regarded as an exemplary Fifties novelist, by the end of the decade his work was changing markedly. In 1960 he published one of his finest books, *Take a Girl Like You*, where the reference point is not Henry Fielding but Samuel Richardson, the author of *Clarissa*. Amis took the classic story of Richardsonian romance, seduction and near-rape, traditionally leading to repentance and virtue, and set it in relation to the *mores* of an age of shifting moral values. The story is seen largely through the eyes of its heroine, the interesting Jenny Bunn, and confronts questions of post-war moral change, shifting gender relations and sexual habits in the age of the pill. The male "shit-hero" Patrick Standish is associated with another key theme, mortal fear, the grasping of life because of the fear of death. The book is morally strange and ambiguous, but in it Amis began unlocking some of the key themes that would feed his later work. His novels of the Sixties – like *I Want It Now* (1968) and *Girl, 20* (1971) – were portraits of rapidly changing manners in the decade of sexual liberation.

The troubled sense of human mortality developed into the fine ghost story *The Green Man* (1969) and the moving *Ending Up* (1974). In later works, like *Jake's Thing* (1978) and *Stanley and the Women* (1984), he examined the growing gender conflicts between men and women and their impact on the family and on male psychology. And his prizewinning *The Old Devils* (1986) showed his cantankerously mortal sensibility, still capable of sustaining what was now the long dark comedy of life into later years, in which the once angry young man had turned into a yet more angry and mortal old one.

The real revolution represented by *Lucky Jim* was primarily a cultural one; it represented a significant alteration in the register of fiction, a paradigm shift of clear importance. It was left to other writers of the later Fifties to document the variety and the detail, explore the shifting social structure, the new landscapes and cityscapes, the general eyeline taken from lower-middle-class or working-class life, the revival of local and regional cultures, the note of dissent that rose as the decade unfolded. By the second half of the decade, the sound of protest grew. Even now, though, the dominant air was not exactly that of rebellion, rather the often half-cynical exploration of a new order of society, where a new affluence was emerging, but a sense of alienation remained. Thus John Braine's *Room at the Top* (1957), the story of Joe Lampton, who exploits his looks and his body to ensure his personal success and his greedy social ascent in the Yorkshire town of Leddersford and beyond. It is a grossly material fiction, its best rhetorical energies being spent on descriptions of very expensive cars and suits, a fiction of commodification. It is just saved from being a male version of female popular romance (or s. and f., pointless shopping, pointless fornication, written in a glow of bodily parts and commodities) by the self-conscious relevance of the theme. Joe is the Fifties version of the Stendhalian opportunist (like Julien Sorel in *The Red and the Black*) whose ascent exploits a vacancy in a society that grants new exploitative opportunities in an age of competition and material success. Braine's was one of a significant group of powerful regional novels that appeared in the later Fifties, when provincial life indeed became, as Wain suggested, an alternative source of renewal in literary culture, and a wealth of new writers – Alan Sillitoe, Keith Waterhouse, Stan Barstow, Bill Hopkins, David Storey – voiced its cultural tones and attitudes.

Sillitoe's *Saturday Night and Sunday Morning* (1958), a work by an author who had already written seven novels before this was published, is one of the most notable – the powerful working-class story of Arthur Seaton, a newly affluent worker on a capstan lathe in a Nottingham bicycle factory, who still hangs on to an older, instinctive working-class anarchism and a gut resentment of all authority ("don't let the bastards grind you down"). He means to have his fun, take his pleasures, and cheat the world before it cheats him. His weapon is his cunning, but his paypacket, his sexual amusements, his expensive suits and working-class codes limit his rebellion. The novel is split between weekly assembly-line slavery, Saturday-night pleasures, and Sunday-morning repentance – a tale of a hungry desire for a freedom stifled in the end, as he becomes a caught fish, readjusted to society through marriage. Sillitoe was, and still is, a vigorous and vivid novelist. And the novella that followed, *The Loneliness of the Long Distance Runner* (1959), an excellently imagined fable about a young Borstal boy's struggle against the powers of authority and for freedom of spirit, showed his metaphorical as well as realistic strengths. Just as remarkable was David Storey's first novel *This Sporting Life* (1960), on its surface a grainily realistic novel about Arthur Machin, a northern working-class boy who wins fame playing professional rugby-league football, though it is also about the conflict of the physical and the aesthetic, the body and the spirit, the masculine and the feminine. These themes, ambitiously expanded, would be the basis of his powerful third novel *Radcliffe* (1963), a panoramic, original work about the struggle of good and evil unfolding in a northern landscape, which rewrites the Gothic novel of the Brontës and the psycho-cultural drama of Lawrence for the divided modern day. Storey's novels, including the excellent *Pasmore* (1972), about a miner's son who becomes a university teacher, and *Saville* (1976), are stories of social and moral disintegration in a changed condition of England, driven by a powerful sense of emotional division and an urgent feeling for art.

The later Fifties saw a number of important works – from Stan Barstow's humane *A Kind of Loving* (1960), set in the quickly changing Northern community of Cressley, to Raymond Williams' *Border Country* (1960) – which looked at the new borderlands of working-class life. Williams' novel is set not only on the borders of Wales and England, but on those of class and classlessness, history and change, the borders where, as his own study *Culture and Society* (1958) and Richard Hoggart's *The Uses of Literacy* (1957) showed, the meanings and changes of contemporary culture could best be read. One reason why realism flourished in the late Fifties was indeed that it became a significant document for the making of new social records and the understanding of new social attitudes. With its strengths came its weaknesses – for, without a strong aesthetic spine, a powerful sense of history, or a real social urgency, it quickly disintegrates into anecdote, documentation, autobiography, as in many fictional works thereafter it did. The best writers of the Fifties would thus prove to be those who, once the new social and cultural records had been begun, drove the form onward into strong aesthetic inquiry; in consequence they would finally prove to be very doubtful realists. But then realism had never been the only tone of the period. In fact many of the most important writers of the Fifties had been moving in a quite different direction from the start.

9.

In 1954, the year of *Lucky Jim*, William Golding – a major writer who would eventually win the Nobel Prize for Literature in 1983 – published *Lord of the Flies*, hardly a work of realism, or in the conventional sense a Fifties novel, since, though its subject was timely, it possessed all the timelessness of myth.

The book belonged, if anything, to the tradition Robert Louis Stevenson called "romance," and drew on the boys' book adventure – to which Stevenson greatly contributed – for its story, though the chief Victorian book that lay in the background was R. M. Ballantyne's *The Coral Island* (1857), a story of a resourceful group of boys marooned by shipwreck on an isolated island. But Golding's version of the story, which added a metaphysical dimension absent from the original, was as much occasioned by the moral crisis brought about by the war, when, Golding once observed, we acquired "a terrible desperate knowledge of what human beings are capable of." Golding takes similar schoolboy characters, though they are now marooned not by shipwreck but by a plane-crash, and the time is the future, in the aftermath of a nuclear war, moving their fortunes further away from society. They attempt to construct their own self-sufficient social order on the island, but this founders in the face of terror, sin and evil, leading to the awareness, on the part of one of the boys, of "the end of innocence, the darkness of man's heart." Golding's late modern story is not a tale of young resourcefulness but a deeply pessimistic vision of human evil, and it lies far beyond Victorian optimism or indeed conventional liberal dreams of human progress. He once flatly observed that "man's nature is sinful and his state perilous," and in fact all his novels are set somewhere beyond "the end of innocence." They rarely deal directly with the social world, show little concern with manners or social morals, and take place in distinctive, enclosed, neo-allegorical spaces, often on the borders of the social and the non-social, or history and pre-history. *The Inheritors* (1955) is about the encounter of Neanderthal Man and *Homo sapiens*, its story being seen from the point of view of the Neanderthals, and thus summoning up the very origins of speech, and sin. *Pincher Martin* (1956) is about a torpedoed sailor (alive or dead?) marooned alone on a desolate rock in the mid-Atlantic, his social past displayed in illusory flashback, "islanded in pictures" like "a row of trailers of old films." *Free Fall* (1959), also told in flashback, does move through the world of modern artistic society, and involves a Gestapo interrogation in a prison camp, where questions of the very nature of being and consciousness, sin and guilt, body and soul, are explored. *The Spire* (1964), a powerful allegorical tale about the building of a cathedral spire (like that at Salisbury) on shaky foundations, is about the ambiguous nature of human art and aspiration. In 1967 came *The Pyramid*, the closest he came to writing a social novel.

Like Graham Greene, but in a quite different theological frame, with a stronger literary education and a more vividly internalized sense of human consciousness, Golding addressed fundamental questions of good and evil, being, wholeness and creative aspiration in a godless age. His stories were, he once said, not fables but myths – fable being "an invented thing out on the surface whereas myth is something that comes out of the roots of things in the ancient sense of being a key to existence, the whole meaning of life, and experience as a whole." The large claim was fair: Golding's works have a timeless air, but they are also struggles of creation, works in which the character and the subject are shaped not by naive representation but by strongly felt notions of being and becoming. They have a realism of vivid specificity; they also have a quality of timeless allegory. In middle career Golding fell silent for several years. Then in 1979 he produced *Darkness Visible*, a novel "about England," filled with Miltonic and apocalyptic allusions – a work which, despite or because of its technical complexity, its time-shifts and wide varieties of viewpoint, remains his most obscure and confusing. It was followed by the group of "maritime" novels formed by *Rites of Passage* (1980), *Close Quarters* (1987) and *Fire Down Below* (1989), set on an old sailing ship voyaging out to colonial Australia during the Napoleonic Wars. They are still about the ambiguity of human nature, the tug of primitivism, the presence of evil, the formlessless of experience, the uncertainty of progress; but more than ever they suggest the value of quest, creativity, order and aspiration, however strangely founded in humanity these things may be. The late trilogy is probably his most optimistic and also his finest work, a careful questing toward Utopia, whose deceptive horizons unfold one after another. Golding's work challenges many of the liberal and humanistic conventions of much British fiction, and there is a certain timelessness about the prose – though not the technique – which makes it stand monumentally apart from much contemporary writing. But it is and will surely remain a central contribution to the modern British novel.

Golding's *Lord of the Flies* was not the only novel that pointed to another impulse going through British fiction in 1954. For this was the year Iris Murdoch (having written five unpublished fictions already) brought out her first published novel *Under the Net*. It was promptly identified as the work of "an angry young man," even though Murdoch was none of these things. The story was, it is true, told by a male narrator, a dissident, drifting intellectual anti-hero, an "outsider," in a cycle of downward social descent; and there were indeed a few surface similarities between it and the work of Amis and Wain. But it might have been noted that the book takes its title from Wittgenstein, and is dedicated to Raymond Queneau, whose surrealist influence is everywhere apparent. There are innumerable allusions to Sartre, on whom Murdoch, herself a philosopher, had published an excellent study the previous year. There was evidence of the influence of the early Beckett, and Murdoch went out of her way to praise Camus' fiction as "a serious attempt on the truth." In short the book drew a good deal on the tradition of French surrealism, and was also philosophically contemporary with the French existentialist novel, with which it conducts a kind of debate. In the manner of surrealism, the novel is set in two Londons, one "necessary" and the other "contingent," but also in a mime theatre, a film studio, and in a surreal Paris itself. An important character is a film-star dog called Mister Mars, and there are many debates about the nature and limits of language, the relationship between word and silence, act and image, figure and referent. The hero, or anti-hero, Jake Dona-ghue, is a writer concerned with his own silence and his relation to the world, and he is engaged on an obscure and absurd quest which results finally in some form of revelation about language and creativity, and his own relation to the vigour of the world. Jake's discovery is as much philosophical as it is social or moral, though it might in its sense of revelation remind us of the more realist aspects of George Eliot or James, and it has far more to do with knowing the truth than it does with moral competence. If it is not quite a "philosophical novel," and maybe challenges whether there can really be one, it is a novel where contemporary philosophical questions are central. The "realistic" elements that link the book with other "angry" novels – the sense of alienation, the drifting and down-and-out existence, the air of protest, the concern with money and left-wing political problems – seem superficial only.[11]

Under the Net is surely one of the most important novels to come out of the Fifties, and one of the most considered. It also opened a career that would move through many phases and many different modes for testing the ways in which art has to do with the true and the good. Elsewhere Murdoch was debating the fate and nature of the liberal novel, most significantly in her 1961 essay "Against Dryness." "We no longer see man against a background of values, of realities which transcend him," she wrote, noting the deep difference between Victorian and modern fiction: "We picture man as a brave naked will surrounded by an easily comprehended empirical world. For the hard idea of truth we have substituted a facile idea of sincerity." Modern fiction had become divided between the "journalistic" novel, realistic and contingent, straightforward stories enlivened with empirical facts, and the "crystal-

---

[11] As Murdoch explained to Frank Kermode, the book "plays with a philosophical idea. The problem which is mentioned in the title is the problem of how far conceptualizing and theorizing, which from one point of view are absolutely essential, in fact divide you from the thing that is the object of the theoretical attention." And, she also said, social detail was not an essential concern: "That was just self-indulgence. It hadn't any particular significance." See Frank Kermode, "The House of Fiction: Interviews with Seven Novelists" (1963), reprinted in Malcolm Bradbury (ed.), *The Novel Today: Contemporary Writers on Modern Fiction* (London, rev. ed., 1990). The seven novelists are Iris Murdoch, Graham Greene, Angus Wilson, Ivy Compton-Burnett, C. P. Snow, John Wain and Muriel Spark, and collectively offer a rather different view of the contemporary novel from that of the period's critical convention. Murdoch's "Against Dryness" (1961) is also reprinted in this volume.

line" novel, consoling quasi-allegorical objects portraying the human condition, but without "characters" in the nineteenth-century sense. Murdoch has consistently linked the task of the modern novel with the recovery of a new moral philosophy, the need to sustain "the sovereignty of good." In an earlier essay ("The Sublime and the Beautiful Revisited," 1959), therefore, she spoke of the importance of remembering that the novel is a portrait of human personality written in words, that "A novel must be a fit house for free characters to live in; and to combine form with respect for reality with all its contingent ways is the highest art of prose." Many of these concerns are laid down in her very earliest novels – *The Flight from the Enchanter* (1956), *The Sandcastle* (1957), *The Bell* (1958) – which represent a move away from a Sartrean existentialism and toward an exploration of the movement toward the "unutterably particular," the distinctiveness of individual life set against the powers of enchantment, fantasy and dream. With *A Severed Head* (1961), she changed her tone toward romantic comedy, and wrote a satire on Bloomsburified "personal relations" (Antonia, one of the central characters, is a minor figure from Bloomsbury, has "a sharp appetite for personal relations," and possesses "a metaphysic of the drawing-room"), which finally shifts the characters into a space beyond the "gentler world" and into one "remote from love and remote from ordinary life." As Robert Scholes later observed, with a wisdom greater than most of her early critics, Murdoch's fiction was a writing not of realism but of what he called "fabulation," constantly dispensing with realistic elements, drawing on fantasy and symbolism, on ornate decor and dramatic pastiche, in the interests of constructing an original myth.[12] And Murdoch's fiction thereafter has clarified the view that her works deal with a vast imaginary theatre of human drama where the spectacle and action test and tease the power and nature of art and goodness.

Murdoch was not the only novelist whose work was hard to

[12] See Robert Scholes, *The Fabulators* (London and New York, 1967), later extensively revised and extended as *Fabulation and Metafiction* (Urbana, Chicago, London, 1979).

see in the dominant critical climate. "No Angry Young Woman?" demanded one disappointed reviewer when Muriel Spark's novel, *The Comforters*, came out in 1957. In fact the book was a blatant dissent from fiction's realist illusion, from a writer newly converted to Catholicism who had already established herself as an important poet. Drawing on Waugh and Graham Greene, especially the self-conscious Greene of *The End of the Affair*, Spark was adding to the complex metaphysical sum of modern Catholic fiction, while adding a few notes that were entirely her own. Though one part of the plot of the book is her own movement from raffish London bohemia (a cityscape she would frequently return to) into the no less strange world of Catholic companions, and though the book is decorated with an extravagant apparatus of occultism, smuggled diamonds and blackmail, it is particularly concerned with the metaphysics of novels. The book, she explained in an interview with Frank Kermode, was "a novel about writing a novel"; she also observed, "I don't claim that my novels are truth – they are fictions out of which a kind of truth emerges."[13] It is no wonder Caroline Rose, writing in the story a solemn study called *Form in the Modern Novel*, is "having difficulty with the chapter on Realism," or that the book frankly explains "the characters in this book are all fictions." Caroline also feels that someone is typing her story up above (she is), and she persistently questions her position in the novel, raising the question of higher and lower plotters; as in *The End of the Affair*, the paradoxes of modern faith and free will become the paradoxes of modern fiction ("I intend to stand aside and see if the novel has any form apart from this artificial plot. I happen to be a Christian," declares Caroline). Evelyn Waugh admired the book, and it is not hard to see why: this is extension of his own black humour into new and experimental quandaries. In 1958 Spark wrote *Robinson*, which is closer to Golding-like allegory, and owes something to *Robinson Crusoe*. Then in 1959 came *Memento Mori*,

---

[13] See Frank Kermode, "The House of Fiction: Interviews with Seven Novelists," cited above, note 11.

a wonderful black farce about a group of elderly people trying to live absurdly youthful lives who are rung up by Death on the telephone. Golding was writing sombre fables of darkness in human nature; Spark was writing about similarly large themes with a buoyant and wicked humour. She too had learned to see the novel itself as a metaphor of the contemporary human condition, and to regard its fundamental elements – creator and created, plot and ending – as figures for the black comedy of the human condition itself. And in her books the fictional play and meta-fictional enquiry that would affect the fiction of the next decade are already predicted.

The fact was that the period that reaffirmed realism was also the period of its dissolution, and with benefit of hindsight it is possible to see that many of the first novels of the Fifties – a decade remarkable for its first novels and opening careers – need to be reconsidered and reinterpreted as stages on the way to something else. In the fiction of Anthony Burgess, another writer of Catholic background, the early, delightful, comic, linguistically playful "Malayan Trilogy" (*Time for a Tiger*, 1956; *The Enemy in the Blanket*, 1958, and *Beds in the East*, 1959) was an opening step in the extraordinarily rich, inventive and experimental career that was to come. The return to the liberal novel had generated a renewal of fiction, and renegotiated the relationship of contemporary British fiction to its history. But the new history the writers had begun to record posed its own problems of relationship to the tradition, and that would become very apparent in the course of the Sixties. As time passed, nearly all of the most interesting writers – Angus Wilson, William Golding, Doris Lessing, Iris Murdoch, Muriel Spark, David Storey, Anthony Burgess, and more – would prove very doubtful realists. The debate about liberal realism that ran through the Fifties, when, they said, the novel was no longer novel, proved a way of looking back and stepping forward. It had brought fiction back to questions of character and representation, continuity and cultural change, and this had important implications for the writers who began to work away from it, as many did – toward more fantastic, self-examining, fabulatory or allegorical views of the novel. The door beyond realism was already opening out into the paradoxes of fiction. And that was to become one of the strongest concerns of the British novel in the Sixties.

SIX

The Sixties and After
1960–1979

This story I am telling is all imagination. These characters I
create never existed outside my own mind. If I have pretended
until now to know my characters' minds and innermost
thoughts, it is because I am writing in (just as I have assumed
some of the vocabulary and "voice" of) a convention universally
accepted at the time of my story; that the novelist stands next to
God. He may not know all, yet he tries to pretend that he does.
But I live in the age of Alain Robbe-Grillet and Roland Barthes;
if this is a novel, it cannot be a novel in the modern sense of the
word.

John Fowles, *The French Lieutenant's Woman* (1969)

Realistic novels continue to be written – it is easy to forget that
most novels published in England fall within this category – but
the premise of scepticism on the aesthetic and epistemological
premises of literary realism is now so intense that many
novelists, instead of marching confidently straight ahead, are at
least considering the two routes that branch out from the
crossroads. One of these routes leads to the non-fiction novel,
and the other to what [Robert] Scholes calls "fabulation."

David Lodge, "The Novelist at the Crossroads" (1969)

1.

"The Sixties" have now ceased to be a historical decade at all.
Probably they never were, even at the time – rather a state of
mind and body, of political and cultural revolt, which could be
laid across the historical clock in several different ways and at
a number of different dates. But there was a historical Sixties,
which both preceded and more or less outlasted that Sixties

state of being. In world affairs the decade began clearly: at the end of 1960 President John F. Kennedy was elected to office, declaring his age of the "New Frontier" was now about to start. The youngest president ever, the first clearly post-war American leader, he ran his flamboyant "Camelot" presidency from 1961 until his tragic assassination in November 1963. Over that period he and his administration changed, for good or bad, the whole climate of world politics. His "New Frontier" often seemed less a hopeful than a uniquely dangerous place – "a frontier of unknown opportunities and perils," as he warned in his Inaugural. The perils grew greater, for now the Cold War intensified. The first man in space, Russian, circled the earth as the Sixties began; thereafter the space race accelerated not just toward the dream-like goal (achieved in 1969) of putting a man on the moon, but toward rising nuclear threat. Tension grew in Europe, when the Communist authorities attempted to seal off Berlin; the barbed Berlin Wall was erected across the city, a symbol of the prison-like order now growing in Eastern Europe, and it would stay in place for the next thirty years. Nearer home, in the wake of a new wave of anti-American and Marxist revolutions and movements in Latin America, Castro had taken power in Cuba, and when the Kennedy administration permitted a futile CIA assault at the Bay of Pigs, crisis grew here too, as the Russian leader Khrushchev decided to test Kennedy's resolve. The Cuban missile crisis that followed was to be the most frightening and apocalyptic of all Cold-War confrontations, raising the climate of fear and nuclear terror across the world. It was a reminder to everyone everywhere that the cold, dangerous winds of history were still blowing – and they would continue to do so through the Johnson and Nixon presidencies, through "the Great Society" and the escalation of the war in Vietnam, and on to the Watergate political scandals of 1974, which probably mark the real ending of the Sixties both as political decade and state of mind.

At home Kennedy's celebration of the "New Frontier" summoned up high expectations and delivered considerable change – new Civil Rights legislation, for instance, which desegregated the South and improved opportunities for black American people, though not enough to prevent the decade becoming a time of black protest and urban riots. But by the Sixties, as post-war cautions gave way to future hopes, everyone was expecting more. Students in the West demanded more "Free Speech," the "Beat" and "Hippie" movements that had emerged out of the Fifties turned into a general "counter-culture," demanding peace, love, drugs, revolution, and instant Utopia. As the Fifties began, the sociologist David Riesman had published a gloomy portrait of post-war affluent America, *The Lonely Crowd*, about an age of alienated affluent conformity. Over the decade sociology came to seem the best way of exploring a new order growing, first in the USA, then in Europe, in which mass society, corporate systems, material reward and personal alienation were the norm. In 1958 J. K. Galbraith published *The Affluent Society*, a liberal economist's critique of the culture of private wealth and public squalor; in 1960 the political scientist Daniel Bell brought out *The End of Ideology*, arguing that the new Western affluence was producing a new post-ideological consensus, founded on consumer gratification and improved social prospects. Events at once conspired to prove him wrong. Student riots in Tokyo, the Aldermaston marches of CND in Britain, the rise of a "New Left" movement in Europe and the United States, growing anti-Americanism even among young Americans, marked the appearance of a radical "youth intelligentsia" who saw themselves as harbingers of social change. A rising movement of disaffection and protest spread through the Sixties. The Black Power movement expanded and grew more violent, student revolt troubled nearly every Western campus, opposition mounted to the escalating war in Vietnam and the "military-industrial complex" that sustained it, and everything seemed under challenge – including the process of history, or reality, itself.

Out of this spirit of protest – which reached throughout the Western world – many things came. It was a time of rock music, mass concerts, drugs, improvised events, public happenings, street theatre, love-ins, all part of the counter-cultural "revolution of consciousness" that would grow ever more vigorous during the decade. It reached its peak – which was the beginning of its end – in the *événements* of Paris in May 1968, when students and workers tore up the streets to challenge the dominant state. It was the fateful year, the year too of the Russian suppression of the Prague Spring and of the assassinations of Martin Luther King and Robert Kennedy, as well as of the riots that broke up the Democratic Convention in Chicago, ironically helping Richard Nixon to win the American presidency. "The Sixties," as a self-creating historical idea, increasingly came to stand for this international spirit of "new consciousness" and "liberation": the life-style revolution, the happenings, sit-ins and love-ins, the underground activities and protests, the drugs and psychedelic experiences, the communitarian gatherings and the utopian expectations, the trips and galactic space-age dreams, that seemed to bring all things together: politics and the arts, high culture and pop, America and Europe, the older *avant garde* and the young. In the mythic sense, the "Sixties" was this generational and cultural rebellion – a revolution of rising expectations, founded not on poverty but on affluence, not on oppressed workers but on students and young people, not on demands for material reward but for the rewards of new consciousness. A ferment of ideas, old and new, sophisticated and naive, idealistic and brutal, developed, not least in the arts. For now the arts – especially the communal, improvisational arts, new theatre and street theatre, the situation and the happening, the immediate communitarian event, the random voyage in consciousness – came to seem central. In a variety of different ways they galvanized the spirit of artistic change itself, forming, perhaps, the most important and long-standing aspect of the half-illusory Sixties revolution.[1]

But there was a second, and deeper, revolution of the Sixties, which lay exactly in the rising affluence, the new commodification, the application of modern systems, the rise of international

---

[1] A useful contemporary study of all this is Theodore Roszak, *The Making of the Counter-Culture* (New York, 1969)

products and communications. Whether the counter-culture liked it or not, and it often did, their revolt was as much a part of this as it was of psychic independence. And it was this that was becoming the inescapable system of late modern experience in the Western nations: becoming, in fact, the postmodern condition itself. By the start of the Sixties, both these revolutions had arrived in Britain. The nation may have been losing yet more of its world role in the anti-colonial trend of the time, and the abortive intervention at Suez had made its impotence plain; it also brought politics back in the movement of the "New Left," which played its large part in the revolt of the Sixties. But the austerity days were now well over; at last there was full employment, real wages improved enormously, leisure increased, the stores were full, modern appliances were entering most homes, and the worker was now the consumer. The modern commodity culture was taking shape, with its rewards and expectations, alienations and anxieties. When in 1962 Anthony Sampson, in his *Anatomy of Britain*, gave an influential progress report on the present "Condition of England," he saw a nation changing uncertainly in an era of "galloping consumption": "Within two years, the credit squeeze ended, skyscrapers rushed up, supermarkets spread over cities, newspapers became fatter or died, commercial TV began making millions, shops, airlines, even coal and banks had to fight for their lives. After the big sleep many people welcomed any novelty; any piece of Americanization seemed an enterprising change . . ." The "Condition of England" was at issue again; many studies came out to chart the state of a nation seemingly trapped between a declining, traditional imperial past and an accelerating, Americanizing, maybe even a Europeanizing future. With the new commodities came the new technologies, the modern media; a television set had now appeared in around ninety per cent of homes. It opened a wide window on the state of the nation, the crises of the world, the varied lives of others. And with mass society and communications came mass culture – a collectivity, it was said, unique to modern technological society. The age of mechanical reproduction was here, and the window on life was an endless technological serial of random images, in which the old stratifications of "high" and "popular" culture either disappeared or were re-incorporated within the new seamless technological frame. "Mass culture" had its own distinctive accompaniments: ephemerality and rapid stylistic consumption, speedy generational obsolescence, cultural and social collage. The growing demographic and economic power of new groups, especially the young, fed it, commercially and culturally, and it was soon challenging the familiar social images and the existing hierarchies. Thus, through everything from pop culture to pop art, flamboyant new fashion to new styles of film, and from satire to socially critical drama, it assimilated or accommodated the counter-culture as a force for change and cultural dissent. Gradually the arts and the media, the underground and the general behavioural revolution, merged. Meanwhile the rise of radical theatre and the underground and "alternative" press somehow suggested that the *avant garde* and the counter-culture were one and the same.[2]

2.

In Britain, the liberal, moral, austere culture mood of what became known as the "tranquillized" Fifties was soon transforming into the liberationist, amoral, provisional, counter-cultural spirit of what – thanks to *Time* magazine – became known as the "swinging" Sixties. In fact London was soon being declared the cultural capital. "It swings; it is the scene," announced *Time* in 1966, scanning the pop music, the underground theatre, the shops of Carnaby Street and the prevailing cult of youth. The excitements were real, though hardly universal, and a good deal else was happening; in any case, if the Sixties was a style going somewhere, it took most of the decade to get there. Certainly moral matters were still much in the

[2] On the rise of mass culture in this period see in particular David Manning White and Bernard Rosenberg (eds.), *Mass Culture: The Popular Arts in America* (Glencoe, Ill. 1957).

forefront when, in 1963, the Profumo sex-and-spy scandal broke, embarrassing the then Conservative government ("It *is* a moral issue," said *The Times*), or when in the same year John Robinson, the liberal Bishop of Woolwich, published his humanistic version of Christianity, *Honest to God*. But the times were indeed a-changing; cultural debate and plurality grew, rock music boomed, psychedelic colours glared, the underground found its voice, youth culture claimed its rights of access. In 1961 (the year of the Pilkington report on the future of British broadcasting, the founding of the first "new" universities, and the disappearance of the farthing from the currency), the oral contraceptive pill became available, giving women a new control over their bodies they seemed quite willing to use. According to Philip Larkin, in his much-quoted poem "Annus Mirabilis," sexual intercourse began in 1963, "rather late for me – /Between the end of the Chatterley ban/And The Beatles' first LP."

All the items Larkin mentioned, including his own Fifties suspicions, were indicators of a new mood. Sexual politics had appeared, and the term meant something different from its later meanings. The "end of the Chatterley ban" followed a trial in which Lawrence's sexually frank, socially critical novel of thirty years earlier was tested for obscenity (it was the first of many obscenity trials that punctuated the decade). The 1960 publication of the novel might be thought to represent a belated victory for the Modern movement, but it opened doors to much else, not all of which Lawrence himself would have relished. Other exiled "obscene" works broke through the barrier, like William Burroughs' "cut-up, fold-in" drug-induced random *The Naked Lunch* (Paris, 1959), a bitter open-plan satire on codes of order and systems of repression that went back to the surrealist anarchism of the Thirties, and influenced many works thereafter, or the Glasgow-born Alexander Trocchi's no less drug-powered *Cain's Book* (1962). Old anarchist gurus from the pre-war *avant garde* like Herbert Marcuse and Wilhelm Reich offered vitalist visions of libertarian revolt against the age of mechanical reproduction and "one-dimensional man." Sex itself became a means of revolt against everything from control and parenthood to science, international corporations and the military-industrial complex; one went to bed for a great deal in the Sixties – until the issues shifted to a mood more resembling post-coital depression, and a reckoning with the decline of the excitements and the publication of new feminist works like Kate Millett's *Sexual Politics* at the end of the decade.[3]

Literary criticism (now elevating itself into literary theory) was not slow to acknowledge a significant cultural change was occurring – not surprisingly, since cultural politics were central to the Sixties, and the mood of revolt was disproportionately derived from artists, painters, actors, film-makers, music-makers, dramatists, poets, and novelists, rather than political figures. Contemporary forms were changing fast; so were the underlying structures. The strong moral note, and the accompanying disapproval of mass culture, that had shaped the Leavisite Fifties, when matters of standards were central, gave way to the much more descriptive, sociological, permissive views of the Sixties. Developing the "New Left" argument of the Fifties, Raymond Williams observed in *The Long Revolution* (1961) that the whole British way of life, "from the shape of our communities to the organization and content of education, and from the structure of the family to the status of art and entertainment, is being profoundly affected by the interaction of democracy and industry, and the extension of communications." He and Richard Hoggart saw themselves fighting an older cultural élitism; they also found themselves defending the importance of critical standards and judgements against the anything-goes spirit of the Sixties. The New Left itself was looking to popular, mass and youth culture as a force for radical change – "the imaginative resistance of people who live within

---

[3] Among the influential "liberationist" texts were Norman O. Brown, *Life Against Death* (Middletown, Conn./London, 1959) and Herbert Marcuse, *One-Dimensional Man: Studies in the Ideology of Advanced Industrial Society* (Boston/London, 1964). Equally influential were the British psychiatrist R. D. Laing's *The Divided Self* (London, 1960) and *The Politics of Experience* (London, 1967). The best analysis of all this is Philip Rieff's *The Triumph of the Therapeutic* (New York/London, 1966).

capitalism," as Stuart Hall put it in the first issue of the *New Left Review*, in 1960. The politico-sociological approach prevailed: culture was everything it chose to be, from the football chant to the Theatre of Cruelty, and everything was a sign waiting to be read. Some, though, saw more fundamental and irrevocable processes at work. Marshall McLuhan, in *The Gutenberg Galaxy* (1962) and *Understanding Media* (1964), proposed that what was happening was far more than a change in social, political and cultural attitudes. The era of linear, humanist book-based culture itself was ending, giving way to an electronic age of the technological stimulation of consciousness. The medium, and not its content, was the message, and "culture" now meant the signs, structures and technologies of modern media and processes themselves – into which the revolution of consciousness was itself being incorporated. McLuhan expressed both dismay and optimism: the end of humanism, yes, but the beginning of the new tribalism of the electronic global village.[4]

By the end of the Sixties, it was obvious enough that a deep underlying transformation had reshaped life and culture in the late bourgeois Western world. The new revolution in technology and organization had gone along with a "cultural revolution" – aided by the changing demographic and economic pattern and the new generational attitudes that went with it, stimulated not just by "counter-cultural" values but by the consumer boom and rising aspirations. It was a time of style as assertion, badge, declaration of identity. In this the arts themselves, custodians of linguistic and cultural change, played a very large part. This had stimulated a climate of new experimentalism, some of it "counter-cultural," but much of it simply to do with the release of forms and cultural inhibitions, in a time hungry for new interpretations and concepts of reality. By the decade's end many of the issues that have concerned cultural commentators and artists ever since were in play. By

---

[4] See Marshall McLuhan, *The Gutenberg Galaxy: The Making of Typographic Man* (Toronto, 1962), and *Understanding Media: The Extensions of Man* (New York, 1964).

now we had heard of cultural pluralism and provisionality, the breakdown of forms and cultural hierarchies, and their replacement by a new technological culture (which frequently then reappropriated the older forms and hierarchies through adaptation, quotation, pastiche, parody, and stylistic mockery), the rise of the "consciousness industry" and the pervasive influence of the global village, which was less a village than a high-tech international conglomerate. Now no style seemed single, no form seemed permanent, no tradition seemed stable, and everything and everyone borrowed freely from everything and everyone else.

But for the moment this seemed not so much a troubling condition as a radical provocation, stimulating a fresh experimental enquiry right through the arts. Forms opened out, conventions relaxed into provisionality and play, the novel began to lose its stable frame. The novel was dead, of course, along with the book itself; writers were left with what John Barth called "the literature of exhaustion," which exposed "the used-upedness of story." In Britain, B. S. Johnson similarly explained that the nineteenth-century narrative novel was now "exhausted, clapped out," and a new random literature from the age of chaos was needed. But if old stories were used up, the times provoked many new ones – generic crossovers, crossings of borders, easy passage between the high and the popular forms, or the literary and the media arts. Novelists looked back into the labyrinths of narrative to explore new or different paths, and – in a time of unstable realities, when history itself seemed more like a fiction – "fictionality" became a value on its own account. To many it seemed that the postwar cultural revolution the Fifties had somehow been too cautious to deliver was now in play. Theatre flourished on new relations, poetry turned toward performance, the novel took on a destabilized form. The result was a period of considerable innovation in which – perhaps for the first time – it seemed that a new late twentieth-century style was being formed: that, as the critics increasingly began to put it, the arts had entered on a period of "postmodernism."

3.

Philosophy and theory appeared to agree. In Paris, 1968, the year of the *événements*, was also the year when the philosophy of Structuralism – an assemblage of linguistic theory, anthropology, philosophy and psychoanalysis – began giving way to the yet more latter-day philosophy of Deconstruction, with its universe of gaps, slippages and absences, its signs eternally deferred, its centres permanently vacated. Sartre's "empire of signs" had already entered post-imperial crisis as early as 1953, when Roland Barthes published *Writing Degree Zero* (not to appear in English until 1967). Barthes was anti-Sartrean: "the Sartrean novel gives the novel the ambiguity of a testimony that may well be false," he said. But he was certainly a citizen of the empire of signs, indeed a semiotic critic, a sceptical reader for whom culture was a world of shifting signs, awaiting critical interpretation. Indeed Barthes duly read everything – a plate of steak, a sauce-bottle, a wrestling bout – as proof of the fact that the world was a text, the text was a world, and writing was not *lisible* but *scriptible*: not what we see *through*, but what we see. As the contemporary writers of a world of self-absenting meaning responded to this awareness, literature was, he said, becoming "openly reduced to the problematics of language, and that is all it can now be." Fiction was now post-humanist; incapable of reconciling word with object, humanism with history, it was returning to its pure nature as writing itself: "man's direct experience of what surrounds him without his being able to surround himself with a psychology, a metaphysic." Character had withdrawn into consciousness, consciousness into fragmentation, world into text, its relation with reality endlessly deferred. In a later, very influential essay in the key year of 1968, "The Death of the Author," he went further, arguing that there was no way the writer could locate him or herself in the larger textual machine to become writing's subject, the controlling, authoritative "author." In the world of signs, where literature was text, the writer was written, by language itself.[5]

Novelists do not always read critics, or critical theorists; they could well be wise. Still, much of what Barthes – or the text that signed itself "Barthes" – meant was reinforced by the appearance, around this date, of the French *nouveau roman*, in which a flattened, textualized, *scriptible* writing was indeed a dominant manner. Alain Robbe-Grillet's *Les Gommes* (*The Erasers*), a detective story that disappears into the labyrinth of its own signs, came out in that same year, 1953. The following years saw important and exemplary "new novels" by Michel Butor, Nathalie Sarraute, Marguerite Duras and Claude Simon. These were fictions from what Sarraute called "the era of suspicion," when simple representations seemed no longer possible. The "new novel" showed, said Robbe-Grillet, we simply live alone with "the smooth, meaningless, amoral surface of the world." Its offence was to present this not as a humanist tragedy but as the normal state of affairs; the "crime," he said, "consists of stating that there is in existence in the world something that is not man, that takes no notice of him, and has nothing in common with him. The supreme crime . . . is to record this separation, this distance, without doing anything to sublimate it." The *nouveaux romans* dismissed or problematized traditional narrative, dispensed with character and conventional psychology, disintegrated the conventional human subject, offered no gratification of fulfilled plot. They came ever closer to Samuel Beckett's notion of a writing of "nameless things" and "thingless names." These were novels as texts, halted in the middle of the process of becoming, enquiries into narrative in its difficult relation to

---

[5] A much fuller account of these complex matters is to be found in John Sturrock (ed.), *Structuralism and Since: From Lévi-Strauss to Derrida* (Oxford, 1979). Also see Roger Fowler, *Linguistics and the Novel* (London/New York, 1977) and Terence Hawkes, *Structuralism and Semiotics* (London/New York, 1977), which argues that "We live in a world of signs, and of signs about signs. A growing awareness of this situation has involved modern man in a momentous change of perspective which has gradually forced him to accept that in such a world 'reality' inheres not in things themselves, but in the relationships we discern between things . . ."

reality. As Michel Butor putit, in another key essay of 1968, "The Novel as Research," they turned the novel into "the laboratory of narrative" and in so doing set the novel off on a new quest for reality. For, he added, such technical and philosophical enquiry, "far from being opposed to realism, as short-sighted critics often assume, is the *sine qua non* of a greater realism."[6]

As the Sixties started, similar notions, often more playfully expressed, were emerging in other places. "The obtaining of such local ingredients as would allow me to inject a modicum of average 'reality' (one of the few words that mean nothing without quotes) into the brew of individual fancy" was how the Russian-born Vladimir Nabokov described the way he set about "inventing America" in his novel *Lolita*. *Lolita*, a work of decadent fantasy as well as high fictional play, was Nabokov's first book in English, though thanks to its erotic content it was first published in Paris, in 1955, reaching its American audience in 1958. William Burroughs' "cut-up, fold-in" *The Naked Lunch* suffered a similar delay, coming out in Paris in 1959, then in the USA in 1962. It too emphasized the necessary unreality of fiction: "the world cannot be expressed, it can perhaps be indicated by a mosaics of juxtaposition," Burroughs wrote. Both books had great influence on American fiction, and by the early Sixties the spirit of fictionalist self-consciousness was well settled into American writing. This was partly a revolt against anti-experimental realism, and a revival of the experimental *avant garde*. Perhaps more importantly, it was a response to the absurdities and dismays of a contemporary America where, wrote Philip Roth in an essay of 1961, "the actuality is continually outdoing our talents, and the culture tosses up figures almost daily that are the envy of any novelist."[7] In a

[6] For a detailed analysis of this, see Vivian Mercier, *A Reader's Guide to the New Novel from Queneau to Pinget* (New York, 1971). For Michel Butor's comments on the novel as a new "reality," see his essays in *Inventory: Essays*, edited by Richard Howard (London, 1970). Also see his essay in Malcolm Bradbury (ed.), *The Novel Today*, cited above.

[7] Philip Roth, "Writing American Fiction" (1961), reprinted in *The Novel Today*, cited above.

347

time of historical absurdity and powerful and exterior technological systems, plots of abstract history, the newer American
writers increasingly began to explore the difficult border
between fiction and history, imagination and actuality. Authors
like John Hawkes, Thomas Pynchon, John Barth, Donald
Barthelme, Robert Coover, William Gass, Richard Brautigan
and Raymond Federman began, in various forms, to write a
playfully self-examining fiction, a "metafiction," which challenged its own representation, multiplied narrative, questioned
the nature of the text, and the authority of its creator.

It is important to stress that these writers were not all
discarding history as their subject: a significant number of these
works were "about" the Second World War or the present cold-
war situation. But they asserted the independent reality of
fiction, the revolt of the imagination, the oddly fictional nature
of so-called actualities themselves. Their books were fantasies
about realities, refusing to salute the flag, honour the sign, or
function as stable texts, playing with, deferring and parodying
the funds of narrative, the laws of story, the categories of genre.
Fiction was plainly departing from the familiar centres of
realism and naturalism, breaking the borders, and the terms of
the strategies it used began to multiply. It was "fictive" and
"fabulatory," "hyper-real" or "meta-fictional," and we now had
the "faction" or the "non-fiction novel." Though to some this
indicated a fundamental crisis of narrative in the face of
contemporary unreality, to others it represented a fresh assertion of the power of fictions and narratives, as imaginary tales
contested for domination with those other fictions and narratives that were called history, society, politics or news. As John
Barth put it, the "literature of exhaustion" was also the
"literature of replenishment." Or, suggested Ronald Sukenick
in his aptly-titled *The Death of the Novel and Other Stories* (1969),
when reality is in doubt, writing is renewed: "The contemporary
writer – the writer who is acutely in touch with the life of which
he is a part – is forced to start from scratch: Reality doesn't
exist. God was the omniscient author, but he died; now no one

knows the plot . . .". As criticism said, what is now called "postmodern fiction" had plainly arrived.[8]

Similar issues arose in British fiction too, though here the answers were often somewhat different. As the writers of the Fifties had fairly claimed, realism did have a peculiarly strong place in the English novel. The tradition had always been more empirical, socially curious, narratively rich than most; in fact it sometimes seemed that the novel was what the British had instead of philosophy, empiricism in imaginative action. By the mid-nineteenth century the "Victorian novel" had become the great, exemplary repository of social and cultural narrative – stabilized by its Whiggish or liberal fit between individual lives and historical progress, or character and story, and by its narrative authority. Those novelists of the Fifties who had reacted against both Modernism and aesthetic subjectivity had found it natural to return here, and they had reinstated what perhaps had never really gone away: plot and character, strong social setting, onward chronological storytelling, with its evolutionary logic, and the sense of an ending. They had presented sympathetic and identifiable characters, the world as familiarity, recuperating the long-term and probably lasting conventions of fictional narrative. By the Sixties, many of these narrative archetypes were being looked at again, under the influence of social change and literary theory. Beckett and the *anti-roman* – the place where, said Sartre, the novel contests with itself – acquired a new importance; the spirit of "meta-fiction" entered the British novel too, though on its own terms. It was generally less concerned with the crisis of the sign that French writers, in the wake of Flaubert, were examining; nor, despite an ever-increasing concern with crisis and apocalyptic themes, did it have the sense of historical extremity present in much experimental American fiction. Nor did it seem entirely willing to let humanism and the fictional character go so easily; even

[8] I have discussed this in far more detail in my *The Modern American Novel* (London/New York, rev. ed., 1992).

in British meta-fiction the gravitational tug of liberal realism frequently remains.[9]

Still, the displacement was clear enough, as the tradition came to be variously questioned by many writers, including Wilson, Lessing, Spark and Murdoch. In part this challenge could be seen as a matter of personal artistic development, but it also coincided with a climate of change, as writers felt returned to those crises of consciousness and representation that had marked the passage from the nineteenth to the twentieth centuries, on which this present narrative began, when notions of reality, identity and aesthetic representation changed so deeply. But it was also clearly shaped by the climate of change, and shifting subjectives, the new alienations, of the Sixties. The developments of British fiction over the Sixties certainly relate to, even if they are not identical with, those taking place in other fictional traditions – American, French, Italian – at the time. They show a changed attitude to the familiar constituents of a fiction – a new obsession with the nature of a genre, the status of a text, the shape of a plot, the weight of a character, the burden of narrative, the sense of an ending. And they were soon showing a wider view of fiction, examining narrative play, expanding their subject matter, turning to fantasy and Gothic, pastiche and parody, with a freedom that had hardly seemed possible in the Fifties. This was plain from the work of the leading figures: Wilson and Murdoch, Muriel Spark, Anthony Burgess and more. And it was very apparent in two remarkable works of the decade, one from the beginning of it, one from the end, which suggested how the fictional climate was changing.

[9] A point very usefully developed by Patricia Waugh in her examination of different types of meta-fiction in *Metafiction: The Theory and Practice of Self-Conscious Fiction* (London, 1984). Waugh also makes the point that meta-fiction does not, as is sometimes said, simply express or represent a crisis of the novel but a means for its replenishment.

4.

In 1962 Doris Lessing published *The Golden Notebook*, in 1969 John Fowles published The *French Lieutenant's Woman* – two exemplary novels of the British Sixties. Lessing interrupted her sequence "The Children of Violence" (1952–69) – the realistic story of Martha Quest's quest for a meaningful life in Africa and Britain – after the third volume to write a work that was clearly meant as a creative pause for artistic, emotional and political self-examination. *The Golden Notebook* was, she said, a novel that "would talk through the way it is shaped." Its central character, Anna Freeman Wulf, is a writer who has herself written a successful novel about Africa, and is clearly very close to her author. Anna is no longer satisfied with the work she has done, any more than she is satisfied with the framework of her life as a woman; indeed she is passing through both a literary and a psychological breakdown, and seeking a higher self-consciousness. When she sets out to record her life and her literary situation in her "black notebook," she notes that the present-day task of fiction has somehow changed and narrowed. The large novel in the tradition of Thomas Mann – "who used the novel for large philosophical statements about life" – has given way to the flat contemporary novel of social information: "Most novels, if they are successful at all, are original in the sense that they report the existence of an area of society, a type of person, not yet admitted to general literate consciousness." Anna, dissatisfied, hopes for a new kind of book, "powered with an intellectual or moral passion strong enough to create order, to create a new way of looking at life." However the first task is dissolution, an understanding of how consciousness and language understand life, and so she turns to a "formless account" that will capture life as it feels before it becomes literature: "Why not, simply, the truth?" But the truth of contemporary historical existence is sterile and chaotic, and its elements – the social, the historical, the political, the sexual, the sociological, the pyschological, the autobiographical – cannot cohere as a whole, especially in a time when female personality itself is fragmenting, under the pressures of modern change and fresh emotional and existential expectation. Anna's need is to find a changed morality of life, a search for truths that do not simplify, categorize, sanitize, conventionalize, impoverish. The completeness she hunts is the completeness of art itself, but also a completeness of identity. And the crisis she explores is also a crisis of her own inventor.

The Golden Notebook – where, one critic said, Lessing "took narrative apart and laid it out to find a new beginning" – is a work of very complicated structure, which Lessing endeavours to explain in the highly interesting preface she added to it. There is the frame-story, *Free Women*, which is about – and, it will also turn out, by – Anna Wulf, who can no longer unify her life. The sections of this are intercut with the records Anna keeps in four notebooks: black, for her African life; red, for her political life, first in and then out of the Communist party, which has its own notion of history and narrative; yellow, an aborted attempt to write a story about herself; blue, about her psychological breakdown and psychoanalysis. These stories frequently mirror, echo, or interlock with each other, and they consider factuality, fictionality, self-deceit and literary lying. Lessing's preface explains that Anna has to separate things out for "fear of chaos, formlessness – breakdown," but that the drive of the work is through fragmentation and breakdown toward a new reality. The goal is to attain "the golden notebook," though when this appears late in the text it is a story of Anna's affair with another writer, the American Saul Green, who cannot settle with her but whose storytelling merges with hers. Saul inherits a story from Anna, and she a story from him, which becomes *Free Women*. This completes the circle, through paradoxically, since her story is the story of the crisis and it unravels again back into the story of the making of the story. The result is obviously a work of "meta-fiction," though the term does something less than justice to the complexity of the task – both an attempt to explore the multiple facets of a single personality, and to struggle toward a new way of writing appropriate to the consciousness that might come from a recovered wholeness. But at this point in the quest writing reverts to being writing, becomes "meta-fictional," though, while challenging the codes of realism and representation, it is hardly an "anti-novel" either. Anna revolts, for instance, against the "anti-humanist bullying" that tells us that fiction cannot today have a coherent subject, and challenges the notion of linguistic breakdown, which she sees as analogous to psychological breakdown, requiring an act of healing. The aim is the bringing forth of a new form and a new reality, and the book seeks both literary and communitarian wholeness, "for an end to the split, divided, unsatisfactory way we all live." Conventional realism is insufficient for the task, which means that *Free Women* is not itself the answer; the novel for the moment remains suspended in its own writing, while suggesting that further steps must and will be taken.

The Golden Notebook is one of the most powerful of late modern British novels, a complex literary text which is also a vivid portrait of a remarkable woman for whom the elements of personal identity and psychological incompleteness create a crisis of self and discourse. So it has rightly been seen as an important work of feminist sensibility; certainly it is the most remarkable work by a woman to appear in British fiction since Virginia Woolf, though in some ways it is far closer to George Eliot. But it is not hard to see why Lessing herself largely chose to resist this reading. It is not simply about a crisis of discourse, subjectivity, social and sexual identity; it is also an attempt to create and explore, as she thought the novel should, a vision of the intellectual and moral crisis of the age. That produced its ambitious completeness, its multiplicity of codes (historical, personal, political and aesthetic), its androgynous merging in "The Golden Notebook" of male and female narratives. Lessing herself described the writing of the book as a traumatic passage, and it was certainly a transformation in her sense of herself as a writer, a step on the way to other things. It can be seen as the turning point of the "Children of Violence" sequence, which changed radically in form and attitude. The final two volumes

353

are no longer realistic political and personal tales from the past, but stories about the apprehension of the future. A very Sixties, Laingian notion of redemption through illness and breakdown now takes over. So, as society moves toward some ultimate future apocalypse, the sequence concentrates on those who, like Martha, are acquiring new awareness, those who "have included history in themselves and have transcended it." And from this point on Lessing's fiction generally departs from social and political realism. It looks to new, more fantastic and hallucinatory methods of writing, fresh sources of vision, an apocalyptic sense of a double breakdown, of social collapse and the disintegration and reintegration of consciousness.

In her next book, *Briefing for a Descent Into Hell* (1971), another visionary story of breakdown and quest, a Cambridge professor has a hallucinatory crisis in which his wandering consciousness transcends the earth, then is strangely, and satirically, briefed for his descent back into it. *The Summer Before the Dark* (1973) tells of another breakdown, of a forty-five-year-old woman who feels life, social and sexual opportunity have passed her by, and is driven to break free, making a passage through hallucination into a higher, though more resigned, consciousness. The most successful of this group of books is *Memoirs of a Survivor* (1974), which examines both an outer world, a city trying to recover from a nuclear explosion, and an inner one, in a room where the wall opens out into more and more rooms, of the past and the future, a world of consciousness in transformation and recovery, so that it becomes possible to walk "Out of this collapsed little world into another order of world altogether." And by now Lessing was taking her own fiction out of this collapsed little world into another order of world together. Her concerns were now less political than cosmic, less individual than apocalyptic; she had something bigger to do than please us with stories. So came the late ambitious project of her "space fiction," the "Canopus in Argos" sequence (1979–1983). "I feel I have been set free both to be as experimental as I like, and as traditional," she said about this five-volume sequence.

Perhaps what now seems most traditional about it now is its

use of the ever more familiar conventions of science and future fiction, with its tricks, devices, narrative mechanics, and high apocalyptics, in what is plainly a visionary fiction written from a state of transcendent consciousness. As she explained: "I found a new world for myself, a realm where the petty fates of planets, let alone individuals, are only aspects of cosmic evolution . . ." "Cosmic evolution" was indeed the theme, and the intergalactic cosmos of science fiction and new consciousness fantasy, much cultivated in the Sixties – the age when space was "conquered," consciousness acquired planetary aspirations, and apocalyptic feeling ran high – provided her with grandly epic materials. Three galactic empires are attempting in different ways to control the earth, which is itself seen as a small instant in the evolution of cosmic time and consciousness. Lessing uses the form freely, not to tell dramatic stories but to engage both in local satire and in a large meditation on human existence. The point is to create a "new" fiction, set beyond realism, political explanation, conventional identity and subjectivity. But she had not entirely left such themes behind. Cloaked as "Jane Somers," she wrote two social novels that reverted toward her earlier manner. Then, in *The Good Terrorist* (1985), she wrote of contemporary politics, and ideological utopianism turned to terrorist violence, with her now cosmic, bitingly moral sense of existence. Lessing had made a very Sixties passage out of politics and into an art of consciousness. But it is the book that makes the transition, *The Golden Notebook*, a fragmentary work that is meant simply as a step toward a new writing, that stands as her deepest exploration of the novel and its contemporary problems, in the age of changing political, social, historical and gender realities, when, to so many, a general and cosmic revolution of consciousness in the time of the space age seemed in process.

However there were other ways of breaking out from the established conventions of realism, as John Fowles showed in the most interesting novel to appear at the decade's end. Fowles, born in 1926, emerged as a novelist at the start of the Sixties with his short novel *The Collector* (1963), a rather Nabokovian work of decadent-aesthetic atmosphere dealing with the theme of possession and enchantment, the obscure object of desire and the enigmatic symbol. A young clerk, Frederick Clegg, first collects butterflies and then entraps a girl, Miranda, with whom he has fallen in love. The double narrative tells the story from both points of view – that of the collector of the elusive, and the prisoner, who resists containment. The story develops mythically and formally, but ends realistically and grimly; it also feels like a decadent's bridge between realism and a more fantastic form of writing. It was followed in 1966 by the far more ambitious *The Magus*, a book the British critics, still hunting realism, found hard to understand and, at the time, appreciate. It is about a limited young Englishman, Nicholas Urfe, who tries to purge a failed love affair by going to take a teaching job on the Greek island of Phraxos. The novel starts realistically, but once again moves into the world of enchantment, possession, and, it might be said, alternative forms of narrative; here "second meanings hung in the air, ambiguities, unexpectedness." Urfe is taken up by Conchis, the "magus" of the title, the Prospero of the island, which indeed proves to be full of noises, sounds, and "mysteries." Indeed Conchis himself constructs an elaborate web of "god-games" around Urfe. Many of the dramatic illusions, "happenings," he creates are about himself, and engage Urfe with the complex mysteries and atrocities of twentieth-century history, from which his own British life has separated him (Urfe is described as standing for something "passive, abdicating, English in life"). But if Urfe needs to be acquainted, by "magic," or just a different kind of "narrative," with the moral and political history of his century, he also needs to be exposed to his own psychological flaws and the limitations of his own male sexuality. The dramas increasingly become psycho-dramas, exposing him to his own desires, illusions and existential limitations.

It is important that this book, like most of Fowles' later works, is about the complex power of fictions. Conchis, the magus, is, amongst his other protean qualities, a figure of the author himself, "a sort of novelist sans novel." He is the novelist as creator, magician, inventor, weaver of games, but also trapper of souls, forger, counterfeiter, the man of deceptions with his own share of bad faith and historical and emotional guilt. Urfe, the narrator, acknowledges that he has been caught in an ambiguous, if purgative, fiction, a fantasy even more fantastic than he is able to declare (after all there can hardly be a "realistic" reason why Conchis should devote himself to creating his complex magic charade, which involves many others). What Conchis does, though, is what psychologists do when they want to construct psycho-dramas, magicians when they wish to create illusion and the suspension of disbelief, what novelists do when they create fiction. Nicholas finally acknowledges that "all here is illusion" and that the "masque is only a metaphor," but ambiguity remains. Fowles remained somewhat doubtful about the novel, and significantly revised it in 1977; it was, though, one of the more remarkable works of the British Sixties, not least for its historical scope and its psychoanalytical intensity, its steps beyond the "Englishness" of British fiction and ideas of character and representation. This was the book that established Fowles as a major novelist, even though many critics were slow to see the point. But it was in 1969 he published what remains his masterpiece, when he appeared with *The French Lieutenant's Woman*.

This is a work which both reconstructs and deconstructs the Victorian novel, and by implication all that goes with its continuing presence: its ideas of character and society, historical progress and evolution, chronological narrative and God-like storytelling. The Victorian novel Fowles reconstructs or pastiches is not that of any single Victorian novelist – Dickens, Trollope, Wilkie Collins, George Eliot, Thomas Hardy, though all these contribute elements – but the Victorian novel as archetype, the sum of the writings of and indeed about the idea of Victorianism. Fowles constructs Victorian fiction in terms of many of its own conventions and interpretations; he also probes their doubts, inconsistencies and hidden spaces from the standpoint of one who can know what they could not, placing the characters and their world back in a distinctive stage of that

357

historical evolution in which we all, eventually, find ourselves. Fowles seizes on all the Victorian novel has to offer to a successor – its narrative capaciousness, its scale, its massive detail, its sense of opening and closure – even while acknowledging that no contemporary author can write as the Victorians did. The story borrows many Victorian manners, though these are probed and teased with the doubts and questions of an author who knows his modern existentialism, and acknowledges that he belongs to the age of Barthes and Robbe-Grillet. The result is a superb pastiche, telling one of the era's key fables (the male hero faced with the choice between the fair and the dark lady, between sentiment and sensuality, social reaffirmation and danger), often assuming the manners and types of the Victorian narrator, while imposing on this chameleon a modern author who no longer "stands next to God," but is magus, forger and impresario. The story, though, is undermined from within as well as without. The central character, Sarah Woodruff, "the French Lieutenant's woman," is self-created; she wills herself to be an outsider, a *femme fatale*, apart from convention and history, with an independent life greater than the determining age itself could allow: "No insult, no blame, can touch me," she says; within the story she creates her own story. She is granted an independent discourse, and the existential will she is assigned breaks open the narrative, prevents its closure, is itself constructed as a challenge to the role of the author.

The French Lieutenant's Woman is a remarkably doubled work: an endeavour by a distinguished author to recover, examine and question the value of the Victorian novel for his own day, while seeing his own time in the light of its Victorian origins. The historical intimacy is real; Fowles sets the bulk of the story just a hundred years before the time of writing, in 1867, in an age of doubt and contradiction, after Darwin and Marx – at the moment, he said, when the twentieth century was born. The fable itself traces a deep historical change, the break-up of the Victorian world, and moves from the realm of mid-Victorian respectabilities to the aesthetic and decadent spaces of the Pre-Raphaelites. Sarah reappears in the studio of the Rossettis, and in the era of the New Woman; the post-Victorian new has already begun by the story's end. The book functions both as homage and critique: it can itself be read as a very Whiggish novel, about the unfolding laws of progress, which evolve through historical emancipation, Victorian hypocrisy and contradiction yielding, through the application of art, decadence, Marx and Freud, to an age of modern authenticity. It can, though, also be read as a novel that makes no such claim on the past, the modern emancipations being as much social loss as individual gain (Fowles suggests that in destroying the Victorian "other," the labyrinthine realm of the forbidden, the modern world has also destroyed much of its pleasure). Similarly if the playful modern text challenges the illusion of authenticity and identification so important to realistic Victorian fiction, that fiction – which Fowles so effectively impersonates – also questions the depthless surfaces, high self-consciousness, and narrative thinness of much postmodern fiction (one reason why many readers of the book prefer to follow its inner story and ignore the author's interventions). It is in the much discussed Chapter 13 that Fowles first begins to break the illusion so carefully created: "Who is Sarah? . . .," he asks. "I do not know. These characters I create never existed outside my own mind. If I have until now claimed to know my characters' minds and thoughts, it is because I am writing in (just as I have assumed some of the vocabulary and 'voice' of) a convention universally accepted at the time of my story; that the novelist stands next to God." This task, apparently, can no longer be performed: changes in history, gender and identity, and linguistic slippage, are too great.

Yet the very impossibility of the task seems to provoke it; despite all, it can be done. The author continues to present us with a narrative as substantial as that of any of the great Victorians, even while he presents and represents himself in various modern impostures: as structuralist critic, sceptical historian, fop, pasticheur, impresario, cheat, faker. He enters the text, stops and starts the action, intrudes on his world from the standpoint of later historical or sociological knowledge. He achieves a conclusive Victorian ending in the middle of the book – hero sacrifices *femme fatale* for virtuous lady, and lives on not happily but satisfactorily ever after ("They begat, what shall it be – let us say seven children"); but of course it will not now do, because of the existential drive of the character, modern sexual conventions, while the belief that Victorian fiction sacrificed truth to prescriptive modern codes makes it untenable. A second stage of the action begins, the quest for Sarah resumes, the discourse grows more random and critical. That opens up to two more endings, side by side at the close; the characters are free to emerge as "modern" figures, freed from the domination of the "omniscient" author. The famous endings offer less a choice to the reader than a granting of existential independence to the characters, given the chance to "emerge" beyond the story. Of course the fictional paradox remains; there is nowhere for characters made only of words to go next, unless into the reader's willing imagination. "Fiction is woven into all," Fowles explains, as he does elsewhere in his tales, ". . . I find this new reality (or unreality) more valid." But in fact the book remains profitably suspended between the "Victorian" mode – where by intensity of imagination and collusory identification we acknowledge the fictive reality of person and place – and the self-critical meta-fictional novel. The implication is clear. Like many another late modern British writer, Fowles is concerned to retain something of the Victorian novel – its narrative scope, its identification with character, its social breadth and realism – even while acknowledging that, as he says in the story "The Enigma" (in *The Ebony Tower*, 1974), "Everything is fiction." Fowles' ending, poised between a sense of postmodern fictionality and a notion of the eternal inwardness of character, is an ending from the middle ground, where most British novelists seemed inclined to settle.

Were Lessing and Fowles "postmodern" novelists, writing "meta-fiction"? Perhaps not quite, though Fowles' attempt to make the Victorian novel a "pre-text" for a late modern fiction comes close. Fowles' answer is perhaps best implied by his portrait of the artist, Breasley, in the long short story "The Ebony Tower" (1974). He makes an art of the present by appropriating what he usefully can from the art of the past: "Behind the modernity of many of his surface elements stood both a homage and a kind of thumbed nose to a very old tradition." Both homage and thumbed nose are easy to see in *The French Lieutenant's Woman*. When, though, Fowles turned to a contemporary subject in his next novel *Daniel Martin* (1977), a portrait of the modern (screen-) artist, it was the book's traditional elements the critics emphasized: its density of social representation, concern with character, the anxiety about personal identity, its deliberate "Englishness" (Fowles himself said the book was "an exploration of what it means to be English"). With the playful allegory *Mantissa* (1982) he again examined the plural modes of modern writing, teased by an exotic, erotic female muse who knows all about fictions. But when, in *A Maggot* (1985), he returned to his historical subject, to do with the eighteenth-century beginnings of the Shaker sect, his use of document and historical fact was different and far more representational, resulting in a powerful work of historical recuperation. Fowles' enquiries pointed the way to a problematic recovery of the historical subject; his books appear to have exercised a very considerable influence on British fiction since. The attempt to build a serious artistic bridge between the deconstructing present and the difficult past has remained very important to contemporary British novelists, as works from Lindsay Clarke's virtuoso *The Chymical Wedding* (1989) to A. S. Byatt's *Possession* (1990), Peter Ackroyd's *Hawksmoor* (1985) to Adam Thorpe's *Ulverton* (1992), show. These are novels of what Byatt nicely calls "greedy rewriting," recovering the past – "The past is a foreign country; they do things differently there," L. P. Hartley had memorably said in *The Go-Between* (1953) – as a hidden narrative reusable for the present. "Furtive nostalgia," this has been called; but it is more, a complex way not just of recovering the life of the past but of relating fiction itself to an earlier tradition. Thanks, surely, in part to Fowles, the complex novel of historical recuperation was one of the chief concerns of the fiction of the Eighties.

Lessing and Fowles were, though, certainly writing works

that were co-equal with the self-conscious fiction emerging in other countries just around this date. Both writers foreground the process of composition, reflect on the nature of fictionality, the nature of the author, the task of narrative, the nature of the "character" as a stable centre of fiction. They challenge the fictional illusion of reality, and the canon of fiction itself. But it may be part of the distinctive "Englishness" of both writers that, though they question realist conventions, they do not dispense with them entirely. Lessing acknowledged the moral power and scale of the novels of George Eliot – even though "the penalty she paid for being a Victorian woman was that she had to be shown to be a good woman even when she wasn't . . ." Fowles pays his corporate homage to the social and narrative density of Victorian fiction, as, in other ways, did writers like Murdoch and Angus Wilson. These are not novels aspiring to be pure texts. Anna takes on not less but more complexity and solidity as the text she creates or is in begins to fragment; Sarah Woodruff transcends the text she is in as an existentially independent character. The aim of Lessing's fracturing is both to mime the breakdown in contemporary experience and create out of it a new reality; Fowles likewise creates his "godgames" so that a new reality can emerge once the play is over. Both writers represent their central female characters as generative imaginative principles, matching a revolt of the narrative imagination which seeks through fictionality to deliver a deeper reality. Both push realism into problematic status, into the realm of the self-examining, the fleeting, the androgynous, but do not dispense with it entirely. Their works are both novels and anti-novels – part, in fact, of a new compendium of fiction that was emerging internationally as the issues left behind both by Victorian and "modern" fiction started to intersect.

5.

The retesting of realism and narrative Lessing and Fowles were in their different ways of performing found many parallels in the fiction of the decade. And if they were not writing "meta-fiction," others felt they were. Christine Brooke-Rose has complained that in the British tradition the experimentalists and "anti-novelists" made "a sparse alignment compared with the vast body of 'straight' novelists," and that is true. But during the Sixties a good many writers attempted some version of it, trying to break open the frame of the familiar, look again at the complex relation of the world and book. "Experimental" novels appeared in significant numbers. There was – to make an appropriately random list – the work of Ann Quinn in *Berg* (1964) and *Passages* (1969), John Berger's *The Foot of Clive* (1962), Eva Figes' feminist experiments *Equinox* (1966), *Winter Journey* (1967) and *B* (1972), Brigid Brophy's *Flesh* (1962) and *In Transit* (1969), Paul Scott's *The Corrida at San Feliu* (1964), Nicholas Mosley's thoughtful and excellent *Accident* (1965) and *Impossible Object* (1968), Angela Carter's *Shadow Dance* (1966) and *The Magic Toyshop* (1967), Robert Nye's *Doubtfire* (1967), Gabriel Josipovici's very textual *The Inventory* (1968), Julian Mitchell's *The Undiscovered Country* (1968), Alan Sheridan's *Vacation* (1972), Alan Burns' *Europe After the Rain* (1965), *Celebrations* (1967) and *Babel* (1969). These were all works that differently draw on random methods, present hard surfaces or complex textual interweavings, show some obvious debt to Beckett and the *nouveau roman*, some of them by writers who would have considerable influence in fiction thereafter.

There was also, for that matter, the fiction of Christine Brooke-Rose herself. A translator of Robbe-Grillet, a good, witty Structuralist and Deconstructionist critic of fiction who has had special interest in the intertextual, the uncanny and the fantastic, she has lived, and taught, mostly in France; and her books always make some virtue of their cross-Channel dimension, some being written in a kind of inter-language between English and French. Her first novel *The Languages of Love* (1957) is a light satirical comedy set around London University, but declares an interest in language and interpretation that would mark her later work. Her chief fiction is the group of highly textual, sometimes pictographic, novels formed by *Out* (1964),

Such (1966), *Between* (1968) and *Thru* (1975), later to be collected together in 1986 as *The Christine Brooke-Rose Omnibus*. The Parisian point is to emphasize that the book is indeed a text, a book of signs, a language open to the complexities of interpretation. *Thru*, a very texty text indeed, uses language charts, considers linguistic problems of noise and redundancy, looks at conflict on the linguistic borders, and abounds in "intertextual" references, incorporations of other texts. Her most recent fiction to date, *textermination* (1991) (the abstract, punning title is typical), is a comic *tour de force* of woven intertextualities, a critical fiction set around a congress on the late modern novel, and dedicated to the shrine of the implied reader. It is, perhaps, the ultimate campus novel – this one possibly best read on a campus. It certainly helps a good deal in reading her to know the changing climate of French literary theory in which she has worked, on which her fictions form a witty meta-commentary. That said, she is an important figure, who has brought the self-critical novel closer to the heart of British writing.

But far more homegrown and British versions of the anti-novel were on offer in the decade. "Literary forms do become exhausted, clapped out," declared B. S. Johnson, a highly interesting writer whose tragic suicide in 1973 cut off a promising career: "That is what seems to have happened to the nineteenth-century narrative novel too . . . No matter how good the writers are who now attempt it, it cannot be made to work for our time, and the writing of it is anachronistic, invalid, irrelevant and perverse."[10] Johnson explained he was "besotted by Irish writers like Sam Beckett, James Joyce and Flann O'Brien," though when he published his first novel *Travelling People* (1963), the ghost in the machine was Laurence Sterne, the parent of them all, and the inventor, near to the novel's

---

[10] He adds: "Present-day reality is markedly different from, say, nineteenth-century reality. Then it was possible to believe in pattern and eternity, but to-day what most characterizes our reality is the probability that chaos is the most likely explanation; while at the same time recognizing that even to seek an explanation represents a denial of chaos." See B. S. Johnson, "Introduction to *Aren't You Rather Young to Be Writing Your Memoirs?*" (1973), in Bradbury (ed.), *The Novel Today*, cited above.

beginnings, of the first British anti-novel. Typographical play, blank pages, comic interruptions of the fictional illusion, self-conscious reference to his novel-writing problems all make their way into the book. But Johnson was less devoted to making his books into texts than to breaking through the realistic and narrative illusion of the conventional linear novel; his following works used ever more complex devices to break the stranglehold of chronology and echo modern randomness and chaos. *Albert Angelo* (1964) has holes in the page, to let the story leak from one narrative section to another. In *The Unfortunates* (1969), the very intimate story of the death by cancer of a close friend, the novel came in a box, twenty-seven unbound sheafs to be shuffled by the reader (though in fact there does seem to be one "right" and obvious way to read the story). *Christie Malry's Own Double Entry* (1973), a surreal black comedy about a man revolting against the slights of life, and one of his most effective books, was printed in two columns: external life and violent reaction to it. In fact there was something quixotic about the endeavour, which was not to make the novel more fictional, but to break fiction's "lie" and bring it closer to document, to autobiographical and social truth: "fuck all this lying look what im really trying to write about is writing . . .," he suddenly declares in *Albert Angelo*, "im trying to say something not tell a story telling stories is telling lies and i want to tell the truth . . ." The problem was that the "truth" is no easier, probably less easy, to tell in a self-consciously fictional work than in a work of conventional realism, and he seemed to realize this in his later novels. *See the Old Lady Decently* (1975), about his mother and England, both of them in process of dying, manages an effective passage between his two interests: "experiment" on the one hand, rejection of fiction for autobiographical truth on the other. Alas, the book, the first volume of a projected "Matrix trilogy," was his last; his sudden death halted a promising experimental career just coming into its stride.

Like Lessing, Johnson saw himself writing in a chaotic, disintegrative age, which did not produce a coherent narrative. So did other writers. "Having begun with an interest in the fragmentary nature of remembered experience I have found myself increasingly involved in the making of new connections," explained Eva Figes in Giles Gordon's important anthology of British experimental writing, *Beyond the Words: Eleven Writers in Search of a New Fiction* (1975), representing her work both as an assault on the English tradition, which "trades in reassurances," and "patriarchal attitudes." Meanwhile, in the same collection, Alan Burns explained his experimental *Babel* (1969) as an endeavour to employ the "cut-up method," promoted by William Burroughs, to explore "the network of manipulations that envelops the citizens and makes them unaware accomplices in the theft of their liberty." Burns' experiment was, increasingly, a protest fiction, a satire on history, a disaster story. That became ever clearer in his *Dreamamerika!* (1972), subtitled "a surrealist fantasy," a collage text about the Kennedys, and *The Angry Brigade* (1973), subtitled "a documentary," and a sympathetic collage portrait with interviews of a British terrorist group. In other writers from David Caute to John Berger, "experiment" became a way of letting the brute facts of history leak into the frame of fiction. So it was appropriate that another place where experiment surfaced was in science fiction, where the leakage of scientific and military fact into hyper-real or fantastic worlds was a readily accepted convention. In the hands of such expert "new wave" practitioners as J. G. Ballard, who published his first "disaster sequence" in the early Sixties, Brian Aldiss (*A Report on Probability A*, 1968) and the prolific Michael Moorcock, SF was becoming an ever more self-conscious instrument for exploring the unease, the sadness, the anomie, the mechanical massing, the blanked-out hostile environment of the day, in a fiction where, as Julio Cortazar put it, "nothing is missing, not even, and especially, nothingness, the true solidifier of the scene." The anti-novel was indeed part of something else, and larger: a growing resort to fantasy, to grotesque writing, a writing about an uncanny and hostile world, stable neither in time nor space, always open to unreality. Indeed, as in Lessing's later "space fiction," the *avant-garde* and the "straight" novel, the experimental work and popular fiction, were growing closer together. Released, whether by formal experiment or by a sense of historical pressure in an age of violence and space adventure, from the codes of conventional signification and familiarity, novelists were widening the repertory of forms, turning toward fantasy and fictional play, the strange and the grotesque, to the indeterminate text, to pastiche and parody. The habitual genres and categories no longer stood secure, and in the "literary" and the popular novel alike the boundaries were changing, leading, in fact, to a quite different inheritance for the novelists who came along in the Seventies and Eighties.

6.

Of still greater importance was the re-examination that was going on among serious "literary" novelists, the writers of what was becoming the fictional mainstream. As I have said, the notion that British writers in the Fifties refused to pass beyond surface realism was always far too simple; but if a good many writers in the Fifties turned toward realism many changed direction markedly in the Sixties. "But the English novel is not an aesthetic novel, it is a social novel," protests the dutiful Herr Birnbaum, a passing character who appears in Angus Wilson's panoramic *No Laughing Matter* (1967), "*The Forsyte Saga* has great importance as a mirror of the British bourgeoisie." The comment is clearly self-conscious; Wilson's own early fiction had been a "social" novel rather than an "aesthetic" novel, a fiction of speculative liberalism about a time of sharp social change. His tactics of irony and mimicry, his awareness of evil and anarchy, had also disturbed the seemingly moral order of his novels, which had always questioned themselves. In *Late Call* (1964), he returned to these themes in his story of a very ordinary, elderly woman, Sylvia Calvert, who was moved from the class-based world of an older England to the postwar socialist Utopia of a New Town, an emblem of contemporary Britain itself. And *No Laughing Matter* itself was no less encompassing and social a story, in which the modern history and fortunes of British life are followed through the saga of a single family, the Matthews family, the lives of whose six children are tracked from before the First World War to the Sixties world of "hire-purchase Hoovers and sleeping-pill salvation." Thus the story incorporates two World Wars, the Fascist marches of the Thirties in London, the Suez crisis, and the contemporary global village, and is in its way a Galsworthyan bourgeois novel. But, as many dismayed readers discovered, Wilson had taken the type only to disestablish it. The story begins at the Kensington Wild West show of 1912, when the new kinemato-scope on display establishes the age of the mechanical reproduction and the global village; the dominant image of the book is the Hall of Mirrors the Matthews family then visits, where they see their identities distorted, multiplied and parodied. The text similarly refuses to lay down a stable realistic surface, and much of the book is done as pastiche or parody, entire segments told in the manner of other writers: Jane Austen, Bernard Shaw, Noël Coward, Samuel Beckett, Harold Pinter. If life is a stage of distorting mirrors, the Matthews children become very self-aware actors in the unreliable theatre of modern society. By the end of the book their old stable identities have gone, and, dispersed to various parts of the world, they have become inhabitants of a postmodern world of mirrors, the world of fragmentary, multiple selves and the global village.

In his next novel *As If By Magic* (1973), Wilson took this even further, writing a book about the polymorphous modern world, an international, indeed global, novel. Its younger characters are Sixties students, hunting for the wisdom of foreign gurus; its central figure, Hanno, is a scientist hoping to bring a new "miracle" rice that will solve the problems of the Third World, and finding that it is an ambiguous salvation. Much of the novel is set abroad, in Japan, Borneo, Morocco, Sri Lanka and Goa, and Wilson was consciously trying to break the provincial framework of the British novel. Hanno is also homosexual, and looking for freedoms British culture refuses to permit. The book considers the pluralization of cultures and meanings, and the crisis and violence that underlies it. Wilson brought this theme home to England again in his next and, as it would turn out, his last novel, *Setting the World on Fire* (1980). England is now seen in the light of a complex and operatic metaphor, and this is Wilson's most poetic and allusive novel. The theme is the chaos and violence out of which, nonetheless, the sense of civilization and the impulse of art arises; again, in the plot, violence and evil explode apocalyptically, but are contained by the desire to create and "set the world on fire." Wilson was able to complete no more novels before his death in 1992, but his work had a complete logic. The liberal satirist of the Fifties had become the complex myth-maker of the pluralizing, troubled world of the later twentieth century, when notions of stability, images of Englishness, had to be re-examined and rewritten. He remained, nonetheless, a liberal writer, concerned to the last with the need for human maturity and self-awareness, for the recovery, in a dividing world, of the moral sense of identity. And his "English" novel was no longer a purely social but an aesthetic one, asking how form and virtue are delivered from chaos.

As for Iris Murdoch, it had been absolutely clear from the start that she did not regard the novel as a form of simple imitation. She valued the realist history of fiction, and considered it should be a fit house for free characters to live in; but the house itself could always be peculiarly ornate and strange. Robert Scholes called her novels "fabulations," and explained what he meant: "Fabulation, then, means a return to a more verbal kind of fiction," he wrote in *The Fabulators* (1967): "It also means a return to a more fictional kind. By this I mean a less realistic and more artistic kind of narrative: more shapely, more evocative; more concerned with ideas and ideals, less concerned with things." Murdoch's various novels of the Sixties certainly fulfilled the prescription. There were many of them; indeed it came to seem no year would go by without a novel from her, and she had produced eight by the time the decade was done. They were certainly "artistic" rather than "realistic," and Murdoch used a kitty of forms with the greatest freedom:

the Jamesian novel of manners, the love romance, the Gothic fantasy, the historical tale. If *A Severed Head* (1961) was a Bloomsbury parody, another novel of the same year, *An Unofficial Rose*, is a serious love romance, seeing love as an unofficial passion which creates havoc and might confer freedom; it is also much concerned with what the books calls "the invigorating presence of shapely human wills." *The Unicorn* (1963), set in Ireland (Murdoch was an Anglo-Irish novelist, born in Dublin, educated in Britain), is a near-parodic Gothic romance with a metaphysical meaning; *The Italian Girl* (1964) is more realistically a love story. *The Red and the Green* (1965), set around the Easter Rising in Dublin in 1916, is an unusual mingling of an historical novel and a complex and allegorical love story; *The Time of the Angels* (1966) and *The Nice and the Good* (1968) are returns, with a new air of philosophical seriousness, to what was now familiar as the Murdochian novel. Though the forms were various, there was indeed something called Murdochland, as distinctive as Greeneland. It was largely a middle-class world, filled with recognizable types of character: the Near-Saint and the Failed Priest, the Strange Enchanter and the Love Prisoner, the Haunted Child and the Deathbed Contemplative, the Bookish Bureaucrat and the Radiant Woman. It was a baroque and highly sexual world, where love relationships served to elicit certain quasi-symbolic themes: the nature of power and possession, the way we create or destroy realities, the need for the beautiful, the good and the true. Murdoch's was an imagination of ornate gifts and very metaphysical passions, in which tales of relationship and love are ritualized and made ceremonial; meanwhile symbol, metaphor and an obscure allegory shape her stories into a complete and distinctive vision.

Murdoch's best book of the Sixties was *Bruno's Dream* (1968), much darker and far less playful, a meditation on memory, love and death in a world without religious certainties, though "love still existed and it was the only thing that existed." It led the way into her late novels, where she faced large themes and directly analysed the Platonic themes of reality, art and decep-

370

tion. Now the important analogy was with theatre, particularly
the drama of Shakespeare. In *A Fairly Honourable Defeat* (1970),
Othello provides a parallel for a story of jealousy and deceit. *The
Black Prince* (1973) is a meditation on *Hamlet*, as well as
Murdoch's most "meta-fictional" novel, containing various
narrators and narrative deceptions, and six different and self-
contradicting postscripts. *The Sea, The Sea* (1978), the story of a
theatre director who has given up his stage, draws greatly on
The Tempest, and directly reflects on Shakespeare's marvellous
theatre, in which "magic does not shrink reality and turn it into
tiny things to be the toys of fairies." Murdoch's fiction was itself
turning into a speculative theatre, where narrative is an illusion
through which are constructed serious rituals of reality and self-
discovery, and where the deceptions involved in creating the
illusion are themselves carefully explored. In more recent novels
still – *The Philosopher's Pupil* (1983) and *The Message of the Planet*
(1989) – it is the oracular powers of the philosopher and the
prophet that are examined and challenged. Murdoch had
started as a philosopher, and to some degree she was choosing
to end as one. But it was as the philosopher who had chosen to
work through art's illusion to explore and envision something
about the conduct of human life and the nature of reality in the
world. Her novels might be set at a certain remove from reality,
and affirm the distinctive laws of the realm of the imagination.
But they dealt with the problems of the real: the value of
individual lives, the roundedness of identity, the encounter with
the darker illuminations of love and death, the danger of illusion
unless it leads toward self-understanding and the understanding
of others. That process had driven her fiction into ever greater
self-examination; her novels are complex explorations of
modern experience in a world where the conventional defini-
tions provided by religion, philosophy and art require a fresh
examination. The human being, Murdoch has said, is a verbal
animal, a word-child, whose only means of understanding is
through language: "the quality of a civilization depends on its
ability to discern and reveal truth, and this depends on the
scope and purity of its language." Her books are meant as

journeys in this direction – not to take us into the realm of pure fictionality but to return us to contact with the real, not meant as texts of an age of language in crisis but as wise encounters with the density of experience and otherness.

7.

If Wilson and Murdoch were re-examining the conventions of the humanist and realist novels in a new social and artistic climate, Muriel Spark was plainly doing much the same for the Catholic novel, and with no less self-consciousness. From *The Comforters* on, Spark had shown herself preoccupied with the nature of fiction, at the same time developing her own hard manner of writing, which avoided psychology, did little to solicit sympathy and identification with the characters, and concentrated on the power of plot. In 1961 she produced what remains her most famous book, *The Prime of Miss Jean Brodie*, the story of a charismatic Edinburgh teacher who, in her "prime" in the Thirties, contrives to turn her entire class of chosen girls into an élite, a cadre, until she is finally betrayed by one of them. The novel is a powerful evocation of pre-war Edinburgh; it is also a formidable work of style. If psychology is absent, time is ever-present; time as it was, is, and will be. The novel uses the device of flash-forward to indicate that all is pre-determined, that what begins must end, and all plotters exist within a larger plot. *The Girls of Slender Means* (1963) recreates, just as vividly, London in the hiatus between VE and VJ day, when the war is over, and not, when "all the nice people in England were poor," and even nice girls have only slender means. This is another black allegory of the arbitrariness of plots and destinies: when an unexploded bomb goes off in the grounds of the May of Teck Club, where the nice girls stay, it is only those with the slenderest of means – the thinnest – who escape through a small window. Evidently it was in the strange arbitrariness of stories, and the novelist's power to administer it, that Spark took delight; she used her author's power of life and death with grim wit and black humour. Hence it was a surprise when she produced her next book, *The Mandelbaum Gate* (1965), long, contingent and near-autobiographical, and set in the contemporary world of Jerusalem, city of many conflicting faiths, at the time of the Eichmann trial. The book seemed to repudiate her earlier hard manner; it also contained an attack on the *nouveau roman*, as "repetition, boredom, despair, going nowhere for nothing." It was true that their books were plotless, hers highly plotted; but there had always seemed a comparison between the French new novel and her own very textual novels, with their hard surfaces, their refusal of liberal sympathy, and their amoral, unpsychological view of an arbitrary world.

In the event Spark decided to write no more long novels, and perhaps the most interesting group of her works are three brief, pared-down novels that followed – *The Public Image* (1968), *The Driver's Seat* (1970) and *Not to Disturb* (1971). Essential parables of late modern fiction, they sit at the centre of her art; by now Spark was plainly sure of her own powers, and the paradoxes of the form she used. These are works of almost pure plot and the most precise economy, so that the text lays all its causalities bare, and becomes a presence; no writer was ever surer of where things are going, how they will work out, why these words are here. They are also chilly tales of moral absence, where lives are conducted in a world of empty things, robbed of humanism, where the self is little more than a public image designed for consumption. There is now a real analogy to be had with the *nouveau roman*; these are texts that see characters as objects in a world of other objects, the essential difference being that Spark's fiction holds to a religious–absurdist view of the world, where the plots always end, normally in death, and the meaning of stories and lives is pre-determined. But though the world is already scripted, the characters know it, and behave accordingly. They generally know they live in an alien fiction: sometimes they speculate about their role in the story, sometimes they challenge or collude with their confident author for control of their fates. Annabel Christopher, in *The Public Image*, is a cinema actress who accepts her hollow role as a fiction, but by getting pregnant contrives to query her fate. Lise in *The Driver's Seat* sets out to manage and control the death that the author – who has decided she will be found dead with stab-wounds – plots for her at the start of the story. In *Not to Disturb* even the servants are informed and writerly enough to turn away unexpected strangers who might interrupt the outcome of the pre-determined Gothic plot. Endings, being usually death, cannot be changed, but the way to them, or their meaning, sometimes can. Indeed the characters are readers in the text, and, as Frank Kermode said, have done most of the interpretative work before the critic even gets to it. Spark's later novels, like *The Takeover* (1976) and *Territorial Rights* (1979), stories of a blank Euro-world where emptiness is the only essence, and life a materialistic parody of divine intentions, indicate that there is a historical reason for the general vacancy and absurdity. Perhaps mindful of Graham Greene's point that "with the death of James, the religious sense was lost to the English novel, and with it the importance of the human act," Spark creates a world of sombre ironies where decadence is universal, and to her cool eye no more than might be expected. Spark may be a virtuoso of the arts of fictionality, but she is more. Her grids, plots and self-conscious fictions are not only knowing texts but satires, showing a real urgency about the meaning or meaninglessness of life, and the moral and religious truths that contingent reality masks. If Murdoch is a late modern metaphysician of character in fiction, Spark is the eschatologist of modern plot.

There could be no doubt that British fiction in the Sixties was going through a period of rising self-consciousness, as could also be seen in the work of Spark's co-religionist Anthony Burgess. In the Fifties, his "Malayan Trilogy" had shown him to be a clever comic realist with a preoccupation with languages and etymologies; then the threat of death from a brain tumour produced a period of frenzied literary production which has never ceased since. The early Sixties saw a whole row of novels of astonishing fertility, including, in the one year of 1962, two of his finest, *A Clockwork Orange* and *The Wanting Seed*. Both are dystopian future fables, apocalyptic tales (there were many just now) of human disaster, satires of human absurdity. Otherwise they take quite different forms. *A Clockwork Orange* has an Orwellian theme; in a dulled socialist society where language has declined into "droog" argot (Burgess creates it inventively), violent teenage gangs rule, requiring "rehabilitation," a moral concept Burgess questions from his Catholic faith. In *The Wanting Seed* the crisis is one of overpopulation; in a Malthusian England contraception is obligatory and homosexuality encouraged, until a counter-revolution brings about a no less unpleasant era of open libertarianism. Burgess looked like joining the ranks of the science-fiction writers, a form that other writers, including not only Doris Lessing but Kingsley Amis, were also beginning to test. But in 1963 came the first of the Enderby novels, *Enderby Inside*, a portrait of the post-Joycean artist as lecher-poet, obsessed with art, death, language and his own insides. He would duly return in future novels. Many of Burgess' chief themes were now in place: a Catholic sense of sin and a social sense of disaster, a fascination with the polymathic and polyglot artist and the strange and often gross and unbidden sources of art. Nor had Burgess taught languages or studied Joyce for nothing, though where Joyce sought the final consolation of form he sought those of prolixity; he was also a very effective literary critic, obsessed with language and punning. The adventures of Structuralism soon entered his novels; *MF* (1971) drew on Lévi-Strauss' anthropology and his fascination both with codes and incest taboos to produce a novel of riddles so complex it took Frank Kermode to decode it. Later came large, wonderfully capacious books like *Earthly Powers* (1980), about papal sins and modern history, *The End of the World News* (1983), which takes Freud and Trotsky into its vast collage, and *The Kingdom of the Wicked* (1985), an historical novel on the grand scale. Burgess was happy to describe himself as a craftsman and not an aesthetician of writing; he is a Joycean without the formalism or indeed the restraint. But it is a serious flaw of modern British criticism that his work has not really been acknowledged in its inventive prolixity and its gifts of linguistic and technical discovery; Burgess is a great postmodern storehouse of contemporary writing, opening the modern plurality of languages, discourses and codes for our use.

The remarkable quality of the mainstream British novel in the Sixties was its rising self-consciousness; indeed we could fairly say a rediscovery of the novel was in process of occurring. Realism came in for examination in Wilson and Fowles, character and vision in Murdoch, plot in Spark, language and play in Burgess. Where was it all leading? According to David Lodge, a formidable critic and novelist, in an essay first published in 1969, the contemporary novelist now stood at a crossroads: "the pressure on the aesthetic and epistemological premises of literary realism is now so intense that many novelists, instead of marching confidently straight ahead, are at least considering the two routes that branch off in opposite directions . . ." One path pointed toward neo-documentary, the non-fiction novel; the other showed the way to fabulation. But Lodge suggested the paths frequently met again further on, and he affirmed his own modest faith in realism. The comments were part of his invaluable reading of the language of fiction; they were also commentaries on his own novels, which seemed themselves to divide neatly between realism and meta-fiction. His first novel *The Picturegoers* (1960), about Catholic life in South London, and his second, *Ginger, You're Barmy* (1962), about the pains of National Service, were clearly realistic works. *The British Museum is Falling Down* (1965), though about Catholic attitudes to contraception, took on the other hand a decidedly playful form. Adam Appleby, a research student working at the British Museum (in, of course, that ur-literary landscape, Bloomsbury), finds himself inside the fictions he studies. The book contains, as did other works of the Sixties, a delightful series of parodies, of Woolf, Lawrence, Kafka, Hemingway and more. It also contains a mythic acceptance of the fact that literature is amended by life. "Literature is mostly about sex and not much about having children; life is the other way round," Adam acknowledges, and the book ends with a parody of Molly Bloom's modernist soliloquy, ending though not on the great life-affirming "yes" but an ironic, postmodern "per-haps." Lodge's later work moved freely between the two methods, seeking different kinds of reconciliation, and he can perhaps be best defined as an experimental realist, a place where, in fact, a good many British writers in the Sixties seemed to settle.

By the close of the decade, the British novel had become a broad and eclectic church. The manners of realism had cer-tainly not died, and some of the most interesting new writers of the period espoused it in one form or another. There was Margaret Drabble, whose early novels – *A Summer Bird-Cage* (1963), *The Garrick Year* (1964), *The Millstone* (1965) – are portraits of intelligent young women entering the world of marriage and career, and are shapely early works of feminism. Drabble would later write a biography of Arnold Bennett, and assert that she would "rather be at the end of a dying tradition which I admire than at the beginning of a tradition which I deplore," and her later work went on to offer a dense, challeng-ing socio-moral portrait of her age. There was Melvyn Bragg, whose first novel, *For Want of a Nail* (1965), was a powerful portrait of a Cumberland scholarship boy, and who has retained a firm faith in the value of the realist novel, despite an energetic interest in the contemporary spectacle of Modernism and Postmodernism and an intense engagement with the media arts. Many other writers, like Julian Mitchell and John Berger, shared Lodge's eclecticism, moving not only between realism and experiment, but between the contemporary novel and the apocalyptic fantasy. Meantime, though, fantasy and Gothic had been decisively restored to the fictional repertory: thus Angela Carter, a writer who would do much to recuperate the spirit of modern fantasy, published her first, grimly flamboyant novel *Shadow Dance* in 1965, and the surreal *The Magic Toyshop* in 1967. The unreal, destabilizing methods of pastiche, intertex-tuality and parody had taken their place in fiction, in Wilson's and Lodge's work, and the critical novel, aware of its own fictionality, self-conscious about its own mode of being, was in place, not least in the form of the "campus novel" itself. The tradition of the novel had widened, new reference points, French and American, had plainly been incorporated, and British fiction was part of the changing experiment of the novel elsewhere. The stable entities of realism began to dissolve, narrative methods multiplied, and novels increasingly refracted a hard, chaotic, random world. If fiction increasingly asserted its fictionality, it also incorporated the fictionality of the supposedly descriptive and documentary forms, journalism, history-writing and autobiography, or any related narrative forms on which it now felt free to draw.

Self-consciousness had come, the fictionalist view had flourished, the sign had wavered, but humanism had not necessarily departed. Many of the most interesting experiments of the Sixties may be experiments in fabulation, metaphoric parables, or texts that declare themselves as texts; but they are also about the need to sustain fiction's humanist authenticity, or preserve the realm of social, moral and metaphysical truth. In an age of historical uncertainty and randomness, realism might have been challenged, considered as a provisional aspect of form, but it was rarely completely disavowed. Fiction now ranged from the minimalism of Beckett to the flamboyant play of Fowles, from Lessing's fragmentary notebooks to Iris Murdoch's ornate and baroque forms, from Wilson's mimicry to Spark's black irony. But in all these writers the task of fiction remained that of finding a structure for wisdom, or truth, or experience. The human figure had not disappeared, and the concern for character was one of the distinctive features of British fiction. These novels were not the meta-texts of the *nouveau roman*, but experimental mediations between liberal realism and new forms. They bequeathed a new fictional freedom to the novelists of the Seventies, which showed a far stronger impulse toward fantasy and an imaginative use of historical forms, as well as a great widening of subject. It was, suggested Lodge, an "aesthetics of compromise," which began to diminish the distinction between "realism" and "experiment" which had so concerned the writers of the Fifties and early Sixties. Twenty years onward, in 1992, Lodge revisited his essay again, and felt that things had changed little. What he called "crossover fiction," which merged the realistic and the experimental, has become, he said, "a salient feature of writing today," when a supermarket of styles seemed freely on offer. And not only in the British novel: the various compound terms that have been common since – "magical realism," "hyper-realism," "dirty realism" – suggest that this has been the way of the novel in the era of late twentieth-century doubts and discoveries, and that the sharp antitheses that dominated the aesthetic argument for two decades have become ever less tenable.[11]

8.

After the swinging Sixties, the sagging Seventies. Rarely has a decade acquired less obvious character, historical or stylistic, than the Seventies – a period that now seems more like a brief historical bridge between the long dying of the Sixties and the sharp and sudden coming of the entrepreneurial Eighties. The confident political and cultural mood of the Sixties declined gradually, first through one crisis and then another: the defeated withdrawal from the Vietnam War, the political scandal of Watergate and the resignation of an American president, the international oil crisis leading to a worldwide economic recession, which meant that the prospects of automatic growth in living standards no longer seemed certain, even the ageing of the participants, gradually dissolved the issues and energies that had been powerful in the previous decade. In Britain the mood seemed one of decline, especially once recession grew: growing conflict and terrorism in Northern Ireland, a miners' strike, and then a serious balance-of-payments deficit, weakened

[11] Lodge's essay "The Novelist at the Crossroads" (1969) appeared in his *The Novelist at the Crossroads and Other Essays on Fiction and Criticism* (London, 1971); it is also reprinted in Bradbury (ed.), *The Novel Today*. His essay "The Novelist Today: Still at the Crossroads?" appears in Malcolm Bradbury and Judy Cooke (eds.), *New Writing* (London, 1992), where he also observes: "The astonishing variety of styles on offer today, as if in an aesthetic supermarket, includes traditional as well as innovative styles, minimalism as well as excess, nostalgia as well as prophecy."

successive governments, and all culminated in the Winter of Discontent of 1978, which opened the way to Mrs Thatcher and Thatcherism. The radical expectations of the Sixties diminished progressively, and political questions moved elsewhere. The Seventies was, it was said, the "me" decade: "After the political turmoil of the Sixties, Americans have retreated to purely personal preoccupations," Christopher Lasch reported in an influential book, *The Culture of Narcissism: American Life in an Age of Diminishing Expectations*, in 1979. The preoccupation he noted included an increased acceptance of postmodern culture, indifference to history and larger political forces, a concern with the cultivation of consciousness and bodily development, an emphasis on the environment rather than on the system, and an intensification of sexual warfare as "relational" concerns grew. Certainly the strong issues of the Seventies came in these areas. In particular, feminism flourished, in the United States after the publication of Kate Millett's *Sexual Politics* in 1969, and in Britain after Germaine Greer's *The Female Eunuch* and Eva Figes' *Patriarchal Attitudes* came out in 1970. Narcissism or not, these issues all had a strong influence on the British fiction of the decade.

In 1969, the founding of the annual Booker Prize for Fiction had a considerable impact, focusing public attention on the serious fiction coming not only from Britain but from other countries (it covered fiction written by citizens of "the Commonwealth, Eire, Pakistan, Bangladesh or South Africa"). The prize was and remains contentious; to its critics it seemed to shift the "serious novel" from the realm of art to that of commerce, bring an unnecessary atmosphere of rivalry into the literary scene, and encourage the writing of a mannerist prize-oriented fiction. That said, it also had the effect of encouraging publishers to support the serious novel at a time when there was a belief that its audience was dying, and of making good fiction a matter of public interest and debate; in both those aims it succeeded. It also drew attention to the breadth of contemporary fiction in English, and many of the early winners or shortlisted works were famously about or from the post-imperial experience (some said you had to write about India to win the prize). In 1971 V. S. Naipaul, the remarkable Trinidadian novelist, whose early fiction (*The Mystic Masseur*, 1957; *A House for Mr Biswas*, 1961) dealt with Caribbean experience, won the prize for his novel *In a Free State*, part document and part fiction, a novel of three multicultural stories, set in the USA, Britain and Africa, and a world perspective; his *A Bend in the River*, a latter-day rewriting of Conrad's *Heart of Darkness*, would be shortlisted in 1979. In 1973 J. G. Farrell won with *The Siege of Krishnapur*, about the Indian Mutiny; in 1974 the South African writer Nadine Gordimer won for *The Conservationist*, a symbolic novel about the possession of African land; in 1975 Ruth Prawer Jhabvala won for her Indian novel *Heat and Dust*, and in 1977 Paul Scott for his novel about the end of the Indian Raj, *Staying On*. All this suggested that the subjects of fiction were widening, the tradition growing a good deal more free and various; many of the novelists now associated with "British fiction" were British neither in birth nor subject. Other signs of British fiction's growing variety were also made apparent. John Berger's *G.*, which won the prize in 1972, is an experimental rewriting of the Don Juan story for modern times, and other complex works like Nicholas Mosley's *Impossible Object* (1969) or David Storey's *Saville* (1976) either won the prize or appeared on the shortlist. The choices of the ever-changing judges were and will remain disputable; thus the most significant work of 1969, John Fowles' *The French Lieutenant's Woman*, did not even reach the shortlist, and other very important writers and works have been strangely absent since, occasionally leading to the production of alternative lists. But anyone trying to keep the accountancy of good recent fiction will find the record of the Booker – so long as one includes shortlisted titles as well as winners – a useful, illuminating chart of good fiction published from Britain from the turn of the Seventies onward.

A notable feature of the Seventies was the return to what Bernard Bergonzi called "fictions of history." Some of the most notable were about the decline and close of the British Empire, finally signalled, said J. G. Farrell, "when the Labour Prime Minister, Harold Wilson, announced the final homecoming of the British legions" in January 1968. Farrell, who had written three interesting novels in the Sixties – including *The Lung* (1965), about his own experience as a polio victim – took up the theme for his "Empire trilogy." Each is set at a key moment of imperial crisis: *Troubles* (1970) deals with the Irish struggle for independence from Britain over 1919–21; *The Siege of Krishnapur* (1973) concerns the Indian Mutiny of 1857; *The Singapore Grip* (1978) is about the Japanese invasion of Malaya in 1941. They are works of contemporary consciousness as well as large-scale historical re-creation (the "troubles" had newly resumed in Northern Ireland, in a violent chaos of bitter remembered history), works of elaborate form and complex metaphor as well as descriptive writing. *Troubles* to some degree echoes the Anglo-Irish novel of Elizabeth Bowen, Henry Green, Iris Murdoch or William Trevor, but it has its own Gothic and hallucinatory intensity, and is dominated by a compelling metaphor, that of the declining, malignly disintegrating Majestic Hotel itself. *The Siege of Krishnapur*, a story set in Victorian times, poses larger problems of re-creation; it is a tale, sometimes parodically told, of disintegrating Victorian confidence, one of its strong metaphors being the Great Exhibition of 1851, another the pervasive sicknesses that spread through the story. *The Singapore Grip* is both a history of Pacific colonialism and a novel of a strange and fantastic society, its ambiguities multiplying from the title onwards – which variously refers to influenza, the hold of colonialism on the region, and the sexual grip of a Singapore whore. Farrell died in an accident in 1979, leaving behind the manuscript of a last novel, *The Hill Station*, which returns to India and is set in Simla in 1871. Now sickness is the dominant metaphor, as it had been by implication through all these novels. They are fictions of a vast historical disintegration, not simply chronicled but imagined from within, given fictional shape and meaning by what is plainly a symbolic imagination, and interlocking the worlds of past and present.

No less powerful was the "Raj Quartet" of Paul Scott,

consisting of *The Jewel in the Crown* (1964), *The Day of the Scorpion* (1968), *The Towers of Silence* (1971), and *A Division of the Spoils* (1975). Scott had served in the Indian Army during the war, and of his thirteen novels most are set in, or refer to, India, and explore the divided culture of those who have passed time there. His books increasingly came to depend on a division, or multiplication, of perspective, personal subjectivities and complex time-schemes being set against shifting historical events. (Scott had written what is plainly a "postmodern" fiction in *The Corrida at San Feliu*, 1964). "The Raj Quartet," set in 1942–47, the last five years of British rule, starts from a metaphor drawn from Forster's *A Passage to India*, and rendered more fundamental and complex. "This is the story of a rape, of the events that led up to it and followed it and the place in which it happened," the opening page of the first book tells us: "There are the action, the people and the place; all of which are interrelated but in their totality incommunicable in isolation from the moral continuum of human affairs." India is presented as a dense reality, almost unimaginable; but also a vast illusion, through which Britain had reflected an image of itself. The novels are also meditations on history, and the different types and conditions of consciousness through which it is experienced, subjectively, in motion, as maze, as labyrinth, as disaster or hope, but always in fragments which together make up the greater sum. As the first book notes: "Only from the air can one trace a pattern, a design, an abortive, human intention." In the late book *Staying On* (1977), for which he won the Booker Prize just a year before his death, Scott looked at the last stage of the British illusion; it is the tragi-comic story of two minor characters from the larger Quartet who stay on in India and try to retain their lives and positions as their world dissolves and the new India takes shape. Offering tantalizing glimpses of the greater whole, it is a significant coda to a major and comprehensive enterprise, unusual in modern fiction.

These were fictions of history in its larger sense, not as faded past but as continuing, shaping process; and among other things these books pointed the way onward to others which dealt with the world beyond imperialism – the novels of V. S. Naipaul, Ruth Prawer Jhabvala's *Heat and Dust* (1975), Anita Desai's *Clear Light of Day* (1980), and on to Salman Rushdie's *Midnight's Children* (1981) and Vikram Seth's *A Suitable Boy* (1993), or, for that matter, novels of Northern Ireland, like Bernard McLaverty's *Cal* (1983), or Glenn Patterson's *Burning Your Own* (1988). But there were other crucial scenes of history to explore, in the divided history of Europe, no less agonized than ever. This was when the Cold War spy novel became an important and revealing form. Len Deighton had published *The Ipcress File* in 1962, and John Le Carré *The Spy Who Came in from the Cold* in 1963, and both quickly became highly successful popular writers. But Le Carré in particular now seemed a significant heir not just of John Buchan but of Graham Greene; his sombre novels of Cold War intrigue came to seem not just a complex allegory of two systems conspiratorially interlocked with each other under modern codes of secrecy, but an enquiry into the moral state of the nation. His novels of the Seventies – *The Naive and Sentimental Lover* (1971), *Tinker, Tailor, Soldier, Spy* (1974), *The Honourable Schoolboy* (1977), and later *The Perfect Spy* (1986) – looked into the state of the British establishment, the moral chaos left by the confused allegiances of the Thirties, the nature of British identity, the postwar obsession with rivalry and secrecy, the nature of treachery and betrayal, with a scope that made them important interpretations of late twentieth-century sensibility. As the climate of the Cold War changed, and finally became a matter of retrospect, Le Carré's fiction would hand on its influence to mainstream fiction. The same was true of science fiction. In surreal works like J. G. Ballard's *Concrete Island* (1974), *High Rise* (1975) and *The Unlimited Dream Company* (1979), or the hyper-productive Michael Moorcock's *The Condition of Muzak* (1977), it was coming ever closer to the dismays and darkness of contemporary history. In fact, in his highly realistic memoir *Empire of the Sun* (1984), about a child learning the primitive arts of survival in a Japanese prison-camp in Shanghai, where he witnesses at a distance the atomic explosion in Nagasaki, Ballard wrote one of the strongest works of the Eighties. To most of these writers recent and contemporary history was now more grotesque than any fantasy; and it was provoking novelists into striking new acts of the imagination.

9.

There were other important histories to tell. In the Fifties and early Sixties, Doris Lessing and Margaret Drabble had explored – Lessing with an ever more expansive invention, Drabble with a balanced moral realism – the story of women's lives in a time of social and moral change. Along with the admirable South African novelist Nadine Gordimer, Lessing increasingly read these concerns in the light of a larger – indeed cosmic – history of the troubled age. Drabble wrote far more intimately, more realistically, of thoughtful middle-class female lives, with their aspirations, opportunities, and disappointments. Her first books were fascinating and often amusing miniatures, about young, well-educated people making their early domestic and professional careers, and discovering their sexual needs and identities. But in the Seventies Drabble's moral realism widened into a sober and thoughtful culture-reading of an age sinking into ever deeper materialism. *The Needle's Eye* (1972) made it plain that her concern was to make a moral reading of the state of society, and the relationship between personal and private lives and larger public matters; the spread of the book takes in different social classes, the divided world of Southern and Northern England, and extends to cover an international stage. Like Angus Wilson's *Anglo-Saxon Attitudes*, her *The Realms of Gold* (1975) takes archaeology as a metaphor to explore the underlying structures of contemporary British life, and the different traditions of women's lives in it. Her chief novel of the Seventies is *The Ice Age* (1977), a large and chilly vision of a Britain of increasing social collapse and sterility in an era of "property development," financial scandals, and growing political stagnation. With *The Middle Ground* (1980), to be followed by an extended trilogy that would span the Eighties, she began a fiction of "shapeless diversity" that would look at women's issues and difficulties in the light of the broader society, its moral emptiness, its failure of trust, its dangerous texture. Critics began to see her increasingly in the light of the tradition from George Eliot, another novelist who used realism to look at the "middle ground" of society, the space between private and public, individual and society, youth and age, men and women. And her work would become ever more powerful in the Eighties, a time of growing social and moral dismay.

Drabble consciously reconstructed her fiction in the light of nineteenth-century realistic fiction, though she was as aware as any writer of the anxious self-consciousness of current writing. So was her sister A. S. Byatt, who published her first novel *Shadow of a Sun*, a realistic story about a daughter growing up in the shadow of a novelist father, in 1964. Her second book, *The Game* (1967), which is unmistakably an interpretation of her own competitive relationship with her sister, is intensely felt but also highly literary, involving a reversion to the world of the Brontës; Byatt was to remain a novelist of intense and intelligent literariness, a modern writer, as she said, "greedily" reading her own relationship to the novels of the past in order to sustain the fiction of the present. Her most ambitious (and still continuing) project, a sequence of multi-layered novels about the second "Elizabethan Age," began with *The Virgin in the Garden* in 1978. The project merges contemporary narrative and many literary and artistic references, and has a Proustian texture. Some of Byatt's best work would come in the Eighties, when her interests widened and her fictional variety increased. Like many of our best contemporary novelists, Byatt is also a serious and interesting literary critic, who has chosen, she has explained, to explore in her work the "symbolic relationship" that exists between traditional forms and texts and the present, testing "the ambiguous power and restrictiveness of the tradition" for the contemporary writer. That task, both sisters considered, demanded a thoughtful and scrupulous attitude from female writers. As Margaret Drabble put it, "We live in an uncharted world, as far as manners and morals are concerned, we are having to make up our morality as we go. Our subject-matter is enormous, there are whole new patterns to create."

"New patterns" were a chief concern of the many women writers who – encouraged by feminism, and re-invigorated by the growing republication and re-analysis of the female tradition in fiction – were the source of many of the more important novels of the Seventies and the Eighties. And while some, like Maureen Duffy and Nell Dunn, saw the task as largely one of realism, others looked to more fantastic forms to pursue the re-engendering of fiction. Surely the most notable was Angela Carter, whose methods merged with that spirit in fiction that came, as a result of the work of South American writers such as Gabriel García Márquez, to be called "magic realism" – fiction, that is, where elements of dream, fantasy, fairytale and magic mingle with social and historical narrative. In her early work like *The Magic Toyshop* (1967) and *The Infernal Desire Machines of Doctor Hoffman* (1972), she declared her interest in the machinery of fairytale and in strongly erotic themes; *The Passion of the New Eve* (1977) shifted the setting to a future America. Increasingly the task involved a postmodern recuperation of fantasy and fairy-story, the place where the borders of convention and experience broke down; she was also rewriting the tradition in feminist terms, brilliantly restructuring the heritage of fairytale in the stories of *The Bloody Chamber* (1979). Her fiction began to establish a fantastic, new Gothic contemporary iconography – a panoply of dolls and toys, puppets and clowns, humans and animals, mythic figures from Dracula to bizarre Hollywood movie queens – that would allow her anti-patriarchal, frequently transsexual stories to move into the realm of radical surrealism. Fantasy was the form of freedom, worth taking seriously, and she made it serious; her new way of writing was to find its finest expression in the two large novels that came toward the end of her career, *Nights at the Circus* (1984) and *Wise Children* (1991). Female and feminist fantasy was becoming one of the strong voices of the decade. No less wicked, rather more frankly comic, was Beryl Bainbridge, whose first novel *A Weekend With Claude* appeared in 1967. Over the Seventies she published some of her finest work, rooted in commonplace realism, yet breaking out into surprise and comic fantasy. In the stories of *Harriet Said* (1972), *The Dressmaker* (1973), *The Bottle Factory Outing* (1974), *Sweet William* (1975), *Injury Time* (1977), and the marvellous *Young Adolf* (1978), nuclear families collapse, sieges interrupt domestic life, violence explodes, the strange constantly enters the familiar. In *Young Adolf*, the penniless young Adolf Hitler proves to have a familiar Bainbridge lower-middle-class upbringing, and it is his Northern sister-in-law who makes him his brown shirts. Bainbridge's comic gift is to normalize and domesticate the world of strangeness and violence, while at the same time undomesticating what we used to think of as the family novel.

Many notable female and feminist careers flourished or developed over the Seventies, and on into the next decade. Novels by Elaine Feinstein and Alice Thomas Ellis, Penelope Fitzgerald and A. L. Barker, Bernice Rubens and Susan Hill, Emma Tennant and Rose Tremain widened the power of female representation, enriched the range of feminist discourse, in modern fiction. Amongst the most striking of these writers was Fay Weldon, whose *Down Among the Women* (1971) and *Female Friends* (1975) laid claim to a radical, generally professional female territory that she explored to fascinating and savage effect over her best books: *Praxis* (1978), *Puffball* (1980), and *The Life and Loves of a She-Devil* (1983). Several of these are hard, sure stories of female revenge on a world that has diminished or mis-identified them, and they show in detail the world of female concerns and changing gender *mores*. At best her works are also interesting explorations of the limits of fictional technique. The tone is cool and ironic; the dialogue is carefully stylized; tales are seen from inside and without – "watching me, watching you." Stories are folded into stories; *Praxis*, her most ambitious novel, crosses between first-and third-person narration, pictures taken from within and without. Later books, like *The Cloning of Joanna May* (1989), about genetic engineering and a girl who finds she has four identical sisters, and set "in a year of strange events," went for even greater extravagance and satirical commentary on the "temporary nature of our lives." Though Weldon's fiction suffers from over-productivity and repetition, her vision at best is a strong one, maybe best explained by the near-closing lines of *Praxis*: "She wrote, she raged, grieved and laughed, she thought she nearly died; then, presently, she began to feel better." Praxis' revolt into writing and new feeling was one that was passing through the fiction of the Seventies, producing a widening of gender representation and, in several of these writers, a feeling that the very tone and form of the novel was altering remarkably.

10.

Indeed by the middle of the Seventies the climate of British fiction was changing fast, as a new generation of writers far less bound by the conventions of realism, increasingly interested in the grotesque and the fantastic, made their mark. The change was strongly signified by two very young writers who quickly made their reputations, Martin Amis and Ian McEwan. Amis was twenty-four when he published his first novel *The Rachel Papers* in 1973, and Ian McEwan twenty-seven when he made his mark in 1975 with his first volume of short stories, *First Love, Last Rites*. Martin Amis was the son of Kingsley Amis, though no two writers could, on first inspection, have seemed more different; in time the similarities appeared greater. *The Rachel Papers*, the story of the adolescent Charles Highway, exploiting sex on his way to Oxford, was a savagely bitter portrait of contemporary society, and also technically disturbing; if the Angry Young Man had come back, it was as a disturbed and perhaps malevolent child, a troubled and extravagant fantasist. Amis' second novel *Dead Babies* (1975) confirmed, from its title onward, a willingness to shock, with its savage and disturbing portrait of intelligent young people engaged in a self-destructive orgy of drugs and sex. Meanwhile the short stories of Ian

McEwan's first volume were just as willing to take on troubling and grotesque themes: death, perversion, violence, madness, extreme fantasies of adolescent desire. Both writers generally started with everyday subjects, the drab realms of "normal" life, and carried them into darkness, psychological strangeness, grotesquerie. Both were also technically complex writers, confidently opening their stories out from the realism their surface methods at first promised to pursue. Like the novels and stories of Angela Carter, theirs were oddly macabre works, fictions where forms became hybridized, and the secure borders that kept fiction in the realm of realism and familiarity collapsed. *The Rachel Papers* is filled with a clear narrative self-consciousness, and various clever tricks of literary deception; *Dead Babies* has direct addresses from self-conscious author to self-conscious reader; this "postmodern trickiness," as Amis called it, would become part of the extraordinary technical theatre of his later and finer fiction of the Eighties. McEwan's work explored the fictional boundaries of the perverse and uncanny, shifting the levels, breaking the frame, admitting the forbidden. There was also a clear sense in which both writers were satirists, indeed troubled moralists, of an increasingly grotesque and alien world, a world in which perverse inner fantasy and grotesque outward reality were forced to meet in new mixtures.

Their later work soon began to confirm their sophistication as well as the grotesquerie of their vision. Amis' third novel, *Success* (1978), is another highly decadent text, but is also a critical portrait of the solipsistic, narcissistic self. His fourth, *Other People: A Mystery Story* (1981), powerfully deals with displaced identity, and follows the course of a girl's breakdown, in which the gap between herself and other people becomes obscured; her death and dissolution are throughout prefigured. Thereafter the question of the boundary line of identity, the failing edges of self, the breakdown of the character, would become a key theme of Amis' fiction, along with a sense of an ever more corrupted and decaying material world. McEwan's second collection of short stories, *In Between the Sheets* (1978), contained more views of perverse sexuality and psychic extremity; now, though, there were growing hints that the "shocking" material was under the control of something very like reticence, that the author was a recorder of a world of an increasing disintegration that could provoke only alienation, nausea and "desolate couplings." The finest story of the volume, "Psychopolis," is set in Los Angeles, postmodernism's true "unreal city," and portrays its chaotic, meaningless pluralism. McEwan's first novel *The Cement Garden* (1978) is a grimly Gothic tale, told from the child's-eye viewpoint, of a household where the parents die and are buried in the garden, leaving the children to a world of incest, transvestism and regression. McEwan's concern, emphasized by his use of the child's-eye view, is with the way innocence is lost, the sense of initiation as darkness comes; these too would be themes in his later fiction. In *The Comfort of Strangers* (1981), McEwan signalled a change, at least of underlying perspective. The story, set in an imaginary city which is plainly Venice, is an impressionist, nightmare fable of labyrinthine and dangerous realationships, shading from initial normality toward an ever more ominously promised moment of the fulfilment of "a violence that is in the air," and is born out of a fundamental dislocation of sexual and gender feeling that "distorted all relations, all truth."

By the turn into the Eighties, both Amis and McEwan had established themselves as major writers, troubling, self-conscious, experimental visionaries of a world where the methods of the grotesque, the mechanisms of fantasy and extremity, seemed all that would serve to encompass the disordered psychic and social landscape of an age where actuality leaked into the world of the thriller, self leaked into social disorder, and the moral wholeness of the times was set in doubt. Both displayed a new attitude growing in fiction, as writers crossed its known frontiers and broke its limits, attempting to link the social aspects of British fiction with the underground psychic and sexual realms where the sense of contemporary crisis was most strongly felt. During the Seventies, in a great many texts, fantasy was merging freely with realism, deconstructive new mythologies were undermining the old structures and surfaces, and the novel was eroticized. John Berger's most powerful novel, *G.* (1972), was a technically complex eroticization of history, a historicizing of eroticism, the Don Giovanni story retold in the setting of the *belle époque* and the Great War, and exploring the way sexual desire relates to cultural and political crisis. Fantasy is a mode of artistic dissolution, breaking down the borders of familiarity and identity, opening the door into otherness, acknowledging unconscious forces, at times admitting to fiction an ultimate loss of order and signification. It was also a way of opening British fiction to forms that lay beyond the realism in which the framework of a consensual and familiar society had been sustained. That evolution had been taking place for some time; it would continue into the novel of the Eighties, when British fiction, growing ever less British, would come to see reality and history less as a recognizable given than a reality in dream-like disorder, to which the novelists had to attend.

As the Seventies closed, a familiar convention was resumed; two important attempts were made to test the condition of the contemporary English novel. In a closing issue of *The New Review* in 1978, fifty-six writers and critics of fiction were summoned to reflect on the state of fiction. Given the history of this particular form of accountancy, it was probably predictable that the bulk of the answers would be depressing. No one now read novels, it seemed generally agreed; no good new writers were appearing, the critics remained as blind as ever, and British fiction was failing to respond either aesthetically or in breadth of vision to the changing, widening, internationalizing world. In 1980 the new (or rather renewed) magazine *Granta* ran a similar symposium at longer length. Similar concerns were proclaimed; British fiction remained parochial, a tiny parish with its own well-defined rules, clear boundaries, and eternal class preoccupations, while elsewhere, above all in the USA and Latin America, a great postmodern experiment was flourishing. There was, though, some acknowledgement that British fiction was widening, being jolted from within as well as without, and at least one critic noticed the variety of nationalities, the multiplicity of different Englishnesses, the new feminist energies, that had come into the novel. Meanwhile, the same issue, the magazine was printing a segment of Rushdie's *Midnight's Children*, a parodic fairytale by Angela Carter, a fragment of Russell Hoban's *Riddley Walker* (a novel of self-creating language which begins "On my naming day . . ."), a "postmodern" speculation by Christine Brooke-Rose – as well as a wise, useful warning by the American critic James Gindin that the view that American fiction was in much better shape than British should not be taken for granted. Perhaps something was indeed ending: a familiar notion of Englishness and the literary conventions that had come to express it. What was not ending was the British novel. As the Eighties began, it was actually in a state of considerable revitalization, from new writers, new viewpoints, new styles, new experimental attitudes, and all of this would go on to flourish in the expanded marketplace of the new decade.

SEVEN

Artists of the Floating World:
1979 to the Present

Our time is different. All times are different, but our time is *different*. A new fall, an infinite fall, underlies the usual – indeed traditional – presentiments of decline. To take only one example, this would help explain why something has gone wrong with time – with modern time: the past and the future, equally threatened, equally cheapened, now huddle in the present. The present feels narrower, the present feels straitened, discrepant, as the planet lives from day to day. It has been said – Bellow again – that the modern situation is one of *suspense*: no one, no one at all, has any idea how things will turn out.

Martin Amis, *Einstein's Monsters* (1987)

". . . Sensei, it is my belief that in such troubled times as these, artists must learn to value something more tangible than those pleasurable things that disappear with the morning light. It is not necessary that artists always occupy a decadent and closed world. My conscience, Sensei, tells me I cannot remain forever an artist of the floating world."

Kazuo Ishiguro, *An Artist of the Floating World* (1986)

1.

In May 1979, Margaret Thatcher, newly elected the British Conservative Prime Minister, marched into 10 Downing Street, declaring 'Now there is work to be done.' A year later, across the Atlantic, Americans elected Ronald Reagan, the "film-star president," and one of the oldest ever, to preside in the Oval Office. A new and happy marriage of political minds came to be celebrated, and on each side of the Atlantic the Eighties started in step. These new administrations took office with a fresh and conservative mandate, and they marked a fundamental change of political direction, a determination to reject or overcome the misdirections, declines and faded dreams of the decade just gone. The Seventies had seemed little more than the dull aftermath of the Sixties, robbed of direction by an oil crisis that had destabilized Western growth and brought international recession. In a Britain where economic growth was feeble and weakening in competition with other developed powers, continuous sterling crises and balance-of-payments problems stripped the decade of real prospects. This was, as Margaret Drabble put it in her Seventies novel of this title, *The Ice Age*, when "the flow had ceased to flow: the ball had stopped rolling." The conflict between ever-rising hopes of affluence and the problems of a deteriorating economy came at the decade's end, when public service workers went on strike in the "Winter of Discontent"; this helped to weaken the then Labour government and bring Mrs Thatcher to power. A similar sense of impotence prevailed in the USA, as inflation rose, unemployment grew, the Great Society overspent itself. There were greater humiliations: effective defeat in Vietnam, the Watergate scandal, the imminent impeachment of a president, and finally the Iran Hostage crisis, which the decent but weak Democrat president, Jimmy Carter, seemed unable to resolve. The Seventies closed on lost hopes, growing social division, and fast-fading liberal dreams. The impatient voters on each side of the Atlantic agreed the Eighties must be different. There certainly was work to be done, though, in a time of continued economic downturn and needed political restructuring, you were lucky if you could find it.

Still a new agenda of social, economic and cultural interpretation was already on offer to help the Eighties on their way. It was essentially born from the reaction against the Sixties – with its utopian myths, its instinctive anarchism, its own distinctive repressive tolerance, its dreams of a great libertarian consciousness-revolution that unending Western affluence would readily finance. But now the dominant cultural language changed radically. If the Fifties had largely read culture with a moral vocabulary, the Sixties with a sociological one, the Seventies with the language of personal consciousness, the Eighties quickly introduced a new discourse founded on myths of money. It was no longer the radical sociologists and the consciousness-gurus, but the post-Keynesian economists who provided the times with their going rate of exchange. The theory they delivered, "monetarism", came to dominate not only the economic and political but the cultural spirit of the day. The welfare-state consensus of the post-war years was now proving both intellectually and economically overspent. New economic realities – no less fictional than any other interpretative realities – took over; fiscal interpretation was applied to all manner of things, and not least to matters of culture and art. The age of the "free market" (which proved not as free as all that) and the commodification of culture had come, and the climate had changed. Like it or not – and most writers and intellectuals, reared both on welfare-state liberalism and the radical agenda of the Sixties, did not – "Thatcherism," as it came to be called, proved an influential and dominant philosophy, and the "Thatcher Revolution" a real revolution, which quickly transformed the social, political and cultural climate, and brought a well-established liberal consensus to an end.

Mrs Thatcher was not one to consent to consensus; as she had remarked in the 1979 election campaign, Old Testament prophets did not say "Brothers, I want a consensus." The Eighties required, she held, firm leadership and a "conviction politics" out of which a different version of late twentieth-century society and the individual would emerge. The word "liberal" lost severely in credit; and if most post-war Western intellectuals had instinctively assumed that the direction of late twentieth-century social order was toward the egalitarian welfare society, the Eighties indicated that it was not. The revolution that revived the capitalist West in the post-war years was less a proletarian than a new bourgeois revolution, based on private affluence and ownership, and not on labour-intensive manufacturing but on new technologies and services. Industrialism no longer dominated as it had, its operations passing to the speeded-up economies of the Second and even the Third

396

World; the class and labour demarcations that had defined British society were in change, and so were the ideologies that came out of them. Where the traditional liberal–left view had stressed the modern collectivity, the "great society" that redistributed wealth to all its members, the new view emphasized individualism and sought to roll back the frontiers of the state. The bourgeois individual was reconstructed, the moral self (imperfectly) recovered, rules of individualism and entrepreneurialism were applied to most aspects of life. Society, said Mrs Thatcher in a phrase much quoted against her, "did not exist." But her meaning was perfectly clear: society consisted not of a "nanny state" organizing all in the presumed best interests of each, but was the sum of its individualisms, the achievement of its most energetic selves. In the Eighties, in a period of increasingly triumphant late capitalism, society patently did exist. Its monuments rose in high tower-blocks of commerce, shopping malls and science parks, multi-national corporations and operations. Beside them stood the ever more vacant lots of culture – declining universities, closing theatres, a complaisant media, a disappearing *avant garde*, and a view of the arts not as critique but as commodity.[1] The public spaces of cities deteriorated, crime rates rose, problems of drugs and urban violence intensified, and sociologists noted the rising problem of the "underclass," those who did not share in the entrepreneurial opportunities the Eighties increasingly offered.

Writers are often imperfect historians, and at first they seemed slow to grasp the scale of the change taking place, or acknowledge that this marked a considerable shift in the direction of the post-war world. In fact during the Eighties the post-war world was ceasing to be the post-war world, and the intellectual map was reshaping. For a period at the beginning of the decade, the Cold War intensified, as Ronald Reagan dramatically condemned the Soviet "evil empire" and the spirit of détente waned. In fact fundamental changes were taking

[1] For a useful study of the Thatcher era, see Dennis Kavanagh, *Thatcherism and British Politics: The End of Consensus?* (Oxford and New York, 1987).

place within the Marxist system, and the Soviet hegemony was beginning to fail. Russia was over-extended in power, had dangerously committed itself in Afghanistan, and Western technological advance was raising the stakes of military challenge too high. The Marxist command economies had also suffered severely in the Seventies world recession; the boom now reviving the Western economies was spilling across the borders, aided by new satellite technologies; both the cruelty and the inbuilt corruption of the police-run Marxist states were becoming ever more intolerable. When in 1984, Mikhail Gorbachev came to power in Russia, he acknowledged this, and a new period of *glasnost* and *perestroika*, openness and restructuring, began. The social and ideological stasis of the post-war era in Eastern Europe and Russia itself began to dissolve. Meanwhile in Western Europe the material boom of the Eighties gave a new impetus to the notion of a European economic and political community. It was in the Eighties that the dream of a united Europe became real. These changes gave real meaning to the free market values of the decade, and, to the dismay of some and the benefit of others, Thatcherite Britain became a major player in the cultural formation of the day.

And, whatever the view of Mrs Thatcher, work had indeed been done. In Britain the social map had been transformed. In some parts of the country, especially the South, gentrification, hi-tech and service industries, traffic, motorways, shopping, leisure, gourmet eating and fast food prospered. Where the Sixties had been the age of the hippie, the Eighties was the age of the yuppie. Psychedelic shapes gave way to straight lines, flared jeans to sharp suits, sex, now tainted by the AIDS epidemic, to money as a source of erotic gratification. It was no longer the old hard money, money as specie; it was plastic, it was the share portfolio, the cash dispenser, the world money-game that flickered on the VDU screens in the dealing-rooms of the City of London, as the erotics of trading grew. In 1986 came, at last, the Big Bang, as Stock Exchange dealing was deregulated, opening the free market and encouraging an economic boom, to be followed not too long after by a deep-seated slump. But for the moment the buzz of the dealing-room, the noise of the mobile telephone, the thrill of the home computer, the chatter of the wine-bar, the delight of gourmet eating, the deal on the Docklands apartment, was the spirit of the Eighties. So too was Mrs Thatcher, who was elected for two further terms. When she was ousted from office in 1990, her fall came not at the hands of the electorate or the parliamentary opposition but at the hands of her own party, dismayed by her ever-increasing authoritarianism and Old Testament prophecy and her instinctive, English reaction to another of the essential motors of Eighties change, the expanding, incorporating and increasing post-nationalist European Community.

In Britain her fall felt like the end of an era. But by now another, much vaster era had ended too. In Eastern Europe the dismays of those who felt imprisoned in Marxism and the tired command economy could no longer be contained. The free market and Europe beckoned, and the conception of entrepreneurial liberty spread. In November 1989 the Berlin Wall came down, the Communist leaders were dislodged in many of the Middle and Eastern European states, and forty-five years of frozen history came to an end. The monuments fell, and the political statues of the century tumbled; streets, squares and entire cities were renamed. New or lost states came into being, frontiers unravelled; the map of nations changed. The mental as well as the geographical maps that had explained the world and its ideological directions for half a century or more no longer served. It was, said the politicians, the New World Order; historians announced "the End of History." "What we may be witnessing is not just the end of the Cold War, or the passing of a particular period of post-war history, but the end of history as such: that is, the end point of mankind's ideological evolution and the universalization of Western liberal democracy as the final form of human government," wrote Francis Fukuyama in 1989 in a famous essay of that title.[2] The Nineties had

[2] See Francis Fukuyama, *The End of History and the Last Man* (London, 1992). I have quoted from his original essay "The End of History?", which appeared in the American magazine *The National Interest* in Summer 1989 (pp. 3–18).

started, at first on a brief plateau of hope which was soon to turn again to doubt and anxiety; the post-war world had truly come to an end. And instead we were in the post-post-war world, which was the pre-twenty-first-century world, shapeless, unprophesied, profoundly insecure, and plainly a new challenge to all its writers.

2.

In British terms, "The Eighties" is in effect the well-marked period between Mrs Thatcher's election in 1979 and her fall from grace eleven years later. It was a time of many reappraisals and restructurings, and of rising doubts, dark prophecies and apocalyptic feelings among a good many of its artists and intellectuals. "It's suddenly chic to be rich, and unchic to be a socialist," noted Margaret Drabble, remarking on the fading of the liberal–left consensus that had played a large part in British post-war intellectual life. Now it was, she pointed out, considered "bad taste" to complain that all was not well, and yet writers always did have "a natural curiosity to know what's going on underground." That "natural curiosity," that look "underground," became one central theme of Eighties fiction, and not least in Drabble's own work. This was the era of some of her largest, bleakest and most weightily realistic novels about the state of the nation and the world, works in which the security of decent liberalism is constantly broken down by the late-modern chaos. The title of her first novel of the Eighties, *The Middle Ground* (1980), suggests the position her fiction had always sought to inhabit; her long expanding sequence *The Radiant Way* (1987), *A Natural Curiosity* (1989) and *The Gates of Ivory* (1991) went on to portray, gloomily, critically, and almost chaotically, a world in which the public and private have split, contemporary cities grow ever more apocalyptic, death, far-flung global crisis and a sense of impending catastrophe impinge ever more on the decent, reforming middle-class lives which form the centre of her fiction, as they too begin to splinter in the social and moral confusion.

Drabble was hardly alone in her vision; many writers of the age of Thatcherism and social discommunity saw it as a time of division, decay, human neglect and lost wholeness. Salman Rushdie's *The Satanic Verses* (1988) won its author a tragic fate for its sceptical, fictionalist's view of the sacred text of Islam; but a main theme of the book was the fragmentation, violence and disorder of a multi-cultural but incoherent Britain, ruled by a "Mrs Torture." As if in return to the mood that had shaped the work of the Naturalists and Decadents of just a hundred years earlier, the spirit of urban apocalyptics reappeared in British fiction (as it did in contemporary American fiction, where the great cities were turning into apocalyptic bonfires of the vanities). London, as the great disorderly city, was everywhere in the novel. Peter Ackroyd's *Hawksmoor* (1985) is a form of London Gothic, where strange serial crimes stalk the city churchyards. Paul Bailey's fine *Gabriel's Lament* (1986) recreates it as a city of Dickensian depth and density. Michael Moorcock's symphonic *Mother London* (1988) links the remnants of Dickens' city through the blitz to the Eighties. Martin Amis' *London Fields* (1989) depicts it as a failed Arcadia, a murder-haunted metropolis on the eve of an ecological holocaust ("If you are interested in ugliness and sleaze, London is the place to be," he commented), Geoff Dyer offered a streetwise version of its chaos and decline in *The Colour of Memory* (1989), Justine Cartwright's *Look at It This Way* (1990) explores it as a carnivorous jungle, Iain Sinclair's *Downriver* (1991) surrealistically represents a place of weird extremities and violent intersections. Angela Carter's *Wise Children* (1991) begins by calling up London as a city split in two like Budapest, two different versions of life being led on the right and the wrong side of the river, the right and wrong side of the tracks, and Jim Crace's ironically titled *Arcadia* (1992) is a poetic portrait of the universal modern city in its darkness and its light.

The Britain of Mrs Thatcher did gradually begin to find its record in fiction. The Eighties was a vigorous and productive period in the novel, and in the course of the decade the genre went through a very considerable change of subject, personnel, style and mood. The newer styles and manners were often elegant carapaces over social dismay. Even before 1979, Martin Amis had seemed to specialize in ironically Thatcherite titles, like *Success* (1978). And in the following few years no writer of fiction better caught the note of the British Eighties, with its immediate gratifications, its apocalyptic anxieties, its cynicism and its underlying alarm. *Money: A Suicide Note* (1984) was a perfect title for the times. "As Saul Bellow said, it seemed for a while in the Eighties that money was the one thing that didn't stink," Amis wrily explained; "Everything was questionable, but money was a vital substance you knew where you were with." In fact money was in many of the titles; one of the most successful stage plays in the (failing) theatre was Caryl Churchill's *Serious Money* ("Sexy greed *is* the late Eighties"). "While making love, we often talk about money," reports the grabby, grubby anti-hero of *Money*, John Self. "I like it. I like that dirty talk." Self is an artist of the tacky TV commercial and the violent film-script who lives firmly in the present ("The future's futures have never looked so rocky. Don't put money on it. Take my advice and stick to the present. It's the real stuff, the only stuff"), and anti-hero of the age of junk food, junk money, junk nature and the junk self. Treated in the novel as a fascinated victim of Amis' disappointed moralism, he is also – as his name suggests – a version of the fragmenting contemporary self. Amis took his own advice and mostly stuck to the present, and his hard style, mordant wit and vividly rolling constructions became an exemplary and much-imitated style of the day. So did the dark note of Ian McEwan's chilling Eighties fables, tales of an imperfect innocence ever more corrupted by bad history, failed politics, and sexual and gender anxiety. In fiction the Eighties generally comes out as an era of dismay.

There was, though, a paradox to be noted in all of this. In the age of highly commercialized culture, drama was declining, the serious social play yielding to the special effects of the

402

musical spectacular, television drama moving off into romance and historical nostalgia (one of the great successes of the early Eighties was television's elegant revisiting of Evelyn Waugh's *Brideshead Revisited*, its story told as a nostalgic spectacular of an age of wealth and class). By contrast, fiction was undergoing a considerable revitalization; the book was back. New and user-friendly bookshops filled the busy highstreets, less user-friendly but well-financed publishing takeovers were increasing the worth of literary properties, the expanding newspapers grew noisy with cultural chatter, and the hype of literary prizes was raising the profile of authors, especially those young authors who directly appealed to the mood of the new generation. Some writers (though not all, or most) began to acquire something of the energetic celebrity of Thatcherite entrepreneurs, enjoying the rewards of high financial success, becoming as famous for their advances or their film sales (or the film-scripts they had been hired by Hollywood to write) as their novels themselves; indeed the novel became a form exploited by media celebrities for decorating their fame. The novel was sexy again, its works increasingly offering a streetwise portrait of changing and divisive times, or providing an escape, into the historical past or to other countries, where the present did not oppress. Novelists themselves became living evidence of the Thatcherite miracle, with its preoccupation with "life-style," its culture of eclecticism, its material competitiveness and its cult of glossy, stylish "success." For once, literary fiction competed with blatantly commercial fiction in the charts, and "postmodern-ism" became not an obscure experiment but, like the smart new upmarket foreign foods, an elegant commodity. And all that no doubt contributed to the distinctive mood – perhaps best characterized as a streetwise note of bitter post-liberal irony – that ran through a good deal of the period's serious writing, which was certainly not in short supply. In fact the Eighties compared with the Fifties in its flourish of new writers, and its strong fictional energy and air of stylistic and stylish discovery.[3]

---

[3] In his interesting but extravagant polemic, *A Vain Conceit: British Fiction in the*

Meanwhile, if some writers and critics shared John Self's opinion that the present was "the real stuff, the only stuff," many novelists began looking back to history. Retrospective fiction now became highly popular; indeed the return to the past began to assume near-epidemic proportions during the decade. The modernist quarrel with the Victorian age was evidently over and done. In a time when Mrs Thatcher sought to restore "Victorian values," and Charles Dickens and Victorian classics enjoyed a striking publishing revival, a good number of writers – encouraged, perhaps, by John Fowles' art of self-conscious retrospect – took to revisiting the era when individualism seemed stronger, the social realities clearer, and our modern history was shaping, frequently pastiching past novels or writers in this recuperative process. The End of the Empire remained a dominant theme: in, for instance, the novels of Barry Unsworth, whose *Pascali's Island* (1980) looked at the aftermath of the Ottoman empire, his *Stone Virgin* (1985) at the fate of imperial Venice, his *Sugar and Rum* (1988) at the dying of Liverpool, a city founded on the slave trade, while in *Sacred Hunger* (1992) he wrote a large and notable epic about those slave voyages themselves. Dying empires and fading lives likewise filled the delicate novels and stories of the excellent, observant Anglo-Irish author William Trevor, whose *The Silence in the Garden* (1988) looked sharply at the trauma of Irish history, and the wickedly witty fiction of Molly Keane, in her novels of the fading Irish Protestant ascendancy like *Good Behaviour* (1981) and *Loving and Giving* (1988). J. L. Carr's *A Month in the Country* (1980) returned to the Britain of just after the Great War in a subtle story of moral and historical archaeology; Isabel Colegate's *The Shooting Party* (1980) was set, like a good number of novels of the time, in 1913, and is about

Eighties (London, 1989), D.J. Taylor argued that newer and younger writers who were breaking through toward a wider vision of contemporary society were largely neglected critically in the Eighties. Almost the opposite seems to me true; new writers broke through with a speed unusual in the novel's history, and it was often notable and discovering work by the older generation that was neglected.

the dying of an aristocratic age as war impends. These are all fine writers, and these are novels of great craft. But they also encouraged the critical complaint that British novelists were steadily returning to tired verities, both of subject-matter and form: ". . . it seems to me that the main thrust of the best new writing of the first years of the Eighties has been backwards, into the past," complained one critic, Hugh Hebert, adding that most writers now seemed to be reverting to "the traditional novel, with its burgher-like literary virtues."

In fact these revisitings were often a good deal more complicated than that, and many of them were far from being conventional returns to the realistic tradition or to the burgher-like forms of the novel. In 1980, in his pictographic *A Humument*, the painter Tom Philips took W. H. Mallock's late Victorian social novel *A Human Document* (1892), and, by painting over some of the words and highlighting others, created a brilliantly teasing, randomized narrative that was also a postmodern multi-media collage. In *The Great Fire of London* (1982), Peter Ackroyd, who was to write a new biography of Dickens, took his *Little Dorrit* and constructed a new version of its story on and off a contemporary film-set. In *Nice Work* (1988), David Lodge went back to the Victorian "Condition of England" novel and the industrial fiction of writers like Mrs Gaskell to look at the divided North-and-South Britain of his own day. A Marxist feminist lecturer at Rummidge University who knows just how to deconstruct the Victorian industrial novel with her students is asked to shadow the managing director of an engineering firm; two Englands and two ideologies meet. So do two styles of fiction, the self-conscious and the realistic, the novel of intertextual pastiche and the novel of social concern and morality. But the styles met often in Eighties fiction, post-modern experiment frequently mixing and merging with traditional narrative. In her ambitious *Possession* (1990), A. S. Byatt intelligently built similar bridges between Victorian art and sensibility and contemporary gender-conflict, feminism and deconstructive thinking, using both effective poetic pastiche and dense social storytelling to look at the way they lived then and the way we

405

live now. A powerful, indeed Umberto Eco-like version of historical reconstruction appeared in Lawrence Norfolk's *Lemprière's Dictionary* (1992), an admirably learned novel where an eighteenth-century project of writing a classical dictionary is interrupted by mysterious global plots (to do with the East India Company), a vast cast of characters spread across the world, and various Gothic horrors. Perhaps it was less that novelists were returning to the fictional verities of the past than making the relations of past and present narratives a matter for self-conscious literary examination. Among novelists, as among historians themselves, the question of the nature of history and history-writing was at issue. "There are times when you have to disentangle history from fairy-tale," wrote Graham Swift in one of the best of these books, *Waterland* (1983), a tale of the unreliable layers of history in which present lives are lived. There was indeed some sign of a return to traditional forms, to a conventionalized literariness, to a fiction of pure historical recreation or sentimental nostalgia. But serious questions of narrative history and fictional "archaeology" – the term acquired a considerable importance in the decade – were an important part of the experiment of the Eighties novel.

3.

Perhaps the best way to explain what was happening is to observe that the "traditional" novel went through both a significant revival and a powerful testing during the decade, which was, as is now evident, not a period of traditionalism but of considerable exploration and much new and original talent. Many of the most interesting novels stood somewhere between anxious return to history and the fictional tradition and what Martin Amis called "postmodern trickiness" – the quality, he thought, that most distinguished his and his generation's work from that of his father Kingsley Amis. A fair number of the serious younger writers were themselves graduates in literature, and they had imbibed the lessons of late-twentieth-century fictionalist experiment. That was perhaps best displayed by Peter Ackroyd, who studied and worked at Yale, then the heartland (if heart it had) of "Deconstruction" and who, on returning to Britain, published an interesting polemical book, *Notes for a New Culture* (1975), which attacked his British fictional predecessors and contemporaries for lack of interest in current philosophy and literary theory. They were, he complained, stultified by the British tradition of humanism and empiricism, trapped in a reified Englishness, dependent on "a false aesthetic of subjectivity and a false context of realism." Hence British novelists were, he claimed, no longer able to "invest created forms with our own significance" (Professor Terry Eagleton could hardly have voiced this commonplace complaint any better). Ackroyd then went on to produce some of the more interesting novels of the Eighties, marked alike by high fictional self-consciousness and a powerful historical re-creation which duly went on to display its own amended version of Britishness. In his intellectual preoccupations, which included the new Francophilia and contemporary science, Ackroyd was hardly a voice crying alone. "Postmodern trickiness," along with the conviction that they now wrote in post-humanist times, was to become a well-established convention among the more serious young writers. "The self is not a steady voice that has needs for itself any more," Amis said, explaining the complex frame of *Money*, in which "John Self" encounters in the text not only his own author Martin Amis but also the author's female double, Martina Twain. "It's a babble, various gibbering needs and envies." He also observed the breakdown of the conventional borders of genre and narrative type, generating a new form of grotesque comedy: "all sorts of things are getting into the comic novel that shouldn't be there, like rapists and murderers. There's a kind of promiscuity of style which is perhaps characteristic of the collapse of various structures in society and fiction."

Stylistic promiscuity – the mixing and merging of various styles, genres, and cultural levels, the intertextual layering of free play with traditional narrative – had in fact been one of the

407

marks of the "postmodern" American writers since the Sixties, writing in the age of what John Barth called "the used-upedness" of the modes of fiction, of lost tradition and late-modern stylistic glut and variety. And similar manners, of heightened factionality and literary play, now became part of the going convention of contemporary British fiction. "Texts" regularly asserted their self-conscious "fictionality," authors intruded into their stories, fiction merged with fact, old tales crossed with new ones, and literary high culture with streetwise pop styles; what Lodge had called "crossover fiction" had evidently come to stay. There was no want of works that proclaimed their refusal of liberal realism, worked the borders of the grotesque and the fantastic, borrowed in style and spirit from the multi-cultural, multi-media plenitude. (No wonder that in Angela Carter's *Nights at the Circus* (1984), a mixed-form performance about the breaking of gender roles and boundaries, the heroine Fevvers has for her motto "Is she fact or is she fiction?") But the term "postmodernism" was itself a movable feast, and its theoretical associations were changing again. Now, according to the many philosophical and sociological volumes on the matter that were beginning to jostle even the hip-and-thigh diets off the bookstore shelves, it meant not so much the fictionalist self-consciousness of artists, or the latter-day taste for parody and quotation, as an overall cultural situation – nothing less than "the postmodern condition" itself.

The scale of this epochal notion was made clear in the more recent news from Paris. The "postmodern condition," explained the philosopher Jean-François Lyotard, meant that there were no Grand Narratives left on which thinkers, or writers, could depend. No totalizing explanations set the scene, the world's big meanings and totalist ideologies had gone, leaving only a seamless mix of small ones, an eclectic and random variety of narratives ("Simplifying to the extreme, I define *postmodern* as incredulity toward meta-narratives"). We now lived in the age of "hyper-reality," argued another influential French philosopher, Jean Baudrillard, when surfaces had no depths, images no content, selves no centre; so in the multi-media theme-park future "power will only belong to those with no origins and no authenticity, who know how to exploit the situation to the full." A yet vaster overview of the Disneyland of modern experience came from the American critic Fredric Jameson, a late-modern Marxist from the age of affluence, who, pretending "to take postmodernism for what it says it is," gave dense accounts of its variegated, Americanized, mass-cultural phenomena: glitz architecture (LA's Westin Bonaventura hotel), shopping fever, endless serial film and video, computer culture and cyberpunk, theme-park history, and "blank parody," the cannibalization of the styles of the past. Jameson explained a substanceless world where life had become life-style, images replaced people, statement became quote, history was instant nostalgia, the apocalyptic became the decorative, and every new building was scaffolded in pastiche. It was, he said, a process of "global gentrification," where everything is digested depthlessly, and represented to us as style.

If pastiche or "blank parody" was, as Jameson claimed, the typical style of an eclectic, globalized age without clear cultural or moral standards, then it certainly acquired a strong voice in contemporary British fiction. The culture, as it appeared in fiction, and was voiced in the language of fiction, seemed to be fragmentary, pluralistic, multi-cultural and depthless; it was also split, violent and self-destructive. Where George Orwell had famously described England as a family with the wrong members in control, it now seemed there was no family at home at all, no familiarity, nothing in control. When writers looked back to history, it was generally not to some steadily evolving cultural continuity, but to shards and fragments, which often stood in some strange, dislocated, "archaeological" relationship to the present. Alternatively they looked back to the morbid ghosts of more recent and pressing history: the Second World War, the Holocaust, the Nuremberg Trials ("It is this ordinariness I must capture," notes the narrator of Graham Swift's *Out of this World*, 1988), the atomic explosions at Hiroshima and Nagasaki ("the light was a premonition of his death," J. G. Ballard writes in *The Empire of the Sun*, 1984), the chilly mirror-world of Cold

War hostilities, the prison-house of Eastern Europe, the endless and irresolvable troubles of Ulster, the trauma of South Africa were constant themes, and on their way to becoming conventional tropes. Forty-five years of cold peace had done nothing to drive away the nuclear horrors, which cast their disturbing shadow over much of this fiction, as for example in Maggie Gee's *The Burning Book* (1983). Martin Amis' story-collection *Einstein's Monsters* (1988) speaks of a world where "the children all feel sick and want to go home," and where, on a planet showing its age, "the past and the future, equally cheapened, equally threatened, now huddle in the present."

Indeed the apocalyptic note became a familiar feature of an Eighties fiction in which culture was random and "junk," time frequently dislocated, and oppressive hints of disaster and crisis seemed universal. The sense of recent history as a sequence of past disasters pointing to some further coming catastrophe, a note which had been present in a good deal of fiction since the 1950s (in the novels of William Golding and Anthony Burgess, for example), intensified, multiplied, came closer. Science fiction, which over previous decades had been moving closer toward the fictional centre, now exercised a growing influence on the literary novel. With *Empire of the Sun* (1984), a novel which points to the birth of the nuclear age and his own ironic and surreal vision, J. G. Ballard became an important mainstream novelist, and his work and that of newer experimental writers like Ian McEwan or Iain Banks no longer seemed far apart. For the degraded cities, ravaged fields and dying clouds that were once the world of science fiction and fantasy now filled many of the novels. "Flies get dizzy spells and bees have booze problems," Amis notes in one of the fine black-comic perorations of *Money*. "Robin redbreasts hit the deck with psychosomatic ulcers and cholesterol overload. In the alleys, dogs are coughing their hearts out on snout and dope." Ian McEwan's *The Child in Time* (1988) portrays a near-future where the Thatcher Right has gone to extremity, but the rot is in the weather too, which is strangely disordered, and creates "a sense of crisis and excitement." Rushdie's *The Satanic Verses* has a

410

surreal London going crazy in a period of extravagant heat-wave; some critics called this the most improbable feature of the book. So common was the end-of-the-world news, the catastrophic gloom, the disaster vision, that it became a relief to turn to those writers who practised the art of sceptical and critical comedy: Rushdie himself, Anthony Burgess, the admirable William Boyd, Angela Carter, Michael Frayn, David Lodge and Howard Jacobson, who were capable of suggesting that even the age of apocalypse deserved satirical attention, and might even have a comic silver lining.

In America, "postmodern fiction" had also moved through the cycle from Sixties fictionalist playfulness to grotesque, experimental, heightened realism, and become much concerned with a contemporary and usually urban scene observed as far more violent, abrasive and estranging than familiar (Don DeLillo, Bret Easton Ellis).[4] British Eighties fiction, especially that from younger writers, generally displayed a similar temper. A good deal of it felt like a *fin-de-siècle* fiction, and it was in fact filled with strong, self-conscious echoes from the previous *fin de siècle*, when the clock seemed to stop on the edge of danger. Angela Carter set *Nights at the Circus* on the transforming moment of the turn into the twentieth century, and its heroine Fevvers is a garrulous refraction of the different images that can be associated with the "child of the century." In his preface to *London Fields* (1989), Amis explains he thought of calling the book *The Millennium*, but *"everything* is called *Millennium* just now." So it was; in Eighties fiction, apocalyptic visions, corrupted Utopias and threatened cities were everywhere. Gothic violence, the uncanny, the fantastic and the grotesque, were back; here innocence is generally corrupted, violence erupts suddenly, psychic extremities are explored, danger stalks the dead world, and there is an unstable relation between "real

---

[4] I have discussed this direction in recent American fiction – toward a late modern realism where "reality is a decadent and absurd fantasy in the midst of plenitude" – in detail in *The Modern American Novel*, cited above. The parallels are considerable, not least because British and American writers have increasingly influenced each other, and their works are now regularly published in both countries.

411

life" and art. Dracula, Vlad the Impaler, Jekyll and Hyde, Jack the Ripper – now in the changed guise of the "the serial killer," the marauding mobile man who represents the dangerous urban darkness – were all dusted down from their role in popular myth, and popular movies, and recycled for the service of modern narrative. Freaks and monsters, incest and sexual violence, all the devices of the uncanny, estranging and deceptive on offer in the rich stock of Gothic reappeared in profusion. Clive Sinclair called his youthful and very Nabokovian first novel (which incorporates Vlad the Impaler) *Bibliosexuality* (1973), and his more recent books, like *Blood Libels* (1985) and *Cosmetic Effects* (1989), exploit both the grotesque and the fictionalist devices of Gothic for exploring brooding, violent modern sexuality and the conflicted Anglo-Jewish heritage. Iain Banks played with a wide array of bizarre psycho-sexual horrors in *The Wasp Factory* (1984) and *Walking on Glass* (1985); Patrick McGrath economically titled one of his highly mannered and amply Gothic novels *The Grotesque* (1989). Gender conflict, violence and confusion added to the scene; in the extravagant, unstable, carnivalesque fictions of Angela Carter, fantasy, narrative superfluity and protean transformation break down gender referents along with the fixed and stable forms, and her work is self-consciously written in an "illegitimate" tradition.

In fact – just as happened in the 1890s – all these destabilizing notes of Gothic gloom, outsider vision, historical dismay, psychic disturbance and general victimization were accompanied by a spirit of literary replenishment, and an avaricious reaching out to all the genres, all the forms, the international panoply of styles. In addition to Gothic mannerism, there was a strong influence from Latin American "magic realism," and the related styles of fantastic realism that had developed in Eastern Europe in reaction against the official norms of fiction and "progressive" notions of history. "Magic realism" distorts but does not deny the power of historical reality, or remove fiction from the political world; it is, explained the Czech novelist Milan Kundera, a fiction marked by "our special humour: a humour capable of seeing history as grotesque." In

412

fact these very locations became familiar settings in British fiction too. South America appeared in Lisa Saint Aubin de Teran's haunting novel of domestic imprisonment in Venezuela, *Keepers of the House* (1982), in Nicholas Shakespeare's *The Vision of Elena Silves* (1990), as an imaginary fictional playground in Louis de Bernières' *The War of Don Emmanuel's Nether Parts* (1990) and *The Troublesome Offspring of Cardinal Guzman* (1992). Troubled, dark Eastern Europe was a recurrent theme, in novels ranging from Brian Moore's *The Colour of Blood* (1987) to Bruce Chatwin's haunting *Utz* (1988) and Tibor Fischer's *Under the Frog* (1992). In the era of "Europe," European subject-matter became ever more important, in the fiction of Ian McEwan and Anita Brookner, Julian Barnes and Penelope Lively.

But then the geography of contemporary fiction was widening greatly, and many other of the world's trouble-spots became part of the familiar landscape of fiction: Africa in the admirable fiction of William Boyd (*A Good Man in Africa*, 1981; *An Ice-Cream War*, 1982; *Brazzaville Beach*, 1990), South Africa in Christopher Hope (*Kruger's Alp*, 1984; *The Hottentot Room*, 1986), Arabia in Hilary Mantel (*Eight Months on Ghazzah Street*, 1988). As in the Thirties, travel writing again became one of the success stories of the decade, some of the best performers, like Bruce Chatwin, Paul Theroux, Colin Thubron and Jonathan Raban, also being among the notable novelists; this was the jumbo-jet age, the age of the novelist as frequent flyer, and the United States in particular became a familiar setting. And if the underlying map of fiction was widening – as, said Martin Amis, the English novel "started to go into places where the English novel didn't go, and was being too fastidious about" – so was the range of cultural resources and traditions from which it took its styles and stories. British-based writers came, as in the earlier part of the century, from a much wider variety of origins: some, like Paul Theroux, Russell Hoban and Rachel Ingalls, all American-born, were transatlantic performers, at home on either side of the ocean. Above all, writers began to display the growing multi-culturalism of contemporary British

413

life, and some of the most important novelists of the Eighties were themselves bi-cultural in origin: Salman Rushdie was born in India, Adam Zameenzad in Pakistan, Timothy Mo in Hong Kong, Kazuo Ishiguro in Japan, Ben Okri in Nigeria, Caryl Phillips in St Kitts in the Caribbean. The new aesthetic prolixity was fed by many things: not just multi-culturalism and the growth of a post-colonial intellectual culture, but the widening of the marketplace, the changing cultural texture and mixture of British life, the role of London as, increasingly, a key publishing centre for international fiction in the English language, the sense that the contemporary novel was, as Rushdie put it, sailing freely on "the sea of stories."

And if the international dimension of fiction was expanding, so was its regional dimension. Ireland had of course long been a major centre of important fiction in the English language, to the point where its tradition now seemed distinct and independent. Still, a significant part of the best fiction read in Britain came from there. To the work of well-established notables like William Trevor and Molly Keane were now added the novels of John Banville (*Kepler*, 1980; *Mefisto*, 1986; *The Book of Evidence*, 1989; *Ghosts*, 1993), John McGahern (*The Pornographer*, 1979; *Amongst Women*, 1990), Claire Boylan (*Black Baby*, 1988), Deirdre Madden (*The Birds of the Innocent Wood*, 1988), Neil Jordan (*The Past*, 1980; *The Dream of a Beast*, 1983), Roddy Doyle (*The Commitments*, 1988), Patrick McCabe (*The Butcher Boy*, 1992), and more. It was not surprising that the accumulating horrors and conflicts of Ulster provoked important fiction – from Brian Moore, Carlo Gebler, Bernard McLaverty (*Lamb*, 1980; *Cal*, 1983), Alan Judd (*A Breed of Heroes*, 1981), Maurice Leitch (*Silver's City*, 1981), Glenn Patterson (*Burning Your Own*, 1988; *Fat Lad*, 1992), Mary Beckett, Robert Liam Wilson, Russell Celyn Jones (*Soldiers and Innocents*, 1990), and others. Scots fiction prospered, some of it self-consciously regional, some of it powerfully experimental. Alan Massie has written variously on international, historical and Scots subjects, most notably in *One Night in Winter* (1984). Alasdair Gray has been both a powerful, teasing postmodernist and a writer who has stayed close to

Glasgow materials (*Lanark*, 1981; *1982, Janine*, 1984, and his "up-to-date 19th century novel" *Poor Things*, 1992), James Kelman has brought an experimental, stream-of-consciousness vernacular to working-class Scots life (*The Busconductor Hines*, 1983, and above all *A Disaffection*, 1989), Jeff Torrington in *Swing Hammer Swing* (1992) records the Glasgow Gorbals, and the fiction of Janice Galloway and A. L. Kennedy detailed contemporary Scots life. Kate Roberts wrote fiction in the Welsh language, Bruce Chatwin looked at recent Welsh history in *On the Black Hill* (1982).

And, perhaps, in part encouraged by the rise of "green" issues, regionality in a different sense was returning: as in the 1890s, the rural novel was coming back. In their different ways Graham Swift's remarkable and experimental Fenland story *Waterland* (1983), Lindsay Clarke's East Anglian *A Chymical Wedding* (1989), D. J. Taylor's inventive mixture of urban and rural in *Great Eastern Land* (1986), followed by Adam Thorpe's complex narratives of the historical layers of rural life in *Ulverton* (1992), demonstrated the fact that the regional novel, self-consciously rewritten in a greening age, still plays an important part in the British fictional mythology. For all the firm leadership of Mrs Thatcher, the Eighties was notably a time when the cultural centre was fragmenting, the spirit of nationalism was declining, and rising internationalism (and Europeanism) was paralleled by an intensified sense of place and region. The British fiction of the Eighties felt less like the writing of a common culture than of a multiplying body of cultures, adding to the mixed fund of myths, the surging sea of stories, and extending and varying the prevailing notions of what the British novel might be.[5]

[5] Interesting surveys of 80s fiction are to be found in two essays, Peter Kemp's "British Fiction of the Eighties" and Valentine Cunningham's "Facing the New," in Malcolm Bradbury and Judy Cooke (eds).), *New Writing* (London, 1992), to which I am indebted.

4.

Perhaps, once again, there was no better indicator of the way the spirit of British fiction was changing, in style, mood and generation, at the start of the Eighties than the Booker Prize for Fiction. The Prize in 1980 was, in the public eye at least, essentially a battle of two of the established giants of the Fifties generation, the two books chiefly in contention being Anthony Burgess' *Earthly Powers* and William Golding's *Rites of Passage*. Both were highly ambitious works by writers of continuing power. Burgess' vast novel was told over eight-one chapters by an eighty-one-year-old pederast Catholic writer-narrator, and summed up the literary, social and moral history of the century with comic richness as well as encyclopedic knowingness. Golding's novel was rightly seen as a new breakthrough in his work, and its story of an historical voyage to Australia in the time of the Napoleonic wars would form the first volume of the "maritime trilogy" that was to be Golding's major late-life achievement (he died in 1993); this was the book that eventually won the Prize. A year later, and the two books chiefly in contention were by much younger writers virtually unheard of beforehand; they were works written in a quite different spirit, with a flamboyant air of new experiment, and suggested the appearance of a new fictional generation. One was D. M. Thomas' *The White Hotel*, a surreal psychological work from an author who had chiefly made his name as a poet, though he had published two previous novels, including the lively surrealist *The Flute-Player* (1979). The other was Salman Rushdie's *Midnight's Children*, a novel from an Indian-born, British-educated author who had previously published one little-noticed, rather dry novel, *Grimus* (1975).

The two books shared a good deal in common. Both could be described as works of "magic realism," and were written with great formal freedom and invention; they also dealt with major historical events – Thomas' with the dark psycho-history of Europe as it culminated in the massacre at Babi Yar, Rushdie's

416

with post-Independence India – with strong political and historical awareness. They also appeared in a year when the novel looked particularly exciting, when there were other obvious signs of a new fictional generation, and a strong sense of reviving experiment. Thus the judges of the prize (I was one) had for their contemplation what felt like a burst of radical new writing and considerable stylistic activity. Alasdair Gray's *Lanark*, Maggie Gee's *Dying In Other Words*, Gabriel Josipovici's *The Air We Breathe*, Graham Swift's *Shuttlecock*, Christopher Priest's *The Affirmation*, George Steiner's *The Portage to San Cristobal of A. H.*, J. G. Ballard's *Hello America*, Michael Moorcock's ambitious *Byzantium Endures*, Martin Amis' *Other People*, Ian McEwan's *The Comfort of Strangers*, A. N. Wilson's *Who Killed Oswald Fish?*, William Boyd's *A Good Man in Africa*, and John Banville's *Kepler* were among the books considered; it was plainly a lively year for fiction.

Still, the work of Thomas and Rushdie stood out as remarkable books of the year. *The White Hotel* interweaves documentary "fact" with fictional fantasy, and pastiche reportage with original poetry, to tell the story of Lisa Erdman, a one-time patient of Sigmund Freud in Vienna who finally perishes in the massacre of Ukrainian Jews at Babi Yar in 1941. The story reaches across the psycho-sexual and political history of an agonized century, and includes a brilliant fictional Freudian analysis, a notable erotic poem, "Don Giovanni," and a sequence of surreal erotic imaginings that are intricately linked with the horrors slowly accumulating in the European and Russian experience of the century. Sexual Utopia, and the regression toward the womb (the white hotel itself) are in conflict with death-bringing powers; the conflict and intricate relation between modern love and modern death are a chief theme. The result is a mode of writing that subverts the code of realism and brings a poetic insight and a psychological intensity to the predominantly unpsychological tradition of the British novel. Thomas' concern with the psychological history of the century links with his technical fascination with multiple storytelling, with improvisation and open narrative, with dream and fantasy. The themes of the book were to continue, into a later, very Russianized sequence of interlinked and "improvisational" novels drawing on Pushkin, and entitled "Russian Nights." That sequence, which to date consists of *Ararat* (1983), *Swallow* (1984), *Sphinx* (1986), *Summit* (1987) and *Lying Together* (1990), juggles with a group of international storytellers, and a variety of modes of storytelling, excitingly playing with the idea of narrative improvisation; it also reflects seriously on the nature of art and the erotics of the imagination and incorporates many important twentieth-century stories from the age of modern massacre, international espionage and Cold-War conflict. Thomas' more recent work (*Pictures at an Exhibition*, 1993, etc.) has continued to deal with highly important themes – Kennedy's assassination, the Nazi death camps, modern massacre and political corruption – though with rather more contrived and mechanical invention. But the creative fluency and invention of the early work – *The White Hotel*, the opening volumes of "Russian Nights" – stand as quite remarkable endeavours to widen, internationalize, poeticize and above all psychologize the spirit of British fiction.

Salman Rushdie – born of a liberal Muslim family in Bombay in 1947, educated and writing in Britain – brought even more that was new and original into the spirit of the British novel. In several senses *Midnight's Children* marked a new narrative start. If the dying of British imperial India had become a familiar subject in the history of the Booker novel, Rushdie's book turns on the moment of India's post-imperial rebirth. The centre of the story is the midnight of independence in 1947 when, the novel proposes, one thousand and one children endowed with various magical powers were born to change the history of the nation. It had plainly not slipped Rushdie's notice that *The Arabian Nights* – that ur-book of storytelling, where the cunning narrator Scheherazade delays her own death by telling more and more stories, each story spawning more stories – consists of one thousand and one tales told over one thousand and one nights; and the children of midnight are themselves stories, the multiplication of new tales being one of India's best hopes. One of these children, Saleem Sinai, is the book's narrator, devious, cunning and inventive. He eventually splits into fragments in the course of his own tale, perhaps reflecting E. M. Forster's observation that no one story can ever capture the "many-headed monster" of India. The book makes much of its own free power of invention and fantasy, but it is also a serious political satire; Saleem tells how the magical powers are finally castrated by India's tragic history of ethnic conflict and the role of "the widow," Mrs Gandhi, who becomes the wicked witch of the fable. But essentially the novel is a celebration of stories and their power, and becomes a many-headed monster itself, as Rushdie draws not only on the Indian tradition of oral storytelling, the multiple narratives of *The Arabian Nights*, but also on the experimental tradition of European and Latin American fiction: the influences of Cervantes' *Don Quixote*, Sterne's *Tristram Shandy*, of Joyce and Beckett, Borges and Márquez all link the novel with the European anti-novel, with modernism, postmodernism and "magic realism." The vast interweaving – of narratives, cultures, voices, traditions, languages, of political and historical realism and free fantasy, of the free digressiveness of the oral story and the verbal and structural precision of written narrative – was also a new start for the late-twentieth-century novel, and with it Rushdie established himself as a major writer of great originality and experimental excitement, one of the most important novelists to emerge anywhere in the early Eighties. This was the book that duly won the Prize.

Rushdie followed the novel with the no less ambitious *Shame* (1983), told by a "sidelined hero" who has not one but three mothers, and set in a Pakistan which is both strangely imaginary and highly real and contemporary. It is a repressed, tragic country that puts the very narrator to "shame," since he cannot change it, except through an act of the imagination: "Realism can break a writer's heart," he explains. But there are other methods of writing, other ways of telling useful stories. "Like all migrants, I am a fantasist. I build imaginary countries and try to impose them on the ones that exist," he acknowledges, adding that he is "only telling a sort of modern fairy-tale, so that's all right; nobody need get upset . . ." People in power did however get upset, and each of Rushdie's early Eighties novels was banned or driven undercover in various countries for their mixture of extraordinary fantasy and significant political allegory. They became even more upset when Rushdie published his next and even more ambitious novel, *The Satanic Verses* (1988), which is described as a "burlesque for our degraded, imitative times." It was another "migrant's tale," and Rushdie has described the migrant situation, in which no single world seems real, as the typical sensibility of the late twentieth century. It is also another story about storytelling, opening, in the magic descent to earth of its two central characters from an exploded airliner, with a post-Miltonic, and postmodern, metaphor of how messages, angels and devils come to us with stories from the heavens, how prophecies, good and bad, descend, how divine and diabolic narratives contend and constantly confuse us, how we fall out of one world and into another. Out of this comes the task of the storyteller, which is to "name the unnamable, to point out frauds, to take sides, to start arguments, shape the world and stop it from going to sleep." A fable from and for migrant and multi-cultural times, the book is set in India, Arabia, a hybridized, racially-tense, multi-ethnic Britain, and above all in the world of the wandering imagination, much of it being presented in the form of fantasy and dreams. Once more a variety of narrative traditions, fables, fictions, myths and sacred texts, the theologies of life and death, heaven and hell, interfuse, and the work celebrates the critical scepticism of all tale-telling, presuming that the storyteller's task is to sail on the sea of stories and imagine the world afresh, creating a new imagination and a new cultural belonging. In the event, the book, and its author, moved toward a tragic fate. The book's sceptical use of the so-called "satanic verses" of the Koran, and his treatment of the prophet Mahommed as an historical figure, offended Moslem fundamentalists, and as a result of their opposition the Iranian Ayatollah Khomeini pronounced in February 1989 his infamous *fatwa*, a religious edict of death on its secular British author, and encouraged his assassination.

This is not the right place to explore the religious and political issues of that tragic situation, which, ironically enough, drew international attention to the significance of Rushdie as a major late-modern writer, comparable with Márquez, Eco, or Calvino. It also shocked Western minds into some sober reflection about what our fictions are for, where their essential value lies. Ever since its origins in the European Renaissance, the Western novel has always been intimately linked with the growth of our humanism and our scepticism. It tells stories of individualized lives through the playful god-games of narrative. Its works are not sacred truths or instruments of power but conscious fictions that say they are fictions – imaginary things that better help us understand the nature of the real. In our present commodity culture, novels can be, and frequently are, trivial, toy-like and self-serving, cheap stories hawked for profit or celebrity. But they can equally be amongst the most fundamental explorations of contemporary experience – essential means by which we come to a moral and metaphysical understanding of our situation, discover the nature of our cultural belonging, give some order and shape to our far from completed history. If in recent years a good many of our finest modern writers – Rushdie among them – have explored the fictionality of our fictions, the plenitude of our stories, the multiplicity of our narratives, and the way we rewrite past ones for our present understanding, then this is a central part of that fundamental, sceptical and long-standing human enquiry. Rushdie is a major late-twentieth-century international author, a self-consciously "migrant" writer who works in the hybrid world of stories in the age of transit, the age after the death of God where there are no longer any grand narratives, simply a multiplicity of human fictions. As he has put it himself: "those of us who have been forced by cultural diplacement to accept the provisional nature of all truths, all certainties, have perhaps had modernism forced on us." His is a fiction of the English language, but written at a time when those who use it no longer directly inherit or acknowledge all its narrative conventions and traditions, and look to new ones, as many modernist writers have over the course of the exiling century. He is, as he put it himself in 1982, after the publication of *Midnight's Children*, an "international" writer, writing at a time when the novel had never been a more international form; as he said, "it is perhaps one of the more pleasant freedoms of the literary migrant to be able to choose his own parents. My own – selected half consciously, half not – include Gogol, Cervantes, Kafka, Melville, Machado de Assis; a polyglot family tree, against which I measure myself, and to which I would be honoured to belong."[6] The world is a sea of stories, sacred and profane, on which we voyage beyond the familiar boundaries and frontier controls in order to make our own contemporary moral and metaphysical discoveries. What Rushdie has inherited from the Western tradition is not only modernist plurality, but the humanist faith in the power of imaginary fictions to explore our place, and fate, in the fissured, schismatic, pluralistic world, and the belief that through art and the imagination we can seek some larger human wholeness – the liberal aim that E. M. Forster expressed in *A Passage to India* some sixty years earlier. If the present tragic situation of Salman Rushdie has any merit, it must be to remind Western novelists of the deeper purpose of the fictional tradition, and its role in exploring and shaping our heritage of moral discovery, humanistic exploration, and intellectual freedom.

5.

Rushdie is an international writer in the larger sense of the term; he is also part of a new spirit of ethnic and stylistic multiculturalism that has been widening the vision and range of what, in the Eighties, it became ever harder to define as the British novel. It was a decade when a considerable number of

---

[6] See the title essay of Salman Rushdie, *Imaginary Homelands: Essays and Criticism, 1981–1991* (London, 1991).

bi-cultural or pluri-cultural novelists emerged in Britain, writers whose work drew on a wide variety of traditions and forms of experience. Thus Timothy Mo – who was born in Hong Kong, and came to Britain at the age of ten – is plainly a novelist of two empires, the Chinese and the British, and has written of the crossing-points of both of them first with a lively, observant comic vision, and more recently with a vast epic sweep. His first novel *The Monkey King* (1980) is set in Hong Kong, and is a wry portrait of a society, doubly seen from the standpoint of Chinese and European experience, where ancient traditions and networks live side by side with speedy modernization. His second, *Sour Sweet* (1982), deals with another divided culture, this time that of London's Chinatown, where the Chen family are subjected both to the ancient claims of the gangland triads and to the whims of the unpredictable English. With his third novel, *An Insular Possession* (1986), Mo displayed a striking change in scale and tactics. The book re-creates the story of the nineteenth-century Opium Wars, which led to the imperial founding of Hong Kong, recounting it through a multiplicity of perspectives, angles and ironic contrasts. Invented letters and newspaper reports are interwoven with huge action scenes of great dramatic vividness. There is a similar grand sweep to *The Redundancy of Courage* (1991), the story not of the founding of an empire but of its moment of collapse. The story is set in "Danu," evidently East Timor, at the point when the Portuguese withdraw from their colonial occupation and violence and massacre erupt, as new political forces are unleashed and the neighbouring Indonesians attempt a murderous intervention, leading to a guerrilla war. The central character, Adolph Ng, observes both the violence and the moral transformation of his contemporaries; the story is a modern historical tragedy, told with comedy, anger, and deep moral dismay.

Nothing could seem further away from Mo's wide and panoramic intentions than the restrained and economical fiction of Kazuo Ishiguro, another writer plainly writing in the Western tradition, but whose Anglo-Japanese inheritance has been quite as powerful as Mo's Anglo-Chinese one. Ishiguro was born in Japan, and came to Britain at the age of six; his three novels to date could well seem to have acquired their reticence from the tradition of the Japanese novel, though they owe just as much to Ishiguro's own aesthetic invention. His books too touch large historical events, but always very indirectly, and from the standpoint of chosen moments from closely perceived individual lives. *A Pale View of Hills* (1982) is set in England, though the essential story returns us to devastated Nagasaki shortly after the War; the atomic horror is never plainly mentioned, though it is everywhere implied. The story, which is modestly told by the narrator Etsuko, reflects on her widow's life in a confusing and alien England and takes us back to her memories of a summer in Nagasaki when the city is being reconstructed and individual lives are being re-made. Somewhere, as an unexplained consequence of all this, a daughter has committed suicide; meanwhile her stories of other people bear a curious similarity to the only half-revealed events of her own. A similar indirection of method governs the story of *An Artist of the Floating World* (1986), this time entirely set in a Japan Ishiguro had not revisited since childhood. It is another first-person narration, a collage of memories and experiences recorded by Masuji Ono, an artist who has won fame in the Thirties and who is now both respected and, evidently, suspected. Amongst other things, the story is a meditation on different kinds of art. Ono has once been "an artist of the floating world," catching impressions from life's underside, "pleasurable things that disappear with the morning light," "things intangible and transient." But as Japanese imperial and military ambitions grow, Ono has obeyed the mood, and done his duty in "troubled times." Again it is what the story does not say, the details that are not revealed that matter; both aesthetic and moral betrayal are everywhere implicit, and the heart of the story must be deduced – after all, Ishiguro, too, is an artist of the floating world, of impressions rather than fully revealed plots. With *The Remains of the Day* (1989), his most successful novel, Ishiguro strikingly shifted his subject from Japan to class-bound England, making his narrator a respectful British butler who follows a near-Japanese code of reticence, self-effacement and obedience. As he travels across the Britain of 1956 (the year of the Suez invasion) on a late-life journey, he too has his memories, of class-bound England in the Thirties; we gradually come to understand the way he has respectfully colluded in the Fascism of his employer, Lord Dartington, as a result of his dutiful obedience. As with Ono, a code of engrained respect has made him passive before large historical events; the price is paid in his personal life, where he has always suppressed his feelings and affections, even neglecting his father's death to serve the demands of his employer. His late-life journey brings home, and less to him than to the reader, the rule of civil suppression by which he has lived, by a leaving of things unsaid. The same rule is ironically followed by the controlled reticence of this tightly and precisely told story, in which Jamesian exactitude and Japanese economy merge naturally together.

Ishiguro has remarked that he too aims to contribute to the making of "the international novel," and in that aim he undoubtedly belongs with a number of other writers, from V.S. Naipaul, Ruth Prawer Jhabvala and Anita Desai to Timothy Mo, who have married British with other forms of fiction to create an international, late-modern fictional voice that is, like Henry James', larger than any individual culture. Other writers have found the marriage of cultures a more difficult task; thus the Kenyan author Ngugi wa Thiong'o, who published several important English-language novels in the Seventies (*Petal of Blood*, 1977), has found it necessary to revert to his own language to find access to a tradition and a vision. Others (here again Rushdie is notable) have questioned the notion that nationality or ethnicity is the prime source of fiction. Writers like the Nigerian author Chinua Achebe, whose first novel *Things Fall Apart* appeared in 1958, and whose *Anthills of the Savannah* (1987) was shortlisted for the Booker Prize, have been able to write intensely about their own culture while opening their fiction both to English and to international influences. Achebe's most notable heir has been Ben Okri, born in Nigeria, though educated and resident in Britain. Okri's first novel, *Flowers and Shadows* (1980), a story of a boy's painful growing up in a small Nigerian town, appeared when he was twenty-one. His second, *The Landscapes Within* (1981), about a Nigerian painter, is the book in which he begins to release some of the free and imaginative poetry that would fill his later work. *The Famished Road* (1989), which won the Booker Prize, is narrated by a "spirit child" and is, in the manner of magic realism, a vast and inventive celebration of magic and dream, and the imagination's power of struggle against fate and death. Also Nigerian and living in Britain, Buchi Emecheta realistically records – most effectively in *Second-Class Citizen* (1974) and *Destination Biafra* (1982) – not only the conflict of tribes in Nigeria, and the experience of racism in London, but the war of the sexes and the battles between tradition and modernity in both native and migrant culture.

Much of this writing represents the powerful role the novel has come to play in a post-colonial world, and many of the most important English-language novels of the Eighties came from writers in post-commonwealth or post-colonial cultures or from the age of what Rushdie calls cultural "migration." Meanwhile multi-cultural Britain has bred its own distinct and powerful stories. Caryl Phillips' *The Final Passage* (1985) is about young Caribbeans in Britain; the film-maker Hanif Kureishi's *The Buddha of Suburbia* (1990) is a wonderfully comic and inventive tale of a Pakistani boy ("an Englishman born and bred – almost") growing up in suburban London; the poet David Dabydeen's *The Intended* (1991) tells of a Guyanan boy trying to understand his heritage as he grows up in a South London slum. Adam Zameenzad, born in Pakistan, settled in Britain, made his debut with the ironic *The Thirteenth House* (1987), and then with *Cyrus Cyrus* (1990) created, in a similar manner to Salman Rushdie, a work of enormous and prolific invention – a satire of human good and evil set in India, California and London, and described a tale of "images of sex and survival, death and after-death, madness and genius, as relived within the dark, unfathomable recesses of the black hole of his mind

426

by Cyrus Cyrus, one of the most notorious men this century has produced." Vikram Seth, who lives variously in Britain, the United States and Bombay, displays the elaborate contrasts of the new international, multi-cultural fiction; his *The Golden Gate* (1986) is a "novel," told entirely in sonnet form, about California and Silicon Valley, while his *A Suitable Boy* (1993) is a vast chronicle novel of post-Independence Indian life, and one of the more startling works of the early Nineties. Each of these writers has had a considerable impact on the mood of contemporary British fiction, with the result that today it becomes harder to determine its edges, and ask where it ceases and something else, a post-colonial world literature written in English, comes to take its place.

6.

But if, as a result of growing multi-culturalism and the global interpenetration of narrative, a wider spread of storytelling was developing in British fiction, then the tradition was also changing from within. In *Money*, the brutish anti-hero John Self confronts his own creator, "Martin Amis," and remarks: "If I stare into his face I can make out the areas of waste and fatigue, the moonspots and boneshadows you're bound to get if you live in the 20th century." The younger Amis was plainly a writer who, unlike his father, did not like it here, who wrote of a placeless, aimless world of what he called the late-twentieth-century "suspense," whose own fictional tradition was international and whose strongest influences were American. He wrote, too, of cultures that afford no identity, and his central characters – John Self, Nicola Six, Keith Talent – are no longer the rounded characters of traditional realist fiction, but traumatized, fragmentary, rootless figures, suffering from a contemporary waste and fatigue, and living in collapsing urban jungles on both sides of the Atlantic in an age of globalism, afflicted by nameless crisis. In their world nothing is real or whole, the present is perpetual, without a real past or future ("Something

427

has gone wrong with modern time"), and identity is incomplete: "I am a thing made up of time lag, culture shock, zone shift," is how John Self explains "himself." *Money* is an Anglo-American story of a transitory, self-fictionalized Western world made of pornography, drugs, videos, space-awareness and refracted images, many-cultured and cultureless at once. The novel is a tale of two refracting cities, London and New York; and when Self shuttles across the Atlantic, he finds a Martin Amis on each side, waiting with language, imagery and literary references to match. The book, and Amis' other later novels, are narrated in a highlit Anglo-American discourse of extraordinary invention – with rolling tropes, extravagant, apocalyptic images, street-slang crossed with all kinds of high literariness and knowing intertextual references.

Amis, who has some claim to be the most influential British stylist of his generation, has acknowledged that he draws some of his late modern manner and his vitalized, illuminated rhetoric from Saul Bellow, and the influence of Vladimir Nabokov, the great magician and ironist of late modern fiction, is here too. But there are also important British debts, and not the least of them to Muriel Spark, whose ironic distance from her stories, and her concern with the relation of author to characters, fictional time to real time, present tense to future tense, is also highly apparent. Amis' later novels are not only clever readings of contemporary instant culture; they are also allegories about their own devising, elaborate combinatorial games playing with the fictional elements – author, character, progression, outcome, narrative time – and the ways they can be manipulated and made metaphorical. *London Fields* (1989) is set ten years on, in 1999, on the cusp of the millennium and some unnamed apocalyptic disaster. The book's aspiring narrator, Samson Young, who is American, comes to London to write a story, thinking that he knows what will happen already: "This is the story of a murder," he says. "It hasn't happened yet. But it will." But (as in Spark's *The Driver's Seat*) the central character and murder victim, Nicola Six, who is British, knows the plot perfectly well too, and is prepared to manipulate it in her own destructive self-interest and as part of the general will to destruction. The book counts on the postmodern assumption that the walls of fiction are never solid; that various characters can become the surrogates of the author, that the relation of author to characters, narrator to action, preplanned plot to outcome, can all be kept negotiable. Stories can break loose from their frames, and "time's arrow" – this was one of several possible titles Amis had for the book – can be fired in several directions.

In fact Amis' next book *was* called *Time's Arrow* (1991), and in it he reverses time's direction entirely, setting the narrative clock in reverse. In his surreal novel *Slaughterhouse-Five*, Kurt Vonnegut proposes that such are the horrors of modern life that in the interests of humanity what we need are "Tralfamadorian novels" where the laws of cause and effect are reversed; bombs do not fall to earth but rise back into their bomb-bays, and modern destruction is eliminated. *Time's Arrow* is Amis's Tralfamadorian novel, the story of a Nazi war criminal escaped to America who lives his life in reverse, from death to birth; in the course of this his holocaust victims are restored from extermination to survival. The book is a formidable exercise in literary skill; resisting the onward code of narrative, the pressure of the sentence, food is regurgitated, garbage men do not collect but strew garbage, and the scenes of the Auschwitz extermination camps become reconstructed as resurrection tales. The moral passion is plain, and the desire to reverse guilt and restore innocence is evident; in this the book has the power of a moral satire. But it does remain an exercise, a virtuoso enterprise in postmodern technical skills, and in it the Holocaust becomes a trope, as indeed it has in a good deal of modern writing. Amis' own style has been defined as one of "adoring revulsion," developed from a pained consciousness of living in a monstrous age; it is also, more uncomfortably, an experimental and playful technique just waiting to pounce. Amis is a pained postmodern ironist, and perhaps the nearest thing to a latter-day Swift the age has produced; but he is also a novelist of the "unpresentable," a writer of late modern Gothic, a novelist of extreme black comic knowingness, a writer of uncomfortable ambiguity, a moralist virtually driven out of business by an age that seems incapable of registering its own moral centre.

During the Eighties, the work of Martin Amis and Ian McEwan was increasingly compared. McEwan's best work came in the Eighties, and it too is freighted with the same abiding sense of historical unease; he was however, far less concerned with fiction's combinatorial games, and growing increasingly concerned with inner emptiness and the oppressive moral weight of violence. *The Comfort of Strangers* (1981) is a disturbing work of Venetian Gothic, where sexual tension and hidden gender conflict turn suddenly into self-gratifying violence; it was followed by the writing of several important screenplays. Then came *The Child in Time* (1988), a work of far greater sensitivities. In some respects it is where the two writers come closest; the setting is, again, a degraded, Thatcherized Britain in the apocalyptic near-future – there is licensed begging, private ambulance services, armed policemen – and the plot also depends on a striking "time-slip." It is also McEwan's most social novel so far, a work where previously private and psychic concerns become directly public and political ones. Childhood is the central theme; no longer an observation of the hard world from the child's amoral point of view, it sets the life of children in the frame of adult and parental life. The book deals both with the abduction of a child from a supermarket, and the regression of an adult to his failed, tattered boyhood. Meanwhile the welfare of children becomes (as in the real world, where concerns with child abuse was growing) a matter of social policy. The theme is solemn; the proper re-integration of the child within the adult, and regeneration, the reconciliation of male and female, through love.

Some of these themes return in *The Innocent* (1990), otherwise a very different book, which responds to the changing climate of the end of the decade, and above all the coming down of the Berlin Wall. In it McEwan goes back in time to the mid-Fifties, and in form to the mode of the cold War spy thriller, taking a true conspiratorial event, a CIA attempt to construct a spying

430

tunnel beneath the Berlin Wall, as its central myth. Against it McEwan tells the story of a personal initiation – that of "the innocent," Leonard Marham, twenty-five and a virgin, a "kind and gentle Englishman who knew so little about women and learned so beautifully." His initiation comes at the hands of the German girl Maria, and his growing sexual awareness uncomfortably displays to him his own instinct for domination. When Maria's husband returns, the story reaches a grim and violent culmination. The husband is killed and his body dismembered; the two stories reunite when Leonard disposes of the corpse in the Berlin tunnel. A coda set thirty years later as the Wall comes down suggests a possible renewal of the loving relationship that violence has destroyed. *The Black Dogs* (1992), McEwan's most recent, plainest, and best novel, returns to the same post-war period in the form of a disturbing fable. Focused around a woman's sight, in rural France, of two black dogs that have been used to intimidate prisoners of the Gestapo, and the influence this has had on her consciousness ever since, it acknowledges "A malign principle, a force in human affairs that periodically advances to dominate and destroy the lives of individuals and nations." Subtly and gently told, the story finally reflects on the need for the human spirit to confront and acknowledge these malign powers from history that come back, again and again, to haunt us. McEwan's own account of his view of fiction was that it was both a formal and a social discovery: "as a work unfolds, it teaches you its own rules, it tells how it should be written; at the same time it is an act of discovery, in a harsh world, of the extent of human worth."

7.

"Writing novels is more like writing history than we often choose to think," Frank Kermode once wrote. "The relationship between events, the selection of incident, even, in sophisticated fictions, the built-in scepticism as to the validity of procedures and assumptions, all these raise questions familiar to philosophers of history as problems relating to historical explanation." It has also increasingly been observed that writing history is more like writing novels than we often choose to think, since, as the historian Hayden White once said, real events never present themselves to us in the form of a story, and do not narrate themselves; it is the historians who do that. Certainly exploring past and recent history, at a time when its progress seemed either ambiguous or disastrous, and many of the progressive dreams of the earlier part of the century had plainly died, did become a central theme of Eighties fiction. Indeed by the beginning of the Nineties it came to seem that no novel would do unless it somehow went back to wartime, the end of Empire, or the age of the Edwardian wonderland before the twentieth century went so wrong. None of this was new, of course; from Fielding's *The History of Tom Jones* to Joyce's *Ulysses*, a one-day history of Dublin, to *Midnight's Children* and onward, the novel has always been a form of history. But what we understand by history, the means by which we construct significant histories, and the way we relate those histories to our understanding of our own situation, are constantly in change, and such conerns are likely to sharpen when writers feel they come toward the close of an epoch, near the end of history – as, it seems, many contemporary writers do.

"We have to keep scooping, scooping up from the depths this remorseless stuff that time leaves behind," says Tom Crick in Graham Swift's *Waterland* (1983), one of the best of the many novels of the Eighties where the recuperation of the past is a matter of concern. Swift established himself as a novelist in 1980 with *The Sweet Shop Owner*, a story, set in a northern town, about a man who feels himself to be a feeble, powerless witness to the larger dramas of wartime, love, and modern history. Since then, in his work, the theme has grown persistently more complicated. *Shuttlecock* (1981) is a psychological thriller about a police archivist who works in the department of "dead crimes," and who gradually comes to understand that there is a dead crime in his own personal history; his father, who has left an heroic record of his work with the French resistance

432

during the war, is suspect. Untrustworthy fathers and the various dead crimes that litter the twentieth-century world were to be the main themes of the fiction to follow, in which contemporary characters always live in the "aftermath," in the shadow of some suspect or corrupted history. The triumphant treatment of the theme came in *Waterland*, Swift's next and still most intricate and thoughtful book, set in the flat, flooded, secretive Cambridgeshire Fenlands – "a landscape, which of all landscapes, most approximated to nothing." The central figure is the history teacher Tom Crick, and history is the chief subject of the story. The very word means, as the book acknowledges, many things: an inquiry; a narrative about the past; simply a story. The book itself is all these things, playing the different notions of history against each other. As for the past itself, it is indeed a "waterland," which yields up not a stable past but a wealth of buried and suppressed pasts, drowned corpses, "dead crimes." Tom explores all these layers, and ways of exploration, not just with his pupils, but in the strange history of his own life, seeing the deceptive ambiguity of all record. The chapter titles tell the problem: "About the Question Why," "About the Explanation of Explanation," "Who Says?" Swift's book shares the fascination with fiction as history, history as fiction, that had been important in the novel certainly since the Sixties. But it is essentially about recuperation, about rediscovering what the past and memory have left for us to use.

With *Out of This World* (1988), Swift moved his theme closer to the larger historical events of the twentieth century, to the ambiguity of the modern record, and the difficulty of finding the right means to make it. Harry Beech, the central figure, is an aerial photographer, a photo-journalist, who has learned to fly above history, out of this world. Born shortly after the Great War, he takes aerial photographs of the bombings of cities during the Second World War, and also makes a photographic record of the "ordinariness" of the Nuremberg Trials. As he acknowledges, all records depend on the perspective from which they are seen, and also on the nature of the recording instruments. Even photographs change over time, from the sepia monochrome of wartime photography to the bright, flaring colour-images of the stressed post-war world. Through the complicated technique of the photographer, different layers of long, dark, twentieth-century history are set into a postmodern collage – the wartime bombing raids and the Apollo mission, the Nuremberg trials and the war in Vietnam. But Beech too is in history, and not out of this world. His father, an arms manufacturer, is another betrayer; meanwhile his daughter is going through her own psychic crisis. Dead crimes, questions of guilt and responsibility, the sense of living in history's after-math, are all examined; above all the question of the "bomb damage" we somehow can no longer escape, however high we try to fly "out of this world." Swift's most recent novel *Ever After* (1992) is a further endeavour in creating a layered archaeology, an angle of approach to the past, with its endless mirrors of betrayal. Its central figure is an emotionally damaged Oxford don, again "betrayed" by a father, who has killed himself because of his wife's, the narrator's mother's, infidelity. Meanwhile he attempts to break through his own deadened life by researching the story of a Victorian ancestor, who in turn has destroyed his own happiness in the search for truth. The traces of what has gone continue, and lives are lived in the aftermath; our lives come after, and the novel is a late history, a search for the way of access, to what has gone before.

If fictional histories were indeed a preoccupation of the Eighties, they were very inclined to move toward methods of fragmentation, strange contrasts between the past and the uncomfortable and apocalyptic present. There was, for instance, the fiction of Peter Ackroyd, with its complicated methods of late-modern literary archaeology, its structuralist fascination with layers and levels, codes and intertextualities. Ackroyd's theme was less the relation between individuals and their history, more that of the present writer and a previous text or author. Ackroyd's first novel *The Great Fire of London* (1982) proved to be deceptively titled; its "pre-text" is not London's seventeenth-century conflagration (which in fact appears in other of his novels) but Charles Dickens' *Little Dorrit*. That earlier novel haunts the texts, points to many of the locations (the Marshalsea prison, etc.), disturbs several of the characters, provokes the making of a film of the book (a notable version was actually made in the Eighties), and steers Ackroyd's Gothic evocation of present-day London, filling it with Dickensian threads and allusions. This was the first of a number of works of experimental homage, where Ackroyd proved himself not just a playful tracer of connections and disconnections, obscure layerings of past and present, but a remarkable impersonator of past literary styles. His next novel, *The Last Testament of Oscar Wilde* (1983), gives us a virtuoso version of Wilde's own story of his last days in Paris, which Wilde himself had somehow failed to write. But Ackroyd's first major work was *Hawksmoor* (1985), which remains to date his most brilliant and complex novel. Nicholas Hawksmoor (1661–1736) was a real figure, a former clerk to Sir Christopher Wren who became a famous eighteenth-century architect, and built some of London's finest neo-classical churches. In the book Ackroyd transforms him into Nicholas Dyer, an eighteenth-century architect who believes in satanic lore, and builds human sacrifices into the plans of his neo-classical churches. Meanwhile – by, presumably, a punning transposition – Ackroyd's own Hawksmoor is a twentieth century detective who is investigating a series of twentieth-century killings that take place in or around "Dyer's" churches (which are actually Hawksmoor's). Once more Ackroyd gives us some brilliant literary impersonation, presenting the eighteenth-century narrative in Dyer's "own" learned and often occult prose, and the twentieth-century narrative in a contemporary voice. The two stories, and their two distinct languages, trickily layered into each other, continually and strangely intersect, and the book possesses both great intellectual wit and a powerful Gothic strangeness.

Ackroyd's next book *Chatterton* (1987) is based on the life and death of Thomas Chatterton, the young late eighteenth-century poet and forger, an expert in faking and pastiche, and is told not in two layers but three. The lying of texts and their ambiguous relation to the ambiguous truth (maybe even Chat-

435

terton's death was faked) open the way to a Victorian tale
about the production of a famous sentimental painting of
Chatterton's death, and there is also a contemporary story
about art and forgery. Like many notable late modern works –
from Fowles' *The French Lieutenant's Woman* to the American
writer William Gaddis' brilliant *The Recognitions* (1955) – this
is not just an historical recreation but a meditation on art as
lying, cleverly unfolded. *First Light* (1989) shifts the scene from
the city to Dorset and the ghost in the background to Thomas
Hardy. The story is about different "archaeologies"; it is set
around the excavation of a neolithic barrow, but takes place
close to an astro-physical observatory. Earth and sky, the
human and the stellar universe, the sense of eternity and the
topical ideas of modern science of the era of quarks, black holes
and new views of time (two of the chapters are titled "The
Uncertainty Principle") are all under investigation; like several
contemporary writers, Ackroyd displays his fascination with the
theories of modern science and of the earth's origins. Ackroyd
had made the case for an experimental, post-realist fiction; his
own complicated, patterned books, interplaying past and present, are also explorations of the relation between traditional
codes and modern ones. Ackroyd is a playful user of fiction,
well aware of all the contemporary devices in the postmodern
novelist's repertory: pastiche, parody, punning, intertextuality.
He is also the writer as scholar-antiquarian, and a powerful
writer of modern Gothic. Still, from a writer-critic who had
once complained that British fiction was in danger of falling in
love with its own Englishness, his most recent novel to date,
English Music (1992), was to prove a surprise. It is a work of
complex structure, and its writer remains an anxious metaphysician of the age of the uncertainty principle. But part of its
pleasure is that it does celebrate the complicated repertoire of
English myths, motifs and traditions, which are evidently
capable of recuperation after all – as other writers, like Adam
Thorpe in *Ulverton* (1992), suggest.

Ackroyd's work plainly owes a great deal to modern French
ideas and theories. So, in a different way, does the work of

Julian Barnes, another writer of great stylistic vigour as well as high critical intelligence. Barnes – who has interspersed his "serious" novels with several sharp, streetwise mystery stories written under the name of Dan Kavanagh – set his first novel, *Metroland* (1980), in Paris during the *événements* of 1968, and the book, essentially a story of love and sentimental education, declares his interest in French life, culture and ideas, as well as in the lucid novel of sentiments developed by Flaubert. That interest came to its furthest flower in *Flaubert's Parrot* (1984), to date his best book. It is half critical text, half a human narrative, all based around the life and artistic impulse of the great nineteenth-century French realist, who also opened the door to fictional Modernism. Flaubert worked with a stuffed parrot on his desk; and he ended one of the most famous tales, *Un Coeur Simple*, with an extraordinary metaphor of the Holy Ghost as parrot ("as she breathed her last breath she thought she saw, as the heavens opened for her, a gigantic parrot hovering over her head"). "Flaubert's parrot" provides the crux of the book, as the narrator discovers numerous copies of it. Meanwhile the text itself takes multiple forms: it is a research, a meditation, an examination paper, a playful latter-day commentary, on Flaubert's own ambiguous realism, and on the strange stimuli of art. It busily plays with notions of the real and the fictional, makes its own rules, breaks up its own discourse, leaves behind its own ambiguities: a postmodern "text" indeed. *Staring at the Sun* (1986) seems to take a firmer stance ("This is how it was," it begins), and – like Graham Swift's fiction – it returns to a crucial question of the impact of the Second World War, starting from the airman's angle of vision. But the realities soon become ambiguities, for the novel has several time-layers, including the future; this is yet another novel that looks onward to the twenty-first century for its apocalyptic outcome. *A History of the World in 10½ Chapters* (1989) returns to the question of history in its larger sense: history is "just voices echoing in the dark; images that burn for a few centuries then fade; stories, old stories that sometimes seem to overlap; strange links, impertinent connections." Barnes plays with the limits of fiction, the borders of reportage, the laying and mixing of styles. Starting from the story of Noah's Ark, told, for once, from the wood-worm's point of view, various seaborne tales are spun: literary fabulations, analytical essays (on Géricault's painting *The Raft of the Medusa*), autobiographical recollections, parodies. All are tied by obscure connection to the Ark, linking together by metaphoric or mythic rather than conventional narrative associations; the narrator reflects on the randomness of history, the confusion of its deposits, the need for "love." "Love," or the different voices of lovers, provide the triangular structure of *Talking It Over* (1991), a story of a sexual threesome which is, as one of the characters says, "my word against everyone else's." Barnes' most recent book is *The Porcupine* (1993), one of the earlier novels to address the European world after the coming down of the Berlin Wall. It is the story of the trial of a deposed East European leader (plainly Todor Zhivkov of Bulgaria, where the book was first published), a dispute about history, a struggle of contemporary fictions, a novel of the Nineties. Like Swift's and Ackroyd's, Barnes' fiction is both highly readable and intensely clever, written by an author self-consciously seeking a style appropriate to his times.

Meanwhile other writers were building their own Eighties relationship to history and the tradition with similar critical self-consciousness. David Lodge – a writer, theoretical critic and former academic well used to working with Structuralism – offered in *Changing Places: A Tale of Two Campuses* (1975) and *Small World* (1980) two splendidly comic and satirical portraits of the contemporary academic world in its frantic Francophilia and its love affair with Structuralism, Post-Structuralism and Deconstruction. *Changing Places* contrasts two quite different academic worlds, the drab English Midland campus of Rummidge, and the ludic campus of Euphoria State, in West Coast America. The book is technically ambitious; American fictive playfulness and postmodernism also crosses over with British social realism, and the book ends in mid-air over the Atlantic, and in the mode of the film-script. *Small World* is a version of the medieval quest romance, where the heroes and heroines no longer go on pilgrimages but on academic conferences. It contains not only an intricate and allusive sexual pursuit, but much powerful satire of contemporary literary and critical ideas, displayed in the activities of two critics, the hotshot American Morris Zapp and the sinister French Deconstruction- ist Michel Tardieu, who play their own part in deconstructing the complicated plot. In the much more sober *Nice Work* (1985), Lodge put his two worlds – of critical fictions and drab realities – into a very different relation. The book moves between the age of contemporary post-feminism and the era of the Victorian industrial novel, telling the story of a feminist university teacher who takes part in an industrial "shadow scheme" and is brought into contact with the realities of factory experience, while a male businessman is brought to confront the lore of contempor- ary critical theory. In *Paradise News* (1991), mostly set in Hawaii, the idea of Utopia as a paradisaical holiday resort is tested against the facts of death and fading religious faith.

Lodge is a writer knowing and informed enough to see the limitations as well as rewards of contemporary literary theory, and his highly readable books offer some useful and considered dismantlings of the age of academic *chic*. So does the more recent work of A. S. Byatt, another leading novelist-critic, and, as a writer, less than completely impressed by many of the Deconstructive ideas, the notions of the Death of the Author and the Death of the Subject, that have lately preoccupied so many fine minds. *Possession: A Romance* (1990) is, like *Small World*, a latter-day version of the romance quest, and a consider- able step away from her earlier novels. It is also a thoughtful work about two contemporary academics researching the lives and romantic relations of two mid-Victorian romantic poets, Randolph Ash and Christine La Motte. Through a plot of complicated literary detection, and a multiplication of stories and texts, the novel explores the relation between romance and reality, lies and truths, the Victorian conception of the romantic self and the modern notion of the self as "a discontinuous machinery and electrical message-network of various desires, ideological beliefs and responses, language-forms and hormones and pheromones." Amongst its other qualities, the book is a criticism of the drab impersonality of a good deal of modern literary thought and theory, and a strong inward argument for the recovery of the creative principle – the fire of art and the imagination that should, indeed, restore romance to the disconnected, over-textualized world of the late-modern novel.

8.

Byatt's novel *Possession* was also part of something else: the new energy that was apparent in the feminine and feminist fiction of the Eighties, when the radical female voice found a wide new variety of forms. British fiction has never been short of women writers, but it may well have been short of a women's tradition, if only because so many of the most notable figures – Jane Austen, the Brontës, George Eliot, Virginia Woolf – had been among the most important shapers of the wider androgynous tradition. The post-war years had seen the emergence of many remarkable women writers – Doris Lessing, Iris Murdoch, Muriel Spark, Margaret Drabble, Fay Weldon, Penelope Fitzgerald, Barbara Pym, Beryl Bainbridge, Maureen Duffy, Nell Dunn – but, during the Seventies and into the Eighties, they also saw a period of self-conscious invention of a newly feminist fiction, which meant, amongst other things, a reappraisal of what was on offer, and what had been repressed, in the female tradition. The scene in women's writing of the Eighties was one of a vigorous rewriting of that tradition, and in that no writer was more inventive than Angela Carter, both as a novelist and a lively and challenging theoretician of modern styles. Her fiction now seemed to go through a fundamental sea-change, the earlier work serving as a platform for the increasingly epic and fantastic intention of the later. *The Passion of the New Eve* (1977) – a book which in title reached back to Villiers de l'Isle Adam's *L'Eve future* of a hundred years earlier – is a work of the postmodern world, a story about a man–woman "living legend," set in a future America disintegrating into its own dream-fantasies nd movie-myths, mirrored selves and doubled images, "a series of enormous solipsisms," though from its chaos new myths, new Eves, can be born. The making of new myths out of the shattering images of modern style was to be the groundwork of her highly Gothic and inventive fiction of the Eighties and early Nineties, when she produced two novels, *Nights at the Circus* (1984) and *Wise Children* (1991), which are some of the most inventive myth-forming writing of the time.

Nights at the Circus was certainly her most ambitious novel to date – a story set on the turn from the nineteenth century to the twentieth, much as *Midnight's Children* was set on the moment of Indian independence, a moment when the world transforms and when the imagination seems ready to release itself into new possibilities and the making of new myths. The central character is the Cockney music-hall trapeze-artist Fevvers, who possesses magical powers; she has grown wings, and can fly free, she can stop the clock, and belongs to "the New Age in which no woman will be bound down to the ground." She is also a frank and down-to-earth version of the female of Nineties myths, a public legend, a focus of erotic ambiguities, the object of sexual narcissism, the mystery woman who means to make her mysteries real. She is pursued to a London which is described as the home of two principal industries – the music hall and the confidence trick – by an American newspaper reporter, Jack Walser, who, in trying to get her "story," is at once confronted by not one but two Scheherazades telling him fantastic versions of her tale. He is soon pulled out of the world of realities into her world of legend, the land of nights at the circus. By various forms of trickery, some manipulated by Fevvers and many more by her author, the story unravels, through slippage and literary metamorphosis, from London to Saint Petersburg to Siberia, from city to forest, each Russian doll proving to contain another inside. The book is an extraordinary fantasy, filled with an overplus of characters and creature, a refusal of fixity, a willing redundancy, a feeling that Carter's writing – like Fevvers herself – is alive with an invention that has no need ever to stop.

Her next book *Wise Children* is even more ambitious. It's said to be a wise child that knows its own father, and the Chance twins, Dora and Nora, have an ambiguous relationship with theirs. They are the love-children of a famous father, Sir Melchior Hazard, the famous "legitimate" Shakespearean actor, but the two girls are "illegitimate in every way – not only born out of wedlock, but we went on the halls, didn't we!" They live on "the wrong side of the tracks," in South London, across the river, and are "Chance by name, Chance by nature"; they make their way in the theatre of music-hall, vaudeville, panto-mime, and movies, in antiphonal relation to the serious drama. Carter says elsewhere that pantomime is "the carnival of the unacknowledged and the fiesta of the repressed," and the book tests the limits of the serious literary heritage, though it also alludes to it. It is, amongst other things, a rumbustious rewriting of Shakespearean drama, not, as in Iris Murdoch, in order to rediscover the moral and transcendental dignity of art, but to open its limits and shatter its frame ("There was singing and dancing all along Bard Row that day and we'll go on dancing and singing till we drop in our tracks"). As in all pantomime – and Shakespearean theatre too – theatrical per-formance and impersonation opens the Utopian forest of story out into cross-dressing and the ambiguities of role and gender. Like Rushdie's, Carter's novels have been associated with "magic realism," and understandably: her use of the fantastic and its looking-glass world is vigorous and inventive, but it implies no lack of concern with society and history. Fantasies intermingle everywhere with the controlling realities; clocks stop on command, toys turn into trains, Fevvers "really" does have wings. The magic freedoms of myth and fairy-tale are on offer in her world of what criticism came increasingly to call the word of the "carnivalesque"; reality and history are rewritten, fractured, taken over the edge, and so is the role of her female characters and their female narrator. This was, alas, Angela Carter's last novel; she died at the age of fifty-two in 1992. She left a last book of stories, *American Ghosts and Old World Wonders* (1993), late pieces which continue to illustrate her great and fantastic invention and imaginative variety.

442

Carter is one of several women writers whose work over the Eighties made great use of the uncanny and the marvellous, the mirrored and the refracted, to break home fiction's conventional borders and the safe house of its domesticity and challenge the fixity of women's roles in fiction and in life. Gothic methods – Gothic has long been a way to transgressive images – became important for doing this, not least in the fiction of Fay Weldon; her *The Life and Loves of a She-Devil* (1983) turns on the invention of the rival as double, and *The Cloning of Joanna May* (1989) is a latter-day reworking of Mary Shelley's Frankenstein myth. The heritage was seized by some fine younger writers, like Jeanette Winterson, who established herself with two works both published in 1985: *Oranges Are Not the Only Fruit*, a vivid account of growing up within the confines of a strict Pentecostal sect in the North of England, from which the heroine escapes through a series of outrageous lesbian relationships, as well as a gift for fantasy, and sets out to be a prophet of the imagination; and *Boating for Beginners*, a travesty of the story of Noah's Ark, narrated in Thatcherite discourse, where Noah tries to make an entrepreneurial success of his boating business while still following the obscure will of Yahweh the Unpronounceable. The much more ambitious and exciting *The Passion* (1987) is a fantasy, a mirrored and doubled story, set in the early nineteenth century on Napoleon's march on Moscow and in the city of Venice. The method is one of elaborate and often comic fantasy: one of the key characters is the chicken chef to Napoleon, the other a bi-sexual woman who is born with webbed feet and can walk on water. History becomes a playfield for the strange, the uncanny, and mysterious, and for burlesque, cross-dressing and sexual ambiguity. The narrative is held under cunning verbal and technical control, the two plots at last wittily and mysteriously brought together. *Sexing the Cherry* (1989) travels freely not only in space but in time, between the seventeenth century of the English Civil War and the present. Meanwhile the narrative opens out frequently from the world of history into the realm of fairytales, grimly and cleverly rewritten to match present anxieties. Amongst other things Winterson's work is a powerful exploration of the borders of gender, and deals freely with androgyny and lesbian sexuality. *Written on the Body* (1992) is both a crude and a romanticized meditation on this, a postmodern, sexually ambiguous love-story narrated by an unidentified, sexually hyper-active narrator whose female lover is dying of leukemia.[7]

If the reworking of the romance and Gothic traditions afforded important ways for feminist writers to find a new identity and form during this period, another was to rework and subvert old myths and patriarchal tales from the feminist perspective. Michèle Roberts revised the story of Mary Magdalene in *The Wild Girl* (1984), and then used, again, the Noah's Ark story for feminist purposes in *The Book of Mrs Noah* (1987). Marina Warner explored the myth of Shakespeare's *The Tempest* from the standpoint of Caliban's mother, the witch Sycorax, in *Indigo* (1992); Emma Tennant re-examined both Thomas Hardy and his women in *Tess* (1993). Meanwhile writers like Ruth Rendell and Joan Smith appropriated feminist angles and issues for their detective fiction, while, in her guise as "Barbara Vine," Ruth Rendell produced some powerful psychological novels of contemporary life during the decade, such as *The Dark-Adapted Eye* (1986). Other novelists like Zoë Fairbairns, in *Stand We At Last* (1983), and Sarah Maitland, in *Virgin Territory* (1984), wrote a more directly polemical feminist fiction. Women writers also contributed significantly to the "postmodern" experiment of the decade. So Maggie Gee's powerful experimental novel *Dying in Other Words* (1981) is a sombre portrait of the violent death, through words and deeds, of the central female character, and the novel is alike an exploration of the nature of fictional form and language and the problems and blanknesses of female representation.

One important consequence of all this was its broad effect on sexual and gender representation in the novel, even in the work of those authors who did not choose to acknowledge an identi-

[7] Several of the writers discussed above, and the surrounding issues, are excellently explored by Lorna Sage in her *Women in the House of Fiction: Post-War Women Novelists* (London, 1992).

fication with a feminist tradition of fiction. Rose Tremain – an important novelist who established herself in the mid-Seventies with *Sadler's Birthday* (1976), the bleak story of a elderly butler who has sacrificed his life for others, and who is dying in the stately home he has inherited – has resisted the classification of "woman writer." Her fiction, which includes *Letter to Sister Benedicta* (1978), *The Cupboard* (1981), and *The Swimming Pool Season* (1985), has always been notable for its moral understanding of the pains and discords of all human life, and its striking and androgynous sympathy. Her most powerful book, *Restoration* (1989), is an historical novel, restoring the world of the court of Charles II to fiction. It is also notable for the depiction of its remarkable male narrator, Robert Merivel, a much exploited favourite of the unreliable king, and a man obsessed by unhappy lusts and a pained sense of mortality. Aware of the strange ambiguities of the human heart, he finds himself in "the middle of a story which may have a variety of endings, not all of them to my liking," and his unfolding fate and his discovery both of the pain and the small rewards of life is told with great compassion. Just as compassionate and understanding is Tremain's *Sacred Country* (1992), set in Britain and finally in Tennessee over the period following the death of King George VI, when the "new Elizabethan age" begins. At the centre of the story, which has echoes of Virginia Woolf's *Orlando*, is a Suffolk girl who grows up wanting to be a boy, and finally satisfies her desire to be a trans-sexual – a desire that, we realize, curiously resembles the androgyny of vision the novelist usually aspires to as a part of the creative task.

In the end what distinguishes the women's writing of the Eighties is not only its feminist concerns, and its intensive and fresh exploration of the feminine viewpoint, but its great narrative range and its discovering variety. Anita Brookner's fiction is as far away from the "carnivalesque" quality and creative overspill of Angela Carter as is possible; there is a notable modern fiction of restraint. From, her first novel *A Start in Life* (1981) at the beginning of the decade on, through works like *Hotel du Lac* (1984) and *A Misalliance* (1986), Brookner produced a developing sequence of portraits of the lives of intelligent, lonely, generally self-sacrificing and often *émigrée* women that are above all notable for their cool thoughtfulness and irony, the Jamesian precision and careful reticence of their writing. Penelope Fitzgerald showed a similar precision of tone as well as a biting sense of comedy in her very varied novels; *Human Voices* (1980), about working at the BBC in wartime, and *The Beginning of Spring* (1988), a story of pre-Revolutionary Moscow, are two of the best of them. Penelope Lively has made memory one of her essential themes, most strongly realized in *Moon Tiger* (1987), which concerns an ageing woman historian whose recollections of her life in Egypt turn into a mélange of different voices, telling the tale of the past in a variety of different ways. Marina Warner, in *The Skating Party* (1982) and *The Lost Father* (1988), writes with the sure knowledge that fiction belongs not just to the world of life and its seasonal problems, but also to that of art and myth. Lisa Saint Aubin de Teran moved from the powerful magic realism of her Venezuelan novel *Keepers of the House* (1983) and its Italian successor *Slow Train to Milan* (1984), through a number of splendidly high-Gothic tales, to the larger span of her generational novel *Joanna* (1990). The reinvigoration of women's fiction had an obvious consequence; the later years of the Eighties and the turn into the Nineties saw the emergence of a large number of new women writers – they included Elspeth Barker (the vivid and Gothic *O Caledonia*, 1991), Hilary Mantel, Georgina Hammick, Candia McWilliam, Lucy Ellmann, Jenny Diski, Helen Simpson, Kathy Page and Esther Freud (*Hideous Kinky*, 1992) – who drew widely on the new freedoms that had developed, both in the freer depiction of sexuality and gender and in the openness to fantasy, formal play, and generic intermingling. The same was true of the surge of strong gay and lesbian fiction, in the work of Jeanette Winterson, Adam Mars-Jones and Alan Hollinghurst (*The Swimming Pool Library*, 1988), that came during the decade.

By the end of the Eighties, the climate of British fiction had again altered markedly, and not least because of the deeper

social, cultural and sexual changes that underlay the period of
the "Thatcher Revolution." It now most closely resembled the
situation in the last two decades of the nineteenth century,
when the well-established and solid tradition of the Victorian
novel was coming to its end. Then, too, no one single and clear
movement seemed to be in place, and there was no plain
certainty about what the novel was for, nor what distinguished
the serious from the sensational. No one standard or cultural
impulse appeared to draw together the different kinds of book
on offer: "They are as various as the temperament of man, and
they are successful in proportion as they reveal a particular
mind, different from the others," Henry James observed of this
plurality in his essay "The Art of Fiction" in 1884. As he also
noted: "It must be admitted that the field at large suffers
discredit from overcrowding. I think, however, that this injury
is only superficial, and that the superabundance of written
fiction proves nothing against the principle itself." What struck
critics, then as now, was not the direction of the novel, but its
contentious variety. Aesthetic argument pointed in many different and seemingly contradictory directions: on the one hand
toward the scientific analysis and reportage of Naturalism, on
the other toward the inward, psychologizing self-consciousness
and artistic play of Aestheticism. Traditional forms continued,
but novelties, and outrages, abounded; Gothic fiction grew
popular again, both as a form of literary sensationalism and
a serious treatment of a culture in change. New media and
magazines, new readers with new educations and new social
attitudes, were changing the cultural environment; some
thought this promised the end of the serious novel. At the same
time, the British arts were going through a process of interna-
tionalization, and foreign writers, like James and Conrad, or
British writers born abroad, like Kipling, were changing the
writing climate and the literary subject. Issues of sex and
gender were important, and as Elaine Showalter said of this
time of what she calls "sexual anarchy," when sexual certainties
break down, fictional certainties change as well. What is quite
clear in retrospect is that these artistically plural, confusing,

and troubled times were radically productive, and a new stylistic era, the era of "modern fiction" itself, was born. The 1980s were also historically confusing, culturally various, and aesthetically plural, a time when fiction took on a much greater variety of voices and a wider spread of styles and manners. Postmodern ways increasingly entered British fiction, which grew far more open to the fantastic, the Gothic and the grotesque. So did the postmodern problem, which is an acceptance of the catholicity of all styles, along with a doubt and indeterminacy about their use and authority. Directions grew confusing, as writers looked back selectively at history and the past tradition, yet at the same time drew on a much wider range of international influences, from contemporary American to Latin American fiction, and came out of a much wider variety of cultural sources. Styles and identities were borrowed from other forms and other media, from film and music and television; issues of sex and gender raged; the apocalyptic feelings familiar to the end of a century were strong. Yet, for all the historical gloom, the urban depression, the political despair, the confusion of manners and styles, the vigour of fiction was apparent; and there seems little doubt (indeed it has already begun to happen) that the Eighties will be looked at as a vigorous, discovering, expanding period of the British novel.

Coda:
An Afterword from the Nineties

A word about the title. Several alternatives suggested
themselves. For a while I toyed with *Time's Arrow*. Then I
thought *Millennium* would be wonderfully bold (a common
belief: *everything* is called *Millennium* just now). I even flirted, late
at night, with *The Death of Love*. In the end the most serious
contender was *The Murderee*, which seemed both sinister and
deeply catchy. And I wavered and compromised with things like
London Fields, or The Murderee: Final Version . . .

Martin Amis, "Note" to *London Fields* (1989)

As I finish this book, the world most of us have grown up in,
the world of the final phase of the twentieth century, bumps on
unhappily toward its millennial end. A hundred years after the
Eiffel Tower went up, the Berlin Wall came down, and in the
brief period since it has grown very clear that a good deal more
than a Cold War era came to a close. One of the chief guiding
ideologies of the twentieth century, Marxism, had reached a
point of terminal exhaustion; the other, liberal capitalism,
enjoyed only a brief episode of free-market triumph before the
economic boom and pan-European dreams of the later Eighties
slid into recession, slump, and budget deficit. Four years on,
many of the high historical expectations that swept the world
in November 1989 have already faded. The disintegration of
the Soviet Union, the Gulf War, genocidal conflict in former
Yugoslavia and a growing uncertainty within the European
Community soon turned the New World Order into the New
World Disorder. The End of History proved to be a return to
the last hundred or so years of European history, a reversion to

449

the unfinished crises of a century of conflict. In disturbing replay, the flashpoints and troublespots of the European past came back once again to the centre of international consciousness: the Baltic states, Czechoslovakia, Sarajevo. The issues of 1945 and 1939, of 1918 and 1914, of 1879 and 1848, are back on the agenda of post-national Europe; tribal, ethnic, regional and national hatreds frozen since 1945 are again released. Once more, European cities are bombarded, and the refugees and shattered, shocked victims of genocide and "ethnic cleansing" wander the roads and cross the frontiers of a world plainly less stable than it had been. Our political leaders seem helpless and enfeebled; our historians and our philosophers, like our businessmen and bankers, appear only short-term prophets, offering no new political philosophies or guiding ideas to interpret the times to come.

Indeed, if the raising of the Eiffel Tower represented an abstract, triumphal, technological celebration of the great project of the Modern (and so it was seen at the time), a vision of the twentieth-century destiny, then the fall of the Eastern European order in November 1989 seems in many ways to mark its exhaustion. It is the dreams and goals of high modernity – the break with the past that would produce the historical originality of the present, the great idea of universal world progress, salvation through science and discovery to create higher human possibilities and prospects – that have been left in question as the century comes toward its end. If Marxism had failed, much else in the idea of the Modern had failed too. Indeed the spirit of Postmodernism had deconstructed its predecessor only too well. The failure of the grand narratives, the prevalence of styles without centres, the sense of history without depth, awareness of endless relativity and uncertainty; these were what the West seemed to have on offer by the end of the Eighties. Meanwhile, despite the fading of the nuclear threat from the Cold War, Einstein's Monsters had in no sense gone away. Other nameless terrors – ozone holes and global warming, sexual plague and mass starvation, choking cities, dying fields, drug-sodden cultures, mass migration of

450

peoples, fundamentalist religious wars – soon took its place. Seen in the long retrospect from its end, the twentieth century looks less an era of high human promises and discoveries than a time of terrors, of human crimes and scientific horrors, wasteland vanities and Kafkaesque futilities, etched into the human consciousness far more deeply than the revolutionary and redeeming new becoming with which it all began. The century's achievements and discoveries have been many, the energy behind its progress has not ceased, a significant proportion of human lives, especially in the West, have been vastly improved by modern development and discovery. Yet the new technologies have persistently proved as destructive as they have been inventive, the new frontiers as disillusioning as they have been promising, the social Utopias have turned into dark, oppressive dystopias. For the moment at least, the brilliant expectations and high hopes that many brought to the modern age have turned into historical weariness; even the mythic excitement that even a few years ago attached to the year 2000, when new interplanetary prospects and post-human hopes were in sight, appears, if our literary records are a good guide, to have been displaced by visions of planetary decay and moral disaster.[1]

The familiar tremors that have generally accompanied any of the great turnings of the historical clock are all too evident, and they will no doubt accumulate as the end not only of another century but of the second millennium of the Christian calendar comes closer. The close of all the modern centuries has been marked by deep historical changes, fundamental revolutions in culture, consciousness and sensibility, accompanied by powerful transformations in the arts. The eighteenth century ended on the American and French revolutions, and the birth of the age of libertarianism and romanticism; the nineteenth closed on a radical vision of the age of the modern and the new, accompanied by great changes in the literary and artistic forms. Just twenty-five years after the Eiffel Tower went up, the Great War

---

[1] An exciting example of this hopeful interpretation of the modern is to be found in O. B. Hardison, Jr., *Disappearing Through the Skylight: Culture and Technology in the Twentieth Century* (New York, 1989; London, 1990).

came; the European order in which the first modern hopes and the key modern ideas had been forged began to dissolve. Twenty-five years after that, a Second World War came, and much of the impulse of the Modern movement died; an Age of Anxiety and of human guilt began which has never gone away. Twenty-five years onward from that, in the mid-Sixties, a "post-modern" idea of radical new liberation was still in its age of innocence, soon to fade in the events of 1968. The changes of 1989 come at the end of a hundred years of modern and postmodern history, and at a time marked by the fading of many hopes and certainties. The ending of a century generally concentrates the human mind wonderfully; to its process the arts have indeed usually been a significant witness, and it is to them that we usually turn to read the shifting of our conscious-ness and the deeper tremors of change. But so far what most seems to mark our own end-of-century are the weakness of our hopes, the depth of our unease, the intensity of our nostalgia, even for the worst. One part of the power of the Modern is that it has rendered what followed as an era still in its shadow, a postmodern time, lacking both Modernism's certainties and the conviction of being something truly new itself. Our own times seem to be closing on political uncertainty, guilty nostalgia, a depthless sense of history, a mood of apocalyptic dismay: a "postmodern condition" indeed.

What does the climate of the British novel tell us, as the Nineties start and the century closes? Not, it should be said, a great deal about the changed world order since 1989; novels take time to capture such things. On the other hand, as Martin Amis says, most books could be called *Millennium* just now. In several different senses our current fiction still indeed seems "postmodern": experimental, exploratory and retrospective all at once. What the Modernist writers of the early part of the century explored or darkly predicted, present-day writers mostly look back on, writing in what Graham Swift calls the "aftermath," pressed on as much by what has been as what is to come. Again and again they have returned to the prime sites of contemporary fictional archaeology: the Victorian disintegration, the Edwardian anxieties that prefigured the Great War, the world of the trenches, the crisis in Ireland, the Second World War and the Holocaust, the nuclear dawn, the end of Empire, the coming of the post-colonial world. In the Booker Prize of 1992, five out of the six novels selected for the shortlist dealt with "historical" subjects, quite a few of them with recent history in its most forbidding guise: above all with the Second World War and is now familiar themes and motifs, the extermination camps, the destruction of identity, the loss of historical significance, the taints and guilts of the period that followed. The dominant mood is retrospective rather than experimental; most are written in a tone of poeticized nostalgia that suggests these themes have become conventional literary tropes. The novel is, amongst other things, a history; but we expect it also to be a prophecy, a prefiguration, a reaching out toward new forms, an instrument of discovery. The contemporary problem faced by our writers is that they have begun to reach the end of postmodern times, if not the postmodern condition, and are entering an age that has no clear shape, no clear prospects, no clear name. It already becomes interesting and urgent to ask how our fiction and our arts will explore not just our past and immediate cultural present but our larger future. The last decades of centuries are notorious for their twilight feeling, their instinct that an order is fading and something new is waiting to be born. In such times we live our lives, and our writers write, in a state of great stylistic uncertainty – wondering again about the relation of art to life, our literary forms and ideas to the changing history to which they should be the imagination's response.

In British fiction, the Eighties opened in an atmosphere of political dismay but great artistic excitement. The Nineties started on a note of gloom, perhaps the inevitable bitter reflection of an increasingly recessionary time which has affected the marketplace, making publishers cautious, readers fewer, critics more savage. When, in 1993, the magazine *Granta* announced its second select list of the twenty "best of young British novelists," the familiar gloomy reports did not take a

long time to come in. "Contemporary British fiction, as everyone knows . . . is in a sad state," announced the *Guardian*
newspaper darkly. Other critics and newspapers echoed the
despondency; "we have failed even to produce a handful of
novelists of any real stature," noted one young writer (Nick
Hornby) of his contemporaries. The now usual complaints were
widely rehearsed: British fiction was poor in comparison with
American or Latin American writing, had no sense of world
history and no wide view of contemporary Britain, no social
and reportorial excitement, no strong voice, no moral force, no
deep themes. Some of this was understandable and justified;
some of it plainly reflected the habitual self-laceration that has
become a British cultural commonplace. If the list was intended
to display writers of experimental vigour or long-lived promise,
it certainly had its limitations, serious omissions and tokenisms;
on the other hand it also drew attention to a significant number
of young novelists of high quality (like Lawrence Norfolk) who
had largely gone unnoticed. There were too many works of
mannerist chic, too many novels that seemed designed to win
literary prizes, and the influence of Martin Amis and Ian
McEwan was everywhere to be seen. Eighties innovations were
showing signs of becoming Nineties conventions; "postmodern"
experiments that would have been exciting ten years earlier
now seemed as traditional as the traditional fiction that had
plainly survived postmodernism's challenge. At the same time
the "postmodern" and multi-cultural mood had dissolved the
novel's tradition and its sense of cultural centrality; and, as
another young critic put it, "postmodern craft work" now
seemed the order of the day. In other respects the mood was
narrower; a sombre literary solemnity seemed to have thinned
a British tradition generally noted for its social abundance,
comic variety and satirical vigour (never more needed than in
an age given to *bien-pensant* pieties and the politically correct).
The novel, some observers proposed, was no longer a central
form of expression; young writers who had grown aware that
the large rewards that had gone to their Eighties predecessors
(they were an aberration in the history of fiction's economics in

any case) were unlikely to be repeated were looking elsewhere, to music, film, and literary journalism – even to the writing of articles about the death of the novel.

In fact the gloom was excessive. For, in the larger prospect, contemporary British fiction is hardly in a sad state (as is generally acknowledged in other countries where the vigour of the British novel compares well with what is on offer there). There are three striking generations still powerfully at work. Many of the best writers from the strong generation of the Fifties and early Sixties – Doris Lessing, Iris Murdoch, Kingsley Amis, Anthony Burgess, Muriel Spark, John Fowles, David Storey, Alan Sillitoe, Stanley Middleton, William Trevor, Margaret Drabble, A. S. Byatt, Beryl Bainbridge, David Lodge, Fay Weldon – continue to produce important fiction. Out of the equally strong generation of the Seventies and early Eighties – Martin Amis, Salman Rushdie, Ian McEwan, Julian Barnes, Peter Ackroyd, William Boyd, Graham Swift, Rose Tremain, Marina Warner, Alasdair Gray, Timothy Mo, Kazuo Ishiguro, John McGahern and more – comes much remarkable writing. The later Eighties and early Nineties saw the emergence of another lively literary generation – to risk a few names, Jeanette Winterson, Alan Hollinghurst, Justin Cartwright, Hilary Mantel, Gilbert Adair, Michael Ignatieff, Jim Crace, Esther Freud, Lawrence Norfolk, James Kelman, Roddy Doyle, Glenn Patterson, Elspeth Barker, Geoff Dyer, Lindsay Clarke, Adam Thorpe, Bernard McLaverty, Hanif Kureishi and Adam Zameenzad – who at the least display remarkable promise. Britain remains a major centre for the publication of literary fiction, serious fiction, some of it magnificent, some aspiring, some of it too smart and easy, but amounting to a substantial culture of the novel. It is a country where some six thousand new fiction titles are published every year, and where, despite the pressure of the media age, the novel remains central reading matter and an important aspect of British self-understanding. Many books of small merit are published, and some gain celebrity; the fact remains that in fictional variety and support for literary fiction, Britain, despite a recent economic recession and a mood of historical gloom, retains a powerful fictional scene.

If critics do have any use (and at times we do well to wonder), then one of the things they can usefully do is to remind us that we have been here, or somewhere like here, before. A hundred or so years ago, when this account starts, many of the hopes of the nineteenth century were themselves disintegrating. The European empires were in fundamental disorder, and as the race toward technological, commercial and imperial domination accelerated much that was central to Victorian culture dissolved. A previous world – the "Victorian world" – was dying, and another was struggling to be born. As new philosophies of uncertainty and indeterminacy undermined religious faith and scientific positivism, the era's Grand Narratives were yielding to what the American historian Henry Adams called "the modern multiverse." The world of economic and imperial competition was leading to political unrest, and fears of the coming collapse of institutions, systems, states and empires. New technologies were organizing social and individual life in unprecedented ways, and suppressing what was "natural" or "communal," and consciousness felt overwhelmed by the forces compelling it. Cities were falling into disorder and political ungovernability, nameless terrors and violences stalked their streets. Sexual and gender roles were rapidly shifting, destabilizing domestic life. Decadence and "degeneration" reigned, as the changing world threw up perverse new values and identities. The laws of time and space were altering too. Life seemed lived between two worlds, the dying world of the old, the shapeless world of the new. The arts of the day began to dispense with familiar realism, and filled with strangeness and self-consciousness, impressionism and nuance, prophecies of the shapes of things to come. There seemed a lack of intention and rigour, a disintegration of writing, as the tradition gave way to random influence coming in from everywhere. Then as now people anxiously awaited the trembling of the veil, the coming of the new. For them too a system of historical, social and religious ideas was dying, and whether in decadent despair or futurist anticipation they looked to the turning of the times.

That sense of an ending was also the beginning of the Modern century, and the beginning of a new age of writing, as disquieting to some as it was exciting to others. Out of this came the Modern novel, whose complicated history in Britain over the following century I have here tried to tell. A hundred years is a long time in history, and in the history of a literary form. Ours has been a painful, an accelerated century, when every new decade saw its own social, technological, and artistic innovations, its own crises and disasters. Even so, we can still read a long continuity from the early coming of the modern in fiction to the present, from tea-time with George Eliot to the novel of today. "Modern fiction" was born from the process of late-Victorian change, in a time of fracturing and intense artistic self-consciousness. Its greatest and most powerfully imagined works – James' final studies, Conrad's ambiguous and cosmopolitan fiction, Lawrence's, Joyce's and Woolf's exploration of the limits of both consciousness and literary form – remain to this day intensely "modern," intimate with ourselves. The dying of the Modern movement around the time of the Second World War brought another remarkable wave of fiction, itself telling a story that is now almost fifty years long. Its achievement has been just as varied, and at its finest just as great. What comes next is now in question; nothing repeats itself exactly. But the novel, nationally and internationally, remains a discovering medium. It has survived; it still is, as it was a hundred years ago, an imaginative exploration of time and consciousness, of living history and of lives lived in relation to that history. It locates us in relation to our past, and reaches into our prospect for the future. It examines our morals, explores our psychologies, excites our fantasies. It is a research into our reality, which is always changing and transforming, as must the novel too. It intersects with all the other narratives we tell ourselves, or have told to us – our journalism, our politics, our philosophy – and it reminds those who think they have narratives of absolute truth that these too are part of fiction. It tells us stories of the

457

intimate and the cosmic, of the local and the global; it is an expression of a region or a nationality, and a vision of a world far larger. For a long time we have read or written in Modernism's shadow; maybe we are now about to pass beyond it. A hundred years back Holbrook Jackson saw the dying decade of the last century, the 1890s, as "a renascent period characterized by much mental activity and a quickening of the imagination," a period of re-creation in the arts. And though nothing, indeed, does repeat itself exactly, we have no less reason to hope that a similar mental activity, another quickening, will provide the fictional companion to our transition through the end of the modern and into another millennium.

The British Novel since 1876:
A List of Major Works

The following list of authors and titles is intended to indicate the wide variety as well as the quality of the British fiction published since the 1870s. It reaches well beyond the authors it has been possible to cover in the text, but, though full, it remains, of course, personal and selective. Not all works by each author are included.

ACKROYD, PETER (1949   )
The Great Fire of London (1982), *Hawksmoor* (1985), *Chatterton* (1987), *First Light* (1989), *The House of Doctor Dee* (1993).

ALDINGTON, RICHARD (1892–1962)
Death of a Hero (1929), *The Colonel's Daughter* (1931).

ALDISS, BRIAN (1925   )
A Report on Probability A (1968), *The Hand-Reared Boy* (1970), *A Rude Awakening* (1978), *Helliconia Spring* (1981), *Remembrance Day* (1993).

AMBLER, ERIC (1909   )
The Dark Frontier (1936), *Epitaph for a Spy* (1938), *Journey into Fear* (1940), *The Night-Comers* (1956), *The Intercom Conspiracy* (1970), *Doctor Frigo* (1974), *The Care of Time* (1981).

AMIS, KINGSLEY (1922   )
Lucky Jim (1954), *That Uncertain Feeling* (1955), *Take a Girl Like You* (1960), *One Fat Englishman* (1963), *The Anti-Death League* (1966), *The Green Man* (1969), *Ending Up* (1974), *Jake's Thing* (1978), *The Old Devils* (1986), *Difficulties With Girls* (1988).

AMIS, MARTIN (1949   )
The Rachel Papers (1973), *Dead Babies* (1975), *Success* (1978), *Money* (1984), *London Fields* (1989), *Time's Arrow* (1992).

ARLEN, MICHAEL (1895–1956)
The London Venture (1920), *The Green Hat* (1924).

BAILEY, PAUL (1937   )
At the Jerusalem (1967), *Trespasses* (1970), *A Distant Likeness* (1973),
Old Soldiers (1980), *Gabriel's Lament* (1986), *Sugar Cane* (1993).
BAINBRIDGE, BERYL (1934   )
A Weekend with Claud (1967), *Harriet Said* (1972), *The Bottle Factory
Outing* (1974), *Sweet William* (1975), *Injury Time* (1977), *Young Adolf*
(1978), *An Awfully Big Adventure* (1989).
BALLARD, J. G. (1930   )
The Atrocity Exhibition (1970), *Concrete Island* (1974), *High Rise*
(1975), *The Unlimited Dream Company* (1979), *Empire of the Sun*
(1984), *The Day of Creation* (1987), *Running Wild* (1988).
BANKS, IAIN (1954   )
The Wasp Factory (1984), *Walking on Glass* (1985), *The Bridge*
(1986), *The Player of Games* (1988).
BANVILLE, JOHN (1945   )
Kepler (1981), *Mefisto* (1986), *The Book of Evidence* (1989), *Ghosts*
(1993).
BARKER, A. L. (1918   )
John Brown's Body (1969), *Relative Successes* (1984), *Zeph* (1993).
BARKER, PAT (1943   )
Union Street (1982), *Century's Daughter* (1986), *The Man Who Wasn't
There* (1989).
BARNES, JULIAN (1946   )
Metroland (1980), *Flaubert's Parrot* (1984), *Staring at the Sun* (1986),
A History of the World in 10½ Chapters (1989), *The Porcupine* (1992).
BARSTOW, STAN (1928   )
A Kind of Loving (1960), *Joby* (1964), *The Watchers on the Shore*
(1966), *A Raging Calm* (1968), *Just You Wait and See* (1986).
BATES, H. E. (1905–1974)
The Fallow Land (1932), *Thirty Tales* (1934), *My Uncle Silas* (1939),
Love for Lydia (1952), *The Purple Plain* (1947), *The Darling Buds of
May* (1958).
BATES, RALPH (1899   )
Lean Men (1934), *The Olive Tree* (1936).
BECKETT, SAMUEL (1906–1989)
More Pricks Than Kicks (1934), *Murphy* (1938), *Molloy* (Paris,
1951), *Malone Dies* (Fr., Paris, 1951, trans. 1956), *The Unnamable*

(Fr., Paris 1953, trans. 1959), *Watt* (Paris, 1953), *How It Is* (Fr., Paris, 1961, tr. 1964).

BEDFORD, SYBILLE (1911   )
A Legacy (1957), *A Compass Error* (1968).

BEERBOHM, MAX (1872–1956)
Zuleika Dobson, Or An Oxford Love Story (1911).

BELL, ADRIAN (1901   )
The Cherry Tree (1932), *The Balcony* (1934).

BELLOC, HILAIRE (1870–1953)
Four Men (1911), *The Green Overcoat* (1912).

BENNETT, ARNOLD (1867–1931)
A Man From the North (1898), *Anna of the Five Towns* (1902), *The Grand Babylon Hotel* (1905), *The Old Wives' Tale* (1908), *Clayhanger* (1910), *Hilda Lessways* (1911), *Riceyman Steps* (1923).

BERGER, JOHN (1926   )
A Painter of Our Time (1958), *The Foot of Clive* (1962), *Corker's Freedom* (1964), *G.* (1972), *Pig Earth* (1979).

BOWEN, ELIZABETH (1899–1973)
Encounters: Stories (1923), *The Hotel* (1927), *The Last September* (1929), *Friends and Relations* (1931), *The Cat Jumps and Other Stories* (1934), *The House in Paris* (1935), *The Death of the Heart* (1938), *The Heat of the Day* (1949), *A World of Love* (1955), *Collected Stories* (1980).

BOYD, WILLIAM (1952   )
A Good Man in Africa (1981), *An Ice-Cream War* (1982), *Stars and Bars* (1984), *The New Confessions* (1987), *Brazzaville Beach* (1990).

BRADBURY, MALCOLM (1932   )
Stepping Westward (1965), *The History Man* (1975), *Rates of Exchange* (1983), *Doctor Criminale* (1992).

BRAGG, MELVYN (1939   )
For Want of a Nail (1965), *The Hired Man* (1969), *A Place in England* (1970), *The Nerve* (1971), *The Silken Net* (1975), *Love and Glory* (1983), *The Maid of Buttermere* (1987), *Crystal Rooms* (1992).

BRAINE, JOHN (1922–1986)
Room at the Top (1957), *The Vodi* (1959), *The Jealous God* (1964), *The Queen of a Distant Country* (1972), *The Pious Agent* (1975), *The Two of Us* (1984).

BRIERLEY, WALTER (1900–1972)
Means-Test Man (1935), *Danny* (1940).

BROOKE-ROSE, CHRISTINE (1926   )
The Languages of Love (1957), *The Dear Deceit* (1960), *Out* (1964), *Between* (1968), *Thru* (1975), *Amalgamemnon* (1984), *Xorandor* (1986).

BROOKNER, ANITA (1928   )
A Start in Life (1981), *Look at Me* (1983), *Hotel Du Lac* (1984), *Fraud* (1992), *A Family Romance* (1993).

BROWN, GEORGE MACKAY (1921   )
A Time to Keep (1969), *Greenvoe* (1972), *Magnus* (1973), *Time in a Red Coat* (1985).

BUCHAN, JOHN (1875–1940)
Prester John (1910), *The Power House* (1913), *The Thirty-Nine Steps* (1915), *Greenmantle* (1916), *Mr Standfast* (1919).

BURGESS, ANTHONY (1917   )
Time for a Tiger (1956), *The Enemy in the Blanket* (1958), *The Wanting Seed* (1962), *The Clockwork Orange* (1962), *Nothing Like the Sun* (1964), *MF* (1971), *Abba Abba* (1977), *Earthly Powers* (1980), *The End of the World News* (1982).

BURN, GORDON (1948   )
Alma Cogan (1991).

BURNS, ALAN (1929   )
Celebrations (1967), *Babel* (1969), *Dreamamerika!: A Surrealist Fantasy* (1972), *Revolutions of the Night* (1986).

BUTLER, SAMUEL (1835–1902)
Erewhon, Or Over the Range (1872, enlarged 1901), *Erewhon Revisited* (1901), *The Way of All Flesh* (1903, post.).

BYATT, A. S. (1936   )
Shadow of a Sun (1964), *The Game* (1967), *The Virgin in the Garden* (1978), *Still Life* (1980), *Possession: A Romance* (1990), *Air and Angels* (1992).

CARR, J. L. (1912   )
A Day in Summer (1964), *A Month in the Country* (1980), *The Battle of Pollock's Crossing (1985)*, *What Hettie Did* (1987).

CARTER, ANGELA (1940–1992)
Shadow Dance (1965), *The Magic Toyshop* (1967), *The Infernal Desire*

Machines of Dr Hoffmann (1972), *The Passion of New Eve* (1977),
Nights at the Circus (1984), *Wise Children* (1991).
CARTWRIGHT, JUSTIN (1945   )
Interior (1988), *Look at it This Way* (1990), *Masai Dreaming*
(1993).
CARY, JOYCE (1888–1957)
Aissa Saved (1932), *The African Witch* (1936), *Mister Johnson* (1939),
Herself Surprised (1941), *To Be A Pilgrim* (1942), *The Horse's Mouth*
(1944), *A Fearful Joy* (1949), *Prisoner of Grace* (1952).
CAUTE, DAVID (1936   )
At Fever Pitch (1959), *The Decline of the West* (1966), *The Occupation*
(1971).
CHATWIN, BRUCE (1940–1989)
On the Black Hill (1982), *The Songlines* (1987), *Utz* (1988).
CHAUDHURI, AMIT (1962   )
A Strange and Sublime Address (1991), *Afternoon Raag* (1993).
CHESTERTON, G. K. (1874–1936)
The Napoleon of Notting Hill (1904), *The Club of Queer Trades* (1905),
The Man Who Was Thursday: A Nightmare (1908), *The Innocence of
Father Brown* (1911).
CHILDERS, ERSKINE (1870–1922)
The Riddle of the Sands (1903).
CHRISTIE, AGATHA (1890–1976)
The Mysterious Affair at Styles: A Detective Story (1920), *The Murder of
Roger Ackroyd* (1926), *The Mystery of the Blue Train* (1928), *Lord
Edgware Dies* (1933), *Death on the Nile* (1937), *Ten Little Niggers*
(1939).
CLARK, LINDSAY (1939   )
Sunday Whiteman (1987), *The Chymical Wedding* (1989).
COMPTON-BURNETT, IVY (1892–1969)
Dolores (1911), *Pastors and Masters* (1925), *Brothers and Sisters*
(1929), *A House and Its Head* (1935), *Manservant and Maidservant*
(1947), *A Father and His Fate* (1957), *The Mighty and Their Fall*
(1961), *A God and His Gifts* (1963).
COLEGATE, ISABEL (1931   )
Orlando at the Brazen Threshold (1971), *News from the City of the Sun*
(1979), *The Shooting Party* (1980), *Deceits of Time* (1988).

COMYNS, BARBARA (1909–1992)
Our Spoons Came from Woolworths (1950), *The Juniper Tree* (1985), *Mr Fox* (1987).

CONRAD, JOSEPH (JOSEF KORZENIOWSKI) (1857–1924)
Almayer's Folly (1895), *The Nigger of the "Narcissus"* (1897), *Lord Jim* (1900), *Nostromo* (1904), *The Secret Agent* (1907), *Under Western Eyes* (1911), *Chance* (1913), *Victory* (1915), *The Shadow Line* (1917), *The Arrow of Gold* (1919), *The Rescue* (1920).

COOPER, WILLIAM (HARRY HOFF) (1910)
Trina (as H. S. Hoff) (1934), *Scenes from Provincial Life* (1950), *The Struggles of Albert Woods* (1952), *Disquiet and Peace* (1956), *Young People* (1958), *Scenes from Married Life* (1961), *Memoirs of a New Man* (1966), *Scenes from Metropolitan Life (1982)*, *Scenes from Later Life* (1983), *Immortality at Any Price* (1991).

CRACE, JIM (1946)
Continent (1986), *The Gift of Stones* (1988), *Arcadia* (1992).

DABYDEEN, DAVID (1956)
The Intended (1991), *Disappearance* (1993).

DAY LEWIS, CECIL (1904–1972)
The Friendly Tree (1936), *Starting Point* (1937), *Child of Misfortune* (1939).

DEIGHTON, LEN (1924)
The Ipcress File (1962), *Spy Story* (1974), *The Berlin Game* (1983), *The Mexico Set* (1984), *London Match* (1985).

DENNIS, NIGEL (1912)
Cards of Identity (1955), *A House in Order* (1966).

DOUGLAS, NORMAN (1868–1952)
Siren Land (1911), *South Wind* (1917).

DOYLE, ARTHUR CONAN (1859–1930)
A Study in Scarlet (1887), *The Sign of Four* (1890), *The White Company* (1891), *The Adventures of Sherlock Holmes* (1892), *The Memoirs of Sherlock Holmes* (1894), *The Return of Sherlock Holmes* (1905).

DOYLE, RODDY (1958)
The Commitments (1988), *The Snapper* (1990), *Paddy Clarke Ha Ha Ha* (1993).

DRABBLE, MARGARET (1939)
A Summer Bird-Cage (1963), *The Garrick Year* (1964), *The Needle's Eye* (1972), *The Realms of Gold* (1975), *The Ice Age* (1977), *The*

Middle Ground (1980), *The Radiant Way* (1987), *A Natural Curiosity* (1989), *The Gates of Ivory* (1991).

DUFFY, MAUREEN, (1933   )
That's How It Was (1962), *The Paradox Players* (1967), *Capital* (1975), *Londoners* (1983).

DU MAURIER, DAPHNE (1907–1989)
Jamaica Inn (1936), *Rebecca* (1938), *Frenchman's Creek* (1941), *The Flight of the Falcon* (1965).

DU MAURIER, GEORGE (1834–96)
Peter Ibbotson (1892), *Trilby* (1894).

DURRELL, LAWRENCE (1912   )
The Black Book (Paris, 1938), *Justine* (1957), *Balthazar* (1958), *Mountolive* (1958), *Clea* (1960), *Monsieur, Or the Prince of Darkness* (1974).

EGERTON, GEORGE (MARY CHAVELITA BRIGHT) (1859–1945)
Keynotes (stories, 1893), *Discords* (stories, 1894), *Symphonies* (stories, 1897).

ELLIS, ALICE THOMAS (1932   )
The Sin Eater (1977), *The Twenty Seventh Kingdom* (1982), *Unexplained Laughter* (1985), *The Clothes in the Wardrobe* (1987).

ENRIGHT, D. J. (1920   )
Academic Year (1955), *Figures of Speech* (1965).

FARRELL, J. G. (1935–1979)
A Man From Elsewhere (1963), *A Girl in the Head* (1967), *Troubles* (1970), *The Siege of Krishnapur* (1973), *The Singapore Grip* (1978), *The Hill Station* (1981, post.).

FEINSTEIN, ELAINE (1930   )
The Circle (1970), *Children of the Rose* (1975).

FIGES, EVA (1932   )
Equinox (1966), *Winter Journey* (1967), *B.* (1972), *Ghosts* (1988).

FITZGERALD, PENELOPE (1916   )
Offshore (1979), *Human Voices* (1980), *At Freddie's* (1982), *Innocence* (1986), *The Beginning of Spring* (1988).

FITZGIBBON, CONSTANTINE (1919   )
The Arabian Bird (1949), *When the Kissing Had to Stop* (1960).

FIRBANK, RONALD (1886–1926)
Caprice (1917), *Valmouth* (1919), *Prancing Nigger* (1924), *Concerning*

the Eccentricities of Cardinal Pirelli (1926), *The Complete Firbank* (1961).

FLEMING, IAN (1908–1964)
Casino Royale (1953), *Thunderball* (1961).

FORD, FORD MADOX (FORD MADOX HUEFFER) (1873–1939)
The Brown Owl: A Fairy Story (1892), *The Inheritors* (with Joseph Conrad, 1901), *The Fifth Queen* (1906), *A Call* (1910), *The Good Soldier* (1915), *Some Do Not . . .* (1924), *No More Parades* (1925), *A Man Could Stand Up –* (1926), *The Last Post* (1928), collected as *Parade's End*.

FORSTER, E. M. (1879–1970)
Where Angels Fear to Tread (1905), *A Room with a View* (1907), *Howards End* (1910), *The Celestial Omnibus and Other Stories* (1911), *A Passage to India* (1924), *Maurice* (1971, post.)

FOWLES, JOHN (1926   )
The Collector (1963), *The Magus* (1965: rev. ed., 1977), *The French Lieutenant's Woman* 1969, *Daniel Martin* (1977), *A Maggot* (1985).

FRAYN, MICHAEL (1933   )
The Tin Men (1965), *The Russian Interpreter* (1966), *Sweet Dreams* (1973), *The Trick of It* (1989), *Now You Know* (1992).

FREUD, ESTHER (1963   )
Hideous Kinky (1992), *Peerless Flats* (1993).

FRY, STEPHEN (1957   )
The Liar (1991).

GALSWORTHY, JOHN (1867–1933)
The Man of Property (1906), *The Country House* (1907), *In Chancery* (1920), *To Let* (1921), *The Forsyte Saga* (1922).

GARNETT, DAVID (1892–1981)
Lady Into Fox (1922), *A Man in the Zoo* (1924).

GEBLER, CARLO (1954   )
The Eleventh Summer (1984), *Work and Play* (1987), *The Glass Curtain* (1991).

GEE, MAGGIE (1948   )
Dying in Other Words (1981), *Light Years* (1985), *Grace* (1988).

GERHARDIE, WILLIAM (1895–1977)
Futility (1922), *The Polyglots* (1925), *Of Mortal Love* (1936).

GIBBON, LEWIS GRASSIC (JAMES LESLIE MITCHELL) (1901–1935)
Sunset Song (1932), *Cloud Howe* (1933), *Grey Granite* (1934), all reprinted as *A Scots Quair* (1945).

GIBBONS, STELLA (1902–1992)
Cold Comfort Farm (1932).

GISSING, GEORGE (1857–1903)
Workers in the Dawn (1880), *The Unclassed* (1884), *Demos* (1886), *Thyrza* (1887), *The Nether World* (1889), *New Grub Street* (1891), *The Odd Woman* (1893), *In the Year of the Jubilee* (1894).

GLAISTER, LESLEY (1956   )
Honour Thy Father (1990), *Trick or Treat* (1991).

GLANVILLE, BRIAN (1931   )
The Reluctant Dictator (1952), *The Bankrupts* (1958), *A Second Home* (1965), *The Financiers* (1972).

GLYN, ELINOR (1864–1943)
Three Weeks (1907), *Elizabeth Visits America* (1909), *It* (1926).

GOLDING, WILLIAM (1911–1993)
Lord of the Flies (1954), *The Inheritors* (1955), *Pincher Martin* (1956), *The Spire* (1964), *Darkness Visible* (1979), *Rites of Passage* 1980), *The Paper Men* (1984), *Close Quarters* (1987), *Fire Down Below* (1989).

GORDON, GILES (1940   )
The Umbrella Man (1971), *Girl with Red Hair* (1974).

GOSSE, EDMUND (1849–1928)
The Secret of Narcisse (1892), *Father and Son* (autobiography, 1907).

GRAND, SARAH (FRANCES MCFALL) (1854–1943)
The Heavenly Twins (1893), *The Beth Book* (1897).

GRAVES, ROBERT (1895–1985)
I, Claudius (1934), *Claudius the God* (1934), *Antigua, Penny, Puce* (1935).

GRAY, ALASDAIR (1934   )
Lanark (1981), *1982, Janine* (1984), *The Fall of Kelvin Walker* (1985), *Poor Things* (1992).

GREEN, HENRY (1905–85)
Blindness (1926), *Living* (1929), *Party-Going* (1939), *Caught* (1943), *Loving* (1946), *Concluding* (1948).

GREENE, GRAHAM (1904–1991)
The Man Within (1929), *It's a Battlefield* (1934), *Brighton Rock*

(1938), *The Power and the Glory* (1940), *Nineteen Stories* (1947), *The Heart of the Matter* (1948), *The End of the Affair* (1951), *The Quiet American* (1955), *A Burnt-Out Case* (1961), *The Comedians* (1966), *The Human Factor* (1978), *Monsignor Quixote* (1982).

GREENWOOD, WALTER (1903–1974)
Love on the Dole: A Tale of Two Cities (1933).

HAGGARD, H. RIDER (1856–1925)
King Solomon's Mines (1885), *She* (1887), *Allan Quatermain* (1887), *Montezuma's Daughter* (1893), *Heart of the World* (1896).

HANLEY, JAMES (1901–1985)
Boy (1931), *Sailor's Song* (1943), *Winter Song* (1950), *Collected Stories* (1953), *The Welsh Sonata* (1954), *Say Nothing* (1962), *A Woman in the Sky* (1973).

HARDY, THOMAS (1840–1928)
Under the Greenwood Tree (1872), *Far From the Madding Crowd* (1874), *The Return of the Native* (1878), *The Mayor of Casterbridge* (1886), *The Woodlanders* (1887), *Wessex Tales* (1988), *Tess of the D'Urbervilles* (1891), *Jude the Obscure* (1896).

HARKNESS, MARGARET ("JOHN LAW") (1861–1921)
A City Girl (1887), *Out of Work* (1888), *A Manchester Shirtmaker* (1890).

HARRIS, WILSON (1921   )
The Guyana Quartet (1960–3), *Black Marsden* (1972), *Carnival* (1985).

HARTLEY, L. P. (1895–1972)
Simonette Perkins (1925), *The Shrimp and the Anemone* (1944), *The Go-Between* (1953), *The Hireling* (1957), *Facial Justice* (1960), *The Betrayal* (1966).

HILL, SUSAN (1942   )
Strange Meeting (1971), *Bird of Night* (1972), *In the Springtime of the Year* (1974), *Air and Angels* (1991).

HINES, BARRY (1939   )
Kestrel for a Knave (1968), *The Gamekeeper* (1975), *Looks and Smiles* (1981).

HOLLINGHURST, ALAN (1954   )
The Swimming Pool Library (1988).

HOLTBY, WINIFRED (1898–1935)
The Land of Green Ginger (1927), *South Riding* (1936).

HOPE, CHRISTOPHER (1944   )
Kruger's Alp (1984), *The Hottentot Room* (1986), *Black Swan* (1987),
My Chocolate Redeemer (1989), *Serenity House* (1992).

HOPKINS, BILL (1928   )
The Divine and the Decay (1957).

HOWARD, ELIZABETH JANE (1923   )
The Beautiful Visit (1950), *The Long View* (1956), *After Julius* (1965),
Odd Girl Out (1972), *Getting It Ready* (1982).

HUDSON, W. H. (1841–1922)
The Purple Land That England Lost (1885), *A Crystal Age* (1887),
Green Mansions (1904).

HUGHES, GLYN (1935   )
Where I Used to Play on the Green (1981), *The Hawthorn Goddess*
(1984), *The Antique Collector* (1990).

HUGHES, RICHARD (1900–1976)
A High Wind in Jamaica (1929), *In Hazard* (1938), *The Fox in the
Attic* (1961).

HUNT, VIOLET (1866–1942)
The Workaday Woman (1906), *White Rose of Weary Leaf* (1908), *The
Tiger Skin* (1924).

HUXLEY, ALDOUS (1894–1963)
Crome Yellow (1921), *Antic Hay* (1923), *Those Barren Leaves* (1925),
Point Counter Point (1928), *Brave New World* (1932), *Eyeless in Gaza*
(1936), *Time Must Have a Stop* (1945).

ISHERWOOD, CHRISTOPHER (1904–1986)
All the Conspirators (1928), *The Memorial* (1932), *Mr Norris Changes
Trains* (1935), *Goodbye to Berlin* (1939), *The Berlin Stories* (collection,
1946), *The World in the Evening* (1954), *Down There on a Visit* (1962),
A Single Man (1964).

ISHIGURO, KAZUO (1954   )
A Pale View of Hills (1982), *An Artist of the Floating World* (1986),
The Remains of the Day (1989).

JACOBSON, DAN (1929   )
The Trap (1955), *The Price of Diamonds* (1957), *The Beginners*
(1966), *The Rape of Tamar* (1970), *The Confessions of Joseph Baisz*
(1977).

JACOBSON, HOWARD (1942   )
Coming from Behind (1983), *Peeping Tom* (1984), *Redback* (1986).
JAMES, HENRY (1843–1916)
Roderick Hudson (Boston, 1876; 1879), *The American* (1877), *The Europeans* (1878), *Washington Square* (1881), *The Portrait of a Lady* (1881), *The Bostonians* (1886), *The Princess Casamassima* (1886), *The Tragic Muse* (1890), *What Maisie Knew* (1897), *The Awkward Age* (1899), *The Wings of the Dove* (1902), *The Ambassadors* (1903), *The Golden Bowl* (1904), *The Art of the Novel* (prefaces, ed. R. P. Blackmur, 1934), *The Future of the Novel* (essays, 1956).
JAMES, P. D. (1920   )
Cover Her Face (1962), *Unnatural Causes* (1967), *The Black Tower* (1975), *Death of an Expert Witness* (1977), *Innocent Blood* (1980), *The Skull Beneath the Skin* (1982), *A Taste of Death* (1986), *Devices and Desires* (1989), *The Children of Men* (1992).
JAMESON, STORM (1891–1986)
The Single Heart (1932), *Women Against Men* (stories, 1933), *Love in Winter* (1935).
JHABVALA, RUTH PRAWER (1928   )
To Whom She Will (1955), *The Householder* (1960), *A New Dominion* (1972), *Heat and Dust* (1975), *Three Continents* (1987).
JOHNSON, B. S. (1933–1973)
Travelling People (1963), *Albert Angelo* (1964), *Trawl* (1966), *The Unfortunates* (1968), *House Mother Normal* (1971), *Christie Malry's Own Double Entry* (1972), *See the Old Lady Decently* (1975).
JOHNSON, PAMELA HANSFORD (1912–1981)
World's End (1937), *Too Dear for My Possessing* (1940), *An Impossible Marriage* (1954), *The Unspeakable Skipton* (1959), *Night and Silence, Who Is Here?* (1962), *Cork Street, Next the Hatters* (1965), *The Bonfire* (1981).
JONES, RUSSELL CELYN (1955   )
Soldiers and Innocents (1990), *Small Times* (1992).
JORDAN, NEIL (1950   )
The Past (1982), *The Dream of a Beast* (1983).
JOSIPOVICI, GABRIEL (1940   )
Mobius the Stripper (1974), *The Echo Chambers* (1978), *In the Fertile Land* (1987).

JOYCE, JAMES (1882–1941)
Dubliners (1914), *A Portrait of the Artist as a Young Man* (New York, 1916, London, 1917), *Ulysses* (Paris, 1922: New York, 1934, London, 1936), *Finnegans Wake* (New York, 1939; London, 1946).

KELMAN, JAMES (1946   )
The Busconductor Hines (1984), *A Chancer* (1985), *A Disaffection* (1989).

KING, FRANCIS (1923   )
The Dividing Stream (1951), *The Widow* (1957), *The Last of the Pleasure Gardens* (1965), *A Domestic Animal* (1970), *The Action* (1978), *Frozen Music* (1987), *Woman Who Was Good* (1988).

KIPLING, RUDYARD (1865–1936)
Plain Tales from the Hills (Calcutta, 1888; 1890), *The Light That Failed* (1890), *The Jungle Book* (1894), *The Second Jungle Book* (1895), *Stalky & Co.* (1899), *Kim* (1901), *Just So Stories* (1902), *Puck of Pook's Hill* (1906).

KOESTLER, ARTHUR (1905–1983)
The Gladiators (from German, 1939), *Darkness at Noon* (1940), *The Age of Longing* (1951).

KUREISHI, HANIF (1954   )
The Buddha of Suburbia (1990).

LARKIN, PHILIP (1922–1985)
Jill (1946), *A Girl in Winter* (1947).

LAWRENCE, D. H. (1885–1930)
The White Peacock (1911), *The Trespasser* (1912), *Sons and Lovers* (1913), *The Prussian Officer and Other Stories* (1914), *The Rainbow* (1915), *Women in Love* (New York, 1920; London, 1921), *The Lost Girl* (1920), *Kangaroo* (1923), *The Plumed Serpent* (1926), *Lady Chatterley's Lover* (Florence, 1928; London, 1932), *The Virgin and the Gypsy* (1930), *Phoenix* (essays) (1936, post.), *Mr Noon* (1985, post.).

LE CARRÉ, JOHN (DAVID CORNWELL) (1931   )
The Spy Who Came in from the Cold (1963), *The Looking-Glass War* (1965), *Tinker, Tailor, Soldier, Spy* (1974), *The Honourable Schoolboy* (1977), *The Little Drummer Girl* (1983), *A Perfect Spy* (1986), *The Night Manager* (1993).

LEHMANN, JOHN (1907   )
Evil Was Abroad (1938).

LEHMANN, ROSAMUND (1903   )

A Dusty Answer (1927), *A Note in Music* (1930), *An Invitation to the Waltz* (1932), *The Weather in the Streets* (1936), *The Ballad and the Source* (1944), *The Echoing Grove* (1953).

LE QUEUX, WILLIAM (1864–1927)

Guilty Bonds (1890), *A Madonna of the Music Halls* (1897), *The Invasion of 1910* (1906).

LESSING, DORIS (1919   )

The Grass Is Singing (1950), *Martha Quest* (1952), *The Golden Notebook* (1962), *Briefing for a Descent Into Hell* (1971), *Memoirs of a Survivor* (1974), *Shikasta* (1979), *The Good Terrorist* (1985), *The Fifth Child* (1987).

LEVERSON, ADA (1862–1933)

Love's Shadow (1908), *Tenterhooks* (1912), *Love at Second Sight* (1916), collected as *The Little Ottleys* (1962).

LEWIS, C. S. (1898–1963)

Out of the Silent Planet (1938), *Voyage to Venus* (1943), *That Hideous Strength* (1945).

LEWIS, NORMAN (1908   )

The Day of the Fox (1955), *The March of the Long Shadows* (1987).

LEWIS, WYNDHAM (1882–1957)

Tarr (1918), *The Childermass* (1928), *The Apes of God* (1930), *Snooty Baronet* (1932), *The Revenge for Love* (1937), *Rotting Hill* (1951), *The Human Age* (1955).

LIVELY, ADAM (1961   )

Blue Fruit (1988), *The Burnt House* (1989), *The Snail* (1991), *Sing the Body Electric* (1993).

LIVELY, PENELOPE (1933   )

The Road to Lichfield (1977), *Judgement Day* (1980), *Next to Nature, Art* (1982), *According to Mark* (1984), *Moon Tiger* (1987), *Passing On* (1989).

LODGE, DAVID (1935   )

Ginger, You're Barmy (1962), *The British Museum Is Falling Down* (1965), *Out of the Shelter* (1970, rev. ed. 1985), *Changing Places* (1975), *How Far Can You Go?* (1980), *Small World* (1984), *Nice Work* (1988), *Paradise News* (1991).

LOWRY, MALCOLM (1909–1957)
Ultramarine (1933), *Under the Volcano* (1947), *Dark as the Grave Wherein my Friend is Laid* (1968 post.), *Lunar Caustic* (1968, post.), *October Ferry to Gabriola* (1971, post.).

MACAULAY, ROSE (1881–1958)
The Furnace (1907), *Told By an Idiot* (1923), *Crewe Train* (1926), *Keeping Up Appearances* (1928), *Staying With Relations* (1930), *The Towers of Trebizond* (1956).

McEWAN, IAN (1948   )
First Love, Last Rites (stories, 1975), *In Between the Sheets* (stories, 1978), *The Cement Garden* (1978), *The Comfort of Strangers* (1981), *The Child in Time* (1987), *The Innocents* (1990), *Black Dogs* (1992).

McGAHERN, JOHN (1934   )
The Barracks (1963), *Nightlines* (1971), *The Leavetaking* (1974), *The Pornographer* (1979), *Amongst Women* (1990).

MACHEN, ARTHUR (1863–1947)
The Great God Pan (1894) *The House of Souls* (stories, 1906).

MACINNES, COLIN (1914–1976)
To the Victors the Spoils (1950), *City of Spades* (1957), *Absolute Beginners* (1959), *Mr Love and Justice* (1960).

MACKENZIE, COMPTON (1883–1972)
Carnival (1912), *Sinister Street* (1914), *Extraordinary Women* (1928).

MACLAVERTY, BERNARD (1942   )
Lamb (1980), *Cal (1983)*.

McWILLIAM, CANDIA (1955   )
A Case of Knives (1988), *A Little Stranger* (1989).

MADDEN, DEIRDRE (1960   )
The Birds of the Innocent Wood (1988), *Hidden Symptoms* (1988).

MANNING, FREDERIC (1882–1935)
Her Privates We: By Private 19022 (1930).

MANNING, OLIVIA (1911–1980)
The Wind Changes (1937), *School for Love* (1951), *A Different Face* (1953), *The Doves of Venus* (1955), "The Balkan Trilogy" (1960–65), "The Levant Trilogy" (1977–8).

MANSFIELD, KATHERINE (1888–1923)
In a German Pension (stories, 1911), *Bliss and Other Stories* (1920), *The Garden-Party and Other Stories* (1922).

MARS-JONES, ADAM (1954   )
The Waters of Thirst (1993).
MASSIE, ALAN (1938   )
Change and Decay in All Around I See (1978), *The Death of Men*
(1981), *A Question of Loyalties* (1989), *The Hanging Tree* (1990).
MAUGHAM, W. SOMERSET (1874–1965)
Liza of Lambeth (1897), *Mrs Craddock* (1902), *Of Human Bondage*
(1915), *The Moon and Sixpence* (1919), *Cakes and Ale* (1930), *The*
Razor's Edge (1944).
MAYOR, F. M. (1872–1932)
The Third Miss Symons (1913), *The Rector's Daughter* (1924).
MEREDITH, GEORGE (1828–1909)
Modern Love (1862), *The Egoist* (1879), *The Tragic Comedians* (1880),
Diana of the Crossways (1885).
MIDDLETON, STANLEY (1919   )
A Short Answer (1958), *Harris's Requiem* (1960), *Two's Company*
(1963), *Apple of Eve* (1970), *Holiday* (1974), *In a Strange Land*
(1979), *Recovery* (1988).
MITCHELL, JULIAN (1935   )
Imaginary Toys (1961), *A Disturbing Influence* (1962), *The White*
Father (1964), *The Undiscovered Country* (1968).
MO, TIMOTHY (1950   )
The Monkey King (1978), *Sour Sweet* (1982), *An Insular Possession*
(1986), *The Redundancy of Courage* (1991).
MORGAN, CHARLES (1894–1958)
The Fountain (1932), *The Voyage* (1940), *The River Line* (1949).
MOORCOCK, MICHAEL (1939   )
The Chinese Agent (1970), *Byzantium Endures* (1981), *Mother London*
(1988), *The Laughter of Carthage* (1984), *Jerusalem Commands* (1992).
MOORE, BRIAN (1921   )
The Lonely Passion of Judith Hearne (1955), *The Luck of Ginger Coffey*
(1960), *An Answer from Limbo* (1963), *The Emperor of Ice Cream*
(1966), *Catholics* (1972), *The Doctor's Wife* (1976), *Cold Heaven*
(1983), *The Colour of Blood* (1987), *Lies of Silence* (1990), *No Other*
Life (1993).
MOORE, GEORGE (1852–1933)
A Modern Lover (1883), *A Mummer's Wife* (1885), *A Mere Accident*

(1887), *Esther Waters* (1894), the "Hail and Farewell" trilogy (1911–14).

MORRIS, WILLIAM (1834–1896)
The Dream of John Ball (1888), *News from Nowhere* (1890), *The Wood Beyond the World* (1895).

MORRISON, ARTHUR (1863–1945)
Tales of Mean Streets (1894), *A Child of the Jago* (1896), *To London Town* (1899), *The Hole in the Wall* (1902).

MOTTRAM, R. H. (1883–1971)
The Spanish Farm (1924), *The Spanish Farm Trilogy, 1914–18* (1927).

MOSLEY, NICHOLAS (1923   )
Spaces of the Dark (1951), *The Rainbearers* (1955), *Accident* (1965), *Impossible Object* (1968), *Natalie, Natalia* (1971), *Imago Bird* (1980), *Hopeful Monsters* (1990)

MUNRO, H. H. ("SAKI") (1870–1916)
The Chronicles of Clovis (1911), *The Unbearable Bassington* (1912).

MURDOCH, IRIS (1919   )
Under the Net (1954), *The Bell* (1958), *A Severed Head* (1961), *An Unofficial Rose* (1962), *The Red and the Green* (1965), *The Nice and the Good* (1968), *The Black Prince* (1971), *A Word Child* (1975), *The Sea, The Sea* (1978), *The Philosopher's Pupil* (1983), *The Book and the Brotherhood* (1987), *The Green Knight* (1993).

MYERS, L. H. (1881–1944)
The "Clio" (1925), *The Near and the Far* (1929), *The Root and the Flower* (1935).

NAIPAUL, V. S. (1932   )
The Mystic Masseur (1957), *A House for Mr Biswas* (1961), *The Mimic Men* (1967), *In a Free State* (1971), *Guerrillas* (1975), *A Bend in the River* (1979), *The Enigma of Arrival* (1987).

NEWBY, P. H. (1918   )
A Journey to the Interior (1945), *Picnic at Sakkara* (1955), *The Barbary Light* (1962), *Something to Answer For* (1968), *Leaning in the Wind* (1986).

NORFOLK, LAWRENCE (1963   )
Lemprière's Dictionary (1991).

NYE, ROBERT (1939   )
Doubtfire (1967), *Falstaff* (1976), *Faust* (1980), *Voyage of the Destiny* (1982).

O'BRIEN, EDNA (1932   )
The Country Girls (1960), *Girls in Their Married Bliss* (1964), *August is a Wicked Month* (1965), *The Love Object* (1968), *Johnny I Hardly Knew You* (1977).

O'BRIEN, FLANN (BRIAN O'NOLAN) (1911–1966)
At Swim-Two-Birds (1939), *The Dalkey Archive* (1964), *The Third Policeman* (1967).

O'FAOLAIN, SEAN (1900 – 1991)
A Nest of Simple Folk (1933), *Midsummer Night Madness (1982), The Heat of the Sun (1983).*

OKRI, BEN (1959   )
Flowers and Shadows (1980), *Incidents at the Shrine* (1986), *Stars of the New Curfew* (1988), *The Famished Road* (1991), *Songs of Enchantment* (1993).

ORWELL, GEORGE (ERIC BLAIR) (1903–1950)
Burmese Days (1934), *A Clergyman's Daughter* (1935), *Keep the Aspidistra Flying* (1936), *Coming Up for Air* (1939), *Animal Farm* (1945), *Nineteen Eighty-Four* (1949).

"OUIDA" (MARIE LOUISE DE LA RAMÉE) (1839–1908)
Moths (1880), *Wanda* (1883).

PATTERSON, GLENN (1961   )
Burning Your Own (1988), *Fat Lad* (1992).

PEAKE, MERVYN (1911–1968)
Titus Groan (1946), *Gormenghast* (1950).

PHILIPS, TOM (1937   )
A Humument: A Treated Victorian Novel (1980: rev. ed., 1987).

PHILLIPS, CARYL (1958   )
The Final Passage (1985), *A State of Independence* (1986), *Cambridge* (1992), *Crossing the River* (1993).

POWELL, ANTHONY (1905   )
Afternoon Men (1931), *Venusberg (1932), From a View to a Death* (1933), *What's Become of Waring?* (1939), "A Dance to the Music of Time" (12 vols., 1951–75), (1971), *The Fisher King* (1986).

POWYS, J.C. (1872–1963)
Wood and Stone (1915), *Wolf Solent* (1929), *A Glastonbury Romance* (1933), *Weymouth Sands* (1934, 1963).

POWYS, T. F. (1875–1953)
Mr Weston's Good Wine (1927), *Unclay* (1931).

PRIEST, CHRISTOPHER (1943   )
Indoctrinaire (1970), *Inverted World* (1974), *The Affirmation* (1981).

PRIESTLEY, J. B. (1894–1984)
The Good Companions (1929), *Angel Pavement* (1930), *Festival at Farbridge* (1951), *Lost Empires* (1965), *The Image Men* (1968).

PRITCHETT, V. S. (1900   )
Dead Man Leading (1937), *Mr Beluncle* (1951), *Key to My Heart* (1963), *Collected Stories* (1982), *More Collected Stories* (1983).

PYM, BARBARA (1913–1980)
Some Tame Gazelle (1950), *Excellent Women* (1952), *Less Than Angels* (1955), *A Glass of Blessings* (1958), *Quartet in Autumn* (1977), *The Sweet Dove Died* (1978), *An Academic Question* (1986, post.).

QUIN, ANN (1936–1973)
Berg (1964), *Three* (1966), *Passages* (1969), *Tripticks* (1972).

RABAN, JONATHAN (1942   )
Foreign Land (1985).

RAPHAEL, FREDERIC (1931   )
Obbligato (1956), *The Trouble with England* (1962), *Glittering Prizes* (1976), *After the War* (1988).

RAVEN, SIMON (1927   )
The Feathers of Death (1959), the "Alms for Oblivion" sequence (1964–75).

READ, PIERS PAUL (1931   )
Game in Heaven With Tussy Marx (1966), *The Junkers* (1968), *The Professor's Daughter* (1971), *A Married Man* (1979), *The Villa Golitsyn* (1981), *A Season in the West* (1988).

REID, FORREST (1875–1947)
The Kingdom of Twilight (1904), *Uncle Stephen* (1931), *The Retreat* (1934), *Young Tom* (1944).

RENDELL, RUTH (1930   )
Shake Hands for Ever (1975), *Make Death Love Me* (1979), *An*

Unkindness of Ravens (1985), *A Dark-Adapted Eye* (as Barbara Vine, 1986), *Heartstones* (1987), *Talking to Strange Men* (1987).
RHYS, JEAN (1894–1979)
Postures (1928, reissued as *Quartet*), *After Leaving Mr Mackenzie* (1930), *Voyage in the Dark* (1934), *Good Morning, Midnight* (1939), *Wide Sargasso Sea* (1966).
RICHARDSON, DOROTHY (1873–1957)
Pointed Roofs (1915), *Backwater* (1916) and further volumes collected as "Pilgrimage" (4 vols., 1938, 1967).
ROBERTS, MICHÈLE (1949   )
A Piece of the Night (1978), *The Wild Girl* (1984), *The Book of Mrs Noah* (1987), *Daughters of the House* (1992).
ROLFE, FREDERICK ("BARON CORVO") (1860–1913)
Hadrian the Seventh (1904), *The Desire and Pursuit of the Whole* (1934, post.).
RUBENS, BERNICE (1927   )
Set on Edge (1960), *The Elected Member* (1969), *Spring Sonata* (1979), *Birds of Passage* (1987).
RUMENS, CAROL (1944   )
Plato Park (1987).
RUSHDIE, SALMAN (1947   )
Grimus (1975), *Midnight's Children* (1981), *Shame* (1983), *The Satanic Verses* (1988).
SAINT AUBIN DE TERAN, LISA (1953   )
Keeper of the House (1982), *Slow Train to Milan* (1983), *The Tiger* (1984).
SANSOM, WILLIAM (1912–1976)
Fireman Flower (1944), *Something Terrible, Something Lovely* (1948), *The Body* (1949), *The Face of Innocence* (1951), *A Bed of Roses* (1954), *The Cautious Heart* (1958), *The Stories of William Sansom* (1963).
SAYER, PAUL (1955   )
The Comforts of Madness (1988), *The Absolution Game* (1992).
SAYERS, DOROTHY (1893–1957)
Clouds of Witness (1927), *Lord Peter Views the Body* (1928), *The Nine Tailors* (1934), *Gaudy Night* (1935), *Busman's Honeymoon* (1937).
SASSOON, SIEGFRIED (1886–1967)
Memoirs of a Fox-Hunting Man (1928), *Memoirs of an Infantry Officer*

(1930), *Sherston's Progress* (1936), collected as *The Complete Memoirs of George Sherston* (1937).

SCHLEE, ANN (1934   )
The Vandal (1979), *Rhine Journey* (1980), *Laing* (1987).

SCOTT, PAUL (1920–1978)
Johnnie Sahib (1952), *The Alien Sky* (1953), *A Male Child* (1956), *The Birds of Paradise* (1962), *The Jewel in the Crown* (1966), *The Day of the Scorpion* (1968), *The Towers of Silence* (1971), *A Division of the Spoils* (collected as *The Raj Quartet*, 1976), *Staying On* (1977).

SCHREINER, OLIVE (1855–1920)
The Story of an African Farm (1883), *From Man to Man* (1927, post.).

SELF, WILL (1961   )
Cock and Bull (1992), *My Idea of Fun* (1993).

SETH, VIKRAM (1952   )
The Golden Gate: A Novel in Verse (1986), *A Suitable Boy* (1993).

SHAKESPEARE, NICHOLAS (1957   )
The Vision of Elena Silves (1990), *The High Flyer* (1993).

SHARPE, TOM (1928   )
Riotous Assembly (1971), *Indecent Exposure* (1973), *Porterhouse Blue* (1974), *Wilt* (1976), *The Great Pursuit* (1977), *Vintage Stuff* (1982).

SILLITOE, ALAN (1928   )
Saturday Night and Sunday Morning (1958), *The Loneliness of the Long-Distance Runner* (1959), *The Ragman's Daughter* (stories, 1963), *The Death of William Posters* (1965), *The Flame of Life* (1974), *The Storyteller* (1979), *Out of the Whirlpool* (1987).

SINCLAIR, ANDREW (1935   )
The Breaking of Bumbo (1959), *My Friend Judas* (1959), *Gog* (1967), *Magog* (1972), *King Ludd* (1988).

SINCLAIR, CLIVE (1948   )
Bibliosexuality (1973), *Hearts of Gold* (stories, 1979), *Blood Libels* (1985), *Augustus Rex* (1992).

SINCLAIR, IAIN (1943   )
White Chappell, Scarlet Tracings (1987), *Downriver* (1991).

SINCLAIR, MAY (1863–1942)
The Helpmate (1907), *The Three Sisters* (1914), *The Tree of Heaven* (1917), *Mary Oliver: A Life* (1919), *The Life and Death of Harriett Frean* (1922), *A Cure of Souls* (1924).

SMITH, STEVIE (1902–1971)
Novel on Yellow Paper (1936), *Over the Frontier* (1938), *The Holiday* (1949).

SNOW, C. P. (1905–1980)
Death Under Sail (1932), *The Search* (1934), *Strangers and Brothers* (1940), *The Masters* (1951), *The New Men* (1954), *Homecomings* (1956), *Corridors of Power* (1964), *The Sleep of Reason* (1968), *Last Things* (1970), *The Malcontents* (1972).

SPARK, MURIEL (1918   )
The Comforters (1957), *Memento Mori* (1959), *The Ballad of Peckham Rye* (1960), *The Prime of Miss Jean Brodie* (1961), *The Girls of Slender Means* (1963), *The Public Image* (1968), *The Driver's Seat* (1970), *Not to Disturb* (1971), *The Hothouse by the East River* (1973), *Territorial Rights* (1979), *Loitering With Intent* (1984), *The Stories of Muriel Spark* (1986), *A Far Cry from Kensington* (1988).

STEVENSON, ROBERT LOUIS (1850–1894)
The New Arabian Nights (1882), *Treasure Island* (1883), *The Strange Case of Dr Jekyll and Mr Hyde* (1886), *Kidnapped* (1886), *The Black Arrow* (1888), *The Master of Ballantrae* (1889), *Catriona* (1893), *Weir of Hermiston: An Unfinished Romance* (1986, post.).

STOREY, DAVID (1933   )
This Sporting Life (1960), *Flight into Camden* (1960), *Radcliffe* (1963), *Passmore* (1972), *Life Class* (1974), *Saville* (1976).

SWIFT, GRAHAM (1949   )
The Sweetshop Owner (1980), *Shuttlecock* (1981), *Waterland* (1983), *Out of This World* (1988), *Ever After* (1992).

TAYLOR, D. J. (1960   )
Great Eastern Land (1986), *Real Life* (1992).

THOMAS, D. M. (1935   )
The Flute-Player (1979), *The White Hotel* (1981), *Ararat* (1983), *Swallow* (1984), *Sphinx* (1986), *Summit* (1987), *Pictures at an Exhibition* (1993).

THORPE, ADAM (1956   )
Ulverton (1992).

THUBRON, COLIN (1939   )
The God in the Mountain (1977), *Emperor* (1978), *A Cruel Madness* (1984).

TOLKIEN, J. R. R. (1892–1973)
The Hobbit (1937), *The Lord of the Rings* (3 vols., 1954–5), *The Silmarillion* (1977).

TOMLINSON, H. M. (1873–1958)
Gallion's Reach (1927), *All Our Yesterdays* (1930).

TREMAIN, ROSE (1943   )
Sadler's Birthday (1976), *Letter to Sister Benedicta* (1978), *The Cupboard* (1981), *The Swimming Pool Season* (1985), *Restoration* (1989), *Sacred Country* (1992).

TRESSELL, ROBERT (ROBERT NOONAN) (1870–1911)
The Ragged-Trousered Philanthropists (1914, post.).

TREVOR, WILLIAM (1928   )
The Old Boys (1964), *The Boarding House* (1965), *Mrs Eckdorf in O'Neil's Hotel* (1969), *The Children of Dynmouth* (1976), *Fools of Fortune* (1983), *The Stories of William Trevor* (1983), *The Silence in the Garden* (1988), *Two Lives* (1991).

TROCCHI, ALEXANDER (1923–1984)
Cain's Book (1962).

UNSWORTH, BARRY (1930   )
The Hide (1970), *Mooncranker's Gift* (1973), *The Rage of the Vulture* (1982), *Pascali's Island* (1980), *Stone Virgin* (1985), *Sugar and Rum* (1988), *Sacred Hunger* (1992).

UPWARD, EDWARD (1903   )
Journey to the Border (1938), *In the Thirties* (1962), *The Railway Accident and Other Stories* (1969), *The Rotten Elements* (1969), *No Home But the Struggle* (1977).

WAIN, JOHN (1925   )
Hurry On Down (1953), *Living in the Present* (1955), *A Travelling Woman* (1959), *Strike the Father Dead* (1962), *A Winter in the Hills* (1970), *The Pardoner's Tale* (1978).

WALPOLE, HUGH (1884–1941)
Mr Perrin and Mr Traill (1911), *Rogue Herries* (1930).

WARNER, MARINA (1946   )
In a Dark Wood (1977), *The Skating Party* (1982), *The Lost Father* (1988), *Indigo* (1992).

WARNER, REX (1905   )
The Wild Goose Chase (1937), *The Professor* (1938), *The Aerodrome* (1941).

WARNER, SYLVIA TOWNSEND (1893–1978)
The Espalier (1925), *Mr Fortune's Maggot* (1927).

WAUGH, EVELYN (1903–1966)
Decline and Fall (1928), *Vile Bodies* (1930), *A Handful of Dust* (1934), *Scoop* (1938), *Brideshead Revisited* (1945), *The Loved One* (1948), *Men at Arms* (1952), *Officers and Gentlemen* (1955), *Unconditional Surrender* (1961), (these three collected and revised as *Sword of Honour*, 1965), *The Ordeal of Gilbert Pinfold* (1957).

WEBB, MARY (1881–1927)
Gone to Earth (1917), *Precious Bane* (1924).

WELDON, FAY (1931   )
The Fat Woman's Joke (1967), *Down Among the Women* (1971), *Female Friends* (1975), *Praxis* (1978), *The Life and Loves of a She-Devil* (1984), *The Shrapnel Academy* (1986), *The Rules of Life* (1987).

WELLS, H. G. (1866–1946)
The Time Machine: An Invention (1895), *The Invisible Man: A Grotesque Romance* (1897), *The War of the Worlds* (1900), *Kipps* (1905), *In the Days of the Comet* (1906), *Tono-Bungay* (1909), *Ann Veronica: A Modern Love Story* (1909), *The History of Mr Polly* (1910), *The Country of the Blind and Other Stories* (1911), *The New Machiavelli* (1911).

WEST, REBECCA (CECILY FAIRFIELD) (1892–1983)
The Return of the Soldier (1918), *The Judge* (1922), *Harriet Hume* (1929), *The Thinking Reed* (1936), *The Fountain Overflows* (1956), *The Birds Fall Down* (1966).

WHITE, T. H. (1906–1964)
The Sword in the Stone (1938), *The Once and Future King* (1958).

WILDE, OSCAR (1854–1900)
The Happy Prince and Other Tales (1888), *The Picture of Dorian Gray* (1891).

WILLIAMS, CHARLES (1886–1945)
Descent into Hell (1937), *All Hallows' Eve* (1945).

WILLIAMS, NIGEL (1948   )
My Life Closed Twice (1977), *Class Enemy* (1982), *Black Magic* (1988), *The Wimbledon Poisoner* (1991).

WILLIAMS, RAYMOND (1921–1988)
Border Country (1960), *The Volunteers* (1978), *The Fight for Manod* (1979), *Loyalties* (1985).

WILLIAMSON, HENRY (1895–1977)
The Beautiful Years (1921), *Dandelion Days* (1922), *The Dream of Fair Women* (1931), the "A Chronicle of Ancient Sunlight" sequence (1951–1969).

WILSON, A. N. (1950   )
The Sweets of Pimlico (1977), *The Healing Art* (1980), *Who Was Oswald Fish?* (1981), *Wise Virgin* (1982), *Scandal* (1983), *Love Unknown* (1986), *Incline Our Hearts* (1988).

WILSON, ANGUS (1913–92)
The Wrong Set and Other Stories (1949), *Such Darling Dodos* (1950), *Hemlock and After* (1952), *Anglo-Saxon Attitudes* (1956), *The Middle Age of Mrs Eliot* (1958), *The Old Men at the Zoo* (1961), *Late Call* (1964), *No Laughing Matter* (1967), *Collected Short Stories* (1987).

WILSON, ROBERT McLIAM (1964   )
The Dispossessed (1992).

WINTERSON, JEANETTE (1959   )
Oranges Are Not the Only Fruit (1985), *Boating for Beginners* (1985), *The Passion* (1987), *Sexing the Cherry* (1989), *Written On the Body* (1992).

WODEHOUSE, P. G. (1881–1975)
The Man With Two Left Feet (1917), *My Man Jeeves* (1919), *The Clicking of Cuthbert* (1922), *The Inimitable Jeeves* (1923), *Young Men in Spats* (1936), *Summer Moonshine* (1937), *The Code of the Woosters* (1938).

WOOLF, VIRGINIA (1882–1941)
The Voyage Out (1915), *Night and Day* (1919), *Jacob's Room* (1922), *Mrs Dalloway* (1925), *To the Lighthouse* (1927), *The Waves* (1931), *The Years* (1937, *Between the Acts* (1941); *The Common Reader* (essays, 1925; 2nd series, 1932).

ZAMEENZAD, ADAM
The Thirteenth House (1987), *Love, Bones and Water* (1989), *Cyrus, Cyrus* (1990).

Select Bibliography

This list concentrates on general works on the modern novel and modern literary culture, on studies of periods and particular literary tendencies and groupings. The modern British novel, especially for the period between 1890 and 1939, is very well studied ground. There are innumerable thorough studies of the individual authors, many specialist works of textual analysis, biography and literary theory. Readers looking for more of this will need to go to other bibliographies. The chief source for twentieth-century British literature in general is the indispensable I. R. Willison (ed.), *The New Cambridge Bibliography of English Literature, Vol 4: 1900–1950* (Cambridge, 1972). But see also E. C. Bufkin, *The Twentieth Century Novel in English: A Checklist* (Atlanta, Ga., 2nd ed., 1984), and Randall Stevenson, *The British Novel in the Twentieth Century: An Introductory Bibliography* (London, 1988).

Valuable guides to more recent writers and writing are two volumes in the *Dictionary of Literary Biography* – Jay Halio (ed.), *Vol 14, British Novelists Since 1960* (2 vols., Detroit, 1983), and Bernard Oldsey (ed.), *Vol 15: British Novelists: 1930–1959* (2 vols., Detroit, 1983). And also see Leslie Henderson (ed.), *Contemporary Novelists* (Chicago and London, 5th ed., 1991), James Vinson (ed.), *Twentieth Century Fiction* (Chicago and London, 1983), Virginia Blain, Patricia Clemens and Isobel Grundy (eds.), *The Feminist Companion to Literature in English* (London, 1990), Lionel Stevenson, *The History of the English Novel, Vol II: Yesterday and After* (New York, 1967) and Hans Bertens *et al.* (eds.), *Post-war Literatures in English* (Groningen, 1988), all invaluable both for general information and bibliographical material.

On Modernism in general, there is an extensive bibliography in

Malcolm Bradbury and James McFarlane (eds.), *Modernism, 1890–1930* (Harmondsworth, rev. ed., 1989), while the invaluable background book is Richard Ellmann and Charles Feidelson (eds.), *The Modern Tradition: Backgrounds of Modern Literature* (New York/London, 1965). There are also useful bibliographies in Boris Ford (ed.), *The New Pelican Guide to English Literature, Vols 7 & 8* (London, 1988) and A. C. Ward, *Longman Companion to Twentieth Century Literature* (London, 1981), and recurrent bibliographies in *English Literature in Transition, Twentieth Century Literature, PMLA, The Year's Work in English Studies*, etc. There is more detailed background on individual authors or individual texts in volumes in the "Macmillan Casebooks," the "Prentice-Hall Twentieth Century Views," the Methuen "Contemporary Writers" series, the Macmillan "Women Writers" series, and the "Critical Heritage" series. Also see the Harvester "Key Women Writers" series and the Penguin "Lives of Modern Women" series, ed. Emma Tennant.

Some useful general studies of the modern British novel – especially in the earlier part of the century – are Walter Allen, *The English Novel: A Short Critical History* (Harmondsworth, 1954) and *Tradition and Dream: A Critical Survey of British and American Fiction from the 1920s to the Present Day* (Harmondsworth, 1965), Malcolm Bradbury, *Possibilities: Essays on the State of the Novel* (Oxford/New York, 1973) and (on more recent writing) *No, Not Bloomsbury* (London, 1987), Anthony Burgess, *The Novel Now: A Student's Guide to Contemporary Fiction* (London, 1967), David Cairns and Shaun Richards, *Writing Ireland: Colonialism, Nation and Culture* (Manchester, 1988), Margaret Crossland, *Beyond the Lighthouse: English Women Writers in the Twentieth Century* (London, 1981), David Daiches, *The Novel and the Modern World* (Chicago, rev. ed., 1960), G. S. Fraser, *The Modern Writer and His World* (Harmondsworth, rev. ed., 1970), William C. Frierson's *The English Novel in Transition, 1885–1940* (Norman, Okla., 1942), Martin Green's quirky *The English Novel in the Twentieth Century: Doom of Empire* (London, 1984), Geoffrey Hartman's *Beyond Formalism: Literary Essays 1958–1970* (New Haven, 1970), Douglas Hewitt, *English Fiction of the Early Modern Period, 1890–1940* (London, 1989), Frederick R.

Karl and M. Magalaner's *A Reader's Guide to Great Twentieth Century English Novels* (New York/London, 1959), John Orr's *The Making of the Twentieth Century Novel* (London, 1988), Mark Schorer's edited collection of essays *Modern British Fiction* (Oxford, 1942), Elaine Showalter's *A Literature of Their Own: British Women Novelists from Brontë to Lessing* (London, 1978), J. I. M. Stewart's *Eight Modern Writers* (Oxford, 1963) (with good bibliography), and George Woodcock (ed.), *Twentieth Century Fiction* (London, 1983).

More general studies of the period include Harry Blamires' *Twentieth Century English Literature* (London, 2nd ed., 1982), Malcolm Bradbury, *The Social Context of Modern English Literature* (Oxford, 1971), Irving Howe's collection *The Idea of the Modern in Literature and the Arts* (New York, 1967), Frank Kermode's brilliant *Essays on Fiction, 1971–82* (London, 1983), Jose Ortega y Gasset, *The Dehumanization of Art and Other Essays* (London, 1972), P. Meisel, *The Myth of the Modern: A Study of British Literature and Criticism since 1850* (New Haven/London, 1989), John Oliver Perry (ed.), *Backgrounds to Modern Literature* (San Francisco, 1968), Stephen Spender's *The Struggle of the Modern* (London, 1963), Wylie Sypher's *Loss of the Self in Modern Literature and Art* (New York, 1962), William York Tindall's *Forces in Modern British Literature, 1885–1946* (New York, 1947), and Raymond Williams, *Culture and Society, 1780–1950* (London, 1959). Also useful are Edmund Wilson's splendid internal study of the Modern movement, *Axel's Castle* (New York, 1931), and Cyril Connolly's pleasant and personal guide *The Modern Movement: 100 Key books from England, France and America, 1880–1950* (London, 1965).

There are many useful books on a variety of key themes, topics and developments running through modern British fiction. For instance, see Kingsley Amis, *New Maps of Hell: A Survey of Science Fiction* (London, 1961), Nicola Beauman, *A Very Great Profession: The Women's Novel, 1914–1939* (London, 1983), Glen Cavaliero, *The Rural Tradition in the English Novel, 1900–1939* (London, 1977), Claud Cockburn, *Bestseller: The Books that Everyone Read, 1900–1939* (London, 1972), C. B. Cox, *The Free Spirit* (London, 1963), Gail Cunningham, *The New Woman and the Victorian Novel* (London, 1978), A. E. Dyson, *The Crazy Fabric: Essays in Irony* (London,

1965), Mary Eagleton and David Pierce, *Attitudes to Class in the English Novel From Walter Scott to David Storey* (London, 1979), Leon Edel, *The Psychological Novel, 1900–1950* New York, 1955), Melvin Friedman, *Stream of Consciousness: A Study in Literary Method* (New Haven, 1955), Daniel Gunn, *Psychoanalysis and Fiction: An Exploration of Literary and Psychoanalytic Borders* (Cambridge, 1988), W. J. Harvey, *Character and the Novel* (London, 1965), Jeremy Hawthorn (ed.), *The British Working Class Novel in the Twentieth Century* (London, 1984), Frederick J. Hoffmann, *Freudianism and the Modern Literary Mind* (Baton Rouge, La., 1957), Irving Howe, *Politics and the Novel* (New York, 1957), Gabriel Josipovici (ed.), *The Modern English Novel: The Reader, The Writer and the Work* (London, 1976), David Lodge, *Language of Fiction: Essays in Criticism and Verbal Analysis of the English Novel* (London, 1966) and *The Modes of Modern Writing: Metaphor, Metonymy and the Typology of Modern Literature* (London, 1977), Giorgio Melchiori, *The Tightrope Walkers: Studies of Mannerism in Modern English Literature* (London, 1956), A. A. Mendilow, *Time and the Novel* (London, 1952), Sharon Spencer, *Space, Time and Structure in the Modern Novel* (New York, 1971) and Julian Symons, *Bloody Murder: from the Detective Story to the Crime Novel* (London, 1972), and, on the thriller, Colin Watson, *Snobbery With Violence* (London, 1971).

For an invaluable study of the history of the entire period, see James Joll, *Europe Since 1870: An International History* (London, 4th ed., 1990), and other important historical works are E. J. Hobsbawm, *The Age of Empire: 1875–1914* (London, 1987), Norman Stone, *Europe Transformed: 1878–1918* (London, 1983), Barbara Tuchman, *The Proud Tower* (London, 1966), and David Thomson, *England in the Twentieth Century* (Harmondsworth, 1970).

Chapter 1

On the fiction of the period 1876–1900 in general, a recent, central background study is Peter Keating's *The Haunted Study: A Social History of the English Novel, 1875–1914* (London, 1989), which also contains a useful listing of the chief fiction published between 1875 and 1915; and also see John Sutherland, *The Longman Companion to Victorian Fiction* (London, 1988). On the much-discussed "transition" of the novel, some of the chief books are Alan J. Friedman, *The Turn of the Novel: The Transition to Modern Fiction* (New York and London, 1966), John A. Lester, *Journey Through Despair, 1880–1914: Transformations in British Literary Culture* (Princeton, 1968), Stephen Kern, *The Culture of Time and Space, 1880–1918* (London, 1983), D. R. Schwarts, *The Transformation of the English Novel, 1890–1930* (London, 1989), David Trotter, *The English Novel in History, 1895–1920* (London, 1993) and Raymond Williams, *The English Novel from Dickens to Lawrence* (London, 1970).

On the 1890s, see Malcolm Bradbury, David Palmer, and Ian Fletcher (eds.), *Decadence and the 1890s* (London, 1979), Barbara Charlesworth, *Dark Passages: The Decadent Consciousness in Victorian Literature* (Madison, Wis., 1965), Holbrook Jackson, *The Eighteen Nineties* (London, 1913; reissued 1988), Elaine Moers, *The Dandy* (London, 1960), Roger Shattuck, *The Banquet Years* (London, 1969), Elaine Showalter, *Sexual Anarchy: Gender and Culture at the Fin de Siècle* (New York, 1990/ London, 1991), and John Stokes, *In the Nineties* (New York/London, 1989). On fantasy and Gothic, see David Punter, *The Literature of Terror* (London, 1980) and Victor Sage, *Horror Fiction in the Protestant Tradition* (London, 1988). On fiction and imperialism, see Martin Green, *Dreams of Adventure, Deeds of Empire* (London, 1980), and Alan Sandison, *The Wheel of Empire: A Study of the Imperial Idea in Some Late 19th Century and Early 20th Century Fiction* (London/New York, 1967). On fiction and the new feminism, see Patricia Stubbs, *Women and Fiction: Feminism and the Novel, 1880–1920* (London, 1981). On "future fiction" see I. F. Clarke, *The Pattern of Expectation: 1644–2001* (London, 1979) and *Voices Prophesying War: Future Wars 1763–3749* (London, rev. ed., 1992).

For the changing ideas of the period in general, see Leo Henkin, *Darwinism in the English Novel, 1860–1910* (New York, 1963), and H. Stuart Hughes, *Consciousness and Society: The Reorientation of European Social Thought, 1890–1930* (London, 1959). Also see, for one important broad historical overview, E. J. Hobsbawm, *The Age of Empire, 1875–1914* (London, 1987).

Chapter 2

Several of the works cited above also deal with the fiction of the period 1900–1914. More detailed studies of the Edwardian period include Richard Ellmann (ed.), *Edwardians and Late Victorians* (New York/London, 1960), and his *Eminent Domain: Yeats Among Wilde, Joyce, Pound, Eliot and Auden* (London, 1968), Samuel Hynes, *The Edwardian Turn of Mind* (Oxford, 1969), and his *Edwardian Occasions* (London, 1972), and Simon Newell Smith (ed.), *Edwardian England, 1901–1914* (Oxford, 1964). On the Edwardian novel as such, see John Alcorn, *The Nature Novel from Hardy to Lawrence* (London, 1977), John Batchelor, *The Edwardian Novelists* (London, 1982), William Bellamy, *The Novels of Wells, Bennett and Galsworthy, 1890–1910* (London, 1971), Jefferson Hunter, *Edwardian Fiction* (Cambridge, Mass., 1982), and Frank Kermode's *Essays on Fiction: 1971–82* (cited above).

The pre-war development of the Modern movement has been extensively studied (again see the large bibliography in Malcolm Bradbury and James McFarlane (eds.), *Modernism, 1890–1930* (cited above)). Among the interesting recent general studies are Hugh Kenner's highly polemical *A Sinking Island: The Modern English Writers* (London, 1988), Stan Smith, *The Origins of Modernism* (Brighton, 1988), and Julian Symons, *Makers of the New: The Revolution in Literature, 1912–1939* (London, 1987). Also see Allon White, *The Uses of Obscurity: The Fiction of Early Modernism* (London, 1981). The rise of psychological fiction and "stream of consciousness", and the general evolution of the "modern" novel, are explored in a number of the titles listed in the "General Studies" section above. On the importance of women writers to the Modernist movement see Gillian Hanscombe and Virginia L. Smyers, *Writing for Their Lives: The Modernist Women, 1910–1940* (London, 1987).

Some more specialist works well worth noting are M. Chelford *et al.* (eds.), *Modernism* (Urbana, Ill., 1986), Joseph Chiari, *The Aesthetics of Modernism* (London, 1970), Richard Cork, *Vorticism and Abstract Art in the First Machine Age* (London, 1976), Donald Gordon, *Expressionism: Art and Idea* (New Haven, 1987), Hilton

Kramer, *The Age of the Avant Garde* (London, 1974), Michael Levenson, *A Genealogy of Modernism* (Cambridge, 1984), Marjorie Perloff, *The Futurist Moment* (Chicago, 1986) and Stella K. Tillyard, *The Impact of Modernism* (London, 1988).

Chapter 3

An important work on the changed cultural mood of the Twenties is Paul Fussell, *The Great War and Modern Memory* (New York/London, 1975); also his *Abroad: British Literary Travelling Between the Wars* (New York/London, 1980). Other important works on the post-war situation are Bernard Bergonzi, *Hero's Twilight: A Study of the Literature of the Great War* (London, 1965), M. S. Greicus, *Prose Writers of World War I* (London, 1973), Frederick J. Hoffmann, *The Moral No: Death and the Modern Imagination* (Princeton, 1964) and Holger Klein (ed.), *The First World War in Fiction* (London, 1976). On the general climate of the time, useful books are Cyril Connolly's *Enemies of Promise* (London, 1938), Frank Swinnerton's analysis *The Georgian Literary Scene* (1938: rev. ed., London, 1969) and A. C. Ward's *The Nineteen-Twenties: Literature and Ideas in the Postwar Decade* (London, 1930). Two important studies from our contemporary perspective are Martin Green's *Children of the Sun: A Narrative of 'Decadence' in England After 1918* (London, 1977) and Humphey Carpenter's *The Brideshead Generation: Evelyn Waugh and His Friends* (London, 1989).

There are now many works on "Bloomsbury," but the early study by J. K. Johnstone, *The Bloomsbury Group: A Study of Forster, Strachey, Woolf and Their Circle* (London, 1954), usefully shows how it was once seen; also note Leon Edel, *Bloomsbury: A House of Lions* (New York, 1979). The best close record is Anne Oliver Bell, *The Diaries of Virginia Woolf* (London, 5 vols., 1977–84), while Virginia Woolf's *A Room of One's Own* (London, 1927) remains a central work on women and fiction. On the broader world of the Twenties Modern movement, see Noel Riley Fitch, *Sylvia Beach and the Lost Generation: A History of Literary Paris in the 20s and 30s* (London, 1984).

Twenties Modernism has been extensively explored; some of the chief references are already listed above. Studies concentrating on the fiction of the 1920s include some of the essays in Frank Kermode's *Puzzles and Epiphanies: Essays and Reviews, 1958–61* (London, 1962), S. J. Greenblatt's *Three Modern Satirists: Waugh, Orwell and Huxley* (New Haven, 1965), and Sean O'Faolain's *The Vanishing Hero: Studies in Novelists of the Twenties* (London, 1956). Edwin Muir's *Transition: Essays on Contemporary Literature* (London, 1926) and Edgell Rickword's two volumes of *Scrutinies* (London, 1928, 1931) are important contemporary critical records.

Chapter 4

The best single work on the literature of the Thirties is Valentine Cunningham's marvellously documented *British Writers of the Thirties* (Oxford and New York, 1989) (with excellent bibliography) and Samuel Hynes, *The Auden Generation: Literature and Politics in England in the 1930s* (New York, 1972: London 1976), is also an excellent analysis. Other important studies are John Lehmann's *New Writing in Europe* (Harmondsworth, 1940) and Stephen Spender's *The Thirties and After* (London, 1978). Also note Valentine Cunningham (ed.), *The Spanish Front: Writers on the Civil War* (London, 1986). The period also has been plentifully covered in memoirs by its participants: of special note is Lehmann's *The Whispering Gallery* (London, 1955), Graham Greene's *A Sort of Life* (London, 1971), Christopher Isherwood's *Lions and Shadows* (London, 1938) and *Christopher and His Kind* (London, 1997), and Spender's *World Within World* (London, 1951). Also note the essays of George Orwell, in Sonia Orwell and Ian Angus (eds.), *The Collected Essays, Journalism and Letters of George Orwell* (London, 4 vols., 1968), and W. H. Auden, *The Dyer's Hand and Other Essays* (London, 1963).

Some other important works, most emphasizing the dominance of political issues in the period, are Bernard Bergonzi, *Reading the Thirties: Texts and Contexts* (London, 1978), David Caute, *Illusion: An Essay on Politics, Theatre and the Novel* (London, 1971), J. Clark *et al.* (eds.), *Culture and Crisis in Britain in the Thirties* (London, 1979), Frederick Grubb, *A Vision of Reality: A Study of Liberalism in the 20th Century* (London, 1965), Jeremy Hawthorn (ed.), *The British Working Class Novel in the 20th Century* (London, 1984), Richard Johnstone, *The Will to Believe: Novelists of the 1930s* (Oxford, 1982), Jack Lindsay, *After the 'Thirties: The Novel in Britain and Its Future* (London, 1956), John Lucas (ed.), *The 1930s: A Challenge to Orthodoxy* (Brighton and New York, 1978), Hena Maes-Jelinek, *Criticism of Society in the English Novel Between the Wars* (Paris, 1970), John Mander, *The Writer and Commitment* (London, 1961), J. A. Morris, *Writers and Politics in Modern Britain* (London, 1977), Malcolm Muggeridge, *The Thirties* (London, rev. ed., 1967), George Orwell, *Collected Essays, Journalism and Letters* (London, 4 vols., 1968), Julian Symons, *The Thirties: A Dream Revolved* (London, rev. ed., 1975), Alan Swingewood, *The Novel and Revolution* (London, 1975), and George Woodcock, *The Writer and Politics* (London, 1948).

Other important dimensions of the period are examined in Paul Fussell, *Abroad* (cited above), Peter Gay, *Weimar Culture: The Outsider as Insider* (London, 1969), Robert Graves and Alan Hodge, *The Long Weekend: A Social History of Great Britain, 1918–1939* (London, 1940), Robert Hewison, *Under Siege: Literary Life in London, 1939–45* (London, 1977), C. L. Mowat, *Britain Between the Wars, 1918–1940* (London, 1955), and A. J. P. Taylor, *The Origins of the Second World War* (London, 1964).

Chapter 5

Some of the main studies of British fiction after 1945 are Bernard Bergonzi, *The Situation of the Novel* (London, 1970), and *Wartime and Aftermath: English Literature and Its Background, 1939–1960* (London, 1993), Malcolm Bradbury and David Palmer (eds.), *The Contemporary English Novel* (London, 1979), Malcolm Bradbury, *Possibilities: Essays on the State of the Novel* and *No, Not Bloomsbury*, both cited above, James Gindin, *Postwar British Fiction: New Accents and Attitudes* (London, 1962), Alfred Kazin, *Contemporaries* (London, 1963),

Frederick R. Karl, *A Reader's Guide to the Contemporary English Novel* (London, rev. ed., 1965), Richard Kostelanetz (ed.), *Contemporary Literature* (New York, 1964), Gabriel Josipovici, *The World and the Book* (London, 1971), Alan Kennedy, *The Protean Self: Dramatic Action in Contemporary Fiction* (London, 1974), Frank Kermode, *Puzzles and Epiphanies* (cited above), *Continuities* (London, 1968) and *Modern Essays* (London, 1971), David Lodge, *The Novelist at the Crossroads and Other Essays* (London, 1971), *The Modes of Modern Writing* (cited above), and *The Art of Fiction* (London, 1992), Neil McEwan, *The Survival of the Novel: British Fiction in the Later Twentieth Century* (London, 1981), Rubin Rabinowitz, *The Reaction Against Experiment in the English Novel, 1950–1960* (New York, 1967), Lorna Sage, *Women in the House of Fiction: Post-War Woman Novelists* (London, 1992), Margaret Scanlan, *Traces of Another Time: History and Politics in Postwar British Fiction* (Princeton, 1990), Alan Sinfield (ed.), *Society and Literature, 1945–70* (London, 1983), Randall Stevenson's thorough *The British Novel Since the Thirties: An Introduction* (London, 1986), Patrick Swinden, *Unofficial Selves* (London, 1973) and his *The English Novel of History and Society, 1940–1980* (London, 1984), and D. J. Taylor's recent, interesting and wide-ranging *After the War: The Novel and English Society Since 1945* (London, 1993).

The British Council has produced a frequently updated sequence of invaluable guides to contemporary British fiction; they include Henry Reed, *The Novel Since 1939* (London, 1946), P. H. Newby, *The Novel 1945–50* (London, 1951), Walter Allen, *The Novel Today* (London, 1955), Anthony Burgess, *The Novel Today* (London, 1963), Michael Ratcliffe, *The Novel Today* (London, 1968), etc. Statements by contemporary novelists are collected in Malcolm Bradbury (ed.), *The Novel Today: Contemporary Writers on Modern Fiction* (London, rev. ed., 1990), in Heide Zeigler and Christopher Bigsby (eds.), *The Radical Imagination and the Liberal Tradition: Interviews with Contemporary English and American Novelists* (London, 1982), and in the various *Paris Review* "Writers at Work" interviews. The major reference books are Lesley Henderson (ed.), *Contemporary Novelists* (London and Chicago, 5th ed., 1991 (also see earlier editions)).

On the climate of Existentialism, see especially Walter Kaufmann (ed.), *Existentialism from Dostoevsky to Sartre* (New York,

1956), and William Barrett, *Irrational Man: A Study in Existentialist Philosophy* (New York, 1958; London, 1961).

Also see Kenneth Allsop, *The Angry Decade* (London, 1958), Al Alvarez, *Under Pressure* (London, 1965), Robert Hewison, *In Anger: Culture in the Cold War, 1945–1960* (London, 1981), Richard Hoggart, *The Uses of Literacy* (London, 1957), Peter Lewis, *Th. Fifties* (London, 1978), Tom Maschler (ed.), *Declaration* (London, 1958), Harry Ritchie, *Success Stories: Literature and the Media in England 1950–59* (London, 1988), Richard Titmuss, *Essays on the Welfare State* (London, 1958), and Raymond Williams, *Culture and Society, 1780–1950* (London, 1958) and *The Long Revolution* (London, 1961). There is an excellent overview of the whole "post-war" period to the present in Bryan Appleyard, *The Pleasures of Peace: Art and Imagination in Post-war Britain* (London, 1989). Also see Peter Hennessy, *Never Again: Britain 1945–1951* (London, 1993).

Chapter 6

Not surprisingly, good studies of British fiction from the 1960s on still remain limited, though accounts improve yearly. The British Council maintained its accounts of the contemporary novel with Ronald Hayman's excellent general survey *The Novel Today 1967–1975* (London, 1976) and its successor, Alan Massie, *The Novel Today: A Critical Guide to the British Novel, 1970–1989* (London/New York, 1990). The British Council and the Book Trust together also publish a very useful series of "Contemporary Writers" pamphlets on the individual authors. Bibliography can be found in Irving Adelman and Rita Dworkin, *The Contemporary Novel: A Checklist of Critical Literature on the British and American Novel Since 1945* (Metuchen, N.J., 1972). Also see Henderson (ed.)., *Contemporary Novelists* and Halio (ed.), *British Novelists Since 1960*, both cited above (and equally relevant to the next chapter).

For some useful general essays on contemporary fiction, see Anthony Burgess' *Homage to QWERTYUIOP* (London, 1986), John Fletcher's *Claude Simon and Fiction Now* (London, 1975), Frank Kermode's *Modern Essays* (cited above), David Lodge's *The Modes of Modern Writing* (cited above) and his *After Bakhtin: Essays on Fiction and Criticism* (London, 1990), Gabriel Josipovici's *The World and the Book* (cited above), and Angus Wilson's *Diversity and Depth in Fiction: Selected Critical Writings* (ed. Kerry MacSweeney) (London, 1983). Also see Richard Kostelanetz (ed.), *On Contemporary Literature* (New York, 1964), for an international overview.

For the rise of experimentalism, see Patricia Waugh's *Metafiction: The Theory and Practice of Self-Conscious Fiction* (London/New York, 1984), which has useful judgements on British fiction. Other important studies are Robert Alter, *Partial Magic; The Novel as a Self-Conscious Genre* (Berkeley, 1975), Robert Scholes, *The Fabulators* (New York, 1967), later substantially revised as *Fabulation and Metafiction* (Urbana/Chicago/London, 1979), David Lodge (cited above) and Linda Hutcheon, *Narcissistic Narrative: The Metafictional Paradox* (Waterloo, Ont., 1980). An important context is explored in Vivian Mercier, *A Reader's Guide to the New Novel from Queneau to Pinget* (New York, 1970).

There have been a number of important studies on the role of history in contemporary British fiction, including David Leon Higden, *Shadows of the Past in Contemporary British Fiction* (Athens, Ga., 1985), Neil McEwan, *Perspective in British Historical Fiction Today* (Wolfeboro, N.H., 1987), Margaret Scanlan, *Traces of Another Time: History and Politics in Postwar British Fiction* (Princeton, 1990), and Patrick Swinden's *The English Novel of History and Society, 1940–1980*, cited above. See also David Rubin, *After the Raj: British Novels of India Since 1947* (Hanover, N.H., 1986).

On literary culture in the Sixties, see Peter Ackroyd, *Notes for a New Culture: An Essay in Modernism* (London, 1976), A. Alvarez, *Beyond All This Fiddle: Essays* (London, 1968), Bryan Appleyard, *The Culture Club: Crisis in the Arts* (London, 1984), Paul Barker (ed.), *Arts in Society* (London, 1977), Christopher Booker, *The Neophiliacs* (London, 1969), Giles Gordon (ed.), *Beyond the Words* (London, 1975), Dick Hebdige, *Subculture: The Meaning of Style* (London, 1979), Robert Hewison, *Too Much: Art and Society in the Sixties: 1960–1975* (London, 1986), George Melly, *Revolt into Style* (London, 1970), Jeff Nuttall, *Bomb Culture* (London, 1968), and C. H. Rolph (ed.), *The Trial of Lady Chatterley* (Harmondsworth, 1961).

Changing cultural theory is found in works by Richard Hoggart and Raymond Williams, already listed; also Marshall McLuhan, *Understanding Media: The Extensions of Man* (New York/London, 1964), and David Manning White and Bernard Rosenberg (eds.), *Mass Culture: The Popular Arts in America* (Glencoe, Ill., 1957). On other aspects of the thought of the period, see Philip Rieff, *The Triumph of the Therapeutic* (New York/London, 1966), Christopher Lasch, *The Culture of Narcissism* (New York, 1978), and Theodore Roszak, *The Making of the Counter-Culture* (New York, 1969). Also see John Sturrock, *Structuralism and Since: From Lévi-Strauss to Derrida* (Oxford/New York, 1979). And on the rise of feminism, see Kate Millett, *Sexual Politics* (London, 1969), Germaine Greer, *The Female Eunuch* (London, 1970), and Mary Ellmann, *Thinking About Women* (London, 1979), as well as works listed in the following section.

On the British background of the period, see Anthony Sampson, *Anatomy of Britain* (London, 1962). Also useful are Eric Butterworth and David Weir (eds.), *The Sociology of Modern Britain* (London, 1970), Vernon Bogdanor and Robert Skidelsky, *The Age of Affluence, 1951–1964* (London, 1978), Alan Sked and Chris Cook, *Postwar Britain: A Political History* (Harmondsworth, 1979), and Elizabeth Wilson, *Only Halfway to Paradise: Women in Postwar Britain, 1945–68* (London, 1980).

Chapter 7

On the fiction of the 80s, see D. J. Taylor's polemical but interesting *A Vain Conceit: British Fiction in the Eighties* (London, 1989). A number of the more recent volumes cited above also include discussion of the fiction of the decade. For recent women's writing, see Lorna Sage, *Women in the House of Fiction*, cited above.

On the period of "Thatcherism," see Dennis Kavanagh, *Thatcherism and British Politics: The End of Consensus* (London, rev. ed., 1988) and Hugo Young and Anne Sloman, *The Thatcher Phenomenon* (London, 1986). Also see Anthony Sampson, *The Changing Anatomy of Britain* (London, 1972).

As the chapter indicates, one striking feature of contemporary fiction is the surrounding theoretical debate, much of it conducted by academic critics, for whom key themes have been "postmodernism" and "feminism." For the general intellectual situation, see Jonathan Culler, *Structuralist Poetics* (London, 1975) and *On Deconstruction: Theory and Criticism After Structuralism* (London, 1983). Important studies reflecting the growing influence of "Postmodernism" both on fiction and on literary theory itself are Robert Alter, *Partial Magic: The Novel as a Self-Conscious Genre*, cited above, Catherine Belsey, *Critical Practice* (London, 1980), Christine Brooke-Rose, *A Rhetoric of the Unreal* (Cambridge, 1981), Christopher Butler, *After the Wake: An Essay on the Contemporary Avant Garde* (Oxford, 1980), Susi Gablik, *Has Modernism Failed?* (London, 1984), Linda Hutcheon, *Narcissistic Narrative: The Metafictional Paradox* (Waterloo, Ont., 1980) and her *A Theory of Parody* (London/New York, 1985), Brian McHale, *Postmodernist Fiction* (New York/London, 1987), Alison Lee, *Realism and Power: Postmodern British Fiction* (London, 1990), E. J. Smythe, *Postmodernism and Contemporary Fiction* (London, 1991), Patricia Waugh, *Metafiction: The Theory and Practice of Self-Conscious Fiction*, cited above, *Feminine Fictions: Revisiting the Postmodern* (London/New York, 1989) and *Practising Postmodernism/Reading Modernism* (London/New York, 1992), Hayden White, *Metahistory* (Baltimore, 1973), Alan Wilde, *Horizons of Assent: Modernism, Postmodernism, and the Ironic Imagination* (Baltimore/London, 1981). A good introduction to the overall issue of postmodernism is Steven Connor, *Postmodernist Culture: An Introduction to Theories of the Contemporary* (Oxford, 1989).

On feminism and theory, see Janet Todd, *Gender and Literary Voice* (London, 1981), Michelene Wandor, *On Gender and Writing* (London, 1983), Dale Spender (ed.), *Feminist Theories: Three Centuries of Women's Intellectual Traditions* (London, 1983), Toril Moi, *Sexual/Textual Politics: Feminist Literary Theory* (London, 1985), and Elaine Showalter (ed.), *The New Feminist Criticism: Essays on Women, Literature and Theory* (London, 1986).

For new writing emerging at the present time, useful sources are the volumes *First Fictions*, published irregularly by Faber (London), *New Writing* (London, for the British Council), published annually from 1992, and the issues of the magazine *Granta*.

Index

A figure 2 in brackets immediately after a page reference means that there are two separate references to the subject on that page. The letters *e.* and *n.* after page references indicate epigraphs and footnotes.

Blasting and Bombardiering, 68
Childermass, The, 142, 194
Tarr, 138, 193
Wild Body, The, 194
liberalism, 72, 115, 268, 276, 282
Lively, Penelope, 413, 446
Lodge, David, 4, 66, 376–7, 378–9,
    411, 438–9
British Museum is Falling Down, The,
    376–7
Changing Places, 438
Ginger, You're Barmy, 376
Nice Work, 5, 405, 439
"Novelist at the Crossroads, The",
    335e., 376, 378–9
Paradise News, 439
Picturegoers, The, 376
Small World, 438–9
London, 11–12, 23, 24–5, 53–4, 78,
    81, 99, 113, 401
London, Jack, 53
Longrigg, Roger, 318
Lowry, Malcolm, 256–7, 282,
    300–303
*Dark As the Grave Wherein My Friend
    is Laid*, 302
In Ballast to the White Sea, 257
Lunar Caustic, 257, 302
October Ferry to Gabriola, 302–3
Ultramarine, 256, 300–301
Under the Volcano, 257, 282, 301–2,
    303
Lukacs, George, 223
Lyotard, Jean-Francois, 408

Macaulay, Rose, 141, 259
McCabe, Patrick, 414
McEwan, Ian, 389–91 *passim*, 402,
    413, 430–1
Black Dogs, The, 431
Cement Garden, The, 391
Child in Time, The, 410, 430

Comfort of Strangers, The, 391, 417,
    430
First Love, Last Rites, 389, 389–90
In Between the Sheets, 390–1
Innocent, The, 430–1
McEwan, Neil, 279n.
McGahern, John, 414
McGrath, Patrick, 412
MacInnes, Colin, 318
Maclaren-Ross, J., 221
McLaverty, Bernard, 384, 414
McLuhan, Marshall, 343
MacNeice, Louis, 210, 211
McWilliam, Candia, 446
Madden, Deirdre, 414
"magic realism", 387, 412–13, 442
Mailer, Norman, 272
Maitland, Sarah, 444
Malamud, Bernard, 272
Mann, Thomas, 100, 109, 151
Mannheim, Karl, 7
Manning, Frederic, 204
Manning, Olivia, 286
Mansfield, Katherine, 77, 81, 139,
    140, 190
Mantel, Hilary, 413, 446
Marinetti, E. F. T., 79
Mars-Jones, Adam, 446
Marsh, Edward, 82
Marxism, Communism, 210–11,
    217–18, 221, 222–3, 267
Masefield, John, 71
Massie, Alan, 414
Masterman, C. F., 71, 74
Maugham, W. Somerset, 23, 53
Maupassant, Guy de, 21
Melville, Herman, 93
Meredith, George, 13–14, 115
Merriman, Henry Seton, 71
Mew, Charlotte, 22
Miller, Henry, 220, 299–300
Mitchell, Julian, 377

507